LATIN AMERICA 1810–2010

Dreams and Legacies

LATIN AMERICA 1810–2010

Dreams and Legacies

Claude Auroi
The Graduate Institute, Switzerland

Aline Helg
University of Geneva, Switzerland

editors

ICP Imperial College Press

Published by

Imperial College Press
57 Shelton Street
Covent Garden
London WC2H 9HE

Distributed by

World Scientific Publishing Co. Pte. Ltd.
5 Toh Tuck Link, Singapore 596224
USA office: 27 Warren Street, Suite 401-402, Hackensack, NJ 07601
UK office: 57 Shelton Street, Covent Garden, London WC2H 9HE

British Library Cataloguing-in-Publication Data
A catalogue record for this book is available from the British Library.

LATIN AMERICA 1810–2010
Dreams and Legacies

ISBN-13 978-1-84816-846-6
ISBN-10 1-84816-846-2

In-house Editors: Samantha Yong and Catherine Yeo

Typeset by Stallion Press
Email: enquiries@stallionpress.com

Printed in Singapore by Mainland Press Pte Ltd.

Contents

Acknowledgments

The essays included in *Latin America, 1810–2010: Dreams and Legacies* were presented at a conference held in March 2010 at the Graduate Institute of International and Development Studies in Geneva. Organized by Claude Auroi and Aline Helg, the conference received major funding from the Swiss Society of Americanists (SSA) and the Swiss Academy for the Humanities and Social Sciences (ASSH) as well as from the Graduate Institute of International and Development Studies, the Pierre Du Bois Foundation, the Faculty of Arts (Faculté des Lettres) and its Department of History at the University of Geneva, and the European Association of Research and Training Institutes for Development (EADI). We express our profound gratitude to these institutions that made the conference — and thus this book — possible.

We are grateful to the contributors to this volume and to all the participants who made the conference a rewarding and enjoyable experience, notably Isabelle Milbert, professor at the Graduate Institute of International and Development Studies, and Yasmina Tippenhauer, Director of the Cultural Center Tierra Incógnita in Geneva, who kindly agreed to moderate some sessions; Irina Du Bois, President of the Pierre Du Bois Foundation, for her enthusiastic support, as well as Nicole Anliker, Tzinti Ramírez, and Leonardo Rodríguez for their expert organizational skills.

Some texts had to be translated from French and Spanish and we are very grateful to Maya Ostrofsky and Andrew Philominraj for their work.

We also extend our thanks to Imperial College Press, particularly Commissioning Editor Elena Nash and Senior Editor Jacqueline Downs, for their commitment to transforming this conference into a book.

Claude Auroi and Aline Helg
Editors

Notes on Contributors

Claude Auroi

He is Professor emeritus at the Graduate Institute of International and Development Studies in Geneva. He has been teaching rural development and the history of Latin American development for more than 30 years. In the 1980s he worked as a scientific adviser at the International Potato Center in Lima. A Doctor in International and Political Sciences, he has undertaken extensive research on agrarian issues in Peru, Bolivia, and West Africa and has been a consultant for the Swiss Development Corporation, UNESCO, and other organizations and NGOs. Recently he has also dealt with problems of governance, migration, and integration in Latin America. He is the author of *Des Incas au Sentier Lumineux, l'histoire violente du Pérou* (Georg, Geneva, 1988), and editor of *Latin American and East European Economies in Transition: A Comparative View* (Frank Cass, London, 1998), among others. He is the President of the Swiss Society of Americanists. He was also the Executive Secretary of the European Association of Development Research and Training Institutes (EADI) between 1989 and 1999.

Oscar Corvalán Vásquez

He is a Professor at the Institute for Research and Development of Education at the University of Talca, Chile. His training includes sociology, a PhD in History from the University of Concepción (Chile) and a PhD in Educational Sciences from the University of Toronto. His research areas are technical and professional education, the urban informal sector, the sociology and economics of child and teenager education and the teaching of social sciences and economics. Since the 1990s he has also studied and evaluated projects on the interaction between the workplace and the world of education. He was the designer of the curriculum of the Euro-Chilean Institute of Tourism at the Universidad de la Frontera. He has served as an adviser for the programs of Technical Education of the Ministries of Education of Chile and Uruguay. He has published *El aprendizaje en la industria: Evaluación de una experiencia chilena* (CINTERFOR/OIT, Montevideo, 1980) as well as various articles on adult education and the formation of disadvantaged young people.

Philippe De Lombaerde

He is Associate Director at the United Nations University Institute on Comparative Regional Integration Studies (UNU-CRIS) in Bruges (Belgium). Previously he was an Associate Professor of International Economics at the Universidad Nacional de Colombia (Bogotá), a Researcher and Lecturer at the University of Antwerp, and a Researcher at the National Institute of Development Administration (NIDA) (Bangkok). He has been a consultant for the governments of Belgium, Flanders, France, Colombia, and Thailand as well as the UN, the International Labor Organization, the Organisation for Economic Co-operation and Development, and the European Commission. His research interests include regional economic integration, international trade, monitoring tools and indicators, comparative regionalism, Latin American regionalism, EU external policy, and cross-border micro-regions. His books include *Regionalisation and Global Governance: The Taming of Globalisation?* with A. Cooper and C. Hughes (Routledge, London, 2008); *Del regionalismo latinoamericano a la integración interregional*, with S. Kochi and J. Briceño (Siglo XXI, Madrid, 2008), and *Integración asimétrica y convergencia económica en las Américas* (Universidad Nacional de Colombia–Antropos, Bogotá, 2002).

Christian Deblock

He is Professor of International Political Economy at the University of Québec in Montréal, Director of the Center for Integration and Globalization Studies (CEIM), and co-editor of the journal *Papers in Political Economy*. He earned his MA and PhD in Economics from the University of Montréal and the University of Louvain. He has been a visiting professor at various universities, such as the Institut des Hautes Etudes de l'Amérique latine in Paris and the Universidad Nacional Autónoma de México (UNAM). He has also worked as a consultant on matters of economic integration and trade negotiations, notably for the International Organization of La Francophonie. His research focuses on regional economic integration, US trade policy, and international economic institutions. He has co-authored numerous books and articles, including *Nord-Sud: La reconnexion périphérique*, with Henri Regnault (Athena, Montréal, 2006); *L'ALENA: Le libre-échange en défaut*, with Dorval Brunelle (Fides, Montréal, 2004); and *Le bien commun comme réponse à la mondialisation*, with Olivier Delas (Bruylant, Brussels, 2004).

Katherine Del Mar

She is a PhD candidate in international law at the Graduate Institute of International and Development Studies, Geneva, and a Teaching and Research Assistant at the Faculty of Law, University of Geneva. She holds a BA and a JD from the University of Queensland, Australia, and an LLM (mention très bien) from the Geneva Academy of International Humanitarian Law and Human Rights. She is researching proof before the International Court of Justice and has published a number of articles in international law, including 'The Requirement of "Belonging" under International Humanitarian Law', *European Journal of International Law*, 21/1 (2010).

Oscar Guinea Ibáñez

He is currently an intern at the European Commission–DG Trade in Brussels, having previously worked as a researcher at UNU-CRIS. He is an economist with degrees from the College of Europe (Belgium), Sussex University (UK) and the Universidad Autónoma de Madrid (Spain). He has also spent research time at the UN Economic Commission for Latin America and the Caribbean (Chile) where he was working on the links between Food Security and Biofuels in Latin America. His research interests lie largely in the field of Development Economics, especially in issues between EU and ACP countries. He is also interested in the spatial analysis of poverty, inequality, trade, and regional integration. He is co-author of 'Systems of Indicators for Monitoring Regional Integration Processes: Where Do We Stand Anno 2010?', published in *Köz-Gazdaság — Economic Theory and Policy* (2010).

Aline Helg

She is Professor of History at the University of Geneva. She has taught as an Associate Professor at the Department of History and the Teresa Lozano Long Institute of Latin American Studies of the University of Texas at Austin (1989–2003), and at the Universidad de Los Andes in Bogotá. She has been a resident scholar at the National Humanities Center in North Carolina. Her areas of specialization are independence and nation building, the African Diaspora in the western hemisphere, ethnicity, and racism, on which she has published journal articles and chapters. Her books include *Liberty and Equality in Caribbean Colombia, 1770–1835* (University of North Carolina Press, Chapel Hill, 2004) and *Our Rightful Share: The Afro-Cuban Struggle for Equality, 1886–1912* (University of North Carolina Press, Chapel Hill, 1995), both winners of prizes from the American Historical Association, and *La educación en Colombia, 1918–1957: Una historia social, económica y política* (CEREC, Bogotá, 1987; reprint, 2001). She is currently writing a comparative study of slavery and abolition in the Americas.

Marc Hufty

He is a Professor at the Graduate Institute of International and Development Studies in Geneva. He has a doctorate in Political Science from the Graduate Institute of International Studies (HEI) and the University of Geneva. He specializes in the areas of public policy and governance applied to biodiversity, protected areas, forests and social movements. He has conducted research for the Swiss National Fund and taught in Argentina, Bolivia, Peru, and Madagascar, and he coordinates several research projects. He has published several books on Argentina and Bolivia, and most notably he is the co-editor of *A donde va Bolivia? Gobernancia, gobernabilidad y democratización* (Plural, La Paz, 2005).

Alan Knight

He is Professor of Latin American History at Oxford University and a Fellow at St Antony's College. He previously taught at the University of Essex and the University of Texas at Austin, and he was a visiting fellow at the Center for US–Mexican Studies at the University of California, San Diego. His chief interest is twentieth-century Latin American history, with a focus on Mexico, agrarian society, state-building, revolutions, popular movements, education, and culture, on which he has published several articles. He is the author of the award-winning *The Mexican Revolution* (2 vols, Cambridge University Press, Cambridge, 1986) and has co-edited *The Mexican Petroleum Industry in the Twentieth Century*, with Jonathan C. Brown (University of Texas Press, Austin, 1992). After the publication of the first two volumes of a general history of Mexico, *Mexico: From the Beginning to the Conquest*, and *Mexico: The Colonial Era* (Cambridge University Press, Cambridge, 2002), he is completing its third and last volume, *Mexico Since Independence,* and doing research for a socio-political study of Mexico in the 1930s.

Marcelo G. Kohen

He is Professor of International Law at the Graduate Institute of International and Development Studies in Geneva. He has also served as a counsel and advocate for a number of states before the International Court of Justice and has been a visiting professor at several European universities. He is generally interested in research related to international law theory, territorial and border disputes, as well as international dispute settlement. His most notable publication is *Possession contestée et souveraineté territoriale (Adverse Possession and Territorial Sovereignty*, PUF, Paris, 1997), which was awarded the Paul Guggenheim Prize in 1997. His other publications include various articles and book chapters, and he edited or co-edited the following: *Secession: International Law Perspectives* (Cambridge University Press, Cambridge, 2006); *State Practice Regarding State Immunities /La Pratique des Etats Concernant les Immunités des Etats*, with Gerhard Hafner and Susan Breau (bilingual, Martinus Nijhoff, Leiden, 2006); and *Promoting Justice, Human Rights and Conflict Resolution through International Law: Liber Amicorum Lucius Caflisch* (bilingual, Martinus Nijhoff, Leiden, 2007).

Sabine Kradolfer

She is an Anthropologist and a Sociologist. She has a doctorate from the University of Lausanne and University of Paris III. Her doctoral thesis focused on the social organization of Mapuche communities in the province of Neuquén in Argentina. Between 2000 and 2009, she taught at the University of Lausanne successively as an assistant and a substitute professor, and was also the director of a research project. She is currently conducting post-doctoral research at the University of Barcelona and the National University of Rio Negro (Argentina), thanks to a research grant from the Swiss National Fund. Her research is entitled: 'Indigenous claims and assertions of identity in Latin America: how the respect of differences generates differences'. She has published *Quand la parenté impose, le don dispose. Organisation sociale, don et identité dans les communautés mapuche de la province de Neuquén (Argentine)* (Peter Lang, Bern, 2011) and 'Les autochtones invisibles ou comment l'Argentine s'est "blanchie"', *Cahiers ALHIM* 16 (2008; available online: http://alhim. revues.org/index3028.html).

Magnus Jesko Langer

He is a Teaching and Research Assistant at the International Law Unit of the Graduate Institute of International and Development Studies (Geneva). He is a PhD candidate in International Law at the Institute, and holds an MA in International Law (HEID), a Licence in International Relations (HEI), and a Bachelor in Law (University of Geneva). His research focuses on the fields of international environmental law and international investment law. His thesis analyses the question of how international environmental law has impacted the entitlements that states enjoy over their natural resources. He has written, with J.E. Viñuales, 'Managing Conflicts between Environmental and Investment Norms in International Law', in *International Law Faced with Environmental Problems* (Hart Publishing, Oxford, 2011).

David Lehmann

He is a sociologist and an anthropologist. After teaching at the Institute of Development Studies of the University of Sussex, UK, he moved to Cambridge University where he served as the Director of the Centre for Latin American Studies for ten years. His research focused first on agricultural development and land reform, especially in Chile and Ecuador, and later shifted to Brazil and to the role of Catholic intellectuals and activists in such popular movements as Liberation Theology and the People's Church. Recently, he has turned his attention to evangelical Protestantism and ultra-Orthodox Judaism. He is currently working on the diffusion of multiculturalism (*interculturalidad*) in Latin America (especially Mexico, Peru and Brazil), with the aim of using the Latin American example to cast light on the political and philosophical issues arising from cultural relativism and multiculturalism in Britain and Europe. His major publications include *Democracy and Development in Latin America: Economics, Politics and Religion in the Post-War Period* (Temple University Press, Philadelphia, 1990); *Struggle for the Spirit: Religious Transformation and Popular Culture in Brazil and Latin America* (Polity Press, Oxford, 1996); and *Remaking Israeli Judaism: The Challenge of the Shas* (Hurst Co., London, 2006) (written with Batia Siebzehner).

José Marín Gonzáles

He is an independent scholar with a PhD in Anthropology from the University of Paris I-Sorbonne and an MA from the University Institute of Development Studies in Geneva. From 1971 to 1987 he has participated in research projects on the Andean and the Amazon regions in association with the Central University of Peru, the University of Manchester, and the Institute of Advanced Studies of Latin America in Paris. He has taught at the University of Geneva and collaborates with the School of Social and Pedagogic Studies in Lausanne and the Institute of Social Studies in Geneva. He is the author of *Peuples indigènes, missions religieuses et colonialisme interne dans l'Amazonie Péruvienne* (Svenska Institutet för missionsforskning Uppsala Universitet, Uppsala, 1992), and of contributions such as 'Histoire de l'Etat Nation : de la politique d'intégration en Europe et en Amérique latine' in *Intégrations et migrations: Regards pluridisciplinaires*, edited by Christiane Perregaux (L'Harmattan, Paris, 2001).

Edgard Moncayo

He is Director of the Center of Economic Studies in the School of Economics of the Universidad Central, Bogotá, and an Associate Research Fellow at the United Nations University Institute on Comparative Regional Integration Studies (UNU-CRIS) in Bruges. He was previously the Director of the Colombian Delegation at the United Nations Economic Commission for Latin America and the Caribbean (ECLAC), a member of the Andean Pact Board, the General Director of the Colombian Institute of Foreign Trade, the Economic Secretary of the President of Colombia, and the Economic Counsellor of the Colombian Embassy in Washington DC. He has also been involved in consultancy with international organizations such as the International Development Bank, and is a visiting fellow at Oxford University. His areas of interest are international trade and economic integration, industrial development, and regional and urban economics. His books include *Impactos territoriales de la globalización: Una perspectiva macro-sectorial* (Universidad Autónoma de Colombia, Bogotá, 2007).

Corinne A. Pernet

She has a Swiss National Fund Research Professorship at the University of St. Gallen. Holding a PhD from the University of California, she undertook research at the Universities of Illinois and Texas. After three years as Assistant Professor at the University of Oklahoma, she joined the History Department of the University of Zurich, also as Assistant Professor. Her interests focus on twentieth-century Latin American and international history, with an emphasis on transnational movements. Having worked on cultural relations between the United States and Latin America, she is currently completing a book on the cultural aspects of Latin American engagement in the League of Nations and UNESCO. She is also beginning research for a project on food policies in Latin America in relation to development and cultural heritage. She is the author of several articles and book chapters as well as of *El MEMCH hizo Historia* (Fundación Biblioteca y Archivo de la Mujer, Santiago de Chile, 1997).

Dennis Rodgers

He is Senior Research Fellow in the Brooks World Poverty Institute (BWPI) at the University of Manchester, UK, and Visiting Senior Fellow in the Crisis States Research Centre (CSRC) at the London School of Economics and Political Science, UK. A social anthropologist by training, his research focuses on issues relating to gang violence and urban development in Nicaragua, and the politics of democratisation in Argentina. He is the author of 'Living in the Shadow of Death: Gangs, Violence, and Social Order in Urban Nicaragua, 1996–2002', *Journal of Latin American Studies,* 38/2 (2006); 'Slum Wars of the 21st Century. Gangs, Mano Dura, and the New Urban Geography of Conflict in Central America', *Development and Change,* 40/5 (2009); and he has co-edited, with G. A. Jones, *Youth Violence in Latin America: Gangs and Juvenile Justice in Perspective* (Palgrave Macmillan, New York, 2009).

Leonardo Rodríguez Pérez

He holds an MA in History from the University of Limoges (France) and an MA in the History of Alien Worlds and International Relations from the University of Paris I Sorbonne. He is currently working on a Doctoral thesis on the indigenous discourse in Colombia between 1970 and 2000, at the Graduate Institute of International and Development Studies in Geneva. He is interested in indigenous peoples and the history of Latin America in general, and is the recipient of the Pierre du Bois scholarship granted to doctoral students from Latin America attending the Graduate Institute. His MA thesis is entitled 'Les Discours politiques dans la guerre civile de 1854 en Nouvelle Grenade' (Paris, Latin American and Spanish Cultures Research Centre, CRALMI, University of Paris I).

Alain Rouquié

He is Research Director emeritus at the French National Foundation of Political Science and President of the House of Latin America in Paris. He is a political scientist, specializing in contemporary Latin America. He has been the Ambassador of France to El Salvador, Mexico and Brazil. He has published numerous books and articles on Latin America, such as *Pouvoir militaire et société politique en République argentine* (Presses de la Fondation nationale des sciences politiques, Paris, 1978); *L'Etat militaire en Amérique latine* (Seuil, Paris, 1982); *Amérique latine: Introduction à l'Extrême-Occident* (Seuil, Paris, 1987); *Guerres et paix en Amérique centrale* (Seuil, Paris, 1992); *Le Brésil au XXIe siècle: Naissance d'un nouveau grand* (Fayard, Paris, 2006); and, most recently, *A l'ombre des dictatures: La démocratie en Amérique latine* (Albin Michel, Paris, 2010).

Pierre Salama

He is an economist and specialist in Latin America. He is a Professor at the University of Paris XIII, and a member of the editorial board of several journals; he was scientific director of the journal *Tiers Monde*.

His main areas of research concern the dynamics of underdevelopment and the modes of economic financing of emerging countries, and poverty. He specializes in drug economy, and presented a report to the Council of Europe on violence in Latin America. The Chair, Julio Cortázar, named him a Doctor Honoris Causa of the Autonomous University of Mexico and the University of Guadalajara (Mexico). He has published numerous books and most have been translated into Spanish and Portuguese. Among his individual works are: *Sur la valeur: Elément pour une critique* (François Maspero, Paris, 1975) and *Le défi des inégalités: Amérique latine/Asie — une comparaison économique* (Editions La Découverte, Paris, 2006). He has also directed various collective works such as: *Mesures et démesure de la pauvreté* (2002) and recently *Les Suds dans la crise*, with Philippe Hugon (2010).

Yvette Sánchez

She is Professor of Hispanic Cultures and Literature at the University of St. Gallen, and Director of the Centre for Latin American Studies (CLSHSG). She has studied Spanish and English Language and Literature and Anthropology, and received her PhD from the University of Basel, with a thesis published as *Religiosidad cotidiana en la narrativa reciente hispanocaribeña* (Hispánica Helvética, Lausanne, 1992). She is now conducting research for projects on Latin American cultural topics, especially on US Latinos. She is also involved in the fields of Interculturality, TransArea and Hemispheric Studies. Her literary interests focus on the poetics of failure, collectionism, and visuality and on the Spanish author Enrique Vila-Matas. Her second monograph is *Coleccionismo y literatura* (Cátedra, Madrid, 1999). She has also edited or co-edited several books, such as *Poéticas del fracaso*, with Roland Spiller (Gunter Narr/A. Francke, Tübingen, 2009), *Fehler im System. Irrtum Defizit und Katastrophe als Faktoren kultureller Produktivität*, with Felix Philipp Ingold (Wallstein Verlag, Göttingen, 2008), and the anthology *Cuentos de humo* (Siruela, Madrid, 2001).

Jorge E. Viñuales

He is Assistant Professor at the Graduate Institute of International Studies, Geneva. He received his PhD from the Institute of Political Sciences in Paris. He is also a Counsel with the law firm Lévy Kaufmann-Kohler in Geneva, as well as the Executive Director of the Latin American Society of International Law. Before joining the Graduate Institute, he was a full-time practitioner specializing in international investment law. He has worked on many cases under ICSID, UN CITRAL, PCA, ICC, or LCIA rules, including several high profile inter-state and investor-state disputes. He has also served as consultant or provided advice on different matters of international law to private companies, governments, international organizations and major NGOs. His research currently focuses on the interface between environment and investment, a topic on which he has published several articles in leading journals; his forthcoming book, *Foreign Investment and the Environment in International Law*, will be published by Cambridge University Press.

Yannick Wehrli

He is a PhD candidate at the Department of History of the University of Geneva and holds an MA in History and Spanish and Portuguese cultures. He has previously been a teaching assistant in Contemporary History at the University of Geneva, and in 2006 he was awarded a one-year fellowship from the Swiss National Fund to conduct research in several archives in Latin America and the United States. His forthcoming PhD dissertation focuses on Latin American states' foreign policy regarding conflict prevention and resolution during the inter-war period, with special emphasis on Latin American participation in the League of Nations and the pan-American movement. His areas of interest are political history and international relations of Latin America in the twentieth century as well as the history of international organizations, on which he has published articles and book chapters, such as 'Les délégations latino-américaines et les intérêts de la France à la Société des Nations', *Relations Internationales* 137/1 (2009).

United States
Mexico
Gulf of Mexico
North Atlantic Ocean
North Pacific Ocean
South Pacific Ocean
South Atlantic Ocean
Caribbean Sea
The Bahamas
Cuba
Haiti
Dominican Republic
Honduras
Guatemala
El Salvador
Nicaragua
Costa Rica
Panama
Venezuela
Guyana
Suriname
Colombia
Ecuador
Peru
Brazil
Bolivia
Paraguay
Chile
Argentina
Uruguay
Scale 1:50,000,000
Azimuthal Equal-Area Projection

Figure 1

Introduction

Aline Helg

The celebration of the bicentenary of Latin American independences in 2010 comes as a special invitation to look back at the last two centuries from the viewpoint of today's Latin America. Huge changes have taken place in the world, in the western hemisphere, and in Latin America itself over these 200 years, but in some domains continuity seems the rule. To take a few examples, all Latin American countries are now predominantly urban, in the sense that most of the people live in cities, but their economies continue to depend on agricultural and extractive industries located in the countryside or new frontier areas as before 1810. At the onset of independence, Native Americans and Afro-descended peoples were legally discriminated against, and today they are recognized as full citizens of their nations. But economically, politically, and socially they still are overrepresented among the poor. Moreover, although levels of education and health have greatly improved with time, Latin America continues to be the most unequal region in the world.

The following essays stem from a conference held in March 2010 at the Graduate Institute of International and Development Studies in Geneva, organized by Claude Auroi and Aline Helg. Its purpose was to better identify the distinct, always complex, and often contradictory processes that took place in Latin America over the last two centuries by using a thematical approach, followed as well by the division of this volume into four parts. The book starts with an international perspective, looking at Latin America in world geopolitics and international relations. The second part focuses on state formation and political change as well as on the related issues of citizenship and governance at the national, local, and hemispheric levels. The third part of the book revisits the economic history of the region, beginning with its rural/urban divide and ending with questions about current and future economic models. The fourth part examines religion, culture, and the changing place of the Other in Latin American societies.

Part One examines Latin America in world geopolitics and international relations, going back to the independence processes. It analyzes the twentieth-century subcontinent's fragmented and sometimes conflictive attempts to overcome US domination through active participation in international organizations and South–South relations up to today's challenge of globalization.

Alain Rouquié explores the evolution of the international status of Latin American states since the 1900s in order to evaluate their strategic ambitions at the beginning of the twenty-first century. At the time of the celebration of the region's first centenary of independence, Latin America seemed an El Dorado to Europeans and capital, with millions of people emigrating to its southern countries and US and European investments pouring into the region. Today these trends have reversed, at least demographically, with millions of Latin Americans emigrating and contributing through their remittances to some 15% of the region's GDP. Simultaneously, however, unlike in the 1900s, democracy seems to be entrenched everywhere, no doubt partly due to the relative neglect of the United States for the region since the end of the Cold War and 11 September 2001. Also, several Latin American countries have been able to resist more solidly the 2008 financial crisis than the whole subcontinent did after the 1929 and 1973 crises, for example. Yet, despite economic and social progress, Latin America continues to be the most unequal region in the world, and its participation in the global trade continues to be modest (about 5% in 2008).

Despite a common historical and cultural heritage, Latin America is undergoing important geopolitical shifts. In the twentieth century, the region was commonly thought of as one entity, dominated by the United States, even though the Mexican Revolution exercised considerable cultural and political influence on many countries, and the Cuban Revolution prompted continental shock waves and myriad guerrillas. Today, northern Latin America — Mexico above all — continues to be tied to the United States, a link that has increased for Mexico since the establishment of the North American Free Trade Agreement (NAFTA). The south is trying to create its own alternative center in Brazil, but old intracontinental tensions, the development of South–South exchanges, and Venezuelan President Hugo Chávez's initiative of a "Bolivarian Alliance" (ALBA) tend to exacerbate Latin America's fragmentation. According to Rouquié, although the diversification of external partnerships is positive for the economic future of the region, it is also imperative that it integrates and exists collectively to count in the global world.

Marcelo G. Kohen and **Katherine Del Mar** go back to the process of decolonization in Latin America in the 1820s from the perspective of international law. They see it as a vanguard phenomenon, as, for the first time, the partial collapse of two colonial empires — the Spanish and the Portuguese — produced a plurality of nations. Of course, unlike Spain's continental vice-royalties and captaincies, Brazil did not fragment but became one federal empire. Until the emergence of Latin American independences, European public law dominated international relations. But after 1820 an "American international law" began to take shape in the western hemisphere that progressively modified current international law. As the authors show, the first contribution of the former Iberian colonies was the rule of *uti possidetis*: the principle according to which each independent state disposes of the same territory as the one established by the colonial administration (denying, I might add, the fact that the periphery of the colonial vice-royalties and captaincies was not colonized but the home of Native American peoples). In other words, the former colonies were not considered *terrae nullius*, and their colonial borders became the international borders separating the new states. This did not prevent several frontier wars and disputes between Latin American countries from the second half of the nineteenth century on, but still the rule of *uti possidetis* has served as the international legal principle for the process of African independences in the 1960s as well as for the dissolution of the former Socialist Federal Republic of Yugoslavia, the former Soviet Union, and Czechoslovakia. In all cases, the aim of *uti possidetis* was to provide stability in the relations among newly independent states. It also aimed at guaranteeing the respect of their territorial integrity and at prohibiting conquest. In sum, Latin American independences have paved the way for the predominance of law over force and the demise of colonialism.

Next, **Yannick Wehrli** focuses on the participation of Latin American states in the League of Nations, the ancestor of the Organization of United Nations, in the 1920s and 1930s. After a brief discussion of Simón Bolívar's attempt to create a Congress of the former Spanish colonies in Panamá City in 1826, he draws a parallel between this Congress and the League of Nations, as both sought to form a system of collective security as well as of prevention and resolution of international conflicts. He explains why, at a time of intense US Marine intervention in Central America and the Caribbean, Latin American nations enthusiastically joined the League of Nations in order to have a forum to express their views outside of the realm of the United States. This common goal did not prevent frontier conflicts among South American nations that were then arbitrated by the international organization. Nor did it stop competition among delegates of specific countries to influence the League. Yet, through their important presence — 17 of the 42 states' members of the League of Nations were Latin American — Latin American delegates learned to work together as a "family" and to reduce tensions within the subcontinent.

Corinne A. Pernet moves on to Latin America's initiatives at the United Nations during the early years following the Second World War. Like Wehrli, she stresses the role of the UNO as an arena for

Latin American diplomats to express self-determination and self-articulation when, with the Rio Treaty of 1947, the United States imposed hemispheric solidarity against the Soviet Union. But simultaneously, decolonization in part of Asia and the Middle East offered the opportunity for Latin America to develop a South–South perspective that has been understudied. As Pernet notes, this meant that Latin American delegates had to recognize their countries as "underdeveloped" and subjected to neo-colonialism, which did create resistance. Nonetheless, the fact that UN attention was entirely turned to post-war reconstruction in Europe and Asia prompted their reaction. Some Latin American countries mobilized to question the validity of the cultural and economic models the United States and Western Europe wanted to impose on the world. A first sign of Latin Americans' response to their marginalization was their protest against their US engineered exclusion from the Dumbarton Oaks meetings that prepared the proposals for the creation of the UNO. It resulted in the pan-American 1945 Chapultepec Conference in Mexico that produced few results. Nevertheless, Latin American delegates did manage to make an important contribution to the UN Universal Declaration of Human Rights by successfully struggling, together with the delegates from the Philippines, China, and Lebanon, for a declaration that not only guaranteed political and civil liberties, but also social, economic, and cultural rights. Another meaningful Latin American contribution to the UN's first years of activity was the creation of the Economic Commission on Latin America (ECLA, or CEPAL) in 1948, thanks to the support of India and Lebanon. With its headquarters located in Santiago de Chile, ECLA rapidly developed a series of recommendations for the development of Latin America that criticized current models and theories of international trade through a periphery-based approach that promoted industrialization and social policies aimed at integrating the region. ECLA was linked to a new Latin American school of economists that established South–South links prefiguring the Third World movement.

Part One ends with an examination by **Yvette Sánchez** of the new transcontinental configurations created by the presence of renewed generations of Latin American immigrants (Latinos) in the

United States. Indeed, from a minority subculture, Latino culture is now recognized as a parallel culture in the northern nation. Demographically, today Hispanic Americans account for about 60 million (77% of them US citizens or legal immigrants) out of a total population of 310.5 million. They have become the largest "minority", followed by African Americans. The Spanish language is increasingly spoken in the United States, and in several areas English is completely marginalized. As Sánchez shows, in addition, both Spanish and English languages never cease to mutually modify and influence each other. As for Latin American migrants, they commute between their region of origin and regions in the United States, constantly affecting culture in the north and the south. These complex and profound changes have enhanced Latinos' self-esteem and self-affirmation. Sánchez illustrates this evolution by an examination of some artistic expressions that exemplify borderless cross-influence, such as performance, comics, fiction, and art installations that vividly show a new culture in the making.

The contributors to **Part Two** focus on the political process of independence and the construction of nation-states. They compare the sociopolitical results of Latin America's twentieth-century revolutions and military dictatorships. This part also closely studies governance and participatory citizenship through the insightful perspectives of public education, indigenous peoples, and forest management.

Alan Knight opens this section with a sweeping study of Latin American patterns of protest and revolution from 1810 to 1910 and the second half of the twentieth century. Contrary to analysts who posit that revolutions follow clear-cut patterns, he demonstrates that in Latin America, revolutions were not only scattered in time and place, but generally came unexpectedly. There was no logical chain of events, nor any specific structure or conjuncture that ineluctably led to revolution in one country rather than in another at a given time. Yet, revolutions did happen, and thus Knight proposes to define what constitutes a modern revolution. According to him, a social revolution includes a major polarization around rival projects that leads to armed conflict and violence; and an outcome resulting in fundamental structural change in regime and/or society. The latter nuance is important, as some revolutions, such as the Latin American wars of independence, were primarily political. Others, such as the Mexican, the Bolivian, the Cuban, and the Nicaraguan revolutions were both political and social (or socioeconomic): they created new forms of government, they established national control of natural resources, and they changed property rights as well as class (and ethnic or racial) relations. Knight then turns to a closer examination of continental Latin American independences. The movement was undoubtedly triggered by the Napoleonic invasion of the Iberian Peninsula, but it was generated by a series of grievances against the colonial state and its agents. It also included socioeconomic protests coming from the middling and lower, often non-white, strata who participated in the movement without being able to impose their views on the elite leaders, resulting in a political revolution without much social outcome. In contrast, external factors had little impact on Latin American twentieth-century revolutions. Their main causes were internal: extreme personalist authoritarian rule and export-led economies with racist assumptions about a substantial part of the popular classes. In each case, the overthrow of the state was necessary to reorder the economy and society. Nevertheless, other Latin American nations with similar conditions did not experience revolution, a fact that confirms the unpredictability of the latter.

Oscar Corvalán Vásquez follows with a focus on the role public education has played in the construction of citizenship and democracy in Latin America. In his view, democracy cannot be achieved without the development of public education, and the colonial legacy had a long-lasting influence on the whole process. Under Spain, no public education existed, and only some whites and *mestizos* had access to the few existing elementary schools, whereas higher education was restricted to the white elite and run by the Catholic Church. After independence, the new Latin American states had little revenue to implement their laws promoting public education, and throughout the nineteenth century less than 20% of the school-aged population, generally the upper to middle strata, had access to it. From 1900 to 1950, most countries made an effort to develop public education, but their principal goal was not to develop the sense of citizenship but to prepare children for the labor market. Literacy rates varied greatly in connection with the average per capita income: on top, in Uruguay, Argentina, and Chile, between 80 and 85% of the population could read and write, and the annual average per capita income reached about US$400; at the bottom, in Bolivia and Guatemala (without taking Haiti into account), about 30% were literate with an average per capita income of $100 to $150. Whereas the Second World War fostered the need for educated technicians, Corvalán Vásquez shows that the dictatorships and the economic model of neo-liberalism that prevailed in the Southern Cone during the Cold War undermined public education and annihilated the few existing efforts to build a participative citizenship. Today, despite two decades of democracy in the region, there is still a long way to go until a public education centered on citizenship develops, and thus until Latin Americans can fully participate in the local and regional development of their nations.

José Marín Gonzáles adopts a global historical approach to history and analyzes Latin America's tensions between the nation-state and multicultural society as a continuing effect of its dependency on Europe. He states that during the last two centuries, colonial and postcolonial Europe has considered Latin America as a political laboratory. It has imposed on this region as well as on others its political models, particularly the nation-state with its concomitant perverse effects: intolerance, racism, exclusion, and the denial of fundamental rights. After a presentation of the evolution of the idea of "nation" in Europe, Marín Gonzáles shows how there the construction of nation-states has denied cultural and linguistic diversity. In the Americas, the same process has been devastating from the extreme north to the extreme south, destroying the ancestral rights of various indigenous peoples while at the same time excluding them from citizenship. In some cases, it led to ethnocide or genocide, but more generally, states have promoted the "national integration" of their indigenous population, in reality subjugating them as supposedly inferior. Marín Gonzáles then turns his attention to Peru from the early fifteenth century to the 1780s Tupac Amaru rebellion and the mid-twentieth century before studying today's policies of evangelization, alphabetization, and assimilation. He focuses particularly on the Amazonian Basin, where indigenous organizations are increasingly developing bilingual and intercultural education while opposing neo-liberal endeavours to exploit their lands and subsoil. To him, whether Peru can respond to indigenous demands and create a new multicultural and pluri-national state will have consequences for the multicultural societies of Europe as well.

Also interested in indigenous rights and the state is **Leonardo Rodríguez Pérez's** study of Colombia in the 1990s. Beginning with a discussion of the tensions existing in international law between state sovereignty and indigenous peoples' right to self-determination, Rodríguez Pérez examines how the ratification in 1991 by Colombian Congress of the International Labor Organization's Convention 169 on indigenous self-determination and the adoption of the 1991 new Colombian constitution, which recognizes the ethnic and cultural diversity of the nation and protects minorities, have affected the relationships between the state and indigenous communities. He does it by summarizing several legal cases, such as one involving oil drilling on the territory of the U'wa people; another, the construction of a dam on Embera-Katio lands; a third on the construction of an Evangelical church on Arhuaco territory; and the installation of a US anti-drug radar on Wuitoto and Muiname Amazonian lands. All these cases were brought to Colombia's Constitutional (or Supreme) Court. The court rulings show that indigenous peoples' right to self-determination was recognized only in the case involving religious freedom: the Evangelical church would have violated Arhuaco cultural autonomy. In all other cases, the court concluded that national interest or national security should prevail over indigenous self-determination. In Colombia, the ILO Convention 169 meant little change for those it aimed to protect.

Marc Hufty looks at Latin America through the angle of forests. Indeed, half of the territory of the subcontinent, from Mexico to Tierra del Fuego, is covered by forests that together represent one quarter of all the Earth's forests. Yet, despite the establishment of conservation mechanisms and the legal protection of indigenous lands, Latin America lost 10% of its forests between 1990 and 2010. Relying on political ecology and environmental history, Hufty surveys the diversity of Latin American forests. He explains their rapid destruction through proximate causes (infrastructure expansion, logging, land conversion to agriculture, ranching, extractive industries, etc.) and underlying factors that can be economic (such as the world demand for palm oil, soybeans, and sugarcane), demographic, sociocultural, institutional, or technological. Deforestation produced the loss of biodiversity and ecosystem services, the loss of the livelihoods and identities of local and indigenous peoples as well as urban migrations, and increased inequalities and diseases. Hufty then turns to a history of precolonial forests that challenges the view of unspoiled Latin American forests and the stereotype of small indigenous groups of hunters and gatherers. Before the sixteenth century, Native Americans densely inhabited and exploited parts of these forests, not only in Central America. But their large settlements disappeared with most of them after the European invasion, through massacre, new diseases, slavery, and abuse. Still, continental tropical forests and their native people never ceased to have an aura of mystery fed by centuries of travel stories and fictional narratives still influential today. Finally, Hufty examines the politics of forest conservation that have translated, all over Latin America, to the establishment of nature reserves or protected areas as the best response to the perceived biodiversity and forest crises. Simultaneously, the legal recognition of indigenous territories has been promoted as the major solution to indigenous claims. Yet participatory conservation is still far from being entrenched. Indigenous and local populations are increasingly associated with the protection of forests and biodiversity, but less because of their inside knowledge than because partisans of sustainable use see them as valuable allies in their fight against the predatory party. Hopefully this alliance will eventually result in more participation in the public space and a new citizenship from below.

Part Three is dedicated to Latin America's rapid demographic shift from mostly rural to mostly urban populations. Despite this change, Latin America stands out as the continent with the greatest social inequalities as well as high rates of poverty among its population. Moreover, as two centuries ago and despite the implementation of different models of development, its economies continue to depend on exports of raw materials and agricultural products.

In his contribution on rural areas vs. cities, **Claude Auroi** reminds us that today the immense majority of Latin Americans live in cities, whereas 200 years ago they were predominantly rural. After discussing the multifaceted concept of rurality, he traces back the rural–urban complex to the early colonial period, showing how several types of links progressively tied the rural and the urban worlds together: people, goods, and money. Still existing today, the rural–urban complex does not form a network but a hierarchical relation in which the city dominates, and the rural areas both feed the cities but above all produce for exports. However, cities range from small towns with 2,000 inhabitants living according to quite rural standards to megacities, such as Mexico and São Paulo, whose metropolitan areas count about 20 million inhabitants, and intermediate cities of one or two million inhabitants each. But in the interstices of these cities, a rural lifestyle can coexist with fully urbanized customs. Similarly the "countryside" and land tenure are diverse, but two extremes dominate: the large landholdings with an underpaid labor force on the one hand, and small peasant landholdings on the other. In some countries, the nineteenth-century haciendas have evolved toward agro-industrial conglomerates, whereas in Bolivia, Peru, and, above all, Cuba, agrarian reforms have limited or nationalized the *latifundios*. Despite these changes, Latin American rural areas have continued to produce mostly agricultural and mining products, although over time some of these products have been replaced by others. Auroi also examines the psychological divide between urban and rural dwellers that dates back to the colonial era. In the nineteenth century, Argentinian Domingo Sarmiento equated the city with civilization and the countryside with barbarism, in his book *Civilization and Barbarism* (1845). Although in the 1870s, José Hernández struck back with epic poems featuring the idealized character of Martín Fierro as a means of exalting Argentina's rural *gauchos*, today negative stereotypes still stick to the Latin American very diverse "peasantry". All things considered, the future of rural Latin Americans looks rather gloomy, as the expansion of agribusiness, megaprojects, and deforestation pushes most of them toward overcrowded cities with few job opportunities.

Pierre Salama offers an elaborate discussion on whether growth driven by external demand can be a solution to economic crises. Looking back at the crisis of the 1930s that sharply reduced exports of primary commodities and thus imports of manufactured goods, he notes that for relatively large national economies, such as those of Argentina, Brazil, and Mexico, the crisis led to a phase of "unplanned industrialization". In all three countries, the transition from light to heavy import substitution was also made possible by populist regimes led by powerful and charismatic presidents. By the end of the Second World War, this model was in rapid decline despite its support by ECLA. Following the 1973 crisis that had an acute impact on the region, Latin American economies opened to free trade and financial flows; they also tended to return to a model of exports of raw materials and agricultural products to the detriment of industrialization. In the 1990s, the Washington Consensus reinforced this orientation and led to further reduction in social spending. Salama switches then to the 2008 crisis that had a deep but relatively brief negative impact on several Latin American economies. He attempts to assess the likelihood of success of the "domestic market bet" in a world context that differs greatly from the 1930s, because it is characterized by trade openness and competition with the new booming economies of China and South Korea, among others. He sees Latin America at a crossroads. Today the region's trade openness is still relatively moderate, and although exports have increased, Latin American share in international trade remains modest. One of the principal reasons for this is the very high income inequalities that characterize most Latin American societies and limit the size of their domestic markets. In Salama's opinion, it is time for the largest countries, such as Brazil and Argentina, to take advantage of their rapid recovery from the 2008 crisis to contribute to sustainable growth by fostering the domestic demand through the creation of a true welfare state — otherwise the region will most likely return to its nineteenth-century position of supplier of primary commodities.

Next, **Jorge E. Viñuales** and **Magnus Jesko Langer** study how, after independence, the quest for economic emancipation compelled Latin American countries to seek foreign investment while simultaneously trying to limit the disruptive impact of such investments on their social and political development. By turning to foreign loans, the newly independent nations tied their economies to foreign interests, and faced foreign state intervention — including military occupation and naval blockade — to protect foreign nationals and assets. The tension between Latin American host states and the home states of capital not only gave rise to foreign intervention but also to competing legal doctrines. Viñuales and Langer focus on two types of legal concept: the methods for solving investment conflicts, and the rules potentially applicable to solving such disputes. They also define four different historical phases for which they analyze these two types of legal concept: (1) 1810–1907, when European, mostly British, powers used a "gunboat diplomacy" to enforce on Latin America the claims of their nationals. Latin American intellectuals responded with legal doctrine, notably the "Calvo doctrine" based on the sovereign equality of states and the ensuing territorial jurisdiction; (2) 1907–1948, when the intervention of foreign states to defend their nationals became more limited (with the exception of the United States in Central America and the Caribbean) and gave way to the exercise of diplomatic protection before international tribunals; (3) 1948–1990, when the decolonization process in Asia and Africa led to a new balance of powers at the UN General Assembly that favored Latin American countries. It resulted in a resolution guaranteeing the permanent sovereignty over natural resources to each state, but at the same time tensions between capital-importing and capital-exporting countries increased, and most Latin American countries gained little from the new balance of powers; and (4) after the failure of the import-substitution industrialization model, several countries turned to investor-friendly treaties and most-favored-nation clauses as means of developing their economy and public services. These strategies have increased the possibilities of arbitration but can generally be considered to benefit the capital-exporting countries more. Although there are major differences between Latin American countries, most of them still depend on foreign investment.

As for **Edgard Moncayo**, **Philippe De Lombaerde**, and **Oscar Guinea Ibáñez**, they focus on the often neglected, yet crucial role played by the UN ECLA in the development of Latin American regionalism from the Second World War to 2010. As already mentioned in Pernet's contribution, ECLA launched a systemic and coherent approach to the development of Latin America at the end of the 1940s. The three contributors detail the principal phases of ECLA's policies, starting with the choice of industrialization in order to enlarge national markets, correct the balance of payment, and create employment and better living standards for the popular classes. The 1960s were ECLA's golden age, as economic integration schemes based on trade complementarities strengthened Latin America as a region. However, the 1973 oil crisis and the neo-liberal paradigm imposed by US president Ronald Reagan and British prime minister Margaret Thatcher initiated the dissolution of industrialization policies, first in the military dictatorships of the Southern Cone. Progressively, policies of privatization of the public sector, fiscal orthodoxy, and market deregulation swept the whole region, leading in the late 1980s to a second phase characterized by ECLA's waning influence. Still, some of its economists renewed proposals for industrialization based on the formation of an endogenous core of technical progress. But initiatives for a "new regionalism" rested now on US controlled financial institutions and on diverse free trade agreements. Among them, the neo-liberal and US promoted project of a Free Trade Area for the Americas (FTAA) was paramount, and NAFTA was its first full materialization. According to Moncayo, De Lombaerde, and Guinea Ibáñez — and in agreement with Salama — ECLA has now entered a third phase, as disillusion with neo-liberal policies seems to mark the return to active policies of Latin American integration in order to face external shocks and to improve the region's international competitivity.

Christian Deblock pursues the examination of these issues with a focus on the north, more specifically on NAFTA, signed in 1992 by the United States, Canada, and Mexico. He asks if it has been a springboard or trap for Canada and Mexico. After defining the objectives of the treaty (mostly to eliminate trade barriers, to facilitate the cross-border movement of goods, investments, and services — but not persons — and to promote fair competition between the associated countries), Deblock notes that in reality each partner pursued different goals, as the three countries had profound economic, political, social, and cultural differences. He then analyzes what has been achieved by NAFTA generally and from the perspective of Canada and Mexico. Undoubtedly, NAFTA has broadened and secured access to each country's market; it has also increased trade. But the latter remains bilateral and polarized on the United States. Investments, still coming principally from the United States, have lagged behind. Growth has been modest, and both Mexico and Canada have continued to export mostly oil, not manufactured goods, to the United States. Deblock concludes with a relatively bleak perspective for NAFTA, especially now that China has increasingly become the principal supplier of manufactured goods in the whole region, putting Mexico's hope of industrialization through a secured access to the US market in jeopardy.

Part Four examines Latin America's religions, cultures, and ethnic identities. After the social disruption initiated by the Columbian Encounter and amplified by African slavery, modern Latin American societies have undergone a process of laicization that has marginalized the Catholic Church as a dominant institution. New constitutions have also recognized the cultural contribution of previously denigrated populations — Native (Amerindian) and Afro-descended peoples — who are organizing at the continental level. Yet, if Sarmiento's barbarians have ceased to be equated with the non-white frontier people, they are currently being reincarnated as the youth of urban gangs.

David Lehmann opens this last section with an examination of the religious field in Latin America. He focuses on the erosion of Catholicism and the concomitant demise of the hegemonic position of the Catholic Church in society. He links this evolution to increasing secularization and a religious renewal among the faithful. The restructuring of the Latin American religious field is brought about by the changing demography of the Catholic priesthood, the increasing prominence of devotional and quasi-monastic movements, and the Catholic hierarchy's own preoccupation with securing the Church's moral and ideological frontiers. Although Lehman recognizes the parallel growth of Native American and African-derived religions, he focuses on Catholicism and Protestant Evangelism. He reminds us that official and alternative practices have always coexisted in Latin America since the Columbian Encounter — without producing a schism in the Catholic Church. Yet some nineteenth-century millenarian movements did prompt deadly military responses supported by the Catholic hierarchy. Lehman then revisits the Vatican's pre-Second World War doctrine and policies to prevent the rise of socialism, before turning to postwar Latin American Catholic engagements, notably Liberation Theology and its preferential option for the poor, which he sees as a minority phenomenon when compared with devotional movements. Indeed, simultaneously Pope John Paul II encouraged Opus Dei and the Mexican-born Legion of Christ, whose lay and clerical members pursued a conservative agenda in universities and high political spheres. In parallel, a quasi-Pentecostal Catholic movement created in the United States in 1967, the Catholic Charismatic Renewal, became a mass organization in several Latin American countries and was eventually recognized by the Pope in 1993. Like Evangelical churches, the Catholic Charismatic Renewal uses TV and mass rallies, promotes the religiosity of instant emotional gratification, and militates for conservative societal issues, such as the outlawing of abortion. All these religious associations do not hesitate to mobilize their members in political elections. Together, they are reshaping the field of religion, redefining what religion is and who has the power to lead the faithful, and redrawing the relationship between religion and politics.

Sabine Kradolfer analyzes the recent resurgence of Latin American indigenous or native peoples, with a special emphasis on the Argentinian case. Using a variety of traditional and "postmodern" strategies, they are now at the forefront of many socioeconomic, political, and environmental struggles. With pride and strength, they disprove the fallacious racial determinism of the nineteenth century that predicted their disappearance in the name of the "natural selection of the fittest". After a description of Spanish colonial policies that evolved from genocide to ethnocide through forced Christianization, Amerindians were recognized as members of humanity — but assigned to "republics of Indians" segregated from the "republics of Spaniards". By the seventeenth century, separation had obviously failed, and racial mixing between Amerindians, Spaniards, and Africans was so widespread in the colonized areas that the colonial authorities began to promote *mestizaje*, a policy followed by Latin American countries after independence. Nevertheless, before and after independence, huge portions of the territory remained unconquered and under the actual sovereignty of indigenous peoples. This was particularly the case in southern South America. Kradolfer, thus, examines the brutal incorporation of the Mapuche into the Argentinian State in the last third of the nineteenth century, following a series of treaties with and attacks by Argentinian caudillos. The infamous "Campaign of the Desert" launched by General Julio A. Roca in 1879 began a process that lasted until the 1930s, in order to extend the frontier westward and southward by exterminating or forcedly "integrating" indigenous peoples. Supposedly reduced to 0.7% of the total population by 1895, indigenous Argentinians were thought to definitely belong to the past. Yet, following long years of dreadful military dictatorships, in 1994 Argentina's new constitution recognized the existence of indigenous peoples in the nation and guaranteed the respect of their distinct cultures and languages as well as their participation in the management of the natural resources in their territories. Furthermore, the 2001 census showed the presence of tens of thousands of native peoples not only in the periphery but in the main cities as well. Not only were the Mapuche very visible, but other peoples thought to be extinct, such as the Ona, demonstrated their resilience.

Aline Helg surveys 200 years during which Africans and Afro-descended people contributed to Latin America's economic, political, social, and cultural development. She shows that at the onset of the independence process, race mattered. Whereas whites, Indians, and their *mestizo* offspring were credited with *limpieza de sangre* (blood purity), African slaves and their free or enslaved, mixed or unmixed, descendants were attributed a permanent "depraved origin" that excluded them from higher education and most civil, military, and church positions. At the same time, in every Spanish American city, most domestic workers were slaves, as were the producers of Spanish American main exports, such as gold from the Pacific Coast, sugar from Peru, and cocoa from Venezuela. Everywhere, however, free Blacks and Afro-descendants outnumbered slaves, with the result that together they were an important component of society, even in regions with an indigenous majority. Therefore, when the tiny minority of white Creoles launched the independence wars against Spain in continental America, in order to be able to win they had to enlist in their armies high numbers of slaves with the promise of freedom, and of free people of color with the promise of equality. Helg then analyzes three crucial moments in Latin American history to test the limits of equal rights in Latin America's multiethnic and multiracial societies: first, the independence process of the 1810s–1820s, when Latin American patriots fought for freedom from Spain and Portugal while at the same time maintaining slavery. The second period runs from 1889 to 1912, just after the abolition of slavery in Brazil and Cuba, when the elites in power granted legal freedom and equality to all, but simultaneously championed positivism, pseudoscientific racism and European immigration. In Cuba, then, Afro-descended citizens founded the only successful black political party in the hemisphere, which was annihilated in a massacre in 1912. Finally Helg examines the years from 1990 to 2010, when, in several countries from Colombia to Brazil, as Kradolfer noted in Argentina, new constitutions recognized land rights and some autonomy to Native American and Afro-descended communities, while at the same time governments ignored or sponsored their forced displacement so that national and global corporations could exploit their territories.

Finally, **Dennis Rodgers** examines the recent phenomenon of Central American gangs through the lenses of Sarmiento's aforementioned *Civilization and Barbarism*. He recalls that Central America has always being characterized by violence, from the genocide of the Conquest through the brutal dictatorships and civil wars of the twentieth century. Contemporary gangs date back to the rapid urbanization of the region in the 1940s, but the demobilization of large numbers of militarily trained youth in the 1990s gave *pandillas* a new impulse, reinforced by the lack of local governance. As for the *maras*, they are linked to two-way migratory patterns involving Mexicans moving to Los Angeles in the 1960s, Salvadoran and Guatemalan refugees following their path in the next two decades, combined with the forced repatriation of many of them to Central America after they served their prison terms in California. Now a mostly locally self-sustaining phenomenon, gangs probably count a total of up to 200,000 members in Central America, a number that exceeds that of the military and the police. Although they commit murders, thefts, and muggings, they are not the only authors of violence in a region characterized by high levels of poverty, unemployment, and social marginalization. Yet, they have become for the authorities easily targetable scapegoats for states' failure to provide a decent alternative to the citizenry. According to Rodgers, gang members' adaptation to Central America's urban modernity and oligarchic regimes questions the definition of "civilization". It tends to demonstrate that Sarmiento's dichotomy was less a utopia for Latin America's future than a telltale sign of the long-lasting dystopian nature of Latin American societies that continue to need barbarians to claim their civilization.

Part One

LATIN AMERICA IN WORLD GEOPOLITICS AND INTERNATIONAL RELATIONS

Chapter

1

Latin America in 2010: Geopolitical Shift and Strategic Ambitions

Alain Rouquié

1.1. INTRODUCTION

The bicentenary celebration in 2010 of Latin American independence comes as a special invitation to look back and take stock. Latin America sets an example in this regard. Indeed, those countries for which the year 1810 marked the beginning of their emancipation process are today commemorating this date without pomp or complacency. It is no longer a time for euphoria and delusions, as it was in 1910 with the First Centenary, when the religion of progress led the ruling classes to a kind of 'delirious optimism' (Lanus, 2001). Looking beyond separate national 'snapshots', the present time of reflection and even introspection, though sometimes disenchanted, is an opportune moment to focus on Latin America's presence in the world, on its role and the place of its states in international relations.

First, this chapter will examine the international status of the Latin American states in this first decade of the twenty-first century, seeking to identify the current perception of the continent in centres of global power. Next, I will analyse the impact on Latin America of changing political and economic developments in the global system, particularly in the structuring of regional space. Finally, I will attempt to analyse the strategic ambitions of its various national stakeholders.

1.2. INTERNATIONAL STATUS AND AUTONOMY

This much we can assert: In 2010, although the image (and reality) of Latin America as a whole does not, as it did in 1910, inspire self-congratulatory lyricism, it is more positive than it has been in 80 years, since 1930. In this respect it shatters stereotypes and pre-conceived notions. Three sets of major factors seem to have configured this 'new Latin America': political stability, economic and social progress and resilience to external shocks.

This continent, better known for its dictatorships and chronic instability than for its respect of constitutions, today has more representative governments and leaders elected in a pluralistic context than any other continent. Never in the history of Latin America have there been so many democratic regimes, for such long periods. For the past two decades, in continental America, one finds no exception. It should be added that democracy seems entrenched everywhere, including countries that had never experienced it previously (as is the case in countries of Central America such as El Salvador, Paraguay and Mexico), or that had practised it only intermittently in the twentieth century. Argentina, Bolivia and Brazil belong to this category of 'episodic democracies'. Even if its quality is not the same everywhere and many threats still hang over its development, almost a quarter century of democracy does reflect both the consolidation of institutions and the progress of citizenship. On a continent that had long favoured political violence as a means of provoking or preventing change, there is now strong belief in the power of the vote (Rouquié, 2010).

In the twenty-first century, this political stability has been accompanied by extraordinary progress in economic and social development. While the growth of Latin America has been relatively slow in the past 30 years (World Bank, 2005; IDB, 2010), the states of this region enjoyed a period of strong prosperity between 2003 and 2009, with high growth rates, reaching 5% on average and even 8–9% in some countries that particularly benefited from Asian demand and the rising cost of raw materials.

Although the per capita income dropped five times in a row between 1980 and 2000, it now appears to be on the rise in all countries throughout Latin America during the period we are concerned with, and by up to 3% in the richest countries. The Latin continent is an area with a high concentration of poverty. It is also the most non-egalitarian region in the world, far ahead of Africa or Asia in this regard. On this rich continent, in the late twentieth century, more than 40% of the population lived below the poverty line. Though poverty has not disappeared in the twenty-first century (there are still some 180 million poor people across the continent), it has dropped significantly from 44% to 33% of the population (ECLAC, 2008). In some countries like Chile, it has been reduced by half and is now below 15%. This means that tens of millions of Latin Americans have become consumers and gained access to the middle classes of their society, up until 2009 at least. Even in the matter of inequality, after the spurt of social inequalities of the 1990s, there is marked improvement in 12 out of 18 countries.

The third relevant feature as we step into the bicentenary is conjunctural rather than structural, but no less significant. It has to do with Latin America's relative resistance, with some exceptions, such as Mexico, to the consequences of the subprime financial crisis. For once (thinking back on 1984, 1994 and 1998), we can say that Latin America is in no way responsible for a crisis that emanates this time from the centre and not the periphery. This crisis proceeds from the heart of the system, that is to say (from the perspective of Latin Americans), from the givers of lessons in the North and the creators of the 'Washington Consensus'. It is 'their crisis', as the president of Brazil has not hesitated to assert in vivid terms.

This sudden crisis certainly did not spare Latin America. The 'decoupling' was a dream or a myth. But it has shown the resilience and response capacity of most Latin American states when faced with a major external shock. Thus, Latin America, after recording a good growth rate in 2008 (+4%), and a slight decline in 2009 (–1.5%), has resumed a steady growth rate in 2010. In their momentum, four countries even experienced a 1 to 3% expansion of their GDP in 2009. In 2010, the growth rate should be around 3%. The forecast for Brazil exceeds 5%. Moreover, unlike what happened with the indigenous crises of the past, we have not seen any flights of capital from Latin America in 2009, or any speculative attack against its currencies.

Because their finances were in order and their prosperity at the turn of the millennium had been adequately managed, several countries were able to react to the present crisis in a countercyclical manner, through recovery plans and financial stimulus measures. Obviously, the global recession did not spare the continent. Unemployment increased, and per capita GDP receded at times, but there was no disaster putting economies on the brink of bankruptcy or forcing governments to seek external financial support.

These three sets of factors clearly alter Latin America's status and position within the international hierarchy of the post-Cold War era. Indeed, its states could hardly be respected on the diplomatic scene when they were ruled by violent dictatorships, and saddled with unmanageable external debt and high inflation. To quote the title of a visionary and influential book (Mende, 1952), Latin America has 'entered the stage' and is no longer destined to exit. This seems to have been reflected by the inclusion in a G20 (expanded from the G7), of three major countries in the hemisphere: Brazil, Mexico and Argentina. This opening of the club of rich countries means, among other things, that Latin American countries in their diversity have become essential for directing the outcome of this recession and for legitimising concerted multilateral efforts to improve global governance.

This new respect for Latin America, whose maturity is now being recognised, is not simply a source of prestige, but is accompanied by concrete results. A number of states on the continent have thus acquired a specific weight and significant leeway to diversify their foreign relations and vigorously defend their national interests. This autonomy of sovereign decision is particularly illustrated by the failure of the proposed Free Trade Area of the Americas (FTAA). This pan-American grand plan, presented by Washington, was politely but firmly rejected (and buried) by Brazil and Argentina at the Summit of the Americas in Mar del Plata in 2005. The FTAA did not reappear at the next Summit of Trinidad and Tobago in 2009. Moreover, the signing of trade agreements with the European Union and with Asian countries, the active presence of Latin American nations in the Association for Asia-Pacific Economic Cooperation (APEC) and the decisive role played by China, which has become the subcontinent's second largest trading partner in the economic vitality of South America, bear witness to the magnitude of the changes. The time for a 'closed hemisphere in an open world' dreamed by the State Department in the immediate postwar era is completely over. The myth of the 'American family' has lost its appeal. And could there still be today a top diplomat for Latin America who, like one of his predecessors of the 1960s, would say that 'What is good for the US is good for Latin America'?

Further, the foreign policies of Latin American states reflect something more than their economic and trade priorities. Their advocacy of the principles of international law against North American unilateralism in the Middle East attests to this. Thus, two Latin American states, Chile and Mexico, opposed the 2003 vote by the UN Security Council on a resolution legitimising a military intervention of the United States in Iraq. Yet unlike France, these two states, though among the most pro-American on the continent, were not made to suffer from Washington's displeasure. And what to think of North America's lack of reaction, even silence, towards the Venezuelan president's inflammatory rhetoric against the 'Empire'? Is it a realistic attitude towards an oil-producing country where anti-American oratory flourishes, but in which, paradoxically, the United States remains first client and supplier? Should this attitude be interpreted more broadly as the ultimate and significant expression of a lack of interest by the first world power in a whole subcontinent that it once looked upon as its own backyard? Or has Latin America become the 'forgotten continent', as per Michael Reid's apt formula, amidst ruthless global competition?

1.3. GEOPOLITICS AND GLOBALISATION

Could it be that Latin American states have won unprecedented international respectability, only to cease to be among the priorities of their natural partners? Admittedly, where the United States is concerned, the importance it attaches to its southern neighbours is, as we know, discontinuous. Phases of active intervention alternate with ones of 'benign neglect' or even simply 'inattention' as dictated by the security priorities of the hegemonic power. Thus the 'friendly neighbour' policy was inspired by the early signs that preceded the Second World War. In the 1960s, John Kennedy replied to the Castro threat with the 'Alliance for Progress', a micro Marshall Plan of social aid and propaganda. In more recent times, one will remember Ronald Reagan's obsession with Central America and his distorted view of the hemisphere, where Sandinista Nicaragua's 'serious threat to US security' eclipsed the great Brazil.

In the twenty-first century, the Texan president George W. Bush announced that Latin America would be one of his priorities. For this purpose, he had attempted to get closer to Mexico. This was before the attacks of 11 September 2001. Everything changed thereafter. The Mexican border was integrated into the frame of the 'War on Terror' and of Homeland Security. The armed intervention in Iraq has become the central axis of North American foreign policy. Today the 'United States of Obama' is faced with the uncertain outcome of two armed conflicts: a threatening Middle East, and extremely serious economic and social problems at home. In this context, Latin America appears as a blind spot in North American policy.

It was, in fact, the arrival on the continent of the Cold War and the convulsions of the Central American Isthmus that placed Latin America on the geopolitical map of the world and gave its states new influence. Let us recall that it was initially for political reasons that the European Community became institutionally interested in Latin America in the 1980s. The first 'dialogue', the one of San José in 1984, was intended to support a peaceful and negotiated solution to Central American conflicts at a time when the US military wanted to eliminate the regional revolutionary movements at the risk of causing a general conflagration and destabilising the fragile democracies just restored in South America (Rouquié, 2005).

The bi-regional dialogue was born of this European concern. The Rio Group, an informal discussion forum (established in 1986 by a merger of the group known as the Contadora, formed of neighbouring states of the Isthmus, and its Support Group) became Europe's vis-à-vis in 1990, for the purpose of promoting consultation and political cooperation between the two regions. This dialogue took a new step in Rio de Janeiro in 1999 with the first Summit meeting of the Heads of State and Government of Latin America and the European Union, joined by the countries of the Caribbean (ALCUE). However, these biennial summits, the last one held in Madrid in May 2010, now appear to be losing momentum — if we can judge by the level of representation of some European countries and the disillusioned comments of the Latin American press.

One cannot help thinking that with the end of the Cold War and the restoration of peace in Central America, Latin America has been somewhat downgraded on the international agenda of the 'great powers'. In fact, it is not inconceivable that a continent of peaceful, largely disarmed and nuclear-free democracy is of less interest and has fewer means of influence than a region or countries that exhibit the opposite characteristics. Indeed, all the Latin American states (except Cuba) ratified the Treaty of Tlatelolco in 1967, thereby renouncing nuclear weapons. As for military expenditures, they are low in all countries of the continent as compared with those of Asian states or of some European countries.

Furthermore, it is clear that the Latin America of the Second Centenary is less attractive than the Latin America of the First Centenary. During the 'first globalisation' (1880–1918), the region had indeed seemed like an El Dorado for capital and men. The globalisation of today appears much less favourable to the Latin American continent, especially when judging by the direction of migration flow. Between 1860 and 1930, Latin America attracted millions of immigrants, mostly from Europe. Argentina received 3.5 million of these and Brazil 5.6 million, to mention just these two favoured destinations. Since the late twentieth century, millions of Latin Americans now migrate to industrialised countries. In the United States, Latinos now outnumber Afro-Americans. Emigration in some countries of Latin America touches 10% of the workforce, while financial transfers from emigrant workers represent up to 15% of national GDP.

Also, contemporary globalisation, characterised by the accelerated circulation of financial and industrial products and the standardisation of production lines, is not favourable to Latin America. This 'trade war of all against all' is in fact diametrically opposed to the comfortable 'international division of labour' of the Belle Epoque, which witnessed the continent's first period of economic success. In the new context of the twenty-first century, Latin America as a whole is not in the best position. Its participation in world trade is relatively modest and mostly stable. It was 4% in 1980 and did not exceed 5% in 2008 (a percentage which is nearly equal to the contribution of the French economy alone), while Asia quadrupled its contribution over the same period. This obviously does not reflect the wealth of the Latin American continent in terms of natural and human resources.

The continent is also a prisoner of its initial success as a supplier of raw materials and agricultural products. In fact, according to the logic of extroversion and 'comparative advantage', Latin American countries became industrialised by force of circumstance, to meet the demands of their domestic markets, and have since developed highly protected and non-competitive industries. While international trade from the 1970s onwards became the main engine of global growth, with several Asian countries implementing policies to promote industrial exports, Latin America remained basically faithful to the self-centred 'substitute' model of industrialisation, while its productivity regressed inexorably.

Certainly, the major states of the continent have a diversified, sometimes highly integrated industrial base, from heavy industry to finished products, but the legacy of the *hacia afuera* growth model and of 'self-centred development' has marked their recent economic history. And the solutions adopted to overcome the distortions of a closed economy have not always yielded the best results. The liberal shock treatments and unilateral openings have sometimes resulted in the destruction of part of the industrial system under the impact of imports (as in Argentina between 1976 and 1983, then from 1990 to 2000) or led to the development of subcontracted manufacturing, which is highly dependent and has very low value added (as in the Mexican *maquiladoras*, for example).

This is why, with some notable exceptions, the continent still exports mainly primary commodities, more or less processed. The recent prosperity driven by Chinese demand has not favoured the diversification of foreign trade towards products of medium or high technology. Thus 75% of Brazil's exports to China, which has become its primary market, consist of agricultural commodities or minerals. This is hardly a concern for the Brazilian giant, but could be one in some less complex South American countries, which are at risk of becoming mono-exporters and suffering from the extreme volatility of international prices for commodities. Thus, Argentina's recent transformation into a 'Soya Republic', sacrificing everything to the current 'king product' (ECLAC, 2009), is noted with concern by some observers.

It is true that economic models do not have a direct impact on international stratification or, indeed, on the foreign policies of states. They do, however, contribute to the attractiveness of these states, to the continuity of their resources and hence to their place on the world stage. Nonetheless, against this economic backdrop, a balanced account of a pluralistic continent must also adopt other approaches.

1.4. THE RESTRUCTURING OF REGIONAL SPACE

Despite a common cultural background and the parallelism of their histories, the diversity of the continent's countries is a permanent feature. Today we note the emergence of two distinct and coherent geopolitical entities. The current crisis has helped in this regard to exaggerate and magnify that image. Accordingly, at the beginning of the twenty-first century, two Latin Americas clearly appear — a northern and a southern one — that seem to be drifting apart.

To the north, Mexico, Central America (including Panama) and the Caribbean are economically and politically turned towards the United States — their main market, first investor, magnet for their migrant workers and middle classes alike and source of their intellectual references. The emergence of free trade agreements has institutionalised and, in a certain way, cemented the exclusivism of this relationship, which goes beyond the economy in shaping a freely acknowledged North–South dependency. Indeed, the countries of this region have sought free trade treaties as a means of securing their access to the world's largest market. Thus, after the coming into effect in January 1994 of the Treaty establishing the Free Trade Area of North America (NAFTA), which links Mexico and Canada to the United States, the states of Central America, joined by the Dominican Republic, signed and ratified in 2005 the agreement known by its English acronym CAFTA-DR.

Historically, all these countries belong to the traditional security zone of the United States. As is known, it is in this strategic area (and not elsewhere in Latin America) that the hegemonic power has intervened militarily on several occasions in the twentieth century. Moreover, apart from Mexico, which is painfully attached to the United States that lopped off half of its territory in 1848, this northern area includes only states of modest size and which are therefore very vulnerable.

The 2008 financial crisis and the international recession that followed did not (far from it) cause this geopolitical shift, but revealed it more clearly. Thus Mexico, which sends more than 80% of its exports to its great northern neighbour since NAFTA took effect, against less than 70% previously, saw its GDP drop by 7% in 2009. In Brazil, by comparison, with the US market absorbing only 15% of its foreign trade, the consequence of the crisis was zero growth only. Looking at the sharp contraction of the Mexican economy we see that it comes from an accumulation of factors originating in the North American market. To a decline in oil revenues, one should add the collapse of industrial and agricultural exports, the decline in remittances from emigration and the drying up of tourism, primarily American.

By contrast, the geographic situation and resources of the states of South America (on the whole and with a few exceptions such as Venezuela) allow them to enjoy pluralistic trade relations. Most of them share ties with Europe and Asia. They have greater economic and political autonomy. Unlike the northern states of Latin America, the large countries of the southern hemisphere, Brazil and Argentina, have shown total hostility to the extension of NAFTA to the whole continent. To defend their economic interests and especially the agricultural ones, they blocked the proposed Free Trade Area of the Americas (FTAA).

South American states, whether they succeed or not, generally seek to diversify their export markets, which do not exclude the United States but are clearly incompatible with near monopolies. The model in this respect, and many others, is Chile, whose foreign trade is divided roughly into four almost equal parts between Asia, Europe, North America and Latin America. But from now on the evolution of South America and even her destiny is closely tied to the rise of Brazil, which alone accounts for more than 50% of GDP in the region.

In Washington in 1971, President Nixon had declared to President General Medici:

'South America will go where Brazil goes'. At the time, this protocolar platitude shocked the whole continent. Nowadays, empowered by the strength of its economy, its stability and the attractiveness of its large domestic market, democratic Brazil has been trying since 2000 to rally its neighbours into some sort of federation, to build with them a vast entity of which it would be the centre and no doubt the main beneficiary. Since the first South American Summit was convened in Brasilia on 1 September 2000, successive governments have sought to reconcile and merge the two existing bodies of integration: Mercosur and the Andean Community of Nations, both of which, individually, are at a standstill. The first, more recent one is paralysed by the huge asymmetry of its member states. The second, with its variable geometry and composition, suffers both from the weak complementarity of its economies and from chronic ideological conflicts.

In Cuzco, in December 2004, the South American Community of Nations was founded between these two blocs; and this entity has been joined by three states, including Chile, that belonged to neither of the blocs. In March 2008 this new entity became UNASUR, the

Union of South American Nations. One may have wondered whether this was intended to expand on the other integrations that were underway but in crisis, or whether it marked their dissolution into a disparate union. In fact, UNASUR is more of a political project than an economic or commercial one. Its two major projects have to do with defence and road infrastructures. The Continental Infrastructure Initiative (IIRSA) is tasked to build land transportation routes between the two oceans. Indeed, in the highly fragmented South American region there is as yet no consolidated connector roadway linking east to west. The South American Defence Council is intended to ensure independent security for the subcontinent and regional peace, free from outside interference.

Nevertheless, the page for Latin American unity is not yet turned. Unitary rhetoric never loses its rights. Moreover, it is intertwined with the awareness that Latin Americans have of themselves. It is true that the institutional mechanisms set up in the 1980s, in the wake of the Central American conflicts and the foreign debt crisis, are still active. The Rio Group continues its statutory initiatives and, in particular, its consultative summits. It even included Cuba in 2009, under the rotating presidency of Mexico, giving this North American state the opportunity to remind everyone of its Latin American identity. In Cancun in February 2010, Mexico even presided over the creation of a common organisation between this Group and the countries of the Caribbean (CARICOM), which the media interpreted as an act of independence from the United States.

It is clear, however, that the geopolitical split of the region would have been impossible without diplomatic action, and therefore the political will of a unifier: the United States to the north, Brazil to the south. Washington's hegemony of the American 'Mare Nostrum' is old, dating back to the late nineteenth century and the war with Spain. It has adopted a more economic form in recent times, which has attenuated its Imperial virulence. As for Brazil, it has only recently and by very different means imposed itself on its reluctant rivals, including Argentina, its 'historic adversary'. Brazil's continental clustering strategy, as the most powerful state in this region, is not without arousing fears and suspicions. Some of its neighbours fear that North–South relations might be imposed, with the Brazilian giant playing the role of a northern industrial power, buying raw materials or sensitive assets and supplying manufactured goods. This situation is especially feared by Argentina, which was richer than Brazil just half a century ago and whose GDP is today only a fifth of that of its 'historical enemy', now an imposed partner.

But Bolivia, the first supplier of gas to Brazil, and Paraguay, a major exporter of electricity (from the bi-national Itaipu dam) have also often criticised Brazil's asymmetrical relations with them, even deeming them 'neo-colonial'. In these three cases Brazil, rather than uphold its short-term interests, has acceded to the concerns and demands of its neighbour-partners. By accepting major concessions it has favoured the strengthening of its regional influence. Brazil has thus implemented 'constructive restraint' as the mark of its diplomacy. *Primus inter pares*, it tries to downplay its natural supremacy and to convince its neighbours of its desire to cooperate without pursuing hegemonic interests.

As is apparent, ongoing developments in the western hemisphere are not outcomes of inevitable fate but actions of states, on the basis of their resources, their capabilities and their strategic ambitions.

1.5. REGIONAL POLICY AND STRATEGIC AMBITIONS

Although they have improved their lot and acquired political stability and relative predictability, Latin American states today are not characterised by the dynamism of their foreign policies and strategic projects. As we know, this has not always been the case. The extreme example in this regard is Cuba, which assumed a global role in the 1970s and 1980s. Its soldiers even intervened in Africa, where Cuba had friendly relations with certain revolutionary governments. Back then, Havana was looked upon as a Mecca of 'Third World socialism'. During the same period, Mexico too had become a new centre of regional power whose diplomatic activism proved particularly audacious. After playing a decisive role in the creation of SELA (Latin American Economic System), a kind of continental OECD, Mexico reopened the North–South dialogue in Cancun (October 1981) while supporting, against Washington, a negotiated end to Central American conflicts.

But then Cuba, losing its Soviet patron, fell into economic difficulties while seeking to ensure the survival of its anachronistic and isolated 'revolution'. As for Mexico, democratised since 2000 and with an open economy that is strongly integrated into North America, its diplomacy is again defensive, attached to some basic principles of international law that form a coherent and unchanging doctrine. In other words, it presents a low profile with modest activity.

With regard to all the countries of the region, their overall diplomatic ambitions now appear very limited and mainly focused on development. In fact, external policies beyond the multilateral forum are limited to managing trade relationships and territorial disputes. Indeed, on one hand we have witnessed an increase in international trade and cooperation agreements, yet there also appears to be an awakening or emergence of many bilateral disputes that exacerbate the continent's fragmentation. In recent times Peru and Chile faced some tense moments over the sharing of territorial waters. The presence of FARC guerrillas in Ecuador, and Colombia's military intervention beyond its borders, has created conditions for serious conflict between the two countries. Between Colombia and Venezuela, ideological differences and personality clashes have revived their age-old rivalry. Finally, since 2003 a new type of conflict has arisen between two member states of Mercosur, Argentina and Uruguay, which are the closest in all respects, around the environmental impact in Argentina of a cellulose plant located on Uruguayan territory.

Two states, however, Venezuela and Brazil, depart from the norm by the extent of their international ambitions. This situation is not new — as can be seen from the past foreign policies of both countries since the 1960s at least. For that reason, to explain their external actions, we cannot rely on the easy interpretation of rivalry between these countries for regional leadership. For one thing, these two neighbouring states do not have any disputed claims, and instances of cooperation between them are strong and numerous. Furthermore, Brazil represents the equivalent of about six times Venezuela in domestic product and population.

Venezuela's international aspirations are made possible by the presence of oil on its territory and the high prices of crude oil. In the early twenty-first century, this mono-producer state was able, thanks to its huge oil revenues, to counter the United States' Bush Administration without risk. It has had the means to assist friend states and political parties — and to create, as a challenge to the Pan-American Free Trade Area of the Americas (ALCA), a 'Bolivarian Alliance' (ALBA), that brings together a diverse group of countries. Beside Bolivia and Ecuador, whose governments have some affinity with the Venezuela of Chavez (i.e. nationalism and hostility to neo-liberalism), one also finds, amongst this group, clients of Caracas that receive aid, including oil, under exceptionally favourable conditions. These include Cuba, Nicaragua, Dominica and Honduras, even though the latter was traditionally pro-American until June 2009.

Venezuela, despite the drop in oil prices, has remained faithful to Cuba as its foremost economic and trading partner. It subsidises the weak economy of the island and provides 65% of its oil consumption at low 'solidarity' prices. For its part, Cuba pays its debt by sending thousands of aid workers to Venezuela, especially in the field of health. But aside from ALBA, Caracas is pursuing a global course of action that is confrontational and risky, but also potentially fruitful, in order to legitimise the 'socialism of the twenty-first century'. Its strategy consists of fostering a climate of international tension, even trying to resurrect an era that ended with the fall of the Berlin Wall.

Indeed, Venezuela's almost mimetic alignment with the Cuban Revolution of yesteryear, the support it has provided for the return to power of a non-updated Sandinista regime (itself a pure product of the East–West conflict), the partnerships forged by Hugo Chávez with various states considered disreputable by Washington (e.g. Syria, Belarus, Libya), and especially his close relationship with Iran's President Ahmadinejad and his rapprochement with Russia (and purchases of Russian weapons) — all seem to indicate a nostalgia for global confrontation and a bipolar world.

No doubt this is why President Chávez, in continuity with his anti-Western logic and much to the displeasure of NATO, did not hesitate to recognise the 'independence' of Abkhazia and of South Ossetia during a visit to Moscow in September 2009. Apart from 'Bolivarian' Nicaragua, it is true that Venezuela is the only state in the world to have ratified the Russian protectorate over these Georgian provinces.

With the arrival of Barack Obama in the White House, the Venezuelan government, for a moment helpless, quickly exploited some false moves by Washington in Honduras or Colombia, and regained its footing by attempting to give credence to the idea that the 'Empire' had not changed. With the departure of George W. Bush, Chávez may have lost a useful enemy, but not the 'structuring antagonism' that justifies his domestic policy, directs his action in the international sphere and forms the basis of his grand 'Bolivarian' project of continental unity cemented by 'anti-imperialism'.

Brazilian foreign policy is less tied to circumstances or to the personality of a leader than to the quasi-natural rise to power of a country-continent that has had global ambitions for a century (Rouquié, 2006; Grabendorff, 2010). With a GDP that places it, in current dollars, on a par or even above Russia and India, forecasters believe that Brazil could become the world's fourth largest economy in 2050, or earlier (it is the ninth today). Once known for its cyclical prosperity and its glaring contrasts, Brazil has enormous resources and is an agricultural giant as well as an industrial country in the world of high technologies (civil aviation in particular). It also has its place among the emerging greats of BRIC, an arbitrary gathering of peripheral powers to which the government in Brasilia is, in fact, attempting to give life.

Since 2000, Brazil, an unrivalled leader in South America and proponent of a regrouping of the subcontinent, has advocated a major strategic project for South American integration, of which Mercosur seems to have been one phase. But, conscious of its place and its role on the world stage, Brazil is also claiming a permanent seat on the United Nations' Security Council, alongside Japan and Germany. Indeed, Brazil's leaders feel that their country is the only one in Latin America with the attributes and skills needed to enter the restricted inner circle of 'great powers' in the Council. Its role in Haiti (at the head of MINUSTAH) and its interest in the Middle East are intended to show that Brazil can assume global responsibilities.

For Brazil is a state opposed to status quo, a revisionist of the international order. This old orientation is even a permanent feature of its foreign policy, becoming apparent as the country's economic situation permits. President Lula has expressed this in practical terms, for internal use, declaring that he wanted to 'change the map of world trade'. This is why his country, which in its way is 'a nation indispensable' to multilateral trade negotiations (as was seen in August 2003 at the conference of the Doha Round of WTO in Cancun), seeks to bring together the countries of the South, beyond the Americas.

This South to South approach, which some see as a resurgence of 'Third Worldism', inspires the great diplomatic initiatives of twenty-first-century Brazil, and of the Lula presidency in particular. The rapprochement with India and South Africa in a Forum for Three (G3 or IBSA), the Arab–South American summits (the first of which took place in Brasilia in May 2005), the will to ensure a political presence in sub-Saharan Africa and the exchange of high-profile presidential visits with China, are all manifestations of a determined policy of 'peripheral solidarity'.

What should we make then of Brasilia's active sympathy towards the barely re-elected Iranian president, or its hostility to possible sanctions from the international community against Tehran's opaque nuclear projects? How can we explain Brazil's strong commitment in favour of the Honduran president, ousted in a coup, which contradicts the basic principles of its diplomacy and drags it outside of its traditional sphere of influence? Without excluding the possibility that such attitudes may be for internal use on the eve of a difficult presidential succession for his party, one can also construe them as a demonstration of independence from the major powers or the desire to avoid a division of South America, where Bolivarian countries have clearly taken sides with Ahmadinejad and Zelaya.

In fact it is not always easy to grasp the true meaning of Brasilia's diplomatic activism in recent years. The most likely explanation is that Brazil is now trying to emerge as undisputed leader of Latin America, to finally be recognised as a new 'great power'. But we cannot rule out that it wishes to establish its role as a global player, so as to ensure its undisputed regional leadership. Could it be simply that Brazil now finds itself at a crossroads, in search of a role that is equal to its aspirations and of a sustainable status in a deconstructed world order?

1.6. CONCLUSION

What conclusion should be drawn from the contrasting and paradoxical panorama of bicentenary Latin America in today's world? Insofar as we look back on its past, to say that Latin America no longer exists comes as a truism more than as a 'shock formula'. Nonetheless, the geopolitical divide is an undeniable reality. The divergence of national paths and the fragmentation of the continent have increased. This is due less to political or ideological factors (between right- and left-wing governments, or between 'Bolivarian' states and others) than to strong external constraints as well as deliberate policy choices.

Thus, driven by Asian demand, the boom in exports of raw materials that seemed to have awakened unitary dreams has in fact contributed to 'reprimarise' the economies of Latin America (Cypher, 2009). This has put extroverted development back on the agenda, thereby blocking the dynamics of regional integration — as states that are often barely complementary have sometimes become competitors in the global market.

Although unitary initiatives and the rhetoric that goes with them have flourished in the last period, they lack substance. Indeed, salvation is no longer expected from a stalling regionalism, but from the international market. Countries that created economic, political and even social ties with each other in the past are now inclined to turn their backs on one another. Not even the improvement of Latin America's status or Brazil's triumphalist momentum can counter this tendency.

It is not forbidden, however, to take the risk of forecasting and to consider the future of the continent within the next 10 or 20 years, at the dawn of the third century. All things being equal, we can imagine two possible scenarios.

The first is an extension of current trends: fragmentation and everyone for himself on one hand; two poles of attraction and aggregation, in the North and South, on the other. In such a context of development, Brazil stands to distance itself even more from the rest of the continent. Mexico, for its part, would be more and more incorporated into North America, either in a kind of 'subsidiary' dependence, or, as some have dreamed, according to an evolutive and less asymmetrical approach, taking inspiration from the model of the European Community.

The second scenario could come from an awareness of the new geography of world power, and the common nature of the challenges faced by states in this region. In a world that is economically and politically multi-polar or 'a-polar', and therefore fluid and uncertain, there no longer exist any privileged circuits or a single centre. The time has come for diversification of external partnerships. But Latin America must also exist collectively for its sovereign interests to be taken into account in a future global economic architecture. For this, a new approach to integration must arise, no longer limited to trade and institutional inflation but led by concrete and ambitious joint projects, less sensitive to economic conditions and able to create a strong dynamic. To change the nature of regional clusters would fundamentally change the weight of Latin America on the world stage and give it the role it deserves in a new global configuration. This is one of the possible futures of the Latin Americas. It seems the most desirable for tomorrow's equilibrium and for our common future. It is not the most probable outcome, but if it became reality, the Old Europe of suicidal contradictions would certainly have a lot to learn from the other shore.

BIBLIOGRAPHY

CEPALC (Comisión Económica para América Latina y el Caribe) (2008). *Panorama social de América Latina*, CEPAL, Santiago de Chile.

CEPALC (Comisión Económica para América Latina y el Caribe) (2009). *L'Amérique latine et les Caraïbes au seuil du troisième millénaire*, CEPAL, Santiago de Chile.

Cypher, J. M. (2009). ¿Vuelta al siglo XIX? El auge de las materias primas y el proceso de "primarización" en América Latina, *Foro Internacional*, January–March, pp. 119–162.

Grabendorff, W. (2010). Brasil de coloso regional a potencia global, *Nueva Sociedad*, March–April, pp. 158–171.

Inter-American Development Bank (2010). *The Age of Productivity: Transforming Economies from the Bottom Up*, Palgrave Macmillan, New York.

Lanus, L. (2001). *Este Apogeo*, Emecé, Buenos Aires.

Mende, T. (1952). *L'Amérique latine entre en scène*, Editions du Seuil, Paris.

Rouquié, A. (2005). Europe-Amérique latine. Un partenariat stratégique dans un monde unipolaire? *Géoéconomie*, 34, Summer, pp. 33–41.

Rouquié, A. (2006). *Le Brésil du XXIe siècle, Naissance d'un nouveau grand*, Fayard, Paris.

Rouquié, A. (2010). *A l'ombre des dictatures. La démocratie en Amérique latine*, Albin Michel, Paris.

World Bank (2005). *Virtuous Circles of Poverty Reduction and Growth*, Washington, DC.

Chapter

2

Decolonisation in Latin America: Its Trail-Blazing Role for Decolonisation in Other Parts of the World

Marcelo G. Kohen and Katherine Del Mar

2.1. INTRODUCTION

An examination of the process of decolonisation in Latin America in the nineteenth century, compared with the process of decolonisation that took place in other parts of the world at a later stage, demonstrates that many rules underpinning the decolonisation process initially developed at the regional level of Latin America, subsequently to become of universal application. Indeed, it may be said that decolonisation occurred in Latin America in spite of international law, facilitating later decolonisation processes in other regions of the world that benefited from the Latin American experience, and which consequently occurred in line with international law.

Since their emergence as independent states, Latin American states have exerted considerable influence over the progressive development of international law in territorial matters. When they became part of the international community of states in the nineteenth century, Latin American states joined an existing international legal order, which was comprised of many rules governing territorial matters that were not favourable to them. The right of decolonisation, the notion of wars of national liberation and the idea of a right of development, were all concepts that took another century and a half to become firmly entrenched in international law. In contrast, the constitutive character of recognition by so-called 'civilised' states, the colonisation of non-European territories, the principle of legitimate monarchy supported by the Holy Alliance and the use of force in international relations, were all rules which, among others, characterised international law and relations of that era, referred to as 'European public law' or the 'law of European nations' (Heffter, 1881).

'Decolonisation' was not a term employed during the nineteenth century in Latin America to describe the phenomenon of accession to independence. Indeed, this term was not employed in international affairs until the second half of the twentieth century. The decolonisation that took place in Latin America was a vanguard phenomenon: it marked the first time that a plurality of states emerged as a consequence of the collapse of a colonial empire. From an international legal perspective, the struggle for independence in Latin America was viewed as an internal conflict. As a consequence, independence movements were regarded as 'rebels' or 'insurgents', a qualification that held fast until certain powers — in particular, Great Britain in 1822 and the United States in 1825 — recognised Latin American states (Moore, 1906, Vol. I, pp. 83, 174; Smith, 1932, Vol. I, p. 280).

In light of the political and legal context that existed in the nineteenth century, it is not difficult to understand the new states' desire to establish clear rules for the protection of their respective territories. It is quite possible that when they established such rules, Latin American states considered that these would only apply to the subcontinent. In the same vein that one spoke of 'European public law' with respect to the Old World, the notion of an 'American international law' thus began to develop in the context of the New World (Barberis, 1992, pp. 94–96).

Over the course of the nineteenth century, Latin American states almost imperceptibly replaced some of the foundations of the international legal system with their regional transformation of international law governing territorial matters. These rules progressively took on a universal character to become part of the international law of today. This chapter examines the development of the rules that underpin the process of decolonisation: the rule of *uti possidetis* (Part 2), the principle of respect for the territorial integrity of states (Part 3), the prohibition of conquest as a valid mode for the acquisition of sovereignty (Part 4) and the prohibition of colonialism (Part 5).

2.2. *UTI POSSIDETIS*

Uti possidetis is undoubtedly the most well-known international law rule developed in the context of the Latin American legal tradition. Respect for the territorial integrity of states, the prohibition of conquest and of colonialism, are to a large extent corollaries of an application of the rule of *uti possidetis*. The originality of the Latin American rule with respect to the existing law in the nineteenth century is addressed in section 2.2.1. Despite the apparent irreconcilable contradiction between the Brazilian and Hispanic American understandings of the rule of *uti possidetis*, namely whether the rule is *iuris* or *de facto*, these divergent approaches have much in common, as will be discussed in section 2.2.2. Finally, the extension of this regional rule to other parts of the world towards the end of the twentieth century, and its establishment as a rule of universal application, is analysed in section 2.2.3.

2.2.1. The Originality of the Rule of *Uti Possidetis*

South American Hispanic states were the first to invoke the rule of *uti possidetis* in a legal milieu that was not conducive to the establishment of such a rule. Historical reasons account for its emergence: Latin American states refused to obey the royal authorities from 1810 onwards. In 1821, the Central American Republic proclaimed its independence. Brazil followed suit one year later. In 1839, the

Federal Republic of Central America collapsed, and each former member attained independence. The different moments in time that the new states ceased to recognise Spanish authority explains why South American Hispanic states refer to a *uti possidetis* of 1810, whereas Central American states refer to a *uti possidetis* of 1821.

The fundamental idea underpinning *uti possidetis* is that each Hispanic American state disposes of the same territory that belonged to Spain in keeping with the former colonial administrative borders. By immediately defining the territorial sovereignty of each new state as soon as it attains independence, this principle addresses problems that may arise in two different spheres of international relations: (a) the principle provides stability in the relations among newly independent states by defining shared boundaries; and (b) the principle serves to avert future colonialist attempts by states outside the subcontinent. The International Court of Justice stated as much in the *Frontier Dispute* case when it noted that,

> [the] obvious purpose [of *uti possidetis*] is to prevent the independence and stability of new States being endangered by fratricidal struggles provoked by the challenging of frontiers following the withdrawal of the administering power.... Its purpose ... was to scotch any designs which non-American colonizing powers might have on regions which had been assigned by the former metropolitan State to one division or another, but which were still uninhabited or unexplored. (International Court of Justice, 1986, pp. 565–566, para. 20–23)

The rule of *uti possidetis* comprises two constitutive elements. Firstly, it affirms that territories on the American continent were not *terrae nullius*, because these territories were formerly either Spanish or Portuguese territories. Secondly, it establishes the requirement to respect the pre-existing administrative borders, which are transformed into international boundaries when independence is attained, thereby defining the territorial limits of each new state. According to the Argentine jurist José León Suárez, all Hispanic American governments tacitly accepted this principle when the new states gained independence. The Panama Congress formally consecrated the principle in a collective manner in 1826, and the Lima Congress followed suit in 1847–1848, referring to *uti possidetis* as a 'principle of American law' (Suarez, 1918, p. 46; De Lapradelle, 1928, pp. 77–78).

Affirmation of the principle of *uti possidetis* was not an easy task in the nineteenth century. The scant rules governing the succession of states in European legal scholarship at that time did not address the territorial aspect of this issue. Practice and international scholarship did not define clearly the territories that fell under the category of *terrae nullius* (Kohen, 1997, pp. 434–437). The fact that Spain and Portugal did not effectively control the vast spaces that they nevertheless considered to be under their respective sovereignties, the long duration of the hostilities between Spain and the new nations and the final victory of those fighting for independence, could have instigated another wave of colonialism in Latin America by other powers.

In order to define their respective territories, the new states had before them a number of options. They could have rejected the existing administrative borders, arguing that these had been established by the Spanish Crown without taking into consideration the human and geographic realities on the ground and, as was often the case, without any knowledge of the territories that were being delimitated. However, if the pre-existing administrative borders had been cast aside, boundaries would have to be delimited *ex novo*. To do this, the new states could have adopted the theory of 'natural' boundaries — in vogue in the scholarship at the time — or applied the rule of effective occupation, or allowed brute force to settle the question.

In sharp relief to these alternative methods for determining the international boundaries of the newly independent states, *uti possidetis* appeared as a reasonable and peaceful solution that responded to objective criteria. Indeed, the pre-existing administrative borders were the only viable option for determining boundaries at the moment of independence. All other options would have resulted in new states beginning their existence without defined international boundaries. Although the pre-existing administrative borders were arbitrarily established by the former colonial powers, other more seemingly objective methods for determining boundaries were no 'fairer'.

'Natural' boundaries are not easily identifiable in practice. States can have different points of view on what constitutes the 'best' or 'natural' boundary between their respective territories. Even if neighbouring states could reach an agreement on a 'natural' boundary, they would have to adopt concrete criteria for delimitating mountain ranges, water courses and other geographic particularities, which may in turn lead to further disputes. An example of the difficulties that may be encountered in delimitating 'natural' boundaries, is the drawn-out boundary dispute between Argentina and Chile, particularly with respect to the identification of a ridgeline and water divide along the shared boundary, which required five arbitral awards over the course of one century for the boundary to be eventually defined.

As a matter of course, resort by Latin American states to the rule of effective occupation as a way of determining international boundaries would have been a contradictory position for them to have taken. Effective occupation is a method for establishing sovereignty over *terrae nullius*. For Latin American states, this method of determining boundaries was clearly inapplicable for territories that had previously been either Spanish or Portuguese. Hispanic American states thus chose to define their boundaries on the basis of the pre-existing administrative borders — in 1810 for South America, and in 1821 for Central America.

Some scholars at the beginning of the twentieth century criticised this approach (Suarez, 1918; Ayala, 1931, p. 456). These same criticisms were later reiterated by a new wave of scholars (Antonopoulos, 1996; Ratner, 1996; Sorel *et al.*, 1994; Delcourt, 1999; Corten, 1999; Klein, 1999). They argued that instead of resorting to *uti possidetis*, international boundaries should be defined through negotiation between the states concerned. At first blush, this seems like a reasonable suggestion, particularly in light of the auxiliary argument that in many cases it proved almost impossible to determine the administrative borders established by the Spanish Crown. However, the principal problem with this alternative approach, and what these same scholars do not address, is the basis upon which such negotiations would be premised. As outlined above, considerable difficulties arise with respect to identifying 'natural' boundaries, and with occupation and effective possession as methods for defining boundaries. If these options are set aside, and if one simply considers that no boundary exists between the new states at the moment of independence or — even worse — that international law does not provide any legal rules for determining the international boundaries in dispute, then one would have to accept that the whole question must be regulated by negotiation. This suggestion appears to entail more instability than that which it seeks to overcome.

Effective possession was also not a viable criterion for determining the measure of territory under the sovereignty of each of the newly independent states. Hispanic American states rejected this criterion in preference of pre-existing borders, and instances of possession that were contrary to these borders were regarded as usurpation. As Chief Justice Hughes held in the *Honduras/Guatemala* arbitral award,

> [w]hen administrative control was exercised by the colonial entity with the Spanish monarch, there can be no doubt that it was a juridical control.... If, on the other hand, either colonial entity prior to independence had asserted administrative control contrary to the will of the Spanish Crown, that would have been mere usurpation. (Special Boundary Tribunal, *Honduras/Guatemala*, 1933, p. 1324)

This pre-eminence of a 'right to possess' over 'pure possession' is expressed by the addition of the Latin term '*iuris*' to the expression '*uti possidetis*' (International Court of Justice, 1986, p. 566, para. 23)

2.2.2. Different Understandings of *Uti Possidetis*: Brazil and Hispanic America

According to Brazil, and in contrast to Hispanic American states, the rule of *uti possidetis* is grounded on effective possession. As a result, the Brazilian approach to understanding *uti possidetis* is sometimes referred to as '*uti possidetis de facto*'. Unfortunately, the divergent interpretation of *uti possidetis* taken by Brazil, compared with Hispanic American states, has led to a regrettable misunderstanding in legal scholarship, and in the beliefs held by the peoples of the states concerned, that the two approaches are irreconcilable. This is not the case. Although clear differences exist, these approaches to understanding *uti possidetis* are reconcilable, and indeed, regardless of the interpretation adopted, the rule of *uti possidetis* remains at its very core, fundamentally the same.

If one examines in detail the general position taken by Brazil in territorial matters, and particularly with respect to its shared boundaries with neighbouring states, it is apparent that Brazil does not reject the principle of *uti possidetis iuris.* Indeed, Brazil has affirmed the exclusive application of this principle in relations among Hispanic American states — see the letter from Baron de Rio Branco, Brazilian Minister of Foreign Affairs, addressed to his Ecuador counterpart, Carlos Tobar (Cançado Trindade, 1986, Vol. I, p. 265). Whilst it is evident that territorial decisions taken by the Spanish Crown are not opposable to Brazil, Spanish domestic legislation nevertheless may assist in establishing the administrative borders of the former Spanish colonial empire.

The fundamental difference in their respective understandings of the rule of *uti possidetis* by South American Hispanic states and Brazil, resides in their differing attitudes towards the Luso–Spanish treaties of 13 January 1750 and 1 October 1777, which defined the boundaries of the two Iberian Crowns in South America. For Hispanic American states, these treaties were in force at the moment of their independence and, as a consequence, they provide the legal basis for defining the shared boundaries between these states and Brazil, both before and following the independence of Brazil in 1822. In contrast, Brazil contends that the two treaties in question are no longer in force following the war between Spain and Portugal that took place from March to June 1801 (Brazilian memorial submitted in the context of the *Territorio de Misiones* Arbitration, 1894, Vol. II, p. 10; Buarque de Hollanda, 2000, pp. 368–379). Brazil's interpretation of *uti possidetis* as effective possession should be understood as a reflection of Brazil's attitude towards the Luso–Spanish treaties. According to the Brazilian authorities, there was no relevant legal title in force at the moment of independence (Accioly, 1935; Kohen, 1993, pp. 951–952; Kohen, 1997, pp. 446–447; Barberis, 1999). For this reason, in the absence of a legal title, Brazil views the principle of *uti possidetis* as being premised on effectiveness.

The issue of whether or not the above-mentioned treaties of 1750 and 1777 were in force at the moment that Brazil attained independence will not be addressed here (Kohen, 1997, pp. 448–449). Despite their differences in opinion, Brazil and Hispanic American states nevertheless agree on the following fundamental issues: there were no *terrae nullius* in South America; new states in South America succeeded the territorial sovereignty of Spain and Portugal; and boundary agreements concluded by the former colonial powers were applied for the purpose of defining the boundaries of the newly independent states (*Territorio de Misiones Arbitration*, 1894, Vol. II, p. 9).

The convergence of views with respect to *uti possidetis* held by Brazil and Hispanic American states is most apparent in the boundary disputes that have arisen between Brazil and European states. In the context of a dispute with France, Brazil invoked Article 8 of the Treaty of Utrecht of 1713 that established the Luso–French boundary in the Guyana region (see text of the agreement between France and Brazil, and the arbitral award by the Swiss Federal Council, in La Fontaine, 1902, pp. 36–45). Similarly, in the dispute concerning the boundaries with British Guyana, the Brazilian government invoked the Luso–Spanish treaties of 1750 and 1777 (*Fronteiras do Brazil e da Guyana Ingleza*, in Cançado Trindade, 1986, Vol. I, p. 269). See also Brazilian arguments made in relation to the dispute with Great Britain over Trinity Island (Calvo, 1887, pp. 29–34).

Although differences of views between Hispanic American states and Brazil concerning *uti possidetis* have some important implications in practice, on the theoretical level the differences are less apparent. Brazil's position concerning effective possession is grounded essentially in the absence of a legal title in a treaty that could apply to its relations with its Hispanic neighbours. The Brazilian position is in keeping with the general understanding that effectiveness plays a residual role in the settlement of territorial disputes, in the absence of a legal title, as well as in the interpretation of an unclear legal title.

2.2.3. The Universal Applicability of *Uti Possidetis*

The International Court of Justice affirmed the universal applicability of the rule of *uti possidetis* in 1986. The Court stated that although 'the principle of *uti possidetis* seems to have been first invoked and applied in Spanish America … the principle is not a special rule which pertains solely to one specific system of international law. It is a general principle which is logically connected with the phenomenon of the obtaining of independence, wherever it occurs' (International Court of Justice 1, 1986, p. 565, para. 20). The decision of the Court also served to quell scholarly debate concerning the legal normative value of *uti possidetis*. Following the handing down of the *Frontier Dispute* judgement, the bulk of European and North American scholarship ceased to question the legal character of *uti possidetis*. An excellent account of this doctrinal shift is provided in Shaw, 1996.

The extended reach of the principle of *uti possidetis* beyond the subcontinent of Latin America first occurred on the African continent. In its Resolution 16(1) adopted in Cairo on 21 July 1964, the Organisation on African Unity made reference to *uti possidetis* under the guise of the 'principle of the intangibility of frontiers'. Like Latin America, the new African states defined their international boundaries in accordance with the pre-existing administrative borders established under colonial rule. The application of *uti possidetis* on the African continent could have been understood simply as a new regional application of a rule established in Latin America. However, as the Court made clear, '[t]he fact that the new African states have respected the administrative boundaries and frontiers established by the colonial powers must be seen not as a mere practice contributing to the gradual emergence of a principle of customary international law, limited in its impact to the African continent as it had previously been to Spanish America, but as the application in Africa of a rule of general scope' (International Court of Justice 1, 1986, p. 565, para. 21). The application of *uti possidetis* in Africa is thus viewed as the first application of a principle with universal scope.

The application of the rule of *uti possidetis* to situations outside the context of colonialism has been discussed at great length in legal scholarship, with most authors agreeing that the rule applied to the states that emerged from the former Soviet Union, the former Socialist Federal Republic of Yugoslavia, the dissolution of Czechoslovakia and the hypothetical secession of Quebec from Canada (Sorel *et al.*, 1994; Torres Bernardez, 1994; Antonopoulos, 1996; Ratner, 1996; Delcourt, 1999; Corten, 1999; Cot, 1999; Klein, 1999; Kohen, 1999). The universal application of *uti possidetis* is not difficult to explain. It reflects the logical necessity for a territorial basis at the moment of independence of new states. The rule plays an important stabilising and pacifying role in international relations. Contrary to the opinion expressed in some of the doctrine, *uti possidetis* does not promote secession. It applies immediately once independence is attained, but it does not itself provide a legal basis for the creation of states under international law.

2.3. THE PRINCIPLE OF RESPECT FOR THE TERRITORIAL INTEGRITY OF STATES

Respect for the territorial integrity of states was affirmed in the New World long before the principle was consecrated in Article 10 of the Covenant of the League of Nations, and later in Article 2§4 of the Charter of the United Nations (Kohen, 1997, pp. 369–379). The Treaty of Union, League and Perpetual Confederation, adopted by the Panama Congress in 1826, is cited by some authors as the first multilateral affirmation of the principle; however, the principle is not explicitly mentioned in the text of this treaty (Yepes *et al.*, 1934, Vol. I, p. 281).[1] In contrast, Article II of the treaty of confederation, adopted by the Lima Congress in 1847, provided a system of collective security in the event that the territorial integrity of a contracting state was threatened (*Conferencias Internacionales Americanas*, 1838, p. 42, note 3).

On 9 November 1856, the representatives of the eight Latin American states meeting in Washington adopted a treaty that

[1] See treaty text in *Conferencias Internacionales Americanas*, 1938.

affirmed the mutual respect for the territorial integrity of each state (Yepes, 1930, p. 41). Article I of the Treaty of Union and Defensive Alliance, approved by the Lima Congress in 1864, undoubtedly constituted the most developed collective organisation for ensuring respect for the territorial integrity of states. It stipulated that the contracting states would unite in defence against an act of aggression whether carried out by a foreign power, one of the contracting states or foreign forces not acting on behalf of a recognised government (*Conferencias Internacionales Americanas*, 1838, p. 42, note 4). Article II obligated the contracting states to take action if the guarantee of territorial integrity of one of the contracting states was violated.

The political climate in the nineteenth century explains why Latin American states sought to establish mechanisms for ensuring the respect of the territorial integrity of their respective territories. In the early 1830s, Great Britain occupied the Malvinas/Falkland Islands and usurped power from the Argentine authorities. During the 1840s, Spain was thought to have made plans to re-colonise the Pacific coast of South America. A war between Mexico and the United States resulted in the former losing part of its territory to the latter. In the 1850s, the American buccaneer William Walker took control of Nicaragua and affirmed his wish to control the whole of Central America. In 1861, Spain reconquered the Dominican Republic. In 1862, France intervened in Mexico in order to depose the ruling government. Finally, the United States developed its hegemonic policy for the American continent. There were thus many reasons motivating Latin American states to affirm the existence of a principle of respect for territorial integrity.

Latin America was not simply a pioneer in the establishment of a treaty-based principle for the respect of territorial integrity, but it also contributed to its development. The first step in this evolution was Article 11 of the Montevideo Convention on the rights and duties of states of 26 December 1933, adopted by the Seventh International Conference of American States, which consecrated the inviolability of state territory, and affirmed that a state could not be occupied, nor could force be used against it either directly or indirectly.

The second step in the development of the principle is more recent. At the universal level, the principle of respect for the territorial integrity of states has developed to govern inter-state relations, as the International Court of Justice recognised in its advisory opinion on Kosovo on 22 July 2010 (International Court of Justice 3, 2010, para. 80). Whether this principle can be generally invoked *vis-à-vis* non-state participants remains disputable at the general level. In contrast, within the context of the Charter of the Organization of American States (OAS), the principle has developed also to apply explicitly to secessionist movements. Article 8 of the Charter of the OAS limits admission of new members to independent states from the American continent that were members of the United Nations before 10 December 1985, and to Non-Self-Governing territories listed in the OAS document AG/doc.1939/85 of 5 December 1985, which have since attained independence. Article 8 of the Charter of the OAS thus reinforces the principle of respect for the territorial integrity of states in two ways. On the one hand, it ensures that territories belonging to Latin American states that are colonised cannot invoke their purported independence before the OAS. On the other hand, Article 8 prohibits secessionist entities from becoming members of the OAS.

2.4. PROHIBITION OF CONQUEST AS A VALID MODE FOR THE ACQUISITION OF TERRITORIAL SOVEREIGNTY

The affirmation of the rule of *uti possidetis*, and the principle of respect for the territorial integrity of states, led naturally to the prohibition of conquest as a valid mode for the acquisition of territorial sovereignty. Only two years after the Berlin Conference of 1888, on the basis of a joint proposal by Argentina and Brazil, the First International Conference of American States that met in Washington on 18 April 1890 adopted a resolution entitled 'Right of Conquest', which solemnly affirmed in the first operative paragraph that 'the principle of conquest shall not be recognized as admissible in American public law'.

The second operative paragraph of the same resolution went even further: conquest cannot be 'laundered' through a treaty agreeing to the separation of part of the territory of an American state. For some 80 years, this article was the precursor to Article 52 of the 1969 Vienna Convention on the Law of Treaties (Busch, 1973, pp. 21–22). This firm stance on prohibiting conquest as a mode for the acquisition of territorial sovereignty has its roots in the war that Argentina, Brazil and Uruguay waged against Paraguay in 1870. The Argentine government proclaimed that 'victory does not give rights' (Whitaker, 1964, p. 38), a statement that was later reproduced word-for-word in Article 3(g) of the Charter of the OAS.

These declarations on the prohibition of conquest by Latin American states challenged existing international law, which at that time recognised conquest as a valid mode for the establishment of territorial sovereignty if all the conditions required under the law of nations were present. In this respect, the Permanent Court of International Justice acknowledged in *Legal Status of Eastern Greenland* that:

> [c]onquest only operates as a cause of loss of sovereignty when there is war between two States and by reason of the defeat of one of them sovereignty over territory passes from the loser to the victorious State. (Permanent Court of International Justice, 1933, p. 47)

The American Republics that met in Washington on 3 August 1933 issued a declaration marking the northern Chaco war between Bolivia and Paraguay, which declared the non-recognition of a settlement of a dispute that was not obtained by peaceful means, and the non-recognition of territorial acquisition obtained by force (Eighth International Conference of American States, 1938, No. 2, p. 107). Thirty-seven years later, the 'Declaration on Principles of International Law concerning Friendly Relations and Cooperation among States in accordance with the Charter of the United Nations' contained in General Assembly resolution 2625 (XXV) of 24 October 1970 reiterated this declaration.

These general formulations were consecrated in the form of a treaty in the Rio de Janeiro Anti-War Treaty of Non-Aggression and

Conciliation, concluded in Rio de Janeiro on 10 October 1933, also know as the 'Saavedra Lamas Treaty' after the Argentine Minister of Foreign Affairs. This treaty was open for ratification by all states. Contracting states agreed in Article II that 'territorial questions must not be settled by violence, and they will not recognize any territorial arrangement which is not obtained by specific means, not the validity of the occupation or acquisition of territories that may be brought about by force of arms'.

Article 11 of the Montevideo Convention on the Right and Duties of States of 26 December 1933, adopted at the Seventh International Conference of American States, also contained an affirmation of the principle, specifying that '[t]he contracting states definitely establish as the rule of their conduct the precise obligation not to recognize territorial acquisitions or special advantages which have been obtained by force whether this consists in the employment of arms, in threatening diplomatic representations, or in any other effective coercive measure'.

Latin American states were thus the pioneers of the declaration of the prohibition of conquest as a valid mode for establishing territorial sovereignty well before the Kellogg–Briand Pact outlawed war as an instrument of national policy in relations among contracting parties, and before Article 2§4 of the Charter of the United Nations consecrated the prohibition of the use of force, and General Assembly resolutions 2625 (XXV) and 3314 (XXIX) consecrated the prohibition of the acquisition of territorial sovereignty by force as a corollary of the principle enshrined in Article 2§4 of the Charter of the United Nations.

2.5. THE OUTLAWING OF COLONIALISM AND THE RIGHT OF DECOLONISATION

The sum of all the norms discussed above leads logically to the prohibition of colonialism in Latin America. The Monroe doctrine theoretically shared this objective, even if the attitude adopted by the United States was contradictory in practice. This prohibition on the creation of new colonies did not require existing situations of colonialism to be brought to an end. It was only during the first half of the twentieth century that it was possible to identify a series of elements in the practice of inter-American states that could be viewed as precursors to what has since become the law of decolonisation.

The first identifiable element of the emerging law of decolonisation was the fact that Latin American states did not consider the principle of non-intervention in the internal affairs of states to apply to colonies on the American continent. This constituted a significant precursor to later developments that occurred within the United Nations system, leading the International Court of Justice to imply that situations of colonialism were not matters that fell within the reserved domain of colonial powers (International Court of Justice 2, 1986, p. 108, para. 206).

The outbreak of the Second World War triggered renewed interest in the Inter-American system with respect to existing colonies. Only one month after the invasion of Poland by Nazi Germany, the First Consultative Meeting of the Ministers of Foreign Affairs of the American Republics, which met in Panama, adopted Resolution XVIII, on 3 October 1939, according to which all changes in the sovereignty of an American territory by a non-American state would be qualified as a danger for the security of the American continent as a whole (*Conferencias Internacionales Americanas*, 1838, p. 127). This resolution had in mind a possible Nazi occupation of British, Danish, Dutch and French colonies in the region.

The Act of Havana and the Convention on the provisional administration of European colonies and possessions in the Americas, adopted in 1940 at the Second Consultative Meeting of the Ministers of Foreign Affairs of the American Republics, marked an important normative development for the emerging law of decolonisation. For the first time, an international instrument invoked the right of peoples to exercise self-determination and it envisaged the establishment of a temporary international administration for those territories at risk of being subject to an attempt to alter their sovereignty. The Convention established an Inter-American Commission for Territorial Administration, which had the power to elect a state to the role of administrator of a territory. The Commission was a precursor to the Trusteeship Council established in San Francisco under Chapters XII and XIII of the Charter of the United Nations.

A further catalyst for the emergence of a law of decolonisation was the adoption of resolution XXXIII by the Ninth International Conference of American States in Bogotá in 1948, which proclaimed that colonialism and occupation of American territories by extra-continental countries must cease. This resolution established an American Committee on Dependent Territories, the purpose of which was to 'centralize the study of the problem of the existence of dependent and occupied territories, in order to find an adequate solution to that question' (*International Conferences of American States*, 1958, pp. 271–273). Twelve years later, on 14 December 1960, the United Nations General Assembly adopted resolution 1514 (XV), considered to be the 'Magna Carta of Decolonisation', and on 27 November 1961 in resolution 1654 (XVI), the General Assembly established a Special Committee on the Situation with regard to the Implementation of the Declaration on the Granting of Independence to Colonial Countries and Peoples.

The Inter-American system thus clearly differentiated between two situations of colonialism: the domination of a people, and the occupation of a territory belonging to an American state by an extra-continental state. With respect to the former situation, the Inter-American system proclaimed the right of peoples to exercise self-determination. With respect to the latter, the system encouraged the parties concerned to negotiate in order to bring an end to the situation. This distinction is manifested by the treatment accorded even today to non-self-governing territories and other American territories linked to extra-continental states. As discussed above, according to the OAS Charter, only those territories explicitly mentioned in the OAS document AG/doc.1939/85 may be admitted as members of the OAS. This document examines the constitutional situation of the British, French, Dutch, Danish and US possessions in the western hemisphere, but it does not take into account the Malvinas/Falkland Islands, South Georgia and the South Sandwich Islands, which form the object of a dispute between Argentina and the United Kingdom.

This practice followed in the Inter-American system may be distinguished from the practice of the United Nations. The

Malvinas/Falkland Islands, South Georgia and the South Sandwich Islands are not analysed in the context of the Inter-American system because the OAS does not address territorial colonialism, in contrast to the United Nations which addresses both forms of colonialism (see Ros, 1964). Conversely, and in contrast to the United Nations, the French Overseas Departments and Territories situated in America, Greenland and the Netherlands Antilles, are addressed by the OAS, which could be regarded as taking a broader approach to the phenomenon of colonialism than the United Nations. For the United Nations, these territories have ceased to be 'non-self-governing territories' as this expression is understood under Chapter XI of the Charter of the United Nations. Indeed, the administrative powers of these territories no longer provide the information requested in Article 73(e) of the Charter of the United Nations. The particularity of the situation of Puerto Rico, clearly the result of strong political undercurrents, is not addressed by the Inter-American system even though it remains an active question for the United Nations Special Committee on decolonisation.

2.6. CONCLUSION

Decolonisation in Latin America can be said to have challenged the international law in force at the time, and it spurred the development of international law in a direction that would later benefit decolonisation processes in Africa, in vast regions of Asia, in the Pacific and in the Caribbean during the twentieth century. The practice of this subcontinent testifies to the strong commitment of Latin American states to international legality, and the fundamental role that this region played in the universal consecration of fundamental principles pertaining to territorial matters.

Latin American states were pioneers in establishing an 'American public law', as opposed to a 'European public law', which was successful in becoming of universal application, and thus forming part of the international law of today. This Inter-American practice was often not limited to South American states, but as a number of regional instruments demonstrate, it also encompassed the United States. The

Americas forged a series of norms that served to alter the foundations of the international legal order through their development and application at the regional level. They were the rule of *uti possidetis*, the principle of respect for the territorial integrity of states, the prohibition of conquest as a valid form for the acquisition of territorial sovereignty and the outlawing of colonialism leading to the law of decolonisation. The consecration of these norms demonstrates the coherent Latin American approach to territorial matters.

The stabilising and pacifying principle of *uti possidetis* emerged as the only viable method for determining the international boundaries of the newly independent states on the Latin American subcontinent. By immediately defining the boundaries of each new state as soon as it attained independence, this principle served to provide stability in the relations among newly independent states by defining their shared boundaries, and it served to prevent future colonialist attempts by states outside the subcontinent in a particularly tumultuous period in the history of Latin America. The principle of respect of the territorial integrity of states was recognised and developed in inter-American instruments long before the principle was consecrated at the universal level. The prohibition of conquest, as an affirmation of the predominance of law over force, and the emergence of the law of decolonisation, were logical developments on the back of these normative forerunners.

BIBLIOGRAPHY

Treaties

Charter of the Organization of American States (1948). Signed in Bogotá in 1948 and amended by the Protocol of Buenos Aires in 1967, by the Protocol of Cartagena de Indias in 1985, by the Protocol of Washington in 1992 and by the Protocol of Managua in 1993.

Charter of the United Nations (1945). 26 June 1945, entered info force on 24 October 1945, 1 UNTS XVI.

Covenant of the League of Nations (1919). 28 April 1919.

Convention on the provisional administration of European colonies and possessions in the Americas (1940). Adopted at the Second Consultative Meeting of the Ministers of Foreign Affairs of the American Republics, 21–30 July 1940.

Kellogg–Briand Pact (1928). Treaty between the United States and other powers providing for the renunciation of war as an instrument of national policy, Paris, 27 August 1928.

Luso–Spanish Treaty (1750). Treaty of Tordesillas (Portugal/Spain), 13 January 1750.

Luso–Spanish Treaty (1777). Preliminary Treaty of Peace (Portugal/Spain), 1 October 1777.

Montevideo Convention on the rights and duties of States (1933). Adopted by the Seventh International Conference of American States, 26 December 1933.

Treaty of Confederation (1847). Adopted by the Lima Congress, 8 February 1848.

Treaty of Union, League and Perpetual Confederation (1826). Adopted by the Panama Congress, 15 July 1826.

Treaty of Utrecht (1713). 11 April 1973.

Treaty of Union and Defensive Alliance (1864). Approved by the Lima Congress, 1864.

Vienna Convention on the Law of Treaties (1969). 23 May 1969, entered into force on 27 January 1980, 1155 UNTS 331.

United Nations Documents

General Assembly resolution 1514 (XV), 14 December 1960.

General Assembly resolution 1654 (XVI), 27 November 1961.

General Assembly resolution 2625 (XXV), 24 October 1970.

General Assembly resolution 3314 (XXIX), 17 September 1974.

Cases

International Court of Justice 1, *Frontier Dispute (Burkina Faso/Mali)*, Judgment, *I.C.J. Reports 1986*, p. 554.

International Court of Justice 2, *Military and Paramilitary Activities in and against Nicaragua (Nicaragua v. United States of America)*, Merits, *I.C.J. Reports 1986*, p. 14.

International Court of Justice 3, *Accordance with International Law of the Unilateral Declaration of Independence by the Provisional Institutions of Self-Government of Kosovo*, Advisory Opinion, 22 July 2010.

Permanent Court of International Justice, *Legal Status of Eastern Greenland*, Judgment of 5 April 1933, Series A/B No. 53.

Special Boundary Tribunal, *Honduras/Guatemala*, Opinion and Award of 23 January 1933, *United Nations Reports of International Arbitral Awards*, Vol. II, pp. 1307–1366.

Territorio de Misiones Arbitration (Argentina/Brazil), Exposição que os Estados Unidos do Brazil apresentam ao Presidente dos Estados Unidos da América como arbitro segundo as estipulações do tratado de 7 de setembro de 1889, concluído entre o Brasil e a Republica Argentina, New York, 1894.

Other

Conferencias Internacionales Americanas (1938). Carnegie Endowment for International Peace, Washington D.C.

Eighth International Conference of American States (1938). *Diario de la VIII Conferencia Internacional Americana,* Lima, 7 December 1938.

First International Conference of American States (1890). Resolution on the 'Right of conquest', Washington D. C., 18 April 1890.

International Conference of American States (1958). *Second Supplement 1942–1954*, Pan-American Union, Washington D. C.

Ninth International Conference of American States (1948). Resolution XXXIII, Bogotá.

Organisation on African Unity, Resolution 16(1) (1964). Cairo, 21 July 1964.

OAS documents AG/doc.1939/85 (1985). 5 December 1985.

Doctrine

Accioly, H. (1935). Le Brésil et la doctrine de l'*uti possidetis*, *Revue de droit international*, IX, pp. 36–45.

Antonopoulos, C. (1996). The Principle of *Uti Possidetis Iuris* in Contemporary International Law, *Revue hellénique de droit international*, 49, pp. 29–88.

Ayala, E. (1931). Le principe de l' *uti possidetis* et le règlement des questions territoriales en Amérique, *Revue de droit international*, VIII, 4, pp. 441–456.

Barberis, J. A. (1992). Les règles spécifiques du droit international en Amérique latine, *R.C.A.D.I.*, 235, pp. 81–230.

Barberis, J. A. (1999). 'La conception brésilienne de l'*uti possidetis*', in *Liber Amicorum Mohammed Bedjaoui*, Kluwer, The Hague, pp. 49–62.

Buarque de Hollanda, S. (2000). *História Geral da Civilização Brasileira, I. A época colonial. 1. Do descobrimento à expansão territorial*, 11th ed., Bertrand Brasil, Rio de Janeiro.

Busch, W. (1973). *Die Entwicklung eines Annexionsverbots auf dem amerikanischen Kontinent seit der internationalen amerikanischen Konferenz von Washington (1899/1890)*, Philipps-Universität, Marbourg.

Calvo, C. (1887). *Le droit international théorique et pratique*, 4th ed., Guillaumin *et al.*, Paris, VI.

Cançado Trindade, A. A. (1986). *Repertório da Prática Brasileira do Direito Internacional Público (Período 1899–1918)*, Fundação Gusmão, Brasília.

Corten, O. (1999). 'Uti possidetis et droit des peuples à disposer d'eux-mêmes: deux faces d'une même médaille?', in Corten, O., Klein, P., Delcourt, B. and Levrat, N. (eds), *Des limites administratives aux frontières internationales. L'uti possidetis en question(s)*, Bruylant, Brussels, pp. 299–324.

Cot, J.-P. (1999). 'Des limites administratives aux frontières internationales, rapport général', in Corten O., Klein, P., Delcourt, B. and Levrat, N. (eds), *Des limites administratives aux frontières internationales. L'uti possidetis en question(s)*, Bruylant, Brussels, pp. 17–33.

Delcourt, B. (1999). 'L'application de l'*uti possidetis juris* à la Yougoslavie: règle coutumière ou impératif politique?', in Corten, O., Klein, P., Delcourt, B. and Levrat, N. (eds), *Des limites administratives aux frontières internationales. L'uti possidetis en question(s)*, Bruylant, Brussels, pp. 35–78.

Heffter, A. W. (1881). *Das europäische Völkerrecht der Gegenwart*, 7th ed., Schroeder, Berlin.

Klein, P. (1999). 'Les glissements sémantiques et fonctionnels de l'uti possidetis', in Corten, O., Klein, P., Delcourt, B. and Levrat, N. (eds), *Des limites administratives aux frontières internationales. L'uti possidetis en question(s)*, Bruylant, Brussels, pp. 403–435.

Kohen, M. G. (1993). L'*uti possidetis* revisité: L'arrêt du 11 septembre 1992 dans l'affaire El Salvador/Honduras, *RGDIP*, 97, 4, pp. 939–973.

Kohen, M. G. (1997). *Possession contestée et souveraineté territoriale*, Presses Universitaires de France, Paris.

Kohen, M. G. (1999). 'Le problème des frontières en cas de dissolution et séparation d'Etats: quelles alternatives?', in Corten, O., Klein, P., Delcourt, B. and Levrat, N. (eds), *Des limites administratives aux frontières internationales. L'uti possidetis en question(s)*, Bruylant, Brussels, pp. 365–401.

La Fontaine, H. (1902). *Pasicrisie internationale*, Staempfli, Bern.

Moore, J. B. (1906). *A Digest of International Law*, Government Printing Office, Washington D. C.

Ratner, S. R. (1996). Drawing a better line: *Uti Possidetis* and the borders of new states. *A.J.I.L.*, 90, pp. 590–624.

Ros, E. J. (1964). Las conclusiones y recomendaciones del Comité especial de las Naciones Unidas para la aplicación de la Resolución 1514 (XV) en el caso de las Islas Malvinas. Su análisis, *Revista de Derecho Internacional y Ciencias Diplomáticas*, Rosario (Argentina), XIII, 25/26, pp. 83–103.

Shaw, M. (1996). The Heritage of States: The Principle of *Uti Possidetis Juris* Today, *BYBIL*, LXVII, pp. 75–154.

Smith, H. A. (1932). *Great Britain and the Law of Nations*, King & Son, London.

Sorel, J.-M. and Rostane, M. (1994). L'*uti possidetis* entre la consécration juridique et la pratique: Essai de réactualisation. *A.F.D.I.*, XL, pp. 11–40.

Suarez, J. L. (1918). 'L'*uti possidetis* y los límites americanos', in *Diplomacia Universitaria Americana. Argentina en el Brasil. Ciclo de Conferencias.* Escoffier, Caracciolo y Cía., Buenos Aires, pp. 41–66.

Torres Bernardez, S. (1994). 'The "Uti Possidetis Juris Principle" in Historical Perspective', in Ginther K. (ed.), *Völkerrecht zwischen normativen Anspruch und politischer Realität. Festschrift für Karl Zemanek zum 65. Geburtstag*, Duncker & Humblot, Berlin, pp. 417–437.

Whitaker, A. P. (1964). *Argentina.* Prentice-Hall, Englewood Cliff, New Jersey.

Yepes, J. M. (1930). *El panamericanismo y el Derecho Internacional.* Impr. Nacional, Bogotá.

Yepes, J. M. and da Silva, P. (1934). *Commentaire théorique et pratique du Pacte de la Société des Nations et des Statuts de l'Union Panaméricaine*, Pedone, Paris.

Chapter

3

Latin America in the League of Nations: Bolívar's Dream Come True?

Yannick Wehrli

3.1. INTRODUCTION

During the First Assembly of the League of Nations (LoN) in November 1920, the Venezuelan delegate Manuel Díaz Rodríguez exposed the reasons why his country had joined the young international organization and explained it as a logical consequence of Venezuela's history:

> The idea of such a League of Nations inspired and supported her heroic efforts to achieve her freedom and at the same time gave her the light and leading necessary for the first steps of her independent life. Such a conception, indeed, was the guiding star of the noble career of the Liberator, the Venezuelan Simon Bolivar [sic], who, on many occasions during his brilliant public life, defined and expressed it in the same terms as those in which it found expression 100 years later, amid the tumult of contemporary Europe. (Société des Nations, 1920, p. 166)

Thus the spiritual link between Simón Bolívar and the LoN was already formulated while the work of the Institution had barely started.

After his huge contribution to the independence and constitution of the new Hispano-American republics, Bolívar thought of ensuring the continued existence of his work by strengthening the weight of these new states on the international scene. In December 1824 he called together the former Spanish colonies in Panamá in order to set up a permanent institution endowed with supranational powers in matters of foreign policy and defense. This permanent Congress was also meant to operate as an arbitration court in which the conflicts between states' members could be resolved peacefully. A new common juridical order had thus to be established. The congress convened at Panamá City in summer 1826, did not respond to Bolívar's expectations since the perpetual Pact of Friendship adopted there never came into force due to lack of ratifications.

Comparing Bolívar's project and LoN's Covenant, one cannot help noticing similarities as both texts consider a system of collective security and of prevention and resolution of conflicts. But Bolívar never looked for the establishment of a universal body such as the LoN. In fact, if he looked favorably at a closer relationship with the British Empire, he never trusted the United States and dreamed rather of a Hispano–American Union (Lievano Aguirre, 1968; Collier, 1983 and 2008; Salcedo-Bastardo, 1977 and 1981; Lynch, 2006). Even if the LoN and Bolívar's project are so different in scope, it is reasonable to wonder whether the former could not offer the opportunity to make the latter a reality.

Indeed, the Geneva Institution offered Latin American states an ideal place to build links of solidarity. It is, at least, what the Ecuadorian Minister of Foreign Affairs asserted in his yearly report to Congress, describing Geneva and the LoN as "an ardent center of integral Latino Americanism". He added: "In Geneva the true conscience of our race and of our continent is taking shape" (República de Ecuador, 1935, p. 201). It should be mentioned, however, that such enthusiasm can also be explained by the need of the Ecuadorian Minister to justify, in front of Congress, the recent adhesion of his country to the LoN.

When the LoN was created in 1919–1920, Latin America, and above all the Caribbean area, was suffering several interventions by the United States, which were trying to impose their hegemony in what may be called their "backyard". At first sight, because of the non-ratification of the Treaty of Versailles by the US Senate and the subsequent absence of the Unites States in the LoN, the system of guarantees and of collective security set up by the Covenant could not protect Latin American states against new limitations to their sovereignty. Nevertheless, the League did offer a forum where they could make their voices heard, a place where they could get in touch with the great majority of the nations of the world, and, above all, European ones. Moreover, the absence of the United States from this room allowed a larger freedom of action and the possibility of closer contacts between Latin American delegates.

Certainly, a political organization such as the LoN, whose main task was peacekeeping, could not escape from facing confrontation in the defense of conflicting national interests. Thus several Latin American conflicts were treated there: in 1920–1921 the dispute of the Tacna and Arica provinces between Peru and Chile and of the Bolivian access to the Pacific; in 1933–1934 the conflict between Peru and Colombia about the territory of Leticia; and in 1932–1935 the bloody Chaco war between Bolivia and Paraguay.

The LoN was also the place where several Latin American rivalries arose, mainly between "enemy brothers" when a position of prestige like a non-permanent seat in the Council of the LoN was at stake. Thus Venezuela looked with strong dislike at the Colombian claim for that honor in 1926.[1] The same happened with Peru and Ecuador in 1935.[2]

---

[1] Report of the Chilean delegation on the seventh session of the Assembly, 1926, *Archivo General Histórico del Ministerio de Relaciones Exteriores*, Chile (AGHC), *fondos historícos*, Vol. 1075a.

[2] Peruvian Foreign Ministry to the Peruvian delegation to the LoN, 1 August 1935, *Archivo Central del Ministerio de Relaciones Exteriores*, Peru (ACME), Telegrams and cables, *libro copiador* n° 124 "Consulados y varios, 1935".

Furthermore, the Covenant of the LoN guaranteed the independence and territorial integrity of the member states and gave no supranational power to the international institution. This system, allowing its members to express themselves and to act on an egalitarian basis by voting on questions of world politics, strengthened the individuality of the states. Since the exercise of foreign policy is one of the main attributes of sovereignty, the participation in the LoN represented for a weakened nation — for instance after or even during a territorial occupation by a foreign power — a way to reaffirm its national sovereignty (Wehrli, 2009). The delegates from Panamá, Haiti, or the Dominican Republic took advantage of this opportunity (Société des Nations, 1924, p. 190; Société des Nations, 1927, pp. 100–103; League of Nations, 1930, pp. 42–46).

Even so, the Latin American delegations used the League's gatherings in order to create links of solidarity and to consolidate the conscience of a common identity. This is what this chapter will try to demonstrate.

3.2. FIRST CONTACT BETWEEN LATIN AMERICAN DELEGATES

At the closure of the first session of the Assembly in 1920, the LoN counted no less than 17 Latin American states among its 42 members, and 16 Latin American delegations participated in this first meeting. It suddenly seemed obvious that Latin American delegations constituted a significant weight in terms of votes as long as they were coordinated.

A few weeks before the opening of the 1920 session of the Assembly, the Uruguayan Minister in Paris, Juan Carlos Blanco, invited all the appointed Latin American delegates to forge relationships and exchange ideas and points of view regarding the League's first meeting. His idea, he pointed out, was not the constitution of a regional bloc. Every delegation had to preserve its freedom of action and vote. Nonetheless, the delegations agreed to work together in order to obtain the election of as many Latin American delegates in the committees of the Assembly as possible (Vivas Gallardo, 1981, pp. 99–100). The field on which the Latin American delegations would focus was already looming: the election of the chairman and the vice chairmen of the Assembly and its committees and the election of the non-permanent members of the Council.

The Latin American delegates soon got into the habit of holding private meetings during the sessions of the Assembly. Some of the delegates, above all the Chileans Manuel Rivas Vicuña and Agustín Edwards, were, in 1921, not very keen on participating in such meetings lest the defense of national interest be harmed. At that time they actually had to fight against the Bolivian attempts to involve the League in the revision of the 1904 treaty adopted after the War of the Pacific.[3] But as early as the following year, once the danger had passed, the same delegates considered the framing of a regional group as an efficient way to reduce rivalries. "It is on continental or regional groups that international life tends to settle", they added.[4] In 1923, Edwards even reckoned that Latin American delegates' unity of action, made possible by the holding of regular private meetings, was responsible for their growing influence in the Assembly: "This tight union deeply calls European countries' attention and gives the action of Latin America a strength she would otherwise not have".[5]

The opinion shared by the majority of the Latin American delegates was to ensure the continued existence of such meetings. After the 1923 Assembly, the Salvadorian representative José Gustavo Guerrero suggested that the Bureau of Latin America, the organ of the LoN's Secretariat specifically in charge of the relationship with those countries, be responsible for convening in Paris or Geneva, shortly before the opening of the sessions of the Assembly, a preparatory

---

[3] *Memoria de la delegación de Chile ante la segunda Asamblea de la Liga de las Naciones celebrada en Ginebra del 5 de septiembre al 5 de octubre de 1921*, AGHC, *fondos historícos*, Vol. 881a.

[4] *Memoria de la delegación de Chile, tercera Asamblea de la Sociedad de las Naciones, Ginebra, 4–30 de setiembre 1922*, AGHC, *fondos historícos*, Vol. 881a.

[5] *Quarta Asamblea de la Sociedad de las Naciones, Ginebra, 3–29 septiembre de 1923, Memoria de la delegación de Chile*, AGHC, *fondos historícos*, Vol. 981c.

meeting in which the Latin American delegates could reach an agreement and organize the defense of common interests. The officials of the Bureau of Latin America, with the authorization of the General Secretary, studied Guerrero's suggestion and probed into other delegates' opinions. Most of those pooled declared themselves in favor of the formalization of a practice that had already earned its spurs, but some of them, such as the Chilean Agustín Edwards, the Uruguayan Benjamín Fernández y Medina, or the Colombian Francisco José Urrutia, still feared that such a step could encourage the framing of a regional bloc that would be counterproductive for the work of the Assembly and above all for the defense of national interests. Faced with a lack of unanimity, the Secretariat dropped the idea.[6] As it may be seen, the idea of a limited coordinated action, mainly for electoral purpose, was approved, but there still remained a strong resistance against the possibility of a common political action resulting from the constitution of a political block among the Latin American delegations.

3.3. ELECTIONS AND DEFENSE OF JURIDICAL PRINCIPLES

Even so, the private meetings kept on. They allowed an efficient action in order to improve the representation of Latin American states in the Council. So the proportion of non-permanent seats reserved for Latin American members increased from one quarter in 1920 (one out of four seats) to one third in 1922 (first two out of six and then three out of nine seats in 1926). As early as 1922, the Latin American delegations, during a private meeting, appointed the candidate they presented to the Assembly for one of the reserved non-permanent seats.[7] The Assembly then limited itself to endorse

---

[6] Correspondence from November 1923 to March 1924, League of Nations Archives (LONA), R 1600, 40/32369/32369.

[7] *Memoria de la delegación de Chile, tercera Asamblea de la Sociedad de las Naciones, Ginebra, 4–30 de setiembre* [sic] *1922*, AGHC, *fondos historícos*, Vol. 881a.

this pre-selection. The Latin American countries therefore constituted a distinct group, recognized as such by the rest of the delegations (Fischer, 2001, pp. 254–297).

The defense of juridical principles potentially affecting Latin American interests was also a reason for a coordinated action, as the Corfu incident would demonstrate. After the assassination of an Italian general in Greek territory in August 1923, Benito Mussolini decided on the bombing and the occupation of Corfu, while claiming a heavy allowance to Greece. This country denounced the Italian aggression to the Council, which let the Conference of the Ambassadors deal with the issue (Barros, 1965). But from this political affair emerged a juridical debate that was considered dangerous by the Latin American delegates. Indeed, the Italian representatives deemed that the country was responsible for all political crimes committed on its territory. According to the Italian position, Greece had to pay. Some members of the Council seemed to approve such a doctrine, but the Latin Americans reckoned it was contrary to International Law and it violated the sovereignty of the states. During a private meeting, they put the Uruguayan Alberto Guani and the Brazilian Afranio de Mello Franco in charge of speaking against the Italian position to the Council, where both were representing their countries. The Colombian representative Francisco Urrutia, supported by the Venezuelan and Salvadorian delegates, intervened in the Assembly. As far as the Chilean Alejandro Álvarez was concerned, he redacted a memorandum addressed to the Council and to the Conference of the Ambassadors.[8] The mobilization and the combined action of the Latin American delegates contributed to the appointment by the Council of a committee of jurists in charge of settling the juridical argument. Its final verdict was that a country is not responsible for political crimes committed on its territory (Álvarez, 1924, p. 33; Walters, 1971, pp. 255–257). The juridical principle defended by the Latin Americans was, therefore, upheld.

[8] *Quarta Asamblea de la Sociedad de las Naciones, Ginebra, 3–29 de septiembre de 1923, Memoria de la delegación de Chile,* AGHC, *fondos historícos,* Vol. 981c.

3.4. LOOKING FOR MORE COOPERATION

Despite these successes, some delegates, such as the Colombian Francisco Urrutia and the Venezuelan César Zumeta, complained of lack of unity among the Latin American delegations and of their sole focus on electoral matters (República de Colombia, 1925, p. 151; Perez-Guerrero, 1936, pp. 58–59).[9] They spoke in favor of a better use of the coincidence in Geneva of numerous Latin American delegations in order to improve the defense of common interests. In 1925, the Assembly convoked an economical and financial conference. Pointing out the differences between European and Latin American states in economical matters, the Chilean delegates Eliodoro Yáñez, Emilio Bello Codesido, and Enrique Villegas put to their government that they propose an exchange of views with their Latin American counterparts in order to identify their common preoccupations and set up a coordinated action.[10] This proposition was not followed by any practical move from the Chilean government and the delegates repeated their suggestion the next year without success.[11]

Three years later, their fellow countryman Jorge Valdés Mendeville renewed the idea but in a much more ambitious way. He estimated that Latin American nations would receive greater benefits if the delegations were duly instructed by their governments to work on a common basis, not only on matters dealt with by the League, but also on any questions related to the American continent. He based his proposal on the following observation:

> It must be taken into consideration that not a single city or body in the world gives the opportunity for political, juridical, social, and economical delegations from at least 12 countries of our continent

---

[9] Gilson G. Blake (US Consul in Geneva) to the Secretary of State, 7 November 1929, *National Archives and Records Administration*, College Park MD, RG 59, Decimal file 500.C001/583–1/2.

[10] Report of the Chilean delegation on the sixth session of the Assembly, 1925, AGHC, *fondos historícos*, Vol. 981c.

[11] Report of the Chilean delegation on the extraordinary session of the Assembly, 1926, AGHC, *fondos historícos*, Vol. 1075a.

> to meet with the same frequency as in Geneva. While American international conferences bring us together only sporadically, in Geneva we count on the certainty of periodical contact.[12]

Indeed, the pan-American conferences only took place every five years and, even then, under the supervision of the United States. By contrast, the LoN offered a place where Latin American diplomats could meet on a regular basis. Why not take advantage of this situation, then, and deal with continental issues? Thus Geneva and the League would become a kind of clearing house for Latin American diplomacy.

Again, the Chilean government did not show any sign of interest but the idea thrived among the Latin American delegates the next year during the 1929 session of the Assembly. This session was special as all the Latin American member states, with the noticeable exception of Argentina, were represented, which had not been the case for several years. The Peruvian, Bolivian, and Honduran delegations were making their comeback to the Assembly. Peru and Bolivia had not been represented since 1921 and changed their mind only once the Tacna and Arica issue had been resolved thanks to the mediation of the United States. As far as Honduras was concerned, it participated very irregularly in the League's meetings. At the instigation of the Chilean Enrique Villegas, the Latin American delegates decided to modify the nature of their private meetings. Their main purpose would no longer be the resolution of electoral matters but the discussion of any continental question of social, political, or, above all, economical order. The delegations should try to conduct a coherent and common action inside the League, also taking into consideration the interests of the absent Latin American states. In short, the idea was to set up Latin American diplomacy. Furthermore, added the Chilean, "The situation of sixteen or seventeen American delegations in the LoN, by acting together, would have an extraordinary strength in world debates".[13] The delegates welcomed these proposals with

---

[12] Report of the Chilean delegation on the work of the League of Nations in 1928, AGHC, *fondos historícos*, Vol. 1161a.

[13] Report of the Chilean delegation on the work of the League of Nations in 1929, AGHC, *fondos historícos*, Vol. 1161a.

great enthusiasm and decided to write them down and forward them to their governments.[14]

The idea of a Latin American political block, dismissed in 1923, seemed suddenly to win general approval. But if the delegates' reactions were positive, the opinion in the Ministries of Foreign Affairs was very different. The Latin American governments coolly received the initiative of their delegates and just filed it. For instance, Santiago was totally opposed to it although the first impulse had come from the Chilean delegation. The Minister of Foreign Affairs, Manuel Barros Castañón, thought that the continental issues had to be tackled in meetings convened for that purpose and with the presence of all the American states. Therefore, the League was not an appropriate place. He approved the idea of cooperation, solidarity, and fruitful discussions between delegations, but rejected the principle of sanctioning this practice by a formal agreement between governments that would necessarily restrain the freedom of action of sovereign states. Neither did he deem it advisable to constitute, inside the LoN, a kind of American League of Nations enjoying its own statute.[15] In Montevideo, the Uruguayan government preferred to give priority to pan-American bodies,[16] while in Lima, Augusto Leguía's regime, inclined not to upset Washington at any price, wished first to study the consequences of such a proposal and then obtain the approbation of the United States.[17]

In spite of its failure, this proposed agreement illustrates the awareness of the Latin American delegates that they belong to a distinct community of nations and that they need to work together for the sake of the Latin American "family".

---

[14] Enrique Villegas (President of the Chilean delegation to the LoN) to the Chilean Minister of Foreign Affairs, 27 October 1929, AGHC, *fondos historícos*, Vol. 1205.

[15] Manuel Barros Castañón to Enrique Villegas, 20 December 1929, AGHC, *fondos historícos*, Vol. 1205a.

[16] Instructions to the Uruguayan delegation to the 11th session of the Assembly, 1930, *Archivo histórico diplomático*, Uruguay, section Sociedad de las Naciones, box 1, file 1270.

[17] Peruvian Minister of Foreign Affairs to the Peruvian delegation to the LoN, 14 September 1929, ACME, telegrams and cables, *libro copiador* n° 99 "Legaciones, varios, 1929".

3.5. FREEDOM OF ACTION AND *ESPRIT DE CORPS*

Various factors explain that the delegates felt the need to take, and were given permission for taking, such initiatives. As Villegas had pointed out, the 1929 agreement aimed above all to get more precise instructions from the governments about matters dealt with by the League that presented a continental interest to assert.[18] Indeed, most of the Latin American delegations participated in the works of the League without being duly instructed by their governments on the very diverse and specialized issues tackled, which were largely out of the area of competence of these diplomats. While the European governments appointed numerous technical experts and advisers to assist their representatives, Latin American capitals usually limited themselves to sending a few diplomats recruited among their European legations. Financial and also bureaucratic and administrative reasons are responsible for the lack of preparation of the Latin American delegations (Vivas Gallardo, 1981, p. 10; Rhenan Segura, 1993, pp. 18, 127–128). This situation explains the great frustration they felt[19] (República de Panamá, 1923, pp. 156–164; República de Colombia, 1935, pp. 429; Garay, 1934, p. iv) and their wish to collaborate, but also the broad room for maneuver they enjoyed thanks to the lack of instructions.

Another explanatory element is the constitution of what may be called an *esprit de corps* shared by the Latin American delegates. In the first place should be mentioned their common language, religion, social origins, and juridical and literary culture. The delegates also shared several places of sociability. Most of them resided in the same European capitals, for instance Paris, Rome, London, or Berlin, and met at diplomatic dinners and cultural or literary events. But it was

[18] Report of the Chilean delegation on the work of the League of Nations in 1929, AGHC, *fondos historícos*, Vol. 1161a.

[19] Report of the Chilean delegation on the 13th session of the Assembly, 1932, AGHC, *fondos historícos*, Vol. 1161a; Raúl Amador to Cristobal Rodríguez, 31 December =1925, LONA, S 499, file 4.

above all in Geneva and in the several meetings of the League, sessions of the Council, or of the Assembly, technical commissions or conferences, that the personal links were created as many delegates were appointed by their governments for several years. The private meetings, usually held in the office of the officials of the Secretariat's Bureau of Latin America, also contributed to shape an *esprit de corps* as did the several dinners they organized every year during the Assembly: one offered by the Chilean delegations on the occasion of the national day, 18 September; another organized by the Latin American delegations in honour of the Latin American member elected to the council; or this offered by the Spanish delegation for the sake of Hispanity.

Moreover, the *esprit de corps* was reinforced by the conscience of a common mission: by an impartial attitude, a sincere collaboration to the appeasement of European politics, and by an effort of "regeneration of the international order". According to Latin American delegates, "historical traditions and community of race", but also the adoption of conciliation and arbitration as a means of peaceful resolution of conflicts, had allowed Latin America to live in harmony without secular hatred. As a result, they believed they were invested of the mission to spread around Europe their peace gospel, particularly prevalent on the American continent within the pan-American conferences (República de Colombia, 1924, pp. 101–103; Société des Nations, 1925, p. 190; Société des Nations, 1926a, p. 29; Société des Nations, 1927, p. 100).

The final element strengthening the *esprit de corps* was the reference to a common heritage, that of Bolívar and the 1826 Panamá Congress. As early as the 1919 Paris Peace Conference (US State Department, 1919, p. 303), then during the first session of the Assembly in 1920 (Société des Nations, 1920, p. 166) and again on several occasions between 1926 and 1931 (Société des Nations, 1926b, p. 43; Société des Nations, 1927, pp. 49–52; Société des Nations, 1928, p. 1642; League of Nations, 1930, p. 198; Société des Nations, 1931, pp. 82–83), Latin American delegates evoked in their statements Bolívar, his project of Union, or the Panamá Congress. Most of the time, they pointed out how precursory Bolívar had been when he suggested the setting up of an international body like the LoN and insisted on the American (continental) origin of the idea, finally achieved by president Woodrow Wilson.

It is probably during the 1930 session of the Assembly that Bolívar's spectre hung most insistently over the League: on the commemoration of the centenary of his death. The delegates from the countries liberated by Bolívar grasped the opportunity to invite the Assembly to pay tribute to him. The Colombian Urrutia even managed to make the Assembly vote on a resolution in which it expressed, "its gratitude and admiration for the memory of Bolivar [sic] [···] who, by his initiatives and efforts to ensure the reign of justice and peace between peoples, was a precursor of the League of Nations" (League of Nations, 1930, p. 73). At that moment, delegates from the five Bolivarian republics represented at the Assembly — Bolivia, Colombia, Panamá, Peru, and Venezuela — revealed their intention to cast a bronze plaque reproducing an extract of the letter from Jamaica and destined for the future *Palais des Nations* whose construction had just begun.

Thus, the Latin American delegates, or at least those coming from the Bolivarian nations, stood out as the depositories and protectors of Bolívar's legacy. By putting forward Bolívar as a tutelary figure for the League, they reinforced the self-assigned American continent's role of leader in the promotion of international peace and justice, allowing a Latin American identity to take shape in Geneva in front of the European delegations mired in the impossible settlement of peace in Europe.

3.6. CONCLUSION

In conclusion, by their own sociability, by the conscience of a common mission, and by the worship of Simón Bolívar, the Latin American delegations established a relationship of alterity with the rest of the delegations. This, added to the lack of instructions from their governments and their inability in terms of means and competence to follow all the activities of the League, drove them to study the possibilities of an efficient collaboration in order to defend common interests and to institutionalize this collaboration at governmental level. The ambitious 1929 project also aimed to convert the League into the principal place for discussion of any continental affairs, far away from the influence of the United States. Links of solidarity and unity might thus be created. However, even if they showed their ability to defend some juridical principles and to obtain a larger representation of the continent in the Council, they failed to convince their government to adopt their proposal for a coordinated action. The reason for that failure can be found in the contradiction between their aspiration to present a Latin American united front in the management of several economical, financial, social, or technical issues and the traditional antagonisms of inter-American politics. If there was one moment when governments gave them very precise instructions, it was exactly when national political interests were involved, usually in contradiction to those of neighboring nations. The failure of the Latin American delegates also bore witness on the one hand to their isolation and to the distance that stood between them and the realities of their countries, but, perhaps above all, on the other hand to the lukewarm interest of their respective governments in the activities of the League of Nations.

BIBLIOGRAPHY

Álvarez, A. (1924). *La cinquième Conférence panaméricaine et la Société des Nations*, Alcan, Paris.

Barros, J. (1965). *The Corfu incident of 1923: Mussolini and the League of Nations*, Princeton University Press, Princeton.

Collier, S. (1983). Nationality, nationalism, and supranationalism in the writings of Simón Bolívar, *The Hispanic American Historical Review*, 63(1), pp. 37–64.

Collier, S. (2008). 'Simón Bolívar as Political Thinker', in Buschnell, D. and Langley L. D. (eds), *Simón Bolívar, Essays on the Life and Legacy of the Liberator*, Rowman Littlefield, Lanham, pp. 13–34.

Fischer, T. (2001). *Lateinamerika im Völkerbund: Schwache Staaten und kollektive Sicherheit, 1920–1936*, unpublished *habilitation* dissertation, University of Bern.

Garay, N. (1934). *Año y medio en Ginebra*, Impr. Nacional, Panamá.

League of Nations (1930). Records of the eleventh ordinary session of the Assembly, plenary meetings, text of the debates, *League of Nations Official Journal*, special supplement 84.

Lievano Aguirre, I. (1968). El congreso de Panamá: Bolivarismo y monroismo, *Desarrollo Económico*, 8(30), pp. 193–241.

Lynch, J. (2006). *Simón Bolívar: A Life*, Yale University Press, New Haven & London.

Perez-Guerrero, M. (1936). *Les relations des états de l'Amérique latine avec la Société des Nations*, A. Pedone, Paris.

República de Colombia (1924). *Informe del Ministro de Relaciones Exteriores al Congreso de 1924*, Imp. de La Luz, Bogotá.

República de Colombia (1925). *Informe del Ministro de Relaciones Exteriores al Congreso de 1925*, Imp. de La Luz, Bogotá.

República de Colombia (1935). *Memoria del Ministro de Relaciones Exteriores al Congreso de 1935*, Imp. Nacional, Bogotá.

República de Ecuador (1935). *Informe que el Sr. Ministro de Relaciones Exteriores presenta a la Nación, Junio de 1934–Julio de 1935*, Talleres tipográficos nacionales, Quito.

República de Panamá (1923). *Memoria que presenta el Secretario de Relaciones Exteriores a la Asamblea Nacional Legislativa en sus sesiones ordinarias de 1922*, Imp. Nacional, Panamá, tome III.

Rhenan Segura, J. (1993). *Sociedad de las Naciones y Política Centroamericana (1919–1939)*, Euroamericana de Ediciones, San José (Costa Rica).

Salcedo-Bastardo, J. L. (1977). *Bolivar: A Continent and its Destiny*, Richmond Publishing Co., Richmond.

Salcedo-Bastardo, J. L. (1981). *Visión y revisión de Bolívar*, Monte Ávila Ed., Caracas.

Société des Nations (1920). Actes de la première Assemblée, séances *plénières*, Genève.

Société des Nations (1924). Actes de la cinquième Assemblée, séances plénières, compte rendu des débats, *Journal Officiel de la Société des Nations*, supplément spécial 23.

Société des Nations (1925). Trente-deuxième session du Conseil, *Journal Officiel de la Société des Nations*, février, pp. 120–130.

Société des Nations (1926a). Actes de la session extraordinaire de l'Assemblée, séances plénières et séances des commissions, *Journal Officiel de la Société des Nations*, supplément spécial 42.

Société des Nations (1926b). Actes de la septième session ordinaire de l'Assemblée, séances plénières, compte rendu des débats, *Journal Officiel de la Société des Nations*, supplément spécial 44.

Société des Nations (1927). Actes de la huitième session ordinaire de l'Assemblée, séances plénières, compte rendu des débats, *Journal Officiel de la Société des Nations*, supplément spécial 54.

Société des Nations (1928). Cinquante-deuxième session du Conseil, *Journal Officiel de la Société des Nations*, octobre, pp. 1640–1650.

Société des Nations (1931). Actes de la douzième session ordinaire de l'Assemblée, séances plénières, compte rendu des débats, *Journal Officiel de la Société des Nations*, supplément spécial 93.

US State Department (1919). *Papers Relating to the Foreign Relations of the United States, The Paris Peace Conference, 1919*, Vol. III, US Government Printing Office, Washington, DC.

Vivas Gallardo, F. (1981). *Venezuela en la Sociedad de las Naciones: 1920–1939. Descripción y análisis de una actuación diplomática*, Universidad central de Venezuela, Caracas.

Walters, F. P. (1971). *Historia de la Sociedad de Naciones*, Editorial Tecnos, Madrid.

Wehrli, Y. (2009). Sean Lester, Ireland, and Latin America in the League of Nations, 1929–1946, *Irish Migration Studies in Latin America*, 7(1), pp. 39–44.

Chapter

4

Shifting Position to the Global South: Latin America's Initiatives in the Early Years at the United Nations

Corinne A. Pernet

4.1. INTRODUCTION

Around the world, the end of the Second World War raised hopes for the rise of a postwar order that would foster international justice and peace. Though not affected by military action, Latin America was no exception to this trend. This chapter will emphasize the contingencies of geopolitical positioning and interrogate the connotations of the concept of "Latin America" in the early postwar years, as it examines how Latin American diplomats constructed the region in the changing geopolitical context of that period. The United Nations, a major element of the postwar order, provided an important arena for such attempts at self-articulation. What is presented here is neither an exhaustive nor a definite account, but a first foray into what an examination of Latin American policy at the UN beyond the strictly political has to offer. I argue for a discernible shift from hopeful aspiration to be seated "at the banquet of civilization", as the Mexican diplomat and intellectual Alfonso Reyes put it (Reyes, 1936) to a self-identification with the Global South, albeit with Latin America in a leading role. Of course, "Global South" is a term that I use retrospectively, as the parlance at the time was "underdeveloped countries" or "economically underdeveloped countries".

Historians have frequently described the postwar years as an era of hemispheric solidarity, during which short-lived democratic aspirations soon gave way to repressive regimes. The Rio Treaty (Inter-American Treaty of Reciprocal Assistance, 1947) reaffirmed military solidarity and the reorganization of the Pan-American Union into the Organization of the American States implied that Latin America was firmly placed in the US orbit and accepted Cold War politics (Gilderhus, 2000; Rock, 1994). However, under the surface of a US-led front against international communism, a number of Latin American countries attempted to chart their own course (Cornelius, 1961). The UN was one important venue for such independent ventures, especially in matters other than security policy. Positioning Latin America as part of the Global South meant emphasizing the differences with the United States and with Europe and speaking for the less powerful countries. Latin American leaders called on the UN for expanded protection through human rights regimes. They also garnered the support of the UN to examine their economic situations, established the necessary institutions, and gained access to resources otherwise not available to them. More importantly, they questioned the validity of the economic and cultural models that the United States and Europe had tended to impose abroad. This important aspect of Latin American strategies at the UN has long been neglected. Only recently, historians such as Vijay Pradesh have recognized the openings that these efforts have offered for Asian and African countries and the precedents they set for projects of the "Third World" a number of years later. More research on South–South connections is obviously needed (Pradesh, 2007, 2008).

After a short sketch of the war period, I will highlight the early debates at the UN that illustrate this new alignment. First, I will discuss the Latin influence on the Universal Declaration of Human Rights, which is testimony for the aspirations and world views of Latin American UN delegates. Second, I will examine the establishment of the Economic Commission on Latin America and the positioning — not only implied, but explicit — of Latin America in the "underdeveloped" world. Though authors like Walter Mignolo (Mignolo 2005) attribute the rise of the notion of a unified "Latin" America to European imperial projects, I see a different mechanism at work here. Pursuing their own political and economic aims, Latin American diplomats contributed to the discursive as well as institutional construction of the "developing world" in an international order that ideally should be responsive to its social and economic needs.

4.2. THE WORLD'S GOOD NEIGHBOR, NOT LATIN AMERICA'S

During the early 1940s, Latin American diplomats were hopeful that the postwar international order might signify a new start and expectantly attended the wartime conferences that established the UN's Relief and Rehabilitation Administration, the Food and Agriculture Organization, or the International Bank for Reconstruction and Development (Belaúnde, 1966; Castañeda, 1958; Chile antes las Naciones Unidas, 1956). They avidly participated in the Inter-American Juridical Committee in Rio de Janeiro, which in 1942 passed recommendations for a future international organization. The report[1] reflected long-standing Latin American preoccupations: It

[1] The report was written by the following members: Brazilian lawyer and diplomat Afrânio de Melo Franco (1870–1943), who had led several delegations to the League of Nations in the 1920s and served as Foreign Minister from 1930–1934; Félix Nieto del Río (1888–1954), a lawyer and career diplomat and Chile's Ambassador to Brazil; the Mexican Pablo Campos Ortíz (1899–1963), a professor of international law before joining the diplomatic service with stations in Madrid, The Hague, Rio de Janeiro, and Washington; the young lawyer Carlos Eduardo Stolk who served as Venezuela's envoy to the UN until 1950, and Charles G. Fenwick (1880–1973), a legal scholar and university professor who was the sole US representative on the team.

called for the repudiation of the use of force and paired an unqualified obligation to arbitration with strong international organizations which had means and instruments to foster economic and social justice while suppressing political and economic imperialism (Preliminary Recommendation, 1943). These recommendations served as a blueprint to the goals that the Latin American delegates were going to pursue at the UN.

Their agenda might have gained in urgency as it became clear over the years that the importance of Latin America for the United States would wane once the war ended. Evidence for this was that the US government excluded Latin American representatives from the Dumbarton Oaks meetings and barely consulted them beforehand. Latin American political circles strongly resented the secrecy surrounding the Dumbarton Oaks proposals. When the United States finally revealed the plans for the new UN, the reactions from Latin America were so critical that the State Department unenthusiastically accepted to meet for an Inter-American Conference on Problems of War and Peace in Mexico City in early 1945 to prevent an éclat at the San Francisco Conference. Opinion makers and political leaders were rather pessimistic about the meeting, which they thought would lead to clashes between the United States and its southern neighbors (Cosío Villegas, 1945). Indeed, the Chapultepec Conference, as it is commonly called, revealed a deep gap between the position of the United States and the aspirations of the Latin Americans.

Latin American diplomats argued that the Dumbarton Oaks plans for a postwar UN accorded too much power to the Big Four (USA, UK, USSR, and China). The delegations from Latin America worked together to draft amendments to the proposed charter. These included the strengthening of the General Assembly vis-à-vis the Security Council, a claim to "adequate representation" of Latin America on the Security Council, an extension of the powers of an International Tribunal as well as provisions for a new agency of intellectual cooperation (Report of the Delegation of the United States, 1946, p. 103). Secretary of State Edward Stettinius, for one, increasingly worried that the "Latin American bloc" would formulate policies unfavorable to the interests of the United States.

He complained that he was having "one hell of a time here holding this Latin American situation together" (Campbell and Herring, 1975, p. 280). Indeed, the Latin American delegations at Chapultepec pushed through a resolution that summarized their critiques of the Dumbarton Oaks proposals and announced that they would pursue them, as representatives of sovereign states, at the San Francisco Conference (Conferencias Internacionales Americanas, 1945–1954). Also with regards to the Pan-American Union, the Latin Americans objected to the custom that the Director General was always an American, elected to an indefinite term. The conference decided to limit terms to 10 years and prohibited succession by a person of the same nationality, which diminished the Americans' dominance (Manger, 1961).

Apart from concerns about the postwar political order, economic questions were pressing at the Chapultepec conference. The Mexican Foreign Secretary Ezequiel Padilla expected "practical resolutions, resolutions that relieve the misery, the helplessness of a great section of our masses, that satisfy the desire for permanent security and for a peace based on justice". Raising the standard of living in Latin America took center stage. Latin American governments expected that the United States would support increased industrial investments in Latin America and would give access to US markets for manufactured goods, as they were not willing to cement their wartime position as the provider of raw materials. As Padilla put it, Latin America wanted "to do more than produce raw materials and live in a state of semi-colonialism" (FRUS, 1945, pp. 122–125). Chile and Mexico presented detailed plans for industrialization, Peru suggested a new Pan-American Bank of Reconstruction and Development, and Brazil proposed that "the richer American nations recognize their 'duty' to promote the development of poorer nations". The United States did not appreciate such proposals, and countered with a resolution that condemned "economic nationalism". Instead, the Americans "appeared to regard the economic problems of the regions as essentially internal" (Fitzgerald, 1994, 93). The Conference did issue an Economic Charter that promised an "equitable coordination of all interests" to serve as a "basis for the sound economic development of the Americas", but the declaration was little more than a smoke screen hiding the bitter conflict about the direction of economic policy (Pan-American Union, 1945, pp. 39–40, p. 84; Castañeda, 1958, p. 170). Specific talks on thorny questions such as tariffs were put off again and again, as was the next Inter-American Conference planned for October 1945, which finally took place in 1947. As one State Department official put it: "The United States no longer desperately needs Latin America" (Rabe, 1978, p. 284).

The experience of the last war years and, in particular, the slow death of the Rooseveltian Good Neighbor policy, encouraged Latin American diplomats to position themselves as leaders of the Global South. This involved repeated attempts to make the international system more equitable by empowering the "small nations" at the UN. At the San Francisco Conference, the Latin American delegations proposed many changes to the Dumbarton Oaks proposals: to include a declaration of human rights in the charter, to revise the organization of the security council, to give more weight to the UN Assembly, and to strengthen the Economic and Social Council. While substantial reforms of the Security Council were unfeasible, Latin American countries were instrumental in vesting the UN with a new field of action that went far beyond security concerns to include broadly defined human rights with economic and cultural dimensions. Moreover, they attempted to harness the UN as a means to improve economic conditions in Latin America.

4.3. THE HUMAN RIGHTS TRADITIONS OF LATIN AMERICA AT THE UNITED NATIONS

Critics as well as proponents of the Universal Declaration of Human Rights (UDHR) tend to present it as a straightforward document of classic Western political and civil liberties, its immediate precursors being Roosevelt's four freedoms and the Atlantic Charter. Moreover, the UDHR is frequently pegged as the result of the struggle between Eleanor Roosevelt and a succession of Soviet delegates and viewed as an instrument of US hegemony (Normand and Zaidi, 2008; Morsink, 2000; Evans, 1996). Recent critics of the UDHR seem to be oblivious to the circumstances of its drafting and approval. Many other protagonists, most notably Carlos Romulo from the Philippines, Peng-Chun Chang from China, Charles Malik from Lebanon, and John Humphrey from Canada played key roles. Moreover, the inputs from the Global South had a deep impact on the UDHR. The Latin American delegates to the General Assembly as well as the Latin American members of the UN Commission on Human Rights — especially the Chilean lawyer Hernán Santa Cruz Barceló — successfully fought for the inclusion of social, economic, and cultural rights. To highlight this contribution does not imply a negation of Latin American realities, which were, by all accounts, far from the ideals formulated at the UN. Nor does it detract from the fact that the declaration was neither legally binding nor sustained by an enforcing mechanism. Nonetheless, the anchoring of economic, social, and cultural rights in the UDHR established an ethical standard and opened avenues for future struggles for social justice (Normand and Zaidi, 2008, p. 189).

The active pursuit of economic, social, and cultural human rights by the Latin American delegates had formal regional antecedents. The 1938 Inter-American Conference at Lima had already adopted a resolution that condemned discrimination on racial and religious grounds, and another that called for the expansion of women's rights. Moreover, the Conference also issued a "Declaration in Defense of Human Rights" that made recourse to international law as well as "human sentiments" to call for the protection of basic rights in the case of war (Conferencias Internacionales Americanas, 1938, pp. 468–471). The importance accorded to human rights was reaffirmed at the Chapultepec Conference in early 1945. As the Dumbarton Oaks proposal did not include much in the way of human rights, the Latin American delegates insisted on commissioning a draft for an American Declaration of the Rights and Duties of Man which they wanted to discuss at the San Francisco Conference for inclusion in the UN Charter.

At the San Francisco Conference, the Panamanian delegate Ricardo J. Alfaro submitted a draft declaration of human rights and proposed to have it inserted into the UN Charter, a move that was strongly supported by Cuba, Chile, and Mexico. The Chilean delegation submitted its own proposal, "On human rights and duties", which had been drafted by the Inter-American Juridical Committee.[2] The representatives of Uruguay, Brazil, Mexico, the Dominican Republic, Cuba, Venezuela, but also of Egypt as well as India, demanded forcefully that a significant commitment to human rights be placed prominently in the Charter. These proposals received a decidedly cold reception by both the United States and the United Kingdom, but continued pressure from the Latin American coalition and allies such as General Carlos Romulo from the Philippines, as well as from civil and labor organizations (Korey, 2001) eventually led to the inclusion of several human rights provisions in the UN Charter. The Charter declared that a major purpose of the UN was to ensure fundamental freedoms, "for all, without distinctions as to race, sex, language, or religion", and that member states were obliged to fulfill these provisions (Articles 55 and 56 of the UN Charter). The Charter also established the Economic and Social Council (ECOSOC) to promote human rights as well. Indeed, ECOSOC established the Human Rights Commission in June 1946 with the mandate to draft an international bill of rights (Morsink, p. 14).

A number of Latin American drafts circulated when the Human Rights Commission (18 members, among them delegates from Chile, Panamá, and Uruguay) convened in January 1947. The United Kingdom, too, submitted a draft, which ignored anything beyond civil and political rights, and had "little if any influence on the final outcome" (Humphrey, 1983, p. 1412; Glendon, 2001). After deciding the form of the document, the Canadian John Humphrey, the first director of the Human Rights Division of the UN secretariat, was appointed to write a preliminary proposal that would be discussed by a drafting committee of eight (Roosevelt, Chang, Malik, Cassin, Wilson, Koretsky, Santa Cruz). Humphrey relied heavily on

[2] The draft was elaborated at the American Law Institute and carried the stamp of the eminent Chilean jurist Alejandro Álvarez. It included the right to education, health care, social security, and work. Shortly afterwards, Álvarez was appointed to the International Court of Justice.

the draft sponsored by Panamá, which he considered "the best of the texts" and added economic, social, and cultural rights from the Chilean draft. These drafts came closest to his own ideal "to combine humanitarian liberalism with social democracy" (Humphrey, 1983, p. 415; Yearbook on Human Rights, 1949).

When the small drafting committee met to discuss Humphrey's work, the articles concerning economic, social, and cultural rights caused "considerable opposition" (Humphrey, 1983, p. 412). The final inclusion of articles on a person's right to "just and favorable remuneration, ensuring for himself and his family an existence worthy of human dignity, and supplemented, if necessary, by other means of social protection" (Article 23), or the "right to a standard of living adequate for the health and well-being of himself and of his family, including food, clothing, housing, and medical care and necessary social services, and the right to security in the event of unemployment, sickness, disability, widowhood, old age, or other lack of livelihood in circumstances beyond his control" (Article 25) were the results of tough negotiations. Opponents preferred to state only "broad principles" in the Declaration, while Santa Cruz maintained that these rights needed to be included in such detail to give any real meaning to the Declaration. Santa Cruz and Humphrey managed to retain these rights in the draft that was presented to the General Assembly in 1948 (Morsink, 2000, p. 131).

By April 1948, the Organization of American States had approved the American Declaration of the Rights and Duties of Man, the outcome of the Chapultepec conference. This was the first international human rights instrument and it contained, apart from political and civil rights, the right to the preservation of health and well-being "through sanitary and social measures relating to food, clothing, housing, and medical care, to the extent permitted by public and community resources", the right to free primary education as well as "equal opportunity" in education, a "right to work and to fair remuneration" as well as social security provisions for old age, disability, and unemployment. Ten articles outlined the duties, which included family duties, duties toward the community (education, work), and toward the state (obey the law, pay taxes, vote, serve the community and the nation). The preamble to the OAS Declaration made clear that the responsibility for human rights lay not only with the individual states, but also with the international community: "The international protection of the rights of man should be the principal guide of an evolving American law".

At the UN General Assembly of 1948, the Latin American delegates who had not been involved in the Human Rights Commission were keen on presenting the OAS declaration, which they deemed superior. Santa Cruz worked hard to prevent his Latin American colleagues from demanding a point by point comparison between the Declaration of Bogotá and the Draft UN Declaration (Santa Cruz, 1984, p. 184). But to the dismay of the Human Rights Commission members, the Third Committee, which considered the draft, reopened the discussion on each and every article, which delayed the vote for the declaration considerably while relations between the West and the Soviet bloc were rapidly deteriorating. As expected, the articles on economic, social, and cultural rights were controversial. Delegates like the Mexican Pablo Campo Ortíz and the Cuban Guy Pérez Cisneros, both co-authors of the OAS declaration, or the Uruguayan Jiménez de Arechaga even attempted to amplify them, at times with success (Normand and Zaidi, 2008, p. 190–192). John Humphrey wrote for the public that in the final debates, "it seemed at times that the chief protagonists in the conference room were the Roman Catholics and the communists, with the latter a poor second". In his private diary, he wished Pérez Cisneros to hell for jeopardizing the declaration through his insistence (Glendon, 2003, p. 37).

These goals of the UDHR were not only entrusted to the respective national governments of UN members, but also made reference to the international order: Article 28 gave a broad scope of action to the UN, as it declared that, "Everyone is entitled to a social and international order in which the rights and freedoms set forth in this Declaration can be fully realized". Clearly written for the "small countries", for the underdeveloped, this article made the Declaration more palatable for the Global South. Anchoring economic and social rights in the Declaration of Human Rights and entrusting their vigilance to the international body was one more attempt to protect the interests of the geopolitically disfavored in the new postwar order. Just before the final vote on the declaration in the General Assembly on 10 December 1948, Hernán Santa Cruz pointed to Articles 3, 22, and 28, emphasizing the need "for an effective international cooperation so that people can turn their rights into reality" (Santa Cruz, 1984, p. 198).

But by the early 1950s, the effects of the Cold War had reached the UN. In the discussions about an instrument for implementing the Declaration, the so-called Human Rights Covenant, the support for internationally anchored economic and social rights, began to erode. In the United States, the last holdovers from the Roosevelt administration were marginalized and no Eleanor Roosevelt was there to sway the State Department regarding the "freedom from want". Though the General Assembly, on petition of seven delegations (among them Chile, Mexico, Peru, and Brazil) had, in 1949, decided that political, civil, economic and social rights should all be included in one covenant, two years later the Assembly reversed itself and opted for two pacts: one on political and civil rights only, the other on economic and social rights. At the 1951 General Assembly, Chile's representative, Ana Figueroa, a former school director, voiced her disappointment about the weakened covenant in a language that pointed to the deepening schism:

> We dare to ask: if the high standard of living in the industrialized countries is not dependent on a low standard of living in other countries, why do the former oppose the aspirations of the latter? If we think in terms of an international division of labor, we would say that the covenant should be divided in two because the liberty of the few is financed by the misery of many. (Quoted in Santa Cruz, 1984, pp. 214–215)

Figueroa put into plain words the divisions between North and South. Yet even within Latin America, the consensus to push economic and social rights even against the resistance of industrialized countries had faltered. Bolivia, Brazil, Uruguay, and the Dominican Republic, for instance, now sided with the United States in wishing to separate political from economic rights. Even the eminent Charles Malik had difficulties in moving the two covenants forward — they were finally accepted in the General Assembly 18 years after the Declaration, in 1966 (Normand and Zaidi, 2008, pp. 237–242).

Though commentators have frequently discussed these rights as the result of negotiations between the individualistic US and the collectivist Soviet Union, a strong Latin touch is evident, which was not necessarily socialist in its origins (as Morsink, 2000 states) but also stemmed from Catholic social thought (Carrozza, 2003). When the UDHR was voted on, Malik thanked Santa Cruz specifically because he had, "kept alive in our mind the great humane outlook of his Latin American world" (Malik, 2000, pp. 121). This chapter is not the place to discuss in detail the social struggles in which the UDHR and the covenants have served as instruments, but it's clear that the inclusion of social and economic rights has effects to this day.

4.4. THE CREATION OF CEPAL

Part and parcel of the relocation to the Global South was the recognition of the steep social inequalities in Latin American countries and the hope that international organizations such as the UN could contribute to improving living conditions for the broad masses. In short, Latin American delegates and counselors at the UN were interested in "development". The notion of "development" has been highly controversial in the past 20 years, as it tends to isolate the causes of poverty to the periphery, thereby obscuring the role of (neo-) colonialism in creating these conditions (Sachs, 2007; Cullather, 2000; Escobar, 1994; Sachs, 2002). Its critics imply that leaders of the Third World were coerced into or seduced by developmentalism. However, in Latin America the search for economic progress had a long tradition and the call for development was a modernization of vocabulary that did not imply ignorance of geopolitical factors.

To help implement the economic and social rights he fought to include in the Declaration, Santa Cruz spearheaded another effort at the Economic and Social Council of the UN. In July 1947, he proposed the creation of an Economic Commission on Latin America.

ECOSOC had already instituted such commissions for the European and the Asian regions to coordinate postwar reconstruction. One month later, Santa Cruz was given a chance to make his case and he presented a stark picture of social conditions in the different countries in Latin America — a first at the UN. He highlighted the considerable raw material contributions of Latin America during the war and pointed to the dangers that the high postwar prices for capital goods posed to incipient industrialization. But there were also long-term, structural problems that necessitated intervention. The documentation elaborated for the creation of CEPAL insisted on a "maladjustment" that could only be solved in a regional or even a global context. Santa Cruz pleaded that the great powers were too focused on their own problems and on Europe, and misjudged Latin America as the fortunate region that had not suffered in the war (Santa Cruz, 1995, p. 25). Moreover, the UN charter gave the organization a mandate to improve the living conditions around the world, and for millions in Latin America, these had long been as dire as those in war-torn countries. Alluding to the UN stance on social rights, he commented: "Latin America had the right to demand that the United Nations assist it in the difficult task of raising the standard of living of its inhabitants". His colleagues from Cuba and Venezuela seconded his statement. Carlos d'Ascoli, a Venezuelan, argued that intervention of international bodies such as the UN was necessary to stabilize prices for raw materials, normalize trade, and contribute to diversification of Latin American economies (Santa Cruz, 1984, pp. 147–148).

The proposal faced the outright rejection by the Soviet Union, the United Kingdom, and Canada, while the United States stalled the discussion by insisting that the Pan-American Union pronounce itself on the matter first. But the proposition also had staunch supporters in ECOSOC: not only Peru, Venezuela, and Cuba put in strong words, but also Lebanon, India, China, and Norway favored the project. Finally, on 11 August, the 18 ECOSOC member nations agreed to appoint an ad hoc committee with representatives of Cuba, Chile, Peru, Venezuela, as well as France, China, Lebanon, the UK, and the US to draw up a recommendation on the matter. The Latin American delegates were given a chance to work out a draft resolution, which they presented to the committee in February 1948 (Yearbook of the United Nations, 1947–1948, p. 538).

The ad hoc committee met in October and January to write the first UN report on economic conditions in Latin America. The UN secretariat members David Weintraub, an American, and the Briton Harold Caustin fully agreed with the Latin Americans that the reliance on primary exports was the mark of a "semi-colonial economy" (Toye and Toye, 2004, p. 140). The Cuban representative quoted neo-colonialism as the cause of Latin America's economic problems. The report expanded on Santa Cruz's basic analysis, pointing out that coordination between countries was necessary to diversify the economies, industrialize and modernize agriculture, and foster commerce and capital accumulation in order to finally lift living standards in the region. The report tried to make the commission more palatable to an international audience by arguing that an economically stronger Latin America could help resolve the economic problems of other continents (Yearbook of the United Nations, 1947–48, p. 537).

The insistence on studying Latin American economic problems in relation to the world economy opened CEPAL's door to representatives from the United States, the United Kingdom, France, and the Netherlands. This move was hotly contested among the Latin Americans because it smacked of an acceptance of European colonialism. Apparently, the participation of those countries helped to attain the abstention, rather than the rejection, of the United States and the United Kingdom (Santa Cruz, 1984, pp. 149–150).

The last obstacle was an issue that the United States had raised: that CEPAL should not duplicate inter-American institutions. However, led by the Colombian Alberto Lleras Camargo, the Pan-American Union voiced no objection and explicitly recommended the creation of CEPAL. Thus, the Latin American–Middle Eastern–Indian coalition carried the proposal in the General Assembly. On 5 March 1948, the Economic and Social Council established the Economic Commission on Latin America (CEPAL), to be headquartered in Santiago de Chile. Just three days later, the Latin American delegates supported the creation of an analogous commission for the Middle

East. As CEPAL was established on a temporary basis for three years at first, the United States tried to undermine it by suggesting that it be merged into the structure of the Organization of American States and moved to Washington. Latin American diplomats as well as the CEPAL community resisted such maneuvers successfully; condemning attempts at US "sabotage" and arguing that they needed the UN umbrella and the location in Santiago to protect them from US pressures (FRUS, 1950, 2, pp. 683–686; Pollock *et al.*, 2001, p. 12).

In Santiago, CEPAL rapidly developed into a think tank for alternative economic models. The 1948 report had identified the problems of the agricultural, non-industrial economies with low living standards, but also called for better coordination within the Latin Americas, for complementarity rather than competition. These ideas were taken up by the Argentine economist Raúl Prebisch, who joined CEPAL in 1949. The commission developed its own critique of current theories of international trade. Prebisch pointed out repeatedly that the "intellectual independence" afforded by the institution, which was far from New York or Washington, was a great asset. Moreover, CEPAL became an institutional anchor for Latin Americans working together to turn the region "in the right direction" (Pollock *et al.*, 2001, p. 13; see also Devés Váldes, 2000). Rejecting the fiction of common economic interests with the United States that was underlying pan-Americanism and the postwar Organization of American States, CEPAL focused on terms of trade, import substitution and cooperation among Latin American countries as venues for economic development (Castañeda, 1958).

"Cepalismo" signified the eruption of a specifically periphery-based approach to economic problems as well as the creation of new school of Latin American economists (Devés Valdes, 2000b; Wood and Morales, 1965). The alternative visions that CEPAL elaborated were still visions of development. But they were clearly cognizant of the geopolitical power relations. Neither the Latin Americans nor the UN could change these relations considerably, but they did establish institutions that generated independent knowledge on the economies of Latin America.

4.5. CONCLUSION

Latin American countries have struggled hard, politically, economically, and culturally, to escape (neo-) colonialism and they have done so in different ways. At the conjuncture of the early postwar period, Latin American leaders reassessed the experience of pan-Americanism in the light of continued neglect by the United States and chose a different tack at the UN. In the early years of the UN, being Latin American meant being postcolonial, poor, and in alignment with the emerging "developing world" that demanded inclusion in the international political order as well as resources to overcome its problems. But Latin Americans did not simply accept "development" as "antipolitics" and were quite aware of geopolitical factors that constrained their options. They attempted to harness the UN and its human rights regime as an additional safeguard. Perhaps there was, as North American diplomats frequently pointed out, an element of "speechifying and solemn pronouncements, especially when accompanied by the glamour and spotlight of an international conclave", and certainly, diplomats also thought of their home audiences when talking about social and economic rights, and questions of development (Rabe, 1978, p. 293). Even so, human rights, economic policy, and development models were matters of concern and became the subject of public discussion. As these attempts did not bring success over the years, the critical attitudes multiplied. As this short chapter on human rights and the creation of CEPAL shows, the Latin Americans could not strike back at Empire, but they could — and did — use the UN to establish norms and institutions that would restrain its power.

BIBLIOGRAPHY

Belaúnde, V. A. (1966). *20 años de Naciones Unidas,* Ediciones Cultura Hispánica, Madrid.

Campbell T. C. and Herring, G. C. (eds) (1975). *The Diaries of Edward R. Stettinius, Jr., 1943–1946,* New Viewpoints, New York.

Carrozza, P. G. (2003). From Conquest to Constitutions: Retrieving a Latin American Tradition of the Idea of Human Rights, *Human Rights Quarterly,* 25, pp. 281–313.

Castañeda, J. (1958). *Mexico and the United Nations*. National Studies on International Organization, Carnegie Endowment for International Peace, New York.

Chile ante las Naciones Unidas (1956). Special issue of the *Anales de la Facultad de Derecho Tercera Época (Santiago, Chile)*, 3(5).

Conferencias Internacionales Americanas (1938). Publicaciones de la Dotación Carnegie para la Paz Internacional.

Conferencias Internacionales Americanas (1944). *Primer Suplemento 1938–1942*. Publicaciones de la Dotación Carnegie para la Paz Internacional.

Conferencias Interacionales Americanas (1954). *Segundo suplemento 1945–1954*, Publicaciones de la Dotación Carnegie para la Paz Internacional.

Cosío Villegas, D. (1945). La conferencia de Chapultepec, *Cuadernos Americanos*, May/June, pp. 19–45.

Cullather, N. (2000). Development? Its History, *Diplomatic History*, 24(4), pp. 641–653.

Devés Váldes, E. (2000a). La CEPAL: Red internacional, actor internacional, y promotora de la integración, *Sociologías*, 2(3), pp. 232–233.

Devés Váldes, E. (2000b). *El pensamiento latinoamericano en el Siglo XX: Entre la modernización y la identidad*, Biblos, Centro de Investigaciones Diego Barros Arana, Buenos Aires and Santiago de Chile.

Escobar, A. (1994). *Encountering Development: the Making and Unmaking of the Third World*. Princeton University Press, Princeton.

Evans, T. (1996). *US Hegemony and the Project of Universal Human Rights*, Macmillan, Basingstoke.

Fitzgerald, E. V. K (1994). 'ECLA and the Formation of Latin American Economic Doctrine', in Rock, D. (ed.), *Latin America in the 1940s: War and Postwar Transitions*, University of California Press, Berkeley, pp. 89–108.

Foreign Relations of the United States, 1945, 9.

Foreign Relations of the United States, 1950, 2.

Glendon, M. A. (2001). *A World Made New: Eleanor Roosevelt and the Universal Declaration of Human Rights*, Random House, New York and Toronto.

Glendon, M. A. (2003). The Forgotten Crucible: The Latin American Influence on the Universal Human Rights Idea, *Harvard Human Rights Journal*, 16, pp. 27–39.

Humphrey, J. P. (1983). The Memoirs of John P. Humphrey, the First Director of the United Nations Division of Human Rights, *Human Rights Quarterly*, 5(4), pp. 407–415.

Korey, W. (2001). *NGOs and the Universal Declaration of Human Rights: 'A Curious Grapevine'*, Palgrave Macmillan, Basingstoke and New York.

Malik, H. C. (ed.) (2000). *The Challenge of Human Rights: Charles Malik and the Universal Declaration*, Centre for Lebanese Studies, Oxford.

Manger, W. (1961). *Pan-America in Crisis: The Future of the OAS*, 4, Public Affairs Press, Washington, DC.

Mignolo, W. (2005). *The Idea of Latin America*, Blackwell, Oxford.

Morsink, J. (2000). *The Universal Declaration of Human Rights: Origins, Drafting, and Intent,* University of Pennsylvania Press, Philadelphia.

Normand, R. and Zaidi, S. (2008). *Human Rights at the UN: The Political History of Universal Justice,* Indiana University Press, Bloomington.

Pan-American Union (1945). *Inter-American Conference on Problems of War and Peace, Conference and Congress Series*, 47, Pan-American Union, Washington, DC.

Pollock, D. *et al.* (2001). Raúl Prebisch on ECLAC's achievements and deficiencies: An unpublished interview, *CEPAL Review*, 75, pp. 9–22.

Preliminary Recommendation on Postwar Problems, (1943). *International Conciliation*, 387, pp. 97–125.

Rabe, S. G. (1978). The Elusive Conference. United States Economic Relations With Latin America, 1945–1952, *Diplomatic History*, 2(3), pp. 279–294.

Report of the Delegation of the United States of America to the Inter-American Conference on Problems of War and Peace, Mexico City, Mexico, February 21–March 8 (1945). Conference Series 85, Government Printing Office, Washington.

Reyes, A. (1936). Notas sobre la inteligencia americana, *SUR* (*Buenos Aires*), 24, pp. 7–16.

Sachs, W. (ed.) (2007). *Development Dictionary. A Guide to Knowledge as Power*, Zed Books, London.

Santa Cruz, H. (1984). *Cooperar o perecer: El dilema de la comunidad mundial*, 1, Emece, Buenos Aires.

Santa Cruz, H. (1995). La creación de las Naciones Unidas y de la CEPAL, *Revista Cepal*, 57, pp. 17–32.

Toye, J. F. J. and Toye, R. (2004). *The UN and Global Political Economy: Trade, Finance, and Development*, Indiana University Press, Bloomington.

Wood, B. and Morales, M. (1965). Latin America and the United Nations, *International Organization*, 19(3), pp. 714–727.

Yearbook of the United Nations, 1947–48.

Chapter

5

New Transcontinental Configurations: The US Latinos

Yvette Sánchez

5.1. RECONQUERING SPACE

The intensifying pan-Americanization and decolonization processes in the Latin American regions highlighted by various chapters of this volume may be applicable, if we direct our attention north for a moment, to the following issue within hemispheric studies: the strongly growing participation of Latin American immigrants in North American society, who are gradually turning from a minoritarian subculture into a parallel culture with an increasing sense of self-esteem (and claim of self-representation) subsumed under the label Latinos. Up to 200 years of independence from European colonizers have gradually shifted Latin American nations towards new dependencies and asymmetries in their relationship with the US. Now the topic chosen sheds fresh light on the continental role allocation; it is not as much

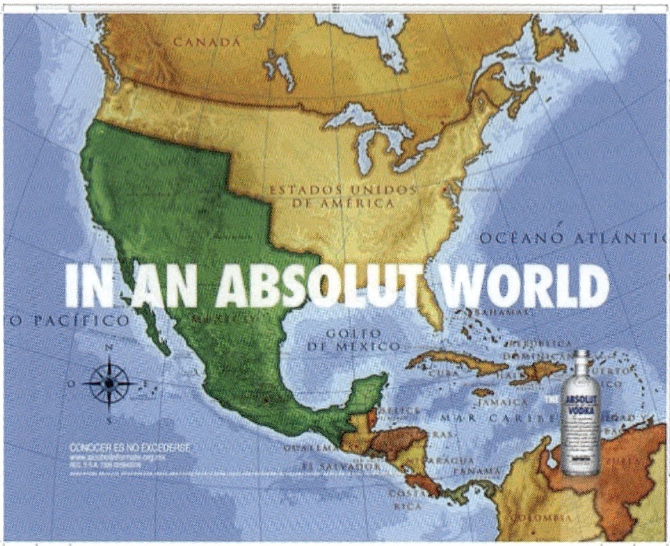

Figure 5.1. A hint of the fear of "Reconquista" plans at the Mexican-American border.

about the unilateral presence of the north in the subcontinent anymore. Latin Americans will be reconquering space within the northern hemisphere and altering the country's cultural, sociopolitical, ethnic, economic — perhaps even geographic profile, as provocatively insinuated in this advertisement for a Vodka brand (Fig. 5.1[1]).

The Spanish language is increasingly widespread on US territory; in Miami one can speak it almost exclusively.

In this respect the different traditions within the US in terms of mono- and bilingual education on the southeastern and the southwestern coast show in the corresponding approaches of the two areas: California has to deal with English Only campaigns, while Miami has tended to partly cultivate bilingual education (English Plus, since

[1] http://consumerist.com/2008/04/is-this-absolut-ad-cheeky-or-distasteful.html [Accessed 25 November 2010].

1987), which obviously affects the language used in daily routine and in literature.[2]

5.1.1. Miami

There is an evident difference between the two main migration axes from south to north. Cuban exiles in Miami arrived in the US wealthy and educated, a substrate with a stronger self-confidence, also in terms of Spanish retention, than the Mexican and Central American immigrants in the southwest.

Although the demographic landscape is more or less the same, with approximately 60% of Latinos, their position and participation in those two regions differs as to political, financial, and legal influence on US society.

In the enclave Miami, the internal decolonizing process is relatively advanced, having achieved more self-determination, with less radical asymmetries and splits between anglophone and hispanophone Americans. Latinos here have much more power than Mexican-Americans in California, who are mainly gardeners, waiters, or unskilled day laborers in the construction industry and agriculture (e.g. flower pickers), maids and nannies. Nowadays Miami serves as an influential center, even a tacit capital of Latin America, and its inhabitants have gone through a diversification process in terms of countries of origin, detached from endogamic nationalism or clustering in national ghettos. Little Havana belongs to the past; the Cuban dominance has been clearly reduced, but the funds brought along half a century ago, after the Revolution, have multiplied and sedimented.

And there has been an exodus of WASPs tired of foreign "infiltration", moving away to other regions of Florida, less dominated by

---

[2] Of two Latino writers I met in spring 2010, the one in Florida is perfectly bilingual (publishing some of his books in Spanish, others in English); the one in Los Angeles uses Spanish only in an oral Latino context, on the soccer field or when talking to his Mexican parents. In the Los Angeles academic community of Chicano/Latino Studies, I even met scholars who don't speak Spanish.

Latinos. We may recall the much quoted ironic car sticker saying: "Will the last American to leave Miami please bring the flag!" Thus when using the generalizing pan-ethnic identity label, Latinos, we always have to keep in mind this fundamental difference between the southwest and the southeast, also in terms of the predominantly Caribbean (Afro-American) population on the one side and the Mexican or Central American inhabitants (of indigenous *mestizo* origin) on the other.

In the context of migration, it is not only a matter of geographies and geopolitics, but also of generational succession in the migratory line, as in the above-mentioned case of the writer from Los Angeles talking in Spanish only to his first-generation parents.

Because of the decisive socio-cultural impact of different layers of first-, second-, third-, and fourth-generation immigrants, numerous denominations reflecting generational affiliation have been created. "One-and-a-halfers", living on a hyphen according to Gustavo Pérez-Firmat (1994), for instance, Mexican-Americans moving back and forth, displaced and in the interstices between the two cultures of their land of origin and the Anglo-American host country, which demands permanent recontextualization, de- and reterritorialization. The Latino label dismisses or lives beyond the hyphen and is applied deliberately by the concerned citizens themselves.

In the Cuban diaspora we have the ABC Generation ("American-Born Cubans" or "Cuban-born, but US raised"). Generation Ñ is bicultural, bilingual, consisting of middle class professionals, not "deculturated", although pro-US, the privileged part of the ABC Generation (Allatson, 2007, p. 9).

Samuel Huntington in his xenophobic book chapter "The Hispanic Challenge" (2004) has completely forgotten about (or intentionally ignored) generational issues when speaking about Latino resistance to assimilation and Spanish-language loyalty and retention as a common index of integration, which also varies geographically, of course. Language displacement and language shift is a more complex issue, analyzed by Hartmut Stösslein in his doctoral thesis on Latino bilingualism (2005). What will thus happen to the second and third Latino generation in language contact situations in the US? According to the three-generation model, how will the language be chosen in bilingual settings?[3] Will there be more retention because of the massive growth of the Latino population?[4]

5.2. DEMOGRAPHIC LANDSCAPE AND COMMUTING NARRATIVES

The statistics of the 2010 census show us some impressive figures. Not many people in Europe know about these radical and massive waves of immigration comparable to some extent, although not quantitatively, to current migratory patterns in countries of the Old World. But while Germans, for instance, deal with 2–3% Turkish immigrants, in the case of the largest minority of the US we have other dimensions, moving towards 20%. We speak of 50.5 million Latinos, plus approximately 11 million without a residence permit (thus a total of more than 60 million). Predictions claim that in the year 2042 every third inhabitant of the US might be of Latin American descent. So the US by the end of this century will turn into a different country, with a grown proportion of bilingual citizens,

---

[3] Based on an enormous corpus of the Latino case, Strössle (2005) furthermore discusses "language choice in bilingual domains, the attitude towards Spanglish and the mainstream language, language pressure, the role and importance of language domains, intersentential code-switching and code-mixing, the dichotomy and results of parental language decisions as well as family language planning (assimilation into the mainstream culture or language maintenance) [...]". According to the 2000 census, approximately 75% of all Hispanics spoke Spanish at home; parts of Texas and New Mexico (and along the border) have language retention rates over 90%, whereas parts of Colorado and California have retention rates lower than 30%. (cf. http://en.wikipedia.org/wiki/Hispanic [Accessed 25 November 2010]). In urban or metropolitan areas (Los Angeles) there is less retention.

[4] Here again I found an interesting phenomenon that connects these mechanisms with territory. Los Angeles writer Salvador Plascencia talked to me in English, but when he took me to East LA by car, and as soon as we crossed the bridge from Downtown to East LA to drive through Latino *barrios*, he started to switch to Spanish, without hardly noticing it.

which supposedly will put into perspective any dogmatic pretensions of homogenous, purist white nativism, also connected, by the way, with imperialistic attitudes towards the former "backyard" in the south. Even the melting pot concept is worn out.

What we are rather faced with is an extreme case of condensed cultural exchange, assembly, and intersection, in a huge contact zone together with a certain "Latin-Americanization" of the US, with the immigrants increasing their active participation in the majority culture, releasing them from their former subaltern status. The hybrid, rhizomatic, transcultural Latino consciousness and identity is also unfolding due to geographic contiguity to their former home countries, increasing mobility and media networking; migrants turn into commuters in Inter-American cultural contact zones.

Along with the massive demographic change goes a paradigm shift. Latinos, because of their sheer number and their feeling continentally domestic, are acquiring cohesion and self-esteem. This has first shown in popular culture: food, sports, music, the entertainment industry (show business, *telenovela* soaps), and media,[5] the latter with a clear concentration in Miami, where, to give an example, in the last few years more CDs have been produced than on the whole Latin American subcontinent.

The Latino hype also shows in a growing claim of self-projection and artistic expression producing thriving works of Latino art, performance, film, and literature, written in Spanish or English, often situated in transit zones, at border crossings between north and south (customs, airports, airplanes, boats, even reservations).[6]

---

[5] More than 800 Spanish-language radio stations were counted in 2008 (Albarran/Hutton, 2008, p. 9), and around 80 TV channels (cf. http://www.multichannel.com/article/80372-Guide_to_Hispanic_TV_Channels.php [Accessed 25 November 2010]).

[6] Luis Humberto Crosthwaite focuses on the twin towns Tijuana/San Diego; Luis Rafael Sánchez on the "flying bus" between Puerto Rico und New York; Roberto Quesada on the customs point at Miami International Airport; Roberto Fernández on a reservation for expelled WASPs in South Beach/Miami or a self-made *balsa* trying to reach the US coast.

These experimental zones of encounters, third spaces, heterotopias or counter spaces seem to provoke interesting situations and images, and stimulate humorous transgressions, full of quaint ideas and comic relief. For example, Elvis Presley's spirit, traveling back from Mexico, where he went to eat an authentic taco, and trying to re-enter the US, senses his comeback on a Las Vegas stage, when persecuted by searchlight reflectors and helicopters of the border patrol. This is a short story, "Marcela y el rey" by Tijuana author Luis Humberto Crosthwaite (1988).

To give further evidence of Latino effervescent aesthetics, one could look at the rich performance scene. In October 2009, in Geneva, we enjoyed Carmelita Tropicana (Tropic Ana, also referring to Havana's legendary cabaret), a queer performance artist acting out transgressive configurations of gender and ethnicity, e.g. representing a hyper-feminine stereotype Latina or her Pingalito Betancourt, a macho bus driver of the M15 route in Havana, who pictures himself as the Cuban Antonio Banderas (Figs. 5.2[7] and 5.3[8]).

Way back in 1992, performance artists Coco Fusco and Guillermo Gómez Peña made a clear postcolonial statement in *Two Undiscovered Amerindians Visit Madrid* simulating two authentic indigenous captives kept in a golden cage (alluding to Christopher Columbus's exhibition of a pair of "Indians" brought along to Spain) (Fig.5.4[9]).

Not only do recent artistic statements question emphatically established and mainstream discourses of asymmetric colonialism, but they also construct their own legitimizing literary tradition *a posteriori*, starting in the colonial era. In Florida we have Cabeza de Vaca's chronicle, which inverts colonial order, or José Martí's and Reinaldo

---

[7] http://www.brooklynmuseum.org/eascfa/feminist_art_base/gallery/carmelita_tropicana.php?i=355 [Accessed 25 November 2010].

[8] http://sitemaker.umich.edu/mdorson/multiple_roles [Accessed 25 November 2010].

[9] http://www.museodeartecarrillogil.com/images/artefusco.jpg [Accessed 25 November 2010].

Figure 5.2. Carmelita Tropicana.

Figure 5.3. Carmelita as Pingalito Betancourt.

Figure 5.4. Performance artists Coco Fusco and Guillermo Gómez Peña.

Arena's texts on Cuban exile in the US.[10] A new dimension in this canon building process comes into play in the 2,500 pages of the *Norton Anthology of Latìno Literature*, edited in 2010 by the scholar and writer Ilan Stavans. Together with a second exponent of Latino culture, comics artist Lalo Alcaraz, he had already published the *Cartoon History of US Latinos* a decade ago.

By now, after having gone through the "linguistic turn" and much questioning of the border between fiction and empirical reality, we know that a literary corpus might not only *illustrate* or *mirror* findings and empirical evidence in social sciences, but directly establish and shape a socio-cultural atmosphere, even enhance certain characteristics of a society. So I may venture to demonstrate the above-mentioned

---

[10] Moreover Nilo Cruz's stage play *Ana en el Trópico* (cf. Tropic-Ana Carmelita), 2003 winner of the Pulitzer Price, evokes the first decades of Cuban Independence after the depression (1929), in a cigar factory with immigrant workers in Ybor City/Tampa. The conflict between a traditional Cuban world and North American "modernity" is transposed to the 1920s, whereby Nilo Cruz shows precisely the historicity of the dilemma of assimilation.

paradigm shift with three narrative plots full of ironic distance and humor, carnivalesque (world upside down) fictions, which distance themselves from the classic emigration saga with its lamenting attitude and problematic topics of failure, migratory dramas, minority existence, solitude, prejudice, social injustice, homesickness, and nostalgically frozen-in-time home countries.[11]

The new narratives are artistically more refined, experimental, unconstrained, dynamic, mandatorily transterritorial, switching, commuting, with an irreverent, picaresque, playful, absurdist, and extravagant humor; in short, sparkling with wit.

A fictional vision of Miami as a decolonized enclave comes from the Cuban-American, bilingual author Roberto G. Fernández.

'La gira' (Fernández, 2001) shows a reservation for expelled WASPs in Miami, in a mangrove forest in South Beach, where Latinos go to see how the former Anglo-natives of the city used to live in earlier times. The reservation is described with discourse patterns of Spanish chroniclers from the period of discovery, conquest, and colonization.[12] Latino visitors hear WASPs singing, "Sometimes I feel like a motherless child/a long way from home and thirsty..." (Fernández, 2001, p. 91). And Anglo-Americans suffer an (inverse) embargo in the reservation, with shortages of food and repair parts for old cars (Fernández, 2001, p. 98). "–Luego que Vds. nos expulsaron, decretaron la prohibición del paso de mercancías a South Miami. Aquí no hay Coca-Cola a pesar de que nosotros la inventamos" (Fernández, 2001, p. 94). After finishing the tour ("la gira"), Latino sightseers are brought back to town on a shuttle bus.

The generational issue is raised in the second plot by the same author, Roberto Fernández, based on an olfactory metaphor. In

[11] We refer to the classical immigration and family sagas in the Latino literature of previous generations, but also to current ones, for example: *When I was a Puerto Rican* by Esmeralda Santiago, Oscar Hijuelos, *The Mambo Kings,* Sandra Cisneros, *The House on Mango Street*, Cristina García, *Dreaming in Cuban*, or even Julia Álvarez's novels.

[12] The singers have "hair of the color of the sun" and their "languid eyes" reflect "the pain of their displaced race" (Fernández, 1997, p. 93).

Tatiana (Fernández, 1997, p. 200), a blind grandfather, on the beach of Miami, asks his granddaughter to indicate to him the approximate direction of Cuba at a distance of 170 miles, wanting to inhale with nostalgia the breeze coming from his home country, whereas the child associates this name of her ancestors' land of origin solely with a cheap beach restaurant, Cuba, whose environment stinks of garlic, onions, and old grease. This is the ultimate breeze the grandfather has to cope with.

Roberto Fernández's third and last story to be mentioned in more detail is entitled *Kon Tiki* (*The Augustflower* in the English translation). Referring to the "wet foot, dry foot policy" established by the Clinton Administration in 1995, which agreed with Cuba that the US would stop admitting people found at sea, so a Cuban caught on the water between the two nations (with "wet feet") would be sent home or to a third country. One who makes it to the shore ("dry feet") gets a chance to remain in the US and later achieve permanent residency status and citizenship. As a consequence, Cubans started to try to immigrate through Mexico ("dusty feet").[13]

Political relationships between the north and different Latin American countries influence US immigration policy to different degrees. Puerto Rico and its oxymoronic status of "Estado Libre Asociado" of the US has had open borders since 1952, thus making it a commuters' nation, but remains stuck in a semi-colonial, subordinate condition, a most obvious example that, even after a century of independence, colonial, subaltern structures stubbornly maintain attitudes submissive to authoritarian domination. In this case of the new imperial player of the nineteenth and twentieth centuries, the US showed its hegemony, e.g. in the Monroe Doctrine or the Treaty of Guadalupe Hidalgo.

The status of the numerous Mexican migrants is limited by a (more or less) repressive policy obliging them to stay in the US illegally. Cuban exiles easily receive a residence permit as political refugees, but are not free to travel back to Cuba.

[13] http://en.wikipedia.org/wiki/Wet_feet,_dry_feet_policy [Accessed 25 November 2010].

In *Kon Tiki*, a first-person narrator tells the story of his attempt to legalize the residency of a Latino hotel staff member in Miami Beach. After having heard of a big raid on "illegals" in a similar hotel in the neighborhood, five persons of Mexican, Honduran, and Haitian origin decide to launch a transnational project, making up very convincing stories, changing identities, names, and nationalities into Cuban inventions, getting sunburnt and mosquito-bitten for three days,[14] and designing, with a perfectionist claim of authenticity, a rudimentary boat of palm lumber, plywood gussets, old truck tires and large plastic bottles (for buoyancy), supposedly arriving at the US coast from Cuba after an "arduous crossing". "Cuban dry feet get to stay, Cuban wet feet go away".[15] But, alas, the lumber of the royal palm trunks were just too much of a Third World simulation: the raft sank before arriving at the chosen coast, because the palm wood was immediately drenched with water.

> In that precise moment, the fucking stage for our American debut was sinking. The tires, tired of keeping the drenched royal palm trunks afloat were giving up. In my great quest for authenticity, I had selected the wrong tree. Our American dream was capsizing in front of our very eyes.[16]

Witty rhetoric plays with the paronomasic tires getting tired; the coast guard cutter is naturally first perceived as a whirlpool by the hotel staff; the "stage of the American debut" reflects the simulated and theatrical orchestration.

One of the false Cuban refugees prepared himself, very wittingly and pragmatically, by covering his feet with more efficient basic materials: two "Publix Supermarket plastic bags fastened to his feet with

---

[14] Jesús Díaz (1998) had created a similar fiction in his novel *Dime algo sobre Cuba*, with the protagonist faking a deep suntan, too, in order to get US residency.

[15] Unpublished manuscript in English supplied by the author. The Spanish original had been edited in *La Gaceta de Cuba* No. 5 (Sept.–Oct., 2004), and also in the anthology *Cuba Entre dos aguas* (Fernández, 2006).

[16] *Ibid.*

two purple rubber bands that had kept broccoli spears in a bundle". This prosaic and sudden end of the story underlines the absurdity of the measures of the US policy.

Such fictional visions contribute to the awareness of decolonizing modifications in (trans)hemispheric culture contacts and relationships on internationalized, and pan-Americanized terrains, and indirectly also to anti-imperialistic and anti-interventionist regional integration on the subcontinent.[17]

Kon-tiki, an old name for Viracocha, the Inca sun god, alludes to the famous expedition of Norwegian explorer Thor Heyerdahl (1914–2002), which in 1947 was to prove the possibility that a simple raft (balsa) of the Pre-Columbian era could make it all the way from the American continent to Polynesia (4,500 miles away). Heyerdahl used local materials (e.g. Peruvian balsa logs) and applied Pre-Columbian, autochthonous construction techniques, handed down by Spanish conquerors. The expedition was successful in crossing the Pacific Ocean safely within 101 days.

Again Fernández impregnates his narrative with a colonial discourse model, but instead of mounting a triumphant Kon Tiki adventure, he makes fun of his protagonist's faked "expedition" and total failure of a romanticizing and homogenizing image such as Heyerdahl's. The narrator and main character with his fake experiment is not even contributing, in the sense of Heyerdahl, to the convergence of the two (geographically closer) American hemispheres or to the reduction of the North–South polarization. Instead of the 4,500 miles, his crossing is a little detour of barely half a mile, furthermore illegal, ridiculous, yet existential for the five crew members.

5.3. LATINO ART AND MOBILITY

Literature, compared to the visual arts, is somewhat slower or less agile in adopting the before-mentioned paradigm shift in terms of

[17] With Brazil as leader of this integration process, which distances itself from US-American interventions in the south, above all the Caribbean, let alone the annexation of Puerto Rico in 1898.

implementing contemporary, experimental, innovative (also international) impulses in contemporary aesthetics. The thriving art scenes of LA and Miami have a lot to offer.

Quite a few artists react to or transform migration and border crossing, showing their experimental interpretation of mobility and of the more or less improvised means of transportation by water or by land.

Besides the cars and tires of Betsabée Romero installed at the authentic Mexican-American border, stuffed with the soft leaves of roses,[18] I discovered at the Walter Macías Gallery in Culver City, LA, the vehicles by Margarita Cabrera, elaborated with a similar contrast of hard topics and facts, and soft materials. Cabrera works with textiles, especially soft vinyl fabric (Figs. 5.5–5.7): the border patrol Hummer is all done with (useless) vinyl replacing a metal or plastic exterior shell and resulting in a cartoon-like, somewhat depressing and surreal form.

Figure 5.5. Hummer, 2006, vinyl, thread and car parts 84″ × 180″ × 96″

[18] http://www.arte-mexico.com/betsabee/ayate-car/ayate.htm [Accessed 25 November 2010].

Figure 5.6. Bicycle (*Maroon and Blue*).

Figure 5.7. *Nopal can Tunas #3*, 2006, border patrol uniform, thread and terra cotta pot.

5.4. RAW MATERIALS AMALGAMATED

There are cactuses of the border zone as well, the flesh of the succulents having been made of worn-out uniforms of border patrol officers. One can still detect the labels. Stitching and seams are left exposed conveying the lack of official care in the handicraft (Fig. 5.7[19]). So again one notices ironic distance, a dark and comic making fun of the officers. But in spite of the irony, the context is to be considered serious, dramatic, tragic. Irony only points to the all too direct 1:1 representation of the highly problematic borderland reality in traditional art and literature.

The same goes for Julio César Morales' *Undocumented Interventions* (Fig. 5.8[20]), which shows fictional designs of possible hideouts for clandestine, "undocumented" border crossings, which could be a goldmine for *coyotes* smuggling people.

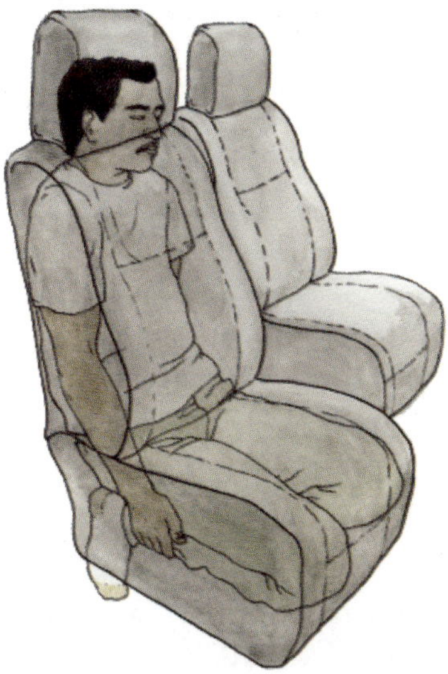

Figure 5.8. ***Undocumented Interventions*, 2007.**

[19] http://m-impressions.blogspot.com/2010/02/margarita-cabrera.html [Accessed 25 November 2010].

[20] http://www.universes-in-universe.de/car/singapore/eng/2006/tour/city-hall/img-27-2.htm [Accessed 25 November 2010].

Figure 5.9. Kcho's *Regata*.

Regata by Cuban artist Kcho collects stranded waste materials at the beach, creating a gap between the playful elaboration of the rudimentary fleet of balsas that look like toys and the traumatic experiences of *balseros* and their precarious vessels (Fig. 5.9[21]).

Finally Armando Moriño in his title *The Raft* (2002) combines both *patera* (playing with the homonym *pata,* "foot") or balsa and car,[22] similar to the authentic variants of real rafts trying to reach one of the *cayos* of Florida near the US coast (Figs. 5.10–5.11).[23]

---

[21] http://piterortega.blogspot.com/ [Accessed 25 November 2010].

[22] http://www.cubanartnews.org/can/P60/ [Accessed 25 November 2010].

[23] These ideas of crossing may find parallels in literature, but there they are rarer than in the arts: e.g. the before-mentioned Luis Humberto Crosthwaite's *Instrucciones para cruzar la frontera*, or *Misa fronteriza*, which all broke new aesthetic ground and manifested attitudes of humor and ironic distance.

Figures 5.10 & 5.11. Authentic balsas close to the coast of Florida.

Eventually the metaphoric meanings of "crossing" (crossbreeding, hybridization, blend) allow us to criss-cross and open our corpus towards the works of humorous amalgamations independent of the geopolitical border, for instance, different raw materials applied by young Miami artist Cristina Lei Rodríguez: the exuberant tropical vegetations (plastic varieties) thwarted and domesticated, spoilt even more by artificial substances, such as hot glue.[24]

María Magdalena Campos-Pons, a Cuban-American artist, does polaroids and, since one of her forefathers was Chinese, learned to draw and paint using Chinese technique on Chinese ceramics but using genuinely Cuban motives (easily recognizable) (Fig. 5.12[25]).

Figure 5.12. My Mother Told Me I Am Chinese: Painting Lesson, 2008.

[24] http://artblog.net/index.php?name=2005-03-01-06-37-rodriguez [Accessed 25 November 2010].

[25] Photo: Yvette Sánchez.

5.5. HEMISPHERIC DYNAMICS

The same hybrid of alienated handicraft material, traditional embroidery, needlepoint of Gobelin tapestry, combined — as a sort of stitched snapshots — with popular icons, celebrities, or nudes of the camp type. The artist María E. Piñeres is Latina, too, from Medellín and currently lives in Los Angeles.

One of her series helps us to round off this tour of Latino art and the rapidly rising series of Latino artistic experiments. I consider *Palindromes* (the example of a duplicated nude entitled *pagegap*, or several doubled portraits of celebrities) a cypher of the cultural situation of Latinos, who have to commute and oscillate constantly along the mirror axis between two cultures (Fig. 5.13).

The bifrontal, switching aspect refers us to several similar metaphors, such as the pendulum or the Möbius strip, which might contribute to illustrate and better understand the culture contact dynamics of US Latinos.

The Inter-American condition today has become somewhat less asymmetric than one (or two) centuries ago, at least in the Latino

Figure 5.13. ***Pagegap,* 2006.**

Figure 5.14. Caution wet floor sign in LA.

enclave of Miami. The new economic status of the so-called emerging countries of origin of the Latinos in the southern hemisphere vis-à-vis the US[26] will increment to some extent continental symmetries and even pan-American utopias. Signs of the strong Latino presence in the US and thus of bilingualism, such as the one in front of a café on Melrose Avenue in LA (Fig. 5.14[27]), are becoming more customary, although some bicultural slip hazard will remain.

BIBLIOGRAPHY

Albarran, A. B. and Hutton, B. (2009). "A History of Spanish Language Radio in the United States", The Center for Spanish Language Media. The University of North Texas. Available at: http://www.arbitron.com/downloads/mcl_unt_history_spanish_radio.pdf [Accessed 10 March 2010].

[26] Cf. the title page illustration of *The Economist* (9 September 2010), which turned upside down the continental cartography, interchanging roles of economic potential and assigning the United States the space in the south respectively transferring the subcontinent to the north.

[27] Photo: Yvette Sánchez at Melrose Avenue, LA.

Allatson, P. (2007). *Key Terms in Latino/a Cultural and Literary Studies*, Blackwell Publishing, Malden/Oxford.

Crosthwaite, L. H. (1988). *Marcela y el rey: Al fin juntos*, Joan Boldó i Climent, México.

Cruz, N. (2004). *Ana en el Trópico* [2003]. Theatre Communications Group, New York.

Díaz, J. (1998). *Dime algo sobre Cuba*, Espasa, México.

Economist (2010). "Nobody's backyard", "A special report on Latin America" and "So near and yet so far", 11–17 September, pp. 13, 22, 35, 48 and 56 [3–18].

Fernández, R. G. (1988/1997). "Tatiana", in *Raining Backwards*, Arte Público Press, Houston, p. 200.

Fernández, R. G. (2000). *En la Ocho y la Doce*, Houghton Mifflin, New York.

Fernández, R. G. (2006). "Kon Tiki", in *Entre dos aguas*, Letras Cubanas, La Habana, pp. 84–92.

Huntington, S. (2004). *Who Are We? The Challenges to America's National Identity*, Simon & Schuster, New York.

Pérez-Firmat, G. (1994). *Life on the Hyphen: The Cuban-American Way*, University of Texas Press, Texas.

Stavans, I. (ed.) (2010). *The Norton Anthology of Latino Literature*, W. W. Norton, New York.

Stavans, I. and Alcaraz, L. (2000). *Latino USA: A Cartoon History*, Basic Books, New York.

Stösslein, H. (2005). *Linguistic attitude of speakers of the first, second and third Latino generation in language contact situations in the United States of America.* Doctoral thesis, University of Bamberg, German Download Available at: http://www.opus-bayern.de/uni-bamberg/volltexte/2005/74/pdf/Tesis_Stoesslein.pdf [Accessed 25 November 2010].

Part Two

THE NATION-STATE, POLITICS, CITIZENSHIP, AND GOVERNANCE

Chapter

6

Patterns of Protest and Revolution in Latin America: 1810–1910–2010

Alan Knight

6.1. INTRODUCTION

The Mexican War of Independence began in 1810, giving rise to a decade of violent civil war before the new regime of the 1820s restored a semblance of stability. Similarly, the Mexican Revolution began in 1910, giving rise to a decade of violent civil war before the new regime of the 1920s restored a semblance of stability.[1] Today, in 2010, the ruling regime may regard these precedents with some concern, especially as it grapples with a seriously depressed economy and extensive narco-violence.[2] But the notion of hectohistorical cycles is surely misleading; historians may repeat themselves (as I will surely do

[1] I have extended this analogy in Knight, 2007, pp. 153–154.

[2] Mexico's GNP fell by 7% in 2009, in which year narco-homicides reached some 8,000 (compared to 3,000 in 2006, before President Calderón's military initiative began). The extra 5,000 implies a 20–25% increase in Mexico's 'traditional' homicide rate.

in this paper); but history doesn't; at least, not in such mathematically regular and predictable patterns (Fischer, 1970, p. 145). In fact, a great many revolutions come as complete surprises: 'I consider general revolution to be out of the question, as does public opinion and the press', reported the German envoy to Mexico in 1909.[3] Furthermore, I am doubtful that revolutions follow clear-cut patterns which can even be discerned *ex post facto*; the 'fundamental law(s) of revolution' which Lenin and Trotsky claimed to discern are probably mythical (as regards both the causality and the trajectory of revolutions) (Halliday, 1999, p. 173; Trotsky, 1967, pp. 15, 19). Revolution may be no more amenable to meaningful comparative analysis than, say, holes in the ground (MacIntyre, 1978, p. 260).

If this sceptical position is valid, it presents a problem when one is called upon to talk about a series of Latin American revolutions; and the problem is compounded when the scope is both temporally and spatially very wide. Thus, I am going to talk about both the revolutions of independence and twentieth-century revolutions; and I will try to resist the temptation to focus strongly on Mexico, the case I know best, and will also allude to cases in South America and the Caribbean, particularly the Bolivian and Cuban Revolutions of the 1950s.

6.2. POLITICAL AND/OR SOCIAL REVOLUTIONS

It is legitimate to cast the analytical net thus wide (as I have been asked to do), because the concept of 'great' or 'social' revolution is, in my view, a valid one. That is to say, within the huge chaos of history, 'revolution' — and particularly 'great revolution' — is a meaningful and limited category. Since 1789, if not before, historical actors and analysts have distinguished between (mere) rebellions and

[3] Even more remarkably, the same envoy, Karl Bunz, 'reiterated that opinion' in December 1910, one month after the revolution had broken out (Katz, 1981, p. 3). The great Andean revolt of 1780 similarly 'took the colonial state by surprise'; while 'the CIA were berated . . . for having reported in 1978 that Iran was *not* in a pre-revolutionary situation' (Walker, 1999, p. 33; Halliday, 1999, p. 172).

(great) revolutions, the latter being distinguished by the scope of their impact, both short and long term (Halliday, 1999, p. 32). Latin America, in particular, has experienced a vast number of coups, *cuartelazos*, rebellions and *pronunciamientos*;[4] but major revolutions have been much fewer, and can probably be counted on the fingers of two hands. Thus, by discussing — necessarily superficially — the revolutions of independence (1808–1825) and the Mexican, Bolivian and Cuban revolutions, I am probably dealing with a majority of this select category.[5]

The latter has been usefully and somewhat consensually defined by several scholars, Samuel Huntington and Theda Skocpol among them.[6] Drawing on their work, and keeping a close eye on historical reality, I would suggest that social revolutions contain two necessary ingredients: a process of major polarisation around rival visions or projects, involving substantial conflict and violence; and an outcome which brings with it a major structural change in regime and/or society (Knight, 1990, pp. 179–180). The scale of the process may vary (the Mexican Revolution was much more extensive and destructive than the Bolivian or Cuban); and the radicalism of the outcome is not necessarily proportional to the scale of the process (the Cuban Revolution produced more radical change than the Mexican). In some cases, what looks like a revolutionary 'process' (for example, the Tupac Amaru revolt in Upper Peru in 1780–1781 or the Colombian Violencia after 1948) fails to yield a revolutionary

---

[4] Professor Will Fowler, of St Andrews University, is currently running an ambitious research programme designed to define and elucidate the Mexican *pronunciamiento*.

[5] Other cases with strong claims to 'revolutionary' status would the Cuban War of Independence (1898) and the Sandinista Revolution in Nicaragua (1979).

[6] 'A revolution is a rapid, fundamental, and violent domestic change in the dominant values and myths of a society, in its political institutions, social structure, leadership and government' (Huntington, 1971, p. 264). 'Social revolutions are rapid, basic transformations of a society's state and class structures; and they are accompanied and in part carried through by class-based revolts from below' (Skocpol, 1979, p. 4). Of the two, I prefer Skocpol's definition, although I think 'basic transformations of . . . class structures' may be asking a lot.

outcome; either repression or implosion occur.[7] And revolutionary outcomes — substantial changes in regime and/or society — may not require a prior revolutionary process (the best example might be the velvet revolutions in Eastern Europe after 1989, at least outside Romania.[8] I am not aware that there have been 'velvet revolutions' in Latin America, unless we define post-1980 democratization — the Continent's 'Third Wave' — as 'revolutionary' (Huntington, 1991). The specificity of great or social revolutions (henceforth, just 'revolutions'), therefore, involves both process and outcome.

As regards outcome, a final clarification is needed. The outcome may be political or social or both. (In reality, I suspect, radical political change is bound to be, in some measure, social and, even more clearly, radical social change is likely to have political consequences; as a result, the social/political dichotomy is, in reality, quite blurred) (Halliday, 1999, pp. 172–173). The revolutions of Independence, as I shall argue, were primarily political: they changed the Spanish-American regimes, substituting republics for a colonial monarchy (outside Cuba and Puerto Rico).[9] They were certainly major revolutions, even though they did not revolutionise Spanish-American *society* as a whole[10] (I shall offer a broad explanation for this outcome shortly). The revolutions of the twentieth century, in contrast, were social — or 'socioeconomic' — as well as political. Even when they did not usher in socialism, as in Cuba, they substantially affected property rights, class (and ethnic) relations and national control of material resources. For some dogmatic analysts of Latin America, wedded to a crude Leninism and, usually, ignorant of revolutions elsewhere in the world, the failure to introduce socialism means that

---

[7] Charles Tilly (1995, p. 239) makes a similar point, albeit with different terminology: 'revolutionary situations sometimes occurred widely in times and places where revolutionary outcomes remained rare'. Tilly's 'situation' is close — but not identical — to my 'process'.

[8] Tilly (1995, p. 235) offers a different interpretation of Eastern Europe.

[9] For want of space and expertise, I will say very little about Brazil, whose trajectory towards independence was quite different.

[10] Here (for once) I agree with Guerra (1999, pp. 47–48).

they were not real revolutions at all, the only proper twentieth-century revolution necessarily being a socialist, i.e. Communist, one. 'Measured by the standards of Lenin', Ramón Ruiz writes, Emiliano Zapata 'falls woefully short of being a revolutionary'.[11]

This seems to be to be unhelpfully narrow and arbitrary. For my purposes, the independence revolutions were, indeed, revolutions (perhaps comparable to 'wars of national liberation' elsewhere in colonial societies), even though they were essentially political; and the Mexican and Bolivian revolutions were also revolutions, in that they achieved the quantum of change — political and socioeconomic — which revolutions are meant to achieve, even if they did not introduce socialism. We can, of course debate — though we can rarely measure — how great that 'revolutionary quantum' should be.[12] But my argument is more conceptual than quantitative. If we deny the independence movements the status of 'revolution', then we should have serious doubt about the French Revolution too; and if, say, Mexico is deprived of its revolution on the grounds that it did not spawn socialism, then, again, France probably had no revolution either; a *reductio ad absurdum* which should make us query its theoretical validity (not least here in Geneva, the birthplace of Jean-Jacques Rousseau).

However, the fact that we can establish a meaningful category of 'great revolutions' and can make strong claims for the inclusion

[11] Similarly, 'the evidence contradicts the view of (Pancho) Villa as a revolutionary'. Yet Ruiz is happy to concede the 'revolutionary' credentials of, say, Danton and Robespierre, since 'the French Revolution upended the Ancient Regime and replaced it with a capitalist state run by the bourgeoisie': a view which not only stands at odds with the great bulk of French historiography, but also embodies the old and nefarious practice of damning Mexico — or Latin America — by invidious comparison with an idealized Europe (or United States); a practice which has its political, cultural and economic variants (Ruiz, 1980, pp. 4, 8).

[12] Cogent studies of both the Mexican and Bolivian Revolutions have shown that, when it comes to per capita income and other indices of welfare, the benefits of 'revolution' are not very obvious (Eckstein, 1988; Kelley and Klein, 1981). This is perhaps not surprising, since income relates to production and productivity, which even revolutions cannot boost overnight, even if they effect some redistribution.

of several Latin American cases, does not necessarily mean that these cases follow common paths in terms of cause, course or origins (still less Lenin or Trotksy's mechanistic 'laws of motion'). This is a descriptive, not an explanatory category. We could similarly define 'wars' and the counterpart of 'great revolutions' — 'total wars' — and such a definition might again help us to order the chaos of history, but it would not follow that wars or 'total wars' follow common patterns in respect of causes, trajectories or outcomes.[13] Many historians, adopting, as historians often do, a narrow, even nit-picking, empirical approach, deny that any general patterns can be discerned in revolutions; hence no comparisons can be meaningful attempted.[14] Faced with a mountain of data, they prefer to 'split' and they regard 'lumping' — framing broad hypotheses or explanations — as risky, ahistorical and fanciful (Hexter, 1979, pp. 241–243). Indeed, 'lumping' may mean surrendering to those grand 'historicist' theories of Hegelian or Marxist provenance against which Professors Popper and Berlin used to warn us, tirelessly and verbosely (Popper, 1961; Berlin, 1969, Part 2). Such theories should certainly be regarded with great caution; though I would suggest that it is 'modernisation' theory, in its several, shape-shifting forms, which has been the most pervasive, enduring and counterproductive metahistorical scheme to afflict Latin American studies.

However, without surrendering to such schemas, we might be able to come up with, 'middle-range' hypotheses, rooted in empirical

---

[13] For a recent discussion of the concept of 'total war', see Bell, 2008, pp. 7–8.

[14] For a characteristic statement of bullish empiricism, see Cobb, 1972, xvi–xvii. In fact, Cobb was too intelligent to live by his own self-denying ordinance: while claiming that his work was merely 'impressionistic', dedicated to showing that 'in this place, things were like this, in that place, like that', he also ventured much broader generalizations: for example, that 'popular history, in France as in India, can be studied with profit only in very limited regional terms' and that, regarding popular movements, 'long-term militancy is a luxury few can afford and that a popular movement may be defeated as much by disease, apathy and economic ruin . . . as by repressive action' (*ibid.*, xv, xvii).

reality (a reality which, in old-fashioned positivistic style, I believe exists)[15] and capable of shedding light on diverse historical phenomena, in this case revolutions. And the risk, if we don't, is that history becomes all splitting and no lumping; 'one damn thing after another'; a universe of endless chaos tending towards entropy. Indeed, the study of the Mexican Revolution (the case I know best), has become so complex and variegated that it is increasingly difficult to produce generalisations — even qualified middle-level hypotheses — without a 'splitter' piping up that it was not like that in the Papagochic Valley or in the career of revolutionary hero Coronel Fulano de Tal (or, nowadays, Coronela Fulana de Tal). The death by a thousand cuts of the French Revolution shows the way its Mexican counterpart is going.[16] And if we cannot generalise about a particular Revolution, then, of course, we have no hope of comparing revolutions across time and space.

While I think we should take sceptical splitting seriously, we should also keep up the effort to lump where we can. In that spirit, I will try to suggest a comparison between the revolutions of independence and the revolutions of the twentieth century (all members, as I have argued, of the common category of 'great revolutions'), and I will particularly address the comparison between the Mexican insurgency and the Mexican revolution, thus, between 1810 and 1910. The most obvious and suggestive difference is that 1810 formed part of a systemic continental crisis, which involved insurgencies from the Mexican Bajío to Buenos Aires, which made the careers of Hidalgo, Morelos, Bolívar, San Martín and O'Higgins, and brought about the collapse of the 300-year-old Spanish empire (outside the Caribbean).

---

[15] In other words, I do not subscribe to the more extreme relativism of some recent — loosely, 'postmodern' — historiography, which tends to see history as a welter of free-floating texts, radically divorced from any knowable reality, insofar as I understand it.

[16] This may be an inexpert exaggeration; at least, it applies to a branch of Anglophone (especially British) historiography of the French Revolution, exemplified by Richard Cobb (see n. 14 above). That there are parallels in the recent historiography of major revolutions seems undeniable (Knight, 1992, pp. 159–199).

In contrast, Latin America's twentieth-century revolutions were scattered in time and place: Mexico's was the 'first great revolution of the twentieth century' (a pretty meaningless accolade, as it happens); and, though the Bolivian and Cuban revolutions both occurred in the 1950s, this chronological contiguity was, I think, largely fortuitous and, of course, the two countries not only were separated by great spatial distance, but also were radically different societies, whose revolutions also produced radically different outcomes. When Che Guevara tried to export revolution, Cuban-style, to Bolivia in the 1960s, he failed completely. Of course, twentieth-century Latin America has experienced common trends: external shocks (1914, 1930 and 1939); the 1980s debt crisis and the political fall-out which these shared experiences tended to produce (the fall of governments c.1930; the democratic opening of post-1945; the 'third wave' democratisation of the 1980s and 1990s).[17] But it is hard to see any common continental pattern to the major revolutions of the twentieth century.

6.3. THE ORIGINS OF REVOLUTIONS

If 1810 is distinctive by virtue of marking a common, pan-Latin American (or, perhaps, pan-Spanish-American) crisis, it poses the basic question, familiar to historians of the period, of whether the causality was external or internal. (Again, this is a slightly false dichotomy, since 'external' actions — e.g. those taken by the Spanish Crown — soon had internal repercussions; and Crown policy was in turn influenced by factors within Latin America. Nevertheless, I think the distinction, while blurred, has analytical validity). Some historians discern profound structural tensions, which made colonial rule fragile if not untenable; the 'external shock' — Spain's international wars,

[17] In 1930, governments were toppled by armed force in Argentina, Bolivia, Brazil, the Dominican Republic, Guatemala and Peru; in 1931, in Chile, Ecuador, El Salvador, and Panama. On the brief postwar democratic opening, see Bethell and Roxborough (eds) (1992); on the recent democratic 'wave' (which has spawned a whole academic industry), see Huntington (1991).

culminating in the Napoleonic invasion of the peninsula[18] — merely supplied the trigger. (Historians of revolutions are, we might say, distinctly trigger-happy, fond of distinguishing short-term 'triggers' from long-term 'causes'. While ostensibly sophisticated, these causal distinctions are rarely defined — when, for example, does a big trigger become a small cause or *vice versa*? — and they tend to breed like rabbits, producing a whole family of 'factors', 'stimuli', 'roots', 'influences', 'impulses', 'catalysts', 'symptoms' and — my favourite — 'prodromes') (Fischer, 1970, pp. 175–176). Not surprisingly, socioeconomic historians, some of Marxist inclination, tend to prefer such structural interpretations.[19] We can call them the 'internalists', who stress internal factors; we could also call them 'societal' theorists, who detect the origins of revolution in mounting social tension. Others, however, see the colony as fundamentally sound; for them, the 'trigger' is much more than a trigger; it is the primary cause, without which colonial rule would have survived, perhaps mutating, in reasonably peaceful and incremental fashion, into a kind of Hispanic Commonwealth.[20] We can call them the 'externalists' or 'state-centric' theorists; for them, external shocks and consequent state failure are the chief causes of independence. It is also not surprising that 'externalists' tend to be more politico-ideological in approach and Hispanophile in intellectual temper. They also draw sustenance from recent theories of revolution which, as against deep socioeconomic (or demographic) factors, stress the impact of external wars and crises (the best known, again, being the theory of Theda Skocpol).

---

[18] It is worth stressing that the 'external shock' argument can itself be deployed in both short-term contingent and longer-term (structural? 'less contingent'?) forms: the first would stress the Napoleonic invasion and the immediate events of 1807–1808, the second would address the cumulative weakening of Spanish imperial power after 1789, as recurrent wars undermined Spanish financial and maritime power. What both explanations have in common is a Eurocentric focus: the causal arrows fly, east-west, across the Atlantic and, absent the French Revolution and its consequences, there would have been no Independence struggle.

[19] A good — in both senses — example is Tutino (1986); Knight (2002, Part 2) probably falls within this camp too.

[20] Rodríguez (1998) is perhaps the best overview of this kind.

These contrasting alternatives can be summed up in the familiar metaphor of the pressure cooker: beneath it is the heat (i.e. social or political tensions); inside is the bubbling liquid (social groups, to varying degrees agitated) and on top there is a strong lid (the state). Greater heat (tensions) agitates the social groups, putting pressure on the lid. If the pressure is too great, or the lid is too weak, the result is a socio-political explosion, a revolution (in processual terms at least; the final outcome is another matter). Obviously, the immediate result — an explosion, or, of the lid holds, quietly contained simmering — is a function of these two factors: pressure and lid.[21] But while 'internalists' stress the pressure, 'externalists' focus their attention on the lid. If the pressure is sufficiently great, no lid can survive (say the former); or, if the lid is unbreakable, any pressure can be withstood (say the latter). As I proceed, I shall apply this simple model to both the independence movements and the revolutions of the twentieth century.

6.4. INDEPENDENCE MOVEMENTS IN EARLY NINETEENTH-CENTURY LATIN AMERICA

There is no doubt that the precise timing of the independence movements was determined by the Napoleonic invasion of Spain; hence the cluster of bicentenaries which we are now commemorating. However, this immediate crisis followed nearly 20 years of international conflict, during which Spain funded, fought and often lost a series of wars, which had the dual effect of weakening colonial control while augmenting colonial exactions. In 1808, a political crisis in the metropolis thus generated a series of colonial crises, as Spanish Americans were forced to decide whether to accept a Napoleonic usurper, recognise the Council of Regency, or proclaim their own independence, as the Thirteen Colonies of British North America had

---

[21] Of course, this is a 'parsimonious' model; in reality, matters are more complicated. The pressure below is a product of both the make-up and volume of the stew, on the one hand, and the level of heat on the other; while the 'lid' represents not just the state but other forms of top-down social control and repression (paramilitaries, vigilantes, slave-hunters, *guardias blancas*, etc.).

done a generation earlier. Furthermore, between the second and third alternatives (the first being by far the least palatable), there were several gradations of 'Home Rule', which involved asserting a measure of colonial autonomy without making a complete break from the metropolis. Portugal, of course, experienced a less severe crisis and no imperial decapitation; the Braganzas sailed to Brazil, shepherded by the Royal Navy, and no outright break occurred. Brazilian independence was achieved peacefully and incrementally, culminating in Pedro I's Grito de Ypiranga in 1822.[22]

Two points regarding this sequence of events need to be stressed. First, the Home Rule option rapidly closed as it became clear that — whoever ruled in the peninsula — Spain was not disposed to make substantial concessions to its American subjects. Even measures which looked liberal and reformist — like so-called *comercio libre* — were designed to enhance imperial control and revenue (Lynch, 1973, pp. 12–13). Furthermore, Spanish intransigence spanned the political spectrum: *mutatis mutandis*, it informed not only the knuckle-headed absolutism of Fernando VII, but also the thinking of the patriotic Cortes of Cádiz and the liberal army which took power in the peninsula in 1821 (Anna, 1990, pp. 22–24). Disaffected colonial subjects concluded that Home Rule within the empire was unattainable: 'Neither the king nor the Spanish patriots could be relied on and "America" would have to go it alone' (Guardino, 1996, p. 67).

Second, it is also worth recalling that Spain had experienced a major crisis 100 years earlier, at the time of the War of the Spanish Succession, when the Bourbon dynasty had fought its way to power in the peninsula, and there had been no colonial response, no assertion of Home Rule, still less of independence. Philip V, the new Bourbon king, inherited a loyal American empire.[23] While the two

---

[22] If the Bourbons had fled Spain and transferred the seat of royal government to Mexico, the latter might have enjoyed a 'Brazilian' transition to independence (see Topik, 1989, pp. 331–338).

[23] 'Spanish America supported the Bourbon succession. The war gave its inhabitants a golden opportunity for independent action, had they wished, but loyalties hardly wavered' (Lynch, 1989, p. 52).

crises were clearly different (one a dynastic struggle, the other a foreign invasion), the contrasting outcomes strongly suggest that, in c.1800, Spanish America was much more socially tense and politically restless than it had been a century before. 'The year 1700', Lynch writes, 'meant little to the mass of Spanish Americans, and the political moment had not arrived when a conjuncture of this kind would raise thoughts of liberation' (Lynch, 1989, p. 53).

By the early nineteenth century the moment had arrived. This conclusion is strongly supported by the recurrent rebellions of the late Bourbon period: the tax revolts in Quito in 1765, the pro-Jesuit riots in Mexico in 1766, the massive Andean insurrection of the late 1770s and early 1780s, and the Comunero rebellion of 1781 in New Granada. These were the major uprisings; but a broader statistical analysis of 'village riots and uprisings' in the colonial heartlands of Mexico and Peru confirms this trend: in the first 50 years of the eighteenth century, Mexico experienced 35 such events and Peru 32; between 1750 and 1810, the respective figures were 95 and 102 (the Peruvian total swollen, it is true, by the cumulative effect of the great Andean revolt of 1777–1782) (Coatsworth, 1988, pp. 32–33). Steve Stern, therefore, sees the period 1742–1782 as 'the Age of Andean Insurrection' (Stern, 1987, p. 35).

What brought about this cycle of violent protest? While causes no doubt varied from place to place — and some regions, such as rural Guatemala and Ecuador, were much less affected — protest sprang from the tensions engendered by the Bourbon reforms and their accompanying socioeconomic context. In the later eighteenth century, as Lynch puts it, the Spanish Crown attempted a 'second conquest' of the Americas (Lynch, 1973, p. 7),[24] designed to assert royal and *peninsular* control, strengthen the creaking machinery of government, increase the colonial yield of bullion and taxation and bolster colonial defences. In order to resist French and — especially — British threats, Spain had to emulate British and — especially — French methods.

[24] This is not to be confused with the 'second conquest' of the late nineteenth century, when Latin America was rapidly inserted into the world division of labour: see Topik and Wells (eds) (1998).

The external shock of 1808 thus impacted upon an empire that was in the throes of administrative, fiscal and economic reform, all of which had provoked serious protest well before Napoleon's invasion.

Thus, the Quito riot of 1765 was provoked by increases in internal customs (*alcabalas*) and an unpopular reform of the *aguardiente* trade (McFarlane, 1990). But the protest did not stop Bourbon fiscal exactions: in 1778 a powerful new official, combining 'political, fiscal, judicial and military power', began to crank up — indirect and regressive — taxes, producing a 'dramatic rise in per capita tax rates in the late colonial period'. Indeed, by the 1800s, Quito taxpayers carried twice the per capita burden that the — more affluent — colonists of British North America had suffered and resisted, while the tax take in Guayaquil — then undergoing a cacao boom — 'dwarfed anything collected in the thirteen English colonies' (Andrien, 1995, pp. 192, 200–202). At the same time, the Tupac Amaru rebellion of 1780 derived partly from fiscal abuses; while the much larger Mexican economy also experienced sharply rising fiscal demands, based on bullion and state monopolies; in Mexico, Spanish extraction of resources culminated in the Law of Consolidation of 1804, which seized church assets, to the serious detriment of the domestic economy (Rodríguez, 1998, p. 34). Thus not only did Spain's colonial subjects face 'taxation without representation' far in excess of what George III's subjects suffered in North America; the returns also flowed across the Atlantic, to be spent by a faltering power in pursuit of vain military objectives. Meanwhile, the defence of the colonies — for example, of Buenos Aires during the English invasions of 1806–1807 — fell to the colonists themselves. The reciprocity, which makes taxation — and other state demands — tolerable, was increasingly absent, hence colonial rule became increasingly illegitimate.[25]

Thus, the principal grievances of Spanish-American protestors — both before and after 1808 — had to do with the colonial state; they can be confidently defined as anti-colonial and anti-state (and, as

[25] See the general principles of reciprocity vs. exploitation outlined by Moore (1979, pp. 455–456).

such, they clearly contrast with the grievances of twentieth-century revolutionaries, as I shall suggest). Five sorts of anti-colonial, anti-state grievance were apparent:

i. *Fiscal* grievances, based on colonial taxation, which had risen sharply (not least in Mexico) and affected a wide range of colonial society and which tended to become more acute as Spain, embroiled in a series of costly wars, turned the fiscal screw, sometimes in highly coercive fashion.[26]
ii. Resentment against the *peninsular* control of government and the exclusion of *criollos*, which had advanced during the later eighteenth century as a result of the 'Second Conquest' (Lynch, 1973, pp. 16–17); a grievance which, of course, chiefly affected the *criollo* well-to-do (not the plebs).
iii. *Commercial* grievances, on the part of (usually *criollo*) business interests who chafed at Spanish mercantilist controls and favoured a measure of free trade, not least with the burgeoning British economy. Again, such grievances were chiefly apparent among *criollo* elites, in regions — like the Atlantic lowlands of the Río de la Plata and Venezuela — where the export of primary products, such as hides and cacao, was buoyant, offering potential profits (Lynch, 1973, 15).[27] In Mexico and Andean America, the *repartimiento* of goods, whereby Spanish merchants engaged in coercive trade with peasant — usually Indian — communities, also rankled.
iv. *Religious* sensibilities, particularly acute in New Spain, which were offended by the incipient anti-clericalism of the Bourbon crown as it expelled the Jesuits in 1767 and sequestrated church wealth in 1804. By way of counterpoint, we may note the build-up

[26] In Quito in 1765 'popular remonstration with the tax collectors evoked an unsympathetic response and threats to erect a gibbet in each parish to deal with complaints' (McFarlane, 1990, p. 220).

[27] Lockhart and Schwartz (1983, p. 336) discern an export-led 'east coast revolution' affecting the Atlantic littoral, especially the Río de la Plata region, in the late eighteenth century.

of the Bourbon army and the Crown's increasing resort to repression, the necessary official response to increasing protest. Thus, as David Brading (1971, p. 27) noted 'where the Habsburgs used priests, the Bourbons employed soldiers'; the regular army replaced the regular orders; and military coercion supplanted religious legitimisation. Popular Catholicism — allied, perhaps, to messianic beliefs — thus fuelled the insurgency in the Mexican heartland, where the two great leaders and martyrs of independence were, of course, the *curas* Hidalgo and Morelos; yet it was in the ranks of the burgeoning royalist army that many of the leading caudillos of the early national period, such as Iturbide and Santa Anna, learned their praetorian trade.

v. Finally, acting as a kind of cultural cement for the anti-colonial cause, was incipient *nationalism* (or, if you prefer, 'proto-patriotism'), a sentiment which historians have long discerned among *criollo* elites, but which is now seen to have penetrated rather deeper into society than previously thought (Brading, 1993, Chapters 14, 20). The negative sentiments of anti-colonialism thus fostered the positive ties of patriotism. In a time of political flux and experimentation, Spanish-Americans groped their way from localised resistance to broader home-rule/autonomist projects, before finally committing to the construction not only of new states, but also of new nations.

All of the above focused on state agents and state abuses, and the independence wars were, very obviously, directed against the colonial state. But the Bourbon reforms also coincided with important socioeconomic trends, which the colonial state in no sense created or controlled, but which it sought to exploit, often in parasitic style; trends which de Vries (1994) has recently summed up as elements of an 'industrious revolution', which an earlier generation of Marxist marxisant historians preferred to call 'the rise of merchant capital'. The eighteenth century, and particularly the later eighteenth century, witnessed a fall in shipping costs, a brisk increase in transatlantic trade and 'windfall' gains for Europe which, as Pomerantz (2000, pp. 264–283) argues, helped it draw ahead of China. This was not (yet) an industrial revolution, nor was it economic 'globalization' in the strict sense (O'Rourke and Williamson, 1999). It was driven by European demand for 'luxury' goods which were becoming items of mass consumption — sugar above all — as well as by the European states' lust for bullion, which, as belligerent mercantilists, they needed in order to prosecute their interminable wars. These processes, too, impacted on Spanish America: in part via the (Spanish) state exactions, already mentioned; in part via more diffuse economic processes, as mining and commerce expanded and Spanish merchant interests found rich pickings in the colonies. To the extent that the Spaniards benefited from Spanish 'imperial preference' — after all, were not the colonies *meant* to serve Spanish economic interests?[28] — resentment against the imperial system grew; but, in addition, Americans — both *criollo* elites and the common people — chafed at the wealth, power and perceived abuses of Spanish merchants: not just the privileged mercantile elite of the *consulados*, but also the hard-nosed traders who controlled local retailing.

Thus, alongside the anti-state and anti-colonial grievances already mentioned, there coursed a current of anti-Spanish socioeconomic sentiment, combining both class and ethnic elements, and which was particularly apparent among the middling and lower orders of society (many of them *mestizos*, *pardos* and Indians). Hence we see protests which went beyond state officials and targeted *peninsulares* more broadly; in Mexico, the massacre of the Alhóndiga in Guanajuato was not limited to Spanish officials; and the cry '*mueran los gachupines*' extended to merchants as well as representatives of the state (Guardino, 1996, pp. 61–64). However, since there had been no industrial revolution — hence no major subversion of the old regime of property and class relations, no wholesale dispossession of the peasantry, no creation of a mass proletariat — this 'socioeconomic' resentment was usually secondary to the primary target: the colonial state. Indeed, given the logic of mercantilism, it was difficult to

[28] For a forthright statement of colonial priorities, see Lynch (1973, pp. 5, 14), quoting Peruvian Viceroy Gil de Taboada in 1781 and Mexican Viceroy Revillagigedo in 1794.

disentangle state power and socioeconomic power. Significantly, the most radical and threatening popular rebellions arose in those regions — like the Mexican Bajío — where economic growth had been most rapid and proletarianisation was most advanced. When Hidalgo, leading his Bajío army, reached the Valley of Mexico (where a robust peasant society still flourished), it received a cool welcome (Tutino, 1986, Chapters 2, 4; Hamill, 1966, pp. 48–49, 135–136, 176).

This emphasis on the political, or anti-state, thrust of the Independence movement, which contrasts with the relative weakness of its anti-seigneurial — or anti-bourgeois? — thrust, is confirmed by its outcome. The revolutions of Independence overthrew the colonial state and created new regimes — usually republics — which governed new countries. But socioeconomic relations were not revolutionised. Economic historians see a distinct continuity between 1750 and 1850 — the so-called 'middle period' of Latin American history — when socioeconomic change failed to match the dramatic innovations which were being attempted in the political realm (Voss, 2002).[29] Commercial ties with the outside world were diversified and strengthened; but there was still no industrial revolution, no mass dispossession of the peasantry, no wholesale conversion to market capitalism. Indeed, a tentative case could be made that the period c.1820–1860 was, for the Spanish American peasantry, something of a silver age (I would not go so far as to term it 'golden'), an age when village resources were retained, when political instability inhibited landlord confidence and estate expansion, while affording the peasantry greater bargaining power; and when the fragile republican state lacked the fiscal power to extract resources from its new citizens (Coatsworth, 1988, p. 55; Tutino, 1988). Low taxation, of course, meant chronic government penury and recurrent bankruptcy (Tenenbaum, 1986). And the careers of a slew of 'populist' political leaders showed that the plebs — urban and (more usually) rural — exerted real leverage in post-Independence politics, by virtue of both

[29] I would query the extension of the 'Middle Period' into the twentieth century, but global historians also seem to favour a c. 1750–1850 periodization (Bayly, 2002).

ballots and bullets: José Artigas, Juan Alvarez, Rafael Carrera, Manuel Belzú.

6.5. REVOLUTIONS IN TWENTIETH-CENTURY LATIN AMERICA

If we now jump ahead a generation or more — to c.1910 — we see a different scenario; one which generated important new tensions and, in the case of Mexico, a major revolution. Furthermore, the tensions and the targets were different from those of 1810. As I have said, there was no continental-wide crisis, hence no cluster of Latin American revolutions in a few short years. The major revolutions were scattered in random fashion: 1910, 1952, 1959 and 1979. Not only was there no metropolitan decapitation; it is also very difficult to argue that external factors in general were crucial in generating revolutions in the twentieth century. The best case would be Bolivia, where the Chaco War of the 1930s contributed to domestic discontent and political mobilisation (Dunkerley, 2003, pp. 143–145). But, in the case of Mexico, efforts to find external causes — such as US machinations or, more plausibly but still unconvincingly, the adoption of the Gold Standard in 1906 or the recession of 1907 — have been largely unsuccessful. Hence, as I have argued elsewhere, Skocpol's revolutionary etiology, which stresses external factors (war, defeat and bankruptcy), does not work well in the Mexican — or indeed, the other Latin American — cases (Knight, 1990, pp. 176–177). In 1910 the Díaz regime was ostensibly stable and solvent, enjoying the confidence of investors and the Taft administration. American tin-purchasing policy had an impact on Bolivia (Lehman, 1999, pp. 77–76); but it is very hard to see how that could have provoked a major social revolution which involved middle- and working-class as well as peasant mobilisation (mobilisation which, in many cases, dated back years if not decades). In the case of Cuba, external — US — influence might be presumed to be significant and US policy did help give Batista a final belated shove late in 1958. But, by then, the triumph of the Revolution was imminent. And no major recession presaged Batista's fall; indeed, in macro-economic terms, 1957 'was Cuba's best year ever' (Domínguez, 1978, p. 121).[30] American policy may have helped radicalise the Revolution after 1959, but that is quite different from US policy causing the Revolution in the first place. Thus, the main causes of these three — or four — revolutions were to be found within the respective countries. As a perceptive US observer in northern Mexico put it in 1913:

> This fight is entirely a Mexican fight. True it is that some of the Mexicans claim to hate all Americans and the United States — but the fact is: it is all Mexican hatred, Mexicans hating Mexicans, and Mexicans fighting Mexicans — ... it is their own family quarrel.[31]

An internalist explanation must, therefore, be sought for this 'family quarrel'. To make sense of a mass of chaotic data, I shall divide the explanations into 'state-centred' and 'societal'; my conclusion is that, in contrast to the independence struggles of a century or more before, the latter — societal grievances and tensions — were much more important. But first, the state, which I see as a secondary issue. The states overthrown by twentieth-century revolutions were, of course, republican regimes, governing nation-states and claiming a kind of 'modern' legitimacy based on popular sovereignty. They were, therefore, substantially different from the Throne-and-Altar colonial state of 1810 which, even in its 'enlightened-despotic' Bourbon incarnation, claimed sacred and prescriptive legitimation. Indeed, it was the shift from one to the other which generated such febrile instability in nineteenth-century Latin America and

---

[30] Domínguez (1978, p. 74) gives deflated figures of (i) Cuban GDP and (ii) GDP per capita for 1952/1957 as: (i) 773m pesos/944 million pesos; (ii) 135/154 pesos. Of course, this does not take into account income distribution.

[31] Consul Hanna, Monterrey, to State Department, 28 November 1913, United States, State Department Records, Internal Affairs of Mexico 1910–1929, 812.00/10301.

which justifies the confident description of the independence movements as 'real' (political) revolutions.

By the late nineteenth century a rough distinction can be made between (i) those states — mainly in the Southern Cone — where the state's official ideology (or 'public transcript', if you prefer) roughly corresponded to reality: that is, where a measure of democratic representation, civil rights, and freedom of expression existed (e.g. Argentina, Chile, Uruguay; perhaps, also, Colombia); and, on the other hand, (ii) states where the public transcript and practical politics widely diverged, where 'artificial democracies' existed, and authoritarianism flourished behind a façade of 'polyarchy'. Significantly, these states were to be found in Andean America and Mesoamerica, where class and ethnic divisions were greater: in Peru, Ecuador, Bolivia, Guatemala and Mexico. These were also the states where social revolutions occurred (Mexico, 1910, perhaps Guatemala, 1944, and Bolivia 1952), or where lesser rebellions assumed more 'social-revolutionary' characteristics (for example, in Peru and southern Bolivia in 1915–1916 and the 1920s) (Jacobsen, 1993, pp. 337–353). In contrast, the countries of the Southern Cone were more stable; and, when rebellions occurred, they tended to be intra-elite political struggles (e.g. the Blanco–Colorado civil wars in Uruguay, or the rise to power of the Argentine Radical Party).

Indeed, the regimes which fell victim to social revolutions were often extreme cases of personalist authoritarian rule: Díaz in Mexico, perhaps Ubico in Guatemala, later Batista in Cuba and Somoza in Nicaragua. The Bolivian *rosca* was not a personalist regime, but was certainly 'too narrow, too rigid and too precarious to cope with socio-political pressures' (Whitehead, 2003, pp. 27). Such regimes allowed little freedom of expression or 'circulation of elites'; even if the lid of the pressure cooker looked strong (as it certainly did in Díaz's Mexico and Batista's Cuba), it lacked an escape valve, so that pressure built up inside, with no way for the steam to get out. Indeed, there is evidence that longstanding tyrants like Díaz, Batista and Somoza became increasingly oblivious to the mounting pressure, which both a censored media and a coterie of sycophantic advisers could not bring to the tyrant's attention. In the case of Nicaragua in the 1970s, even supposed US experts were suckered in to the sycophantic circle.[32]

Of course, the Bourbon regime had also been authoritarian and lacking in mass media (unless we include the pulpit of Catholic churches). But in 1800 the alternatives were fewer: the United States was the only republican counter-example (while Haiti offered a grim warning). But by the early twentieth century democratic models were common, and some — such as Uruguay and Argentina after 1912 — were to be found in Latin America itself. Thus, the more egregious personalist regimes were particularly vulnerable to political protest and rebellion: not because they had been weakened by ill-advised arms races and foreign wars, as Skocpol suggests, but rather because they denied basic forms of expression and representation, thus making a mockery of their formal constitutions, while cocooning the ruling elite in a narrow, self-regarding, camarilla politics. No major revolution has ever toppled a functioning democracy; all victims of such revolutions have been absolutist monarchies or dictatorial presidencies. (To the roster of Latin American examples we can add Charles I, Louis XVII, Nicholas II, the Shah of Iran and perhaps Nicolae Ceauşescu).

However, such regimes do not fall at the flick of a feather. Díaz and Batista both had well-equipped and apparently effective armies; the Porfirian army survived the first revolt of 1910–1911 and was only slowly and painfully ground into defeat during the long campaigns of 1913–1914. Batista's forces nearly annihilated Castro's guerrillas when they landed in December 1956 and the subsequent civil war lasted three years.[33] These regimes fell not because the lids were too weak, but because the pressure inside was too strong (and, I repeat, because the lids lacked effective escape valves, of the kind which more liberal and

[32] James Dunkerley (1988, p. 236) cites the case of Turner Shelton, appointed US Ambassador to Nicaragua in 1970, a 'fawning diplomat' who was capable of 'little beyond adulation of his host', Anastasio Somoza; but who did at least get his portrait on the twenty córdoba note.

[33] The Bolivian Revolution — in its initial armed insurrectionary form — lasted a matter of few days; but the Nicaraguan Revolution more resembled the Mexican and Cuban models.

representative regimes possessed: ultimately, the option of 'kicking the bums out' at an election). The pressure inside, which is in turn a function of both the heat and the contents of the cooker, is, therefore, the key variable. After all, there had been plenty of authoritarian and dictatorial regimes in nineteenth-century Latin America which had survived relatively unchallenged, the classic case being Paraguay's Dr Francia, who died with his boots on after 26 years of draconian personal rule.

But Francia had governed a closed, largely subsistence economy, a prolongation of colonial Paraguay under neo-absolutist rule. By the twentieth century, such a project was anachronistic. The later nineteenth century had witnessed what Topik and Wells call the 'second conquest' of Latin America (not to be confused with Lynch's second — Bourbon — conquest; perhaps we should, therefore, call it the third?). It involved rapid immersion in the world economy at a time when 'globalisation' (for once, this overused term is entirely valid) was forging ahead. Latin America began to export (and, therefore, to import); its credit improved; it attracted foreign investment as well as foreign immigration; its domestic markets also deepened. Cities grew and the countryside — still the home of the majority of the population — underwent commercialisation. Foreign 'enclaves', dedicated to the export of industrial minerals, oil and bananas sprang up in northern and Gulf-coast Mexico, on Colombia and Costa Rica's Atlantic littoral and in the central sierra of Peru; these would eventually produce robust labour movements (Bergquist, 1986). Corporate land tenure gave way to individual freehold property, to the detriment of the Church and peasant, particularly Indian, communities. The demand for labour, instead of pushing up real wages, was offset by proletarianisation, by forms of forced labour (peonage, *enganche* and *mandamiento*), by population growth and, in the Southern Cone, by European immigration. Latin America's landlord class — a staple of society since the colony — grew richer and more entrepreneurial; some branched out in to manufacturing and banking; and the numbers of the middle class swelled. On the other hand, in Latin America as in Europe, the creation of a large urban proletariat provoked concerns about the so-called 'social question' which, by the 1900s, had become the object of both Catholic and liberal debate, as well as radical — including Anarchist — protest.

These processes, powered by the second (or, if you prefer, third) conquest, generated serious social tensions which were quite different from those associated with the independence movements. For one thing, taxation was no longer a major issue; in fact, the Spanish-American states of the early twentieth century were, in fiscal terms, 'pathetically' weak (Bulmer-Thomas, 1994, p. 111); and those which fell victim to revolution — Mexico and Bolivia — were particularly weak (conversely, the more liberal and stable regimes of the Southern Cone — Argentina, Chile and Uruguay — raked in more tax revenue, both absolutely and relatively).[34] After all, these were states largely run by landlords or their allies; they were not going to tax their own rent, property or income; so they relied heavily on foreign trade taxes, especially those which fell on imports.

Thus, tax grievances, the staple of late eighteenth-century rebellions, are largely absent in the great revolutions of the twentieth century. Indeed, we can see a noticeable decline in fiscal protests in mid-nineteenth-century Mexico and about a generation later in the Andean region (Coatsworth, 1988, p. 50). Schematically, we could see this as a secular shift from what Eric Wolf calls a 'tributary' (tax-based) mode of exploitation to a capitalist mode based on private property, private profit and corresponding class divisions (Wolf, 1982, Chapter 3). Nor, of course, was the old resentment at peninsular colonial rule an issue, since states were now, in theory at least, independent self-governing republics; the presence of large quantities of foreign direct investment — such as the 'enclaves' just mentioned — did not turn them into *de facto* colonies.[35] If genuine colonial parallels are to be found, they reside rather in the domestic socio-political sphere: Mexico and, *a fortiori*, Bolivia were racialised republics, in which ethnic divisions reinforced

---

[34] Public revenue per head in 1913 stood at $4 in Mexico and Bolivia, compared to $18 in Argentina, $22 in Chile and $29 in Uruguay (Bulmer-Thomas, 1994, p. 112).

[35] Thus, while 'formal' imperialism, as represented by Spanish viceroys, *consulados* and silver-miners, may share some distant kinship with 'informal' imperialism, the work of United Fruit, Anaconda, the CIA, and diplomats like Ambassador Shelton (see note 32), they are at different ends of a wide spectrum, their respective *modi operandi* are quite distinct, thus the formal/informal criterion remains crucial.

class antagonisms (in Nicaragua race was denied; in Cuba it was glossed over). It is, therefore, certainly possible to see such states as agents of internal colonialism, as the imperious logic of *desarrollo hacia afuera* (roughly, export-led development) fortified racist and positivistic assumptions about lazy natives, feckless Indians and the consequent need for an authoritarian regime which could impose 'order and progress'. However, since ethnic and class divisions overlapped — the plebs were browner, the elites were whiter — the effect was to augment class/ethnic tensions, rather than to provoke the kind of intra-elite divisions which had pitted *peninsulares* against *criollos* in the late colonial period. Colonialism had divided the elites, driving some (such as Bolívar) into an anomalous cross-class alliance with slaves, Indians and *pardos*; 100 years later, 'neo-colonialism' tended to foster elite solidarity, while provoking the resentment of subaltern classes and ethnicities.[36] That, at least, was the pattern which prevailed in the Mexican and Bolivian revolutions, when the landlord class — narrow, oligarchic and closely tied to the old regime — opposed reform, clung to reaction and became the main victims of revolutionary land distribution.

Meanwhile, the *ancien régime* state was targeted by the rebels less because it was the chief agent of exploitation — it did not, as I have said, impose swingeing taxes — than because it was hand-in-glove with the hated elites, especially the landlord class.[37] It had come to

---

[36] In twentieth-century Mexico, the derogatory term *gachupín* has broadened to include Mexican elites who are whiter, richer, and more high-faluting than their fellow-citizens and who, especially in hard times, are therefore equated with the peninsular oppressors of the past (Gilly, 1989).

[37] There is an important qualification to be made. The Mexican Revolution — more than either the Bolivian or the Cuba — also embodied popular revolts by peripheral communities who were protesting against the oppressive powers of the state (both national and regional); I have described these as *serrano* movements (since most, though not all, emanated from highland zones) (Knight, 1986, pp. 115–126). These displayed a kinship with older anti-state revolts, and tended to be led by 'traditional' authorities, like the caciques of the Sierra Juárez of Oaxaca or the Sierra Norte de Puebla. However, they attained only limited, short-term success: over time, the state revived — now in its new 'massified' revolutionary form — and dreams of provincial autonomy were dashed. Thus, *serrano* anti-state revolts, while they played their part in the revolutionary *process*, failed to set their stamp on the revolutionary *outcome*.

resemble Marx's 'agent state', the 'executive committee of the ruling class', in this case, not a progressive bourgeoisie but a powerful conservative and racist oligarchy of landlords and businessmen (including, in Bolivia, the big mining oligarchy). Thus, the Mexican and Bolivian revolutions — and, we could suggest, the kind of revolution which Peru might have experienced in the 1920s or which Guatemala nearly did experience in the 1940s and 1950s — were strongly class-inflected and directed against socioeconomic elites who had the backing of ostensibly strong, but in fact quite brittle, 'agent' states. The overthrow of the state, therefore, was the necessary prerequisite for reordering social relations, by means of land reform, the nationalisation of certain enterprises (tin and oil), and the creation of powerful peasant and working-class organisations, whose relationship to the infant revolutionary state was crucial but contentious (Knight, 2003). Formal and institutional reforms aside, both revolutions also prompted a socio-psychological shift, as plebeian (including Indian) leaders assumed power and old patterns of social and political deference crumbled. On all these counts, therefore, the Mexican and Bolivian revolutions were *social* revolutions, for which the *political* ouster of the old regime was a necessary condition, but not the main objective. In contrast, the Independence movements, targeting the colonial state, were *political* revolutions (but, I repeat, real revolutions nonetheless!) which did not bring with them sweeping social change.

Finally, a word about Cuba. Cuba was not only a *social* revolution; it was also a *socialist* revolution, which subverted both the political and socioeconomic old regime, introducing a command economy. (In highly schematic terms, we could contrast this with the Mexican and Bolivian revolutions which, though *social*, were not *socialist* in their outcomes, even though currents of socialism can be seen swirling amid the turbid waters of revolution.)[38] The Cuban revolution, too, targeted property owners, both Cuban and foreign,

[38] Not least in the 1930s, when the Mexican government instituted 'socialist' education, created 'collective' *ejidos* (land reform communities), and briefly had Marxists running the both the Ministry of Education (Narciso Bassols) and the main labour confederation, the CTM (Vicente Lombardo Toledano).

and soon embarked on a radical land reform and, indeed, wholesale nationalisation. It therefore fits within the broad comparative schema presented here: the revolutions of the twentieth century sought to implement social change, for which the armed overthrow of the state was a necessary prerequisite. But Cuba was, in 1959, more 'advanced' than either Mexico in 1910 or Bolivia in 1952: it had a higher per capita GDP, higher literacy, bigger cities, more industry, thus a more developed capitalist economy.[39] It was also a smaller, more centralised, more secular and more homogeneous country (class and ethic distinctions notwithstanding). And the Cuban state historically enjoyed extensive powers of regulation and intervention (Domínguez, 1978). In its final Batistiano form it was personalist, corrupt, authoritarian and unpopular, an egregious example of what has been called 'mafiocracy', 'kleptocracy' and 'sultanismo' (the Somocista state being another egregious example) (Wickham-Crowley, 1991, pp. 212, 218). But the Cuban state commanded a large payroll and ample 'patrimonial' resources, far beyond anything Díaz or the Bolivian *rosca* had enjoyed. If asked why Castro implemented socialism — when neither the Mexicans nor the Bolivians had done so — one glib but partially true answer might be: 'because he could'. He inherited a state and a country where a socialist experiment was feasible. After all, Marx envisaged socialism being constructed in the advanced industrial societies of Europe (Germany in particular), not the vast, relatively backward, agrarian empires of Tsarist Russia or Manchu China. Cuba was the Latin American equivalent of Germany (in terms of socioeconomic development: I am not entering the risky terrain of political culture or national character!); Mexico more resembled Russia, and Bolivia China. By way of contrast, as the experience of the radical Cárdenas government showed, implementing socialism in a vast, varied country like Mexico, where

[39] Cuban per capita income in 1950 stood at $450 (in 1970 prices) compared to Bolivia's $189; Cuban literacy was 79% compared to Bolivia's 32%; and Cuba had 20 telephones per 1,000 inhabitants compared to Bolivia's 4. I believe Cuba also had the highest ratios of Cadillacs to population in the entire world.

the authority of the state was hedged and contested (not least by a very powerful Catholic Church), was difficult, if not impossible.

Cuba thus differed from Mexico and Bolivia and the differences help explain the island's peculiar turn towards socialism. However, if we gloss over these differences and lump the three twentieth-century revolutions together, we can see how, as a group, they contrast with the constellation of independence revolutions previously discussed. The latter were directed against a formal colonial state and the state was seen as the chief agent of oppression, in its diverse forms: tax, *repartimiento*, anticlericalism, military repression and mercantilist constraints. Spanish landlords and merchants also incurred hostility, but they, in turn, depended on their close and corrupt association with the colonial state, itself a gross example of Wolf's 'tributary' mode. A wide range of groups could unite in opposition to the state whose overthrow — a radical political revolution by any standards — promised benefits for all, or at least for many. More than 100 years later the Latin American economies had been transformed; market capitalism had advanced and erstwhile colonies had become independent republics governed, in many cases, by narrow oligarchies (and, in some cases, by even narrower personal dictatorships). The tributary mode had given way to a loosely capitalist mode, in which exploitation served the interests not of a foreign metropolis (since 'dependency', even if it existed, was radically different from the formal colonialism of the past), but rather of national elites, for whom the state was an ally, usually a congenial and compliant ally. Now, the owners of wealth and property became the chief targets and, necessarily, the revolutionaries became 'social' as well as 'political' revolutionaries; and the ensuing revolutions — in Mexico, Bolivia and Cuba — have a valid claim to belong to that select category of 'great' or 'social revolutions', as I argued at the outset.

BIBLIOGRAPHY

Andrien, K. J. (1995). *The Kingdom of Quito, 1690–1820*, Cambridge University Press, Cambridge.

Anna, T. E. (1990). *The Mexican Empire of Iturbide*, University of Nebraska Press, Lincoln.

Bayly, C. A. (2002). "Archaic" and "Modern" Globalization in the Eurasian and African Arena, c. 1750–1850', in Hopkins, A. G. (ed.), *Globalization in World History*, Pimlico, London, pp. 47–73.

Bell, D. A. (2008). *The First Total War: Napoleon's Europe and the Birth of Modern Warfare*, Bloomsbury, London.

Bergquist, C. (1986). *Labor in Latin America*, Stanford University Press, Stanford, CA.

Berlin, I. (1969). *Four Essays on Liberty*, Oxford University Press, New York.

Bethell, L. and Roxborough, I. (eds) (1992). *Latin America Between the Second World War and the Cold War, 1944–48*, Cambridge University Press, Cambridge.

Brading, D. A. (1971). *Miners and Merchants in Bourbon Mexico, 1763–1810*, Cambridge University Press, Cambridge.

Brading, D. A. (1993). *The First America*, Cambridge University Press, Cambridge.

Bulmer-Thomas, V. (1994). *The Economic History of Latin America Since Independence*, Cambridge University Press, Cambridge.

Coatsworth, J. C. (1988). 'Patterns of Rural Rebellion in Latin America: Mexico in Comparative Perspective', in Katz, F. (ed.), *Riot, Rebellion and Revolution. Rural Social Conflict in Mexico*, Princeton University Press, Princeton, New Jersey, pp. 21–62.

Cobb, R. (1972). *The Police and the People: French Popular Protest, 1789–1820*, Oxford University Press, Oxford.

Domínguez, J. (1978). *Cuba: Order and Revolution*, Harvard University Press, Cambridge.

Dunkerley, J. (1988). *Power in the Isthmus. A Political History of Modern Central America*, Verso, London.

Dunkerley, J. (2003). 'The Origins of the Bolivian Revolution in the Twentieth Century: Some Reflections', in Grindle, M.S. and Domingo, P. (eds), *Proclaiming Revolution. The Bolivian Revolution in Comparative Perspective*, Institute of Latin American Studies, London, Chapter 6.

Eckstein, S. (1988). *The Poverty of Revolution: The State and the Urban Poor in Mexico*, Princeton University Press, Princeton.

Fischer, D. H. (1970). *Historians' Fallacies*, Harper & Row, New York.

Gilly, A. (1989). *Cartas a Cuauhtémoc Cárdenas*, Ediciones Era, Mexico.

Guardino, P. F. (1996) *Peasants, Politics and the Formation of Mexico's National State: Guerrero, 1800–1857*, Stanford University Press, Stanford, CA.

Guerra, F.-X. (1999). 'De lo único a lo múltiple: Dimensiones y lógicas de la Independencia', in McFarlane, A. and Posada-Carbó, E. (eds), *Independence and Revolution in Spanish America: Perspectives and Problems*, Institute of Latin American Studies, London, pp. 43–78.

Halliday, F. (1999). *Revolution and World Politics*, Macmillan, Basingstoke.

Hamill, H. M. (1966). *The Hidalgo Revolt*, University of Florida Press, Gainesville.

Hexter, J. H. (1979). *On Historians*, Collins, London.

Huntington, S. P. (1971). *Political Order in Changing Societies*, Yale University Press, New Haven, CT.

Huntington, S. P. (1991). *The Third Wave. Democratization in the Late Twentieth Century*, University of Oklahoma Press, Norman.

Jacobsen, N. (1993). *Mirages of Transition: The Peruvian Altiplano, 1780–1930*, University of California Press, Berkeley.

Katz, F. (1981). *The Secret War in Mexico*, Chicago University Press, Chicago.

Kelley, J. and Klein, H. S. (1981). *Revolution and the Rebirth of Inequality: A Theory Applied to the National Revolution in Bolivia*, University of California Press, Berkeley.

Knight, A. (1986). *The Mexican Revolution*, 2 vols, Cambridge University Press, Cambridge, v. 1, pp. 115–26.

Knight, A. (1990). Social Revolution: A Latin American Perspective, *Bulletin of Latin American Research*, 9, 2, pp. 175–202.

Knight, A. (1992). Revisionism and Revolution: Mexico Compared to England and France, *Past and Present*, 134, pp. 159–99.

Knight, A. (2002). *Mexico: The Colonial Era*, Cambridge University Press, Cambridge.

Knight, A. (2003). 'The Domestic Dynamics of the Mexican and Bolivian Revolutions', in Grindle, M. S. and Domingo, P. (eds), *Proclaiming Revolution. The Bolivian Revolution in Comparative Perspective*, Institute of Latin American Studies, London, Chapter 3.

Knight, A. (2007). 'Mexico's Three Fin de Siècle Crises', in Servín, E., Reina, L. and Tutino, J. (eds), *Cycles of Conflict, Centuries of Change*, Duke University Press, Durham, pp. 153–183.

Lehman, K. D. (1999). *Bolivia and the United States: A Limited Partnership*, University of Georgia Press, Athens.

Lockhart, J. and Schwartz, S. (1983). *Early Latin America*, Cambridge University Press, Cambridge.

Lynch, J. (1973). *The Spanish American Revolutions, 1808–1826*, Weidenfeld and Nicholson, London.

Lynch, J. (1989). *Bourbon Spain, 1700–1808*, Blackwell, Oxford.

MacIntyre, A. (1978). *Against the Self-Images of the Age*, University of Notre Dame Press, Notre Dame.

McFarlane, A. (1990). 'The Rebellion of the *Barrios*: Urban Insurrection in Bourbon Quito', in Fisher, J. R., Kuethe, A. K. and McFarlane, A. (eds), *Reform and Insurrection in Bourbon New Granada and Peru*, Louisiana State University Press, Baton Rouge, pp. 197–254.

Moore, B. Jr. (1979). *Injustice: The Social Bases of Obedience and Revolt*, Macmillan, London.

O'Rourke, K. H. and Williamson, J. G. (1999). *Globalization and History*, MIT, Cambridge, MA.

Pomerantz, K. J. (2000). *The Great Divergence*, Princeton University Press, Princeton.

Popper, K. (1961). *The Poverty of Historicism*, Harper & Row, New York.

Rodríguez O., J. E. (1998). *The Independence of Spanish America*, Cambridge University Press, Cambridge.

Rodríguez O., J. E. (ed.) (1989). *The Independence of Mexico and the Creation of the New Nation*, UCLA Latin American Center Publications, University of California, Los Angeles.

Ruiz, R. E. (1980). *The Great Rebellion: Mexico 1905–1924*, W. W. Norton, New York.

Skocpol, T. (1979). *States and Social Revolutions*, Cambridge University Press, Cambridge.

Stern, S. J. (1987). 'The Age of Andean Insurrection, 1742–82: A Reappraisal', in Stern, S. J. (ed.), *Resistance, Rebellion and Consciousness in the Andean Peasant World, 18th to 20th Centuries*, University of Wisconsin Press, Madison, pp.34–93.

Tenenbaum, B. (1986). *The Politics of Penury: Debts and Taxes in Mexico, 1821–56* University of New Mexico Press, Albuquerque.

Tilly, C. (1995). *European Revolutions, 1492–1992*, Blackwell, Oxford.

Topik, S. (1989). 'Mexican Independence in Comparative Perspective', in Rodríguez, O., J. E. (ed.) (1989). *The Independence of Mexico and the Creation of the New Nation*, UCLA Latin American Center Publications, University of California, Los Angeles, pp. 331–338.

Topik, S. J. and Wells, A. (eds) (1998), *The Second Conquest of Latin America. Coffee, Henequen and Oil during the Export Boom, 1850–1930*, University of Texas Press, Austin.

Trotsky, L. (1967). *Trotsky's History of the Russian Revolution*, 3 vols, Sphere Books, London.

Tutino, J. (1986). *From Insurrection to Revolution in Mexico*, Princeton University Press, Princeton.

Tutino, J. (1988). 'Agrarian Change and Peasant Rebellion in Nineteenth-Century Mexico: The Example of Chalco', in Katz, F. (ed.), *Riot, Rebellion and Revolution. Rural Social Conflict in Mexico*, Princeton University Press, Princeton, pp. 95–140.

Voss, S.F. (2002). *Latin America in the Middle Period, 1750–1929*, Scholarly Resources, Wilmington, DE.

Vries, J. de (1994). The Industrial Revolution and the Industrious Revolution, *Journal of Economic History*, 54, 2, pp. 249–270.

Walker, C. (1999). *Smoldering Ashes. Cuzco and the Creation of Republican Peru, 1780–1840*, Duke University Press, Durham.

Whitehead, L. (2003). 'The Bolivian National Revolution: A Comparison', in Grindle, M. S. and Domingo, P. (eds), *Proclaiming Revolution. The Bolivian*

Revolution in Comparative Perspective, Institute of Latin American Studies, London, Chapter 2.

Wickham-Crowley, T. (1991) *Exploring Revolution. Essays on Latin American Insurgency and Revolutionary Theory*, M. E. Sharpe, Armonk, New York.

Wolf, E. R. (1982). *Europe and the People Without History*, University of California Press, Berkeley.

Chapter

7

Education, Citizenship, and Decentralization in the Latin American Bicentenary: The Chilean Case

Oscar Corvalán Vásquez

7.1. SUMMARY

This chapter examines the role public education has played in the progress and construction of democracy in a selected number of Latin American countries, in order to demonstrate that the development of both goes hand in hand, that they benefit each other and are mutually dependant. Nevertheless, the analysis is mainly concerned with data related to Chile.

This chapter offers a summary of the consequences that colonial legacy has had for the construction of the fragile democracy that has prevailed in many Latin American republics, their persistent social inequalities, the heterogeneous nature of their production, and the cumulated negative impact these factors have had on the development of civic education. It also analyzes the strategies proposed to Latin American countries in the last 50 years by diverse international organizations, which have emphasized the importance of education for the labor market rather than for civic education. Furthermore, it argues that civic education and regionalization are fundamental to improve forms of governance and reduce the effects of the enormous heterogeneity in economic production and social cohesion.

It concludes with a reflection on the recent education reforms carried out in parallel to economic neo-liberal policies. It makes recommendations in order to achieve a high quality public education which should focus on people's training as much as on the development of the citizenry. It should develop civility, which has been repeatedly neglected or destroyed by past and recent dictatorships and neo-liberalism, two shared inheritances of Latin Americans today.

7.2. INTRODUCTION

The examination of the contribution of public education in the evolution of political institutions and the progress of governance in Latin America raises several questions related to the region's slow development of civic consciousness. The existing productive matrix and the insufficiency of public education correlate during the second century of political independence. Public education during the nineteenth century only benefited less than a fifth of the population. The questions that arose upon further investigation of a more diverse range of sources were the following: Can public education compensate for social inequalities and the historical legacy unfavorable to the democratic development of Latin America? How can this historical legacy be differentiated in the different countries that make up the region? Is it sufficient to offer an education that promotes production and productivity and aims at making exportation more competitive? Why are civic education and regionalization necessary for development? What characteristics should quality public education have to respond to the socio-political changes introduced by economic neo-liberalism? What is the impact of the decentralization of education initiated in the 1980s? What role should education perform in Latin America's third century of independence? What kind of orientation and contents should it have in order to promote employment and a productive framework, and at the same time to institutionalize democracy to secure comprehensive development.

7.2.1. The Limitations and Potential of Public Education to Redress Inequalities and a Historic Legacy Contrary to Democratic Development in Latin America

In this section, we focus on the limitations that public education in Latin America has had in its contribution to civic development. The following sections summarize the potential that quality public education has to improve political institutions and secure regionalization in Latin American countries.

Often when professionals dedicated to economic growth and/or social development meet a problem that does not have a solution within their paradigm of thought, they claim that it is related to a cultural problem that could be solved through educational reform. That is why, for example, economists have difficulty justifying high economic growth with an increase in distributive inequality, as is the case in Chile. Similarly, social scientists attribute the lack of necessity to strive for success among marginalized populations to cultural factors, such as ethnicity or socio-demographic features.

It is insufficient to simply recognize that socioeconomic systems are open and complex. There exists an ethical responsibility for those who are interested in the common good of our societies to re-examine the epistemological bases of our paradigms of knowledge. If we want to be sensitive to the suffering caused by the social injustice that the latter reproduce or amplify, we need to modify the Cartesian and positivist paradigms according to which there is a social cost the poor should necessarily pay. We are waiting for the economists to do their part and revise their epistemological paradigms that brought us to the recent financial crisis and increase in social inequalities and inequities between nations.

Historically, the various and reoccurring authoritarian governments ruling almost all Latin American countries were given the mission of undermining the fundamentals of education for democracy, civic development, and workers' self management of local development. Rarely was public education's real contribution to the construction of citizenship valued. On other occasions it was plainly eliminated for being contrary to the politics of the government in power.

From a theoretic point of view, San Martín (2003) has endeavored to demonstrate that the concept of citizenship in Latin America may not fully embody the classical European notion of civil society. It finds itself *jeopardized* in our continent because of the strong cultural influence of another, more ancestral, type of social organization that was communal, self-managed, and emancipated. That means the liberation of the authority of the *idea* over the *symbolic interaction*. As a result, the construction of Latin American citizenship should endeavor to rescue the valuable elements of the classical idea of civil society and citizenship, and reinterpret them from a different point of view.

The examination of historical data shows that the progress experienced by the education sector in the first century of Latin American political independence was minimal. In Chile until 1880 there were fewer than 500 people (teachers and assistant teachers) involved in public education. It was not until 1930 that the staff reached 12,650. In 1895 the total enrollment reached 150,000 students in 1,300 small public education institutions. Only in the mid-1960s were these numbers tripled (Correa *et al.*, 2001, p. 24). This low enrollment was reflected by the fact that the majority of adults were illiterate during the entire first century of Chilean independence (see Table 7.1).

The best rates of primary retention appear in 1950 in the province of Santiago de Chile with 53% in the sixth grade in urban schools and 22% in rural schools. (Havighurst, 1962, p. 185), Meanwhile, in Cuba the retention rate was 18% in urban areas and 26% in rural areas, and the average (urban and rural) rates were 9% in Ecuador and Paraguay, 11% in Peru, 12% in Puerto Rico, 13% in

Table 7.1. Chile: Evolution of rates of illiteracy 1854–1930

Year	1854	1865	1875	1885	1895	1907	1920	1930
Percentage	86.5	83.0	77.1	71.1	68.2	60.0	50.0	44.0

Source: Labarca, 1939, p. 276.

Table 7.2. Capacity to read and write in Latin America population over the age of 10, by 1950

Country	Percentage of readers and writers	Per capita income in dollars
Uruguay	85%	400+
Argentina	85	400+
Chile	80	300–400
Puerto Rico	76	Idem
Cuba	75	Idem
Costa Rica	75	250–300
Panamá	68	idem
Paraguay	66	100
México	60	200–250
Ecuador	57	100–150
Colombia	53	200–250
Venezuela	53	400+
Brasil	50	200–250
Perú	48	100–150
República Dominicana	43	150–200
Salvador	38	150–200
Honduras	38	150–200
Nicaragua	38	100–150
Bolivia	32	100
Guatemala	28	150–200
Haití	10	10

Sources: CEPAL, *Estudio sobre la mano de obra en América Latina*, CEPAL, La Paz, 1957; UNESCO, *L'alphabétisme dans le monde au milieu du XXème siècle*, UNESCO, Paris, 1957 (see Havighurts, 1962, p. 114).

Costa Rica, and 46% in Venezuela. This is reflected in the educational achievements of each country (see Table 7.2).

In Chile, from the second half of the nineteenth century to 1938, bitter battles rose up between liberal educators and conservatives supported by the Catholic Church, especially around the issue of replacing Latin with the study of sciences, as well as commercial and industrial training in order to train workers as fundamental actors in the strengthening and integration of the nation. Lengthy discussions between educators and politicians and between public and ecclesiastical authorities stemmed from the law of compulsory primary instruction in 1920. However, this law was not enacted in Chile until 1938 (Correa *et al.*, 2001, pp. 40–41). From this period on, the number of students enroled in primary education was over 500,000 in 1925 and rose to 795,600 in 1950. In this period, secondary education's enrollment increased from 63,500 to 148,900 students. At the same time university enrollment almost doubled from 6,200 to 11,000 students. In other words, the construction of a true system of public education at the national level had to wait more than one century after independence to be established. This, at least, made access to education possible for urban students, but rural education centers only began to open in the second half of the twentieth century.

It was the necessity derived from the process of import substitution after the Second World War that led to the development of a State Technical University in 1947. It involved the fusion of the School of Arts and Trade, the School of Industrial Engineers, the School of Mining in Copiapo and la Serena, the industrial schools in Concepción and Valdivia, the Industrial School of Temuco, and the Technical Institute of Pedagogy. At that time the only institutions of higher education that existed were the University of Chile, the Catholic University of Chile, and the University of Concepción, to which we can add the Technical University Federico Santa María in Valparaiso. Nevertheless, in 1947 nearly a third of adults were illiterate and almost half of school-aged children (900,000) did not go to school. Infant mortality was very high; a study by the ministry of public health in the late 1940s showed that 50% of children died before the age of nine (Correa *et al.*, 2001, p. 188).

7.3. PERCEPTIONS OF THE COLONIAL LEGACY IN LATIN AMERICA AND THE EFFECT OF DICTATORSHIPS AND NEO-LIBERALISM IN CIVIC FORMATION

After a description of the effects of the colonial legacy in the construction of democratic republics in Chile and Latin America, this section will examine the concurrent effects of dictatorship and economic neo-liberalism on the formation of citizens and quality public education.

7.3.1. The Colonial Heritage in the New Republics

This section does not present an in-depth examination of the colonial legacy in Latin American republics' political, economic, social, and cultural development; in this chapter it is only possible to address the most important of these. The aim is to shed some light on the consequences that the pre-republican period had in facilitating or limiting public education. It summarizes factors that favored or limited citizens′ development and higher levels of social and labor equality. Explanations of the effect of colonization in the subsequent development of Latin American countries often emphasize geography or political institutions established during the colonial period, or an unfair international commerce. Alternatively, they stress the density and variety of the indigenous population that occupied the territory before colonization. Each of these factors is viewed as an explanation for subsequent underdevelopment. However, what interests us here is the degree to which Iberian colonization affected or could have affected democratic development, which in turn influences social equity and the development of public education.

If we discount the peak period of commerce with the metropolis known to the viceroyalty during the destruction of the Maya and Inca culture and the mining that took place in other countries, during the colonial period the Spaniards did not, to a large extent, manage to create political institutions. Apart from the army and the Catholic Church, the institutions they established did not have a significant effect in the countries′ development of municipal councils and local institutions. The fact is that during Latin America's colonial period nothing was done to promote the participation of the majority of the population in society. Meanwhile, the political role reserved for Creoles remained very limited until the wars of independence. Napoleon's advance in Spain and the capture of the monarch led to the end of the Spanish monopoly of trade with the Ibero-American colonies. The British Navy patrol facilitated illegal commerce with English and North American ships. The colonies had not imported the necessary machinery and technology to provide themselves with industrial resources and instead relied upon the exchange of primary materials obtained from mining and agriculture to obtain these products (Stein and Stein, 1970, p. 181).

After Latin American declarations in the early 1810s, the implementation of a postcolonial model of integration in the international trade system was based on the exploitation and exportation of natural resources and the reception of immigration prior to the First World War. The existence of some institutions that were not very responsive to social changes reinforced the disparities inherited from the colonial period (often associated with large estates) that contributed to social inequality.

In the postcolonial period the social structure was not modified but rather constructed within the framework of colonial institutions. In turn, this had a significant effect on long-term dynamics of growth and inequality in Latin American countries. The route followed in the first century of independence constructed a national history based on inequality, instead of founding the nation on the principles of a democratic republic composed of free citizens, equal under the law.

In addition to the scarce development of political institutions, the determining factors of geography and the availability of natural resources and the type of production easiest to export had a significant influence on the organization of productive organisms. Proprietors ran sugar mills, coffee estates, and mines thanks to the exploitation of indigenous peoples and slaves imported from Africa, and large agricultural estates began to form social organizations with a culture on their own — a culture that was incompatible with democratic and republican ideals: This was far from encouraging "citizens" participation. Latin American former colonies took a century to begin the industrialization process. Later this process gathered speed because of the need to substitute imports during the Second World War. Therefore, the education of the population was not a priority for governments or for an economy that was based on the exportation of primary materials.

In the postcolonial context, the institutional framework was made up of a few formal political institutions and many informal social institutions. Due to increased transparency, the first ones have had an improved capacity to adapt to change and allow upward social mobility

(Alonso, 2007). But in traditional or highly fragmented societies the underprivileged commonly turn to informal rather than formal institutions, something that had negative consequences in the development of the young democracies.

In general, political institutions formed by the nation-state had a significant influence during the first century of independence, but these institutions generally excluded citizens' participation. Most of the population was illiterate because during this period no country provided a system of compulsory public education. Only after the First World War did Latin American countries attempt to combat illiteracy, which in the case of Chile affected more than a third of the population over 15 years old.

For example, in the case of Brazil, a country which became a republic in 1891, with strong decentralization of the state, the establishment of federalism increased local power but led to the extreme "rule of the cornels". As a result, the republic became more autocratic than the monarchy. Generally the title of "cornel" referred to *fazendeiros*, or owners of large estates whose lands were inhabited by people truly subjected to serfdom. In the new regime, "the rule of the cornels" stood out as one of the main reasons that the democratic political exercise was so difficult. Those who exercised power controled elections and always won, and when citizens voted they did so with loyalty to their local cacique. In this way, the oligarchy and these fraudulent procedures were perpetuated. The privileged few abandoned the population submerged in poverty without instruction and medical services (Iglesias, 1994, p. 41).

In Brazil, it was only in 1930 that President Getúlio Vargas ordered Francisco Campos to create and head a Ministry of Education and a Ministry of Health. Campos showed himself to be very active and authoritarian, as was to be expected in Brazil from then on. He introduced education reforms at the elementary, secondary, technical, and university levels under the imposition of special laws (Iglesias, 1994, p. 63). Continuing to face high rates of illiteracy, the government created the Brazilian Literacy Movement (MOBRAL) in December 1957. But it was a populist measure, which produced few effective results.

7.3.2. The Regression Suffered by Public Education During the More Recent Dictatorships

A few decades after Latin American republics were first established, authoritarian governments took over, justifying their necessity as founders of nation-states superior to local *caudillos*' rule and to monarchist attempts to promote counterrevolution. Although authoritarian, none of the nineteenth-century dictatorships compare to those that arose during the Cold War to counter popular initiatives to gain further national independence. Post-1950 dictatorships declared themselves anti-communist and had devastating effects in Latin America. Not only were the crimes they committed unprecedented, but they also led to the disarticulation of civil society, traditional mechanisms of government, and their incipient proposals for democratic education. During the decades of the 1970s and 1980s, Latin American dictatorships set out to impose a climate of terror and suspicion on social networks and liberal education contrary to effective civic education.

In this respect this section will only refer to the emblematic Chilean dictatorship (1973–1990) to illustrate the subsequent difficulties of re-establishing educational systems that contribute to civic formation as well as education for work. It can be remembered that, "throughout the period of military government, there was a systematic effort to take control of patriotic symbols and impose one version of national history, through various programs and curriculum reforms that would produce effects on several generations of Chilean students..." (Correa *et al.*, 2001, pp. 284–285). All teachers in public education who did not adhere to the doctrine of national security were persecuted. As a result, teachers and students who sympathized with and militated in favor of the previous democratic government (1970–1973) were fired.

In political terms, the Chilean military government declared itself nationalist. However, this became distorted over time. It started as a nationalistic project (declaration of principles of 1974) with Catholic, neo-corporatist, and spiritual characteristics rooted in *Hispanidad* and Spanish Francoism. The economic crisis encouraged active participation by Catholic neo-liberal ministers (called "Chicago Boys" because many had been trained by Milton Friedman at the University of Chicago). They insisted in changing the role of the state from previously being the "vertebral column" in the construction of the Chilean nation (Góngora, 1981) to being a mere observer of the free exchange between private participants. The state was supposed to offer some subsidiary programs to those who did not achieve integration into the market. In this way, the Chilean dictatorship fully supported the free market model, privatized public companies, and opened the country to the free flow of exports and imports as a strategy for economic development. At the same time, the military government persecuted all opposition and maintained an iron grip on internal social control, prohibiting all political parties. The economic results of the dictatorship's neo-liberalism were low or negative but in the social sphere the fragmentation of society meant the duplication of the percentage of the poor in the nation, which rose from 28% in 1970 to 44% in 1980.

In Chilean universities repression and intervention started the very day of the military coup. An ideological purge without precedent was unleashed, thanks to the appointment of new rectors who were often retired members of the military and to whom discretionary power over people and organizations was given. These rectors expelled and/or exonerated some 20,000 people by means of the creation of black lists, denunciations, and the presence of agents of the repressive military regime inside the classroom. They also decided to omit academic programs favorable to the development of thought and culture. They closed 23 sections including disciplines such as sociology, languages, and theater, as well as various research centers, especially those related to social sciences. Thousands of books were thrown into fires to prevent people reading books by authors stigmatized by the regime (Correa *et al.*, 2001, pp. 301–302). The quality and prestige of Chilean universities fell considerably after they were deprived of many of their best professors. Some professors went into exile; others became part of one of the 35 independent centers of research and development that had received some 300 researchers by 1984. In 1982, 10 years after the beginning of the dictatorship,

28,000 students were enroled in Chilean universities, a total lower than student enrollment when the dictatorship started in 1973.

Towards the end of the Cold War, Chile and the majority of Latin American countries returned to newborn democracies, facing a legacy of poverty, social segregation, and civic and political distrust. In Chile, as in most of Latin America, it has been necessary to rebuild trust, social networks, and civic and political networks in order to attend to the basic needs of education, health, housing, and work for the impoverished majority. Meanwhile, nearly half the gross domestic product (GDP) was distributed to a privileged few without the slightest remorse about the dictatorial past.

The cruelty of Latin America's recent military dictatorships — self-defined as anti-communist — would not have been possible without the active collaboration of civil political groups. This fact produced the disarticulation of citizens' education and continual violations of human rights. In the case of Brazil between 1974 and 1975, almost 72 million Brazilians (67% of the population) consumed less calories than required per day (Iglesias, 1994, p. 222). In the mid-1970s, Minister Delfim Neto revealed that a large majority of the population did not even consume the minimum necessary for survival, which was physically and intellectually disastrous for children. Of course, in a context in which two thirds of the population was malnourished, it was impossible to offer quality education.

Mexico followed a distinct path in developing its public education due to its revolution in the early twentieth century. In the 1920s, efforts were initiated and designed to eradicate illiteracy, but also to Hispanicize the population as well as to improve teacher training in public education.

In the decades from the 1920s onwards, including ... the 1950s, 10% of the federal budget was directed to education. From 1960 to 1970 the school networks and government spending in education increased impressively ... By extending federal education to the entire republic the standardization of national education was achieved. This put a stop to the tendency observed up to the end of the nineteenth century, according to which each state was entirely responsible for regulating its own educational system. (Hernández, 2000, p. 420)

In the Mexican case it seems that it was necessary to centralize the educational system to improve it, but the long-term results have not been encouraging. In fact, a reform of Article 3 of the 1934 Constitution made a form of socialist education exclusive to the state non-compulsory at primary, secondary, and higher level. It was replaced in 1946 with "the original principles of the Constitution of 1917, for free and secular education ... based in freedom of belief and in democracy. Understood to be a way of life founded in a constant striving for economic, social and cultural betterment for the community ... without competence or exclusivity..., in which the ideals of fraternity and equality are the rights of all the people" (Hernández, 2000, p. 421). The centralization of education created other problems, like the unification of the teachers' union, because the corporate spirit of the PRI (Institutional Revolutionary Party) forced them to unite. Although Mexico did not suffer the same consequences of the Cold War as Chile and other Latin American countries, since 1958 an unachieved reform began there as well, with the aim of de-concentrating education, which remained in the hands of the Secretary of Public Education (SEP) despite the protests of the teaching profession from 1958–1959 and the bloody student insurgency of 1968.

From the point of view of public policies, it should be recognized that education has historically been at the center of efforts to decrease bureaucracy and achieve decentralization, regionalization, and local development, without being able so far to provide the formation of citizens required from a quality education. Despite the recent international financial crisis neo-liberal policies which promote total deregulation of markets, including financial markets, have survived. They do not only represent an economic model but are the basis for a structure of society. This brings us to the mechanisms that make its persistence possible.

In the cases of Chile and Argentina the most lasting effect of the new neo-liberal model has been the change of conscience that started to sweep the country. According to its ideological principles, development is basically understood as economic growth. Supposedly neo-liberalism assures more freedom than the welfare state, which is

Table 7.3. Chile: Percentage of variation in gross national production 1972–1991

1972	1973	1974	1975	1980	1982	1983	1984	1985	1986	1989	1991
−1.2	−5.6	−13.3	7.7	−13.4	−3.5	6.1	3.5	5.6	9.9	7.3	11.0

Economía y Trabajo en Chile 1997–1998. Informe Anual No.7, Programa de Economía y Trabajo (PET). Santiago, June 1998.

inefficient and hampered by traditional restrictions. According to the neo-liberal conception of the state, society, and the market, as José Piñera predicted when he served as a minister of labor under Pinochet, Chile would have reached the status of a developed country by 2010 (Piñera, 1997). But simultaneously he kept silent over the issue of the thousands of Chileans who were "disappeared" and exiled, the high levels of unemployment and poverty, and the small growth of GDP per capita achieved by the military government (see Table 7.3).

According to several historians, in Chile "the economic model could have advocated for liberty, but despite the fact that it was applied with a high social cost, once some success had been achieved, fundamental questioning of the economic model was not permitted (and) the fundamentalist slant of its participants, mostly uncritical, if not participating in the political repression of the dictatorship, made their supposed liberalism questionable in the wide and proper sense of the word" (Correa *et al.*, 2001, p. 299).

From a socioeconomic point of view, the neo-liberal policies imposed by the Chilean dictatorship has led to a society which is divided, profoundly unequal, with low solidarity, prone to crime, and segmented at all levels. As a consequence, it appears to show a regression in political, civic, and social participation. Indeed, the merits of the social and economic development of the past 20 years were not necessarily due to the military government, but rather to the democratic government that promoted policies of growth with equity, achieving the decrease of poverty by a third in this period. Notwithstanding the segmented nature of the structure of production, whether it is oriented to the global or national market, it has not permitted the improvement of highly inequitable income distribution.

From a social and political perspective, Chile, like all Latin American countries, now faces the challenge of offering quality public education in the context of economic, communication, and cultural globalization and the transition towards societies of knowledge and information. In effect, the segmented and heterogeneous characteristics of Latin American societies produce an ambiguous place for them in globalization. Some authors see globalization as endangering future governability and they maintain that "in a world that requires more and more efficient macroeconomic coordination and a more effective redistributive function, it is a regressive tendency" (Bouzas and French-Davis, 1998, p.124). Governability requires a re-equilibrium of the tendencies that exhibit the different ingredients of globalization (Bouzas and French-Davis, 1998). The world financial crisis of 2008 showed these authors to be correct. Until now we have not caught a glimpse of international institutions capable of achieving macroeconomic coordination, which would have a more efficient redistributive function.

From a cultural point of view, a growing number of new or renewed cultural elements are presented through the media. Quality education should integrate the media as a possible ally rather than considering it an enemy. The media not only transmits knowledge and information, but is also the current method preferred by the cultural and entertainment industry.

Both education and the media have significant political consequences in the construction of social consciousness and in the manner of doing politics using these means of communication. Hopenhayn (1994) from CEPAL has called to attention the role that the media can play in a true market of messages that enter a circuit of global exchange and temporary acceleration transforming the limits of heavy and light, high and low, learned and popular, national and international culture.

In Chile and other Latin American countries the unstoppable influence of television on the political arena is unquestionable.

Television has facilitated political practice but making it closer to a public spectacle than a public debate:

> The discussion of real issues has been replaced by competing images that are constructed according to the desires and demands of the consumer in this unique market. Candidates act for these images … looking for scandal instead of debate … in a true political sham they hardly even bother to hide their general disinterest for social questions. (Romero, 1994, pp. 386–387)

Neither private nor state television (still maintained by the profits of publicity) has contributed significantly to the development of citizenship. On the contrary, it appears that the programming negatively affects the formation of willingness to act collectively and weakens the legitimacy of the state as it constantly addresses the consumer instead of the citizen.

From an educational perspective, if we take into account that there is a high inverse correlation between levels of poverty and educative achievements, it can be maintained that educational policy has been simply limited to reproduce the distribution of poverty and inequality. Although poverty has decreased in Chile, inequalities in education have not. Education of higher quality is private and paid for by those who can afford it, and state-financed education is generally of a lower quality. It should be taken into account that inequalities depend to a large extent on economic, social, cultural, legal, and political elements that determine the situation of each family:

> Although poverty is related to insufficient economic resources, this does not necessarily mean that economic factors are the main causes of poverty. Certain cultural, political and judicial practices that facilitate or promote discrimination against certain groups or individuals like women, indigenous peoples or ethnic minorities act as mechanisms for social exclusion which cause or contribute to poverty. (Abramovic, 2006, p. 37)

Following a historical cycle that has focused education exclusively towards production, a proposal for quality education for citizenship in Latin American countries can start from a social ethic and a revitalized human rights perspective, which in turn can contribute to the strengthening of democratic institutions. In fact, currently there is a search for a change of logic in the relation of the poor with the state and its lenders of assets and services. This does not have to do only with people who need and receive social security benefits or discretional loans but with holders of rights, such is the right to quality education (Abramovic, 2006).

This is justified further still by the fact that neo-liberal thought has imposed on public opinion not only suggestions but the agenda of problems to be discussed through purely economic lenses. All public debate is reduced to economics and all economics to "macroeconomic stability" as a means of avoiding the ghost of inflation and its damaging consequences. The goal of full employment has been abandoned and in the best of cases a dignified income is sought, partly from labor, partly subsidized by the state.

Instead of praising "meritocratic behavior", equality of opportunity, right to education, and health and housing, today the political debate revolves around the efficiency of services offered by public and private sectors and the capacity to access these services. Instead of talking about citizens and governance, a society composed of buyers and sellers has been imposed, a society of users and contributors who try to ground ethics in fiscal control, and not in the participation of citizens and workers who claim their part of the product through legitimate association. The social construction of the identity of workers and citizens is each time more blurry, although unemployment does not only affect the poorest of the poor. Also, political leadership is mainly built by appearing on television at whatever price (Romero, 1994).

On the periphery and in some enclaves of each city there are social groups who are poor and impoverished, without access to quality public education. They live side by side with those who have links with drug dealers and consumers. They also have to live alongside juvenile gangs and organized crime groups recruiting young people who see crime as a way out of family unemployment. The problem is more complex when we consider that these groups present behavior adverse to the performance of citizenry practices, and do not develop attitudes or abilities that would benefit from eventual quality education. The educational system is definitely not prepared to integrate them. Therefore, the strategy to improve participation should be socio-political and include a wide range of public policies in which education is just one element, despite its strategic value.

The growing segmentation of society makes it increasingly difficult to organize education for citizens and local territories with the goal of obtaining a better quality of life. The privileged social spheres become isolated and push the poorest people towards marginal spaces in the city, deprived of basic services or public spaces (with the exception of supermarkets for those who still have the capacity to buy).

The social atomization produced by neo-liberalism has destroyed social networks and, in its most basic expression, the family, which finds itself threatened by the absence of mothers and fathers during the day (and often in the evening) as they struggle to provide for their families' subsistence; meanwhile children are undereducated by the media or become involved with gangs in the miserable environment in which they live. In Chile, more than 25% of single-parent families are headed by women who cannot contribute to the education provided by the school because they perform the double function of mother and worker. In addition,

> the public space disappears as a space of common responsibility, constructed and maintained by action based on solidarity not concerned with the search for individual success. Community education, public health, public security, and public spaces, which have been at the center of a strongly integrated society, are being further eroded by the advance of the private sector, with the logic that those who have rights are those who can pay for them. The new society in its practices includes little that can sustain democracy. (Romero, 1994, pp. 385–386)

This is why schools have often had to move away from their mission of education and respond to the need to provide food, clothing, and daycare for children and adolescents with the goal of keeping them away from the dangers they face, including in their own homes. Teachers and public schools act as the last barrier of defense for those who do not want to resort to crime and antisocial conduct. School acts as a kind of social refuge.

In such a context, the question has become whether public policies can go against these trends and whether public education has the tools necessary to redress social inequality. According to Olave, "The levels of poverty existing in Chile today cannot be explained by a lack of economic growth but ... by the existence of structural mechanisms and institutions that tend to increase inequality and social exclusion" (Olave, 2003, p. 230), such as, for example, the use of large estates and the skewed structure of income. Therefore, solutions to social, economic, and political problems are not sought amongst large sections of the urban population and the decreasing rural population. And even an offer of quality public education in schools will be insufficient to generate equality in the country.

7.4. THE PROMOTION OF EDUCATION FOR THE PRODUCTIVE MARKET AND THE LACK OF CONSTRUCTION OF POLITICAL INSTITUTIONS IN CHILE

Traditionally in Chile and in most Latin American countries, governments have stated that education should forge social integration, but fundamentally it should train a workforce with a wide range of qualifications and trades. Rarely do governments offer a proper civic education for democratic and regional development at all levels.

In fact, the economy has always been dominated by Latin America's place on the international level. From the beginning, Latin America was characterized by the type of products the region sold in the world market. Since the postcolonial period, mining and agricultural enterprises such as meat production, and wool and its by-products have been emphasized, without taking into account whether the country was tropical or not. All of these enterprises are characterized by their limited aggregate value and their dependence on the fluctuations of the terms of exchange. The exportation of industrial goods is only a recent phenomenon (in large part within the region), particularly for those countries who can count on an extensive internal market.

This standard of exportation probably had more influence on the organization of national education than the political institutions brought by the colonizers or by the characteristics of the indigenous population. In areas where the indigenous population was not apt or sufficient, slaves were imported from Africa and then the immigration of European technicians and professionals was promoted. In other words, the existing demography rarely determined production. On the contrary, geographic and postcolonial factors led to dependence on the exportation of raw materials.

During the first republican century, the state did little to develop secular public education despite the influence of the French Revolution and of US independence ideals. During the twentieth century in Chile and most Latin American countries, the promotion of secular public education was not exempt from strong and sustained opposition from the oligarchy and the Catholic Church. Even today in Chile most centers of quality education paid for by parents are private Catholic schools. But this is also the case for the private schools and colleges subsidized by the state. Thus, most municipal schools attend to the poorest sectors of the country. In fact, today municipal education enrollments are roughly equal to those in private schools subsidized by the state, and municipal schools are on the decrease. This circumstance makes state action difficult and limited to offering economic incentives for schools to follow its directives.

The development of public education has also been limited because since the 1940s the emphasis was placed on imports' substitution, which led to the promotion of education for the needs of production, industry, and commerce. Half a century later, CEPAL disseminated a new thesis contained in the publication of *Transformation of production with equity* (1990), which overstresses the significance of education for production and productivity and has not placed a strategic importance on civic, local, and regional development.

Up until the 1960s education as a way of forging citizenship was not really a primary objective. According to Havighurst

(1962, p. 228) other goals were favored, such as full coverage of primary education, contacts between teachers and local communities, and the development of a neutral attitude towards religion together with vocational training. Civic education was only promoted in secondary and professional schools, which contributed to the strengthening of the middle class and its aptitude to govern. In other words, the issue was to establish an elitist education that prepared some to govern and others to be governed.

7.4.1. Centralism and the Regional Development of Production

As already mentioned, during the second half of the twentieth century, the priority in Latin American countries was production for competitive exports, which led to the creation of so-called "poles of development" where industries characterized by better management and imported technology were concentrated. The objective of economic policies was to significantly increase the export portion of GDP. However, this strategy failed to contribute to a regionalization capable of giving value to the area in which the industries were located.

The Chilean historian Gabriel Salazar[1] maintains that the Chilean centralization has not been and is not the product of a sovereign decision by the citizens but rather the direct or concomitant intervention of the military apparatus; and this was done with the consent and complicity of the political class and in the presence of large mercantile–financial capitalists. It was not legitimized by citizens but represented a usurpation of their sovereignty in various forms. In this context it is not surprising that all programs for decentralization that proposed that the government act democratically and from below (privileging authorities such as autonomous municipalities, provincial assemblies, or the collective sovereignty of citizens' networks and organizations) have been disqualified as anarchic, or under the pretext

[1] In the Introduction to *Alegato histórico regionalista* (Valenzuela, 1999, p. 6).

that the citizenry lacked maturity to exercise its rights. The individuals who proposed decentralization were sometimes jailed; others were treated like deluded idealists when not ignored.

Valenzuela argues against the thesis of Sergio Boisier, who maintains that the challenge of decentralization is the strengthening of regions while abiding by the central governments' articulation of planning. According to Boisier, regionalism does not exist and must be constructed socially. However, in Chile it was initiated by an administrative act of the state, from the top, as the elitist structure imposed by the military government in 1974. Towards the end of the twentieth century, the proponents of a timid (controlled and conditional) decentralization supported nothing more than an idea. Their mistake was to insist on imposing geographical regions and expect that these regions would socially construct themselves. Decentralization was arbitrarily imposed by decree but did not respect true territorial democratization. To succeed, in Valenzuela's view, decentralization should permit local communities to believe in their political institutions and even to fix their borders without threatening state unity. This can be done without undermining the functions of the nation-state as the guardian of redistribution, external defense and as protector of individual rights. In countries with more advanced democracy, a local community may decide by plebiscite if it wants to belong to another territorial entity or even create a new local government (Valenzuela, 1999, pp. 13–14).

For his part Boisier (2004) holds that even if globalization imposes regionalization upon the citizens, the development of the territory depends on them. But it is evident that this is not a question of volunteerism but rather a long educational process where the cultural and social capital required for local development should be encouraged and formed in the long term.

Today local development is further complicated because it depends on integration in global rather than national chains of production. CEPAL holds that:

> Old policies directed to the promotion of local order (for example the contents of the national requirement) are no longer feasible, not

> only because they are prohibited by multilateral agreements signed with the World Trade Organization but also because they are in direct opposition to the essential logic of global value chains. In other words, to become part of the world market there is no other option but to participate from a local level according to the rules in an international context. (CEPAL, 2009, p. 58)

In addition, at local and national levels, there are many national companies that are not able to position themselves in an international value chain. This is a vast and extremely heterogeneous universe, not only in terms of the different sizes of the companies but also in their technological capacity, their organizational management, and the absence of educational resources available to their workers.

An opportunity for development exists for those who position themselves as providers or lenders of services to local companies having achieved integration in global value chains. Another possibility is to form an association and in this way access the international market on one's own merits. This requires an orientation towards small-scale or niche production of personalized and specialized products while receiving strong support in organization, education, science, and technology. Meanwhile, other companies may reach sufficient levels of productivity to be able to use the special advantage gained from the knowledge of local conditions that allows them to produce goods and services for the domestic market. In any case, the expansion of small and medium-sized companies is essential to increase the framework of production and to generate the employment that integration in global markets does not foster. In order for such a process to take place, it is necessary to mobilize general and specific economic policies for the organization of units of production linking their productivity with the creation and development of productive employment.

Notwithstanding the necessity of the formation of a local base of production Valenzuela reminds us that regionalization is a major player in the regional business world. Regionalization makes it possible to democratize power, to articulate local interests, to produce social pacts within regions, to debate labor and environmental conditions, to revitalize local culture, and value religious and artistic dimensions

(Valenzuela, 1999, p. 64). This cannot be achieved without strong, decisive, committed, and continuous support from an education directed towards the integrated development of citizens ranging from children to adults. Participation can be learned at school but should go further than the system of voting every few years by adults who can only chose between two lists of candidates belonging to the currently dominating binominal electoral system.

7.4.2. The Transformation of Production to Achieve Equality

As shown above, in the last quarter of the twentieth century CEPAL and other organizations have proposed to governments the transformation of the productive system to achieve both social equality and better participation in the international market. More recently, due to a climate favorable to business, innovation, and enterprise, CEPAL has said that:

> The possibility to ascend the value chains is related to national advances in increasing the qualified work force, in infrastructure and appropriate logistics. Also increasingly the capacity to manage the dynamics of absorption, diffusion and creation of innovation and knowledge is expressed in a critical mass of qualified human capital connected to international networks of innovation and supported by public policy that invests in these activities. (CEPAL, 2009, p. 57)

After the so-called lost decade of the 1980s, CEPAL initiated a period of renewal of its economic and social position. Previously it had emphasized policies of import substitution. In 1990 CEPAL launched the document *Productive transformation with equality,* but its proposals were and are of an economic and productive nature. It is also relevant to the design of a strategy for economic reacceleration that allows more equity in Latin American and Caribbean development. At the end of the 1980s the transformation of production and equity were the main issues both in diagnosis and formation of policies and instruments.

The proposed concept of a transformation of production with equality showed a certain degree of optimism. The strategies and tactics defined and applied should bring progressive advances in equity thanks to an increase in the creation of better-paid productive employment and the incorporation and diffusion of technological advances. This strategy would serve not only to combat poverty but also to foster a fairer distribution of income, with the understanding that poverty corresponds to income levels but distribution refers to the prevailing income structure in a given country. But, besides what has been mentioned about the importance of economic and productive aspects, CEPAL's *Productive transformation with equality* barely recognizes and confronts equity and social challenges as priorities.

To overcome the stage of exportation of natural resources, countries such as Sweden and Finland (which started with exportation of natural resources) have introduced a focus on "how to produce" with respect to "what to produce". They have used technologies from other sectors to improve production. This possibility came from a re-evaluation of natural resources in the current cycle of global development, taking into account the structural transformations that characterize it and the development of all-purpose technologies. Well managed, the evolution of knowledge could create a wide range of innovation in products and processes in agriculture, mining, production-related services, and renewable energy, amongst other activities. Profits obtained from natural resources could partly be used to finance innovation in relation to these and other types of production in order to enable them to compete on the international market.

Some Latin American countries have tried to adapt to this challenge by way of policies and institutions efficiently promoting innovation. For example, Brazil has specialized in the management of technologies to exploit petroleum reserves; Chile has started to apply a royalty tax to copper designed to finance universities promoting scientific and technological research, not only directed towards copper mining but other areas as well. Simultaneously, public education has a fundamental role to play in the appropriation and diffusion of new, general and specific, technologies. Among the first, the advance of information and communication technology (ICT) has been spectacular in the last few years. Now access to these technologies should be improved and they should be better utilized in local development. In regard to specialized technologies, universities have an undeniable role to play, such as in the appropriation, development, and diffusion of bio- and nanotechnology, new materials and non-conventional energy resources. Hopefully they will lead to major changes, some of which may mature in the next few decades.

The extent to which companies, governments, and societies can benefit from these trends will depend on the extent to which they are able to take advantage of these technologies and to apply them to concrete situations. The enormous advances in ITC in the last few years should result in better access to these technologies and their productive utilization for national and local development. But their application would require a more educated labor force.

The wide appropriation and diffusion of these technologies should result in workers' enhanced technological capabilities and in the transformation of the productive structure into more equality. This is a process in which public education should play a fundamental role. If this is not the case the importation of technological packages often comprising external technical assistance will continue.

In the last instance, the magnitude of technological benefits for companies, governments, and societies will depend on the manner in which they are able to take advantage of these innovations and apply them to each situation. In this way, it will favor local development. For example, it will be necessary to establish innovative networks that make sustainability of productive transformation possible. Companies already globalized may participate in some of these innovative networks, be they national or foreign. Others will supervise associated local companies dedicated to similar productions (wine, flowers, tourism, furniture, organic products, among others). Evidently these networks should join with universities and responsible public institutions as well as with world centers of excellence in each specific area, so that some of these networks may serve as a base for scientific and technological cooperation between Latin American countries.

Consequently it is possible to use the current productive enclave that dominates all-purpose technologies for the processing of natural resources, taking advantage of their large-scale production (food and beverages, cellulose and paper, copper, petrochemical and others) as well as mid-range production (special materials and personalized products) or smaller production (niche markets). To achieve this, current exports of natural resources would help implement policies in education, science, and technology by reaching two goals: to serve as a platform for the transformation of production and as a source available to finance new initiatives.

7.4.3. The Construction of Social and Political Networks

The big challenge here is to organize civic participation in order to avoid continuing situations in which policy and development programs are exclusively produced by national governments and big corporations. It is necessary to encourage the construction of new national strategies to bring to life advances in the transformation of production in the current context of each nation. This means the mobilization of a wide range of social sectors. In this sense, participative public policy would be beneficial to local groups. First, this requires each country to define a vision of its place in the world in the medium and long terms in order to act as a catalyst for efforts to detect and take advantage of present and future opportunities. Second, the construction of alliances between sectors that are long-lasting, mutually beneficial, and reciprocally committed would make possible the design and implementation of strategies to progressively strengthen this common vision and take advantage of these opportunities. A public/private alliance is inevitable to facilitate an equitable productive transformation, given that the post-neo-liberal state has limited resources.

Centralism has had a profound historical influence on Latin America, particularly in Chile, a country which is known as "the country of order", but order is often confused with homogenization. This is probably the primary psychosocial damage that occurred in the political elite due to the end of democracy in 1973. After the re-democratization of the country, the market was given a dominant role which has led to the continuing goal of stability and consensus as an ideology that does not facilitate reform. Chile, despite having the best macroeconomic indicators in Latin America, is not able to decentralize, to let someone else other than the central government take initiatives — to exercise true democratic politics.

The tension between centralization and de-centralization appears in every policy:

> The latest two reforms which have had certain significance in Chile during the 1990s have been an improvement in the quality of education and, in the judicial area, the creation of independent offices of the public prosecutor. In both cases these reforms were led by the ministers of education and justice, respectively. Regions and communities have to perform [...] goals a-critically. That is to say, the reforms do not accept voices of dissent: for example, a region that prefers to use its budget for the professional development of its teachers by training its teachers in more modern and participative teaching methods, by raising their wages — instead of increasing class time with children under the passive-authoritarian model of teaching that has dominated in Chile. Such reforms would be possible in decentralized systems where innovation is permitted, failure and redesign are tolerated. (Valenzuela, 1999, p. 105)[2]

Bernardo Kliksberg argues that "it may be true that the integration of topics such as social capital and culture make debates about development and the search for adequate designs and strategies more complex. However, it is also true that policies marginalizing these aspects have demonstrated their profound limitations" (Kliksberg, 1999, p. 85). In conclusion, there is no other alternative but to include strategies for increasing social and cultural capital, starting from the strengthening of local social networks with quality public education that supports these networks. Both elements compose the central themes of this chapter.

---

[2] Despite ex-President Ricardo Lagos' good management he was unable to present himself for re-election due to the failure of his plan to reinstall the railway in the south of Santiago. The same could happen to ex-President Michele Bachelet for the defects in her reform of public transport in Santiago.

7.5. EDUCATION FOR THE DEVELOPMENT OF CITIZENSHIP AND REGIONALIZATION

As already discussed, during two centuries of ups and downs in the republican life of Latin American countries, in general, the development of education was successively oriented towards production and the productivity and competiveness of the export sector, but neglected the formation of citizenship and the preparation necessary for taking charge of regionalization projects and management on each country's own territory. At the beginning of the third centennial of independence, it is urgent that this anomaly be rectified, as experience shows continuing this way will fail to create the conditions of social equity and territorial balance indispensible to democratic development.

Chile's recent historical development shows a contradictory pattern in which national per capita income can be doubled in a decade without any changes in income distribution; in this way, it has been possible to reduce poverty by a fourth in two decades, without changing the structure or operation of political power; the consumption of durable goods has augmented considerably at the same time as crime rates have increased even faster; social housing for the majority of the population is provided, but without public spaces or services nearby. Although public education is only one important factor among others in economic, political, social, and cultural development, without its effective contribution no development can be adequately achieved.

The experience of the last 50 years shows that, firstly, training for work has been prioritized over civic education; furthermore, governments have chosen an approach to education that discredited any options leading to alternative forms of development, taking into account the environment and using unconventional technologies requiring different qualifications from the workers. Secondly, during periods of authoritarian governments, public education deteriorated and did not value or integrate the cultural contributions of indigenous populations. Thirdly, although there have been advancements in women's education, their participation in professions founded on mathematics, science, and engineering is still far below their percentage in the active population. Fourthly, despite universal access to 12 years of elementary and secondary education, more than half of workers do not understand what they read.

Furthermore, although it has been possible to enroll almost all children under the age of 18 in (public and private) educational centers, there has been no decline in the rates of drug addiction, teenage pregnancy, and juvenile delinquency. In order to increase enrollment in higher education, progress has been made in offering scholarships and student loans; however, they remain inaccessible for nearly 80% of the graduates of municipal public education where academic standards are too low for university entrance. So, the extreme segmentation of quality of education offered by the system serves as a powerful mechanism that reproduces and legitimizes social inequalities by confining the poor to municipal schools.

Reforms in education carried out in almost all Latin American countries during the past 30 years show that if the coverage in primary and secondary schools expanded, the quality of education did not progress and the pertinence of the education even less. After the reforms launched in the 1990s, the organization of Chile's system has favored educational segmentation, making systematic change more difficult. Keeping the system segmented has important consequences for governance, as it limits the socio-cultural bases of democratic order, from the perspective of the strategy of democratization of a deeply unequal society that manifests itself in terms of differentiated learning. The results of the international PISA test indicate that educational systems with the best results are those whose classrooms are the most socially integrated; on the contrary, the systems that educate a new generation in explicit social segments or implicitly stratified by the family's economic-cultural capital get the worst classification (OECD, 2004). Chile, with its tri-tier — municipal, subsidized private, and private — system of schools, increasingly differentiated according to the family's income, exemplifies a problem of educational segmentation. The latter must be solved from an instrumental perspective — average learning and country competitiveness — and from a perspective of moral integration and democratic quality of the socio-political order. According to García-Huidobro and Bellei (2003), the strong social stratification of the Chilean school system leads to schooling of even more unequal value than in other societies. This is reflected in differentiated learning results, ordered according to the socioeconomic hierarchy of the students set by the type of ownership and financing of the establishments they attend. The first inequality between elite and publicly funded schools, present from the beginning of primary school, increases in high school, and shows a schooling system unable to break away from cultural inequality. However, performance is lower in the municipal sector, which cannot select pupils, than in subsidized private schools, although both are financed by the state at similar levels. Low educational achievements result in a situation where about half of the adult population do not have the basic tools of literacy necessary in the twenty-first century.

By incorporating new social sectors that have been traditionally excluded from education, the Chilean educational system, designed to form elitist groups of various kinds, has proven ineffective. Indeed, it is not possible to increase the reach of education simply by offering a curriculum and methodology designed for selected groups to the popular classes, because the latter are characterized by low social capital and/or cultural elements that are "a-functional" in the current educational system.

Nonetheless, as the state is being held accountable (Abramovich, 2006), it prohibits discrimination and requires the adoption of affirmative measures in order to guarantee the inclusion of groups or sectors of the population traditionally discriminated against. And the principles of equity and non-discrimination should be fundamental criteria in the distribution of budgets and welfare spending. Discrimination in access to rights and liberties can come from the disparity between geographic regions, ethnicities, gender, or any other socio-demographic factor. In the case of Chile and a few other Latin American countries, the decentralization of public education and health has been aggravated by the inequality in access to public services of a comparable quality to those found in other regions. While central state funding per pupil is the same everywhere, local municipalities' average income per capita may vary from simple to more than

10 times — as their capacity to contribute to local schools. In reality, for the quality of the education to be on a similar level everywhere, more investment should be directed to poor areas, and not the other way around.

Regarding the orientation and organization of the contents of education, it is important to point out that this discussion in Chile is as old as the beginning of public education. According to Correa *et al.*, at the end of the nineteenth century there were debates about teaching methods and many innovations were made, such as the adoption of the technique of concentric study, promoted by Valentín Letelier and Diego Barros Arana after their training in Germany. According to this method, instead of teaching each discipline separately from the others, all disciplines should be taught simultaneously, beginning with the most rudimentary notions for each one and gradually expanding the scope of all of them year after year. This technique was presumed to be the expression of a rational and logical structure that, by means of the inductive method, presented an evolutionary and progressive concept of knowledge. This example demonstrates that pedagogical discussion on the best didactics is more than a century old in Chile, but until today it has been unable to change a curriculum structure based on disciplines and separate knowledge, and to solve recurrent problems.

So, today we are still waiting to revise the contents and sequencing of education and to determine the consequences of a focus on the standards on which public education will finally be evaluated. This author has argued that the application of international tests, without taking into account local culture, does not necessarily measure what they are thought to measure (Corvalán, 2009). TIMSS and PISA tests have been applied in Chile and other countries, but the organization of the curriculum still does not have detailed maps of learning progress nor is there any correlation between the methodology of problem solving and the format, contents, and application of the tests. Neither have the appropriate teaching skills been developed. Therefore Chile and other Latin American countries participating in the aforementioned tests do not achieve acceptable results. This is because these tests are incomplete indicators and do not provide a comprehensive vision of the quality of education. A quality education requires evidence not only on learning results, but also on the reach of education, its equality, the contextual conditions of learning, teachers' practice, and learning opportunities structured and sequenced in a form appropriate to the situation of each social group (OECD, 2004, p. 95).

These challenges will be better understood if a mode of education based on standards is adopted at the same time as a program of personal development and civic commitment, including local and regional development. Notwithstanding, according to what Cifali has shown (2005, pp. 243–256), this recent debate takes place in Africa as well as in Latin America. Public education today is under pressure to account to society. In particular, teachers are required to develop the skills necessary to push their students towards higher levels and standards. But the required reorganization of the educational system is still pending.

It is evident that a series of problems must be tackled through quality public education in this period, marked by civility and the economic neo-liberalism imposed on people as the only possible way of providing for the public good. Possible diagnoses and options for development are available. Will the socially disadvantaged sectors be organized in order to achieve quality public education now, as the third centennial begins in each country?

7.5.1. Quality Public Education to Support Local Development

To better assess the challenges Chilean and other Latin American societies face and to outline future processes of local and regional development, it is necessary to summarize the results of three decades of decentralization of the public education system.

The strong segmentation of the Chilean education system manifests itself in the highly unequal performance achieved among students from different schools, which reflects large disparities in the quality of education provided by them. This variation depends greatly on socioeconomic and class differences between students. Between the end of April and June 2006, deficiencies in municipal schools were highlighted by secondary school student protests at the national level, demanding change and improvement in the public education system so that free high quality education could be available to all. Students also demanded free public transportation to schools and free administration of the Test for University Selection as well as participation in the government's decisions affecting education. This students' social mobilization, known as "the march of the penguins" in reference to the school uniforms they must wear, culminated in the formation of a high level commission that recommended improvements in public education to the Parliament (OECD and BIRF, 2009). However, the segmentation of the public education system remained intact, and the state has blocked the possibility of fighting against the social inequality that this very system reproduces.

Despite an average improvement in the quality of life in Chile, the modernization process has been unstable and has not resolved the problem of poverty according to social expectations. Public management has been unsatisfactory, favoring institutional leadership rather than social dynamics, which expresses a tendency towards institutionalization, regulation, and privatization, inside a restrictive framework of local government participation and the predominance of the central public agencies (Davis Toledo, 2009).

So, the persistent centralization and lack of participation by social groups in public management has supported the production of standardized and homogenizing programs and policies based on categories of analysis and actions unrelated to the social contexts in which they are implemented and to the complexity of micro-social dynamics (Correa, 1995).

In Chile, until now, the participation of civil society has been characterized by a certain type of implementation by low-level professionals from the central government, the sub-national government, and segments of the civil society, which resulted in pragmatic, short-term, and depersonalized relationships between different groups, rather than the construction of social projects (Borja *et al.*, 1987).

Furthermore, from the methodological point of view, the evaluation of performance and the assessment of management are problematic in terms of the effective range and relevant quality and appropriateness of public services, programs, and politics (Muñoz in Davis, 2009). Indeed, they show the existence of structural contradictions associated with the juxtaposition of different periods and different levels of social, political, economic, and cultural integration in the distinct social sectors and regional contexts that coexist on a given territory (Garretón, 1993).

During the last two decades following the dictatorship, there has been an effort to promote the social and cultural sustainability of the democratization and modernization of public institutions and of society in general. At the same time attempts were made to reduce and compensate the perverse effects and the externalities — the "social cost" — of the economic model by means of subsidies and public investments channeled through programs and relatively efficient public policies focused on, but not entirely adapted to, local development.

The practice of public management has been oriented towards greater transparency in the system of administration and management of resources. Despite attempts at reinforcing social networks, establishing strategic alliances with the market, and opening public institutions to the participation and control of public management by the citizenry, civil society and sub-national governments have yet to be strengthened. The possibility of reaching an understanding that shows the dynamism, subjectivity and particularities, which are all fundamental for the design of contemporary public policies, remains uncertain.

Therefore, it is time for a serious questioning of public policies, for an analysis of the tangible and intangible bases of the development that is being sought. Such an analysis should integrate, in particular, the idea of social capital (Bourdieu, 1994) and the role of education in the creation of social capital. The concept of social capital points to the normative recovery of values and social practices based on respect, solidarity, and trust, which give social groups a new and greater prominence in the construction of public policy and programs.

The public manifestation of social capital is translated to stable and cohesive societies focused on the common good (Correa, 1995; Garretón, 1993). For this to happen, central public powers need to strengthen local governments through the implementation of strategic policies favoring administrative and financial political decentralization (Bresser, 1999). They need to first create an opening for the participation by regional groups in the design and administration of public policy through practices such as the delegation of strategic tasks from a central to regional level among various political administrations. Second, they need to form networks of groups and points of communication to facilitate synergy in the different instances of decision making — that is, to locally construct what Boisier (2004) calls "synergetic capital".

The recent evaluation of Chile's educative reforms from 1991 to 2006 and the campaign debates of the last presidential election in 2009–2010 pointed out the low quality of education. The new president, Sebastián Piñera, has promised to double the central state's investment in education within a decade and to create some quality municipal high schools. Today, Chile's public investment in education continues to be very low when compared to international standards. According to the Organization for Economic Co-operation and Development (OECD), countries spend an average of 5% of their budget on public education and 0.7% on private education centers. In Chile, these rates are 3.3% on public education and 3.1% on private education (OECD, 2007). On this basis, the specific strategies to be implemented in education can be summarized as follows: (a) to increase state support to public education, and to revise the standardized indicators used to measure both public and private state subsidized education; (b) to promote a public education of higher quality to redress its current low level; (c) to revise the current teaching degree so that it takes into account not only experience acquired over time but also the development of teaching skills; and (d) to guarantee state's financial commitment beyond the four-year term of each elected government.

No consensus has been reached over the strategies needed for the formation of ethical, responsible, committed citizens in order to secure local and national wellbeing. But this includes training citizens for territorial development, caring for the environment, promoting social and political participation, all goals that are linked to the fortification of democracy. Specifically important are the analysis and understanding of complex social systems. In this regard, Jordi Borja *et al.*, (1987) hold that political administrative decentralization is an adequate means of promoting the political socialization of the common people and the development of individual liberties, as well as the socioeconomic changes leading to greater equality. However, in Chile decentralization has been limited to a partial deconcentration of public education and health. It has been understood from the perspective of the development of human capital and restricted to the development of vocational capacities, whereas only from the perspective of the development of citizens can the strategic value of the role that a strong, decentralized public education system could play be fully comprehended.

What is required is a democratic decision to define the type of development sought. But for this it is necessary that, at the very least, the majority of the population should be capable of understanding what they read and of expressing their point of view about the causes and solutions to problems that concern them. Development consists of making individuals and communities the true subjects, generators, and beneficiaries of development. For this to occur, people need to be able to understand these changes and to use them to their advantage. Therefore, good government calls for coherent action to allow for basic social objectives, such as democracy, social integration, and economic growth, to be compatible (PNUD, 1999).

An additional contribution of education consists in its ability to support Boisier's proposal for the development of linguistic constructivism — the use of words applied to conversations that generate consensus about proposals in order to achieve new local powers. The generation of real or latent synergetic capital can enable the whole community to democratically articulate the diverse forms of intangible capital found within it and to give the community direction through knowledge. According to Boisier, in order to produce "synergetic capital" on an adequate territorial and social scale, the reorientation of the country's educational system alone would not be sufficient.

7.6. CONCLUSION

The role played by education in the two centuries of political independence in Latin American nations varies from country to country, according to how early the education systems were organized, to their funding, range and direction, and whether their goal emphasizes responding to the labor market or forming citizens in line with democratic constitutions. In general, these systems were organized during the twentieth century. It is possible to single out some relatively small countries (Costa Rica and Uruguay) that organized public education with a wide outreach at an earlier stage. By the end of the nineteenth century, however, the fight against the illiteracy affecting between a third and half of all adults was enunciated as a priority almost everywhere.

Although the second century of independence saw significant advances in literacy rates, there was still no quality public education which provided both civic education and vocational training for all. Countries which had made advances in this direction such as Chile, regressed as a result of the Pinochet dictatorship and the latter's application of neo-liberalism, and now their educational system is still a reflection of social inequalities. This serves to illustrate the current limitations on the promises of public education to compensate for inequalities and a historical legacy which is contrary to Latin America's democratic development. This is not to say that public education can be neglected in the construction of active citizens, as a tool for social mobility and as a necessary condition for the increase in resources and strategic reform. But today, civic education and regionalization have once again become a priority.

To build quality public education following the socio-political changes introduced by neo-liberalism and globalization, one must act from inside the system. First, it is necessary to define what kind of network organization of local social participants is relevant for a redefinition of the power of the centralized state and its transfer to local and regional levels. Second, public finances should be redefined and distributed according to different criteria. Third, regional and local organizations should be professionalized and trained for tasks encouraging democratization, regionalization, and social participation. Fourth, the direct election of all government bodies, whether they be local and regional, should be achieved — independently from the candidates' affiliation to political party blocks, as occurs in the binominal Chilean system.

Internal changes to the national system of education should from now on have to share their results with society. For this, education ministers should be explicit and accountable in the direction and content they give to public education, and promote appropriate means of evaluation. In this respect the application of international tests that do not take local culture into account should be revised to meet their purpose. Also teachers' skills in these areas need to be developed (Corvalán, 2009). Furthermore, although the TIMSS and PISA tests have been applied in Chile and other countries, the organization of the curriculum still does not provide detailed reports on students' learning progresses. Neither is there any correlation between the methodology used to resolve problems with the format, content, and application of these tests.

These challenges should be met together with promoting education for civic development and providing tools enabling current and future citizens to take charge of their local and regional territory, by procuring more equality and opportunities for personal development for all. Education is far from the process in which local and regional authorities become responsible for producing curriculums that focus on priorities compatible with the local situation, and of establishing goals responding to the joint challenges of the job market and the building of citizenship. Such reforms should also comprise a process on the integration of the extremely segmented current educational system.

BIBLIOGRAPHY

Abramovic, V. (2006). 'Una aproximación al enfoque de derechos en las estrategias y políticas de desarrollo', *Revista de la CEPAL*, 88 (April), pp. 35–50.

Alonso, J. A. (2007). 'Desigualdad, instituciones y progreso: Un debate entre la historia y el presente', *Revista de la CEPAL*, 93 (December), pp. 63–84.

Boisier, S. (2004). 'Desarrollo Territorial y Descentralización', *Eure. Revista latinoamericana de estudios urbano regionales*, 30:90, pp. 27–40.

Borja, J., Valdés, T., Pozo, H. and Morales, E. (1987). *Descentralización del estado, movimiento social y gestión local*, Instituto de cooperación iberoamericana (ICI)-Facultad latinoamericana de ciencias sociales (FLACSO)-Consejo latinoamericano de ciencias sociales (CLACSO), Santiago de Chile.

Bourdieu, P. (1994), *Raisons pratiques: Sur la théorie de l'action*, Ed. du Seuil, Paris.

Bouzas, R. and French-Davis, R. (1998). La globalización y la gobernabilidad de los países en desarrollo. Paper presented to the workshop "Gobernabilidad democrática y participación", organized by Comisión Sudamericana de Paz, Cochabamba (junio).

Bresser Pereira, L. C. (1999). *Reforma del Estado para la Ciudadanía*, Centro Latinoamericano de Administración para el Desarrollo, Buenos Aires.

CEPAL (2009). *La transformación productiva 20 años después: Viejos problemas nuevas oportunidades*, Naciones Unidas, Comisión Económica para América Latina y el Caribe, Santiago de Chile.

CEPAL (1990). *Transformación productiva con equidad: la tarea prioritaria del desarrollo de América Latina y el Caribe en los años noventa*, Naciones Unidas, Comisión Económica para América Latina y el Caribe, Santiago de Chile.

Cifali, M. (2005). 'L´envers et l'endroit d´une «obligation de résultats »' in Lessard, C. and Meirieu, P. (eds), *L'obligation de résultats en éducation: Évolutions, perspectives et enjeux internationaux*, De Boeck Université, Bruxelles, pp. 243–256.

Correa Ríos, E. (1995). 'La Demanda por un Nuevo Estado', in *El Proceso Decisorio Público: Evaluación de impactos y logro de consensos*, ILPES\LC\IP\R, Santiago de Chile.

Correa, S., Figueroa, C., Jocelyn-Holt, A., Rolle, C. and Vicuña, M. (2001). *Historia del siglo XX chileno*, Editorial Sudamérica, Santiago de Chile.

Corvalán, V., O. (2009). 'Perfil de competencias docentes y escalamiento para su desarrollo, *Revista electrónica "Desarrollo de Competencias" REDEC*, 5 (December), Universidad de Talca, Talca, Chile.

COX, C. (2003). 'Las políticas educacionales de Chile en las últimas dos décadas del siglo XX', in Cox, C. (ed), *Políticas Educacionales en el Cambio de Siglo. La reforma del sistema escolar en Chile*, Editorial Universitaria, Santiago de Chile, pp. 19–114.

Davis Toledo, G. A. (2009). *Modernización de los gobiernos sub-nacionales para la implementación de las políticas públicas'*, Postdoctoral paper, Project Fortalecimiento de la Investigación en Políticas Públicas en la Universidad de Talca, Instituto de Investigación y Desarrollo Educacional, Universidad de Talca, Talca, Chile.

Eaton, K. (2004). 'Designing Subnational Institutions: Regional and Municipal Reforms in Postauthoritarian Chile', *Comparative Political Studies*, 37:2, pp. 218–244.

García-Huidobro, J. E. and Bellei, C. (2003). *Desigualdad educativa en Chile*, Universidad Alberto Hurtado, Santiago de Chile.

Garretón, M. A. (1993). 'Aprendizaje y gobernabilidad en la redemocratización chilena', in *Nueva Sociedad*, 128 (November–December), pp. 148–157.

Góngora, Mario. (1981) Ensayo histórico sobre la noción de Estado en Chile en los siglos XIX y XX. Santiago. Ediciones La Ciudad.

Havighurst, R. J. *et al.* (1962). *La sociedad y la educación en América Latina*, Editorial Universitaria de Buenos Aires, Buenos Aires.

Hernández Chávez, A. (2000). *México. Breve historia contemporánea*. Fondo de Cultura Económica, México, D. F.

Hopenhayn, M. (1994). 'Industria cultural y nuevos códigos de modernidad', in *Revista de la CEPAL*, 54, Santiago de Chile (December), pp. 167–178.

Iglesias, F. (1994). *Breve historia contemporánea del Brasil*, Fondo de Cultura Económica, Mexico.

Kliksberg, B. (1999). 'Capital social y cultura. Claves esenciales del desarrollo'. *Revista de la CEPAL*, 69 (December), pp. 85–102.

Labarca, H., A. (1939). *Historia de la enseñanza en Chile*, Imprenta Universitaria, Santiago de Chile.

Lessard, C. and Meirieu, P. (eds) (2005). *L'obligation de résultats en éducation: Évolutions, perspectives et enjeux internationaux*, De Boeck Université, Bruxelles.

OECD (2004). *Chile. Revisión de políticas nacionales de educación*, Organisation for Economic Co-operation and Development, Paris.

OECD (2007). *Education at a Glance: OECD Indicators*, Organisation for Economic Co-operation and Development, Paris.

OECD and BIRF (2009). *La Educación superior en Chile*, Organisation for Economic Co-operation and Development, Paris.

Olave Castillo, P. (2003). *Chile: Neoliberalismo, pobreza y desigualdad social*. Universidad Nacional Autónoma de México, Instituto de Investigaciones Económicas, Mexico.

Ossenbach, S., G. (1993) 'Estado y educación en América Latina a partir de su independencia (siglos XIX y XX)', in *Revista Iberoamericana de Educación*, 1. Available at: http://www.oei.es/oeivirt/rie01a04.htm [Accessed December 22, 2010].

Piñera, J. (1997). *Chile 2010: Libertad, libertad mis amigos*, Economía y Sociedad Ltda., Santiago de Chile.

PNUD (1999). *Índice de Desarrollo Humano en Chile 1990–1998*. Available at: http://www.desarrollohumano.cl/otraspub/Pub03/todo.pdf [Accessed December 22, 2010].

Programa de Economía del Trabajo (PET) (1998). 'Economía y Trabajo en Chile 1997–1998', Informe Anual No. 7, June.

Romero, L. A. (1994). *Breve historia contemporánea de la Argentina*, Fondo de Cultura Económica, Buenos Aires.

San Martín Ramírez, V. (2003). 'Educación y ciudadanía en América Latina: Sugerencias para el análisis y la comprensión', *Revista de Educación* (Ministerio de Educación: Secretaría General de Educación y Formación Profesional), 1 Extra, pp. 83–106.

Stein, S. J. and Stein, B. H. (1970). *The Colonial Heritage of Latin America: Essays on Economic Dependence in Perspective*, Oxford University Press, New York.

Valenzuela, V. T., E. (1999). *Alegato histórico regionalista*, Ediciones Sur, Santiago de Chile.

Chapter

8

Peru: Nation-State and Multicultural Society

José Marín Gonzáles

8.1. INTRODUCTION

If we imagine the history of Latin America as seen through a European window, Europe could be recognized as a *mirror* in which we can identify the structure of a European state political model applied to most American countries with the same consequences in both continents. The lack of competence to respect and manage cultural and linguistic diversity of the multicultural societies, and the incapacity of this type of state model to cope with concrete historical realities, realities that leave the problems of this model uncovered in different contexts: Mexico, Guatemala, Bolivia, Ecuador or Spain — with the emergence of the Catalan nation or the demand for autonomy of the Basque country.

This global approach to history allows us to associate Europe and Latin America over the last two centuries; Latin America is considered to be a political laboratory of colonial and postcolonial Europe.

These facts allow us to understand to what extent political models such as the "nation-state" imposed in this geographical space and on other continents, have finally caused these perverse effects: intolerance, racism, exclusion, and the denial of most fundamental rights.

Beyond the characteristics of historical actors of the European or American societies and their historical and social contexts, there is just one state model and one political determination that influence the integration, assimilation, or exclusion processes.

In history, such influence acts as a mirror that reflects our image as historical actors who belong to a single group: the human race. From this fact a common reflection necessarily emerges on the fundamental principles of respect for pluralism and cultural diversity, which form the core of every human society, as opposed to ethnocentrism that permeates the construction of identity in every culture.

In the European context during the beginning of the nineteenth century and during the twentieth century, the nation-state political model has caused, and still causes, a denial of cultural and linguistic diversity. The victims were the ethnic minorities (such as gypsies in Eastern Europe) or people (such as the Basque in Spain and France) or national minorities (e.g. the Hungarian in Romania and other countries of Eastern Europe) and immigrant colonies in general (Ferrer, 1998; Pérez, 1998; Salvi, 1973; Sanguin, 1993).

In the American continent, from Canada to Chile, the ancestral rights of different indigenous peoples have been rejected, due to the application, against their will, of the authoritarian principles of the nation-state and the denial of citizenship. Such principles leave a trace of racism, exclusion, and marginalization, based on biological, cultural, and legal excuses stated by eurocentrism which has invaded the colonial and neo-colonial political power discourses. In this context, churches and schools became, with the processes of evangelization and alphabetization, the preferred means of forced assimilation, promoted by the policies of "national integration" (Walsh, 2009).

The church and the school will be the ones to prohibit the languages and destroy the indigenous cultures in the name of *occidental and Christian civilization*. These institutions promoted the myths of

Progress and Development (Burga, 1988; Flores Galindo, 1987; Montoya, 1990, 1998).

In the history of the American continent, the situation of the indigenous peoples and the communities that form the multicultural American society reminds us of the reality of the minorities and the immigrants of contemporary Europe. The case of Peru is a historic and a very representative case of this shared history between Europe and America.

8.2. THE NATION-STATE

"The nation-state is both creation and creature of modern Europe" (Edgard Morin, 1991, p. 319), author's translation.

The idea of "nation" emerges as a purely ideological concept and expresses the crystallization of a desire to consolidate a feeling of existence and acknowledgment as a collective identity. It is through an imaginary construction that the (national) consciousness creates the nation. In a historically given space, the repetition and diffusion of the funding myths promoted by a determined language finally allowed the creation of a state that represents a nation. The state uses the nation's myth and discourse to reinforce its political determination of survival.

From the Middle Ages on, nations identified themselves with languages. For example, the German nation has been formed by all the people who speak German. Later on, nations were defined by a language, a territory, an ethnic group, a religion, and traditions. In Greece, Serbia, Bulgaria, and Romania the idea of "nation" precedes the development of the state and motivates the emancipatory fights of the subjugated people to the Ottoman Empire.

The nation-states are never limited by their geographic frontiers. Most of the time, the delimitation of a territory is carried out by the states, through an arbitrary manner which ended up fragmenting the original nations, thus making the history of humanity a succession of dramas. In Africa, the rising states, using colonial delimitations, imposed unreal "nations" over different ethnic groups without shared languages. An extreme case is the one in which the idea of nation not only precedes the formation of a state, but also the occupation of a territory, stimulating the first and then the second one, such as the case of the foundation of Israel in 1948. The case of Zionism is an example of the concretization of an identity, not only religious or ethnic, but also national (Morin, 1991).

The nation-state, as a political model, finds its origins in Europe during the second half of the fifteenth century. The alliance between the kings of Castile and Aragon marks the beginning of the creation of the Spanish state based on the supremacy of a language (Spanish), a religious view (Roman Catholicism), and a connection with the Occidental world: under these conditions, the historical germ of nation-state was born (Attali, 1991; Ferrero, 1994; Marín, 2007).

Historically, Spain was the place where the process of asserting a national identity, based on a political model of state, generated the ideological and legal instruments that led to the rejection of cultural and linguistic diversity on the geographic territory that declared a new state. This principle of institutionalized rejection of distinctiveness and cultural and religious diversity is expressed by the expulsion of a considerable number — 250,000 — Jews from Spain on 31 March 1492. The same year, the Muslims were expulsed too, following their defeat in the battle of Granada, after seven centuries of occupation. The Gypsies, who arrived from northern Africa some decades before the end of the fifteenth century, were persecuted and excluded (Dominguez, 1988; Vilar, 1979).

Until the Middle Ages, the history counted on empires, cities, people, and ethnic groups. The combination nation-state, more widespread than the one of the cities, is more restricted and more unified than that of the empires, in spite of these being polyethnic (Morin, 1991).

The monarchical French state had developed the creation of a "nation" due to the slow imposition of the French language over the conquered ethnic groups. The nation-state concept was formulated by French romanticism against the monarchical absolutism. This revolution strengthened and prolonged with a cosmopolitan conception that goes beyond the identity based on the language (Delannoi, 1991). It is from the revolution, the nation legitimizes the state (Morin, 1991).

The nation-state forms itself slowly, variously, in France, England, Spain, and Portugal, from or around the monarchial power which is transformed by itself in the formation of state-nation.

In North America, after the emancipation of the settlers of the English colony, a federal model of nation-state was created. Since then, based on French principles rather than American principles, the nation-state composes an emancipating, potentially universal, political model. Given this fact, since the beginning of the nineteenth century, the example of the United States encourages the uprise of white and *mestizo* populations, events that will cause the development of new republics in Latin America.

In the nineteenth and twentieth centuries, the European political model of nation-state becomes the model for the constitution of the republics born during the postcolonial period in Latin America, Asia, and Africa from the 1960s.

But, beyond speeches, the political elite in power privileges and imposes, on behalf of cosmopolitism, *a vision of the world*, *a language*, *and a dominant culture*, to the detriment of the other ethnic groups, even when the group in power does not represent the majority. This is a constant fact in the history of Latin America.

The nation-state political model conceived at the beginning of the nineteenth century, after the French Revolution, is based on the construction of the "nation" as a unifying and homogenizing myth of a group of people with their different languages and cultures. These new states claim their sovereignty over the territories that they do not fully control. Despite the proclamation of the principles of *Liberty*, *Equality*, *and Fraternity*, this model turned out to be an ideological and legal instrument that generated an authoritarian policy (Salvi, 1973).

These authoritarian records linked to the foundation of the states, are the origin of contemporary conflicts. In Mexico, for example, current drama of the indigenous peoples from Chiapas still remains despite the 1910 revolution. This revolution had as its primary goal to build an egalitarian society of social justice. A self proclaimed policy of "national integration" intended to consolidate the creation of a Mexican "nation" through the alphabetization by means of the

Spanish language; but in reality, this process degenerated into a process of forced assimilation.

Nowadays, given the differences between state and society, Colombia, a polyethnic and multicultural country, gives us an example of a failed nation-state. As a political model, it is not able to react to the deep social crisis and political violence that divide the society and makes it bleed over its land.

The consequences of establishing this type of political model in contexts where there is an important cultural, linguistic, and religious diversity may cause real ethnocides and genocides, from Canada to present-day Chile. There are eloquent examples of these such as: the loss of territory and the misery of the indigenous peoples in the US; Chiapas' and Guerrero conflicts in Mexico; the recent genocide of 250,000 indigenous peoples in Guatemala; and the displacement and genocide of an indigenous population caused by the political violence and by favoring the interests of multinational companies in Argentina, Brazil, Colombia, Ecuador, Paraguay, Peru, and Chile, to name a few. Of the almost 70,000 victims of political violence reported in the year 2004 by the Truth Commission in Peru, more than 80% were indigenous in origin.

Despite the "Decade Declaration on Indigenous Peoples"* decreed by the United Nations (UN) in 1992, this contemporary drama of economic and social marginalization, racial discrimination, and the systematic rejection of the multicultural character of Latin American societies, constituted, at the beginning of this century, a challenge to be taken particularly in the American continent (Deroche, 2008).

8.3. NATIONAL INTEGRATION

From our historical perception, we can notice that integration is impregnated of multiple dimensions: political, economical, social,

* The following terms are used in this text interchangeably: indigenous people, autochthonous or native communities, to refer to the same population, according to the context without considering or perceiving it as something negative.

and cultural. Our reflection perceives *integration as a real possibility in participating on equal conditions in all the decisions of a determined community or society.*

The political and economical participation in society, schools and everyday life are, among others, the spaces where integration must be carried out. The respect for plurality is essential — all authoritarianism or implicit or declared arbitrariness produces a subtle or forced assimilation. Democracy, as the principle of justice and equality, is only possible if it is capable of integrating all its members. Assimilation and segregation, in all their forms, constitute the contrary of integration. Otherness, difference, and plurality are also the opposite of integration.

The integration of the indigenous peoples of America after the colonial conquest until today has been reduced to a policy statement called, "national integration." This policy was intended to "integrate" the indigenous as "inferiors" under subjugated conditions. This ideological discourse wrongly hides a terrible assimilation.

8.4. A BRIEF HISTORY OF THE NATION-STATE OF MULTICULTURAL SOCIETY AND POLITICAL INTEGRATION IN PERU

At the beginning of the sixteenth century, the Inca state was in control of a vast territory that covered the south of Colombia, Ecuador, Peru, a large portion of Bolivia, one third of Chilean territory, and the north of Argentina. Inca power was based on economic control, tax payment, and political control of the dominated populations — the Incas managed these systems with the help of the elites of the different ethnic groups. Even though Quechua was imposed as the official language, the state allowed the survival of hundreds of indigenous languages, respecting the cultural and religious practices of the dominated people (Rostworoski, 1988; Espinoza, 1986, 1990, 1997).

The colonial period from the sixteenth to the nineteenth century was characterized by a forced assimilation policy, through the evangelization of indigenous peoples. The Holy Inquisition took over the suppression of all the religious and cultural manifestations that differed from the official (Duviols, 1986; Roth, 1989; Zapata, 1990). In the framework of the *School for Young Inca Princes*, the official education destined to the settlers opened a space for the sons of the indigenous leaders, those who collaborated with the colonization. This official education, in Spanish, only promoted the dominant culture.

As an answer to this process of domination, a cultural opposition was organized against the colonization of the so-called indigenous, which was promoted by the oral culture that found support on the preservation of myths and traditions.

Between 1742 and 1781 important indigenous rebellions were developed such as Juan Santos Atahualpa, which started in Los Andes and finished in the Gran Pajonal in the Amazon without being suppressed. Another example could be Tupac Amaru and Tupac Katari, carried out in the Andes region.

At the end of the eighteenth century, following the bloody repression of the indigenous rebellions, access to schools for natives was forbidden due to the formation offered to the main indigenous leaders at the Princes' Schools.

From this period there is a saying: "*indio educado, demonio encarnado*; *indio instruido, demonio perdido*" ("An educated Indian is an incarnated devil and an instructed Indian is a lost devil"). After closing the schools for natives, the myth of education for the indigenous could be transcribed as, "knowing how to read and write is living in the world of lights; not knowing how is like living in the world of shadows." This being a fact, schooling turns out to be a mandatory way to defend their rights in a society that prefers the written culture (Montoya, 1990, 1998).

In 1821, the Republic of Peru was founded over the political model of nation-state and citizenship developed by the French Revolution. Between the years 1823 and 1825, this nation was built by a group of Creole elite, descendants from the settlers who rejected their political dependence from Spain, but neither the exploitation of the territories, nor the domination of the indigenous peoples who lived on the land could declare it as a new state. Native people will be the only ones to economically contribute to this new policy which, in the framework of an *inner colonialism*, will deny them all rights to political and social participation (Arguedas, 1977; Burga, 1988; Flores Galindo, 1987; Marín, 1985; Marín, 1990).

In a republican state, *being a citizen* means: to know how to read, write, and be an individual owner. These are essential conditions for the *integration* to the new republic. However, for the indigenous peoples, these conditions are unattainable. After the end of the rebellions of the eighteenth century, the schools were almost unreachable and the indigenous territories were considered collective properties.

In the year 1856, the Republic established the abolition of the trafficking of African slaves. The Peruvian population of African origin represents a minority group, in contrast to Brazil, Colombia, Cuba, or the Caribbean (Freire, 1974; Guanche, 1983; Romero, 1987). After this prohibition, the traffic of people from southern Asia began. They were mainly Chinese people, who belonged to the Cantonese region, brought with the help of Portuguese traders established in Macao Island. In the year 1986, official immigration of Japanese workers began (Morimoto, 1979; Rodriguez, 1989; Trazegnies, 1994).

After the foundation of the Republic and during most of the twentieth century, the native people were the only ones who paid taxes and worked for a state that excluded them.

During the 1920s, the creation of an intellectual movement for the defense of the indigenous peoples urged the government to create an Indigenous Affairs Office and the Patronage of the Indigenous Race, chaired by the Archbishop of Lima, which turned out to be the first space wherenatives could express themselves. This century was characterized by the continuation of an *assimilation, segregation, and racial discrimination policy* which impregnated all the institutions and everyday life of Peruvian society (Marín, 1985; Portocarrero, 1993).

8.4.1. Evangelization, Alphabetization, and Assimilation

In the mid-twentieth century, the religious missions of the North American Protestant Fundamentalists arrived to Peru, under the academic support of the SIL (Summer Institute of Linguistics), linked to some North American universities. Those universities were financed by several religious institutions, private companies, and programs of the US Department of State.

In 1952, by means of a government decree, the bilingual alphabetization of the indigenous peoples of the Amazon was entrusted to the SIL. The interest of the Peruvian state is to assimilate the indigenous peoples through the alphabetization programs in Spanish, using this language as the basis for the *National Integration* program. For the missionaries, this program was limited to the translation of their religious texts into indigenous languages (Marín, 1992; Marín & Dasen, 2007).

The military revolution in 1968 carried out by a military revolutionary government took the power of the state and ordered an agrarian reform, considered as the most radical reform in the history of Latin America. This law commanded the conversion of large industrial agricultural properties to rural cooperatives. This military government conceived of the *integration* as the participation of all the Peruvian society sectors in political and economic decisions and recognized the multicultural and multilingual character of the Peruvian society. Quechua and other indigenous languages were recognized as official languages, and the government even proposed to include the study of Quechua in school and university programs.

An education reform that follows the previous approaches was trying to consolidate the aforementioned decisions.

Another decree law agreed the participation of the illiterate people in the political elections — a very important disposition since a large group of the population fell under this category.

These measures were taken in 1974 under the law decree 20653, known as the Law of Native Communities and the Agrarian Development of Jungle. This decree opened the possibility of recognizing the territorial rights of these communities. In 1975, the government wanted the expulsion of the SIL.

All these political measures that created a great expectation of openness and political will, to deeply change the structures of the Peruvian society were thwarted by a military coup led by General Morales Bermudez in 1975. This new power rejected all the economic, political, social, and cultural measures that had been enacted, restoring the old neo-colonial order.

Under this government and those which followed, the indigenous peoples continued to face constant assaults on their territories caused by the incursion of multinational companies of gas and petroleum and the lawless illegal chaotic exploitation extended to the entire Amazon mining area, eroding and contaminating their ecosystems.

Peru experienced the emergence of huge political violence between 1982 and 1997, which was an expression of an unresolved social conflict, caused by economic exploitation, racial discrimination, and the marginalization of predominant sectors of the Peruvian society.

The insurrection of armed groups began in the poorest areas with a high density of indigenous population. According to the Truth Commission Report, the indigenous peoples represented four fifths of the 70,000 victims of this conflict.

8.4.2. Multiculturalism and Integration

Integration is the result of respect for plurality; it is the implementation of democracy from the moment the equality of conditions is guaranteed for everybody to cohabit and participate in taking decisions that determine the destiny of a society.

The actual question is: Are we able to open ourselves to the multiplicity of perceptions and points of view considered as valid and accepted by others? If we accept, then we also hope to receive the same respect back from others.

How can we imagine the possibility of keeping cultural diversity and plurality alive? Tolerance must be based on reciprocity; if we are tolerant to others, we expect to be tolerated at the same time. This implies a certain level of acceptance in order to share with others properly. This premise allows us to establish relationships with members of the community, which is the basis for individuals' functioning relations and reciprocity. A group of communities forms civil society, which allows us to imagine a political space that goes beyond authoritarianism, mutations, and the differences among individuals and between the state and society (Sartori, 1994).

Integration implies a process that involves multiple dimensions and can be associated to a state political model.

The state is supposed to represent society, creating conditions for citizens to participate in making fundamental decisions.

Integration implies freedom and respect for the rights of individuals of all the groups involved.

In a multicultural and plurilingual society — the type of societies existing in both Europe and the American continent — the state would have to guarantee respect for cultural and linguistic diversity. From this point of view, education — in a broad sense and in all its forms — is a privileged vehicle to carry out the transmission of world viewpoints, the system of values, norms, and references, and finally, the knowledge that supports a feasible society project.

Administering cultural diversity and plurality, seems to be, from my perspective, the most important challenge for contemporary societies. The current political model of nation-state shows itself as incapable of assuming this multicultural reality that characterizes our American societies.

From this premiss, in the case of multicultural and plurilingual societies, could we imagine a type of state capable of assuming the formulation and application of an intercultural policy that could meet the requirements that we have just provided in evidence?

Our main question is, could a model of confederated state capable of respecting cultural and linguistic diversity would be able to assume the democratic management of the multicultural Peruvian society?

8.4.3. Multicultural Society, Integration, Languages, and Cultures

One of the vital tasks, to make democratic integration a reality, must be assumed by education, which has to promote respect for cultural and linguistic plurality that characterizes Peru and some other countries in Latin America (Marín, 2005a, 2005b).

There are about 50 languages in Peru. Castilian, wrongly called "Spanish", is the official dominant language, followed in importance by Quechua and Aymara in the Andes region, with different dialect variations. In the Amazon region, which is more than half the territory of Peru, about 40 languages are spoken and they belong to 16 linguistic families such as: Arabela, Arahuaca, Bora, Cahuapana, Cantdoshi, Shapra, Harakmbut, Huitot, Jibaro, Pano, Yagua, Simaco, Takana, Ticuna, Tucano, Tupi-Guarani, and Zaparo which are spoken in the region of Peruvian Amazonia (see Fig. 8.1).

In Peru, the descendants from African origin, who came from the traffic of slaves, lost their languages and a considerable part of their cultures due to hard living conditions. During recent years, they have become more active, creating organizations that bring together Afro-Peruvians who participate in the National Commission of Andean, Amazonian, and Afro-Peruvian organizations (Cuche, 1981; Romero, 1987).

To this context of cultural diversity must be added Japanese and Cantonese, spoken by the Asian, Japanese, and Chinese immigrants who lived in Peru from the eighteenth century. Korean immigration is recent and represents a minority. Other cultures and spoken languages also belong to this multicultural and plurilingual environment such as German, Spanish, Italian, English, and others from European origin to which we could add small communities such as Slavonic, Jewish and Middle Eastern (Bonfiglio, 2001; Morimoto, 1979; Rodriguez, 1989; Trasegnies, 1994).

Given the reality of this enormous cultural and linguistic diversity, how can we figure out integration if the state, through official schooling, admits and privileges Spanish in its official program, thus imposing a monocultural and occidental vision of the world arbitrarily?

8.5. NATION-STATE AND MULTICULTURAL SOCIETY: THE AMAZON CASE

Among the achievements obtained by indigenous initiatives, facing a nation-state model incapable of managing a democratic government we could mention:

- The consolidation of Amazon indigenous organizations such as the Consejo de Desarrollo de las Nacionalidades de la Amazonia

PERU: Ethnic and Linguistic Map in the Amazonian and Andean regions

Peru: Total Area 1'285'216 km^2 Population: 27'965'000 (2007 census) 29'496'000 (2010 estimate). Peru is a multiethnic country home of people from many different historical backgrounds. The population includes 45 % Amerindians, 37% mestizos, 15% European, 3% Afro-Peruvians, Japanese, Chinese and other. The Andes and the Amazonian regions is the mainland of the indigenous populations of Peru.

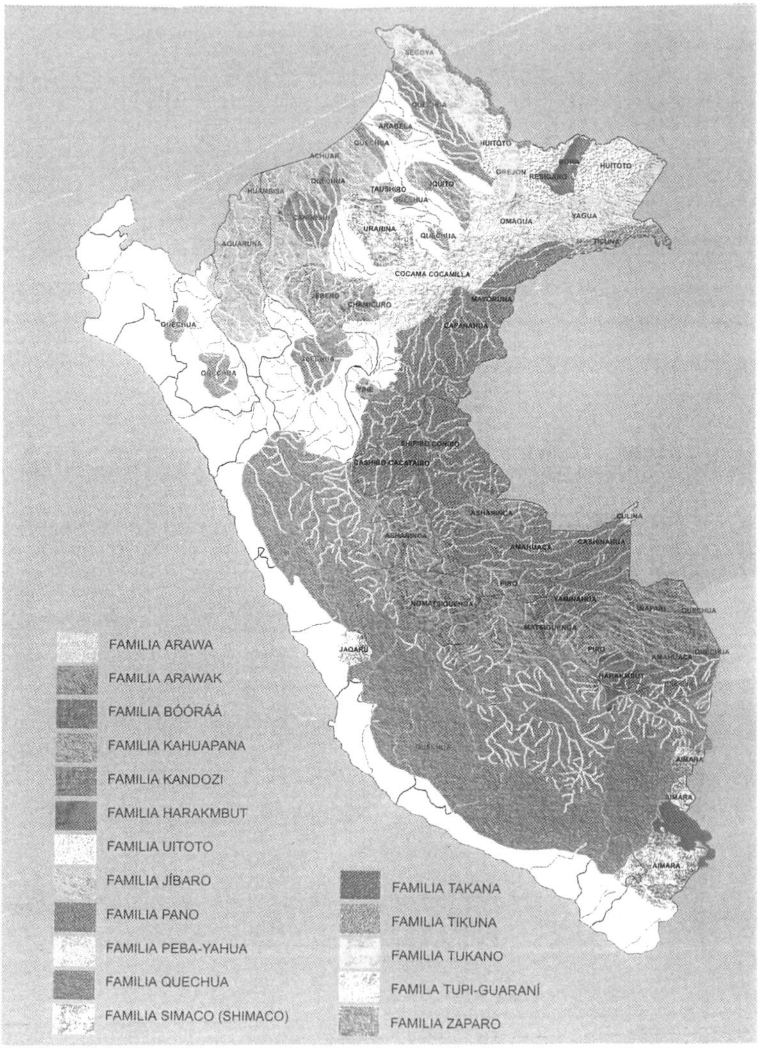

Source : Ministerio de Educación, Unidad de educación bilingue intercultural, *Los desafíos de la diversidad. Materiales para un dialogo nacional sobre la educación*, Lima, 2001.

Figure 8.1.

Peruana (Council of development of nationalities of the Peruvian Amazon, CONAP) and the Asociación Interétnica del Desarrollo de la Selva Peruana (Interethnic Association of the Peruvian Jungle Development, AIDESEP) created in 1980. Today, they lead the opposition to the neo-liberal policy of the government and the defense of their territories — themes that accentuate the conflict between the state and the indigenous peoples.

The AIDESEP is also supported by several indigenous organizations and progressive political and intellectual sectors. Internationally, it is related to the Amazon Confederation of Indigenous Organizations (COICA) which represents all the indigenous peoples from the Amazon basin of South America. This organization is related to several institutions linked to the UN and other international institutions and foundations.

- The legal acknowledgment of its territories as material basis for the preservation of their cultures: rights, currently discussed by the law decrees created by Alan Garcia's government, that break national and international agreements.
- The development of initiatives and the development of a training program of bilingual and intercultural education for teachers (FORMABIAP).

This program proposes a project of revalorization of indigenous languages and cultures. The respect of those peoples to keep their own languages and cultures has been the starting point for democratic and intercultural integration inside multicultural Peruvian society.

At the same time, these features characterize several societies in Latin America (Lopes & Moya, 1989; Montoya, 1990).

The participation of the indigenous organizations in these programs has allowed the debate about the problem of the ownership of territories — without which it is impossible to conceive of development. Without territory, there is no way of preserving culture and neither could one imagine the continuity of societies.

According to the indigenous perception, there is no culture without a territory — culture is built from nature since it is not an abstract conception. The nature and culture axis cannot be divided. This philosophical approach has fed the ecologist way of thinking and its action over occidental society. Nowadays, it is impossible to imagine an economic project that does not consider ecology as the real basis of the concept, *sustainable development* (Gasché, 1989, 1998; Narby, 1990, 1995, 2005).

The central question would be: What is the place of indigenous peoples in the present and future of the economic, social and cultural development of these countries?

This doubt remains as the most important question to answer in every project. This crucial question makes us understand the importance of the political dimension that impregnates education, which acts as the mediator between the society and the state in every integration project (Marin & Dasen, 2007; Walsh, 2009).

In 1988, the first training program of bilingual and intercultural education for teachers (FORMABIAP) was founded in Iquitos, capital city of Loreto District in Amazonian Peru by AIDESEP with the help of the Instituto Superior Pedagógico Loreto and the support of the International Cooperation and other private institutions (Gasché, 1989; Montoya, 1990; Marín, 2005a).

The fundamental principles of the teacher training program of bilingual and intercultural education of Zungarocoha, a town near Iquitos, were the following:

- Association between traditional and occidental education.
- Rejection of a single system of schooling.
- Rejection of an opposition of traditional education with the "modern" school (official school).
- Rejection of policy of social assistance.
- Rejection of a mere conversion of occidental culture in the framework of a bilingual education.
- Approval of an intercultural bilingual education.
- Approval of Spanish learning as a second language.
- Approval of an education linked to ecology.

- Approval of an education associated with the socioeconomic, political, and cultural reality.

Today, this program is blocked by the Supreme Decree 006-2007 ED enacted by the government in the year 2007, through the Education Department. This decree fixes the grade of 14 out of 20 as the condition of allowing applicants to apply for the Superior Pedagogical Institutes. Among these we can find different programs of bilingual and intercultural education, which reduces considerably the option of the young natives to begin pedagogic training.

According to the Office of People's Advocate, this system makes access to education for the indigenous peoples difficult and it does not consider the indigenous capabilities in cultural or linguistic terms, which are the basis for this training. Equally, there are no teachers specially trained to manage the languages and cultures of the children and teenagers of the almost 71 ethnic groups that exist in the country. On 5 April 2010, the Cusco congressman, Victor Mayorga Miranda, presented in Congress bill 3494, which proposes to abolish the Supreme Decree 006-2007 ED, (Available at: Http://Servindi.org/actualidad/25334.morer-25334 [Accessed 3.06.2010]).

Since 2007, this decree has paralyzed many Superior Pedagogical Institutes, including FORMABIAP. Today, these institutes are developing some training activities while they wait to recover their original statute. There is a national mobilization against this arbitrary measure since it was a demagogic decision to disarticulate many programs and institutions of pedagogic training which are not controlled by the government.

The development of educational programs that take into consideration students' mother tongues and the visions of their own cultures and the world, allowed these peoples to reinforce their identities and recover the cohesion of their organizations.

Even though present organizations do not correspond to traditional organizations and caciquism and even though they were adapted to the rules imposed by the state, they are the only legal vehicle that makes defense of their rights possible. The indigenous organizations in the Amazon have been created under the legal frame imposed by the Law of Native (autochthonous, indigenous) Communities enacted by the military government in 1974. Their leaders know how to read and write in Spanish.

Today, we witness the development of a new generation of indigenous professionals who are reinforcing their organizations and creating new programs and institutions adapted to the new socioeconomic conditions.

We could point out certain characteristics of current indigenous organizations, which were perceived by Richard Chase Smith as follows:

> They are alliances built by voluntary decision of the autonomous local communities. The leaders, who represent them, are elected and, in theory, must answer to the will of the members: an organization which associates the political functions of representation of the technical functions (projects), a federation that finds its unity through a particular cultural identity, and above all, a federation that seeks to maintain its autonomy in front of the state, the church, and the political parties. (Chase Smith, 1982, p. 27)

These are the three institutions that generated the triple authoritarian tradition which marked the history of the social, political, and cultural relations in the Peruvian society. This secular authoritarianism, with some shades, is valid until today.

The great challenge today, which is present in indigenous organizations, is to accomplish an autonomous organization that represents the Amazon or Andean indigenous populations as a whole, to avoid the competition and fragmentation suffered by the peasant movements of the Andean and the coastal regions during Fujimori's government (1990–2000). As well as the attacks they have suffered over recent years, these populations also had to bear political violence, which caused 70,000 victims of whom 80% were from indigenous populations, according to the report of the Truth Commission.

Between 1990 and 1998, the beginning of Alberto Fujimori's presidential period was marked by the implementation of a neoliberal political program that brought to discussion the ancestral property of the indigenous communities' lands, particularly in the Amazon region, rich in natural resources such as gold, petroleum, gas, and fine woods, which are valuable resources and in which multinational companies take interest. This economic policy still continues, and it has widened (Chirif, 2010; Montoya, 2010; Varese, 2009).

In the coastal and Andean regions, privatization of the agro-industrial complexes, which were part of the state in 1968, occurred. In this period, socially speaking, we witnessed the dismantling of the social, medical, and educational services and the destruction of the labor market due to the economic restructuration imposed by neo-liberal programs.

This process was the cause of the explosion of the unemployment and precarization rates of the poor and middle-class sectors. The development of a neo-liberal policy produces and emphasizes the authoritarian character of the nation-state, which, as a political model, enters in this perspective. The reduction of large democratic spaces is inherent and the criminalization by the central government of the popular and indigenous opposition characterizes this process.

8.6. NATION-STATE AND MULTICULTURALITY: BETWEEN RHETORIC AND REALITY

Between 2000 and 2001, during the transitional government of Valentín Paniagua, Supreme Decree 015, based on the dialogue between the state and the Amazon indigenous peoples, was enacted; and at the beginning of the government of Toledo, Supreme Decree 111 which created the Discussion Board and the National Commission of Andean, Amazonian, and Afro-Peruvian Peoples (CONAPA) was issued. This decree was presided over by the president's wife, the anthropologist Eliane Karp.

The subscription of the three last international statements carried out in Macchu Picchu, Santiago, Chile and during the meeting of the Rio Group in 2001, was added to the above-mentioned decrees. We must add the Democratic Letter Signing in the framework of the Organization of American States (OAS) to those agreements. We can highlight some of the commissions' agreements from these different events:

- To end the legalization of the indigenous territories.
- To examine the problem of the Amazonian reservation and the pacification in the central zone (conflictive area where some armed groups of Sendero Luminoso linked to drug dealers are still active).
- To develop bilingual and intercultural education.
- To develop a plan for the Amazon.
- To institutionalize the state at a regional level considering the indigenous problems.

All these political statements and the symbolic use of indigenous issues at the service of political demagogy did not crystallize in the daily reality of Peruvian society (Montoya, 2001a, 2001c).

The use of the ethnic factor by political parties in Peru is represented in several episodes. Since the first half of the twentieth century it was represented by indigenism, developed by erudite paternalists, in which natives are not present as historical subjects.

During Augusto B. Leguia's government, the indigenous issue was taken up by state policies. Later, the APRA party got back some indigenous signs to use as the emblem of their political discourse. Between 1990 and 2000, during the Fujimori government, we witnessed the demagogic usage of the ethnic factor for political purposes. In 2001, the Perú Posible party, which took Alejandro Toledo to the presidency, employed a considerable amount of indigenous symbols during the election campaign and also in the presidential investiture ceremony in Macchu Picchu on 28 July 2001. The official investiture ceremony was transmitted internationally, and was carried out in the framework of an indigenous religious ceremony — during its course Apus were invoked (indigenous religion Gods). Also, offerings to the Pachamama (Mother Earth) were presented. These historical facts have been the basis upon which Toledo announced his intention to make his mandate a government of "all bloods." This metaphor, allusive to a government for all Peruvians without considering their origins, belongs to José María Arguedas, as per the title of his novel *Todas las Sangres* (*All Bloods*) published in 1964. He was a Peruvian writer and anthropologist and one of the first to question the multicultural and plurilingual character of Peruvian society (Arguedas, 1977; Marin, 2002a; Montoya, 2001b, 2001c).

It was the same Arguedas, who, in the speech, "I am not an acultured", pronounced during the ceremony of the Inca Garcilaso de la Vega award, for which he was nominated in 1968, that some day in Peru it would be possible and necessary to express the different faces of the cultures and languages, without causing conflicts. He wished for a country in which different national and ethnic identities coexisted, to feel a Peruvian citizen and, at the same time, to be a Quechua, Aymara, or Amazon (Marin, 2002a).

In Arguedas' reflection about Peru, the seed of interculturality was sown as the starting point of a future political project.

However, it is convenient to wonder about the current perspective of the indigenous peoples:

- What are the real chances of crossing the boundaries between simple political discourse and complex reality?
- What are the real chances of creating political spaces in which the different peoples from Peru may express themselves?
- Is it possible to imagine respect for the autochthonous peoples in the modern political context?
- Taking into consideration the multicultural character of current Peruvian society, what is the model of constitution needed by Peru to assume this reality?
- What are the real possibilities of respecting the cultural diversity of the autochthonous peoples, taking into account the interests of the different political movements and the different economic sectors?

8.7. RECENT HISTORY ABOUT THE RELATIONS OF THE NATION-STATE AND MULTICULTURAL SOCIETY

Regarding the Andean region, the First Special Congress of Quechua Peoples in Peru, with participants and guests from

Argentina, Bolivia, and Ecuador, took place in Cuzco between 5 and 9 November 2001.

Among the most important agreements there was a need to develop a constitutional reform that creates a multicultural and plurinational state. This proposal becomes true between 2008 and 2010, with a deep change in the political constitution experienced by Bolivia and Ecuador, in which the decolonization and the refoundation of the state were suggested in order to give a place to the foundation of a plurinational state as a political, social, and cultural space in which the multiculturality that characterizes the societies could live (Montoya, 2001c; Suarez, 2008; Walsh, 2009).

In this meeting in Cuzco, the Quechua peoples demanded political and economical projects that apply to national interests without being subjected to foreign interests and to defend the interests of the country against international organizations such as the World Trade Organization (WTO).

They also proposed the creation of an office to consider the diversity of the different cultures that live in the Peruvian territory, an action that allowed the development of a government of "all bloods" in relation to president Toledo's statements, who ruled from 2001 to 2006 (Marin, 2002a).

On 28 October 2007, Alan García, president of Peru, published an article called "Orchard Dog Syndrome" where he points out that some native communities of Peru keep their lands without production, thus opposing progress. This publication was considered to be an attack on the Amazon peoples (Manrique, 2009).

In December 2007, Congress gave power to the Executive branch of government to legislate on matters regarding the Free Trade Agreement (FTA) with the US. Within the legislation for the FTA, the Executive issued decrees about the indigenous peoples of Peru.

In August 2008, Alberto Pizango, President of AIDESEP, supported the manifestations of Amazon indigenous groups against oil companies that invaded and contaminated their land. According to the director of NGO Survival International, Stephen Corry, "the indigenous Peruvians are being forced to adopt desperate measures to try to save their lands, which during five centuries have been stolen" (http://es.wikipedia.org/wiki/Ley de la Selva en el Per%C3%BA09 [Accessed 06.2010]).

Protests ended when Alberto Pizango and the AIDESEP received support from the Peruvian Congress.

On 20 August 2008, the Peruvian Congress approved the request of the National Commission of Andean, Amazonian, and Afro-Peruvian Peoples to abolish the legislative decrees 1015 and 1073. These decrees made the sale of indigenous territories to private companies easier and opened the access of oil, mining, and agro-industrial companies to the Amazon.

In September 2008, the government did not enact the derogation of the decrees. When the deadline was due, the President of the Congress abolished them as stipulated in the Peruvian Constitution. On 2 September, laws 1015 and 1073 were revoked, re-establishing Articles 10 to 11 of the Law 26505, about the use of the land of native communities.

In March 2009, Congress formed a commission to study other decrees, particularly the points that came into conflict with the Constitution and had a relation with the violation of agreement 169 of the ILO.

On 9 April, since there was no answer, the Amazon strike began, demanding the abolition of six other decrees considered unconstitutional by the Constitutional Commission of the Peruvian Congress, which allowed 60% of the Amazon old-growth forests to be sold to transnational companies for exploitation of hydrocarbons or for growing biofuels.

In May, since the new commission was not established in congress, manifestations extended to the entire Amazon and became more radical with the occupation of some oil facilities, the highway blockade, and other actions.

The Peoples Advocacy acted as a mediator and the president of the UN Permanent Forum of Indigenous Issues (UNFPII) expressed his concern.

The Constitutional Commission of Congress declared unconstitutional the Law Decree 1090 (Forest and Wild Life Law) leaving for discussion at the plenary session of congress.

On 20 May, under a Supreme Decree, the Multisectorial Commission was created to begin negotiations between the government and the indigenous peoples. The President of the AIDESEP, Alberto Pizango, and Yehude Simón, the president of the Cabinet, participated in it. This Commission had the task of analyzing and achieving the search of consensus agreements between the state and the indigenous peoples. The government promised concessions, but in this program, the abolition of Law 1090, which was demanded by the Amazon, was not included. The last meeting was on 30 May.

On 31 May, Pizango declared in the closing ceremony of the "Fourth Continental Summit of the Indigenous Peoples" in Puno that the measures would become more radical, seeking to abolish the decrees, "to defend the indigenous peoples". He decided not to participate in the Discussion Board anymore and demanded an audience with President Alan García, announcing also that he would ask the Constitutional Court to declare those decrees unconstitutional, and warned that, if his demands were not accepted, he would bring a lawsuit in the Inter-American Court of Human Rights. On 3 June he called for a national strike. On 4 June, the Peoples Advocacy brought a lawsuit of unconstitutionality against the Law Decree 1064 in the Constitutional Court as it considered that this Decree violated the land property rights and the one of previous consultation to the native people.

On 5 June, the result of the intervention of security forces in Bagua, ordered by the government, proved to be fatal. A year on from this tragedy, 23 dead policemen and 10 dead civilians were identified. These numbers are corroborated by the People's Advocacy and some Catholic organizations.

On 8 June, Carmen Vildoso Chirinos, leader of the Women and Social Development Ministry, resigned her position as a way to protest against a video that was transmitted by the Peruvian government on the local television station, in which native people were shown to be responsible for the violence. A few days earlier, the prosecutor had requested that Pizango be investigated for crimes of murder and sedition, accusing him of being responsible for the death of the police officers. This situation forced him to ask for political asylum in the Nicaraguan Embassy, and he stayed in Nicaragua until he returned to Peru in May 2010.

On 11 June, a national protest was carried out to demand the abolition of the legislative decrees 1090 and 1064. Several syndicalized organizations and fronts of defence from different regions in Peru called a national strike as a way to reject the political manipulation made by the government in northeastern Peru.

On 15 June, the government proposed the derogation of only two of the seven legislative decrees questioned: the 1090 and the 1064. On 18 June, Congress abolished the two mentioned decrees with a vote in opposition from the Christian Popular Party. (http://es.wikipedia.org/wiki/Ley de la Selva en el Per%C3%BA09. [Accessed 06.2010]).

On 30 June, after having questioned the president of the Cabinet, Yehude Simón, and the Secretary of Home Affairs, Mercedes Cabanillas, Congress decided not to condemn them. A few weeks later, the prime minister would resign his position and the Ministry of Home Affairs would be replaced.

By the end of the first semester of 2010 there had been no substantial changes, so tension prevailed. The government is reluctant to fulfil the agreements to respect the ILO Convention 169.

We witness in modern Peru, a new chapter of the long history of internal colonization with the burden of racist discrimination and the repetition of the colonial tendency in perceiving the indigenous people as *an obstacle for the progress and for the access of the Peruvian nation to the capitalist occidental modernity* (Chirif, 2009, 2010; Levano, 2010; Montoya, 2010; Varese, 2009).

When President García makes reference to the metaphor, "orchard dog", we remember the debate carried out at Colegio San Gregorio de Valladolid (1550–1551) and the thesis of the Priest Dominico Bartolome de las Casas, who defends the humanity of the indigenous peoples against the theologian Juan Ginés de Sepúlveda, who insists on referring to the indigenous peoples as animals to justify the exploitation and genocide suffered in the colonial society (Hanke and Giménes Fernandez, 1954).

Alan García defines the indigenous peoples as second-class citizens and describes them as an obstacle to the transnational privatization of the Amazon indigenous land.

The Peruvian government, by enacting against the Constitution, the 10 Law Decrees, within the framework of the FTA Peru–US, failed to fulfil the ILO Convention 169, to which Peru, being a signatory country, is obligated. Likewise, these decrees do not comply with the UN Declaration for the Rights of Indigenous Peoples, particularly with Articles 26, 29, and 32 among others, and with the jurisprudence of the Inter-American Court of Human Rights, about the land rights of the indigenous peoples.

As an example, we could mention the Legislative Decree 1090, enacted by the Executive Power on behalf of Congress, which deals with the provisions of the forest areas for timber purposes. The problem of this norm is that it violates the Peruvian Magna Carta which gives special protection to the Amazon for the preservation of all natural resources, considering that any disposition about the exploitation and use of natural resources must be enacted by Organic Law. Another constitutional precept indicates that the termination of Executive Power is not possible; thus, the enactment through Legislative Decree is unconstitutional.

The ILO Convention 169, states that the native peoples must be consulted about laws. The norms enacted by Alan García's government go against the Public international Law. The ILO convention, which refers to the indigenous and tribal communities, orders the signatory states (Peru has signed an agreement) to listen and specify the opinions of the native peoples that could be affected by any law.

Article 6 stipulates:

1. In applying the provisions of the following convention:
    (a) The governments must ask the interested peoples through appropriate procedures and in particular through their representative institutions whenever consideration is being given to legislative or administrative measures which might affect them directly.
    (b) The queries carried out in the application of this convention must be made in good faith and in an appropriate way according to the circumstances, with the purpose of reaching an agreement or achieving consent about the proposed measures (ILO Convention 169, 27 June 1989).

At the end of the first half of 2010, the indigenous organizations formed mainly in CONAP and AIDESEP continue their fight with the complete support of many sectors and are reinforcing their organizations. At the same time, they focus the protest against the governmental decrees enacted by the government of Alan García in the framework of Free Trade Agreement (FTA) with the US. This agreement makes the privatization of large geographic areas easy and lets multinational companies exploit natural resources, particularly the concessions, allowing them to make use of petroleum, gas, wood, and agro-industry.

8.8. WHAT IS THE FUTURE OF THE MULTICULTURAL SOCIETY AND ITS DEMOCRATIC INTEGRATION?

Integration is the result of respect for plurality; it is the implementation of democracy, from the moment when everybody is guaranteed equal conditions to coexist and participate in the decision making process, that determines the fate of a society.

The current question is: Are we able to open ourselves up to the multiplicity of perceptions and views considered valid and accepted by others? If we accept, do we also expect to receive the same respect back?

How can we imagine the possibility of making cultural diversity and plurality a reality? Tolerance must be based on reciprocity — if we are tolerant with others, we expect to be tolerated the same way which implies certain acceptance and the opportunity to share with others. All these premises allow us to establish relationships with community members, which is the basis for the implementation of relationships and reciprocity of individuals. Groups of communities form a civil society and allow us to imagine a political space that goes beyond the authoritarianism and mutations and gaps among individuals and also between the state and society (Sartori, 1994; Touraine, 1997).

Integration implies a process that involves multiple dimensions and can be associated with a political model of state.

The state is intended to represent society, which must create conditions for the citizens to participate in principal decisions.

Integration involves freedom and respect for the rights of the individual and for all involved groups.

In a multicultural and plurilingual society — the type of societies existing in both Europe and in the American continent — the state would have to guarantee respect for cultural and linguistic diversity. From this point of view, education — in a broad sense and in its different forms — is the privileged vehicle to carry out the transmission of the world's viewpoints, values, norms, references and, finally, knowledge that supports a feasible society project.

Managing cultural diversity and plurality seems to me the most important challenge for contemporary societies. The current political model of nation-state shows itself as incapable of assuming this multicultural reality that characterizes our American and European societies.

From these premises, in the case of multicultural and plurilingual societies, could we imagine a type of state able to assume the formulation and application of an intercultural policy that satisfies the demands we raised?

Would a model of confederated state — able to respect cultural and linguistic diversity — be capable of assuming democratic administration of a multicultural Peruvian society?

Peru, in the current political context, is unable to offer the needed conditions for socioeconomic integration, and to respect the cultural diversity that permeates its society.

BIBLIOGRAPHY

Arguedas, J. M. (1977). *Relatos completos*, Lozada, Buenos Aires.

Attali, J. (1991). *1492*, Fayard, Paris.

Bonfiglio, G. (2001). *La presencia Europea en el Perú*, Fondo Editorial del Congreso, Lima.

Burga, M. (1988). *Nacimiento de una utopía. Muerte y resurrección de los Incas*, Instituto de Apoyo Agrario, Lima.

Chase Smith, R. (1982). *Las comunidades nativas y el mito del Gran Vacío Amazónico*, Documentos — Aidesep, Lima.

Chirif, A. (2009). No es tiempo de permanecer callados, revista *Que Hacer N° 174, Lima*, abril–junio, pp. 58–63.

Chirif, A. (2010). El perro glotón y su misterioso capital, revista *Que hacer N° 176, Lima*, enero–marzo, pp. 86–93.

Cuche, D. (1981). *Pérou Negre*, L'Harmattan, Paris.

Delannoi, G. (1991). "La théorie de la nation et ses ambivalences", in Delannoi, G. and Taguieff, P. A. (eds), *Théories du nationalisme*, Editions KIME, Paris, pp. 9–14.

Deroche, F. (2008). *Les peuples autochtones et leur relation originale à la terre. Un questionnement pour l' ordre mondial*, L'Harmattan, Paris.

Dominguez, A. (1988). *Los judeoconversos en España y América*, Istmo Editores, Madrid.

Duviols, P. (1986). *Cultura Andina y represión*, Ed. Centro Bartolomé de las Casas, Cusco.

Espinoza, W. (1986). *La destrucción del imperio de los Incas*, cuarta edición, Amaru Editores, Lima.

Espinoza, W. (1990). *Los Incas, economía sociedad y Estado en la era del Tahuantinsuyo*. Segunda edición, Amaru Editores, Lima.

Espinoza, W. (1997). *Amazonía del Perú. Historia de la Gobernación y comandancia General de Maynas*. Fondo Editorial del Congreso — Banco Central de Reserva — PROMPERU, Lima.

Ferrer, F. (1998). "L'Espagne des communautés autonomes et les droits linguistiques", in Pérez, S. (ed.), *La Mosaïque linguistique. Regards éducatifs sur les pays industrialisés*, L'Harmattan, Paris, pp. 21–40.

Ferrero, M. (1994). *Historie des colonisations. Des conquêtes aux indépendances XIIIe–XXe siècle*, Seuil, Paris.

Flores Galindo, A. (1987). *Buscando un Inca. Identidad y utopía en los Andes*, Instituto de Apoyo Agrario, Lima.

Freyre, G. (1974). *Maîtres et esclaves. La formation de la société Brésilienne*, Gallimard, Paris.

Gasché, J. (1989). A propos d'une nouvelle expérience d'éducation bilingue au Pérou. L'indigénisation d'un programme; sa critique de l'anthropologie, *Bulletin de la société Suisse des Américanistes*, 53–54, pp. 131–142.

Gasché, J. (1998). Revalorisation culturelle et structure du programme de Formation d'instituteurs interculturels et bilingues de la Fédération indienne amazonienne AIDESEP et de l'Institut Supérieure pédagogique de Loreto. DiverCité Langues. En ligne, Vol. III. {Reprise 22 November}, du World Wide Web.

Guanche, J. (1983). *Procesos etnoculturales de Cuba*, Editorial Letras Cubanas, La Habana.

Hanke, L. and Giménez, M. (1954). Bartolomé de las Casas, 1474–1566, bibliografía crítica y cuerpo de materiales para el estudio de su vida, escritos, actuación y polémicas que sucedieron durante cuatro siglos. Fondo de Cultura Económica, México.

La ley del Selva (http://es.wikipedia.org/wiki/Ley de la Selva en el Per%C3%BA09 [Accessed 30 June 2010]).

Lévano, C. (2010). Nueva amenaza a la Amazonía, *Diario la Primera, Lima*, 23 June.

López, L.-E. and Moya, R. (eds), (1989). *Pueblos indios, Estado y educación*, PEB — Puno, EBI, ERA, Puno.

Manrique, N. (2009). "Pueblos Indígenas, rezagos de una monarquía", in Informe anual 2008–2009 de Oxfam International, Lima Perú, pp. 66–75.

Marin, J. (1985). Peru: Problema nazionale et discriminazione razziale, *Latinoamerica. Analisi et testi debatiti*, 19–20, Roma, pp. 68–70.

Marin, J. (1990)."El factor étnico en el Perú", in Alvarsson, J.-A. and Horna, H. (eds), *Ethnicity in Latin America/Etnicidad en Latinoamérica*, Uppsala Universitet Press, Uppsala, pp. 89–112.

Marin, J. (1992). *Peuples indigènes, missions religieuses et colonialisme Interne dans l'Amazonie Péruvienne*, Svenska Intitutet för Missionsforsning, Uppsala Universitet Press, Uppsala.

Marin, J. (1994). "Ethnocentrisme et racisme dans l'histoire européenne dans le cadre de la conquête de l'Amérique et perspective actuelle", in Allemann-Ghionda, C. (ed.), *Multikultur und Bildung in Europa. Multiculture et éducation en Europe*, Peter Lang, Bern, pp.181–196.

Marin, J. (2002a). "Perú Estado e Indigenísmo en mutación. El caso de la Amazonía", in Auroi, C. and Bossio, S. (eds), ¿A dónde va el Perú?, Centro Bartolomé de las Casas (CBC), Institut universitaire d'études du développement (IUED), Cusco-Genève. pp. 123–144.

Marin, J. (2002b). "Une éducation appropriée aux peuples autochtones d'Amérique latine", in Dasen, P. R. and Perregaux. C. (eds), *Pour quoi des approches interculturelles en sciences de l'éducation*, De Boeck Université, Bruxelles, pp. 261–280.

Marin, J. (2005a). "*Globalisation, Néolibéralisme, éducation et diversité culturelle*", in Barlogeanu. L. (ed.), *Identité et Globalisation*, Editora Educatia 2004, Humanitas educational, Collection Recherche et Développement, Bucarest, pp. 128–147.

Marin, J. (2005b). "Prácticas interculturales en Europa y en América Latina: El caso de la Amazonía Peruana", in Leite, R., Zaccur, E. and Giambiagi, I. (Orgs), Cotidiano. Diálogos sobre diálogos, DP&A editora, Rio de Janeiro, pp. 89–106.

Marin, J. (2007a). "Breve Historia del Estado Nación y de la política de Integración en Europa y en América Latina", in Hurtado, J. (ed.), *Derecho penal y pluralidad cultural*, Fondo Editorial de la Universidad Católica, Universidad de Friburgo, Suiza, Lima-Friburgo, pp. 341–356.

Marín, J. and Dasen, P. R. (2007). "L'éducation face aux défis de la mondialisation, des migrations et des droits humains", in Tschopp, M.-C. and Dasen, P. R.(eds), *Mondialisation, migrations et droits de l'homme: un nouveau paradigme pour la citoyennete/Globalization, migration and human rights: a new paradigm for research and citizenship*, Vol. I, Bruylant, Bruxelles, pp. 285–318.

Mato, D., Montero, M. and Amodio, E. (eds). *América Latina en tiempos de globalización: Procesos culturales y transformaciones sociopolíticas*, UCV, ALAS, UNESCO, Caracas.

Montoya, R. (1990). *Por una educación bilingüe en el Perú. Reflexiones sobre cultura y socialismo*, Mosca Azul Editores, Lima.

Montoya, R. (1998). *Multiculturalidad y política*, Ediciones SUR, Lima.

Montoya, R. (2001a). Congreso de los pueblos quechuas, *La República, Lima*, 18 November.

Montoya, R. (2001b). Cultura y poder, *Manuscrito inédito.*

Montoya, R. (2001c). Todos tenemos derecho a ser peruanos, *revista Que Hacer, N° 132, Lima, Entrevista de Abelardo Sánchez León*, pp. 80–89.

Montoya, R. (2010). Desafío político después de Bagua, *Diario la primera, Lima*, 12 June.

Morimoto, A. (1979). *Los inmigrantes Japoneses en el Perú*, TEA, Lima.

Morin, E. (1991). "L'Etat-Nation", in Delannoi, G. and Taguieff, P.-A. (eds), *Théories du Nationalisme*, éditions KIME, Paris, pp. 319–324.

Narby, J. (1990). *L'Amazonie, l'espoir est Indien*, Favre, Paris.

Narby, J. (1995). *Le serpent cosmique et les origines de l'ADN*, Georg Editeur, Genève.

Narby, J. (2005). *L'intelligence dans la nature. Un quête du savoir*, Buchet / Chastel, Paris.

Pérez, S. (1998). (ed.), *La Mosaïque linguistique. Regards éducatifs sur les pays industrialisés*, L'Harmattan, Paris.

Portocarrero, G. (1993). *Racismo y mestizaje*, SUR. Lima.

Rodriguez, H. (1989). *Hijos del Celeste Imperio. Migración, agricultura, mentalidad y explotación*, Instituto de Apoyo Agrario, Lima.

Romero, F. (1987). *El negro en el Perú y su transculturación lingüística*, Editorial Milla Bartres, Lima.

Rostworowski, M. (1988). *Historia del Tawantinsuyu*, IEP, Lima.

Roth, C. (ed.) (1989). *La Inquisición Española*, Martinez Roca, Madrid.

Salvi, S. (1973). *Le nazioni proibite*. Ed. Vallecchi, Firenze.

Sanguin, A.-L. (1993). *Les minorités ethniques en Europe*, L'Harmattan, Paris.

Sartori, G. (1994). *Partidos y sistemas de Partidos*, Alianza Editorial, Madrid.

Servindi (http://Servindi.org/actualidad/25334.morer-25334) [Accessed 23.06. 2010].

Suárez, H. J. (2009). *Bolivie la révolution démocratique*, Editions Couleur livres, Charleroi.

Touraine, A. (1994). *Critique de la modernité*, Fayard, Paris.

Touraine, A. (1997). *Pourrons-nous vivre ensemble? Egaux et différents*, Fayard, Paris.

Trazegnies, F. (1994). *En el país de las colinas de arena*, 2 vols, Pontificia Universidad Católica, Lima.

Varese, S. (2009). Poco ha cambiado para los indígenas amazónicos, revista *Qué Hacer* N° 176. *Lima*, October–December, pp. 27–35.

Vilar, P. (1979). *Historia de España*, octava edición, Grupo Editorial Grijalbo, Barcelona.

Walsh, C. (2009). *Interculturalidad, Estado y sociedad. Luchas (de) coloniales de nuestra época*, Universidad Andina Simón Bolívar. Ediciones Abya-Yala, Quito.

Wieviorka, M. (ed.) (1996). *Une société fragmentée? Le multiculturalisme en débat*, La Découverte & Syros, Paris.

Zapata, R. (ed.) (1990). Imágenes de la resistencia indígena y esclava, Ediciones Wari, Lima.

Chapter 9

Interpretation of Self-Determination Right of Indigenous Peoples in Colombia after Ratification of ILO Convention 169

Leonardo Rodríguez Pérez

9.1. INTRODUCTION

This chapter intends to analyze the way in which the Colombian state has interpreted indigenous peoples' right to self-determination after ratification of ILO convention 169 of 1989. This chapter consists of three parts. First, there is a commentary on the interpretation of indigenous peoples' self-determination in the international context. Second, there is a description of political tensions created by the inclusion of indigenous peoples' self-determination in the Colombian 1991 Constitution. Finally, there are observations from the Colombian Constitutional Court on how indigenous peoples' self-determination has been interpreted in the Colombian case after ILO Convention 169's ratification by the Congress in 1991.

9.2. RIGHT TO SELF-DETERMINATION OF INDIGENOUS PEOPLES IN INTERNATIONAL LAW

The recognition of indigenous peoples' right to self-determination by international law has generated difficulties in the discussion of international standards. States see a challenge to their sovereignty if they accept indigenous peoples' right to political self-determination. This fear was evident when states resisted replacement of the term "native populations" used in ILO Convention 107 of 1957, "on indigenous and tribal populations", with the term "indigenous peoples" in ILO convention 169 of 1989 (Tomei and Swepston, 1996).

Although the term "peoples" was retained by ILO Convention 169, international texts enunciate reservations concerning the right of indigenous peoples to self-determination. Self-determination is understood in a particular sense; indigenous peoples do not have the option of separating themselves from the states whose borders include their territories. This restriction is present in the UN Declaration on the Rights of Indigenous Peoples,[1] and in the draft of Declaration of Indigenous Peoples' Rights from the Organization of American States (OAS);[2] ILO Convention 169 also does not recognize indigenous peoples' right to political self-determination.[3] This

[1] The 3rd article recognizes indigenous peoples' self-determination, which allows them to "freely determine their political status". Article 46(1) explicitly limits this right: "Nothing in this Declaration may be interpreted (···) as authorizing or encouraging any action which would dismember or impair, totally or in part, the territorial integrity or political unity of sovereign and independent States". Doc. ONU A/RES/61/295, September 2007.

[2] Doc. OEA/Ser.K/XVI GT/DADIN/doc. 301/07 March 2008.

[3] Article 1(3) separates the term "people" from any implication related with the international law. http://www.ilo.org/ilolex/cgi-lex/convdf.pl?C169 [Accessed 22nd November 2010]. ILO insists on this restriction in its manual to interpret Convention 169: "The ILO's mandate is social and economic rights. It is outside its competence to interpret the political concept of self-determination (···). What Convention No. 169 does provide for is self-management, and the right of indigenous and tribal peoples to decide their own priorities". *ILO Convention on indigenous and tribal peoples, 1989 (No. 169): A manual.* Geneva, International Labour Office, 2003, p. 9.

limitation on self-determination has produced a distinction between "internal self-determination" that can be exercised by indigenous peoples within their territories and "external self-determination", which includes the right to constitute states (Shulte-Tenckhoff and Koubi, 2000, p. 16).

Most indigenous peoples today are not interested in the constitution of sovereign states (Young, 2000, p. 252). They try to be independent within the states under which they live.[4] States, therefore, might be less concerned about the issue of external self-determination by indigenous peoples. Self-determination might be interpreted according to the approach proposed by James Anaya (2006, p. 29), the UN Special Rapporteur on the Situation of Human Rights and Fundamental Freedoms of Indigenous Peoples. This author separates self-determination from the constitution of states. Such separation would make it easier to recognize indigenous peoples' right to internal self-determination. Anaya supports the idea that human rights are applicable to individuals and societies and are not within the scope of states. It would be a mistake to consider that internal self-determination must be a precursor to the constitution of states. In a humanitarian interpretation of this right, an evaluation of political, economic, and social conditions of indigenous peoples in relation to the values of equality and freedom is pertinent. Reform of a state's structure could be sufficient to guarantee indigenous peoples a right to internal self-determination.

---

[4] Demand to indigenous peoples' self-determination within the states they live is present in Article 5(e) from a draft declaration of principles of the League of Indigenous Sovereign Nations of the Western Hemisphere: "Assert ourselves as separate and distinct peoples under international law and that this recognition be incorporated into the respective nation states". The League of Indigenous Sovereign Nations of the Western Hemisphere Draft Declaration of Principles is available at the New Zealand digital library, the University of Waikato, http://nzdl.sadl.uleth.ca/cgi-bin/library [Accessed 15 May 2009]. The *Movimiento Indigenista Pachakuti* (MIP) is an exception; it looks for a national self-determination with the creation of Collasuyo Republic in Bolivia (Castillo, 2007, p. 17).

9.3. INDIGENOUS PEOPLES' SELF-DETERMINATION WITHIN THE COLOMBIAN LEGAL ORDER

In the Colombian case, ratification of ILO Convention 169 three months before the meeting of the Constitutional Assembly was a favorable signal for the aspirations of indigenous peoples in the country.[5] But powerful representatives from the government in the Assembly (especially the Minister of the Interior) were not inclined toward meaningful recognition of indigenous rights.

A constitutional project was discussed by the Assembly and transmitted to a review commission with the intention of preparing a final document. However, this commission suppressed the text favored by indigenous representatives about autonomy in their territories and accepted instead the text from the Minister of the Interior that stated that, "Indigenous territories will be constituted according to the law". The indigenous representatives then threatened to leave the Assembly and to publicize at national and international levels their frustration with what they perceived to be a farce. It was only after these declarations that the government agreed to negotiate (Castillo, 2007, p. 261).

At the Constitutional Assembly, the Colombian government expressed the same fears as other states had done in the negotiations leading up to the drafting of international texts regarding the rights of indigenous peoples. The Colombian government did not want to put the unity of the state's territory at issue. For the government, this unity would be threatened by the recognition of indigenous peoples' autonomy. The indigenous representatives had to clarify what they meant by political autonomy. They insisted on their intention to exert self-determination within the existing nation-state framework:

> We swear and swear again that we did not seek to undermine the unity of the state. That was not our intention; what we wanted was recognition of the indigenous territories and a level of political/administrative

[5] Law from 4 March 1991 (Gomez Vargaz, 1994, p. 65).

> autonomy, in order to continue developing with our own identity, with our own thoughts.[6]

Negotiations between indigenous representatives and the Colombian government concluded with recognition of the legal autonomy of indigenous peoples within their territories (Article 246 of the Constitution). Nevertheless, indigenous representatives had to renounce their claims regarding control of underground resources in their territories. However, the Constitution recognized the right of indigenous peoples to be consulted before exploitation of natural resources in their lands (Article 330).

9.4. INTERPRETATION OF INDIGENOUS PEOPLES' SELF-DETERMINATION AFTER THE 1991 CONSTITUTION

The recognition of internal autonomy in indigenous territories was obtained despite opposition by the government. This opposition must be considered when examining the application of ILO Convention 169 in Colombia. Article 6 of the ILO Convention affirms that indigenous peoples should be able to participate freely in decisions about developing projects which concern them. The Colombian state elaborated a mechanism to apply this international norm; this mechanism was regulated by decree 1320 of 1998 about "previous consultation" with indigenous peoples (Ministerio del Interior, 2008, p. 241). This decree was denounced at the ILO in Geneva because it contradicts Article 6 of Convention 169. In addition to this problem with the wording of decree 1320, the state also lacked the practical will to apply the decree consistently. For example, petroleum operations in the territory of the U'wa people and the filling of a dam in the territory of the Embera-Katio people were developed without previous consultation of these peoples.[7]

[6] Interview with Lorenzo Muelas, 3 January 2004 (Castillo, 2007, p. 259). My translation.

[7] Doc. ILO GB.276/17/1 (November 2001) and Doc. ILO GB.282/14/4 (November 2001).

Nevertheless, the right to previous consultation is recognized by ILO Convention 169, and is included in Colombian jurisprudence. The T-634/99 sentence from the Constitutional Court deals with another feature of previous consultation. This sentence recognizes that the indigenous peoples' control over their territories is based on international norms integrated in Colombian laws. The indigenous peoples' self-determination obliges the state to consult indigenous peoples about administrative decisions and development projects involving them:

> The right of indigenous peoples to participate in matters relevant to their population and territory is linked to the right to ethnic identity, because this is essential for cultural survival. It is also a basic element of the aforementioned constitution; the right of self-determination of peoples is also recognized in Article 9 of the Political Charter and in Article 1 of the Civil and Political Rights Pact of 1966. It is specifically stated in Convention 169 of the ILO, a Convention that was made part of Colombian judicial order by ratification of Law 21 in 1991.[8]

The internal self-determination of indigenous peoples was tested on two occasions with respect to religious freedom. An individual's right to religious freedom was limited in favor of self-determination, considered as a group right. The T-257 sentence of 1993 deals with the "New Tribes of Colombia Evangelical Association" case. The Association had demanded authorization from the indigenous chiefs in the Vaupes region, in the south of the country, to build a runway in their territory. Even though some individual members of the indigenous group supported the Association, indigenous authorities refused to permit the construction of the runway. The Association considered this denial as an act against religious freedom and started a judicial process, ultimately heard by the Constitutional Court. The Court stated that indigenous chiefs were responsible for managing the

[8] Sentence T-634/99 from Colombian Constitutional. All sentences quoted here are available at: http://juriscol.banrep.gov.co:8080/ [Accessed 22 November 2010].

communal property of land and had the right to control the transit of outsiders in their territory. Therefore, the Evangelical Association had to abandon its project.

The Court also explicitly recognized indigenous peoples' self-determination as a group right, superior to the individual right of religious freedom in sentence SU-510 from 1998. An evangelical church thought that religious freedom was violated by traditional authorities of the Arhuaco people in the north of the country. These authorities prohibited access of protestant priests to their territory, despite the fact that around 300 indigenous individuals were evangelical. The Constitutional Court judged that this prohibition was compatible with prerogatives recognized by ILO Convention 169 regarding the internal autonomy of indigenous peoples. The deliberations of the Court are quoted extensively here:

> ... due to the administrative, budgetary and jurisdictional autonomy that tribal ethnic minorities have, in terms of Convention 169 of the ILO, over the territories they occupy as collective private property, they are conferred with the faculty of internally regulating their own affairs (···) It wouldn't make sense for property rights to be guaranteed constitutionally if anyone could circulate through the property without the consent or permission of the owner. In the final analysis, in the legal action that was initiated under the umbrella of the plaintiff religious institutions, the Church was unaware of the mandates and constitutional principles that protect the general ethnic interests and that have precedence over the particular or individual interests of some members of the tribal group.[9]

Internal self-determination prevailed over religious freedom based on previous considerations about the superiority of general interests over particular interests. This type of consideration has been at the core of the Constitutional Court decisions when national interest has conflicted with an interest of indigenous people. According to the same

---

[9] Sentence SU-510/98 from Colombian Constitutional Court.

logic that favored indigenous authorities in the internal conflicts concerning religious freedom of individuals, the Court considered that internal self-determination of indigenous peoples represented a particular interest in contrast with the more general national interest. Therefore, internal self-determination was subservient to the national interest. The following Court decision illustrates this point. Sentence T-405 from 1993, the "Radar Case", concerned the Wuitoto and Muiname indigenous peoples in the Amazonian forest. These peoples were opposed to the installation of a North American anti-drug radar in their territories. For the Constitutional Court, the national security represented by the radar was in the interest of all Colombian people. Therefore, this national interest trumped internal self-determination of indigenous peoples. The Court rejected indigenous demands to install the radar outside their territories.

The prevalence of national interest over the interests of indigenous peoples is a fact clearly established in Colombian jurisprudence.[10] Despite internal self-determination recognized by sentences T-634/99 and SU-510/98 of the Constitutional Court, indigenous peoples do not have legal means to defend themselves against national security concerns and the right of the state to maintain sovereignty in its territory.

In addition, the government has been unwilling to take seriously its duty to consult indigenous peoples before developing projects in their territories. Embera and U'wa peoples were not consulted about projects that had significant impact on them. The Colombian state has not paid attention to the observations of the ILO Administrative Council in Geneva regarding the non-conformity of decree 1320 (regarding previous consultation) with Article 6 of ILO Convention 169 (regarding free participation in decision making). The Colombian Constitutional Court has made some efforts to recognize the internal self-determination of indigenous peoples within the constraints imposed by the national interests. Despite some degree of self-determination, indigenous peoples, in the final analysis, must submit to the old *Raison d'Etat*.

---

[10] Sentence SU-510 of 1998.

REFERENCE MATERIAL

Colombia

Constitución de Colombia http://www.banrep.gov.co/regimen/resoluciones/cp91.pdf [Accessed 22 November 2010].

JURISCOL http://juriscol.banrep.gov.co:8080/[Accessed 22 November 2010].

Gomez Vargaz, J. (comp.) (1994). *Fuero indígena colombiano*. Ministerio de gobierno, Dirección general de asuntos indígenas, Bogotá.

Ministerio del interior y de justicia. (2008). *La Consulta previa a pueblos indígenas y tribales. Compendio de legislación, jurisprudencia y documentos de estudio*: Ministerio del interior y de justicia, Bogotá.

ILO International Labour Organization

Convention on indigenous and tribal peoples, 1989 (No.169).

Representation alleging non-observance by Colombia of the Indigenous and Tribal Peoples Convention, 1989 (No. 169), made under Article 24 of the ILO Constitution by the Central Unitary Workers' Union (CUT).

Doc. OIT GB. 276/17/1, November 2001.

Report of the Committee set up to examine the representation alleging non-observance by Colombia of the Indigenous and Tribal Peoples Convention, 198 (No. 169), made under Article 24 of the ILO Constitution by the Central Unitary Workers' Union (CUT).

Doc. OIT. GB.282/14/3, November 2001.

Report of the Committee set up to examine the representation alleging non-observance by Colombia of the Indigenous and Tribal Peoples Convention, 198 (No. 169), made under Article 24 of the ILO Constitution by the Central Unitary Workers' Union (CUT) and the Colombian Medical Trade Union Association.

Doc. OIT GB.282/14/4, November 2001.

ILO. *ILO Convention on indigenous and tribal peoples*, 1989 (No. 169) Geneva, International Labour Office, 2003.

Tomei, M., Swepston, L., *Indigenous and Tribal Peoples: A Guide to ILO Convention* No. 169. Geneva, International Labour Office, 1996.

Others

United Nations Declaration on the Rights of Indigenous Peoples
Doc. UNO A/RES/61/295, September 2007.

Proyecto de declaración americana sobre los derechos de los pueblos indígenas Doc. OEA/Ser.K/XVI GT/DADIN/doc. 301/07, March 2008.

League of Indigenous Sovereign Nations of the Western Hemisphere, *Draft Declaration of Principles*. Available at http://nzdl.sadl.uleth.ca/cgi-bin/library [Accessed 15 May 2009].

BIBLIOGRAPHY

Anaya, J. (2006). *Los pueblos indígenas en el derecho internacional*, Editorial Trotta, Madrid.

Castillo Gomez, L. C. (2007). *Etnicidad y nación*, Universidad del Valle, Cali.

Shulte-Tenckhoff, I. and Koubi, G. (2000). Peuple autochtone et minorité dans les discours juridiques: Imbrications et dissociations, *Revue interdisciplinaire d'études juridiques*, 45, pp. 1–26.

Young, I. M. (2000). "Hybrid Democracy: Iroquois Federalism and the Postcolonial Project", in Ivison, D., Patton, P. and Sanders, W. (eds), *Political Theory and the Rights of Indigenous Peoples*, Cambridge University Press, Cambridge, pp. 237–258.

Chapter

10

A Political Ecology of Latin American Forests through Time

Marc Hufty

10.1. INTRODUCTION

My purpose here is to approach the subcontinent, from Mexico to Tierra del Fuego, as a whole, through the angle of forests. I will obviously be looking at Latin American forests from an anthropocentric perspective. There is no other way to do so, since the sole fact of describing forests already implies some form of human intervention (a nod to constructivists). The purpose of this chapter is to present a review of forests in Latin America, their importance in the collective imagination and contemporary economies, the ways they are being governed[1] through mechanisms of protection, indigenous lands, forestry, and an overview of different dynamics of land conversion. What I emphasize here are some elements of the relation between

[1] Governance is defined in a very specific way: decision-making and norm formulation processes related to collective issues in any society, according to the 'Governance Analytical Framework' (Hufty, 2010).

societies and a specific type of ecosystem — tropical forests — from the perspective of political ecology and environmental history. Twelve volumes would not suffice, of course, for such an ambitious project. I admit this chapter cannot be but sketchy, and is to be considered as a first essay.

I begin by justifying the relevance of my object by outlining the importance of Latin American forests. I then turn to history, to underline how some myths about tropical forests still find resonance in our times. I also look at the forests through different social practices: conservation efforts, indigenous struggles, and the rush for natural resources.

Throughout the chapter, I take inspiration from two interdisciplinary[2] approaches. The first one is political ecology,[3] especially the now classic chains of explanation model (Blaikie and Brookfield 1987), for which social practices related to nature at the local level have to be explained by underlying interacting political and economic mechanisms situated at the regional, national, and international levels. It was so from the moment that large political entities such as city-states and empires began to appear in America, imposing their institutions and economies on other societies, and the more so since the colonial venture and globalization, in the sense of Braudel's *économie-monde*. Whereas, for example, the classical "commodity chain" puts the stress on supply and demand, and distribution of profits along the chain from production to consumption, a political ecology commodity chain emphasizes social relations along the chain, assuming an economy embedded in, and not isolated from the social, *à la* Karl Polanyi. The conception of nature — there is obviously a strong contrast between the indigenous view of humanity as an integral part of nature and the Western naturalist view of a nature put at the disposal of humanity — influences these social relations. Politics, the institutional mechanisms created by humanity to govern itself, for my concern, its relations with the natural environment, and the

[2] Broadly defined, interdisciplinarity refers to an approach that uses methodological knowledge and tools from different disciplines, in a coordinated way.

[3] The study of the interaction between human societies and a politicized environment.

capacity to impose some forms of social relations of production to the detriment of others, is a crucial factor. Power, structural and relational (Strange, 1988), as well as resistance to power (Scott, 1985), are therefore central variables for understanding the ways forests are thought, governed, and managed.

Environmental history is a relatively young discipline. It emerged in the 1960s, parallel to global ecology[4] and political ecology. Of course, all disciplines related to the environment (geography, forestry, ecology,[5] etc.) have an historical dimension, but it is the systematic study of social change in relation to environmental change that characterizes environmental history. It can be described as an "interdisciplinary discipline", in the same way as geography (Baerwald, 2010) or history since *l'Ecole des Annales.* It uses the tools and methods of several disciplinary approaches to look at how human societies transform the natural environment for their needs, or conceive nature through beliefs, ethics, institutions, and so on. But "nature" has its own cycles and dynamics, which set limits to human action. These limits can be partially overcome through improved techniques or social arrangements (e.g. the green revolution). But nature also reacts to human activity, emitting feed-backs (e.g. increasing or decreasing crops' productivity) that have to be listened to. Ignoring these signals puts human societies at risk. Nature, therefore, may be considered as an actor in itself, in line with Callon and Latour (1981).[6] Of course, some epistemological and theoretical precautions are required. History is always read according to the questions of the day. Interpreting the past by casting our preoccupations or values on yesterday's societies, as those who, by observing — and interpreting — how past societies

[4] The study of ecological processes at the largest scale.

[5] It is worth mentioning "historical ecology", an interdisciplinary research program on human-biosphere interactions, much influenced by Balée (e.g. Balée, 1998). It is not within the scope of this chapter to discuss the, sometimes subtle, nuances between cultural ecology, ecological anthropology, environmental anthropology, etc. From a social science perspective and for my purpose here, environmental history and political ecology cover the range of human-nature relations common to the definitions of all these scientific fields.

[6] The type of agency of nature and humans is obviously not identical.

"collapsed" or "rose and fell", draw lessons for today, is an unsafe temptation. In Latin American environmental history, the result of this "presentism" led, for example, to the creation of the myth of the "good savage", a sober and healthy indigenous living in harmony with nature, inspired by Jean-Jacques Rousseau, with which the Mayas, Aztecs, Incas, Mochicas, or Tupis (all jaunty human sacrifiers and at times cannibals) would find difficulty identifying.

10.2. WHY LATIN AMERICAN FORESTS?

In general, forests of all types cover around 29% of the terrestrial surface (Schmitt *et al.*, 2008). Over 1.6 billion people depend directly on them, of which 60 million are indigenous people (CBD, 2009). Trade in wood and non-wood products amounts to 148 billion USD per year (FAO, 2005). And besides providing vital ecosystem services (MEA, 2005a), they store 50% of terrestrial organic carbon and contain much of Earth's biodiversity. Tropical forests, covering a modest 6% of the world's surface, are renowned for containing as much as 50% of terrestrial biological diversity (Wilson, 1992).

On average, 47% of "Latin America" is covered by forests (see Table 10.1): South America (see Fig. 10.1),[7] 49%; Central America,[8] 37%; Mexico, 33%; and the Caribbean,[9] 30%. Together, Latin American forests represent 24% of the world's forests and half of the world's primary forests, for 15% of the world's land surface (FAO, 2010). A major reason for being interested in Latin American forests is their relative importance in terms of land surface in the world and in the region.

A second motive for an interest in Latin American forests is, therefore, their importance for biodiversity. Almost all Latin American forests (95%) are tropical. Only Chile (100%), Uruguay (100%), and

[7] Including French Guiana.

[8] Seven countries: Belize, Costa Rica, El Salvador, Guatemala, Honduras, Nicaragua, Panama.

[9] Anglophone countries and foreign territories are included. Cuba and the Dominican Republic alone represent 69% of the Caribbean land surface and 52% of its forests.

Table 10.1. Surface covered by forests, Latin America, per region

Country or sub-region	Land surface ('000 hectares)	Forests surface ('000 hectares)	% of territory covered by forests
South America	1 783 040	864 351	48.5
Central America	52 161	19 499	37.4
Mexico	196 438	64 802	33.0
Caribbean	23 474	6 933	29.5
Total	2 055 113	955 585	46.5

Source: FAO 2010.

Mexico (30%) have a substantial proportion of their forests as subtropical or temperate. And some Latin American forest ecosystems are among the world's richest in biodiversity. The most biodiverse areas can be identified by looking at the overlaps between the centers of endemism for birds, butterflies, and plants (Whitmore and Prance, 1987), which mostly happen to coincide with forest ecosystems. This biological importance is captured by the famous "hotspot" concept promoted by the US NGO, Conservation International, to designate the places where, "exceptional concentrations of endemic species are undergoing exceptional loss of habitat" (Myers *et al.*, 2000, p. 853). Latin America contains eight of the 34 hotspots in the world. And out of the 18 megadiverse countries of the world, eight are in the region (Bolivia, Brazil, Colombia, Costa Rica, Ecuador, Mexico, Peru, Venezuela).[10] To further illustrate the point, 1,200 new species were discovered in the Amazon Basin in the last 10 years, one every three days on average (WWF, 2010).

On a global scale, 13 million hectares (including 6 million hectares of primary forests) have been lost annually to deforestation throughout the last decade (FAO, 2010), of which 97% were in tropical countries (Nabuurs, 2007). This contributes to 18% of global CO_2 emissions (Stern, 2006) but also, clearly, to the global loss of biodiversity. The most alarmist discourses refer to a sixth large historical

[10] See the Like Minded Megadiverse Countries, a group created in Cancún, in 2002. http://www.lmmc.nic.in.

Figure 10.1. Schematic extent of South America's major forested areas (author's elaboration).

wave of extinction (Leakey and Lewin, 1995). The loss of species and ecosystems, while not provoking events as spectacular as tropical storms or glaciers melting, is a real preoccupation (CBD, 2010). The pieces of evidence for that crisis are numerous. As much as 25% of known species are threatened, as measured by their inclusion in IUCN's Red List (IUCN, 2009) and the yearly number of species being extinct is said to be as high as 30,000 species, most of them unknown to science.[11] While our era (anthropocene) is gifted with the highest biological diversity in Earth's history, the actual crisis is also different from the earlier ones: it is human-made.

[11] The estimated total number of species would be between 5 and 30 million. Only 1.6 million are described (MEA, 2005).

A third motive for interest is that most Latin American forests are highly threatened. While the average annual deforestation rate is 0.2% for the world, it is 0.4% for South America and 3% for Central America. According to FAO (2005), an average of 3.7 million hectares of forests were lost annually in South America (13 countries) between 1990 and 2000.[12] There is a huge variation, however, between countries: from a rate of deforestation of 1.2% in Ecuador to 0.1% in Chile.[13] For some Central American countries the situation is dramatic: e.g. the annual rate of deforestation is 1.47% in El Salvador, 2.11% in Nicaragua, and 2.16% in Honduras (FAO, 2010). And Costa Rica, a country widely celebrated for its nature and "good governance", has lost almost all of its primary forests: they covered 67% of the national territory in 1940, 17% in 1988, and 3.53% in 2005 (Sader and Joyce, 1988; FAO, 2005). Although FAO data (2005) show a coverage of over 38% for the country, most are degraded and regrown forests. In Brazil, the Mata Atlântica, the costal Atlantic rain forest,[14] made famous by Darwin himself, has a higher biological diversity than the Amazon. Its endemism (the percentage of species found only in that place) is especially high: as much as 62% for amphibians, 40% for plants, 38% for freshwater fishes, and 27% for mammals (CI, 2010). In some places there are as many as 450 tree species per hectare (against 8–15 species on average per hectare in the most diverse forests natural of Europe and 50–200 in the Amazon). It has the dishonor of being one of the most threatened eco-region of the world. It started with the Portuguese who exploited the Brazil wood (used as a dye — the country was named after the wood) to the point of its quasi-extinction in the costal forests. Under the pressure

---

[12] A precautionary note has to be introduced: there is no universal agreement on what a forest is (what percentage of tree cover is needed for a piece of land to be categorized as a forest? Are natural-canopy shade coffee plantations "forests"?) and on qualifying industrial tree plantations as forests (Gerber, Veuthey, and Martínez-Alier, 2009).

[13] According to the FAO definition of forests, monocrop plantations (pine, eucalyptus) count as forests, even if biologically speaking they are extremely poor in diversity. This is a major contentious issue in the global governance of forests.

[14] It extends to Argentina (Misiones province) and Paraguay.

Table 10.2. **Deforestation rate, 15 selected Latin American countries**

Country	Forests area 1990 ('000 hectares)	Forests area 2010 ('000 hectares)	Annual change rate in % 1990–2000	Annual change rate in % 2000–2005	Annual change rate in % 2005–2010
Costa Rica	2 564	2 605	–0.76	0.95	0.90
Guatemala	4 748	3 657	–1.20	–1.32	–1.47
Honduras	8 136	5 192	–2.38	–1.95	–2.16
Mexico	70 291	64 802	–0.52	–0.35	–0.24
Nicaragua	4 514	3 114	–1.67	–1.91	–2.11
Panama	3 792	3 251	–1.18	–0.35	–0.36
Argentina	34 793	29 400	–0.88	–0.81	–0.80
Bolivia	62 795	57 196	–0.44	–0.46	–0.42
Brazil	574 839	519 522	–0.51	–0.57	–0.53
Chile	15 263	16 231	0.37	0.26	0.23
Colombia	62 519	60 499	–0.16	–0.16	–0.17
Ecuador	13 817	9 865	–1.53	–1.73	–1.89
Paraguay	21 157	17 582	–0.88	–0.94	–0.99
Peru	70 156	67 992	–0.14	–0.14	–0.22
Venezuela	52 026	46 275	–0.57	–0.59	–0.61
Total	1 001 410	907 183			

Source: FAO 2010.

of the timber, cattle, cocoa, and coffee industries, as well as urbanization and plantations, it has been reduced to 6–8% of what it was a century ago, and what remains is severely fragmented (CI, 2010). Half of it is protected, but with unequal efficiency.

Latin America has lost 10% of its forests in 20 years, from 1990 to 2010 (FAO, 2010), without taking into account quality, that is the conversion of primary forest in plantations (Costa Rica, Chile) and forest degradation. The Amazon (seven countries; 5.5 million km^2 of forest), the Cerrado (Brazilian savannah; 438 900 km^2), the Gran Chaco (Argentina, Paraguay, and Bolivia; 647 000 km^2), the Yungas (mountainous rainforests of the oriental slope of the Andes, from Argentina to Venezuela, and the most diverse region of the world; 385 660 km^2), and the Meso-American Corridor (from Mexico to Panama; 226 000 km^2) are all threatened (CI, 2010) (Table 10.2).

The causes are well known (Geist and Lambin, 2001), and traditionally divided into proximate causes (infrastructure expansion, logging, land conversion to agriculture, and ranching, extractive industries), and underlying factors (economic — such as the global demand for soybeans or sugarcane, policy related and institutional, technological, socio-cultural and demographic, etc.). These causes are interlinked: for example, a road built for logging will attract settlers, who will clear-cut forests for conversion to agriculture. The consequences are also known, even if not fully understood (it is too soon to assess the long term impacts) and even less internalized into public policies. They range from the loss of biodiversity and ecosystem services such as water cycles, carbon cycles, climate stabilization, soil regeneration, and stabilization (MEA, 2005), to social consequences such as lost livelihoods and identities for local and indigenous peoples, urban migrations or increased inequalities, as well as new diseases: malaria has increased 50% in deforested Amazon regions (Olson, 2009).

There is widespread agreement on the need to halt deforestation, but globally, despite all the institutional arrangements created for their conservation, forests continue to be poorly managed (Hoogeven, 2008) and sustainable forest management remains insufficiently competitive compared with more destructive uses (van Dijk and Savenije, 2009).

10.3. HUMAN IMPACTS ON FORESTS BEFORE 1492

There is no doubt about the deep impact of some indigenous societies on their environment, despite the usually ecologically sound ways of life of most of them (Martinez-Alier, 2003). There is now an abundant body of work that questions the idea of pristine South American forests and the stereotype of small stone-age indigenous populations. It proposes instead the idea of "cultural landscapes" (Sauer, 1925). Human interventions on tropical forests are ancient, deep, and diverse. What appears as virgin forest is often, with close scrutiny, a garden or a "domesticated landscape" (Heckenberger *et al.*, 2007), altered by indigenous peoples over a long time. Brown and Lugo (1990) estimate that 40% of Latin American tropical forests are secondary, mainly due to swidden fallows (the use of fire for rotating agriculture). Balée (1989) estimates that at least 12% of the Amazonian forest is human-made — modified on purpose.

Indigenous peoples managed the forests by selecting trees species, by purposely planting along their trails food crops and plants they knew for attracting edible insects and game (Posey, 1985). They modified the waterways (Raffles, 2002) and reclaimed land through irrigation, terracing and drainage (Denevan, 1970). They created fertile self-regenerating soils — *terra preta de índio* — throughout the Amazon Basin (Smith, 1980), "garden cities" that included roads, and artificial fisheries (Erickson, 2000) that could withstand periodic inundations (Mann, 2008). In Mesoamerica, the Mayas had cleared large forested areas to create intensive agricultural systems in order to feed a growing population, with the consequence of severe erosion in some regions (Dunning and Beach, 1994). The Aztecs were so fond of quetzal (*Pharomachrus mocinno*) feathers, a tropical altitude bird found in the Maya highland areas, and other forest products, that cloud forests in Central America have been considerably disturbed over hundreds of years (Peterson and Peterson, 1992).

The number of indigenous people in Latin America was drastically reduced by the diseases brought by the Europeans (smallpox reached America in 1518), slavery, and mistreatment. When the

Spanish conquistador Orellana, a propagator of the Amazons — this is how the river was given its name — and El Dorado myths, followed the Amazon River from Quito to the Atlantic coast in 1542, his chronicler Carvajal reported that the lower third of the river was densely and continuously populated. Archeologists researching the mouth of the Tapajós area (Santarém) mention in that case, from 100 to 1400AD, a population of 200 to 400,000 people, as large as the Aztec capital Tenochtitlán. All is left is a large area of black earth (7 by 1 km) and countless ceramics fragments (Mann, 2002). In another case, in the Xingu region, settlements had up to 50,000 people, with city centers, roads, and walls (Mann, 2008). This is far from the idea that only Mesoamerica and the Andes had large urban societies, with the forests being almost empty. These large settlements all disappeared after 1500, like most of the continent's native population. The 40 to 100 million Latin American natives calculated by scholars (eight million in the Amazon Basin) were reduced to less than six million in 150 years (200,000 for the Amazon) (Denevan, 1992). The memory of many native groups or tribes vanished. And some of the bands of hunter-gatherers encountered in the forests years or centuries later may well be refugees, remnants of these larger populations (Mann, 2005), victims of genocide. La Condamine (1745) had already mentioned the fact that the natives living along the Marañon (Upper-Amazon) had left *en masse* for inland refuges after having met the first Europeans. It does not come as a surprise that the continental forests were considered almost empty when the Spanish and Portuguese became more interested in their exploitation in the late eighteenth century, in relation to the rubber boom.

10.4. LATIN AMERICAN FORESTS IN THE WESTERN COLLECTIVE IMAGINATION

There was, and still is, an aura of mystery around tropical forests. In the case of the Amazon, it has its origin in an intentional policy of embargoes on knowledge and travels by the Spanish and Portuguese crowns, eager to maintain their monopoly on these lands and their richness (Hecht and Cockburn, 1990). For many years, the interiors of large forested areas were drawn as blank spots or filled with invented monsters on the maps. It is also linked with the material difficulties and costs of traveling through tropical forests. From an airplane they often appear as a flat green carpet of vegetation, cut out only by rivers. In the field, reaching distant places is difficult in the absence of roads. The only way to travel is often by boat (*peque peque, pecamari, falcas*). And one really has to beware of tree spines, mosquitoes, flies, snakes, spiders, wasps, ants, and other hosts of tropical forests you have to know about to avoid unpleasant surprises. The first exploration parties' human losses were tremendous. Less than 100 of the 220 Spaniards and a handful of the 4,000 Altiplano natives survived the unsuccessful Cortes–Orellana expedition of 1542 to the Napo and Amazon mouths.

The first Europeans who described the forests were impressed by its beauties, but also distressed. Latin American forests generated numerous amazed descriptions from the early travelers, who participated in the construction of enduring myths about the impenetrable jungle (a word deriving from India) and its inhabitants. Numerous travel stories, narratives of lost tribes and marvels magnified the mystery. As a late example of this series, Percy Fawcett came from his 1906–1907 expedition, aimed at delimitating the frontier between Bolivia and Brazil, with tales of a 20 meter giant anaconda and other curiosities. He disappeared in 1925, reinforcing the myth and giving birth to an industry of rescue missions in search of him (Grann, 2009). The character even appeared alive in Hergé's *The Adventures of Tintin: The Broken Ear*, published in 1945. The Anaconda theme was very close to Up de Graff's account of his expedition in 1897 (Up de Graff, 1925). While on the bank of the Yasuni River (Ecuador) he and his companion, *en route* to the Jivaro country, saw a gigantic beast. Its body was as large as a man's chest. Taking their 24 foot dug-out boat as a yardstick, they estimated its length at 50, maybe 60 feet. "The most robust man is a powerless wisp of straw when captured in the coils of such a monster", he wrote. It disappeared swiftly in the river, not leaving them "enough time to shoot" (a white-man-in-the-jungle reflex, no doubt).

The good old tradition of touring the Jivaro-Shuar head-hunters to observe their horrific customs was carried on by many adventurers. Whereas Up de Graff describes the process but denounces their abject absence of morale, Flornoy (1939) indulges in the pleasure compulsion. He details, with a self-proclaimed cultural openness, the craftsman's recipe for the preparation of a *tsantsa* (shrunken head): "With 'sadistic joy' and meticulousness, accompanied by songs, dances, and great libation, the head is detached from the skull, boiled, the mouth sewed, the skin dried with warm sand and rubbed with ashes, to finally conclude with a public presentation of the trophy". The fierce Shuars, who successfully resisted the Jesuit missionaries' offensive and the rubber barons' enslavement, began in the early twentieth century to sell shrunken heads, including some explorers' or priests', made especially for Western freak collectors and museums.

More on the side of reason, many great scientists visited and reported on the forests of Central and South America. Charles Marie de La Condamine explored the Andes and the Amazon Basin from 1736 to 1744. He was the first scientist to descend the river, and he came back to France with maps, as well as precise descriptions of rubber, of the use of curare as a poison, and of quinine against malaria. Alexander von Humboldt (1807) and Aimé Bonpland explored what is now Venezuela, Cuba, Colombia, Ecuador, and Peru between 1799 and 1803, meticulously noting what they saw and measuring everything they could. They were the first to situate precisely the Orenoque–Amazon canal.

Charles Darwin, on the voyage of the Beagle (1832), landed in San Salvador de Bahia and commented on the Mata Atlântica:

> Delight itself, however, is a weak term to express the feelings of a naturalist who, for the first time, has wandered by himself in a Brazilian forest. Among the multitude of striking objects, the general luxuriance of the vegetation bears away the victory. The elegance of the grasses, the novelty of the parasitical plants, the beauty of the flowers, the glossy green of the foliage, all tend to this end. A most paradoxical mixture of sound and silence pervades the

> shady parts of the wood. The noise from the insects is so loud, that it may be heard even in a vessel anchored several hundred yards from the shore; yet within the recesses of the forest a universal silence appears to reign. To a person fond of natural history, such a day as this, brings with it a deeper pleasure than he ever can hope again to experience. (Darwin, 1913, pp. 11–12)

Scientists were the new conquerors of Central American forests. Inspired, among others, by Jean-Frédéric Maximilien de Waldeck's drawings and descriptions of Palenque and Yucatán, John Stephens, well-born in New England, volunteered for the post of American *chargé d'affaires* in Central America. Joined by the English architect Frederick Catherwood, he explored the region, the jungles, and the lost cities of what is now recognized as Maya city-states: Copán, Quiriga, Toniná, Palenque, Uxmal. His talent at telling stories, including travel incidents, is only met with the quality of Catherwood's drawings (Stephens, 1844). Stephens is now seen as the "discoverer" of the Mayas.

These early scientists were followed by hordes of biologists, botanists, and anthropologists, collecting thousands of specimens for European museums, but also by the practitioners of a new special field, land survey, who played a historical role. The limits between the Spanish and Portuguese empires had provoked many tensions after the 1494 Tordesillas Treaty, which made it possible for the Portuguese to colonize Brazil. Frontiers had to be drawn in the middle of the continent, giving rise to a new type of explorer, after the conquistador, the priest, the treasure-hunter, and the scientist: the engineer-soldier. José Solano, a classical character, was a member of the famous *Comisión de Límites* in 1754–1761. He also brought descriptions of the forest and the local customs. Brazil, better endowed with land surveyors, was able to gain territory in territorial disputes by a better knowledge of the field and technical capacity. The engineer-soldiers played a crucial role in taming the vast Brazilian territory for the state. Cândido Rondon, the positivist engineer and army marshal, built telegraph lines across the Amazon between 1890 and 1915, to Mato Grosso, Bolivia, and Peru. In contact with various tribes and influenced by the ideas of Auguste Comte, he soon became an advocate of the natives and helped create in 1910 the *Serviço de Proteção aos Índios* (Indian Protection Agency), the ancestor of FUNAI, until the 1950s. He became famous for "pacifying" numerous indigenous tribes: Bororo, Nambikwara, Botocudo, Kaingang, Umotina, Parintintim, Urubu, Xavante. Among his glories as a Brazilian hero, he was behind the creation of the first national park in Brazil, the Xingu, in 1952.

10.5. THE POLITICS OF CONSERVATION

All over Latin America, nature reserves, or protected areas, (hereafter PAs), have been the major response to the perceived biodiversity and forest crises; and indigenous territories, the major response to indigenous claims. PAs (national and subnational parks, state forests, biological reserves, extractive reserves), represent the main concrete and maybe the most successful mechanism for conserving forests. The first Latin American park was established in Mexico in 1898 (El Chico National Park, Hidalgo). Their number increased rapidly during the twentieth century in general in the south[15] and in Latin America in particular. An average of 25% of the land surface is under protection in Central America (Chape *et al.*, 2003); 30% in South America (WRI, 2010), with extremes such as over 70% in Venezuela and 8% in Argentina.[16] With such a territorial extent, PAs represent a major stake in Latin American environmental policies, mainly for three reasons: their indigenous population, the resources they contain, and their role on a global scale.

As much as 86% of Latin American PAs have human populations living within their limits (IUCN, 2009b), most often indigenous

[15] After 30 years of accelerated expansion, they now number over 110,000 in the world and occupy over 13% of the planet's land surface (Chape *et al.*, 2008; Schmitt, 2008), more than cultivated lands (9.7%) (FAO, 2004; Chape *et al.*, 2003).

[16] Again, a precautionary note. Data differ according to the inclusion or not of private protected areas, biosphere reserves, indigenous conservation areas, and Ramsar protected wetlands. Here, Biosphere, Ramsar, and indigenous areas are included.

populations. Thirty-two per cent of Latin America's tropical forests are owned by local communities and indigenous peoples or designated by governments for their use (Hatcher and Bailey, 2009) and 20% of the Amazon is now under permanent rights of indigenous peoples (Nepstad *et al.*, 2005). Latin American forests are not only hyperdiverse in the species and ecosystems they contain, but also in their human populations. Forest protected areas also contain natural resources highly coveted by private and public economic interests: water, land, tropical hardwood, gold, oil, gas, genetic resources, rare animals, or plants. Thirty-two per cent of Latin American tropical forests are in private hands. But there is tremendous pressure on the public and indigenous lands, and PAs, for the use of resources. Two examples illustrate this pressure at different levels.

Oil exploitation in tropical forests has tremendous environmental impacts for different reasons: seismic surveys, oil spills, pipelines, roads, deforestation, workers camps and their associated economy, including bars, prostitution, poaching, violence, etc. (Haller *et al.*, 2007). The government of Ecuador has proposed a moratorium on the exploitation of a large oil field located under the Yasuni National Park (situated in the Amazon Basin and one of the more diverse place on Earth, also an indigenous territory and a biosphere reserve) against the payment by an international trust fund of an annual rent, to be financed by industrialized countries (Rival, 2009). The argument being that Ecuador needs financial resources for its development and that, by not exploiting its oil reserves in order to conserve biodiversity and carbon, it should be compensated — a logic close to the CDM and REDD mechanisms (Clean Development Mechanism and Reduced Emissions from Deforestation and Degradation, both linked to the Kyoto Protocol). The proposed deal really confronts the industrialized countries with their contradictions: on one side they ask countries with tropical forests to stop deforestation, but on the other side they have not upheld their repeated commitments to provide adequate funding for conservation. As I write, the trust fund is open, but money is not really flowing in.

The second example is Amarakaeri in Peru (Álvarez, 2010). The government has, in contrast to Ecuador, opened 70% of the Peruvian

Amazon, including indigenous territories, for oil and gas extraction by attributing blocks to private oil companies and openly promoting the exploitation of natural resources. One case is the Amarakaeri Communal Reserve (ACR), 402,000 hectares, located in the Madre de Dios region, in front of the famous Manu National Park (again one of the most biodiverse places on Earth, one of the most pristine, and one of the last territories with uncontacted indigenous peoples), on the other bank of the Madre de Dios river but included within the Manu Biosphere Reserve. The ACR was created by the government in 2002, after many years of protest and demands on the part of the local indigenous communities, invaded at that time by loggers and gold-diggers. But for the Peruvian law, as is the case everywhere in Latin America, the subsoil remains a state property, even if the usufruct of the land and its forest is conceded to the natives (something questionable for the ILO Convention 169, ratified by Peru). The Repsol and Hunt oil companies followed a very astute policy, dividing the local *caciques* by cooptation and promises. As I write, seismic exploration has started, amid huge protests and debates.

Finally, protected areas also generate considerable economic activity linked with conservation policies, often financed by international conservation NGOs, bilateral cooperation agencies, and international organizations. The network of practitioners, international organizations, NGOs, and state agencies behind this global phenomenon can be labeled as the "global conservation regime". It defines the norms implemented at the national and local levels in global conferences and research institutions, backing them by numerous, complex, and well-endowed financial mechanisms, such as the GEF (Global Environment Fund) or FFEM (*Fonds Français pour l'Environnement Mondial*).

10.6. PARTICIPATORY CONSERVATION

Latin America is diverse and similar at the same time. Each country has its own *cosmovisón* or *Weltanschauung* — its image of the world — but at the same time Latin American countries have histories in common, and they have followed broadly the same political and economic models, changing models simultaneously. One can think of the great waves of national revolutions, bourgeois liberalism, state development, authoritarian regimes, neo-liberalism, and so forth. In this regard, nature conservation policies can be seen as good modern indicators of political tendencies, more precisely, modes of governance, territorial organization, development priorities, attitude towards ethnic minorities, citizenship, and so on. Observing them is to observe one of the most sensitive edges of Latin American societies and their environmental policies.

While, historically, protected areas policies were based on inflexible borders and rules governing access to resources, generating much resistance (Holmes, 2007; Dowie, 2009), the prevalent discourse — please forgive the jargon — claims that conservation policies must be adaptive and participative in order to meet the combined goals of conservation and livelihoods support in the face of social and environmental change (Adams, 2004; Hufty, 2009). Not only because most states don't have the resources to strictly control all the extensive and often remote PAs they have created (often to please donors and green lobbies), but also because, in most cases, PAs are highly interconnected with local communities. And the ways communities behave towards "nature" and protected resources is determined by their institutions as well as the associated rules and expectations that govern individual and collective behavior. This is plainly understood by the social current of conservation (Galvin and Haller, 2008). Local populations have developed *sui generis* ways for managing socio-ecological systems and adapting to change, including "social technology" in the form of resilient, adaptive, and flexible institutions (Berkes, 2009). But no local community or social institution functions without being influenced and impacted by national and international factors, whether political, economic, or ecological. These levels are interdependent (Blaikie and Brookfield, 1987; Young *et al.*, 2008).

While it appears as something obvious in democratic contexts, participation in Latin American PAs is in fact a battlefield. Its practical implementation is a key space for governance processes to take place, a "nodal point" as I define it (Hufty, 2010), i.e. a social interface where actors, material and symbolic stakes, and power games converge.

Defined by the World Bank as, "a process through which stakeholders influence and share control over the decisions and resources that affect them" (WB, 1996, xi), participation historically came out of a radical stance, as in the work of Paulo Freire (1970), who saw it as a tool for human liberation. The concept was popularized by Robert Chambers (1983) who pointed out the existing top-down bias in the design of development projects in favor of the rich, the educated, the urban, the powerful, and the male. It soon became part of the standard tools of international organizations and bilateral aid agencies, and, as a "metanorm" (Hufty, 2010), it was soon overstretched and overused. In the context of nature protection, besides some sincere attempts to empower local people, it has been mostly used strategically to help improve the social acceptability of PAs (Balasinorwala *et al.*, 2004), for defusing opposition to external interventions, or for gaining funding and political support. For its critics, it has been "co-opted and mainstreamed by governmental and non-governmental agencies, part of a new development 'tyranny' that betrays the concept's populist roots" (Walker *et al.*, 2007, p. 423). And despite some good practice examples, it has rarely meant a real transfer of power to local actors (Cooke and Kothari, 2001; Hufty, 2009). Still, the results shown by most PAs are unsatisfactory for many conservationists (those who work in nature conservation as a main occupation). They complain that this new paradigm helps convert some of the most beautiful PAs into "Indian reserves". They call for strictly enforced PAs as the only way to ensure the sustainability of fragile ecosystems. Many PAs confront a dilemma and a double challenge: neither conservation nor social objectives are achieved. Bordering populations complain, claiming that their situation worsens with the creation of PAs, and conservationists are unconvinced of the effectiveness of the participatory paradigm.

Meanwhile, a series of studies have demonstrated that indigenous territories are effective against illegal logging, mining, fire, and other threats (Neptstad, 2006; Nelson and Chomitz, 2009). Indigenous peoples are said to be "close to nature", especially since Rio in 1992 and the emergence of the participatory paradigm. They appear more and more in conservation programs as "biodiversity guardians". This idea fits with reality in some specific contexts, but it is also a sensitive issue in the debate on global environmental governance, autonomy, identity, and territory. There is a strong risk in assuming that communities are traditional by essence (essentialism) or holders of medical and ecological knowledge concealing extraordinary potentialities. This discourse is used by indigenous as well as non-indigenous actors. On the level of the NGOs and international organizations, this is a situation of "working misunderstanding" (Bohannan, 1958), in which stakeholders agree on a discourse while disagreeing on its purpose. It has, indeed, the double function of legitimating the international forums in which indigenous representatives take part, while allowing them concrete gains in other areas, like land. This is where the real issue is in their eyes: political and territorial recognition and not biodiversity conservation (biodiversity is quite a strange concept for most indigenous peoples). The proximity with nature would, then, be called upon in a strategic way by the indigenous insofar as it makes it possible to create alliances with international actors (NGOs, IOs) against nation-states to gain some political ground. In fact, in the 1990s, and due to substantial transformations of Latin America's "public space", they succeeded in gaining access to politics and citizenship in some Latin American countries, such as Peru, Bolivia, and, to some extent, in Argentina.

This analysis is illustrated by the cases of Amarakaeri Communal Reserve, but also by Pilón Lajas Community Territory and Biosphere Reserve (Bolivia), Pizarro national Park and Yungas Biosphere Reserve (Argentina). Despite the important institutionalization of indigenous movements in these countries, their backing to local people's struggles, and the apparent success of their territorial claims, when citizenship is taken as an analytical framework, results are ambivalent. The national state has taken advantage of the dialogue with these communities, and the environmental organizations' funds, to increase its control on territories that used to be regionally autonomous, and on these communities by promoting their political or ethnic reorganization to gain a place at the negotiation table. The recognition of land usufruct to indigenous communities (which in both cases amounted to a claim for a monopoly on the use of resources) did not imply sovereignty on subsoil filed with oil and gold (Amarakaeri), nor the physical capacity to resist *colonos* land invasion and timber business (Pilón Lajas), or to resist the steamroller of soybeans expansion (Argentina).

Much remains to consolidate this "citizenship from below" (local agency through the use of the public space, in the sense of Habermas) and convert provisional gains in structural advantages. As political ecologists would put it, these indigenous peoples are still politically, economically, and ecologically marginalized, in spite of the real progress regarding citizenship in Latin America.

Meanwhile, governments continue to create PAs at an accelerated pace to impress the world and get funds from the international community, even if they often don't have the management and financial capacity to operate them. From a legal and operational point of view, created too quickly, many protected areas are in a fuzzy legal status, with contradictory national legal norms, insufficient financial means, rare and insufficiently trained personnel, limited support by the people who live within their limits and in the vicinity, and an ineffective governance and a lack of scientific bases.

A major problem is the world vision on which the PAs design and governance rest. It is the same vision that is at the origin of the current crisis of biological diversity and forests: modernistic, dualistic, utilitarian, mechanist, and scientistic (Ingold, 2000). It is intrinsically identical to the colonial perception of a nature available for predation. And PAs are often created on sites where all the ingredients for conflicts are present: historical violent marginalization of local people, superposition of different and conflicting legal regimes and governance processes, and conflicting visions regarding the resources they contain. The creation of PAs in this context is likely to exacerbate the existing conflicts, since the establishment of a protected area implies a limitation of the former uses or possible uses of resources. This might partially explain why the main policy tool for forest conservation is not as effective as it could be.

10.7. CONCLUSION

Much fantasized about, Latin American forests have played an increasingly important role in the governance of global environmental change, in relation to classical mechanisms such as protected areas or the newest global fad, REDD+. They have been the silent victim of the capitalist world-economy predatory expansion for centuries. Colonial Europe and Latin American societies have had a complex relationship with these forests, fascinated but turning their back on them as the barbarian element of the equation "barbaria or civilization". Until the 1950s nobody was concerned with conservation. The main idea was to conquer territory, and with an underpinning sexual vocabulary, to "penetrate" the jungle, to tame it and discover its secrets. Development in the form of increased productivity was the master idea. Forests ended up exploited for their resources.

The local populations, decimated by the European arrival, were given successive identities by the dominant societies: non-humans, slaves, pagans, savages, poor people, local communities, and finally the guardians of biodiversity. They had very little chance to show who they were and decide on their future by themselves. With the help of the conservation regime, they had the chance in the second half of the twentieth century to begin a political and territorial renewal. But again this is because they are seen as useful allies in the fight of the sustainable use party against the predatory party, both utilitarian. At least this has allowed them some breathing space and participation in the public space, as goes the hypothesis of citizenship from below.

The exploratory ideas contained in this chapter still have to be developed. With modesty, much remains to be done.

BIBLIOGRAPHY

Adams, W. H. *et al.* (2004). Biodiversity Conservation and the Eradication of Poverty, *Science*, 306, pp. 1146–1149.

Álvarez, A. (2010). Conservación participativa en la Reserva Comunal Amarakaeri, Perú, *Revista Latinoamericana de Conservación*, 1(1), pp. 18–37.

Baerwald, T. (2010). Prospects for geography as an interdisciplinary discipline, *Annals of the Association of American Geographers*, 100(3), pp. 493–501.

Balasinorwala, T., Kothari, A. and Goyal, M. (2004). *Participatory Conservation: Paradigm shifts in International Policy*, Kalpavriksh: IUCN, Gland, Cambridge.

Balée, W. (1995). 'Historical Ecology of Amazonia', in Sponsel, L. E (ed.), *Indigenous Peoples and the Future of Amazonia*, University of Arizona Press, Tucson, pp. 97–110.

Balée, W. (ed.) (1998). *Advances in Historical Ecology*, Columbia University, New York.

Berkes, F. (2009). Community conserved areas: Policy issues in historic and contemporary context, *Conservation Letters*, 2, pp. 19–24.

Blaikie, P. and Brookfield, H. (1987). *Land degradation and society*, Methuen, London.

Bohannan, P. (1958). On Anthropologists' Use of Language, *American Anthropologist*, 60(1), pp. 161–163.

Callon, M. and Latour, B. (1981). 'Unscrewing the Big Leviathan: How Actors Macro-Structure Reality and How Sociologists Help them Do So', in Knorr-Cetina, K. and Cicourel, A. (eds), *Advances in Social Theory and Methodology*, Routledge & Kegan Paul, London, pp. 277–303.

CBD. (Secretariat of the Convention on Biological Diversity) (2009). *Sustainable Forest Management, Biodiversity and Livelihoods: A Good Practice Guide*, CBD Secretariat, Montreal.

CBD. (2010). *Global Biodiversity Outlook No. 3*, CBD Secretariat, Montreal.

Chambers, R. (1983). *Rural Development: Putting the Last First*, Longman, London.

Chape, S., Blyth, S., Fish, L., Fox, P. and Spalding, M. (compilers), (2003). *2003 United Nations List of Protected Areas*, IUCN/UNEP-WCMC, Gland, Cambridge.

Chape, S., Spalding, M. and Jenkins, M. D. (2008). *The World's Protected Areas*, Prepared by the UNEP-WCMC, University of California Press, Berkeley.

CI — Conservation International. (2010). *Biodiversity Hotspots. Atlantic Forest*, Available at: http://www.biodiversityhotspots.org/xp/Hotspots/atlantic_forest/Pages/default.aspx. [Accessed 20 June 2010].

Cooke, B. and Kothari, U. (eds) (2001). *Participation: The New Tyranny?* Zed Books, London.

Darwin, C. (1913 [1860]). *Journal of Researches into the Natural History and Geology of the Countries Visited During the Voyage Round the World of H.M.S. Beagle Under the Command of Captain FitzRoy*, John Murray, London.

De La Condamine, C. M. (1745). *Relation abrégée d'un voyage fait dans l'intérieur de l'Amérique Méridionale depuis la côte de la mer du sud jusqu'aux côtes du Brésil et de la Guyane, en descendant la rivière des amazones, lue à l'assemblée publique de l'Académie des sciences, le 28 arril 1745.*

Denevan, W. M. (1970). Aboriginal Drained-Field Cultivation in the Americas: Pre-Columbian Reclamation of Wet Lands was Widespread in the Savannas and Highlands of Latin America, *Science*, 169, pp. 647–654.

Denevan, W. M. (1992). The Pristine Myth: The Landscape of the Americas in 1492, *Annals of the American Association of Geographers*, 82(3), pp. 369–385.

Dowie, M. (2009). *Conservation Refugees. The hundred-year conflict between global conservation and native peoples*, MIT Press, Cambridge, MA.

Dunning, N. P. and Beach, T. (1994). Soil Erosion, Slope Management, and Ancient Terracing in the Maya Lowlands, *Latin American Antiquity*, 5(1), pp. 51–69.

Erickson, C. L. (2000). An artificial landscape fishery in the Bolivian Amazon, *Nature*, 408, pp. 190–193.

FAO. (2004). *Land Use Data*, Available at: faostat.fao.org/faostat/collections?subset= agriculture [Accessed 23 September 2004].

FAO. (2005). *Global Forest Resource Assessment*, FAO, Rome.

FAO. (2010). *Global Forest Resource Assessment*, FAO, Rome.

Folke, C. *et al.* (2002). *Resilience and Sustainable Development: Building Adaptive Capacity in a World of Transformations*, Scientific Background Paper on Resilience for the Process of The World Summit on Sustainable Development on behalf of The Environmental Advisory Council to the Swedish Government, Stockholm.

Freire, P. (1970). *Pedagogy of the Oppressed*, Continuum, New York.

Galvin, M. and Haller, T. (eds) (2008). *People, Protected Areas and Global Change: Participatory Conservation in Latin America, Africa, Asia and Europe*, NCCR North-South/Geographica Bernensia, Bern.

Geist, H. J. and Lambin, E. F. (2001). *What Drives Tropical Deforestation? A meta-analysis of proximate and underlying causes of deforestation based on subnational case study evidence*, LUCC Report Series No. 4, University of Louvain, Louvain-La-Neuve.

Gerber, F., Veuthey, S. and Martínez-Alier, J. (2009). Linking political ecology with ecological economics in tree plantation conflicts in Cameroon and Ecuador, *Ecological Economics*, 68, pp. 2885–2889.

Grann, D. (2009). *The Lost City of Z: A Tale of Deadly Obsession in the Amazon*, Doubleday, New York.

Haller, T., Blöchinger, A., John, M., Marthaler, E. and Ziegler, S. (eds) (2007). *Fossil Fuels, Oil Companies, and Indigenous Peoples*, LIT, Zurich.

Hatcher, J. and Bailey, L. (2009). *Tropical Forest Tenure Assessment. Trends, Challenges and Opportunities*, Rights and Resources Initiative-ITTO, Washington-Yokohama.

Holmes, G. (2007). Protection, politics and protest: Understanding resistance to conservation, *Conservation and Society*, 5(2), pp. 184–201.

Hoogeven, H. *et al.* (2008). *Designing a Forest Financing Mechanism: A Call for Bold, Collaborative and Innovative Thinking*, Fletcher School of Law and Diplomacy, Tufts University, Metford.

Hufty, M. (ed.) (2009). *Participation, conservation and livelihoods: Evaluating the effectiveness of participatory approaches in protected areas*, Synthesis Report submitted to the SNIS, Graduate Institute, Geneva.

Hufty, M. (2010). Gobernanza en Salud Pública: Hacia un Marco Analítico, *Revista de Salud Pública*, 12(1), pp. 39–61.

Ingold, T. (2000). *The Perception of the Environment*, Routledge. London.

IUCN. (2009a). *Red List*, Available at: http://www.iucnredlist.org [Accessed 22 November 2010].

IUCN. (2009b). *People and Protected Areas: Equity and Governance*, available at iucn.org/about/work/programmes/social_policy/sp_themes/sp_themes_pan dpa [Accessed 30 November 2009].

Leakey, R.E. and Lewin, R. (1995). *The Sixth Extinction: Patterns of Life and the Future of Humankind*, Doubleday, New York.

Malhi, Y. *et al.* (2008). Climate Change, Deforestation, and the Fate of the Amazon, *Science*, 319, pp. 169–172.

Mann, C. C. (2002). The forgotten people of Amazonia, *Science*, 297, p. 921.

Mann, C. C. (2005). *1491, New Revelations of the Americas Before Columbus*, Knopf, New York.

Mann, C. C. (2008). Ancient earthmovers of the Amazon, *Science*, 321, pp. 1148–1152.

Martinez-Alier, J. (2003). *The Environmentalism of the Poor: A Study of Ecological Conflicts and Valuation*. Edward Elgar, London.

MEA — Millennium Ecosystem Assessment. (2005). *Millennium Ecosystem Assessment Synthesis Report*, World Resources Institute, Island Press, Washington, DC.

Miller, S. W. (2007). *An Environmental History of Latin America*, Cambridge University Press, Cambridge.

Myers, N. *et al.* (2000). Biodiversity hotspots for conservation priorities, *Nature*, 403, pp. 853–858.

Nabuurs, G. J. *et al.* (2007). *Forestry in Climate Change 2007: Mitigation*, Contribution of Working Group III to the Fourth Assessment Report of the IPCC, Cambridge University Press, Cambridge.

Nelson, A. and Chomitz, K. M. (2009). *Protected Area Effectiveness in Reducing Tropical Deforestation: A Global Analysis of the Impact of Protection Status*, Evaluation Brief 7, The World Bank, Washington, DC.

Nepstad, D. *et al.* (2005). Inhibition of Amazon Deforestation and Fire by Parks and Indigenous Lands, *Conservation Biology*, 20(1), pp. 65–73.

Olson, S. H., Gangnon, R., Silveira, G. and Patz, J. A. (2010). Deforestation and malaria in Mâncio Lima County, Brazil, *Emerging Infectious Diseases*, 16, pp. 108–1115.

Ostrom, E. (2005). *Understanding Institutional Diversity*, Princeton University Press, Princeton.

Peterson, A. A. and Townsend, A. (1992). Aztec Exploitation of Cloud Forests: Tributes of Liquidambar Resin and Quetzal Feathers, *Global Ecology and Biogeography Letters*, 2(5), pp. 165–173.

Posey, D. (1985). Indigenous management of tropical forest ecosystems: The case of the Kayapo, *Agroforestry Systems*, 3, pp. 139–158.

Raffles, H. (2002). *In Amazonia: A Natural History*, Princeton University Press, Princeton.

Rival, L. (2009). *The Yasuní-ITT Initiative: Oil Development and Alternative Forms of Wealth Making in the Ecuadorian Amazon*, QEH Working Paper Series 180, University of Oxford.

Sader, S. A. and Joyce, A. T. (1988). Deforestation rates and trends in Costa Rica, *Biotropica*, 20, pp. 11–19.

Sauer, C. O. (1925). The Morphology of Landscape, *University of California Publications in Geography*, 2(2), pp. 19–53.

Schmitt, C. B. *et al.* (2008). *Global Ecological Forest Classification and Forest Protected Area Gap Analysis. Analyses and recommendations in view of the 10% target for forest protection under the convention on biological diversity (CBD)*, Freiburg University Press, Freiburg.

Scott, J. C. (1985). *Weapons of the weak: Everyday forms of peasants' resistance*, Yale University Press, New Haven.

Smith, N. J. H. (1980). Anthrosol and human carrying capacity in Amazonia, *Annals of the Association of American Geographers*, 70(4), pp. 553–566.

Stern, N. (2006). *Stern Review on the Economics of Climate Change*, HM Treasury, London.

Strange, S. (1988). States and Markets, Pinter, London.

Up De Graff, F. W. (1925). *Head Hunters of the Amazon: Seven Years of Exploration and Adventure*, Garden City, New York.

van Dijk, K. and Savenije, H. (2009). *Towards national financing strategies for sustainable forest management in Latin America: Overview of the present situation and the experience in selected countries*, Forestry Policy and Institutions WP 21, FAO, Rome.

Von Humboldt, A. and Bonpland, A. (1807–1834). *Voyage aux régions equinoxiales du nouveau continent,* 30 vol. Paris.

Walker, D., Jones, J. P., Roberts, S. and Fröhling, O. R. (2007). When Participation Meets Empowerment: The WWF and the Politics of Invitation in the Chimalapas, Mexico, *Annals of the Association of American Geographers*, 97(2), pp. 423–444.

Whitmore, T. C. and Prance, G. T. (eds) (1987). *Bio-geography and Quaternary History in Tropical America*, Oxford University Press, New York.

Wilson, E. O. (1992). *The Diversity of Life*, Belknap Press of Harvard University, Cambridge, MA.

World Bank. (1996). *Assessing Aid: What Works. What Doesn't and Why*, Oxford University Press, New York.

WRI — World Resource Institute (2010). *Earthtrends: The Environmental Information portal*, Available at: http://earthtrends.wri.org/text/biodiversity-protected/country-profiles.html [Accesssed 20 October 2010].

WWF (World Wide Fund for Nature) (2010). *Amazon alive. A decade of discovery 1999–2009*, WWF, Washington, DC.

Young, O. R., King, L. A. and Shroeder, H. (eds) (2008). *Institutions and Environmental Change. Principal Findings, Applications, and Research Frontiers*, MIT Press, Cambridge, MA.

Part Three

RURALITY, ECONOMY, AND MODELS OF DEVELOPMENT

Chapter

11

Rural Areas vs. Cities in Latin American History

Claude Auroi

11.1. INTRODUCTION

Today Latin America is an urbanised continent today. In 1910, however, the proportion of rural households was no less than 80% (Del Pozo Vergnes, 1997). Later on, at the beginning of the 1960s, the urban and rural population were about equal. At the end of the last century, already 78% of the population lived in cities and towns (FAO, 2009). Of course, the concepts 'urban' and 'rural' are not very precise, as they depend on national statistics that can vary in their definitions. In most countries, a town has at least 2,000 inhabitants (2,500 in Mexico).

Accordingly, in small towns in the countryside, 'rurality' is still very much present, with cows and sheep regularly invading the streets, marketplaces crowded with peasant families and stray dogs looking for garbage on street corners. We can say that capital cities and big cities of 500,000 inhabitants or more are usually true urban areas, at least in their central parts. The fictitious town of *Macondo*, in various García Márquez novels, is considered an archetype of the

Latin American country town, with a quiet life in general but also many quarrels among neighbours and a clear tendency toward decline.[1] There are also mega-cities like Mexico City, São Paulo, Buenos Aires, Lima and Santiago de Chile, from which rurality has been eliminated. Such capital cities concentrate various forms of power — political, economic, and cultural — and have therefore, since the nineteenth century, increased in population more than other cities in a given country, though there are exceptions like Colombia, where Medellín and Cali are almost as big as Bogotá. Brazil and Argentina also have some important regional centres.

Apart from such mega-cities, and outside the commercial centres of other great cities, rurality is still present in a number of densely built suburban environments, where it takes various forms: horses, carriages, peasants in the streets, agricultural production and animals in backyards, trucks loaded with grain and vegetables, deposits of products and inputs and smells and noises, typical of villages (e.g. hens, roosters and donkeys).

But the visual and auditory environment in Latin America has undergone large changes since 1950 and, in certain countries of the Southern Cone, since as far back as 1930. Even in the countryside, where rurality still dominates because agriculture is the main occupation, changes of infrastructure have been apparent everywhere since the 1960s: notably, the availability of electricity, running water and other facilities, the tarring of streets and better housing.

The rural population is still quite important in a few countries — over 20% in Andean countries, Central America, Mexico and also Paraguay — but is diminishing rapidly, even in relative terms. At the continental level, the rural population was still at 42% in 1970, but had dropped to 29% by 1990, and will be at around 10% in 2020 (Escudero, 1998, p. 37; FAO, 2009). The contribution of agricultural production to GNP also dropped from 20% in 1950 to 10% in 1990 and to 5.7% in 2006 — in which year that sector represented only 17% of the labour force (Escudero, 1998, p. 37; FAO, 2009).

[1] Especially in *Cien años de soledad* (1967), (English version, *One Hundred Years of Solitude*) (García Márquez, 1970).

Nevertheless, in 2010, there are still many peasants of various types and more than 120 million people who live from agriculture and directly related activities, even without reckoning on the number of industrial, labour and service employees involved in the value chain of processing agricultural commodities. Although declining, rurality has been predominant for almost 200 years, with a very strong impact on societies and people, culturally, psychologically and politically. It remains, too, a large component in the mindsets of many rural migrants now settled in the towns and cities.

11.2. WHAT IS RURALITY?

According to the FAO definition (Dixon *et al.*, 2001), the concept of a rural population generally refers to some type of agricultural activity, and to an environment where natural elements dominate over constructed areas. In Latin America, there are many ecosystems and therefore many agro-ecosystems as well. These may be comprised of mountain areas (the Andes, sierras, hilly foots of mountains and surroundings), vast, flat pampas, and semi-arid bushy areas; along rivers, in cleared woods, or in the deltas of Pacific coastal areas. Accordingly, physical setting does not fully describe the rural character of a region, and still less the rural–urban interaction, which is based on various types of relationship: commercial, social, political and (recently) ecological. Thus, ecosystem analysis and factors of technological change seldom suffice to explain the formation of rural settings linked to urban ones — what we can call the rural–urban complex or territorial binomial in Latin America. The constitution and perennial configuration of this binary complex needs a historical analysis of social and power relations during the colonial period and the republican epoch.

11.3. FORMATION OF THE RURAL–URBAN COMPLEX

Under Spanish colonial rule, the rural–urban concept, applied to territorial occupation in conquered areas, involved a distinction between two types of 'Republics': the *República de los Españoles* and the *República de los Indios*. The former would live in cities, the latter in villages. But this apartheid vision of coexistence did not survive for very long, as it clashed almost immediately with social necessities: arranging for the service of Indians in the town mansions of Spaniards, and the control of Indians by authorities (*corregidores*) in their 'home lands'. Furthermore, the property structure imposed was comprised of big farms called *encomiendas*, which later became *haciendas*. In the *haciendas* lived Spanish administrators representing the landowners and Indians subordinated to them as field workers. There were also the 'free' zones of the *Repúblicas de los Indios*, where the Spanish Crown had delegated control — collection of the tribute and recruitment of labour for mines and public works to intermediate Indian nobility, the *curacas*. Indian peasants would also have to carry food and other commodities to the cities, and this movement of persons was the primary physical link between the two poles of the incipient territorial binomial — rural areas and cities — and the first direct link in the formation of a rural–urban complex.

The military, administrative and judicial constituencies, as well as the *encomenderos* were all concentrated in the cities. The territory around these power centres were the *Audiencias*, divided into *provincias*. In each of these administrative settings there gradually developed a concentration of people involved with taxation, commerce and judicial affairs, as well as with the Church, giving rise, over time, to a substantial urban bureaucracy. These emerging classes had to be supplied with goods from the countryside; and, therefore, around the cities *campiñas* developed: areas for gardening and orchards, but also for cereal production, cattle breeding and feeding. This was the second direct link of the complex, based on food production and products, which would alter and order the landscape, shaping it to serve urban demand, with well-defined roads, irrigation channels, deposits, mills and buildings.

In this rural–urban relationship, the law initially rewarded goods delivered by the Indians with 'protection' and 'evangelisation' by the Spaniards. But it also imposed forced labour and service. In the Andes, the forced labour was often a continuation of Inca concepts and practices — like the *mita*[2] taken over by Spanish power for its own benefit. Rapidly, however, money — easily masking unequal exchange practices — was introduced. In this way, money, after man and product, became the third linking element of the rural–urban complex.

This systemic complex did not fundamentally change after independence was achieved, and in many countries and regions it prevailed long into the twentieth century. To this day, there are many rich families in Bogotá, Caracas, São Paulo, Mexico, Rio and Santiago who own land and gain income from its exploitation.

But in 2010 it can be said that this old system is highly residual. In some countries, land reforms expropriated the *haciendas.* This was the case in Bolivia and Peru, and partially in Chile, Ecuador and Mexico. In Cuba, the Revolution of 1959 left no land at all in the hands of big landlords. In many cases, the land has been sold or converted to new, more intensive and agro-industrial uses. Big plantations have been transformed into corporations, with a mix of old patrimonial capital, foreign investment and, in some cases, recycled money from illicit activities such as cocoa and cocaine production. This can be seen, for instance, in Colombia with palm production and cattle raising. It is also the case in the Beni and Santa Cruz areas of Bolivia, with sugarcane plantations. In the department of Santa Cruz there still exist very large *haciendas* of thousands of hectares,[3] which can be compared to the large estates in Brazil and Argentina.

11.4. TRANSPORT AND INTERRELATIONSHIP

The binary complex is a hierarchical relation, not a network. The flows of products, services and information between the cities, the

---

[2] In pre-colonial times, *mita* was a system of compulsory labour that peasants had to perform for the Inca throne, the clergy and the community.

[3] One family owns 115,646 hectares, another 116,647. In the three departments of Pando, Beni and Santa Cruz, nine landlords own 723,649 hectares. Cf. *El Candi socialistal,* La Paz, August 2005. Figures from INRA, *Instituto nacional de la reforma agraria,* Bolivia.

harbours and their hinterland are unilateral, straight from one to the other, with very little intermediate stopovers in small towns. These direct links have been increased by modern transport systems in the late nineteenth and twentieth centuries. The use of steamers and lorries and later, in the twentieth century, refrigeration and deep freezing,[4] have enabled people, goods and information to pass directly to their end destinations, with little need to tranship products from one carrier to another, or for people and animals to remain for any time at a given place.

Such modern transport systems have prevailed only since around 1950. Although trains and steamers appeared in the second part of the twentieth century, automobiles and lorries were in use only after the First World War. But roads were dirt lanes, only accessible in the dry season; and boats were restricted to seas and oceans, and to a few big rivers (e.g. the Amazon, the Orinoco, the Rio Parana and the Magdalena). Trains were indeed the first transport vehicles capable of loading large quantities of agricultural products like sugar cane (Cuba), meat (Uruguay and Argentina) or bananas (Colombia, Guatemala). But train lines were limited in number, and in the Andes they were mainly used to carry mineral ore.[5]

In pre-colonial times, the transport of products was done, essentially, by human porters, and across the Andes on llamas' backs. Huge caravans would transit from one *tambo*[6] to the other on Inca roads, loading potatoes, *chuño*,[7] maize, *quinua* and *charqui*. In colonial times, transport was mainly on mule back. In *Concolocorvo*, written in

[4] Freezing of food was invented in 1876 by Charles Tellier, and Carré sent a ship with frozen meat from Argentina to France the following year. But the system was only intensively used from the 1930s on, when Clarence Birdseye rediscovered deep freezing by observing how North American Indians prepared and conserved their fish in ice (Toussaint-Samat, 1987, pp. 346–48).

[5] Nevertheless, in a small country like Uruguay, at the beginning of the twentieth century, there were eight railroad lines bringing products of all types to Montevideo (Alcock, 1907).

[6] A *tambo* is a place to rest for voyagers. It is an Inca institution, meaning an inn, the name of which remained in use in Peru and Bolivia.

[7] Dehydrated potatoes.

1773, the unknown author describes how long files of hundreds of mules would leave the Argentinian pampas around Buenos Aires where they had been bred, heading towards Salta. There they would be tamed and sold to merchants and peasants, and many of them would proceed to the Andean highlands, transporting a variety of products between Argentina, Cusco and Lima, back and forth. Apart from this inland trade, there was also a coastal trade, from one little harbour to another, and from the main official exporting ports like Lima, Vera Cruz, and some others in the eighteenth century. These harbours were the principal departure points for galleons transporting merchandise to and from Cádiz.

These long-distance exchanges were partly disrupted by the Wars of Independence, and then by the creation of independent states that established border controls and favoured their national economies. But with independence the new states also acquired the right to free trade with other nations of the world, of which Great Britain became the most important. In maritime commerce, unequal relations were established, as the flows of products to and from Europe were of the same kind as they had been under Spanish rule: ore and agricultural goods from Latin America; tissues, garments and luxury items from Europe. Bargaining positions were weak on the American side, as Britain had to be repaid for its financial and material help during the Wars of Independence. The ships were all English or from other European nations, and would follow a route from Liverpool/Amsterdam/Le Havre to Brazil, Cape Horn, Valparaiso and Lima (Alcock, 1907). Of course, this traffic increased enormously when steam power was introduced around 1870 (see Figs. 11.1 and 11.2). Still later, refrigeration facilitated the transport of perishable goods. From then on, meat, leather and furs and all other agricultural goods from Argentina and Uruguay could be shipped safely to Europe and the United States.

Discoveries of the industrial conservation of food (e.g. canned food, pasteurisation, chemical treatment of wool and furs) accelerated the rhythm of the capitalist extractive economy at the end of the nineteenth century: alpaca wool production in South Peru (Burga and Reategui, 1981) boomed and made the fortune of the city of Arequipa; *latifundios* in Cuba expanded their sugar exports to the US

Figure 11.1.

Source: Alcock, F. (1907). *Trade and Travel in South America*, George Philipp and Son, Ltd, London.

Figure 11.2.

Source: Alcock, F. (1907). *Trade and Travel in South America*, George Philipp and Son, Ltd, London.

after the end of the war against Spain; sugar, cattle raising and wheat production took over in the pampas; coffee *fazendas* in Brazil and *haciendas* in Chiapas flourished, agave production in Yucatan intensified (Hargous and Vogel, 1993); banana plantations in Colombia and Guatemala (Asturias, 1954) increased production for the US market; and cacao in Ecuador became highly profitable.

Before that great period and since the Conquest, there had been various product cycles, according to the demand for tropical produce in Europe and the US. Brazil is a good example of this evolution: first wood for tincture (*pao Brazil*) in the sixteenth century on the coast and then gold was extracted in the eighteenth century — in the Minas Gerais area and more specifically in Ouro Preto and Mariana. Sugar was a major crop from the beginning of the seventeenth century, first in the northeast around Bahia and Recife. Olinda was occupied by the Dutch from 1630 to 1654, as a result of the sugar boom in Europe. Then cane production expanded also in the São Paulo area, and remained significant until the twentieth century. The coffee boom which occurred at the beginning of the twentieth century, had its ups and downs, and then sugar cane expanded again, at the end of the twentieth and beginning of the twenty-first centuries, for the fabrication of ethanol. The twenty-first century has also seen an increase in cattle raising and soybean production on land that had been deforested.

Note that a 'boom' in some commodities does not necessarily mean abandoning such basic goods as sugar and mining. Nevertheless, some products, after their bonanza, ceased to be exploited when demand fell. For example, rubber (*caucho*) in the Amazon, in the Manaos region, was displaced around 1910–1913 by more profitable plantations in Malaysia (Serier, 1993, pp. 36–70). About at the same time, the production of indigo and quinine was abandoned or became stagnant due to the invention of synthetic replacement products. These cycles testify to the fragility of agricultural production and forestry extraction in Latin America throughout the independence period. The booms generated huge fortunes and revenues for the rich *fazenderos*, but their doom led to big crashes, and the abandonment of entire *pueblos* and infrastructures (García Márquez, 1970). Political collapses were also triggered by the exhaustion of natural resources like *guano* in Peru and nitrates in Chile, both victims of the increased production of chemical fertilisers in Europe at the end of the twentieth century.

Some products were more stable and perennial than others, notably sugar cane, coffee, bananas and cattle (for meat and by-products in the twentieth century). The increase of sandwich and hamburger consumption in the US made the fortune of big *estancias* in Honduras in the 1950s to 1980s. But in this case as in others, the globalisation of markets brought fierce competition for the Latin American *agro*, and led to the fortune of huge export-import enterprises (e.g. Unilever, Nestlé, Kraft) since the 1920s.

Agriculture, in colonial times, was not the main motivation of the Conquistadores; they went to the Americas mainly to find gold, silver and precious stones. Gold and silver extraction had a pervasive influence on agriculture, as it did not foster the skills, techniques and efforts needed for farm work, preferring to rely on hired and forced labour, and on slaves of African origin for plantation until the middle of the nineteenth century (Thomas, 1997).[8] When Charles Darwin made his voyage around the globe, he visited Argentina, Chile and some parts of Brazil, Uruguay and Peru quite extensively in 1832–1934. He was horrified by the systems of slavery that still prevailed in Brazil and describes with compassion the condition of Black people in the area of Rio de Janeiro:

> While staying at this estate, I was very nearly being an eyewitness to one of those atrocious acts which can only take place in a slave country. Owing to a quarrel and a lawsuit, the owner was on the point of taking all the women and children from the male slaves, and selling them separately at the public auction at Rio. Interest, and not any feeling of compassion, prevented this act. Indeed, I do not believe the inhumanity of separating thirty families, who had

[8] The slave trade was abolished in the 1830s under British pressure, but the use of slaves lasted in Peru and other countries till 1854; in Brazil up to 1889.

> lived together for many years, even occurred to the owner. Yet I will pledge myself, that in humanity and good feeling he was superior to the common run of men. It may be said there exists no limit to the blindness of interest and selfish habit. (Darwin, 1839, pp. 62–63)

Flora Tristan, on her trip to Peru to recover her inheritance from her uncle, also witnessed ill treatments inflicted on the slaves at a sugar plantation, and spoke very harshly to the *hacendado*. He replied that 'Mademoiselle' did not know anything about those people and if they were free they would just remain lazy and do nothing (Tristan, 1837).

11.5. EXTRACTIVISM AS A PERMANENT MODEL FOR LATIN AMERICA

Extractivism is a new term, *à la mode* at the beginning of this century (Bebbington, 2008), but in fact it has been the main economic activity both in colonial times, and in the time of the Republic. The concept is easily understood when referring to the extraction of gold, silver, metal ores and precious stones. It is less clear if we think of renewable products of the biosphere and if we consider agriculture under this label. There are a number of fruits, berries, herbs, leaves, nuts and bark and other biotic elements that can be extracted from plants and especially from forests. This could be called 'pure' extraction while agriculture would be 'artificial' extraction. In any case, and without discussing their environmental impacts, both types of extraction have been practiced in Latin America, but seldom on an intensive basis. Collecting and producing has been adapted to the low grade of demographic settlement and expansion. Even today the human density is only about 25 inhabitants per square kilometre at continental level.

Normally all such natural products are renewable, but not if there is over-extraction and extinction, such as occurs with deforestation, extensive modern agriculture, cattle raising and the use of chemicals.

Modern agriculture still has an extractive character in Latin America, by deforestation or the occupation of idle land. When this happens, the primitive ecosystems are lastingly disturbed, as was the case in Europe from the tenth century onwards, when monks came from Ireland to 'civilise' the continent. In this case, 'extraction' would mean extinction of the former natural resources and their replacement by others. The former natural environment might be 'richer' (with more biodiversity) than the latter; but in other cases, the use of land can add biodiversity and enhance landscapes (as occurred on the Peruvian coast with the irrigation of sandy waste areas for orchards and vineyards).

11.6. MAN AND THE AGRICULTURAL USE OF LAND

As compared with the colonial period, the use of land for agriculture and other activities augmented considerably at the end of the nineteenth and during the twentieth century.

The exploitation of such areas is varied and sometimes complex. It takes the form of 'pioneer fronts' which consist of slash and burn practices and rotating cultivation. This was the case in Peru and Bolivia in the regions of the Yungas, at low altitudes and in a tropical climate. Colonisation there goes back to the Incas. At the beginning of the twentieth century the areas were occupied by *haciendas* and small *fincas* producing coca leaves, coffee, cacao or tea (Valle de la Convención, Cusco) and sugar cane (Santa Cruz de la Sierra, Bolivia). The movement of spontaneous colonisation intensified in the second half of the century. But the *colonos* coming from the heights of the Sierra to these areas normally kept fields, family and friends in their village of origin, and would displace themselves from one area to the other according to labour needs for their own production and for their employment by others. This modern *transhumance* is a continuity of the archipelago mode of production of the Incas described by John Murra (Murra, 2002, pp. 83–132).

In any case, the three-faced character of agricultural settlements and production type remained almost unaltered throughout the colonial and postcolonial era: large landholdings and landlords on one side, (badly) paid labour force for the big *latifundios*[9] on the other, and small landholdings. The big *estancieros* or *hacendados* (*fazenderos* in Brazil) were linked to the cities, and kept the rural–urban system working. But small peasants contributed also, reinforcing the link through local and regional markets.

11.7. ARCHETYPES AND STEREOTYPES OF PEASANTRY

Although there have been large changes in production, and in the value chain of agricultural production for food, feed and industry, causing the poles of the rural–urban complex to grow closer, the psychological divide between urbanites and rural dwellers remains strong. This division stems from the system imposed in colonial times, but was accentuated in the nineteenth century.

In literature, art and music some archetypes have appeared which symbolise the urbanite's contempt for (or, in some cases, praise of) the peasants. As Domingo Sarmiento, writer and former president of the Argentinian Republic (1868–1874), has written in his *Facundo* (Sarmiento, 1845), the city–country split was considered to be between 'civilization or barbarity'. In few words this means that the cities are places where civilisation can expand, while barbarity is found in the countryside, where rude customs, ignorance and violence prevail. 'Country life has, indeed, developed in the *gaucho* his physical faculties, but without any of the ones of intelligence' (Sarmiento, 1845, p. 43, my translation). A careful reading of *Facundo* shows that not only *gaucho* peasants are rude, but also local elites, small landlords, merchants and priests, with Facundo Quiroga, a local *caudillo* of Santiago del Estero, being the archetype of barbarity. But in fact all the *caudillos* were tough and rough.

---

[9] The main system to force peones to stay on the *latifundio* was the *enganche*, a permanent linkage of the worker through credit given to them to buy instruments, food and alcohol at the farm's shop. They usually remained heavily indebted.

In 1833 Charles Darwin, on his *tour du monde* on the Beagle, met General Rosas[10] in the pampas. Rosas then was heading the first 'Campaign of the Desert' against the Indians. Darwin was well received in the general's camp, and heard a few stories about this commander's strictness:

> There are many stories current about the rigid manner in which the laws were enforced. One of these was that no man — on penalty of being put in the stocks — should carry his knife on Sunday. This day being the principal one for drinking and gambling, many quarrels arose which, from the general manner of fighting with the knife, often proved fatal. One Sunday the governor came in great form to pay the *Estancia* a visit, and General Rosas, in his hurry, walked out to receive them with the knife, as usual, stuck in his belt. The steward touched his arm and reminded him of the law; upon which turning to the governor, he said he was extremely sorry, but that he must go into the stocks, and that, till let out, he possessed no power even in his own house. After a little time, the steward was persuaded to open the stocks, and let him out, but no sooner was this done, than he turned to the steward and said, "You now have broken the laws, so you must take my place in the stocks". Such actions as these delighted the *gauchos*, who all possess high notions of their own equality and dignity. (Darwin, 1839, pp. 88–89)

Civilisation is understood by Sarmiento as the influx and adoption of culture and ideas coming essentially from the Old World — Britain and France primarily — with other influences considered as being more or less barbaric. Under this global and simplistic paradigm outlined by Sarmiento, other figures symbolising 'barbarity' arose more specifically for the peasantry: the *gaucho* and *chacarero* for the pampas of Argentina, Uruguay and the Rio Grande do Sul, the *ranchero* in Mexico and countries of Central America, the *huaso* in Chile, *guajiro* in Cuba, *boia fria* in the northeast of Brazil.

[10] Later on, President of the Argentinian Republic.

In fact these terms are not equivalent, and do not translate as, or express the same type of peasantry. The terms *ranchero, huaso, chacarero* and *guajiro* refer to small autonomous or quasi-autonomous peasants producing for themselves and for the market (Bataillon, 1994). The term *boia fria* refers to Brazilian urban people in the Nordeste, employed daily in agricultural work, mainly cane cutting. These people have no land, and on working days they eat cold meats. They would wait in the early morning at a *posto* where trucks would pick them up and bring them back at night (Freyre, 1956; Linhart, 1880; De Moraes Silva, 1999). The *gaucho* type is more ambiguous, mainly employed in cattle raising for the *haciendas*, but often owning a little *rancho* of his own. In all these cases, we are concerned with small peasants, poor people, with or without land.

There is of course a third type of peasantry: those on the Indian communities, which we find scattered mainly in the *cordilleras* and forest lowlands. Their type of land tilling is generally semi-communitarian, but their image is somewhat different in the urban imagination; not so much related to agriculture even if they practice it, but more toward ethnic (and racist) considerations. Others in this volume will analyse this image and treatment of the Native Americans. As for agricultural practice, their economy can be related to that of any small farmer, *mestizo* or other, with certain specific traits (Mayer, 2002; Auroi, 1998).

It must be said, however, that the terms used in various countries do not fully overlap socially, nor do they represent the same environmental situations. Some other terms are more generic and applicable in various environments. For instance, the term *peón* can be understood all over Latin America to mean an agricultural worker mainly employed by big farms, on a more or less permanent basis. The term *campesino* is less precise but more embracing, covering many different types of peasantry.

And then there is a whole terminology referring to the property status of the peasant. Many of them are *braceros*, *labradores* hired as labourers. *Aparceros* have the use of the land and work as shareholders. In the sierra of Peru, before the land reform of 1968, there could be found *yanaconas* who were treated like semi-slaves, but also had a piece of land to till in the *haciendas* (Bourricaud, 1967; Auroi, 1988; Matos Mar, 1976). There are *campesinos* who have no land at all, either owned or leased, but who just occupy idle areas. They are called *precarios*, as they live in great precarity, like the *Sim Terra* of Brazil.

As for the landowners, there is also a range of denominations. In Spain a farmer is a *granjero*, but in Latin America this term is seldom used. A *finquero* owns a *finca*, a farm. This term refers often to small and medium sized landholdings. If they are bigger they are *estancieros*, although this term applies mainly to Argentina, Chile, Mexico and some other countries, not so much for the Andean region. *Hacendero* or *hacendado* is still used, especially in the Andes. The equivalent in Portuguese is *fazendero*. In Peru, before 1968, there was a special class of *hacendero*: the *gamonal*. He was the owner of a relatively poor *hacienda*, or was its *mayordomo* (administrator). The owner class does not belong to the *campesinado*, being considered rich and educated, which in remote areas was seldom the case. The modern and (socially speaking) neutral term would be *agricultor*, literally 'somebody practising agriculture', on a piece of land that he owns or rents.

For hundreds of years, the urban class has traditionally seen all *campesinos* as sharing some stereotypical features (although these images are changing today). The campesino is not educated, but mainly illiterate — and considered, in many cases, to be 'simple-minded'. If we look at the image of the peasant in the Chilean cartoon *Condorito*, we see that the *huaso* makes endless mistakes, and with expressions that provoke hilarity.

The *gaucho's* image has suffered from Sarmiento's judgement, and was relegated by most writers to barbarism: he could neither read nor write; he was lazy, quarrelling all the time, cheating, stealing, beating his woman, drinking too much, and regularly abandoning his family. Caricatures drawn by Florencio Molina Campos at the beginning of the twentieth century exaggerate some physical traits: big red nose, prominent lips, globular, slightly squinting eyes, deformed hands, strange posture, and so on (Gutierrez Zaldivar, 1996). Such terms generally express a contemptuous attitude toward the peasant.

But in some cases the *campesino* can be idealised. He appears then as a man or woman living in an idyllic environment, in a nice little house with a lot of flowers, the *ranchero* himself wearing white clothing (always very clean), with an imposing *sombrero* and a big moustache. He is full of wit and happiness (Skerritt, 1994, pp. 141–152). This is the image that Mexican literature songs and cinema often carry of the *ranchero* — and especially his daughter, the *rancherita*. The *rancherita* is very lovely, but harassed by an awful *estanciero* or *bandido* who wants to possess her and keep her kidnapped. Enter Zorro, the handsome *justiciero*, himself a well-off *estanciero*, generous and clever. He saves the *rancherita* and returns her to her parents who are duly thankful.

In Argentina, where the *Auffassung* of 'civilisation and barbarity' prevailed, there was at the same time an idealisation of the *gaucho*. Two authors in particular made him into a good guy — always a victim of bad people, judges, military officers, merchants and others (Indians included) — who is and remains fundamentally 'good' and full of virile virtues. The archetype of that *gaucho* is Martín Fierro, depicted by José Hernandez (1872) in his book of the same title. *Martín Fierro* and in 1879 *The Return of Martin Fierro* (Hernandez, n.d.) are long epic poems relating the adventurous life of this hero in the army, then as a convict among the Indians of the pampas, eventually finding his children again after having lost them for many years, and always ill-treated by the establishment.

The other 'good' gaucho in literature is the one described by Ricardo Güiraldes (1979) in his well-known *Don Segundo Sombra* first published in 1926. Fabio is the representation of a *gaucho* already integrated into society: no longer a rebel, but very obedient, even submissive, to whom Don Segundo teaches the noble virtues of honour, loyalty and respect. Fifty years after the publication of *Martín Fierro* the *gaucho* has become a respectable *finquero* and *paisano*,[11] which shows that our perceptions of others are not static but evolving. But agricultural conditions had also changed by the end of the nineteenth

[11] In Spanish *paisano* means country fellow, coming from the same village or region — and by extension from the same country, if two nationals meet abroad.

century. Modernisation of meat and leather production had led to the enclosure of the *estancias*, which meant for the *gaucho* that his domain of action had become smaller, and that he had to comply with new techniques. From a permanent nomad, he has become sedentary; from a free rider of the pampas, he has become a *peón de hacienda*. We can return once more to Darwin, who depicts the real *gaucho* in the following, balanced way:

> During the last six months [of 1833], I have had an opportunity of seeing a little of the character of the inhabitants of these provinces (Buenos Aires, pampas, banda oriental). The *gauchos*, or countrymen, are very superior to those who reside in the towns. The *gaucho* is invariably most obliging, polite and hospitable. I did not meet with even one instance of rudeness or inhospitality. He is modest, both respecting himself and country, at the same time being a spirited, bold fellow. On the other hand, there is much bloodshed, and many robberies are committed. The constant presence of the knife is the chief cause of the former. It is lamentable to hear how many lives are lost in trifling quarrels. In fighting, each party tries to mark the face of his adversary, by slashing his nose or eyes; as it is often attested by deep and horrid-looking scars. Robberies are a natural consequence of universal gambling, much drinking and extreme indolence. At Mercedes, I asked two men why they did not work. One gravely said the days were too long, the other that he was too poor. (Darwin, 1839, pp. 143–144)

And there is a fourth type of peasant in ideological representation: the fighting hero. This type is to be found in literature, painting and cinema, especially in Mexico during and after the Revolution of 1910–1920 — figures like Pancho Villa and Emiliano Zapata, coming from the countryside, are surrounded and supported by peasant armies made up of *desperados* who have been expelled from big haciendas. John Reed depicts these *peones* who have nothing to lose but a lot to gain (John Reed, 1914). He shows how Pancho Villa, himself illiterate, learned to read and speak good Spanish in eight months.

Later on, in the 1940s, Diego Rivera and other painters like Siqueiros would make the peasant in arms a main feature of most of their *murales*,[12] also drawing Aztec labourers as fighting victims of the Spanish Conquista. The heroes of the revolution are also to be found in Sergei Eisenstein's movie *¡Que Viva México!* (1933), where their rebellion ends in bloodshed. In the case of Mexico, the peasant can be very proactive, but there are only rare examples to be found of this type. Even in Mexican filmography, in most cases the peasant is a pure victim, not defending himself. In the Andes there were also many rural rebellions, for instance in Bolivia at the end of the nineteenth century (Flores, 1984; Calderón and Dandler, 1986; Rivera, 1987), because land transactions had been declared free, and in Peru in the 1920s (Tamayo Herrera, 1982, pp. 191–248), in the struggle against *haciendas*. But these serious events are rarely taken as a subject for novels and cinema. Of course, the *indigenista* literature has given many examples of the reactions of Indian peasants to bad treatment, through the books of José Manuel Arguedas, Ciro Alegria, Manuel Scorza and José Icaza, but these generally deal with individual cases, on some *hacienda* in the sierra or, at most, in a limited region.

11.8. MINIFUNDIO AND LATIFUNDIO

What, then, will be the future of land use and social progress in the *agro* of Latin America? One thesis put forward in the 1960s imagined that the evolution of Latin American agriculture would go irreversibly toward a concentration of farms, and hence to the disappearance of smallholdings — *minifundios*, under 10 hectares. *Latifundios* would become bigger, and would transform themselves into agricultural concerns linked to agro-industries (Warman, 1988; Hernandez, 1993 Giarraca *et al.*, 1999). The long-lasting duality of *latifundio–minifundio* would vanish and the majority of small *campesinos* would become agricultural workers.

[12] Wall paintings.

A first, statistical consideration is that in Latin America throughout history there has always been plenty of land for agriculture, as demographic growth has been slow and will continue to decline in the twenty-first century. The implication of this favourable man/land relation is that access to land, in general, has not been a major problem. Idle, fallow, uncultivated or ownerless land has always permitted constrained communities in overpopulated areas, or with asymmetrical land access and control, to emigrate to 'empty' areas. Pioneer fronts continue to exist today in the *ceja de selva*[13] and Amazonian regions of South America, in the llanos of Colombia and Venezuela, in the Chaco, Mato Grosso. Of course there are other areas like the Andes, Central America and the Brazilian Nordeste where ecological and economic limits have been reached and where intensification of practices and/or emigration are the only alternatives. The figures, considering evolution of farm size in the twentieth century show a tendency for mean size to drop — exactly the opposite of what has been the development of agriculture in Europe. Mean farm size from 1930 to 1990 falls approximately from 5.5 hectares in 1930 to 4.0 in 1990 (Eastwood, Lipton and Newell, 2004, cited by Hazel *et al.*, 2007, p. 2, Fig. 1). This shows clearly that there has been no trend toward concentration of medium-size holdings in Latin America, and because of the abundance of land, small farms have even been increasing in number.

Another consequence of the abundance of land and the historical process of concentration of big landholdings is that there is still great inequality in land distribution, with Gini coefficients of land distribution over 0.8 for Argentina, Brazil and Venezuela, and 0.62 for Mexico, a country which achieved a land reform between 1920 and 1940 (Piñeiro, 2007, p. 23). Figures for poverty at the end of the twentieth century in Latin America show that the countryside is two to three times poorer than the cities (Dirven, 2004, p. 15). Two thirds of rural dwellers are considered poor, corresponding to small landholdings. Programmes to alleviate poverty in rural areas have given only poor results (Figueroa, 1998, pp. 86–120) because

[13] Between 300 and 2000 meters of altitude.

Andean farmers are not interested in market insertion and lack entrepreneurial spirit.

The general trend for booming agricultural development is clearly export driven, as it has always been since the beginnings of sugar, cotton, coffee and meat production in colonial or early republican times.

Uruguay is a good example of the perennial model of agro-exporting that still prevails in Latin America (see Table 11.1).

Various features of this table are quite interesting, giving an indication of a hundred years of evolution of trade and value for agricultural products exported and imported. In 2005 there still remains a solid basis in natural products exported (about 60%). What is different is that one third of those products is now processed and belongs, therefore, to agro-industry. The main change is in imports, consisting of fuel and combustibles in general, which comprise up to 25% of the total. Considering also the importance of transport means

Table 11.1. Exports and Imports for the Republic of Uruguay — 1905 and 2005

Exports, 1905	Imports, 1905	Exports 2005	Imports 2005
Stocks, horses, mules, oxen, sheep, wool, jerked beef or charqui, hides, extract of beef, slaughter house products, sealskins, etc.	Foodstuff, cereals, species, raw materials and machinery, soft goods, beverages, ready-made clothing, live-stock (from Argentina), tobacco and cigars, timber, sundries.	Meat, wool, fish, milk (30%); Agricultural products, raw and processed (15%); leather and peals, raw and manufactured (8%); textiles (7%)	Fuels, petrol (25%); chemicals and plastics (24%); communication hard and software (17%); transport manufacturing (6%).
Value £ 6,547,712	**Value** £ 6,548,421	**Value** $ 3,421,381,000	**Value** $ 3,878,882,000

Source: For 1905: Alcock, F. (1907) *Trade and Travel in South America*, George Philip and Son, London, p. 264.
For 2005: Central Bank of Uruguay, available at: http://www.ine.gub.uy/economia/externo2008.asp [Accessed 25.10.10].

(cars and other vehicles), the table shows the radical change in mobility that Latin America has undergone in the last century. The importance of chemicals and plastics evidences the need for intermediate and industrial products in a highly urbanised society. The example of Uruguay can easily be transposed to many other small and medium-sized countries, if not to all of them.

Food and feed are now in demand by countries like China and India, but the shift to new importers will hardly alter the fragility of such structural dependence. At the interior level, such exports strengthen the big land holds and, since there have been no agrarian reform prospects since 1980 and the precarity of tenancy is seldom addressed, the poor *finquero*, *peón* and *boia fria* may well continue as the archetypes of backwardness and ignorance.

As we have shown in another text (Auroi, 2008–2009), for a number of years there have been better prospects for some 'niche' peasants — coffee producers, cacao producers, horticulture producers around the cities and cattle breeders in certain areas. In their condition these farm owners are somewhat 'privileged', as are those who have been able to enter into a marketing chain. Such value chains are more and more driven by the supermarkets, which have grown in huge proportion since 1970. There is a dilemma here, and the question is how the small and medium-sized farms can integrate into the chains, given their technical backwardness and lack of training in marketing. As one author writes:

> More worrying are the implications of changes to marketing chains. Supermarket operators are becoming increasingly important in parts of the developing world. The supermarkets impose stricter standards for the quality, consistency, and timeliness of supply. They may also require the ability to trace consignments back to the source to confirm how they have been produced. Supermarkets expect their suppliers to adjust rapidly to changing consumer demands. Small-scale, undercapitalized, and often undereducated farmers find it particularly difficult to meet these requirements, especially those of traceability and credence (that is, characteristics that relate to production methods like pesticide use but cannot be proved by

> examining the produce), even if family labour is often well suited to delivering high-quality products. Will small farms be marginalized from the new supply chains? Much depends on whether they grow produce where credence attributes matter and whether supermarkets can obtain their supplies from large farms. When supermarkets can deal with a few large farms, they will; when credence attributes are less important or there are no alternatives to small farms, then smallholders are likely to become part of the evolving supply chains. Equally important is how quickly supermarkets come to dominate food supply chains. Supermarkets thrive in growing economies, so as their control of marketing increases and some small farmers are excluded, chances are that new jobs are being created for them in non-farm activities. (Hazel *et al.*, 2007, p. viii)

The problem with agribusiness (McMichael, 2002, p. 117) and supermarkets is that these try, by any means, to take advantage of low salaries of workers and low prices paid to peasants for their products. In the long run, this does not enhance the living standard of these people, and keeps them in nineteenth-century conditions — just reproducing the old stereotype of Martin Fierro, the poor *gaucho*.

11.9. CONCLUSION

Is Latin America suffering from an agricultural curse? Or is agriculture, in fact, a permanent comparative advantage acquired from colonisation? If a curse, then this can partly explain why industrialisation has not succeeded on this side of the Atlantic as it did in Europe. If a comparative advantage, on the other hand, then it is an endowment that will flourish over time.

The nineteenth century did not raise such questions of advantage and disadvantage: agricultural exports were a gift of God; they made big fortunes and permitted urbanisation in national capitals and other big cities. On the other hand, as this happened, the countryside remained stuck in backwardness and inequality, because there was plenty of land and enough labour. Progress and intensiveness were not real musts.

In the twentieth century, the exporting model had some problems in the 1930s, and it adopted the ISI industrialisation model (industrialisation by export substitution), which prevailed until the debt crisis of the 1980s. But even during that period, the main income came from agricultural exports, under the same social conditions as before. In the 1960s, with some timid agrarian reforms (Cuba being the exception), labour relations changed, but land distribution much less so.

Socially speaking the curse is in the man/land ratio — too favourable for big social pressures on land distribution, green revolution and mechanisation. Progress remains very slow — but in some countries, for big concerns with plenty of land, the curse is gradually being transformed into a blessing, with agribusiness the bearer of new hopes. However, not everyone can join the fiesta, and many peasants like 'Juan Pérez' remain on the *campo*.[14] The integration of small farms into the agribusiness system will take time, requiring some concentration of land, the institution of an effective rural credit system and the development of new commodity chains linking *finqueros* to the consumption centres. All these are tasks that should have been accomplished 50 years ago but, unfortunately, the political conditions were not ripe.

BIBLIOGRAPHY

Alcock, F. (1907). *Trade and Travel in South America*, George Philipp and Son, Ltd, London.

Asturias, M. (1968 [1954]). *The Green Pope*, Delacorte, New York.

Auroi, C. (1988). *Des Incas au Sentier Lumineux, l'histoire violente du Pérou*, Georg, Genève.

Auroi, C. (1998). 'Les agricultures andines, une lente évolution', in Auroi, C. and Maurer, J. L. (eds), *Tradition et modernisation des économies rurales: Asie, Afrique et Amérique latine: Mélanges en l'honneur de Gilbert Etienne, Presses universitaires de France*, pp. 285–310.

Auroi, C. (2008–2009). Situación alimenticia en América Latina y futuro de la producción agropecuaria para pequeños campesinos, *Anuario Americanista Europeo*, 6–7, pp. 201–214, CEISAL.

[14] Juan Pérez, any anonymous person, comparable to Smith in Great Britain, Schmitt in Germany or Dupont in France.

Barragán López, E., Hoffmann, O., Linck, T. and Skerritt, D. (1994) (eds). *Rancheros y sociedades rancheras*, El Colegio de Michoacan, CEMCA, OrstOM, Zamorra, MI.

Bataillon, C. (1994). 'Los ranchos de hoy, una vision comparativa', in Barragán López, E., Hoffmann, O., Linck, T. and Skerritt, D. (eds), *Rancheros y sociedades rancheras*, El Colegio de Michoacan, CEMCA, OrstOM, Zamorra, MI, pp. 99–108.

Bebbington, A. *et al.* (2008). Contention and Ambiguity: Mining and the possibilities of development, *Development and Change*, 39, pp. 887–914.

Bourricaud, François. (1989 [1967]). *Poder y Sociedad en el Perú*, IEP and Institut français d'études andines, Lima.

Burga, M. and Reategui, W. (1981). *Lanas y Capital Mercantil en el Sur. La casa Ricketts, 1895–1935*, IEP, Lima.

Calderón, F. and Dandler, J. (eds) (1986). *Bolivia, la fuerza histórica del campesinado*, 2da edicion revisada, UNRISD, Ginebra y CERES, La Paz.

Concolocorvo. (1997 [1773]). *El lazarillo de ciegos caminantes*, Emecé, Buenos Aires.

Darwin, C. (1989 [1839]). *Voyage of the Beagle*, Penguin Books, London.

De Castro, J. (1964). Geografia do fome. O cruzeiro, Rio de Janeiro.

De Moraes Silva, M. A. (ed.) (1999). *Errantes do Fim do Século*, UNESP, São Paulo.

Del Pozo Vergnes, E. (ed.) (1997). *Organisations paysannes et indigenes en Amérique latine. Mutations et Recompositions vers le troisième millénaire*, Charles-Léopold Mayer, Paris.

Dirven, M. (2004). Alcanzando las metas del milenio: Una mirada hacia la apobreza rural y agrícola, CEPAL, Santiago de Chile.

Dixon, J., Gulliver, A. and Gibbon, D., Principal Editor: Hal, M. (2001). Farming Systems and Poverty. Improving farmers' livelihood in a changing world, FAO, Rome.

Eastwood, R., Lipton, M. and Newell, A. (2004). 'Farm size', Paper prepared for Volume 3 of *Handbook of Agricultural Economics*, Elsevier, Amsterdam, June.

Escudero, G. (1998). 'La visión y misión de la agricultura en el año 2020: Hacia un enfoque que valorice la agricultura y el medio rural', in Reca y Echevarría, *op. cit.* pp. 21–54.

FAO. (2009). Summary of World Food and Agricultural Statistics, Rome.

Figueroa, A. (1998). 'Pobreza rural en los paises Andinos', in Reca, L. G. and Echevarría, R. G. (eds). *Agricultura, medio ambiente y Problema rural en América Latina*, Instituto International de Investigaciones sobre políticas alimentarias (IFPRI) y Banco Interamericano de Desarrollo (BID), Washington, DC, pp. 84–120.

Flores, G. (1984). 'Levantamientos campesinos durante el período liberal (1900–1920)', in Calderón, F. and Dandler, J. (eds) (1984). *Bolivia, la fuerza histórica del campesinado*, UNRISD, Ginebra y CERES, La Paz, pp. 119–132.

Freyre, G. (1956). *Terres du sucre,* Gallimard, Paris.

García Márquez, G. (1970). *One Hundred Years of Solitude*, Harper and Row, New York.
Giarraca, N. (1999). *Estudios rurales, teorías, Problemas y estrategias metodológicas*, La Colmena, Buenos Aires.
Giordano, P., Falconi, C. and J. M. Sumpsi (Compilers) (2007). *Desarrollo rural y comercio agropecuario en America Latina*, BID-INTAL, Buenos Aires.
Güiraldes, R. (1979 [1926]). *Don Segundo Sombra*, Catedra, Madrid.
Gutierrez Zaldivar, I. (1996). *Molina Campos*, Zurbaran Ediciones, Buenos Aires.
Hargous, S. and Vogel, T. (1993). *Mexique, l'homme et l'algave*, L'Harmattan, Paris.
Hazel, P., Poulton, C., Wiggins, S. and Dorward, A. (2007). *The Future of Small Farms for Poverty Reduction and Growth*, IFPRI, 2020 Discussion Paper 4, Washington, DC.
Hernandez, J. (n.d.) *Martín Fierro y la Vuelta de Martín Fierro*, Obra completa, Buenos Aires y Montevideo.
Hernandez, R. (1993–1994). Teorías sobre campesinado en América Latina, Una evaluación crítica, *Revista Chilena de antropología*, 12.
Linhart, R. (ed.) (1980). *Le sucre et la faim, enquête dans les regions sucrières du Nord-Est Brésilien*, De Minuit, Paris.
Matos Mar, J. (1976).*Yanaconaje y reforma agraria en el Perú*, IEP, Lima.
Mayer, E. (2002). *The Articulated Peasant: Household Economies in the Andes*, Westview Press, Boulder, Co.
McMichael, P. (2002). La restructuration globale des systèmes agro-alimentaires, Mondes en développement, *Tome*, 30, pp. 117–145.
Murra, J. (2002). *El mundo Andino, población, medio ambiente y economía*, IEP y Pontificia Universidad católica del Peru, Lima.
Piñeiro, M. (2007). 'Desarrollo rural en América Latina: Tendencies y políticas', in Giordano, P., Falconi, C. and Sumpsi J. M. (Compilers), *Desarrollo rural y comercio agropecuario en America Latina*, BID-INTAL, Buenos Aires, pp. 1–43.
Pinstrup-Andersen, P. (1998). 'Una vision global de la agricultura, la alimentación y el medio ambiente', in Reca y Echevarría, *op. cit.*, pp. 3–0.
Reca, L. G. and Echevarría, R. G. (1998). *Agricultura, medio ambiente y problema rural en América Latina*, Instituto International de Investigaciones sobre políticas alimentarias (IFPRI) y Banco Interamericano de Desarrollo (BID), Washington, DC.
Reed, J. (1914). *Insurgent Mexico*, D. Appleton and Co., New York.
Rivera Cusicanqui, S. (1987). *Oppressed but not Defeated. Peasant Struggles Among the Aymaras and Qhechwas in Bolivia, 1900–1980*, UNRISD, Geneva.
Sarmiento, D. F. (1998). *Facundo: Civilization and Barbarism*, Penguin, London.
Sarmiento, D. F. (2001 [1845]). *Facundo*, Mestas, Madrid.
Serier, J. B. (ed.) (1993). *Histoire du Caoutchouc*, Desjoncquiéres, Paris.
Skerritt, D. (1994). 'El ranchero: Génesis y consolidación', in Barragán López, E., Hoffmann, O., Linck, T. and Skerritt, D. (eds). *Rancheros y sociedades rancheras*, El Colegio de Michoacan, CEMCA, OrstOM, Zamorra, MI, pp. 141–152.

Tamayo Herrera, J. (1982). *Historia social e indigenismo en el altiplano*, Ediciones Trentaitres, Lima.

Thomas, H. (1997). *The Slave Trade: The History of the Atlantic Slave Trade 1440–1870*, Simon and Schuster, London.

Toussaint-Samat, M. (1987). *Histoire naturelle et morale de la nourriture*, Bordas, Cultures, Paris.

Tristan, F. (1837). *Pérégrinations d'une paria*, Gallica, Bibliothèque nationale de France, Paris.

Warman, Arturo (1988). Los estudios campesinos, veinte años depués, *Revista Comercio exterior* (Mexico) 38, 7, pp. 653–658.

Chapter

12

Is Growth Driven by External Demand a Solution to Economic Crises?

Pierre Salama

12.1. INTRODUCTION

After decades of strong growth, the crisis of the 1980s left Latin America deeply bruised. It took 14 years to restore its 1980 level of GDP, while rising poverty rates during that decade were such that only 25 years later has Latin America recovered the level of wealth it had in 1980 (Jiménez, 2010). A continent marked (with few exceptions) by high inequality, regressive taxation, small social transfers as compared to those effective in Europe and modest trade openness (except for Mexico and a few countries of Central America), was interrupted, in a phase of relatively high growth since 2003–2004, by the international crisis of 2008.

Unlike the crisis of the 1980s, the 2008 crisis is less the product of internal difficulties than the contagion of a crisis that originated in developed countries. In this respect, it resembles the Great Depression of the 1930s. Also unlike the crises of those decades, the crisis of 2008, although severe, appears to be of short duration — since recovery was relatively strong at the end of 2009. However, one should be careful not to confuse a cyclic period with a trend, particularly in referring to a structural crisis. In the current state of international crisis, the sustainability of recovery remains in doubt so long as the international architecture has not been redefined. It is certainly a fragile recovery, but, as with the crisis of the 1980s and especially that of the 1930s, the 'experience' of the crisis is characterised by a mutation of production structures, which, though difficult to read at present, is likely to change existing modes of governance.

The purpose of this chapter is to question whether, after years of increasing openness, a new growth plan, focused on a more equitable distribution of income and subsequent expansion of the domestic market, has a serious chance of contributing to a sustained recovery of growth. This investment in the domestic market, following the bet made on the foreign market with the Washington Consensus in the 1990s, seems utopian given the depth of inequalities and powerful conflicts of interest opposing fiscal reform and a redistributive policy that would be costly to the high social strata. But it is clear that in some countries, like Brazil and to a lesser extent Argentina, this 'utopia' has had some early implementation. The counter-cyclical policies decided in the aftermath of the global crisis are different from those of previous years, which were inspired by the Washington Consensus and characterised by a reduction in social spending at the outset of a currency crisis, thus precipitating a recession. The new policies, inspired by a 'pragmatic Keynesianism', seek to promote support for demand and lead to a decrease in primary surpluses. These measures have mitigated the social cost of this crisis rather than increased it, at least until early 2010.

In at least one respect, these counter-cyclical policies are, to some extent, part of a continuity that can be observed in some countries since the early 2000s: a small decline in inequalities, more sustained social policy and growth recovery. Can we consider, then, that the international crisis, in an underground way, is accelerating a process that had already begun? Or, more pessimistically, should we think that this process is shaky and that a somewhat reshaped version of the previous excluding model will be back in full force, once the illusion of recovery is confirmed? A return of the domestic market, a mobilising utopia or a return to the previous model, more open and less vulnerable because of the increase in international reserves that it entails, but also more fragile with respect to increases in the rate of openness and the content of exports (Salama, 2009a, 2009b)? The first part of this chapter will review the effects of the 1930s' crisis on the industrial structure of the major Latin American economies. The second part will try to assess the likelihood of success of the 'domestic market bet' by focusing on two factors: the degree of openness in that market, and the importance of income inequalities.

12.2. FROM ONE CRISIS TO ANOTHER...

12.2.1. Unexpected Consequences of the 1930 Crisis: An Original Mode of Industrialisation in Argentina, Brazil and Mexico

Because it was assigned to an international division of labour pertaining to the exploitation of primary products by dominant powers, industrialisation was a threat to jobs in the firms of dominant countries. Not only did it complicate the social formation of these countries, it also opened the door to challenges of their domination. This explains the hostility to the industrialisation of the exploited countries and the subsequent small scale of their domestic markets. This relationship of domination was deeply altered, however, first by the First World War of 1914–1918, and then by the Great Depression of the 1930s. Finally, there was a change of hegemony: the United States, in seeking to take the place of a weakened and declining Great Britain, created a more favourable environment for the industrialisation of developing countries.

The crisis of 1930 was a major one, and its impact on developing economies was significant almost everywhere. With the deterioration of trade agreements and the sharp drop in exports of primary commodities, the import capacity of these countries was strongly affected. The duration of the crisis, unforeseen by policymakers, had different consequences in different countries. Some did not experience profound mutations and continued, in a ‘traditional’ way, to take part in the international division of labour, while others, after a more or less prolonged crisis period, experienced a phase of ‘unplanned industrialisation’, an expression aptly used by the UN’s ECLA (Economic Commission for Latin America). This unplanned industrialisation was the result of a series of conditions: (a) the existence of a minimal industrial structure produced by the exporting activity itself (e.g. workshops for repairing steam engines used in the transportation of raw materials, agglomeration economies arising from the construction of ports and cities); (b) a more or less important demand, depending on the nature of exports, arising from the spread of market, and even monetary, relations; (c) finally, the support of exporter incomes through the purchase, in local currency, of a part of their production. Once these conditions were met, the unanticipated extension of external restrictions led to an original mode of industrialisation: a virtuous circle of import substitution of light consumer goods (of low capital intensity) allowing the resumption of strong growth within a context of international crisis, and, in the process, creating a coherent domestic market.

The size of the domestic market increased as the process of import substitution took hold. Investment played a large part in creating jobs, since the capital intensity of goods produced was low. Workers came, in part, from international migration but also, in an increasing proportion, from an internal migration from the countryside to the cities. Their employment led to a process of monetisation, since as peasants their labour had had little monetary value. This process was at the source of an increasing demand for what became known as ‘worker goods’. The increasing monetisation took over the demand of exporters and augmented it, valuing production for the growing domestic market. In this sense the circle was virtuous. The dynamic for growth came from increased demand but, unlike the classical Keynesian process, this increase was more a product of the growing monetisation of a workforce that had hitherto been little monetised, than of an increase in wages. This essential aspect of the process of light import substitution in the years 1930–1940 is often ignored by economists.

The structural crisis of the 1930s gave birth to a new growth regime that was 'pulled from within', in the words of the ECLA. In this sense, the crisis opened up a process of restructuring and surpassing, in which 'the old, not wanting to die (the export economy) gave way to the new, trying to be born (industrialisation by import substitution)'.

In provoking this unplanned industrialisation in certain countries of the periphery, the Great Depression led to the emergence of specific political regimes. The growth of industry changed the social formation and, gradually, new conflicts of interest appeared between the social classes and within them. These were exacerbated when the light import substitution slowed down. On one hand, import capacity did not increase much, if at all; and the international crisis persisted. But on the other hand, the structure of imports became increasingly rigid. To produce equipment goods and intermediate products that could not be imported in sufficient quantities became increasingly difficult for two reasons: firstly, production of goods is more capital-intensive and requires substantial investments; and secondly, there is no stock exchange to accumulate the capital that small individual entrepreneurs cannot raise alone. That leaves the state as an agent capable of investing in these sectors. But it is not because the state should (objectively) intervene that it will necessarily do so. Everything depends on the configuration of social conflicts, and how these are overcome and given meaning. In Argentina, Brazil and Mexico, the emergence of Caesarist political regimes (Péron, Vargas, Cardenas), initiated a passage from growth driven by light import substitution to growth propelled by heavy import substitution, resulting from the state's direct intervention as an investor in these sectors. In a certain way, the state took the place of the private contractor, who found himself in deficit because of insufficient size and absence of financial markets (Mathias and Salama, 1983).

Heavy industry, along with the energy and infrastructure sectors, could continue to grow insofar as the necessary political conditions were in place, which made it possible, for some time, to overcome the quasi-insurmountable obstacles produced by the previous growth model. Thus, the impact of the 1930s crisis on Argentina,

Brazil and Mexico was very important from both economic and political perspectives. Is the crisis of 2008 likely to cause effects of similar magnitude?

12.2.2. The 2008 Crisis

The crisis that began in 2008 is different in its causes from the crisis of the 1930s. Financialisation, this time, appears to takes precedence over other causes. The consequences of financialisation on sluggish labour incomes and household debt in some developed countries are now known. However, we cannot classify the 2008 crisis as a realisation crisis on the grounds that wages do not rise much in developed countries over a long period, because the taking on of debt kept up demand, which would otherwise have been sluggish. Nor can we classify it as a crisis of over-accumulation, because the rate of investment remains generally poor in all developed countries and idle production capacity is low.

The effects of the globalisation of trade and finance on wages and productive investment were instrumental in precipitating the 2008 crisis. The globalisation of trade and external constraints from low-wage countries in Asia led to dissociation between productivity growth and wage increase, causing the latter to stall, not only in developed countries but also in the emerging economies of Latin America. Financial globalisation led to a new organisation of business firms to raise their immediate profitability. If we ignore the soaring incomes of managers, the share between profit and salary has tended to be at the expense of the latter, and, within profits, the share of financial profits (or costs) has increased. This means a two-fold effect on earnings: an external constraint, the financial constraint in the distribution of value added, and the temporary positive impact of the 'construction' of securitised financial products (shares) that have become very attractive.

If the present crisis is structural, as we believe, a cyclical upswing will not overcome the causes that produced it. Only a thorough reform of the international financial architecture and the imposition of new rules governing international trade — that take into account the ethical and environmental conditions of production — can overcome the crisis of 2008. In light of what happened during the Great Depression of the 1930s, with the emergence of a new model of industrialisation and the resumption of growth in major Latin American countries, we can consider that the crisis of 2008 may allow for new growth opportunities in the emerging countries of Latin America. We must be cautious, however, as to the duration and meaning of the recovery in these Latin American economies. Is this a cyclical upswing in a downward trend? Or is it the beginning of a sustainable decoupling: the continuation of a structural crisis in industrialised countries and the beginning of sustainable growth, the premise of a new pattern of growth in emerging Latin American economies? It is difficult to answer these questions because the answer depends, as in the 1930s, on the political responses given to conflicts of interest, especially to distributive conflicts, that arise.

The more or less pronounced openness of Latin American economies to trade and financial flows has created 'transmission channels', promoting the effects of contagion between developed countries, and between them and developing countries (WTO/OECD, 2009; OECD, 2009; IMF, 2009).[1] The 2008 crisis was severe, causing growth rates to drop between five and ten points in emerging Latin American economies (Salama, 2009, 2010). This was followed by a fairly rapid recovery, dependent mainly on a boom in the domestic market of these countries and their continuous supply of exports to Asian economies (China and, to a lesser extent, India). However, should a crisis occur again in developed countries, such as the one now threatening the sovereign debt of some European

[1] Let us recall that in emerging economies in general, banks had few high-risk assets. The beginning of the crisis, triggering a credit crunch in developed countries, led in turn to a drying-up of liquid assets in emerging economies. This occurred mainly because capital 'fled' these countries in order to supply liquid assets to parent companies, multinational banks and international investors, causing a drop in their respective currencies against the dollar. The return of capital, attracted by high returns in emerging stock exchanges, has not, however, led to a significant increase in loans, because state banks are now compelled to take over from failing private banks.

nations, the recovery of Latin American economies could be problematic. The effects of such a crisis would be more or less devastating for emerging economies, depending on their degree of trade openness, the type of goods exported, the intensity of financial globalisation, the stock-flow structure of foreign capital (bonds, equities, direct investments)[2] and the magnitude of their actual net reserves.[3] This is not only because there would be a drop in external demand, a depletion of liquid assets and a scarcity of international credits for export, but also because the possible consolidation of market dynamics in some emerging economies depends on the length of time between crises. The longer this interval, the stronger the opportunities to resist an external crisis.

The scope of this chapter does not allow us to concern ourselves with this eventuality, which seems unlikely to occur in the near future. Our hypothesis is that developed countries will continue to experience low growth as long as structural reforms have not been undertaken. Within this context of weak recovery in industrial countries and potential financial turmoil, we analyse the possible emergence, in the major Latin American economies, of new growth plans focused on boosting their domestic market.

12.3. CAN HISTORY REPEAT ITSELF?

In the 1920s, the share of exports of major Latin American economies in world exports was greater than it is at present, despite

---

[2] The impact of a crisis on developing economies depends on the extent of the globalisation process in different countries. Synthetic indicators can help to assess this. International institutions (IMF, 2009) have been trying to do this with varying degrees of success, since according to the OECD indicator (2009, p. 42), Mexico should suffer less than other countries from the effects of the crisis, which is far from being the case.

[3] This is an important point, but little analysed. The reserves are made up of trade balance surpluses and/or capital balance surpluses. Only the former correspond to actual reserves, while the latter are highly sensitive to economic conditions and may be truncated by a partial return of capital, as was the case in late 2008. On this point, see Bradesco (2009).

years of continued openness. It is common, moreover, to characterise the 1920s as a period of liberalisation of markets and to conclude that economies were more globalised than they are today. This, however, fails to take into account the fact that the world at that time differed from today's world on a key point: *the degree of monetisation*. In developed economies, self-produced consumption was still important in the countryside, where most of the population resided. In Latin American economies such consumption was even more significant. Therefore, the ratio of exports to GDP had only minor significance, as it related entirely to monetised values at a time when a very important part of domestic production was passing through non-monetised channels, and hence not being counted in the GDP. Nowadays, monetisation is almost complete and this ratio is more relevant than it was in the 1920s. The domestic market already exists; the only way to improve it now is to increase wages and social transfers, which, in today's context of globalisation of trade, can only be done if a country's relative competitiveness is maintained. In the absence of sustained competitiveness, imports replace domestic production. Unlike the 1930s, growth today that is centred on the development of a domestic market will have to respect the constraints of competitiveness — unless we assume a significant return to protectionism. Protectionist measures could in fact be 'legitimised' by considerations of respect for ethical and environmental production conditions, even with incentives to buy 'national' products, as can already be observed. It is from this dual context of globalisation and of near-complete monetisation, which was quasi-inexistent in the 1930s, that today's 'bet on the domestic market' must be analysed in terms of two variables: the contribution of foreign trade to growth and the extent of inequalities.

12.3.1. A Stronger (But Still Relatively Weak) Contribution of Foreign Trade to Growth

The contribution of foreign trade to growth can be analysed from two perspectives: one a strictly accounting perspective, the other emphasising economic mechanisms and snowball effects.

In the accounting perspective, the assessment of the contribution of trade to GDP is concerned with the growth of exports and imports, i.e. exports net of imports. The former are positively involved in the growth rate, the latter, negatively. External trade may not contribute positively to a country's growth when its trade balance is negative, even if it is open to the global economy. Conversely, a positive trade balance of exports over imports will have a positive effect on growth. The case of Asian countries, and especially of China, is interesting because it is often given as an example to highlight the beneficial effects of export development on growth. If we consider the period between 2000 and 2008, the average contribution of net exports to the growth rate in China was 10.2%. This means that for a 10.2% average GDP growth rate, this contribution is only 1.1 point, while the contribution of investment is 5 points and total consumption represents 4.1 points. Nonetheless, with China's increasing trade surpluses during this period, the proportion has grown: the contribution of net exports rose by about 5% between 2001 and 2004 to more than 20% between 2005 and 2007, according to Goldstein and Xie (2009).[4]

Contribution in the accounting perspective is not entirely the same as economic contribution, which can sometimes be significant even in situations where, from an accounting perspective, the contribution of net exports to growth is weak or negative. In this way, exports can play a coherent role in growth or, conversely, have little or no effect on it, even if the rate of trade openness is high. Let us consider two examples of highly open economies: Mexico and Korea. In the first case, growth is not pulled from the outside, in the second, it is.

In Mexico, unlike Brazil and Argentina in recent years, the trade balance remains in deficit. The structure of Mexican exports consists, by 10–15%, of the export of oil, the price of which is volatile, with the remainder divided roughly equally between products primarily for the Mexican domestic market and products intended wholly for external

[4] For example, South Korea's net contribution throughout this period is higher (28.6%) and Singapore's also (27.3%); Germany's was 64% (strong trade balance surplus) while in the United States it was -4.3% (trade deficit).

markets (almost exclusively the United States). The sharp increase in Mexico's rate of trade openness over the last 30 years is explained by the growth of exports of manufactured assembled goods, produced in *'maquiladoras'*, where the value added is low, and there is very little cluster effect (Palma, 2005). Here, we see that the economic contribution of exports to growth is reduced: GDP growth remains sluggish despite the vitality of exports. Thus, the multiplier effect is weak (Ibarra, 2008).

In Korea, growth is driven by booming exports, but the relationship is more complex than is generally believed. Following the work of Dani Rodrik (1995) and, contrary to the liberal *doxa*, it was not the development of exports and the marked opening of the economy that allowed the acceleration of growth in the 1960s. Imports of capital goods grew faster than exports, consisting mainly of intermediate products and sophisticated capital-intensive equipment. The sharp increase in these imports mirrored the increase in investments. The latter, therefore, were the real drivers of growth. An important portion of these investments was, in fact, intended for the production of goods to be exported, which would in turn bring in foreign currencies. The sequence is thus: increased investment rate leading to import growth leading to export growth; and it was only later that the balance of trade became positive. From an economic perspective, it is clear that the positive contribution of exports to growth is explained here by the government's industrial policy of encouraging local production of the inputs needed for the manufacture of exported products. It is this policy, designed to increase the value added locally, which explains both the increase in investment and in imports of capital goods. Indeed, efficient investment practices, as reflected here by the imports of sophisticated capital equipment, were equally instrumental in bringing about the desired growth. We are in a scenario, therefore, that is radically different from the Mexican case. The contribution to export growth comes from an intensification of related industry, through a direct increase of investments in the sector producing goods for export, and an indirect increase in sectors producing inputs for these products. From a Keynesian viewpoint, the multiplier effect of increased investment outweighs the negative effect of imports and enhances the positive contribution of exports.

This analysis of the Korean case can be applied to many other Asian economies. Boosting the domestic market through a redistribution of income does not mean neglecting the role played by the foreign market. It is not 'a zero sum game'.

The relationship between external market and internal (domestic) market is, therefore, more complex than appears at first glance. To speak as philosophers, we are dealing with two data that are 'separate but interdependent'. It is a point often overlooked by economists.

This being said, trade openness has been moderate and the contribution of exports to growth in Latin America has been weak over the past 20 years. Contrary to what one might imagine, the emerging economies of Latin America have not experienced an exceptional process of trade liberalisation. Though Mexico and some small countries in Central America are exceptions, Brazil, Argentina and many other countries have maintained their overall participation in world exports.[5] As these have grown on average twice as fast as world GDP during this period, globalisation has increased, of course, but at a rate more or less equivalent to the global average. Thus, despite a substantial increase in Brazil's degree of openness between 1990 (11.7%) and 2004 (26.9%), its weight in international trade remains at a marginal level and relatively stable, hovering around 1.1% between 1975 and 2005 (Kliass and Salama, 2008), although it has since gone up slightly due to the significant rise in the cost of raw materials. By contrast, the growth of exports from China is much faster than the global average. Its share in international trade, which was roughly equivalent to that of Brazil in 1975 (0.9%), has risen sharply: 1.9% in 1990, 3.9% in 2000, to reach 7.4% in 2005 and now soaring at 8.9% (Instituto

[5] As noted by Birdsall and Hamoudi in their criticisms of the work of Dollar and Kraay (2002), this is far from being a perfect indicator for economies whose exports are largely, and even exclusively, made up of primary products, as is the case in the least developed countries (LDCs). Indeed, commodity markets are highly volatile. The numerator of this ratio, and hence the indicator itself, are strongly affected by the fluctuating cost of raw materials. To define certain economies as 'Globalisers' or not, depending on the evolution of this ratio, and seek to establish a relationship with the growth rate of GDP, is therefore inappropriate from a scientific perspective.

económico de desenvolvimento industrial and WTO-OECD). The globalisation of trade is, therefore, faster and more important in China than in Brazil. Although Brazil and Argentina have opened up to the world economy, they are not yet what could be called 'open economies'. However, unlike what can be observed in Asian countries, the globalisation of finance in Latin America has been substantial, much higher in fact than in Asian countries.[6]

However, financial openness did not bring about a significant development of high-risk financial stock share products in banks. For this reason, the latter suffered from scarce liquidity due to the repatriation of capital at the beginning of the crisis, more than from the need to 'clean up' their balance sheets. Although their balance sheets have only been slightly affected by high-risk financial products, the behaviour of private banks in these countries has adapted to that observed in developed countries: credits to the economy have declined, and the financing of investments and exports has become more difficult. Credits to the economy have not entirely collapsed, however, because governments have sought to facilitate access to credit and to charge low interest rates (multiple subsidised rates for the purchase of cars and homes, for export, etc.) through their public banks. This policy has been facilitated in some places by the existence of large state banks such as BNDES in Brazil, and made more difficult elsewhere by their absence, or smaller size.

12.3.2. Strong Inequalities as Barriers to Recovery of Growth by the Domestic Market

Income inequalities are particularly high in the vast majority of Latin American countries (Salama, 2006), though with three exceptions (among them Colombia) they have declined slightly in many countries between 2002 and 2008 (ECLA, 2009; Lopez-Calva and Lustig, 2009; Hopenhayn, 2009; Salvatori Dedecca, 2010).

---

[6] See Galindo, Izquierdo and Rojas-Suarez (2010, p. 12). Today, there is abundant literature on this topic; we cite for its particular interest the article by Titelman, Perez-Caldentey and Pineda (2009).

This development is important, and its causes numerous: change in how the labour market operates, greater social transfers, less regressive fiscal policies, population decline and increase in the employment rate of women — though the contribution of these last two factors to the decline in inequality is relatively modest according to Lopez-Calva and Lustig (2009, p. 40 *et seq.*). Indeed, the number of adults per household accounts for 6.6% of the decline in inequality between 2000 and 2006 in Brazil, 8% in Argentina and 10.3% in Mexico. The reduction of inequalities mostly comes, in fact, from improved working conditions (employment, salary) and only in a relatively small proportion from increases in revenue not generated by labour[7] (26% in Argentina, 15.1% Mexico). The exception is Brazil (45.2%). More precisely, we observe in Brazil that the improvement in labour incomes is stronger for low incomes than for high incomes. The earning ratio of the richest 5% to the most modest 50% of the population went from 14.3 in 1993 to 13.5 in 2008, while the ratio of the richest 5% to the poorest 25% went from 23.6 to 18.6 (Salvatori Dedecca, 2010, p. 16). These data may be surprising.[8] They are partly due to the strong increase in the minimum wage, and thereby the number of pensions paid by the public sector,[9] and partly also to employment growth and the

[7] This is a very heterogeneous category, consisting of social transfers as well as rent and income on capital.

[8] Two remarks are called for here. First, the incomes of the 0.01%, 0.1% and even 1% richest segments of the population are growing much faster than in the remaining population, which indeed is also the case in most Western countries; secondly, income on capital (interest, dividends) is very poorly recorded.

[9] In many countries, there appears to be a link between the minimum wage and amounts paid into pensions. A relative increase in the minimum wage tends to raise total pensions. On a more general note, social policies, as defined in Latin America (education and social transfers as well as social protection, which mainly consist of pensions and health care), are still relatively weak, although increasingly strong in some countries like Brazil. According to research by Afonso and Dain (2009), there are only three countries (Argentina, Chile, Costa Rica) in which social spending exceeded 13% of GDP between 1985 and 1990. There were nine such countries in 2006–2007, including Brazil (24.4% of GDP), but no longer Chile. In Mexico, social expenditure was less than 9% of GDP during the first period but increased during the second period to 11.2% of GDP.

changing structure of jobs (Salama, 2007, 2008). But the bottom line is that social transfers, contrary to common belief, play only a small role in the transformation of inequalities. We shall examine this last point more closely.

The works of the OECD (2008) and of Goni, Humberto-Lopez and Serven (2008) clearly show the very weak influence of social transfers on the concentration level of incomes, as measured by the Gini coefficient. In considering the difference between gross income (including social transfers) and market income in Latin America and Europe, we observe that the impact of these transfers on the concentration of incomes is high in Europe but very low in Latin America. While the Gini, on a scale of 1 to 100, dropped by just over 2 points in Latin America, its decrease in Europe was on average much more pronounced. The impact of direct taxes is, on average, very minimal for the countries of Latin America (less than one point on the Gini coefficient) while here again, the average is much higher in Europe. Overall, then, these differences are much more important once transfers, net of taxes, are included. On average, the Gini in Latin America goes from 51.6 to 49.6 while in Europe it goes from 47.6 to 28.2.

From these data, we can readily understand why many economists, following the work of Celso Furtado, have seen the trend of economic stagnation as being caused by these levels of inequality and low social spending (Salama, 2006, Chapter 1) and, conversely, why the slight reduction in inequalities and increase in social expenditures may have boosted growth in the 2000s and revitalised the domestic market.

12.4. CONCLUSION

It is difficult to discuss the possible futures of Latin American countries without distinguishing the different paths they have followed during the last 10 to 15 years. Brazil, Argentina and Mexico have certain features in common: high income inequality, higher in Brazil than in Argentina; slight reductions in these inequalities; a modest openness to international trade (with the exception of Mexico); primary exports once again making up an important proportion of total exports in Argentina and, Brazil; a difficulty in exporting sophisticated industrial products, less pronounced in Brazil than in Mexico or Argentina and, finally, a trend towards appreciation of the real exchange rate, with the exception of Argentina since 2000. These countries also have different backgrounds. In Brazil and Mexico, the average growth rate of GDP has been modest since 2000. While Brazil's growth rate increased somewhat in 2004, Argentina's appeared to take off in Asian style. In 2009, the drop of the GDP was very sharp in Argentina, but still less pronounced than in Mexico and much less so than in Brazil. Inequality has fallen more significantly in Brazil in the 2000s than in Mexico or Argentina, and, while social expenditures have increased in proportion to GDP in Brazil and Argentina, they have stagnated in Mexico (Alonso and Dain, 2009).

These developments, as well as accelerating growth from 2003–2004 onwards, raise questions as to whether the beginnings of a new growth regime in Brazil (and more tentatively in Argentina) started even before the crisis erupted in 2008, carried by a boom in domestic demand. This boom may have been hidden by the simultaneous growth in primary product exports caused by the rise in their prices.

These countries are at a crossroads. Economic recovery and counter-cyclical policies,[10] decided in the aftermath of the breakout of the international crisis, could serve as a springboard for defining a new growth regime. In so doing, these countries, building on what appeared timidly since 2000, would 'benefit' from the international crisis to further reduce their income inequalities and promote the contribution of their internal market to economic recovery — somewhat like what happened in 1933–1934 after the Great Depression of the 1930s.

The massive return of capital into the so-called 'emerging' markets of Latin America, the resumption of GDP growth, the difficulties

[10] These were characterised primarily by policies to support domestic demand, both at a tax level (reduction of certain taxes), a monetary level (artificially low interest rates for the purchase or sale of certain products), and even a budgetary level (due to the increases in the minimum wage, pensions and social transfers). Counter-cyclical policies were relatively little characterised by policies of major public work on infrastructures, such as occurred in China (Khatiwada, 2009; Jimenez, 2009).

in sustaining demand insofar as it could increase labour costs — all these factors strengthen the political weight of those who would like to 'close the parenthesis of the crisis' and return to the previous excluding growth pattern of early 2000. This temptation is even greater now that the return of capital translates into a new trend of appreciation in national currencies, after their sharp decline in 2008–2009. This trend is favourable to foreign investors but bad for exporters of industrial products, because the decrease in competitiveness caused by rising labour costs, expressed in dollars, is not always compensated for by the decline in value of their imports of intermediate and capital goods.

One might think that Mexico will probably be most tempted by this route, as its foreign trade is almost exclusively directed towards the United States and Canada, and foreign ownership in its banking system is very powerful. Conversely, a resumption of the international crisis would promote the continuation of an anti-cyclical policy favouring demand, stimulate the search for alternative trading partners and enable a further depreciation of the peso, thereby offsetting increases in labour costs.

A continued policy supporting domestic demand is more likely to occur in Brazil and in Argentina. But it suffers from many handicaps. As we have seen, the reduction of inequalities is weak and these inequalities remain at an extremely high level. The absolute size of Brazil's population (which is greater than Argentina's) and the existence of Mercosur allow it to have a sufficiently large domestic market, in terms of capital development, for a wide range of products. This in itself seems insufficient, however, to inspire sustainable market-driven growth as long as the weight of finance and its effects on income distribution have not been contained. Increasing the wages of the least paid social strata, however desirable it may be given the extent of poverty, is not sufficient. The obstacle of regressive taxation must be lifted, which cannot be done without deepening serious conflicts of interest that have been at work for some years already.

In the 1930s, the market was created through a 'forced march' of monetisation, produced by industrialisation and giving it impetus.

Today, the domestic market can contribute to sustainable growth only if a true Welfare State is established. This alone will make it possible for the domestic market to offset the sluggish external demand for industrial products. Not to choose this path is to accept a return to international specialisation in primary commodities on the pretext that the international demand is strong. This is choosing the easy way out today, but also a fragile economy for tomorrow. It is opting for a return to the years preceding the 1930s — a strange reversal of history.

BIBLIOGRAPHY

Afonso, J. R. and Dain, S. (2009). *Dos décadas de la descentralización del gasto social en America Latina: una evaluación preliminar*, Working Paper, Cepal, Santiago, Available at www.eclac.org [Accessed 23 September 2010].

Birdsall, N. and Hamoudi, A. (2002). *Commodity dependence, trade and growth: when "openness" is not enough*, Working Paper n° 7, Center for Global Development, Washington.

Bradesco (2009). Em que medida o elevado deficit externo brasileiro em 2010 sera capaz de conter a apreciaçao do real?, Destaque Depec, 28 December, 104.

Cepal (2009). *Balance preliminar de las economías de America Latina y el Caribe*, Santiago.

Cepal (2009). *Tributación directa en Mexico: equitad y desafío*, *Macroeconomía del desarrollo*, 91. Santiago.

Dollar, D. and Kraay, A. (2000). *Growth is good for the poor*, World Bank Working Paper, Available at: www.worldbank.org/research [Accessed 14 September 2010].

Galindo, A., Izquierdo, A. and Rojas-Suarez, L. (2010). *Financial Integration and Foreign Banks in Latin America, How they impact the transmission of external financial shocks*, IDB Working Papers, April, 116.

Goldstein, M. and Xie, D. (2009). *The Impact of the Financial Crisis on Emerging Asia*, Working Paper No. 9–11, Peterson Institute for International Economics.

Gomez, S. and Rossignoo, D. (2008). *Argentina, análisis de la situación tributaria y propuestas de reformas impositivas destinadas a mejorar la distribución del ingreso*, Working Paper, Universidad de Buenos Aires.

Goni, E., Humberto Lopez, J. and Serven, L. (2008). *Fiscal Redistribution and Income Inequality in Latin America*, Policy Research Working Paper, No. 4487.

Ibara, C. (2008). El paradoja del crecimento lento de Mexico, *Revista de la* Cepal, No. 95.

IEDI (2006). *Carta Iedi*, Brasilia.

IMF (2009). *World economic Outlook: Crisis and Recovery*, Chapter 4, Washington.

Jimenez, J. P. (2010). *Crisis, recuperación y espacios de politica: desafíos de la politica fiscal*, Working Paper, Cepal. Santiago.

Khatiwada, S. (2009). *Stimulus Packages to Counter Global Economic Crisis*, Discussion Paper DP/196, International Institute for Labour Studies, Geneva.

Kliass, P. and Salama, P. (2008). La globalisation au Brésil: responsable ou bouc émissaire? *Lusotopie.*

Lopez-Calva, L. F. and Lustig N. (2009). *The recent decline of inequality in Latin America: Argentina, Brazil, Mexico and Peru*, Working Paper No. 140, ECINEQ.

Mathias, G. and Salama, P. (1983). *L'Etat surdéveloppé*, Edition Maspéro-La découverte, Paris.

OECD (2008). *Perspectives économiques de l'Amérique latine 2009*, Paris.

OECD (2009). *Regional Economic Outlook, Western Hemisphere*, Part 2: Latin American and Caribbean Outlook, Paris.

Palma, G. (2005). The seven main stylised facts of the mexican economy since Trade Liberalisation and NAFTA, *Industrial and Corporate Change*, 14, 6.

Rodrik, D. (1995). Growth policy, getting interventions right: How South Korea and Taiwan grew rich, *Economic Policy*, Manchester, pp. 55–107.

Salama, P. (2006). *Le défi des inégalités, une comparaison économique Amérique latine/Asie*, La Découverte, Paris.

Salama, P. (2007). Pauvreté, le bout du tunnel?, *Problèmes d'Amérique latine*, 66/67, pp. 183–202.

Salama, P. (2009a). Argentine, Brésil, Mexique face à la crise, *Revue Tiers Monde,* 197, pp. 53–70.

Salama, P. (2009b). 'Forces et faiblesses de l'Argentine, du Brésil, du Mexique', in *Les Suds dans la crise* (under the guidance of Hugon, P. and Salama, P.), Armand Colin, Paris, pp. 89–125.

Salvatori Dedecca, C. (2010). *As desigualidades na sociedade brasileira*, Working Paper, Mimeo.

Titelman, D., Perez-Caldentey, E. and Pineda, R. (2009). Como algo tan pequeño terminó siendo tan grande? crisis financiera, mecanismo de contagio y efectos en America latina, *Revista de la Cepal,* 98.

WTO-OECD (2009). *Globalisation and Emerging Economics*, Paris.

Chapter

13

Foreign Investment in Latin America: Between Love and Hatred

Jorge E. Viñuales and Magnus Jesko Langer

13.1. INTRODUCTION

The political independence of Latin American countries from European colonial powers, and particularly from the Spanish empire, in the early nineteenth century, signaled the beginning of another important struggle, namely the quest for economic emancipation. Much like the quest for political independence, the fight for economic emancipation was carried out on many fronts, including the front of ideas. Within the intellectual front itself, one of the most important struggles took place in the arena of legal concepts, and more specifically, in connection with the protection of the economic interests of aliens residing in the newly independent countries.

Since their independence, Latin American countries faced the need to attract foreign investment in its different forms (loans, portfolio investment, and foreign direct investment) while at the same time managing the potential disruptive effects of such investment in the social and political development of the new regimes. Indeed, quite often, such investment carried with it an increased risk of potential intervention, including military intervention, by the investor's home State. In other words, economic development was tied to foreign political intervention. On the other hand, a number of capital-exporting countries, such as the United Kingdom, France, or the United States, saw in such investments a way to increase their influence in a geographical area previously subject to the Spanish colonial monopoly (see Whitaker, 1941, pp. 61–99; Robertson, 1923, pp. 186–279; Smith, 1986, pp. 83–119; Marichal, 1995).

This tension between host States and home States regarding the protection of foreign investment gave rise to competing legal doctrines, which in turn constitute a reflection of how the underlying struggle for economic emancipation historically developed. The purpose of this chapter is to shed light on such struggle through a concise analysis of its legal manifestations over time. We will focus on two types of legal concepts. The first concerns the methods for solving investment conflicts, such as diplomatic consultations, submission to a judicial body, or armed intervention. The second relates to the rules potentially applicable to solving such disputes, which may be derived from the municipal law of the investor's home State or from the host State's legal system or, still, from international law. The evolution of these two types of concepts will be analyzed by reference to four historical phases, which provide the backbone for our discussion. These phases must be understood as analytical categories rather than as historical processes, as neither such processes nor the evolution of legal concepts have followed a linear trajectory. They remain, however, useful analytical tools to understand the evolution of the legal concepts governing foreign investment as well as, more generally, to grasp the realities underlying such legal developments.

13.2. FROM GUNBOAT DIPLOMACY TO DIPLOMATIC PROTECTION (1810–1907)

From the perspective of our analytical framework, the main feature of the period, extending roughly from 1810 to 1907, is the struggle for sovereign equality under international law. Historically, the legal concept of sovereign equality applied only to the relations among European powers as well as, later on, the United States (see in particular Wheaton, 1916, pp. 14–15; Lorimer, 1883, pp. 11–16, 161; Rivier, 1896, pp. 7–18; Oppenheim, 1905, p. 10; Root, 1910, p. 517). It followed that other political units, including independent States such as China or Japan, came to be treated as unequal (Fairbank *et al.*, 1989, pp. 460–461). An apposite illustration of this fact is provided by the so-called, "unequal treaties" imposed on China by the United Kingdom in 1843 and later also by the United States, France, and other European powers (see, generally, Auslin, 2004; Wang 2005). After the Opium War, the United Kingdom forced China to conclude the Treaties of Nanking and Hoomun-Chae, respectively in 1842 and 1843.[1] This new treaty system granted the United Kingdom *inter alia* a number of extraterritorial prerogatives, including consular jurisdiction over disputes between English and Chinese nationals as well as the applicability of English law to such disputes.[2] This type of concessions were obtained through the use (or the threat) of armed force, and their main objective was to open China, Japan, and Korea to Western trade and investment.

A comparable pattern can be observed in the relations between Western powers and Latin American countries, insofar as the European powers endeavored to impose their superiority over Latin American countries — however, by using different means. While some reactionary

---

[1] Treaty between China and Great Britain, signed in Nanking, 29 August 1842, in Parry, C. (1969). *The Consolidated Treaty Series*, Vol. 93 (1842), Oceana Publications, New York, p. 465; and Supplementary Treaty between China and Great Britain, signed in Hoomun-Chae, 8 October 1843, in Parry, C. (1969). *The Consolidated Treaty Series*, Vol. 95 (1843), Oceana Publications, New York, p. 323.

[2] See Article II of the Nanking Treaty and Article VI of the Hoomun-Chae Treaty. As stated by Fairbank, the first settlement "placed British consuls in five ports where British residents were under their consul's legal jurisdiction, that is, they had the right of extraterritoriality. The protection of Western legal procedures covered not only the persons of merchants and missionaries but also their goods and property and sometimes extended in practice to their Chinese servants and assistants" (Fairbank *et al.*, 1989, p. 460).

powers of Central Europe considered intervening in Latin America in order to restore the power of the Spanish Crown, the United Kingdom supported the independence of the newly created States and thereafter profited strongly from the opening of new markets in Latin America (Webster, 1938, pp. 1–79; Whitaker, 1941, pp. 73–78, pp. 396–399; Rippy, 1929; Robertson, 1932, pp. 245–246; Berstein and Milza, 1996, p. 173). Also, the United States favored the independence movements (Whitaker, 1941, pp. 386–395; Robertson, 1932, pp. 244–245; Thomas, 1956, pp. 268–269) and in 1823 President Monroe stood against the European powers' interventionism in the new world.[3] Economic historians have underlined the fact that British investments (either public or private loans, direct investments, or portfolio investments) had the largest share of total foreign capital movements to Latin America during the nineteenth century (Stone, 1977, 690; Jones, C., 1995, pp. 70–95; Richardson, 1972, p. 99; Platt, 1980, p. 1; James, 1980, p. 152; Jones, 1980, p. 437; Stone, 1968, p. 311; Rippy, 1959). These primarily concentrated in countries such as Argentina, Chile, or Brazil, and in sectors such as railroads and other infrastructure projects. Capital flows also came from other countries such as France, Germany, and Belgium (see Mauro, 1995, pp. 53–69; Young, 1995, pp. 96–124; Regalsky, 1995, pp. 193–213; Rippy, 1948). However, since profitability of the capital invested was impaired by factors such as political instability and defaults on debt payments,[4] in a number of cases where the interests of foreign nationals were adversely impacted by measures taken by the newly independent States, European powers launched armed interventions in order to enforce the claims of their own nationals. This policy, known as the "gunboat diplomacy", amounted, essentially, to a power display by sending armored vessels to recalcitrant

---

[3] For general information on the Monroe Doctrine, see: Whitaker, 1941, pp. 464–563; Perkins, 1941; Queuille, 1969; Smith, 1994, pp. 2–40; Dent, 1999, pp. 1–19; Livingstone, 2009, pp. 8–22.

[4] For instance, most Latin American countries defaulted on their debt payments during the 1830s and were unable to service their debt for several decades until 1870. A similar pattern appeared after the economic crises of the 1870s and 1890s (Marichal, 1988, pp. 65–75, pp. 125–146, pp. 173–197).

coastal cities in Latin America. The most notable examples are the French blockade of the Rio de La Plata between 1838 and 1850 (with British support between 1843 and 1848, see Calvo, 1896, pp. 324–336), the French blockade of the port of Veracruz in April 1838 (Smith, 1986, p. 84), the French intervention (initially with British and Spanish support) in Mexico between 1862 and 1867 (Robertson, 1932, pp. 651–653; Calvo, 1896, pp. 337–348), and the Anglo–Italian–German intervention in Venezuela in 1902 (see Tamburini, 2002; Thomas, 1956, p. 519; Rippy, 1932, pp. 443–458). Underlying this policy was the idea that the newly independent States could not be treated on an equal footing with European powers and, more precisely, that their laws and institutions were not capable of granting foreign investors the protection they deserved.[5]

To counter such practices, intellectuals from Latin American countries took argument with the legal concepts underlying the policies of European States and sought to restrain the use of force as a legal tool for protecting the interests of foreign investors. Writing in 1832, the Venezuelan author Andrés Bello provided a

[5] Alphonse Rivier sought to justify foreign intervention in the following terms: "the possessions of individuals, subjects of a State, constitute an element of the wealth and prosperity of that State [···] In case these possessions are endangered by the behaviour of a foreign State [···] which violates its obligations towards them, the State to which the people injured belong to is, of course, allowed to take their interests in hand in a way it considers appropriate; it shall take action either through diplomatic channels, or by way of reprisals; all this according to the principles of the law of reprisals and those of the right to intervention" (Rivier, 1896, p. 272; translated by the authors). Arguing on the basis of the same premise, i.e. the unequal standard applicable to non-Western nations, the United States Secretary of State, Mr Seward, came to a different conclusion by arguing that: "[w]e are unfortunately too familiar with complaints of delay and inefficiency of the courts in the South American Republics. We must, however, continue to repose confidence in their independencies and integrity [···] We cannot undertake to supervise the arrangements of the whole world for litigation, because American citizens voluntarily expose themselves to be concerned in their deficiencies"; Note sent by the Secretary of State, Mr Seward, to the American Minister in Colombia in 1866, cited in: Moore, 1906, p. 660. See also: Wheaton, 1916, pp. 14–15; Lorimer, 1883, pp. 11–16, p. 161; Rivier, 1896, pp. 7–18; Oppenheim, 1905, p. 10; Root, 1910, p. 517.

first affirmation of the obligation of foreign investors to submit their disputes to the domestic laws and jurisdiction of the host State. However, Bello admitted foreign intervention in the form of diplomatic protection in exceptional cases such as an instance of denial of justice by the courts and tribunals of the host State (Bello, 1883, pp. 188–196). As noted by one commentator, this doctrine was "created as part of a framework designed to incentivize foreign investment in the region: foreign investors were offered and provided with full civil (non-political) legal equality, a revolutionary statement for those times and perhaps still for the present times" (Montt, 2009, p. 7; see also Dawson, 1986). A more radical approach, excluding recourse to the mechanisms of diplomatic protection as contrary to the sovereign equality of States, has been attributed to the Argentine Carlos Calvo (Calvo, 1896). Calvo's writings were far more influential on subsequent commentators as well as on the practice of Latin American States than Bello's. The so-called "Calvo doctrine" is based on the sovereign equality of States and the ensuing territorial jurisdiction. The idea of sovereign equality implies that no State should be allowed to intervene in the domestic affairs of another State, whereas the concept of territorial jurisdiction entails that the claims of foreign investors are subject exclusively to the domestic laws and jurisdiction of the host State. According to this doctrine, it would indeed be an exorbitant privilege if foreign investors could claim a different status than the one accorded to the nationals of the host State.

The practical effect of this stance must not be underestimated. Some commentators situate its first manifestation in the note sent in 1873 by the Mexican foreign minister of that time, Lafragua, to the US ambassador, Foster. In this note, Lafragua pointed out that Mexico was not to be held responsible for the damage caused to foreign owners, and he sought to justify his position by referring to the writings of Carlos Calvo. Foster replied that Calvo's views were not universally accepted (Tamburini, 2002), thereby confirming the increasing alignment of the United States position on this specific point with that of European powers. Other manifestations of Calvo's influence can also be found *inter alia* in a "Recommendation on Claims and Diplomatic

Protection", adopted at the First Pan-American Conference of 1889–1890,[6] the "Convention related to the Rights of Aliens",[7] and the "Treaty of Arbitration for Pecuniary Claims",[8] both adopted at the Second Pan-American Conference of 1901–1902, or the "Treaty of Friendship, Commerce and Navigation" between Colombia and Italy of 10 August 1894.[9]

Thus, the first period can be characterized as a time where capital-exporting countries resorted to the use of force to assert the claims of their nationals that invested in Latin America, whereas capital-importing countries sought to limit this practice by expounding the doctrine of territorial jurisdiction and national treatment. By the end of this first period, however, the use of force for the protection of foreign investors lost considerable legal ground. This can be seen as a direct consequence of the idea of the sovereign equality of States, which seemed now applicable to newly independent States as well.

The transition can be located at the turn from the nineteenth to the twentieth century. At the peace conference held at The Hague in 1899 only one Latin American country (Mexico) was present. The situation changed considerably at the second Hague Conference of

---

[6] See: Recommendation on Claims and Diplomatic Protection of 18 April 1890, cited in Scott, 1931, p. 45.

[7] See: Convention relative to the Rights of Aliens, cited in Scott, 1931, p. 91. The Convention was ratified by Bolivia, Colombia, Ecuador, Guatemala, Honduras, Nicaragua, El Salvador.

[8] Article 1 of the Treaty reads: "The High Contracting Parties agree to submit to arbitration all claims for pecuniary loss or damage which may be presented by their respective citizens, and which cannot be amicably adjusted through diplomatic channels and when said claims are of sufficient importance to warrant the expenses of arbitration" (Scott, 1931, p. 104). The Treaty was ratified by Colombia, Costa Rica, Ecuador, Guatemala, Honduras, Mexico, Peru, El Salvador, and the United States. The 1902 Treaty was extended to other Parties through the Convention on Pecuniary Claims adopted at the Third Pan-American Conference of 1906 (Scott, 1931, pp. 132–133).

[9] See: Article 21 of the Treaty of Friendship, Commerce and Navigation and Convention for the Modification of the Claims Protocol of 24 May 1886 between Colombia and Italy, signed at Bogotá, 27 October 1892, cited in Parry, C. (1978). *The Consolidated Treaty Series*, Vol. 177 (1892), Oceana Publications, New York, pp. 499–500.

1907, partly because of the insistence of the United States that Latin American countries be invited as well.[10] The participation of Latin American countries in the second Hague Conference was of critical importance in condemning the use of force for debt recovering. Such influence must be understood in the light of contemporaneous events. In 1902, Cipriano Castro, Venezuela's ruler, refused to deal with the claims of foreign investors outside the domestic context, advancing that such claims were an exclusively domestic matter subject to the jurisdiction of domestic courts.[11] As a result, the German, Italian, and English governments decided to send armored vessels to the port of Caracas. This prompted the Argentine foreign minister, Luis María Drago, to send a note to Martín García Mérou, the Argentine ambassador in Washington, in order to explain that the recovery of contractual debt could not justify armed intervention (Drago, 1907, p. 692). Interestingly, in April 1903, Carlos Calvo, then Argentine ambassador in Paris, addressed a circular to several leading international lawyers requesting their opinion on Drago's note. Out of 10 published opinions, six agreed with the substance of Drago's note (Campos, Férand-Giraud, Moynier, Olivecrona, Passy, and Weiss), while the remaining four were more cautious (Charmes, Fiore, Holland, and Westlake) (Herschley, 1907, p. 37). The Venezuelan affair was eventually submitted to arbitration under the auspices of the Permanent Court of Arbitration[12] created in 1899. More importantly, the efforts of Drago to outlaw the recourse to force in order to recover State debt led to the adoption, at the second Hague Conference in 1907, of the so-called Drago–Porter

[10] For the discussion surrounding this particular issue, see: Scott, 1909, pp. 95–101; Hicks, 1908, p. 530.

[11] On the Venezuelan Affair, see: Scott, 1908, pp. 81–85; Rippy, 1954, p. 65; Platt, 1962, p. 3; Forbes, 1978, p. 317).

[12] *Preferential Treatment of Claims of Blockading Powers against Venezuela (Germany, Great Britain, and Italy v. Venezuela)*, Award, Permanent Court of Arbitration, The Hague, 22 February 1904. In this award, the Tribunal found that the three blockading states had a right to preferential treatment for the payment of their claims against Venezuela. These claims were ultimately resolved between 1903 and 1905 by various claims commissions, see: Ralston, 1904.

Convention.[13] The Convention is significant in several respects, the most important being that a judicial dispute settlement mechanism, international arbitration, was to substitute itself to the use of force. The so-called *Porter clause* nevertheless justified the recourse to the use of force in the cases where the indebted State refused to submit the dispute to arbitration or failed to submit to the award. Efforts from Latin American countries were therefore decisive in bringing about this change which progressively secured the resolution of disputes related to foreign investors by peaceful means.

13.3. FOREIGN INVESTMENT BETWEEN NATIONAL AND INTERNATIONAL PROTECTION (1907–1948)

From this moment onwards, the intervention of foreign States on behalf of their nationals will be increasingly limited to a traditional practice already in existence throughout the nineteenth century, namely the exercise of diplomatic protection before international tribunals.

However, the use of peaceful methods did not solve the underlying controversy as to the applicable law and the competent adjudicatory body. Already at the time of the "unequal treaties", one of the main features reflecting the unequal position of the relevant contracting States was the extraterritorial prerogative of consular jurisdiction and the application of a foreign law to disputes arising in the host State. Capital-exporting countries sought to preserve the essence of such features asserting the need for a special judge (even if no longer consular jurisdiction) and a special law (even if no longer the law of the home State). The special judge was to be the international judge in its different forms, including *ad hoc* or institutionalized arbitration, mixed claims commissions, or the Permanent Court of International Justice created in 1920. The special law was to be

[13] See: Article 1(1)–(2) of the Convention respecting the limitation of the employment of force for the recovery of contract debts, signed at The Hague, 17 April 1907, reproduced in Scott, 1909, p. 357.

international law, and more precisely, the so-called "international minimum standard of treatment", which reflected in practice the domestic laws of capital-exporting countries.[14]

Throughout this second period, Latin American countries will, again, be at the forefront of the opposition, reaffirming what was by then known as the "Calvo doctrine", i.e. the treatment of foreigners on the same footing as nationals and the submission of disputes to the national courts of the host States. The increasing influence of the Calvo doctrine on the practice of Latin American countries can be seen at three main levels. First, the doctrine was enshrined in a number of treaties and international instruments, particularly in the context of the Pan-American conferences. For instance, at the sixth Pan-American Conference, held in 1928, a "Convention relating to the Status of Aliens" was adopted, in which the principle of equality between nationals and foreigners was affirmed.[15] This principle was further affirmed in the "Convention on the Rights and Duties of States" adopted at the seventh Pan-American Conference, held in 1933 in Montevideo, Uruguay. Article 9 of this Convention provided for the following: "Nationals and foreigners are under the same protection of the law and the national authorities and the foreigners may

[14] In a famous excerpt from the *Hopkins Case*, the Commissioners held that, "it not infrequently happens that under the rules of international law applied to controversies of an international aspect a nation is required to accord to aliens broader and more liberal treatment than it accords to its own citizens under its municipal laws. The reports of decisions made by arbitral tribunals long prior to the Treaty of 1923 contain many such instances. There is no ground to object that this amounts to discrimination by a nation against its own citizens in favor of aliens. It is not a question of discrimination, but a question of difference in their respective rights and remedies. The citizens of a nation may enjoy many rights which are withheld from aliens, and, conversely, under international law aliens may enjoy rights and remedies which the nation does not accord to its own citizens", *George W. Hopkins (U.S.A.) v. United Mexican States*, Award, R.I.A.A. Vol. IV, 31 March 1926, pp. 41–47, at 47, par. 16.

[15] Article 2 of this Convention reads: "Foreigners are subject as are nationals to local jurisdiction and laws, due consideration being given to the limitations expressed on conventions and treaties". This Convention was adopted with the support of the United States; see: Scott, 1931, p. 415. See also: Tamburini, 2002.

not claim rights other or more extensive than those of nationals".[16] Also, the Final Act of the Montevideo Conference proclaimed the national treatment principle and limited the exercise of diplomatic protection to the cases of manifest denial of justice.[17] Second, the Calvo doctrine was also incorporated into domestic legislation. Examples include the Mexican Constitution of 1917 (Mexican Constitution, Article 27, 1917), the Constitution of Peru of 1933,[18] and the Constitution of Venezuela of 1947.[19] Third, the main ideas of the Calvo doctrine were introduced into contracts concluded

---

[16] Convention on the Rights and Duties of States, signed at Montevideo, 26 December 1933, in *The International Conferences of American States. First Supplement, 1933–1940*, Carnegie Endowment for International Peace, Rumford Press, Washington, 1940, pp. 121–125.

[17] Point 3 of the Final Act reads: "Reaffirms equally that diplomatic protection cannot be initiated in favor of foreigners unless they exhaust all legal measures established by the laws of the country before which the action is begun. There are excepted those cases of manifest denial or unreasonable delay of justice which shall always be interpreted restrictively, that is, in favor of the sovereignty of the State in which the difference may have arisen. Should no agreement on said difference be reached through diplomatic channels, within a reasonable period of time, the matter shall then be referred to arbitration", in *ibid.*, pp. 91–92.

[18] Article 17 of the Peruvian Constitution provides that: "Domestic and foreign mercantile companies shall be subject without reservations to the laws of the Republic. Any contract between the State and foreigners, or any concessions granted by the former in the latter's favor, shall contain the submission of the latter that they expressly submit to the laws and to the courts of the Republic and that they waive all recourse to diplomatic protest". Article 32 of the Constitution provides that: "Foreigners shall be on equal terms with Peruvians in respect of property and may in no case claim exceptional status in respect thereto nor appeal to diplomatic protest", cited in: ICSID (1968). *Convention on the Settlement of Investment Disputes between States and Nationals of Other States — Documents Concerning the Origin and the Formulation of the Convention*, Vol. II, Part 2, Washington, D.C. (Doc. 46, 8 December 1964).

[19] Article 21 reads as follows: "Aliens in Venezuela have, without prejudice to what is provided in international conventions, the duties and rights that this Constitution and the laws grant to them; but neither the one nor the other may be greater than those of Venezuelans". [Online] Available at: http://www.gobiernoenlinea.ve/legislacion-view/sharedfiles/constitucion1947.pdf [Accessed 24 November 2010].

between a number of Latin American countries and foreign investors to the effect that these later waived their right to seek diplomatic protection from their home States (the so-called "Calvo clause").[20]

This body of practice came under severe criticism from capital-exporting countries. As noted by one commentator in 1907, the Calvo doctrine, "absolutely condemns diplomatic as well as armed intervention as legitimate methods of enforcing any or all private claims of a purely pecuniary nature, at least such as are based upon contract or are the result of civil war, insurrection, or mob violence" (see Herschley, 1907, p. 43). Another contemporaneous commentator drew attention to the fact that States were entitled to see an international minimum standard applied to their nationals abroad, especially in cases where the foreign countries were ridden by bad administration (see Borchard, 1913, p. 518; Freeman, 1946, p. 121). In essence, foreign investors and local nationals were to receive equal treatment only if the host State was able to live up to international standards of treatment (see Root, 1910, p. 523), defined by reference to the treatment afforded in capital-exporting countries. Also in this period, shortly before the 1930 Codification Conference on State Responsibility,[21] an important initiative was launched to neutralize the effects of the waiver contained in a Calvo clause inserted in a

[20] On the content of Calvo clauses, García-Amador explained that "[s]ometimes, it merely consists of a stipulation that the foreign individual concerned will be satisfied with the action of the local courts. In other cases, the Clause embodies a more direct and broader waiver of diplomatic protection, as when it provides that disputes which may arise shall in no circumstances lead to an international claim, or else that the foreign individuals or corporate bodies are to be deemed to be nationals of the country for the purposes of the contract or concession" (García-Amador, 1958, pp. 455–456). In general, one can distinguish four types of Calvo clauses: the first excludes the invocation of diplomatic protection in all circumstances; the second excludes this protection except in cases of denial of justice; the third specifies further on that an unfavorable judicial decision is not in itself a denial of justice; and the fourth provides that foreigners will be treated as nationals for all useful purposes. See: Tamburini, 2002.

[21] See: Acts of the Conference for the Codification of International Law (held at The Hague from 13 March to 12 April 1930), Vol. IV, Minutes of the Third Committee (C.351(c).M.145(c).1930.V), in Rosenne, 1975, p. 1425 *et seq.*; Borchard, 1930, p. 517; Borchard, 1931.

contract. Article 17 of the Harvard Research Draft Convention of 1929 stated the following:

> A state is not relieved of responsibility as a consequence of any provision in its own law or in an agreement with an alien which attempts to exclude responsibility by making the decisions of its own courts final; nor is it relieved of responsibility by any waiver by the alien of the protection of the state of which he is a national.[22]

With a few exceptions, Latin American States did not attend the 1930 Conference and no agreement could be found on this issue.[23]

As the foregoing examples suggest, the second period is characterized by an intense opposition between capital-exporting and capital-importing States regarding the legal framework applicable to foreign investment. A representative sample of the forces and arguments informing such struggle is provided by the consequences of the Mexican revolution. In September 1923, the governments of Mexico and of the United States signed a "General Claims Convention"[24] and

---

[22] Harvard Research Draft Codification of the Law on Responsibility of States for Injuries to Aliens, *in* (1929) *American Journal of International Law, Special Supplement*, 23, p. 162. However, it is to be noted that the comment on the draft articles does acknowledge that the "decisions of various international commissions are by no means uniform. In the 19 cases reported by Moore and Ralston up to 1910, eight upheld the clause as barring the right of the claimant to appear before an international commission without having fulfilled his obligation under the stipulation, and eleven denied the validity of the clause as barring the right of the claimant, or of his government, to bring the claim before an international commission, in spite of the fact that the obligation of the stipulation had not been fulfilled", at 208.

[23] On the Codification Conference, see: Borchard, 1930, p. 517.

[24] General Claims Convention, signed at Washington, 8 September 1923, R.I.A.A. Vol. IV, pp. 11–14. Article II reads: "Each member of the Commission [shall] examine and decide, according to the best of his judgment and in accordance with the principles of international law, justice and equity, all claims presented for decision".

a "Special Claims Convention",[25] providing for the creation of Mixed Commissions mandated to adjudicate, respectively, the disputes stemming from the events after 1868 and those related to the revolutionary events between 1910 and 1920. Other Mixed Commissions were also established to administer the disputes between Mexico and other States.[26] The legacy of these proceedings is of great interest for our analysis. Whereas the possibility for an investor to waive his right to seek diplomatic protection in matters relating to contractual claims was acknowledged by such commissions, some fundamental limits were nevertheless introduced, which, in practice, neutralize the very objective sought by Calvo-clauses. First, it was understood that the investor could only waive his rights arising out of contractual claims, leaving unaffected *inter alia* claims arising out of a denial of justice. Second, the investor's waiver did not affect the inherent right of the investor's home State to intervene in the dispute

[25] Special Claims Convention for the Settlement of Claims of American Citizens Arising from Revolutionary Acts in Mexico from 20 November 1910, to 31 May 1920, signed at Mexico City, 10 September 1923, R.I.A.A. Volume IV, pp. 779–782. Article II reads, in its relevant parts, as follows: "The Mexican Government desired that the claims shall be so decided [in accordance with the principles of justice and equity] because Mexico wishes that her responsibility shall not be fixed according to the generally accepted rules and principles of international law, but *ex gratia* feels morally bound to make full indemnification and agrees, therefore, that it will be sufficient that it be established that the alleged loss or damage in any case was sustained and was due to any of the causes enumerated in Article III thereof". Article VI of the Convention stipulates: "Since the Mexican Government desires to arrive at an equitable settlement of the claims of the citizens of the United States and to grant them a just and adequate compensation for their losses or damages, the Mexican Government agrees that the Commission shall not disallow or reject any claim by the application of the general principle of international law that the legal remedies must be exhausted as a condition precedent to the validity or allowance of any claim".

[26] Mexico concluded claims conventions with France (French–Mexican Claims Convention of 25 September 1924), Germany (German–Mexican Claims Convention of 16 March 1925), Spain (Spanish–Mexican Claims Convention of 25 November 1925), Great Britain (British–Mexican Claims Convention of 19 November 1926), and Italy (Italian–Mexican Claims Convention of 13 January 1927).

advancing its own right to see international law respected in the treatment of its nationals.

Indeed, in the *North American Dredging case* the Commission held that, whereas an "appropriately and carefully phrased" Calvo clause could, under some defined conditions, achieve the "legitimate desire on the part of nations to deal with persons and property within their respective jurisdictions according to their own laws and to apply remedies provided by their own authorities and tribunals", such "laws and remedies in no wise restrict or limit their international obligations, or restrict or limit or in any wise impinge upon the correlative rights of other nations protected under rules of international law".[27] The Commission further added that, "[t]he present stage of international law imposes upon every international tribunal the solemn duty of seeking for a proper and adequate balance between the sovereign right of national jurisdiction, on the one hand, and the sovereign right of national protection of citizens on the other".[28] *In casu*, the Commission held that no rule of positive international law prohibited a foreign investor to waive his right to diplomatic protection subject to the exception of denial of justice. Thus, the particular Calvo clause at stake:

> did not take from him his undoubted right to apply to his own Government for protection if his resort to the Mexican tribunals or other authorities available to him resulted in a denial or delay of justice as that term is used in international law. In such a case the claimant's complaint would be not that his contract was violated but that he had been denied justice. The basis of his appeal would be not a construction of his contract, save perchance in an incidental way, but rather an internationally illegal act.[29]

---

[27] *North American Dredging Company of Texas (U.S.A.) v. United Mexican States*, Award, R.I.A.A. Vol. IV, 31 March 1926, pp. 26–35, at 27, par. 3.

[28] *Idem*, par. 4.

[29] *Idem*, at 30, par. 14.

Moreover, according to the Commission, such a clause could not:

> deprive the government of his [the investor's] nation of its undoubted right of applying international remedies to violations of international law committed to his damage. Such government frequently has a larger interest in maintaining the principles of international law than in recovering damage for one of its citizens in a particular case, and manifestly such citizen can not by contract tie in this respect the hands of his Government.[30]

This conclusion was subsequently confirmed by another Claims Commission, in the *Mexican Union Railway case*, where the Commission held that:

> [i]n holding that under the rules of international law an alien may lawfully make a promise, as laid down in the concession, the majority of the Commission holds at the same time that no person can, by such a clause, deprive the Government of his country of its undoubted right to apply international remedies to violations of international law committed to his hurt. A Government may take a view of losses suffered by one of its subjects different to that taken by such subject himself. Where the Government is concerned, a principle higher than the mere safeguarding of the private interests of the subject who suffered the damage may be involved. For the Government the contract is *res inter alios acta*, by which its liberty of action cannot be prejudiced.[31]

---

[30] *Idem*, at 29, par. 11.

[31] *Mexican Union Railway (Ltd.) (Great Britain) v. United Mexican States*, Award, R.I.A.A., Vol. V, 21 February 1930, pp. 115–129, at 120, par. 10. It is, however, to be noted that this evolution reflects several earlier decisions, most notably in the *Martini case* in 1903, where Commissioner Ralston held that, "Italy and Venezuela, by their respective Governments, have agreed to submit to the determination of this Mixed Commission the claims of Italian citizens against Venezuela. The right of a sovereign power to enter into an agreement of this kind is entirely superior to that of the subject to contract it away. It was, in the judgment of the umpire, entirely beyond the power of an Italian subject to extinguish the superior

In sum, the legacy of these proceedings seemed to favor the position of capital-exporting countries who would secure access for their nationals to an internationalized judge bound to apply national law but only within the limits imposed by international law.

Several years later, at the time when land nationalizations accelerated in Mexico and the government decided to nationalize its oil resources,[32] an intense diplomatic negotiation was engaged between the Mexican foreign minister, Eduardo Hay, and the United States Secretary of State, Cordell Hull, on the issue of compensation for the resulting expropriations. In a letter dated 21 July 1938, Hull stressed that Mexico was required to compensate the expropriated investors in accordance with international law:

> The taking of property without compensation is not expropriation. It is confiscation. It is no less confiscation because there may be an expressed intent to pay at some time in the future. If it were permissible for a government to take the private property of the citizens of other countries and pay for it as and when, in the judgment of that government, its economic circumstances and local legislation may perhaps permit, the safeguards which the constitutions of most countries and established international law have sought to provide would be illusory. Governments would be free to take property far beyond their ability or willingness to pay, and the owners thereof would be without recourse. We cannot question the right of a foreign government to treat its own nationals in this fashion if it so desires. This is a matter of domestic concern. But we cannot admit that a foreign government may take the property of American nationals in disregard for

---

right of his nation, and it is not to be presumed that Venezuela understood that he had done so", *Martini (Italy) v. Venezuela*, Award, R.I.A.A. Vol. X, 13 February 1903, p. 663.

[32] After the nationalization of the oil sector in Mexico, Venezuela imposed on the foreign owned oil concessions a 50–50 profit sharing in 1943 and formally nationalized foreign assets in the oil sector in 1976, see: Bye, V. (1979). Nationalization of Oil in Venezuela. Re-defined Dependence and Legitimization of Imperialism, *Journal of Peace Research*, 16, p. 57. For a general overview of Latin American expropriation phases, see: Wesley, 1971–1972, p. 232).

> the rule of compensation under international law. Nor can we admit that any government unilaterally and through its domestic legislation can, as in this instant case, nullify this universally accepted principle of international law, based as it is on reason, equity and justice.[33]

In his response, Hay counter-argued that international law did not impose an obligation of adequate compensation for the type of expropriation effected in Mexico, but that Mexico would be willing to pay compensation in accordance with domestic law.[34] Secretary Hull's famous response was that international law not only imposed a duty to compensate but that such compensation had to be "prompt, adequate and effective".[35] The issue of compensation will remain, for

[33] Note from the Secretary of State of the United States to the Mexican Ambassador at Washington, Department of State Press Release, No. 354, 21 July 1938. For the complete diplomatic exchange, see: American Journal of International Law, Supplement, 32, pp. 181–207. See also: Lowenfeld, 2008, pp. 475–481; Borchard, 1939–1940, p. 445.

[34] "As has been stated above, there does not exist, in international law, any principle universally accepted by countries, nor by the writers of treatises on this subject, that would render obligatory the giving of adequate compensation for expropriations of a general and impersonal character. Nevertheless Mexico admits, in obedience to her own laws, that she is indeed under obligation to indemnify in an adequate manner; but the doctrine which it maintains on the subject, which is based on the most authoritative opinions of writers of treatises on international law, is that the time and manner of such payment must be determined by her own laws"; Note from the Minister of Foreign Affairs of Mexico to the American Ambassador at Mexico City, Ministry of Foreign Relations of the United Mexican States, Mexico City, 3 August 1938, in *American Journal of International Law*, 32, p. 187.

[35] "The Government of the United States merely adverts to a self-evident fact when it notes that the applicable precedents and recognized authorities on international law support its declaration that, under every rule of law and equity, no government is entitled to expropriate private property, for whatever purpose, without provision for prompt, adequate and effective payment therefore. In addition, clauses appearing in the constitutions of almost all nations today, and in particular in the constitution of the American republics, embody the principle of just compensation. These, in themselves, are declaratory of the like principles of the law of nations"; Note from the Secretary of State of the United States to the Mexican Ambassador at Washington, Department of State Press Release, No. 398, 25 August 1938, in *American Journal of International Law*, 32, p. 193.

many decades, at the centre of the legal struggle over the legal framework applicable to foreign investment.

The foregoing considerations suggest that, by the end of the second phase, the struggle between capital-importing and capital-exporting countries had reached maturity, in that the legal position of each side was clearly established in principle and the focus moved on to the details. This state of the struggle can be illustrated by reference to Article VII of the American Treaty on Pacific Settlement, of 30 April 1948, most often referred to as the "Pact of Bogotá".[36] Article VII states that: "The High Contracting Parties bind themselves not to make diplomatic representations in order to protect their nationals, or to refer a controversy to a court of international jurisdiction for that purpose, when the said nationals have had available the means to place their case before competent domestic courts of the respective state".[37] In other words, resort to diplomatic protection and to international courts was open in case of denial of justice. Article V of the Pact further states that: "If the parties are not in agreement as to whether the controversy concerns a matter of domestic jurisdiction, this preliminary question shall be submitted to decision by the International Court of Justice, at the request of any of the parties". However, by this time, the subtleties surrounding the potential use of such clauses to broaden the access to international tribunals were better understood. Several Latin American countries formulated a reservation to Article V. Argentina stated, for instance, that:

> [t]he compulsory execution of arbitral or judicial decisions and the limitation which prevents the States from judging for themselves in regard to matters that pertain to their domestic jurisdiction in accordance with Article V are contrary to Argentine tradition. The

---

[36] American Treaty on Pacific Settlement (Pact of Bogotá), 30 April 1948, U.N.T.S. Vol. 30 (1949), p. 84.

[37] Comparable to Article VII of the Pact of Bogotá, the Charter of the Organization of American States says in its Article 16 that the "jurisdiction of States within the limits of their national territory is exercised equally over all the inhabitants, whether nationals or aliens"; Charter of the Organization of American States, 30 April 1948, U.N.T.S. Vol. 119 (1949), p. 48.

> protection of aliens, who in the Argentine Republic are protected by its Supreme Law to the same extent as the nationals, is also contrary to that tradition.[38]

The government of Peru also introduced a reservation to the second part of Article V, arguing that, "domestic jurisdiction should be defined by the State itself".[39] The fight over the details would become more intense in the following decades and, as we shall see next, it is the detail and not the principle that eventually prevailed.

13.4. FOREIGN INVESTMENT PROTECTION IN THE ERA OF DECOLONIZATION (1948–1990)

The end of the Second World War signaled the end of the colonial empires of the European powers. The decolonization process unleashed by the decline of the European powers' grip on Africa and Asia changed the balance of powers within the United Nations General Assembly in favor of developing countries. Starting in the 1950s and above all in the 1960s, the tensions between capital-exporting and capital-importing countries over the control of natural resources took a new turn. In this new quest, that will eventually lead to the affirmation of a "New International Economic Order" and, later on, to its demise, Latin American countries played a major role.

The initial step in this process was the adoption by the UN General Assembly of Resolution 1803 (XVII) entitled, "Permanent sovereignty over natural resources",[40] which followed an initiative taken 10 years earlier by two Latin American countries, Uruguay and Chile. This Resolution, which has been considered as an expression of

[38] *Ibid.*, p. 108.
[39] *Ibid.*, p. 110.
[40] UNGA Resolution 1803 (XVII) of 14 December 1962.

international customary law,[41] struck a delicate compromise between the interests of capital-importing and capital-exporting countries. The right to expropriate was recognized under certain conditions, notably the payment of an "appropriate compensation",

> in accordance with the *rules in force in the State taking such measures* in the exercise of its sovereignty *and* in accordance with *international law*. In any case where the question of compensation gives rise to a controversy, the *national jurisdiction* of the State taking such measures *shall be exhausted*. However, *upon agreement* by sovereign States and other parties concerned, *settlement of the dispute should be made through arbitration or international adjudication*.[42]

As is evident from the preceding paragraph, the determination of the "appropriate compensation" to be paid in case of expropriation is governed not only by the domestic law of the host State but also by international law. It then recognizes that, in case of a dispute over the determination of such compensation, the national courts of the host State will take priority, unless an agreement has been reached for the submission of such disputes to international adjudication. Thus formulated, Resolution 1803 (XVII) opened the door for two very different future scenarios.

Throughout the 1960s and the 1970s, the respective positions of capital-importing and capital-exporting countries became polarized. In 1974, the capital-importing countries used their majority to secure the adoption in the General Assembly of two controversial resolutions, i.e. Resolution 3201 (New International Economic Order) and 3281 (Charter of Economic Rights and Duties of States). Article 2 (c)

---

[41] *Texaco Overseas Petroleum Company/California Asiatic Oil Company v. Government of the Libyan Arab Republic* (19 January 1977), 17 International Legal Materials 1978, par. 87; *Libyan American Oil Company (LIAMCO) v. Government of the Libyan Arab Republic* (12 April 1977), 20 International Legal Materials, 1981, p. 103; *Case Concerning Armed Activities on the Territory of the Congo (Democratic Republic of the Congo v. Uganda)*, Judgement of 19 December 2005, International Court of Justice, par. 244.

[42] Emphasis added.

of the "Charter" took up the text of Resolution 1803 (XVII), however with a fundamental difference in that the "appropriate compensation" in case of expropriation was to be determined by the State, "taking into account its relevant laws and regulations and all circumstances that the State considers pertinent", and not on the basis of international law. In addition, disputes were to be settled in accordance with the "domestic legislation" of the host country and by the courts of this country, unless the Parties concerned agreed "freely" to resort to other methods of dispute settlement.[43] Therefore, the applicable law and the competent judge were, in principle, those of the host State. Unsurprisingly, several industrialized countries voted against this Resolution,[44] while others abstained.[45]

It must be noted, however, that these resolutions left open an exception, in cases where an agreement had been reached between the relevant States to use another method. Such exception reflected a strategy that had been actively pursued by the capital-exporting countries from the 1960s onwards in connection with both the applicable law and the competent courts. Regarding the first component of such strategy, the 1960s saw the emergence of bilateral investment treaties (BITs) between capital-exporting and capital-importing countries (see Salacuse, 2010; Dolzer and Stevens, 1995, pp. 1–2; Dolzer and

[43] UNGA Resolution 3281 (XXIX) of 12 December 1974. Although strongly opposed by capital-exporting States, the "Charter" already represents a milder version of the capital-importing states compared to UNGA Resolution 3171 (XXVIII) of 17 December 1973. This latter "[a]ffirms that the application of the principle of nationalization [···] implies that each State is entitled to determine the amount of possible compensation and the mode of payment, and that any disputes which might arise should be settled in accordance with the national legislation of each State carrying out such measures" (par. 3). Another milestone in the Latin American context is the adoption in December 1970 of the Andean Commission Foreign Investment Code, which provides, in Article 50, that member States shall not "grant to foreign investors any treatment more favorable than that granted to national investors"; cited in: Cremades, 2006, p. 57.

[44] Belgium, Denmark, Germany, Great Britain, Luxemburg, and the United States.

[45] Austria, Canada, France, Ireland, Israel, Italy, Japan, Netherlands, Norway, and Spain.

Schreuer, 2008, pp. 1–2).[46] The contents of such treaties have varied over time, but they basically provided for a number of investment protections, including the prohibition of expropriation without appropriate compensation and the obligation of host States to accord fair and equitable treatment to investments of the other contracting State (see, for instance, Dolzer, 2005, pp. 87–106). Such treaties were also important for the second component of the strategy, namely the determination of the methods for solving investment disputes. The main technique in this regard was the inclusion of clauses in such treaties allowing foreign investors from one contracting State to bring an investment claim against the other contracting State before an international arbitral tribunal. The development of such investment tribunals must be understood in the light of at least one major initiative undertaken during the 1960s, namely the creation of the International Centre for the Settlement of Investment Disputes (ICSID) in 1965.[47]

Much like the practice of BITs, the ICSID Convention is an interesting illustration of how the exception carved out in the texts of the aforementioned resolutions from the UN General Assembly would become increasingly important in practice. The balance of powers in the negotiation process of this convention was, however, quite different from the one prevailing in the General Assembly. This translated into a final text that tends to reflect the interests of capital-exporting countries,[48] despite efforts by developing countries, and particularly

---

[46] For a historical analysis of international investment agreements, see: Vandevelde, 2005–2006, p. 157.

[47] Convention on the Settlement of Investment Disputes between States and Nationals of Other States, 18 March 1965, U.N.T.S. Vol. 575 (1968).

[48] On the one hand, Article 25, paragraph 1 *in fine* of the ICSID Convention states that once the host state has given its consent to arbitrate it cannot withdraw its consent unilaterally. On the other hand, however, Article 26 provides that a "Contracting State may require the exhaustion of local administrative or judicial remedies as a condition of its consent to arbitration under this Convention". Furthermore, if a foreign investor consented to submit a dispute to ICSID arbitration, the home state is barred from exercising diplomatic protection. Article 27, paragraph 1 states: "No Contracting State shall give diplomatic protection, or bring an international claim, in respect of a dispute which one of its nationals and another

Latin American countries, to uphold their traditional position regarding national treatment and territorial jurisdiction. Indeed, at the Annual Meeting of the Board of Governors of the World Bank in Tokyo in 1964, where the resolution entrusting the Executive Directors of the World Bank with the task of drafting the future ICSID Convention was being discussed, the Governor for Chile spoke out on behalf of the Latin American States opposing the proposed system:

> [the] legal and constitutional systems of all the Latin American countries that are members of the Bank offer the foreign investor at the present time the same rights and protection as their own nationals; they prohibit confiscation and discrimination and require that any expropriation on justifiable grounds of public interest shall be accompanied by fair compensation fixed, in the final resort, by the law courts. The new system that has been suggested would give the foreign investor, by virtue of the fact that he is a foreigner, the right to sue a sovereign state outside its national territory, dispensing with the courts of law. This provision is contrary to the accepted legal principles of our countries and, *de facto*, would confer a privilege on the foreign investor, placing the nationals of the country concerned in a position of inferiority.[49]

The resolution was nevertheless adopted by the Board of Governors in Tokyo,[50] but with the only exceptions of Guyana and Trinidad

---

Contracting State shall have consented to submit or shall have submitted to arbitration under this Convention, unless such other Contracting State shall have failed to abide by and comply as a condition of its consent to arbitration under this Convention".

[49] Excerpt from the statement by Felix Ruiz, Governor for Chile, in ICSID (1968). *Convention on the Settlement of Investment Disputes between States and Nationals of Other States — Documents Concerning the Origin and the Formulation of the Convention*, Vol. II, Part 1, Washington, D.C., (Doc. 39, 9 September 1964, Tokyo), p. 606.

[50] Resolution No. 214 of the Board of Governors (10 September 1964), in ICSID (1968). *Convention on the Settlement of Investment Disputes between States and Nationals of Other States — Documents Concerning the Origin and the Formulation of the Convention*, Vol. II, Part 1, Washington, DC, (Doc. 39), p. 608. Apart from two other countries, all countries that voted against the resolution came from Latin

and Tobago, none of the Latin American States would become members to the ICSID Convention until the 1980s and especially the 1990s.[51]

Throughout this period, Latin American countries were generally reluctant to sign or ratify international agreements that sought to establish international arbitration procedures or even to ratify international agreements providing for the recognition of foreign arbitral decisions (see Abbott, 1976, p. 131; Summers, 1971–1972, p. 1; Grigera Naon, 1990–1991, pp. 219–225; Guzman, 1997–1998, p. 639). During the 1980s and, especially, the 1990s this reluctance faded away and was replaced with a new policy aimed at attracting foreign investment.

13.5. GLOBALIZATION AND FOREIGN INVESTMENT PROTECTION (1990–PRESENT)

The 1990s signaled the beginning of a profound change in the policies of several Latin American countries with respect to foreign investment. With the failure of the influential import-substitution industrialization model, such countries sought alternative strategies to modernize their economies and reform their public services. As part of such strategies, they took different measures to attract foreign investment, such as the ratification of a number of investor-friendly treaties (see Hamilton, 2008–2009, p. 1099),[52] including the ICSID

America: Argentina, Bolivia, Brazil, Chile, Colombia, Costa Rica, the Dominican Republic, Ecuador, El Salvador, Guatemala, Haiti, Honduras, Mexico, Nicaragua, Panama, Paraguay, Peru, Uruguay, and Venezuela.

[51] See: ICSID, List of Contracting States and other Signatories of the Convention (as of 7 January 2010). [Online] Available at: http://icsid.worldbank.org/ICSID/FrontServlet?requestType=ICSIDDocRH&actionVal=ShowDocument&language=English [Accessed 30 April 2010]. For an analysis of the reasons why the Latin American States refused to sign the ICSID Convention, see: Scasz, 1970–1971, p. 256).

[52] For an analysis of the economic incentives of states to sign BITs, see: Swenson, 2005–2006, p. 131; Hallward-Driemeier, 2003.

Convention,[53] the 1958 New York Convention on the Recognition and Enforcement of Foreign Arbitral Awards,[54] and the 1975 Inter-American Convention on International Commercial Arbitration.[55] Moreover, many Latin American countries also concluded numerous BITs with capital-exporting countries. For instance, between 1990 and 2002, Argentina signed over 50 BITs. A similar pattern characterizes the policies of other Latin American countries as well, including Bolivia (which signed 22 BITs between 1987 and 2002), Venezuela (which signed 22 BITs between 1993 and 2002), and Mexico (which signed 22 BITs between 1995 and 2006). The case of Brazil is somewhat different. Although it signed 12 BITs between 1994 and 1998, none of these treaties has entered into force.[56]

The effects, positive or negative, of this change of policy are still debated among observers of Latin American affairs. It seems clear, however, that such policies were quite successful in attracting foreign investment, but also resulted in a large number of investment claims being lodged against Latin American countries, mostly in the first decade of the twenty-first century (over 50 ICSID disputes against Argentina, 14 against Venezuela, 14 against Ecuador, 10 against Mexico, and 6 against Bolivia).[57] As a result, both foreign investment

---

[53] Notwithstanding significant exceptions, most notably Brazil and Mexico, all Latin American countries have ratified the ICSID Convention. Paraguay ratified the Convention in 1983, El Salvador in 1984, and Honduras in 1989. Chile and Grenada ratified the Convention in 1991, Costa Rica in 1993, Argentina in 1994, Nicaragua, Venezuela, and Bolivia in 1995, Panama in 1996, Colombia in 1997, Guatemala and Uruguay in 2003. Belize signed the Convention in 1986 and the Dominican Republic in 2000, but they did not yet ratify the Convention. Finally, Ecuador has been a party to the Convention between 1986 and 2010.

[54] Convention on the Recognition and Enforcement of Foreign Arbitral Awards, 10 June 1958, U.N.T.S., Vol. 330 (1959).

[55] Inter-American Convention on International Commercial Arbitration, 30 January 1975, U.N.T.S. Vol., 1438 (1996).

[56] See: SICE — Organization of American States Foreign Trade Information System, at www.oas.org. For information on the Brazilian model, see: Da Motta Veiga, 2004; Christiansen *et al.*, 2003; Hiratuka, 2009, pp. 33–51.

[57] A list of ICSID cases is available at: http://icsid.worldbank.org/ICSID/FrontServlet [Accessed 24 November 2010].

and the international legal framework put in place to attract it, have come under renewed criticism from Latin American countries. Some of these latter have therefore undertaken certain measures to reduce the impact of international investment law on their political margin of maneuver.

First, Latin American countries have grown reluctant to sign new BITs, and they are also trying to renegotiate existing BITs. Second, in those investment agreements that they nevertheless agree to sign, they try to avoid reference to investor–State arbitration under the ICSID Convention, providing instead for other types of international arbitration (e.g. *ad hoc* arbitration under the UNCITRAL rules; see García-Bolívar, 2009, pp. 39–41). Third, another indication of a reversal in the investment policy of the 1990s is the denunciation of the ICSID Convention, in accordance with its Article 71, by Bolivia, on 2 May 2007 (entry into force on 3 November 2007) and Ecuador, on 6 July 2009 (entry into force on 7 January 2010).[58] As an alternative to ICSID, some Latin American countries have proposed the creation of a regional centre for arbitration and conciliation within the framework of the UNASUR Treaty, signed on May 23, 2008, by Argentina, Bolivia, Brazil, Chile, Colombia, Ecuador, Guyana, Paraguay, Peru, Suriname, Uruguay and Venezuela.[59] The case of Ecuador is also interesting in another respect. In 1998, Ecuador adopted a new constitution which provides in its Article 14 for an implicit Calvo clause that applies to all State contracts concluded with foreign investors and according to which the investor recognizes the jurisdiction of domestic courts and waives his right to resort to diplomatic protection. This element is interesting to assess the persistence of Calvo's ideas in the policies adopted by Latin American countries. In his report on diplomatic protection, Special

[58] Ecuador has been a party to the Convention between 1986 and 2010. For an interesting discussion on the possible effects of such denunciations, see: Tietje *et al.*, 2008. See also: Cabrera, 2009.

[59] South American Union of Nations Constitutive Treaty, signed in Brasilia, 23 May 2008. Available on the UNASUR website: http://www.pptunasur.com/contenidos.php?menu=1&submenu1=10&idiom=1[Accessed 30 April 2010].

Rapporteur John Dugard analyzed the evolution of the Calvo Clause throughout the twentieth century. In the conclusions, he proposed to the Commission the inclusion in the working draft of a contemporary version of a Calvo clause, as a reflection of regional customary law:

> There are two options open to the Commission. The first is to decline to draft any provision on this subject on the grounds that a Calvo Clause is relevant and valid only insofar as it reaffirms the exhaustion of local remedies rule. To include such a provision would therefore be both unnecessary and superfluous. The second option is to draft a provision which limits the validity of the Calvo Clause to disputes arising out of the contract containing the clause and which recognizes that such a clause may give rise to a rebuttable presumption in favour of the exhaustion of local remedies, even where the compromise referring disputes between the State of nationality of the injured alien and the host State to judicial settlement contains a clause excluding the need to exhaust local remedies. Such a provision would reflect jurisprudence, doctrine, and, possibly, State practice on the Calvo Clause. While the Special Rapporteur accepts that there may be some merit in the first proposal, he prefers the latter, *as it would codify a customary rule of one of the major regions of the world* and provide clarity on the limits of a mechanism that has featured prominently in the history of this branch of the law. It is in this spirit that Article 16 is laid before the Commission. (Dugard, 2002, pp. 17–18, para. 39–40, emphasis added)

It is very difficult to assess whether the aforementioned indications of a policy reversal reflect a new phase of enduring hostility against foreign investors or, rather, are mere manifestations of passing hostility driven by short-term political calculations. From a legal standpoint, however, it appears that the international framework established by means of BITs and arbitration instruments will not be easily dismantled, if it is dismantled at all. It may therefore be interesting to mention briefly some of the techniques that this framework offers to balance the interests of capital-exporting and capital-importing countries. In this regard, one may distinguish between procedural and substantive developments.

Among the diverse array of procedural developments that have sprung from the recent surge in investment arbitration, we would like to focus on two, namely the trend towards more transparency in investment proceedings and the potential use of claims or counter-claims by host States in investment proceedings. In the last few years, the issue of transparency in investment arbitration has received sustained attention (see among others, Van Harten, 2007, pp. 153–163; Knahr and Reinisch, 2007, pp. 97–118). Specifically, several commentators have focused on the intervention of third parties in the capacity of "*amici curiae*" (friends of the court) to provide tribunals with information regarding the public dimension of a dispute (see Stern, 2007, pp. 280–348; Grisel and Viñuales, 2007, pp. 380–432; Triantafilou, 2008, pp. 571–586; Menetrey, 2008). Such intervention operates as a tool for representing sectors of the civil society of the host State that will or could be affected by the decision of the tribunal. At the same time, in practice, it provides support to certain types of arguments (use of regulatory powers, emergency and necessity clauses) most likely to be advanced by host States to justify their conduct towards investors. Another potential avenue would be the use by host States of the very mechanisms provided by international investment law to assert claims against foreign investors. One interesting illustration of this possibility is the claim brought by Nicaragua against a Spanish investor, Grupo Barceló, under the aegis of the ICSID Convention, for damages allegedly suffered in connection with the privatization of a tourist resort in the 1990s. This is a highly uncommon step for a State that, according to its Attorney General, considers ICSID as a pro-investor institution,[60] but it remains very

[60] See: "El Gobierno de Nicaragua demanda al Grupo Barceló por 30 milliones de dólares ante el CIADI", *Diario Nicaragua*, 26 June 2008, available at: http://www.diarionicaragua.es/__n265907__El_ Gobierno_de_Nicaragua_demanda_al_Grupo_Barcelo_por_30_millones_de_dolares_ante_el_CIADI.html [Accessed 24 November 2010].

interesting as a potential avenue to broaden the use of the current investment framework (Laborde, 2010, pp. 97–122).

Regarding substantive developments, we would like to mention two main issues, with different implications for the balancing of the interests of capital-exporting and capital-importing countries. The first issue concerns the increasing use of most-favored-nation (MFN) clauses to broaden access to arbitration.[61] Foreign investors have argued, with considerable success, that MFN clauses may be used to neutralize prior negotiation or domestic litigation requirements appearing in the arbitration clauses of a number of BITs.[62] More recently, it has even been argued,[63] and accepted in at least one case,[64]

[61] Stephan Schill discusses several manifestations of "treaty shopping", in particular the possibilities of circumventing pre-arbitration restrictions by allowing the investors to rely on shorter waiting periods contained in third-party BITs, the possibilities of benefiting from clauses contained in third-party BITs while not being bound by its more restrictive provisions, and the possibilities of asserting jurisdiction on the basis of disputed settlement clauses contained in third-party BITs (Schill, 2009, pp. 151–173).

[62] *Siemens v. Argentina*, Decision on Jurisdiction, 3 August 2004, ICSID Case No. ARB/02/8, par. 79–109; *Gas Natural DSG, S.A. v. Argentina*, Decision on Jurisdiction, 17 June 2005, ICSID Case No. ARB/03/10, par. 24–31, 41–49; *Suez Sociedad General de Aguas de Barcelona S.A., and InterAguas Servicios Integrales del Agua S.A. v. Argentina*, Decision on Jurisdiction, 16 May 2006, ICSID Case No. ARB/03/17, par. 52–66: *National Grid PCL v. Argentina*, Decision on Jurisdiction, 20 June 2006, Ad Hoc UNCITRAL Arbitration IIC 178 (2006), par. 53–94; *Suez, Sociedad General de Aguas de Barcelona S.A., and Vivendi Universal S.A. v. Argentina and AWG Group Ltd. V. Argentina*, Decision on Jurisdiction, 3 August 2006, ICSID Case No. ARB/03/19, par. 52–68.

[63] By Gaillard and Banifatemi (2005). Dolzer and Schreuer assert that "[s]ome BITs indicate whether an MFN clause applies to dispute settlement or not. In the absence of such an indication, there is no convincing reason for distinguishing between substantive standards and dispute settlement. As a matter of treaty interpretation, it is difficult to understand why a broadly formulated MFN clause that refers to 'treatment' should apply only to issues of substance, but not to questions of dispute settlement" (Dolzer and Schreuer, 2008, p. 257). See also: Gallagher and Shan, 2009, pp. 342–350.

[64] *RosInvestCo UK Ltd. v. The Russian Federation*, Award on Jurisdiction, October 2007, SCC Case No. V079/2005, par. 124–133.

that MFN clauses may serve to import altogether an arbitration clause from another "more favorable" treaty concluded by the host State, when the treaty on which the investor's claim is based does not contain one. From the perspective of our previous discussion regarding the arm wrestling between capital-importing and capital-exporting countries over the determination of the competent court, the current trend in the use of MFN clauses is clearly favorable to the latter. The second issue that deserves mention is the quite sophisticated case law that has developed in the last few years with respect to the scope of the necessity defense.[65] In at least two cases,[66] Argentina has successfully argued that the measures challenged by the foreign investors were adopted as a result of a state of necessity and were therefore justified under international law. Irrespective of the details of this case law and of their importance from a technical point of view, what must be emphasized is that international law does provide tools for shielding host States from investment claims. The necessity defense is one such tool, but there are others, including the police powers doctrine (see Christie, 1962, p. 307 *et seq.*; Newcombe, 2005, pp. 25–40) or the margin of appreciation of doctrine (see Arai-Takahashi, 2002; Hutchinson, 1999, pp. 638–650). More importantly, even the most restrictive tools, such as the necessity defense, are becoming operational in practice.

The fourth phase, characterized in the preceding paragraphs, is still open. Although it is difficult to make any predictions, the current trend seems to suggest that the international investment framework is here to stay, which means in turn that, from a legal standpoint, the legal concepts staunchly defended by capital-exporting countries have

[65] For a general overview, see: Reinisch (2007: 191). The most well known ICSID cases are: *CMS Gas Transmission Company v. Argentina*, Award, 12 May 2005, ICSID Case No. ARB/01/8; *Enron Corporation and Ponderosa Assets, LP v. Argentina*, Award, 22 May 2007, ICSID Case No. ARB/01/3; *LG&E v. Argentine Republic*, Decision on Liability, 3 October 2006, ICSID Case No. ARB/02/1.

[66] *LG&E v. Argentine Republic*, Decision on Liability, 3 October 2006, ICSID Case No. ARB/02/1, par. 201–266; *Continental Casualty Company v. Argentine Republic*, Award, 5 September 2008, ICSID Case No. ARB/03/9, par. 160 *et seq.*

for the most part prevailed. As a result, the centre of the legal struggle between capital-exporting and capital-importing countries has moved on to another stage, where international law and international jurisdictions are called to play a dominant role.

13.6. CONCLUSION

In assessing the conclusion that closes part IV of our discussion, the reader may have the impression that the struggle for economic emancipation, at least in its legal dimension, has not turned out well for many Latin American countries. In other words, the foregoing considerations may give the impression that capital-exporting countries clearly prevailed in the historical arm wrestling match engaged with capital-importing countries of Latin America. Whereas such an impression is not fundamentally inaccurate, it must be subject to two important nuances.

First and foremost, different capital-importing countries both within and outside Latin America have undergone different processes. Conclusions cannot be drawn for Latin America or for capital-importing countries as a whole without keeping very clearly in mind that the path followed by each country presents many particular features. For instance, Brazil has not taken part in the fourth phase in the same way as countries such as Argentina or Mexico. The impact of the international investment framework on Brazil's economic development is therefore much more limited than in other Latin American countries. Moreover, some countries that were formerly considered as capital-importers, such as China, now behave as capital-exporters in many respects. The BITs concluded by China throughout the third phase contained clauses restricting the availability of arbitration to disputes over the amount of compensation for expropriation (Schill, 2007, pp. 89–91).[67] Conversely, the more recent Chinese BITs, concluded with a number of capital-importing

[67] For instance, Article 13(3) of the 1985 Sino-Singaporean BIT reads in relevant parts as follows: "If a dispute involving the amount of compensation resulting from expropriation, nationalization, or other measures having effect equivalent to

African States, are much like those model BITs elaborated by capital-exporting countries and provide wide access to arbitration.[68] A similar transformation could also be undergone by some Latin American countries in the future.

Second, the advent of the current regime is largely due to the efforts of capital-importing countries, including many Latin American countries, to attract foreign investment. These efforts were undertaken partly as a result of the failure of the import-substitution industrialization model. The analysis of the reasons explaining such failure as well as of those underlying the new wave of investor-friendly policies must, of course, take into account many country specificities. It is a fact, however, that during the 1980s and, especially, the 1990s foreign investment became an important alternative to the previous model, and that, in seeking to attract investment, each Latin American country established a legal framework according to its particular needs. The specific features of each framework were important in a context where competition for foreign investment was keen. At the same time, a more competitive framework entailed also greater exposure to claims brought by foreign investors. The balance between competitiveness and exposure was thus struck by each country in furtherance of its political and economic strategy.

Thus, whereas the current legal framework governing foreign investment attaches great importance to international adjudication and to the application of international law, this is not to say that capital-importing countries did not play a role, and even a fundamental one, in the shaping of such framework. Whether the choices underlying such framework are a reflection of economic emancipation or, instead, of

---

nationalization or expropriation ... cannot be settled within six months after resort to negotiation ... by the national or company concerned, it may be submitted to an international arbitral tribunal established by both parties" (cited in Schill, 2007: 90). See also: Gallagher and Shan, 2009, p. 39.

[68] See e.g. the Chinese Model BIT (2003), which provides in its Article 9 for arbitral dispute settlement for "any legal dispute" in connection with an investment under the aegis of ICSID, cited in: Dolzer and Schreuer, 2008, p. 357). See also: Gallagher and Shan, 2009, pp. 43–46, p. 301).

economic dependency cannot be determined in general. It is a question that must rather be answered for each specific country at a given point in time. And depending on what the answer is, foreign investment will be the object of love or that of hatred.

BIBLIOGRAPHY

Abbott, A. F. (1976). Latin America and international arbitration conventions: The quandary of non-ratification, *Harvard International Law Journal*, 17, pp. 131–140.

Amador, F. V. (1958). State responsibility. Some new problems, *Recueil des cours de l'Académie de droit international*, 94, p. 369.

Arai-Takahashi, Y. (2002). *The Margin of Appreciation Doctrine and the Principle of Proportionality in the Jurisprudence of the ECHR*, Intersentia, Antwerp.

Auslin, M. R. (2004). *Negotiating with Imperialism: The Unequal Treaties and the Culture of Japanese Diplomacy*, Harvard University Press, Cambridge, MA.

Bello, A. (1883). *Principios de Derecho Internacional*, 1st ed., Imprenta Dubrull, Madrid, Imprenta La Opinión, Santiago de Chile, 1832.

Berstein, S. and Milza, P. (1996). *Histoire du XIXe siècle*, Hatier, Paris.

Bethell, L. (ed.) (1986). *The Cambridge History of Latin America*, Vol. IV, Cambridge University Press, Cambridge.

Borchard, E. (1913). Basic Elements of Diplomatic Protection of Citizens Abroad, *American Journal of International Law*, 7, pp. 497–520.

Borchard, E. (1930). 'Responsibility of States' at the Hague Codification Conference, *American Journal of International Law*, 24, pp. 517–540.

Borchard, E. (1931). La responsabilité des Etats à la Conférence de codification de La Haye, *Revue de droit international et de législation comparée*, XII, Série 3, Bruxelles.

Borchard, E. (1939–1940). The "Minimum Standard" of the Treatment of Aliens, *Michigan Law Review*, 38, pp. 445–461.

Bye, V. (1979). Nationalization of Oil in Venezuela. Re-defined Dependence and Legitimization of Imperialism, *Journal of Peace Research*, 16, pp. 57–78.

Cabrera, F. (2009). Quiborax claim against Bolivia continues; may provide first decision on effects of ICSID exit, *Investment Treaty News*, 3 November 2009.

Calvo, C. (1896). *Le droit international théorique et pratique*, Arthur Rousseau, Paris.

Christiansen, H., Oman, C., Charlton, A. (2003). *Incentives-based Competition for Foreign Direct Investment: The Case of Brazil*, OECD Working Papers on International Investment, Number 2003/1. [Online] Available at: http://www.oecd.org/dataoecd/52/40/2500995.pdf [Accessed 24 November 2010].

Christie, G. C. (1962). What Constitutes a Taking of Property Under International Law, *British Yearbook of International Law*, 38, pp. 307–338.

Cremades, B. M. (2006). Resurgence of the Calvo Doctrine in Latin America, *Business Law International*, 7, pp. 53–72.

Da Motta Veiga, P. (2004). *Foreign Direct Investment in Brazil: Regulations, Flows and Contribution to Development.* [Online] Available at: http://www.iisd.org/pdf/2004/investment_country_report_brazil.pdf [Accessed 30 April 2010].

Dawson, F. G. (1986). The influence of Andres Bello on Latin American perceptions of Non-Intervention and State Responsibility, *British Year Book of International Law*, 57, pp. 253–316.

Dent, D. W. (1999). *The Legacy of the Monroe Doctrine. A Reference Guide to U.S. Involvement in Latin America and the Caribbean*, Greenwood Press, Westport.

Dolzer, R. (2005). Fair and Equitable Treatment: A Key Standard in Investment Treaties, *International Lawyer (ABA)*, 39, pp. 87–106.

Dolzer, R. and Schreuer, C. (2008). *Principles of International Investment Law*, Cambridge University Press, Cambridge.

Dolzer, R. and Stevens, M. (1995). *Bilateral Investment Treaties*, Kluwer Law International, The Hague.

Drago, L.M. (1907). State Loans in Their Relation to International Policy, *American Journal of International Law*, 1, pp. 692–726.

Dugard, J. (2002). *Third Report on Diplomatic Protection, International Law Commission*, Doc. A/CN.4/523/Add.1, 16 April 2002.

Fairbank, J. K., Reischauer, E. O. and Craig, A. M. (1989). *East Asia: Tradition and Transformation*, Houghton Mifflin, Boston.

Forbes, I. L. D. (1978). The German Participation in the Allied Coercion of Venezuela 1902–1903, *Australian Journal of Politics & History*, 24, pp. 317–331.

Freeman, A. V. (1946). Recent aspects of the Calvo Doctrine and the Challenge to International Law, *American Journal of International Law*, 40, pp. 121–147.

Gaillard, E. and Banifatemi, Y. (2005). Establishing Jurisdiction Through a Most-Favored-Nation Clause, *New York Law Journal*, 233, 105. [Online] Available at: http://www.shearman.com/files/Publication/96d2288c-0c69-4fd6-b306-07a676768572/Presentation/PublicationAttachment/4153cee7-3402-4cbf-8631-09c534add1da/IA_060205.pdf [Accessed 10 March 2011].

Gallagher, N. and Shan, W. (2009). *Chinese Investment Treaties. Policies and Practice*, Oxford University Press, Oxford.

García-Amador, F. V. (1958). State Responsibility. Some New Problems, *Recueil des cours de l'Académie de droit international*, 94, p. 369.

García-Bolívar, O. (2009). 'Sovereignty vs Investment Protection: Back to Calvo?', in *50 Years of Bilateral Investment Treaties Conference 2009 — Taking Stock and a Look to the Future*, Session Outlines, Frankfurt am Main, 1–3 December 2009.

Grigera Naon, H. A. (1990–1991). Arbitration in Latin America: Overcoming Traditional Hostility (An Update), *University of Miami Inter-American Law Review*, 22, pp. 203–257.

Grisel, F. and Viñuales, J. E. (2007). *L'amicus curiae* dans l'arbitrage d'investissement, *ICSID Review*, 22(2), pp. 349–401.

Guzman, A. T. (1997–1998). Why LDCs Sign Treaties That Hurt Them: Explaining the Popularity of Bilateral Investment Treaties, *Virginia Journal of International Law*, 38, pp. 639–688.

Hallward-Driemeier, M. (2003). Do Bilateral Investment Treaties Attract FDI? Only a bit ... and they could bite, *The World Bank, Policy Research Working Paper No. 3121*.

Hamilton, J. C. (2008–2009). Three Decades of Latin American Commercial Arbitration, *University of Pennsylvania Journal of International Law*, 30, pp. 1099–1119.

Herschley, A. S. (1907). The Calvo and Drago Doctrine, *American Journal of International Law*, 1, pp. 26–45.

Hicks, F. C. (1908). Equality of States and the Hague Conferences, *American Journal of International Law*, 2, pp. 530–556.

Hiratuka, C. (2009). 'Islands of Possibility: MNCs and Economic Development in Brazil', in Gallagher, K. and Chudnovsky, D. (eds), *Rethinking Foreign Investment for Sustainable Development. Lessons from Latin America*, Anthem Press, London, pp. 33–50.

Hutchinson, M. (1999). The Margin of Appreciation Doctrine in the European Court of Human Rights, *International and Comparative Law Quarterly*, 48, p. 638.

James, C. A. (1980). Great Capitalists and the Direction of British Overseas Investment in the Late Nineteenth Century: The Case of Argentina, *Business History*, 22, pp. 152–169.

Jones, C. (1980). 'Business Imperialism' and Argentina, 1875–1900: A theoretical note, *Journal of Latin American Studies*, 12, pp. 437–444.

Jones, C. (1995). 'Los antecedentes de la moderna corporación transnacional: los grupos de inversión británicos en América Latina', in Marichal, C. (ed.). *Historia de la deuda externa de America Latina*, Alianza Editorial, Madrid, pp. 70–95.

Knahr, C. and Reinisch, A. (2007). Transparency versus Confidentiality in International Investment Arbitration — The *Biwater Gauff* Compromise, *The Law and Practice of International Courts and Tribunals*, 6, pp. 97–118.

Laborde, G. (2010). The Case for Host State Claims in Investment Arbitration, *Journal of International Dispute Settlement*, 1, pp. 97–122.

Livingstone, G. (2009). *America's Backyard. The United States and Latin America from the Monroe Doctrine to the War on Terror*, Zed Books, London.

Lorimer, J. (2005). *The Institutes of the Law of Nations. A Treatise of the Jural Relations of Separate Political Communities*, Vol. I, The Lawbook Exchange, New Jersey.

Lowenfeld, A. F. (2008). *International Economic Law*, Oxford University Press, Oxford.

Marichal, C. (1988). *Historia de la deuda externa de America Latina*, Alianza Editorial, Madrid.

Marichal, C. (ed.) (1995). *Las inversiones extranjeras en América Latina, 1850–1930*, Fideicomiso Historia de Las Américas, México.

Mauro, F. (1995). 'Las empresas francesas y América Latina, 1850–1930', in Marichal, C. (ed.) *Las inversiones extranjeras en América Latina, 1850–1930*, Fideicomiso Historia de Las Américas, México, pp. 53–67.

Menetrey, S. (2008). *L'amicus curiae, vers un principe de droit international procédural?*, Ph.D. dissertation, Université Panthéon-Assas, Paris — Université Laval, Québec.

Montt, S. (2009). What International Investment Law and Latin America can and should demand from each other. Updating the Bello/Calvo Doctrine in the BIT Generation, *Workshop in Global Administrative Law Issues in Latin America.*

Moore, J. B. (1906). *A Digest of International Law as Embodied in Diplomatic Discussions, Treaties and Other International Agreements*, Government Printing Office, Washington, DC.

Newcombe, A. (2005). The Boundaries of Regulatory Expropriation in International Law, *ICSID Review*, 20(1), pp. 1–57.

Oppenheim, L. (1905). *International Law. A Treatise*, Longmans, Green & Co., London.

Perkins, D. (1941). *A History of the Monroe Doctrine*, Little, Brown and Company, Boston.

Platt, D. C. M. (1962). The Allied Coercion of Venezuela, 1902–03, A Reassessment, *Inter-American Economic Affairs*, 15, pp. 3–28.

Platt, D. C. M. (1980). British Portfolio Investment Overseas Before 1870: Some Doubts, *The Economic History Review*, 33, pp. 1–16.

Queuille, P. (1969). *L'Amérique latine. La doctrine Monroe et le panaméricanisme*, Payot, Paris.

Ralston, J. H. (1904). *Venezuelan Arbitrations of 1903, including Protocols, Personnel and Rules of Commissions, Opinions, and Summary of Awards*, Government Printing Office, Washington, DC.

Regalsky, A. (1995). 'Las compañías francesas de ferrocarriles y su repercusión en el desarrollo regional de Santa Fé y Buenos Aires, 1880–1930', in Marichal, C. (ed.), *Las inversiones extranjeras en América Latina, 1850–1930*, Fideicomiso Historia de Las Américas, México, pp. 193–213.

Reinisch, A. (2007). Necessity in International Investment Arbitration — An Unnecessary Split of Opinions in Recent ICSID Cases? Comments on CMS v. Argentina and LG&E v. Argentina, *Journal of World Investment & Trade*, 8, pp. 191–214.

Richardson, H. W. (1972). British Emigration and Overseas Investment, 1870–1914, *Economic History Review*, 25, pp. 99–113.

Rippy, J. F. (1929). *Rivalry of the United States and Great Britain over Latin America, 1808–1830*, The Johns Hopkins Press, Baltimore.

Rippy, J. F. (1932). *Historical Evolution of Hispanic America*, F. S. Crofts & Co., New York.

Rippy, J. F. (1948). *French Investments in Latin America*, Inter-American Economic Affairs, Washington, DC.

Rippy, J. F. (1954). The Venezuelan Claims Settlements of 1903–1905, *Inter-American Economic Affairs*, 7, pp. 65–77.

Rippy, J. F. (1959). *British Investments in Latin America, 1822–1849: A Case Study in the Operations of Private Enterprise in Retarded Regions*, University of Minnesota Press, Minneapolis.

Rivier, A. (1896). *Principes du droit des gens*, Tome I, A. Rousseau, Paris.

Robertson, W. S. (1923). *Hispanic-American Relations with the United States*, Oxford University Press, New York.

Robertson, W. S. (1932). *History of the Latin American States*, D. Appleton and Company, New York.

Root, E. (1910). The Basis of Protection to Citizens Residing Abroad, *American Journal of International Law*, 4, pp. 517–528.

Rosenne, S. (1975). *League of Nations Conference for the Codification of International Law [1930]*, Vol. IV, Oceana Publications, New York.

Salacuse, J. W. (2010). *The Law of Investment Treaties*, Oxford University Press, Oxford.

Scasz, P. C. (1970–1971). The Investment Disputes Convention and Latin America, *Virginia Journal of International Law*, 11, pp. 256–265.

Schill, S. W. (2007). Tearing down the great wall: The new generation investment treaties of the People's Republic of China, *Cardozo Journal of International and Comparative Law*, 15, pp. 73–118.

Schill, S. W. (2009). *The Multilateralization of International Investment Law*, Cambridge University Press, Cambridge.

Scott, G. W. (1908). Hague Convention Restricting the Use of Force to Recover on Contract Claims, *American Journal of International Law*, 2, pp. 78–94.

Scott, J. B. (1909). *The Hague Peace Conferences of 1899 and 1907*, Vol. I, The Johns Hopkins Press, Baltimore.

Scott, J. B. (1931). *The International Conferences of American States (1889–1928)*, Carnegie Endowment, New York.

Smith, R. F. (1986). 'Latin America, the United States and the European Powers, 1830–1930', in Bethell, L. (ed.), *The Cambridge History of Latin America*, Vol. IV, Cambridge University Press, Cambridge, pp. 83–120.

Smith, G. (1994). *The Last Years of the Monroe Doctrine, 1945–1993*, Hill and Wang, New York.

Stern, B. (2007). Civil Society's Voice in the Settlement of International Economic Disputes, *ICSID Review*, 22(2), pp. 280–348.

Stone, I. (1968). British Long-Term Investment in Latin America, 1865–1913, *Business History Review*, 42, pp. 311–339.

Stone, I. (1977). British Direct and Portfolio Investment in Latin America before 1914, *The Journal of Economic History*, 37, pp. 690–722.

Summers, L. A. (1971–1972). Arbitration and Latin America, *California Western International Law Journal*, 3, pp. 1–20.

Swenson, D. L. (2005–2006). Why Do Developed Countries Sign BITs?, *University of California Davis Journal of International Law & Policy*, 12, pp. 131–155.

Tamburini, F. (2002). Historia y destino de la "doctrina Calvo": ¿Actualidad u obsolescencia del pensamiento de Carlos Calvo?, *Revista de Estudios Histórico-Jurídicos*, No. 24, Valparaíso, Chile. [Online] Available at: http://www.scielo.cl/scielo.php?pid=s0716-54552002002400005&script=sci_arttext [Accessed 24 November 2010].

Thomas, A. B. (1956). *Latin America. A History*, The Macmillan Company, New York.

Tietje, C., Nowrot, K. and Wackernagel, C. (2008). Once and Forever? The Legal Effects of a Denunciation of ICSID, *Beiträge zum Transnationalen Wirtschaftsrecht*, Heft 74.

Triantafilou, E. (2008). Amicus Submissions in Investor-State Arbitration after Suez v. Argentina, *Arbitration International*, 24(4), pp.571–586.

Vandevelde, K. J. (2005–2006). A Brief History of International Investment Agreements, *University of California Davis Journal of International Law & Policy*, 12, pp. 157–194.

Van Harten, G. (2007). *Investment Treaty Arbitration and Public Law*, Oxford University Press, Oxford.

Wang, D. (2005). *China's Unequal Treaties: Narrating National History*, Lexington Books, Lanham.

Webster, C. K. (1938). *Britain and the Independence of Latin America, 1812–1830*, Vol. I, Oxford University Press, London.

Wesley, R. C. (1971–1972). Expropriation Challenge in Latin America: Prospects for Accord on Standards and Procedures, *Tulane Law Review*, 46, pp. 232–291.

Wheaton, H. (1916). *Elements of International Law*, 5th ed., Stevens and Sons, London.

Whitaker, A. P. (1941). *The United States and the Independence of Latin America, 1800–1930*, The John Hopkins Press, Baltimore.

Young, G. F. W. (1995). 'Los bancos alemanes y la inversión directa alemana en América Latina, 1880–1930', in Marichal, C. (ed.), *Las inversiones extranjeras en América Latina, 1850–1930*, Fideicomiso Historia de Las Américas, México, pp. 96–124.

Chapter

14

Latin American Regionalism and the Role of UN-ECLAC, 1948–2010

Edgard Moncayo, Philippe De Lombaerde and Oscar Guinea Ibáñez

14.1. INTRODUCTION

The UN Economic Commissions have played an important role in support of regional integration worldwide. Among them, the Economic Commission for Latin America and the Caribbean (ECLAC) has historically been the most prominent and influential.

In this chapter, the role of ECLAC regarding the development of post-Second World War regionalism in Latin America is sketched. We will suggest that three historical periods can thereby be distinguished and we will show how ECLAC has re-adapted its position in the transition from one period to another. And although ECLAC has perhaps not preserved the intellectual leadership that it had in the first historical period, we will argue that ECLAC still has an important role to play in the current period of "post-new-regionalism".

The following section is devoted to the first phase of regional integration in Latin America, a period in which the role of ECLAC is essential to understand the role that was attributed to regional integration within the context of reaching the policy objectives of industrialization and economic development. The third section deals with the second phase of regionalism, which follows the collapse of the import substitution industrialization (ISI) strategy and the "debt crisis", and in which ECLAC proposed a "third way" between the neo-liberal model and the former ISI strategy, defined as "open regionalism". The fourth section presents the current reformulation of ECLAC's position vis-à-vis Latin American regionalism. Finally, the last section presents our conclusions.

14.2. FIRST PHASE: INTEGRATION AS A PLATFORM FOR DEVELOPMENT

Early regionalism in Latin America found its concrete expression in the Latin America Free Trade Association — LAFTA — (1960), the Central American Common Market (1960), the Caribbean Free Trade Association — CARIFTA — (1968), and the Cartagena Agreement (1969). This first generation of integrationist schemes in the region, contemporary to the European integration process, had a common denominator: trade liberalization. Moreover, in the case of the Cartagena Agreement (Andean Group), the Central American Common Market and CARICOM, the ambition to create a common market required the creation of a customs union. These treaties, especially the Central American and Andean ones, pursued long term development goals, based on large scale industrialization and productive complementarities among associated states.

Unlike the European experience, where the political impulse was essential, Latin American postwar regionalism originated from predominantly economic considerations. Structural economic factors such as the narrowness of national markets (even worsened by the unequal distribution of income), difficulties in the balance of payments, and the need to accelerate employment creation in order to absorb the demographic explosion, explain the necessity for regional cooperation to ultimately foster economic growth and social development.

In this regard, the role of ECLAC was fundamental. ECLAC was established in 1948, after a decision of the United Nations in 1947.[1] During the 1950s, ECLAC endeavoured a systematic and coherent approach to Latin American development. Based on the "Economic Survey of Latin America, 1948" and Raul Prebisch's seminal contribution, "Economic Development of Latin America and its Principal Problems", published in 1949, (as a prologue of the "Economic Survey...") and supported by a group of remarkable intellectuals under the leadership of Prebisch himself, ECLAC developed the well known "Latin American structuralism" theory, building a truly integrated concept of development. Thus ECLAC's theoretical framework dealt with growth, capital accumulation, structural change, technological progress, income distribution, and international integration of the peripheral economies (Rodríguez, 2006).

The main ideas of ECLAC at the time were closely linked to the proposals developed by structuralist authors such as Kuznetz, Hirschman, Myrdal, and Kaldor, and therefore industrialization was considered as the most appropriate means to achieve higher levels of development. These common approaches and the influence of those authors in development policies in many peripheral countries (not only in Latin America, but also elsewhere in countries such as Egypt and India), represented what Ranis (2004) called a "Postwar consensus".

ECLAC's understanding of industrialization was justified in different ways: (i) industrialization is an endogenous source of growth thus overcoming the external vulnerability caused by the deterioration of the terms of trade; (ii) it generates endogenous technological changes; (iii) it increases employment thus absorbing the excess of labor supply from the agricultural sector; and (iv) the enhancement of the industrialized sector, full employment and the increase of productivity and wages contribute to improving the income distribution and to overcoming long term structural poverty (Fitzgerald, 1998).

[1] To be more precise, in 1948 the UN Economic Commission for Latin America (UN-ECLA) was established; only in 1984 was a Resolution was adopted, changing its name to UN Economic Commission for Latin America and the Caribbean (UN-ECLAC).

Furthermore, in the four above-mentioned aspects, the participation of the state through trade policies, incentives for production, and the coordination and planning of public investment were all essential elements. The support of Latin American integration followed logically from the economic rationale behind the analytical framework articulated by ECLAC. The Commission strived for the liberalization of commercial exchanges between countries in the region in order to overcome the limitations of domestic markets, to maximize the economies of scale and to widen the scope of import substitution to a regional level (Wionczek, 1964: XVII).

ECLAC's work in that period was compiled in the report, "The Latin American Common Market and the multilateral payment systems", presented by the Executive Secretary in 1959. According to the document "[...] the common market aims at the creation of a new and more suitable model for Latin American trade in order to meet the need for industrialization and reduce external vulnerability"[2] (CEPAL, 1959, pp. 330). It must be emphasized that the document rejects any plan or pretension of self-sufficiency in a clear, categorical, and resolute way. On the contrary, the idea of integration as a platform to improve the international inclusion of Latin America (i.e. beyond the region) is stressed throughout the report (CEPAL, 1959, pp. 334–337). Besides, ECLAC's integrationist proposals were not hostile to foreign direct investment (FDI). For ECLAC, foreign capital inflows should play an important role in facilitating the necessary conditions for endogenous growth (CEPAL, 1959, pp. 345). Nevertheless, the report states that a restructuring of trade policies in the core countries is required in order to achieve the double goal of boosting trade with the rest of the world and within the region (CEPAL, 1959, p. 37).

Regarding operational aspects, ECLAC proposed an integration model with the following characteristics: (i) a common market open to every Latin American country, with a common external tariff and universal product coverage, to be achieved in stages; (ii) the harmonization of industrial policies and industrial agreements in order to

---

[2] Our translation.

encourage an advanced phase of import substitution; (iii) special treatment for relatively less developed countries and for the traditional agricultural sector; (iv) safeguard clauses for sensitive products and compensation mechanisms to assure an equitable distribution of benefits; (v) a multilateral payments agreement; and (vi) a state-run integration with an active role for the private sector.

According to Cardozo (1977), the 1960s were the "Golden Age" of ECLAC. There was a full convergence between its ideas on development driven by industrialization and the need to enhance markets through integration on the one hand, and the policies adopted by policy-makers, on the other. Regional integration was conceived by ECLAC as a tool to finally break with low productivity levels in Latin American economies, and was pursued in order to achieve three interdependent objectives: accelerating growth, expanding and diversifying exports, and moving forward with the process of industrialization (Tavares, 1998, p. 202).

ECLAC's theoretical framework and policy recommendations on regional integration materialized in different regional agreements.[3] However, the scope and intensity of the agreements varied between cases. For instance, the Treaty of Montevideo (1960) establishing LAFTA reflected the majority of elements of ECLAC's proposal, albeit in a shallow version.

The Treaty of Managua, however, was more ambitious and aimed at the creation of a common market, a customs union, an accelerated program of trade liberalization, an industrial development plan, and cooperation in areas such as infrastructure and investment financing. This "General Treaty on Central American Economic Integration" was signed in Managua (Nicaragua) by Guatemala, El Salvador, Honduras, and Nicaragua in 1960, culminating a process that started in the preceding decade with ECLAC's active support.[4] In order to

[3] The ideas concerning the linkage between industrialization and regional integration were also echoed outside the region. In the 1970s, for example, ASEAN countries also embarked upon a common industrial policy. See e.g. ASEAN (1980, 1981), Imada (1993), De Lombaerde (1994).

[4] Costa Rica joined in 1962.

pursue the goals of the treaty, the Central American Bank for Economic Integration was also created in 1960. A multilateral payments system was established in 1961, and in 1964 the Agreement for the establishment of the Central American Monetary Union was formalized, although it was never completely implemented.

During the first years of LAFTA, the liberalization of commercial exchanges was very limited and mainly concentrated on raw materials and foodstuff coming from Argentina and Brazil, and on a smaller scale from Uruguay and Paraguay (Cline, 1983, p. 317). This led Colombia's President, Lleras Restrepo, and Chile's President, Frei, to propose to the other Andean countries a more ambitious sub-regional agreement. In 1969, Bolivia, Colombia, Chile, Ecuador, and Peru concluded the Cartagena Agreement (Andean Group), also joined by Venezuela in 1973 (whereas Chile left in 1976).[5] The Andean Group aspired to become a common market with harmonized economic policies towards third countries. A common external tariff and a common regime for FDI and technology were designed. Furthermore, as one of its major objectives, the Andean Group sought to balance sub-regional growth. Therefore, a regime of preferential treatment for the less developed countries i.e. Bolivia and Ecuador was formalized in the final agreement. Among its main mechanisms, a policy of integrated industrial policies was foreseen to jointly develop new industrial sectors.[6]

In 1973, Prebisch declared enthusiastically that the scheme of the Cartagena Agreement overcame many of LAFTA's limitations. One of the strengths of the Andean Group, underlined by Prebisch, was the existence of an Executive Secretariat which, similar to ECLAC, had the legal and technical capability to act in accordance with the collective objectives and independently from the member states' interests (Prebisch, 1973, pp. 34–35). Prebisch was thereby probably inspired by the neo-functionalist literature on the European integration

[5] Colombia, Ecuador and Venezuela constituted the Great Colombia in the beginning of the nineteenth century.

[6] Puyana (1984) presents a complete analysis of the first phases and achievements of the Andean Group.

process, which also stressed very much the role of supra-national institutions in the integration process.[7] Devlin and Estevadeordal (2001, p. 2) argue that the Andean model of integration is a good synthesis of the first wave of Latin American regionalism.

However, in spite of ECLAC's efforts to support and encourage all these different initiatives, the first wave of regional integration did not perform as expected. Latin American integration met serious difficulties. Firstly, unlike the European Economic Community which departed from relatively homogeneous national structures combined with strong economic interdependence, Latin America showed a high degree of "structural heterogeneity". This term, developed by the prominent ECLAC economist Aníbal Pinto, refers to the coexistence of several "modern clusters" — composed by export activities (primary commodities) and industrial activities, with good productivity performance — and "primitive" economic sectors which had not experienced structural changes since colonial times. Consequently, almost half of the Latin American population was not directly connected to the dynamics of the modern capitalist market integration.

Secondly, the governmental elites of the region showed a lack of commitment regarding the adoption of harmonized macroeconomic policies. In practice, each country continued its exchange rate, fiscal and monetary policies, addressing their domestic needs, disregarding the declared objectives of intensifying cooperation within the region.

Thirdly, difficulties associated with the adopted integration models were noticed, such as: exclusive trade orientation and weak institutional basis in LAFTA; unrealistic objectives in terms of joint industrialization; and very complex institutional structures in the cases of the Andean Group and the Central American Common Market.

Finally, the import substitution strategy was incoherently implemented. Some of the most serious limitations of this strategy in Latin America were: the existence of tariff patterns that provided exaggerated protection to consumer goods at the cost of the internal production of machinery and other equipment; lack of interest in

[7] See Haas (1958, 1961) and others.

export development; excessive intrusion by multinational companies; and absence of endogenous technical progress. In these circumstances, the "modern" industrial sector was unable to deploy Kaldor's virtuous cycles — which had characterized industrialization in advanced countries — at the regional level as it was proposed by ECLAC.

Nevertheless, between the 1960s and 1970s, Latin American economic interdependence — as a measure of the level of integration — achieved some significant successes, at least when measured in trade terms. The intra-regional trade share (measured by exports) in LAFTA's member states went from 6.7% in 1961 to 14% in 1980 (ALADI, 1983),[8] growing even more in the Central American Common Market.[9]

However, one should be careful with the supposed causalities between industrialization, economic interdependence, and regional integration. As explained by ECLAC economist Osvaldo Sunkel (1991), the relative success on the import substitution strategy, at least in large countries such as Mexico and Brazil, was not attained owing to the positive dynamics of regional integration. Between the 1960s and 1970s the inward-looking industrialization process was significantly influenced by foreign direct investment. The widening of the internal market was led by multinational companies which attached to regional integration process — compared to ECLAC's proposals — a completely different logic. These foreign companies did not engage in productive activities with national firms and only short-term growth cycles of investment and consumption were achieved. The effect of industrialization was limited and did not generate the endogenous growth and technological capabilities that were needed; it neither stimulated labor demand nor improved income distribution.

---

[8] The biggest part of these exchanges was operating within the Multilateral Compensation and Reciprocal Credit Agreement, signed in 1969 by the central banks of all contractual parties of LAFTA and the Dominican Republic. On the concept and measurement of intra-regional trade shares, see e.g. Iapadre (2006).

[9] In the CACM, the intra-regional trade share (measured by exports) went from 8% in 1962 to 25.4% in 1980 (Halperin *et al.*, 2002, p. 375).

Industrialization was actively promoted by Latin American governments. However, regional integration was not the driver for economic development that ECLAC had proposed. The advantages of an ISI strategy impulse at a regional level were never accomplished because regional integration — mainly trade liberalization — faced too many difficulties. In ECLAC's proposal, industrialization and regional integration went hand-in-hand. Regional integration was a fundamental condition for industrialization, economic growth, and export diversification. In reality, Latin American governments were more inclined to promote national industries than to accomplish a truly Latin American Common Market.

However, the profound disturbances in the world economy which took place in the 1970s and 1980s led to the final collapse of the first phase of Latin American regionalism. Thus, this period is often identified by ECLAC as "the lost decade" for the development of the region.

In 1973, simultaneously with falling economic activity and productivity, the Organization of the Petroleum Exporting countries (OPEC) unilaterally raised oil prices. The corresponding need for international banks to recycle exceeding funds from oil producing countries led to a massive expansion of the international movements of capital. Under the leadership of President Reagan and Prime Minister Thatcher such process was accompanied by an ideological shift in favor of the free market.

Developed countries faced the emerging challenges with a new range of fossil, energy-saving technological innovations starting the transition towards an information- and knowledge-based economy. On the other side, the South East Asian region succeeded in consolidating its industrial export model benefiting from wide access to the United States market.

Latin America, on the contrary, became trapped by the dynamics of petrodollars that flooded the region with unconditional loans and negative interest rates in the 1970s. Later, in the 1980s, a complete change occurred and massive volumes of financial resources were withdrawn, sinking the region for a whole decade. Besides, high debt service payments, with remarkably high interest rates, were accompanied by deteriorated terms of trade, a reduction of primary commodities demand in the industrialized countries, and, consequently, restricted access to fresh capital resources. Between 1980 and 1990 Latin America experienced on average a tightening of -0.1% of per capita gross domestic product (GDP) and suffered severe regression at all political and structural levels in its development process.

The devastation produced by the Latin American debt crisis during the 1980s seriously damaged the pillars of the development model: industrialization based on import substitution, state intervention, and economic integration.

The dissolution of industrialization policies, which started in the 1970s in the Southern Cone (Argentina, Uruguay and Chile) (Ramos, 1986), became a general trend in Latin America during the debt crisis. These countries were convinced that the industrialization process was exhausted and it had induced serious distortions in the structure of relative prices in their economies. Unilateral trade liberalization was initiated by Bolivia, Mexico, and Costa Rica and spread to the rest of the countries at the beginning of the 1990s (Ffrench-Davis, 2005, p. 50).

As prescribed by the neo-liberal paradigm that began to prevail during that period in Latin America, trade liberalization entailed a reduction of the role of the state. The concept of "developmental state" — with an active role through planning, protection of the internal market, fiscal policy, and direct investment in strategic sectors — was gradually replaced by a "smaller state" via privatization, fiscal orthodoxy, and market deregulation.[10] Thus, the new economic growth strategy was usually captured by the saying, "the best industrial policy is *no* industrial policy" (Ocampo, 2008, p. 47).

In such a context, the integration model aimed at boosting the import substitution strategy at the regional level also entered into question. It was a real "identity crisis" since the integration process lost its way due to the lack of higher industrialization objectives and active state leadership.

---

[10] Salazar (1991) presents a good extensive overview of the paradigm shift on the role of the state in Latin America during this period.

14.3. SECOND PHASE: INTEGRATION AS A "BUILDING BLOCK" FOR TRADE LIBERALIZATION

At the end of the 1980s and the beginning of the 1990s, the academic and political community in Latin America started to realize that the process of regional integration began to have different characteristics and was experiencing a transformation, thus reflecting the above-mentioned transformations in the world economy. Several discourses and writings refer to the "new integration", "new regionalism", the "second regionalism", or the "new wave" of trade agreements.[11]

Carvajal employs the term "neo-integration". With it, the author refers to: "(1) [...] a type of renovated integration that differs from the traditional integrationist scheme in its strategic elements, in the actors that it privileges as catalysts of the process, and in the short and mid-term objectives; thus in this sense, the prefix *neo,* pretends to denote the *new* character of the integration that begins in 1990. (2) In a second sense, which complements but does not exclude the former, the prefix *neo* refers to the integration that 'takes off', encouraged by and within the framework of the neo-liberal development model, generalised in Latin America in 1990 with the election of a series of presidents with such governmental plans" (Carvajal 1993, pp. 107–108).

Rosas (2003, p. 149) uses the set of circumstances surrounding the trade agreements subscribed by Mexico, as an illustration of new regionalism. She mentions the contribution of Hettne and Inotai (1994), but develops a quite restricted definition of new regionalism: "a new set of rules and conditions governing FTAs and customs unions (CUs) established after the Cold War".[12] This is pretty much in line with understandings in multilateral institutions such as the World Bank and the IMF.

---

[11] See, Pardo (1992), Garay (1994), Mattli (1999), and Rosas (2003) among others. For a revision of (the first) bibliographic sources about "new" regional integration processes in Latin America in 1985–1988, see González (1989). This section is based in part on De Lombaerde and Garay (2008).

[12] In Hettne (1999) and related works one finds a broader conception of new regionalism, defined by contrasting it with the old regionalism of the first phase (see

The multifaceted character of new regionalism phenomenon gives rise to the use of different (although related) concepts with different contents, also in Latin America. As argued elsewhere (De Lombaerde, 2003), the concept of new regionalism refers both to quantitative and qualitative aspects. As far as the quantitative aspect is concerned, it is without any doubt present in the new Latin American regionalism. Since the second half of the 1980s, even if the number of agreements was already relatively significant,[13] it witnessed further increases. Initially, the increase was related to new economic complementation agreements in the framework of the Latin American Integration Association (LAIA) (1980), and then followed by the US–Canada FTA (1989), the new impulse of the Central American Common Market (CACM) (1990), the creation of the Common Market of the Southern Cone (MERCOSUR) (1991), the North America Free Trade Agreement (NAFTA) (1994), the progress towards a customs union in the Andean Community (AC) (1995) and its transformation into the Andean Community (1997), and an important number of new bilateral or inter-regional agreements.[14] Especially Mexico and Chile played an active role in the negotiation of such agreements. After joining NAFTA in 1992, Mexico initiated similar schemes with Costa Rica, Colombia, and Venezuela — in the framework of the G-3 — and with El Salvador, Guatemala, and

---

above). Following Hettne (1999, pp. 7–8), new regionalism has been shaped in a multipolar (*not* bipolar) world order; new regionalism is a relatively autonomous process (i.e. *not* top-down), where the nation states and other actors play an important role; economic integration in the new regionalism is generally seen as open and compatible with a global interdependent economy; new regionalism is a more comprehensive multidimensional process (i.e. with less specific economic/security objectives); new regionalism is part of a structural transformation of the world order in which the non-state actors are active participants, present at different levels of the global system (i.e. regionalism is *not* the exclusive concern of states). In the same vein some authors argue that the new wave of regionalization is linked to the transnationalization or globalization of the world economy. (Axline, 1994; Sideri, 1996).

[13] See, for example, De Lombaerde (2001).

[14] For an inventory of the treaties of this new wave, see for example, Devlin and Estevadeordal (2002).

Honduras — constituting the Northern Triangle. Furthermore, Mexico extended its network of trade agreements to all the industrialized countries with whom it shared economical relations — except Japan[15] — through different agreements with the European Union and with the European Free Trade Association (EFTA). In the same way, Chile, already an associated member of MERCOSUR, signed regional trade agreements with Mexico, Venezuela, Bolivia, Ecuador, Panama, Colombia, Peru, Costa Rica, the Central America Common Market, Canada, and the United States. In addition, Chile has also been especially interested in the relations with Asian countries, its main trade partners, and has consequently signed several agreements with Japan, South Korea, China, and India. The outcome is known as the *spaghetti bowl* (Bhagwati 1995): the complex co-existence of partly overlapping bilateral and regional agreements, resulting in an important administrative cost for the different economic agents.

Next to the quantitative aspects, qualitative aspects characterize new regionalism. The new integration agreements in Latin America were qualitatively different from those of the first phase. New regionalism in Latin America had internal and external dimensions as well as political and geo-political ones. In general, we can say that it was seeking to match deeper regional integration with the insertion into the global economy, guided by market economy principles and multilateral institutions and agreements. New regionalism in Latin America can be seen as part of the structural reform plans implemented since the mid-1980s. It is important to observe the political use that has been made of regional integration. The agreements at the regional level must be understood as a means to implement locally (domestically) the structural reforms defended by some factions in the domestic political arena and spurred by international financial institutions. In this sense, regional agreements fulfilled two functions: first, politically they made it easier to take certain measures because the governments could refer to responsibilities created by an external authority or obligation; and second, they incorporated an irreversible element in the policies (Devlin and Estevadeordal, 2001).

---

[15] Nevertheless, Mexico is a member of APEC.

In accordance with these developments, since the 1980s, a dramatic change has been observed in FDI policies. The new agreements showed a new strategy to mobilize capital at the regional level, but also to attract FDI from third countries (Devlin and Estevadeordal, 2001; De Lombaerde and Pedraza, 2005). Regarding trade agreements, a trend developed which incorporated new policy areas such as non-tariff barriers (NTB), intellectual property rights, regulation of the service sector, public procurement, etc. This trend was spurred by the Canada–US agreement as well as by the North American Free Trade Agreement (NAFTA). On the other hand, the special and differential treatment has been relatively limited. Beyond the static effects of trade liberalization, new regionalism also aimed at creating dynamic effects through trade interconnectedness and investment: transformation of production structures, economies of scale, greater levels of competition, changes in company performance, etc.

The most outstanding project of new regionalism in the Americas was undoubtedly the Free Trade Area for the Americas (FTAA) launched in December 1994. The materialization of an FTAA required, on the one hand, the consolidation of the opening and reform process started in LAC countries in the late 1980s, the preeminence of the neo-liberal model in the hemisphere, and, on the other, the adoption of a coherent trajectory for the construction of the hemispheric market and a great degree of convergence between the free trade agreements on course in the hemisphere.

The choice of a trajectory was burdensome, in particular given the ample variety of agreements in vigor in the hemisphere. In the selection of the FTA model resided the principal obstacle to negotiate an FTAA. In effect, this was precisely the reason why it was not possible to accomplish the objective of reaching an agreement on an FTAA by 2005 and why in the late 1990s the United States decided to move into sequential negotiations of several NAFTA-type FTAs with LAC countries: first with Chile, then with Central America in two stages and currently with some Andean countries (Colombia, Ecuador and Peru). The US strategy has been twofold: firstly, to sign strict NAFTA-type agreements with as many countries in the hemisphere as possible as a precondition to obtain enough predominance in possible negotiations of the FTAA in the future (specifically, for the adoption of a new generation type of agreement in contrast with the MERCOSUR model, for example) and, hence, to reinforce its hegemony in the Americas and to gain influence in the world arena (while at the same time having been involved in negotiations with countries of other continents), and secondly, to play an active role in the definition of the negotiating agenda at multilateral and regional levels.

As a consequence, a new development was the negotiation and signature of agreements with a North–South dimension like NAFTA, Canada–Chile FTA, CAFTA, FTAA, Andean and Central American bilateral FTAs with the US, etc. It is in this context that NAFTA has become a "model" for other agreements. This model consisted of a gradual programmed and quasi-universal tariff reduction, combined with an alignment with US standards for non-tariff barriers, services, investment, intellectual property rights, state purchases, rules of origin, etc., within the framework of an inter-governmental process.[16] The importance of reciprocal agreements with the US was not only based on the economic weight of the US *per se*, but also on the anchorage and signaling effects for the implementation of structural reforms. The debate concerning the relative potential benefits of North–South versus South–South integration has become a central theme of a wider debate surrounding the optimal strategies for Latin American countries facing different options of insertion into the global economy. The World Bank (Schiff and Winters 2003) and the Inter-American Development Bank (IDB) presented with insistence the arguments in favor of prioritizing North–South agreements. The critics of this position referred to the unsatisfactory balance of Mexico's integration in NAFTA, and concluded that for countries without a border with the US, deeper integration, following the existing model, was even less convincing.[17]

[16] With minimal inter-governmental structures.

[17] For critical evaluations of Mexico's participation in NAFTA, see for example, Domínguez (2000) and Audley *et al.* (2003). However, recent studies such as Tornell *et al.* (2004) and Kose *et al.* (2004) argue that the lack of growth in the

In the political sphere, new regionalism has contributed to the pacification of the borders within Central America (with positive effects on cross-border trade flows) and to the consolidation of democratic institutions. In some cases, democratic clauses have been incorporated into the agreements, like for example, in the EU–Mexico agreement. Likewise, a multiplication of negotiations and inter-regional agreements has been witnessed. In this context, MERCOSUR and Mexico have played a very active role, up to the point that at a second level, below the US, they can be identified as "sub-hubs" in two different systems of agreements with other Latin American and Caribbean countries: Mexico as a "sub-hub" of new generation NAFTA-type FTAs with Central America and some other countries like Chile, Colombia, and Venezuela (G-3), and Peru; MERCOSUR as a "sub-hub" of "first generation" MERCOSUR-type FTAs with the rest of South America (Garay, 1997). In this sense, new regionalism reflects strategies to participate more actively in the hemispheric and global arena.

Let us now return to the role of ECLAC during the second phase of Latin American regionalism and recall that in the early 1980s the major regional integration initiatives entered in a period of stagnation. In this context, ECLAC's initiatives and proposals were abandoned, which was a clear change from ECLAC's ideas on regional integration as a platform for economic growth towards strategies led by the market and inspired by neo-liberal ideas. The predominant role played by ECLAC in the first phase disappeared. The Inter-American Development Bank (IADB) seems to have taken the leadership in combination with other actors such as the World Bank, the Organization of American States (OAS), the Latin American Integration Association (LAIA/LAFTA), the Latin American Economic System (SELA), and ECLAC itself.

Mexican economy cannot be attributed to signing the NAFTA agreement, but that it is in the first place due to the lack of institutional and structural reforms since 1995, and also, in the short term, to the combined effect of the slowdown of the US economy and the greater dependency of the Mexican economy towards the economic cycle in the United States.

Nevertheless, ECLAC, following its historical-structuralist method, adjusting its position according to the sequence of historical events, continued with the study of the Latin American economy, making important recommendations to tackle the challenges faced by the region. Thus, ECLAC first proposed expansive adjustment policies and debt renegotiation and, afterwards, a new strategy oriented towards long-term growth. ECLAC tried to reposition itself with a new strategic vision for Latin American development. The core of this vision — inspired by the work of Fernando Fajnzylber (1983, 1988, 1990) — was a renewed proposal for industrialization based on the creation of an endogenous core of technical progress,[18] needed in order to achieve "genuine" competitiveness in the international market. The "Productive transformation with social equity" (CEPAL, 1990), which articulated ECLAC's contributions, also granted an essential role to an equitable income distribution, the latter being the determinant of consumption patterns and hence savings and investment rates which influence the relationship between capital and production (Bielschowsky, 1998).

This document and a series of subsequent studies outlined a development path which was neither in line with the former approach on inward-looking industrialization of ECLAC nor with the orthodox programmes of structural adjustment, privatization, and unconditional liberalization promoted by the Washington Consensus.

According to the document *Productive transformation with social equity* (CEPAL, 1990):

> [t]he productive transformation with social equity should be achieved in the context of better international competitiveness. Such competitiveness should rely more on a deliberate and systematic incorporation of technical progress in the productive process (with the corresponding productivity increases) than on the shrinking of real wages. Thus, greater recognition of the learning

[18] Some similarity should be noted between this approach and "endogenous growth theories" which, at that time were being developed by North American academia. See, Romer (1990) and Lucas (1988).

> dimension and of the diffusion of the available knowledge at the international level is needed, a prerogative hardly ever used by the region in the past [...]
>
> Industrialization constitutes the core of the productive transformation, mainly because it supports technical progress, and also because, due to the new circumstances, industrialization has to go beyond the narrow sectoral approach. Instead, industrialization should aim to connect itself with the primary and services sectors in order to integrate the productive system and contribute to the progressive harmonization of productivity levels. The overcoming of sectoral entrapment is one of the keys of the productive transformation and the new stage of industrialization. (CEPAL, 1990:14)

As mentioned before, ECLAC's theoretical approach in the three previous decades was known as "structuralism". Therefore, the new proposals from the 1980s and 1990s were accordingly named "neo-structuralism". This new term was a clear reference to the overcoming of the ISI strategy and also a counterfactual to the predominant neo-liberalism. Neo-structuralism acknowledged macroeconomic stability as a necessary input for development policies. However, in ECLAC's view it was also necessary to establish a partnership between the state, private sector, and private-public enterprise in order to achieve a truly endogenous core of technical progress. Firms were inserted in a network linked with academic institution, transport systems, sources energies, etc. and their "systemic competitiveness" relied on public policies. Thus, neo-structuralism was based on selective policies instead of the theoretically neutral neo-liberal policies (Ffrench-Davis, 1988, p. 39).

Whereas the first phase of Latin American regionalism emerged in the theoretical framework of ECLAC's structuralism, the second phase of regional and sub-regional integration agreements found its conceptual support in the notion of "open regionalism", derived from "neo-structuralism" and developed by ECLAC in the first half of the 1990s. Open regionalism is defined as the conciliation between regional preferential agreements and multilateral trade liberalization. Regionalism is not pursued as a tool for industrialization.

Instead, it is promoted as a "building block" for a free and competitive international market. Therefore, open regionalism intends to reconcile integration policies with international competitiveness (CEPAL, 1994, pp. 12–13).[19] The regionalist ingredient comes from a preference for cooperation between countries with geographic and cultural proximity embracing the advantages as suggested by the "old" regionalism. Thus, the new model of economic integration includes, on the one hand, the traditional mechanism of aggregating demand through the creation of a regional market and, on the other hand, an increase in efficiency due to competitive forces from the export markets.

According to Pizarro (1999, p. 34), this change in ECLAC's point of view transformed Latin American integration into a useful tool for generating economic growth based on international trade, no longer a tool for industrialization based on import substitution. Furthermore, the role of the state — another ECLAC's major principles of integration — was consequently weakened.

Towards the end of the second phase (late 1990s and early 2000s), it seems that ECLAC moved further in the direction of the predominant paradigm, as represented by the IADB. This was illustrated by the fact that, together with the Bank and the OAS, it played a role as technical secretariat during the negotiations of a hemispheric free trade area. Consistent with this role, ECLAC accounted for the cost of multiple incompatible bilateral agreements. Kuwayama, Lima, and Silva (2005) — ECLAC economists — argued that although the benefits of bilateral trade agreements were certain, the cost of its multiplicity had to be weighted. The wide variety of preferential rates, tariff elimination schedules and rules of origin represents a considerable burden for

[19] Towards the end of the 1970s, the concept of "open regionalism" was originally presented by Masayoshi Ohika, at the time Japan's Prime Minister, who proposed to engage in an "open regional cooperation in accordance with the new era of globalization" in order to overcome the political and economic differences between the Asia Pacific countries. This initiative was materialized in a consultation mechanism leading to the Asia Pacific Economic Cooperation — APEC — which includes "open regionalism" as one of its basic principles (Okita, 1992).

economic agents and especially for small and medium-sized firms and small traders.

14.4. TOWARD A THIRD PHASE: BEYOND OPEN REGIONALISM

In the confusing framework with which we were left by the second phase of Latin American regionalism, the real possibilities of achieving a convergence of the different integration processes in the regions, developing an effective South American Community (2007),[20] seemed initially extremely remote, especially with the involvement of "alternative" or "post-liberal" integration initiatives such as the Bolivarian Alternative for the Americas — ALBA — signed in Havana (2004).[21] However, the poor results of the neo-liberal reforms and the debilitation of open regionalism are shifting development and integration policies *on average* again from the neo-liberal postulates and the emphasis on the role of trade and FDI for growth in the direction of more nuanced positions. It remains to be seen whether UNASUR could play a role in consolidating a new model of regional integration, at least at the level of South America.

In this context of a (possible) new paradigmatic shift in regional integration thinking, ECLAC might well find an opportunity to strengthen its position as think tank and technical support agency. In the document *Latin America and the Caribbean in the World Economy 2008–2009* (ECLAC, 2009), ECLAC shows some orientations of what could be the next pillars for a new integration model. After the financial crisis, the world economy and world trade have experienced a reduction in the growth rate, protectionism pressures and a tightening in access conditions for financing. Regional

---

[20] In 2004, in order to improve the convergence of the different regional processes the Third Presidential Summit at Cuzco (Peru) agreed on creating a South American Community.

[21] Venezuela and Cuba established ALBA in 2004. Later, Nicaragua and Bolivia joined. In this framework, the People's Trade Treaty — TCP — was signed in Havana in 2006.

integration should compensate these "external shocks" through the increase in intra-regional trade and regional cooperation. Therefore, ECLAC established among its regional priorities, infrastructure investment, intra-regional trade, innovation, reduction of asymmetries, social cohesion, climate change, and closer ties with Asia-Pacific. In this framework, regional integration is more than a "building block" for free and competitive international markets. Integration is pursued as a means to improve international competitiveness, social cohesion, and a sustained economic development.

From this document the main characteristics of this new model can be outlined. Firstly, there is a rediscovery of "regional cooperation", being the key for the success of the main developmental policies such as infrastructure, international competitiveness, innovation and knowledge sharing, social cohesion, promotion of international and intra-regional production chain, and effective representation in multilateral negotiations. Secondly, trade liberalization is less emphasized. The region should enhance many other areas such as legal certainty or joint infrastructure projects on energy and connectivity. Nevertheless, with respect to trade, the emphasis is not on tariff reduction and liberalization but on trade financing, technical assistance, and capacity building at a regional level. Thus, all these objectives are pursued via cooperation rather than via trade liberalization; as ECLAC highlights, "today regional cooperation is more important than progress in trade liberalization" (ECLAC, 2009, p.83). Thirdly, there is a clear recognition of sub-regional differentiation. For instance, Mexico and Central America, South America, and the Caribbean are particular integration processes with different dynamics. Therefore, the respective optimal integration strategies diverge. Finally, ECLAC argues for a depoliticization of regional integration, regional integration being presented as a matter of finding the lowest common denominator. Besides, regional integration is stressed as a long-term structural commitment rather than a policy preference of a specific government in power. The document also appeals for "programmatic realism" in setting objectives for regional integration, improving the performance of current institutions and building bridges between sub-regional initiatives.

The disillusion with the Washington Consensus and the return of "active policies" in integration are reflected in several "post-neo-liberal" initiatives aimed at transcending the model of open regionalism. In the beginning of this "third phase of Latin American regionalism", two trends can be identified. The first is inspired by a "neo-structuralist" agenda aims at promoting productive transformation in the region and a second trend focuses on the conformation of country blocks with ideological affinities (da Motta and Rios, 2007).

The concrete expression of the above-mentioned first trend is the creation of the South American Community of Nations in 2004, recently (2008) transformed in the Union of South American Nations (UNASUR). UNASUR holds a "positive" vision of integration and focuses on the creation of a new regional production platform, abandoning the emphasis given to mere trade liberalization. Furthermore, UNASUR, led by Brazil, proposes to act preferably in political, social, environmental, and security areas. On the other hand, there is the movement aimed at the development of an "alternative" integration based upon an ideological convergence of Latin American socialist regimes. This is being led by President Chávez of Venezuela, who promotes a "twenty-first-century socialism" and the creation of ample South–South Alliances in order to face US hegemony (Sanahuja, 2009).

Beyond the obvious differences in these approaches, the two initiatives share common elements such as the "return of the state", the concern about the social dimension (poverty, inequality and asymmetries in members' levels of development), military security, energy cooperation and the recovery of a "policy space", in order to implement autonomous domestic policies. However, both proposals fail to present an alternative integration model since they compete between them and suffer from internal contradictions. For instance, UNASUR and ALBA combine ambitious objectives — aiming at every dimension of development and external policy — with intergovernmental decision-making, consensus and presidential diplomacy. In sum, weak institutions, lacking binding legal force and supranational capacity, are further obstacles to move into more advanced stages of integration.

Thus, Latin America is in between the end of the open regionalism model and these two new proposals, strongly differentiated in terms of leadership, scope, and political and ideological orientation. Therefore, given its role in the past as a theoretical and cognitive reference guiding the regional integration policies, a substantial contribution from ECLAC would be desirable. During the last decade, ECLAC has maintained a continuous intellectual production. It has focused on a better understanding of the effects of the neo-liberal reforms, as well as providing reliable information and assistance in the financial crisis and the design of policies on social and productive transformation.[22] ECLAC has not yet expressed a global vision on development properly synchronized with the circumstances of the current times, nor has it suggested any proposal on any systemic integration model in order to overcome this stage of open regionalism, although it has monitored the development of every integration process underway.

14.5. CONCLUSION

As illustrated, ECLAC's role and recommendations on regional integration have changed with the development of the region and the several economic and political events. Following its historical–structuralist method, ECLAC has always been in the frontline of the policy discussion. However, the motivation for encouraging regional integration has moved from a platform for industrialization and development to a "building block" for international competitiveness. Nowadays, integration is perceived as an opportunity to deal with global challenges and socioeconomic development in a more efficient manner. Therefore, integration is *per se* an objective pursued by Latin American countries. UNASUR and ALBA are two proposed frameworks for managing the third phase of regionalism. Having acknowledged their shortcomings, such initiatives still raise political

[22] On this subject, the document *Structural Change and Productivity Growth, 20 Years Later. Old Problems, New Opportunities*, by Fernando Fajnzylber, is an attempt to update ECLAC's work on productive transformation of the 1980s.

and academic debate on integration and its relation with socioeconomic development.

In this context, ECLAC should further contribute to the analysis focusing on topics such as the new generation of productive transformation policies; social rights, citizenship and social cohesion; energetic integration; and the new configuration of the world economy. All these issues are included in the new agenda on regional integration but are in need of consensus (or at least, converging) views. ECLAC can thereby build on the huge amount of analytical, theoretical, and empirical knowledge it has already accumulated in all these different dimensions of integration.

BIBLIOGRAPHY

ALADI (1983). Evolución y estructura del intercambio comercial de los países que integran la ALADI, *Doc/ALADI/Sec /Estudios* 5.

ASEAN (1980). *Basic Agreement on ASEAN Industrial Projects*, ASEAN, Kuala Lumpur, 6 March.

ASEAN (1981). *Basic Agreement on ASEAN Industrial Complementation*, ASEAN, Manila, 18 June.

Audley, J. J., Papademetriou, D. G., Polaski, S. and Vaughan, S. (2003). *La promesa y la realidad del TLCAN. Lecciones de México para el hemisferio*, Carnegie Endowment for International Peace, Washington, DC.

Axline, W. A. (1994). "Cross regional comparisons and the theory of regional cooperation: Lesson from Latin America, the Caribbean, South East Asia and the South Pacific", in Axline, W. A. (ed.), *The Political Economy of Regional Cooperation: Comparative Case Studies*, Associated University Press, New Jersey, pp. 178–224.

Bhagwati, J. (1995). "US Trade Policy: The Infatuation with Free Trade Areas", in Bhagwati, J. and Krueger, A. O. (eds), *The Dangerous Drift to Preferential Trade Agreements*, American Enterprise Institute for Public Policy Research, Washington, DC, pp. 1–18.

Bielschowsky, R. (1998). "Cincuenta años del pensamiento de la Cepal", in CEPAL, *Cincuenta años de pensamiento de la Cepal. Textos seleccionados*, Tomo I, FCE and CEPAL, Santiago de Chile, pp. 9–61.

Cardozo, F. H. (1977). La originalidad de la copia: La Cepal y la idea del desarrollo, *Revista de la Cepal*, 4, pp. 7–40.

Carvajal, L. (1993). *Integración, pragmatismo y utopía en América Latina*, Universidad Externado de Colombia — Universidad de Los Andes, Bogotá.

CEPAL (1959). *El mercado común latinoamericano y el régimen de pagos multilaterales en el mercado común latinoamericano*, Naciones Unidas, Santiago de Chile.

CEPAL (1990). *Transformación productiva con equidad*, Naciones Unidas, Santiago de Chile.

CEPAL (1994). *El regionalismo abierto en América Latina y el Caribe. La integración económica al servicio de la transformación productiva con equidad*, Naciones Unidas, Santiago de Chile.

Cline, W. R. (1983). "El interés de América Latina en la integración económica", in Conessa, E. R. (ed.), *Términos de intercambio y tarifa óptima en América Latina*, BID and Intal, Buenos Aires, pp. 23–33.

Da Motta, P. and Rios, S. P. (2007). O regionalismo pós-liberal, na América do Sol: Origens, iniciativas e dilemas, *Serie Comercio Internacional*, 2, CEPAL, Santiago de Chile.

De Lombaerde, P. (1994). ASEAN Industrial Joint-Ventures (AIJVs) in the Light of the ASEAN Free Trade Agreement (AFTA), *International Trade Law and Practise*, 20, 4, pp. 675–680.

De Lombaerde, P. (2001). "Experiencia de la integración económica en el Asia-Pacífico y perspectivas para la integración transpacífica", in Garay, L. J., Ramírez Leyton, D. and De Lombaerde, P. (eds), *El futuro de Colombia en la Cuenca del Pacífico*, Universidad Jorge Tadeo Lozano, Bogotá, pp. 107–149.

De Lombaerde, P. (2003). Book Review of "New Regionalism in the Global Political Economy", *Journal of Common Market Studies*, 41, (5), pp. 968–969.

De Lombaerde, P. and Garay, L. J. (2008). "El nuevo regionalismo en América Latina", in De Lombaerde, P., Kochi, S. and Briceño, J. (eds), *Del regionalismo latinoamericano a la integración interregional*, Fundación Carolina and Siglo XXI, Madrid, pp. 3–35.

De Lombaerde, P. and Pedraza, E. B. (2005). "FDI Productivity Spillovers in the Andean Region: Econometric Evidence from Colombian Firm-level Panel Data", in Cuyvers, L. and De Beule, F. (eds), *Transnational Corporations and Economic Development: From Internationalisation to Globalisation*, Palgrave Macmillan, London, pp. 165–183.

Devlin, R. and Estevadeordal, A. (2001). "What's New in the New Regionalism in the Americas?", in Bulmer-Thomas, V. (ed.), *Regional Integration in Latin America and the Caribbean: The Political Economy of Open Regionalism*, ILAS — University of London, London, pp.17–44.

Devlin, R. and Estevadeordal, A. (2002). "The New Regionalism in Latin America", in: IDB, *Beyond Borders. The New Regionalism in Latin America. Economic and Social Progress in Latin America 2002 Report*, Inter-American Development Bank, Washington, DC, pp. 23–59.

Domínguez, E. (2000). "Regional Integration on Uneven Terms: The Case of México within TLCAN", in Hettne, B., Inotai, A. and Sunkel, O. (eds),

National Perspectives on the New Regionalism in the North, Macmillan, Basingstoke, pp. 239–264.

ECLAC (2009). Latin America and the Caribbean in the World Economy 2008–2009, CEPAL, Santiago de Chile.

Fajnzylber, F. (1983). *La industrialización trunca de América Latina*, Editorial Nueva Imagen, Mexico D. F.

Fajnzylber, F. (1988). Competitividad internacional: Evolución y lecciones, *Revista de la Cepal*, 36, CEPAL, Santiago de Chile.

Fajnzylber, F. (1990). Industrialización en América Latina: De la 'caja negra' al 'casillero vacio', *Cuadernos de la Cepal*, 60, CEPAL, Santiago de Chile.

Ffrench-Davis, R. (1988). Esbozo de un planteamiento neoestructuralista, *Revista de la Cepal*, 34, pp. 37–44.

Ffrench-Davis, R. (2005). *Macroeconomía, comercio y finanzas*, 2nd ed., Cepal and Mayol, Bogotá.

Fitzgerald, V. (1998). La Cepal y la teoría de la industrialización, *Revista de la Cepal*, (special issue), pp. 47–61.

Garay, L. J. (1994). *América Latina ante el reordenamiento económico internacional*, EUN, Bogotá.

Garay, L. J. (1997). "Regionalismo abierto e integración en las Américas. A propósito del caso del Grupo Andino" in Lanzetta, M. (coor.), *Agenda de largo plazo de la relación Colombo-Venezolana en el marco de los procesos de integración*, CAF, Bogotá, pp. 419–525.

González Fernández, S. (1989). Orientación bibliográfica sobre nuevos procesos de integración en América Latina y Europa: 1985–1988, *Pensamiento Iberoamericano*, 15, pp. 280–286.

Haas, E. B. (1958). *The Uniting of Europe*, Stanford University Press, Stanford.

Haas, E. B. (1961). "International Integration: The European and the Universal Process", *International Organization*, 15, pp. 366–392.

Halperin, T. *et al.* (2002). *Historia Económica de América Latina. Desde la independencia a nuestros días*, Crítica, Barcelona.

Hettne, B. and Inotai, A. (1994). The New Regionalism: Implications for Global Development and International Security, *Research for Action*, UNU-WIDER, 14, pp. 1–24.

Hettne, B. (1999). "Globalisation and the New Regionalism: The Second Great Transformation", in Hettne, B., Inotai, A. and Sunkel, O. (eds), *Globalism and the New Regionalism*, Macmillan, Basingstoke, pp. 1–24.

Iapadre, L. (2006). "Regional Integration Agreements and the Geography of World Trade. Statistical Indicators and Empirical Evidence", in De Lombaerde, P. (ed.), *Assessment and Measurement of Regional Integration*, Routledge, London, pp. 65–85.

Imada, P. (1993). Production and Trade Effects of an ASEAN Free Trade Area, *The Developing Economies*, XXXI, 1, pp. 3–23.

Kuwayama, M., Lima, J. D. and Silva, V. (2005). Bilateralism and Regionalism: Re-establishing the primacy of Multilateralism — a Latin American and Caribbean Perspective, *Serie Comercio Internacional*, 58, CEPAL, Santiago de Chile.

Lucas, Jr., R. (1988). On the Mechanics of Economic Development, *Journal of Monetary Economics*, 22, pp. 3–42.

Mattli, W. (1999). *The Logic of Regional Integration. Europe and Beyond*, Cambridge University Press, Cambridge.

Ocampo, J. A. (2008). "Etapas del Pensamiento sobre el desarrollo de América Latina", in Altimir, O., Iglesias, E. and Machinea, J. L. (eds), *Hacia la revisión de los paradigmas del desarrollo en América Latina*, CEPAL, SEGIB, Santiago de Chile, 31–50.

Okita, S. (1992). *Regionalism and the Asia-Pacific Development Outlook*, Paper presented at International Seminar on the Pacific: An Integral Part of the World, the Ocean of the XXI Century, Santiago de Chile.

Pardo, R. (1992). "Prólogo. Colombia-Venezuela: La nueva integración", in Cardona, D. *et al.*, *Colombia-Venezuela: ¿Crisis o negociación?* Tercer Mundo Editores, Bogotá, pp. 5–14.

Pizarro, R. (1999). Comparative Analysis of Regionalism in Latin America and Asia-Pacific, *Serie Comercio Internacional*, 6, CEPAL, Santiago de Chile.

Prebisch, R. (1973). "La integración económica en América Latina", in Wyndlam-White, E. *et al.* (eds), *La integración latinoamericana en una etapa de decisiones*, BID and Intal, Buenos Aires, pp. 29–45.

Puyana, A. (1984). *Economic Integration among unequal partners. The case of the Andean Group*, Pergamon Press, New York.

Ramos, J. (1986). *Neoconservative Economics in the Southern Cone of Latin America, 1974–1983*, The John Hopkins University Press, Baltimore.

Ranis, G. (2004). "*The Evolution of Development Thinking: Theory and Policy*", Economic Growth Center Discussion Paper, Yale University, 886.

Rodríguez, O. (2006). *El estructuralismo latinoamericano*, Siglo XXI, CEPAL, Mexico, D. F.

Romer, P. (1990). Endogenous Technological Change, *Journal of Political Economy*, 98, (2), pp. 71–102.

Rosas, M.-C. (2003). "Mexico's Foreign Trade Policy in the New Millennium: Achievements and Challenges", in Okamoto. J (ed.), *Whither Free Trade Agreements? Proliferation, Evaluation and Multilateralisation* , IDE, Chiba, pp. 148–174.

Salazar, J.M. (1991). "El papel del Estado y del mercado en el desarrollo económico", in Sunkel, O. (ed.), *El desarrollo desde dentro. Un enfoque neoestructuralista para la América Latina,* El trimestre Económico and FCE, Mexico D. F., pp. 455–493.

Sanahuja, J. A. (2009). Del 'regionalismo abierto' al 'regionalismo post-neoliberal'. Crisis y cambio en la integración regional en América Latina, *Anuario de la*

Integración Regional de América Latina y el Gran Caribe, 7, Coordinadora Regional de Investigaciones Económicas y Sociales, Buenos Aires, pp. 11–54.

Schiff, M. and Winters, L. A. (2003). *Regional Integration and Development*, The World Bank, Washington, DC.

Sideri, S. (1996). "Globalization and Regional Integration", Working Papers Series No. 235 Institute of Social Studies, The Hague.

Sunkel, O. (ed.) (1991). *El desarrollo desde dentro. Un enfoque neoestructuralista para la América Latina*, El trimestre Económico and FCE, Mexico D. F.

Tavares, M. C. (1998). La Cepal y la integración económica de América Latina, *Revista de la Cepal*, número extraordinario, CEPAL, Santiago de Chile, pp. 213–228.

Wionczek, M. (1964). "Historia del tratado de Montevideo", in Wionczek, M. (ed.), *Integración de América Latina. Experiencias y Perspectivas*, FCE, Mexico D. F., pp. 53–93.

World Bank (1998). *Trade Towards Open Regionalism*, Annual Conference on Development in Latin American and the Caribbean 1997, Washington, DC.

Chapter

15

NAFTA: Springboard or Trap?

*Christian Deblock**

15.1. INTRODUCTION

The North American Free Trade Agreement (NAFTA) is often presented as a model of competitive integration to be emulated, and both Canada and Mexico have drawn advantage from their close economic relationship with the United States, at least in terms of economic growth, employment and commercial exchanges. Today, however, the "NAFTA model" is not only faced with international competition and changes on the world's economic map, but is also being put to the test, with many people in Canada and Mexico wondering which way the future lies. Three scenarios are contemplated. The first is a path of widespread bilateralism, accompanied by an intensification of the bipartite relationship with the United States. The second scenario involves the institutional enhancement of NAFTA, accompanied by reinforcement of trilateral cooperation and improvement of joint programs. The third scenario could be described as a transitional phase, consisting for each country of the

* The author would like to thank G. Gagné and M. Rioux for their comments and suggestions.

development of targeted trade partnerships, while leaving NAFTA unchanged and waiting for multilateralism to pick up steam again.

In the following pages, I propose to give a broad outline of NAFTA and its particularities, to assess it, to demonstrate how and why the "NAFTA model" is under stress, and to discuss each of the three scenarios.

15.2. NAFTA IN BRIEF

The North American Free Trade Agreement was signed by the prime minister of Canada and the presidents of the United States and Mexico in December 1992. Two parallel agreements (labour and environment) were signed in September 1993. Following its ratification, NAFTA, as planned, became effective on 1 January 1994.

15.2.1. Objectives

NAFTA follows on the heels of CUSFTA, the free trade agreement that was signed by the United States and Canada in January 1988 and became effective on 1 January 1989. NAFTA takes up, improves and expands on CUSFTA. It should also be noted that, in principle, the agreement is open to other countries. Chile was in fact invited, at its own request, to join the agreement at the Summit of the Americas, which took place in Miami in December 1994. The proposal was not followed up, but Chile nonetheless has free trade agreements with each of NAFTA's three contracting parties.

The objectives of the Agreement (Chapter 1, Article 102) are as follows:

1. eliminate barriers to trade in, and facilitate the cross-border movements of, goods and services between the territories of the Parties;
2. promote conditions of fair competition in the free trade area;
3. substantially increase investment opportunities in the territories of the Parties;
4. provide adequate and effective protection and enforcement of intellectual property rights in each Party's territory;

5. establish effective procedures for the implementation and application of this Agreement, for its joint administration and for the resolution of disputes; and
6. create a framework for further trilateral, regional and multilateral cooperation to expand and enhance the benefits of this Agreement.

Beyond their convergence of interests, each of the three countries nonetheless pursued different goals. In essence, the prime objective for Canada and Mexico was to gain preferential, expanded and safe access to their main market and, relying on this market, to improve their competitiveness so as to boost their own economies and successfully integrate themselves into the global economy. The United States for its part pursued a different set of goals, including that of furthering its new commercial agenda, exercising leverage on GATT, and making Mexico into a model of development. Table 15.1 summarises the main priorities for each country.

Table 15.1. Motivations for negotiating with NAFTA

United States	Mexico	Canada
Expand economic opportunities for US companies increase trade, investment and intellectual property rights disciplines, and take advantage of NAFTA as an incubator for trade liberalization in new areas	Obtain a broad, preferential and secure access to US markets	Protect CUSTA and ensure that Canada kept its preferential access to US markets and remained an attractive location for investments
Add momentum to global trade liberalization and stimulate trade partners to greater participation in the multilateral trade system	Increase export diversification and enhance competitiveness by attracting foreign direct investment	Improve CUSTA's dispute settlement mechanism and obtain clearer rules of origin
Extend the benefits of trade to Mexico, forster its integration into the world economy, and support economic and political reforms	Stimulate economic growth, pursue economic reforms, and reduce poverty	Gain access to the Mexican market

Table 15.2. Key indicators for Canada, Mexico and the United States

NAFTA	Canada	Mexico	United States
Population (millions) (2008)	33.5	106.7	304.
GNI ($US Billions) (2007)	1300	878	13886.5
GNI (PPP Basis, $US billions) (2007)	1164.2	1324.6	13829
Per capita GNI (PPP Basis, $US, 2007)	35310	12580	45850
Life expectancy at birth (2007)	80.6	76	79.1
HDI rank (2007)	4	53	13
GDP per capita rant minus HDI rank (2007)	14	5	–4
Manufactured Exports (% of total merchandise exports, 2006)	56	76	79
High technology exports (% of manufactured exports, 2006)	15	19	30

Source: The World Bank, *The Word Development Report* 2009; UNDP, *Human Develcpment Report 2009.*

15.2.2. NAFTA: A Turning Point for the Three Countries

NAFTA is an agreement involving three very different countries, not only in terms of development but also from political, social and cultural perspectives. It is in fact the first free trade agreement signed by the United States with a developing country. It should also be noted that the agreement was born in pain, particularly in the United States, where debates surrounding its implementation were troubled, and where, unlike CUSFTA, the agreement only garnered a weak majority in Congress. Above all, however, NAFTA marked a turning point in the trade policy of the three countries. In the case of the United States, it demonstrated the seriousness of the country's commitment to a bilateral approach (Deblock, 2010); in the case of Canada it confirmed the entrenchment within North America of its foreign policy; and in the case of Mexico, it completed the break with nationalist policies and confirmed the country's commitment to competitive integration within the global economy (Deblock and Turcotte, 2003) (see Table 15.2).

15.3. THE PARTICULARS OF NAFTA

NAFTA is a free trade framework agreement, accompanied by two parallel agreements: bilateral agreements and exceptions. It is a contractual-style integration agreement, complete with a binding arbitration mechanism in case of dispute. Two points especially merit our attention.

First of all, the Agreement rests on the principles of national treatment, most-favoured-nation treatment and transparency. These principles apply to the three parties, with the result that Mexico does not benefit from any differentiated and preferential treatment. Neither is there a regional development fund. Along with this novel feature, NAFTA has as a second: the principle of non-discrimination is extended to corporations, which basically amounts to recognising their rights, especially the right to sue a state directly (Investor-state mechanism).

Secondly, NAFTA is a very far-reaching agreement. It covers trade in goods, including agriculture and services (Part II. The rules of trade. Part III. Technical barriers to trade). The negative list method is applied, with exceptions and exclusions figuring in the annexes. The main ones involve certain sectors such as telecommunications, petrol, inland waterway transport, water, social services and cultural products. NAFTA also includes rules of origin (North American content), which are reinforced in the case of the automobile, textile and clothing industries. Another particularity is that NAFTA authorises anti-dumping and countervailing procedures, a feature which does not appear in subsequent agreements.

The originality and strength of NAFTA, however, stem above all from Parts IV (public markets–government procurement), V (rules of trade–investment, services, telecommunications, financial services, competition policy, business persons) and VI (intellectual property). In these three areas, NAFTA goes much further than is possible with GATT. Furthermore, the provisions contained in these sections have been applied in subsequent negotiations by partners of the United States, including Canada, Mexico, Chile, etc., and have even served as a starting point, for example in negotiations on the Multilateral Agreement on Investment.

Thus, Chapter 11 on investment (Part V), to mention only that one, defines, in a manner that is as broad as it is precise, the notion of investment (extended to include minority interests), prohibits any prescription of results, recognises the freedom to transfer profits, dividends, gains, sales, or liquidation of assets, the free movement of capital, international arbitration, the investor-state mechanism, etc. For all intents and purposes, the provisions of this chapter grant cross-border economic rights to corporations, challenge the Calvo doctrine with respect to dispute settlements, and effectively bind national economic policies.[1] One may then conclude that NAFTA, through the extent and specificities of its provisions, reflects an in-depth integration model (such as the European model), but that this integration lacks direction, as well as mechanisms, other than national ones, for the allocation of benefits and costs.

Part VII of the Agreement deals with administrative and institutional provisions.

Another institutional characteristic distinguishes this agreement. I have said that it is a contractual-style integration agreement; I would add two things: (1) cooperation, which is intergovernmental, is basically limited to issues of common interests in connection with the Agreement, and (2) the institutions are reduced and of three kinds: ministerial (Free-trade Commission and cooperation commissions in the areas of environment and labour), administrative (three secretariats and coordinators), and technical (working groups, ad hoc or standing committees and expert groups). In sum, the institutional, administrative and judicial (dispute settlement mechanism) framework exists only to ensure the implementation and respect of the Agreement. It is not really an evolutive agreement. Let us now examine its chief results.

---

[1] Canada had chosen to modify its law on investment (FIRA) before engaging in negotiations with the United States. Mexico was already well committed to that direction before starting negotiations, but only modified its law once the agreement had been signed. This being said, the net result was the same, since in both cases, a policy geared towards controlling and directing investment was replaced by a promotion and protection policy.

15.4. THE RESULTS OF NAFTA

Throughout the negotiations leading up to it, NAFTA gave rise to heated debates. Even today, the controversy has far from ended.[2] Polls in the United States show that the agreement rallies only weak support, with 37% of favourable opinions against 53% negative ones according to a Gallup poll in December 2008. Still, according to the same survey, the percentages are reversed in Canada — 51% positive opinions against 39% negative ones — while in Mexico, the undecided ones prevail (39%); a mere 20% of those surveyed had a favourable opinion of NAFTA, against 23% of unfavourable opinions. These results reflect the general mood in the three countries.

In Canada, while concerns about the loss of sovereignty and the erosion of social programs have not been completely lifted, economic growth and foreign investments tend to be reassuring as to the future. In the United States, offshoring to Mexico, clandestine immigration and instability at the border are not reassuring to Americans, for whom, moreover, the effects of NAFTA on their economic status are not apparent. Finally, in Mexico, while the population is sensitive to change and to economic modernisation, distrust towards the United States is still prevalent, results in terms of revenues are still being awaited, and the absence of economic strategies is widely condemned.[3]

As for the economic results in themselves, analyses are just as divided as they were 20 years ago. However, (1) judgements and conclusions are on the whole much less radical and ideological, (2) NAFTA's strong and weak points are today fairly well identified and often agreed upon, and (3) the architecture of the global economy has changed a great deal since. Let us consider the results for each of the great official objectives.

---

[2] A few examples of NAFTA results analyses. Favourable: Schott (2008), Hufbauer and Schott (2008), Schwanen (2003). Unfavourable: Blecker (2009), Faux *et al.* (2006) Noncommittal: Zeda *et al.* (2009), Arès (2005; 2009) For a synthetic literature review, see Hornbeck (2004).

[3] For NAFTA debates and results in Quebec, see Viau and Gagné, 2010.

15.4.1. Trade

One of the important goals pursued by the three partners was a broadened and secure access to markets, a goal that has practically been achieved. Of course, certain epic disputes, such as the timber dispute between the United States and Canada or the sugar and road transport disputes between the United States and Mexico, continue to make headlines regularly. One may also evoke security issues at the borders and the lengthening of customs procedures since 11 September 2001, including visa issues, but on the whole, the business climate between the three countries is relatively good and trade disputes are few and quickly resolved.[4] Another important aspect is that deadlines pertaining to the reduction and elimination of customs duties have been respected, and in many cases even moved forward. As for non-tariff barriers, they are subject to ongoing scrutiny and give rise to regular consultations, whether at the ministerial level, by coordinators or working groups.

A second great topic of satisfaction is the augmentation of trade. The NAFTA area is one of the most intense hubs of trade in the world. Exports of merchandise from Canada to the United States have increased threefold between 1992 and 2008 and by four-and-a-half times from Mexico to the United States, as shown in Fig. 15.1.[5] Imports by these two countries from the United States have increased by two-and-a-half and three times respectively, during the same period. The same is true of trade between Canada and Mexico, which has increased sixfold. Today, approximately three-quarters of Canada's and Mexico's exports go to the United States and half of their imports come from there. As for the United States, a little less than 30% of its exports go to its two neighbours, and a little less than 30% of its imports come from them. It should also be noted that trade has been very favourable for Canada and Mexico since the establishment of NAFTA, with both countries accumulating large trade surpluses (see Table 15.3).

[4] There are in fact six dispute settlement mechanisms. They can be found in Chapters 11 (investment), 14 (financial services), 19 (anti-dumping/countervailing measures), 20 (administration of the agreement), and in the two parallel agreements (labour and environment).

[5] Most of the figures in this text have been rounded off to facilitate reading.

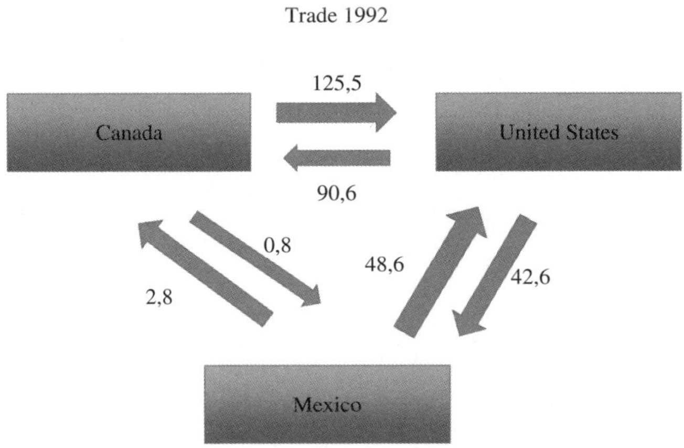

Figure 15.1. Canada — United States — Mexico Exports and Imports, 1992 and 2008, CAD Billions.

Source: Statistics Canada; Bureau of Economic Analysis.

On the downside, we must note first that the three countries depend on each other more for their exports than for their imports. Thus, the proportion of imports from the United States in Canada's total imports changed from 65.4% to 52.8% between 1996 and 2008, and from 60.6% to under 50% during the same period in the case of Mexico. The latter, however, has seen a slight increase of its share in United States imports.

Table 15.3. U.S. merchandise trade balance, Canada, Mexico and China

Deficit, billions of dollars	2005	2006	2007	2008	2009
Canada	76.4	73.2	64.7	74.6	20.2
Mexico	50.1	64.1	74.3	64.4	47.5
China	201.6	232.5	256.3	266.3	226.8

Source: *USITC*.

Another topic of concern is that trade remains bilateral and polarized in the United States. Although trade between Canada and Mexico has increased, as stated previously, Mexico still represents barely 2.5% of Canada's exports and 4.1% of its imports. As for Canada, it represents a little less than 6% of Mexico's exports and less than 2% of its imports.

Moreover, a large part of the trade surplus can be attributed to the weakness of the peso and of the Canadian dollar. With exchange rates on the rise, the competitive advantage is much less clear, notably in the manufacturing sector. The commerce of petroleum products is another dimension of the problem. Canada and Mexico are respectively the first and second suppliers of petroleum products to the United States, a sector in which surpluses mask, in the case of Canada (but of Mexico too), an ever-increasing deficit in the exchange of manufactured goods. Finally, while Canada and Mexico have trade surpluses with the United States, both have deficits with other countries (see Table 15.4).

15.4.2. Investment

In signing NAFTA, an important objective for both Canada and Mexico was to attract foreign direct investments. For a long time, results were very disappointing in Canada. The disappointment was all the more acute because Canada's outward FDI stock, since 1995, has been higher than its inward FDI stock. Canada is currently experiencing a renewal of its attraction, because of its natural resources, among other things, but its share in world inward FDI stocks continues to decline: according to the UNCTAD it fell from 6% to 3% between 1990 and 2008.

Table 15.4. U.S. merchandise trade balance with Canada and Mexico

	Imports		Exports		Trade balance	
	2008	2009	2008	2009	2008	2009
(billions of dollars)						
Canada						
Total trade	334.8	224.6	222.4	171.7	−112.4	−52.9
Petroleum products	111.3	63.7	15.9	9.4	−95.4	−54.3
Other categories	223.5	160.9	206.5	162.3	−17.0	1.4
Mexico						
Total trade	216.3	176.3	131.5	105.7	−84.8	−70.6
Petroleum products	42.6	24.2	11.1	7.7	−31.5	−16.5
Other categories	173.7	152.1	120.4	98.0	−52.3	−54.1

Source: *UNITC*.

Of the three countries, the United States was indisputably the largest FDI recipient: nearly a quarter of world FDI inflows during the 1990s. This said, Mexico could only rejoice in the strong increase of FDI inflows and crossed investments that followed the signing of NAFTA. Between 1992 and 2008, Canada's FDI stock in Mexico increased ninefold and that of the United States sevenfold. By comparison, Canada's FDI stocks in the United States only increased fivefold while the FDI stock of the United States in Canada was only increased by three-and-a-half times, as indicated in Fig. 15.2.

Another interesting indicator, based on UNCTAD data, is Total inward FDI stock as a percentage of the GDP: it went from 7% to 16% between 1990 and 2008 for the United States, from 19.5% to 27.5% for Canada and from 8.5% to 27.1% for Mexico.

As for trade, these excellent results need to be put in perspective. First of all, as attractive as Mexico has become since the implementation of NAFTA, its performance in terms of investment does not really stand out in comparison with that of Brazil, a country that has always held investment treaties at arms' length (see Table 15.5).

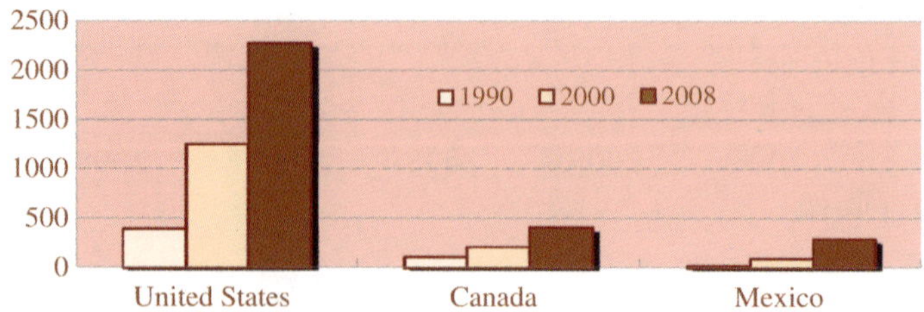

Figure 15.2. NAFTA: Foreign Direct Investment, 1990, 2000 and 2008 (Inward stock, billions of dollars).
Source: CNUCED, WIR 2009.

Table 15.5. Foreign direct investment, Brazil and Mexico. Inward stock, in billions of dollars and as a percentage of GDP

	1990	2000	2008
(Billions of Dollars)			
Brazil	37.1	122.3	287.7
Mexico	22.4	97.2	294.7
		(%)	
Brazil	8.5	19	18.3
Mexico	8.5	16.7	27

Source: *CNUCED, WIR-2009.*

Furthermore, a large number of FDIs are concentrated in the *maquiladora* industry, which has benefited from the restructuring and reorganization of activities by the big American groups (Pacheco-López, 2008; Waldkirch, 2008). An estimated 60,000 to 190,000 jobs have been delocalized from the United States to Mexico.[6] Although these are estimates, the numbers still appear relatively small when contrasted with the number of jobs that have been created and with the advantages for companies in terms of production costs and competitiveness. Another way to evaluate the effects of restructuring is to compare jobs in American subsidiaries in Canada and Mexico. In both cases, the number of jobs has grown between 1997 and 2007,

[6] All these data come from the *Bureau of Economics Analysis.*

going from 800,000 to 1.2 million in Mexican subsidiaries and from some 940,000 to 1.1 million in Canadian subsidiaries. However, in the manufacturing industry alone, the number of jobs has gone from 600,000 to 700,000 in Mexico, but has dropped from 400,000 to 370,000 during the same period in Canada. That said, it should be noted that during this same period, the number of jobs in US Chinese subsidiaries climbed from 180,000 to 730,000 and from 74,000 to 335,000 in US Indian subsidiaries.

Finally, I will note that the United States is still the first investor both in Canada and in Mexico. However, its share is declining: in Canada, it has dropped from 70% to approximately 60% since the beginning of the 1990s; in Mexico, it has dropped from over 60% to 50% during the same period. The reverse phenomenon can also be observed, at least in the case of Canada. From 65% at the beginning of the 1990s, the United States' share in Canadian foreign direct investments has fallen to under 50%. These trends suggest that American investors are now less interested in Canada and Mexico than they were at the beginning of NAFTA, but also that Canadian companies are striving to geographically diversify their foreign investments.

15.4.3. Economic Growth

Consolidating growth was a common goal for the three countries, and the liberalization of trade, promotion and protection of investments and pursuit of economic reforms were the means to achieve this goal. It was also expected that these three policies should conjugate their effects and stimulate investment, productivity and innovation. Of the three countries, it was Mexico that expected the most from NAFTA, just as it was the country whose economy needed to achieve the greatest adjustments.

When it opened its negotiations with the United States, Mexico was already well engaged in reforms, modernization and liberalization of its economy. NAFTA gave these reforms further impetus and, by confirming certain policies, sent clear signals to investors. While NAFTA is not solely responsible for the increase of trade and investment, it nonetheless has widely contributed. One may say the same of adjustment costs. The management of the debt crisis had been painful and, unable to face up to foreign competition, many companies and farming and industrial ventures disappeared. The advent of NAFTA opened up the way to competition to an even greater extent, compelling Mexican companies to adapt — all within an institutional context that forced Mexico to respect the principle of treatment equity and that considerably narrowed the government's leeway, with fair competition rules prevailing.

At the outset, the economic signals were so encouraging that Mexico was even presented by President Clinton as an example to other countries at the Summit of Miami in 1994. The peso crisis that followed two weeks later had dramatic effects, but in spite of this, the Mexican economy reacted better than during previous crises and its rapid recovery, spurred by the depreciation of the peso, augured a new era of growth. Since then, the economy has gone through two more recessions, one in 2000–2001 and the other in 2008–2009, but although in both cases Mexico's economy retreated more than that of its two partners, it did not give rise to any monetary and financial crisis, a fact that seems to demonstrate that overall, the Mexican economy has become more robust while its policies have gained in credibility. That being said, it is in terms of growth that the results are most disappointing. Four points draw our attention.

First, even taking into account the impact of the 1994–1995 crisis, economic growth remains modest, not only by comparison with rates recorded during the oft-criticized period of import-substitution,[7] but also by comparison with other countries in the Americas. The average growth rate of the GDP was thus 2.9% per year between 1993 and 2008, as compared with 3.1% for Canada and 3% for the United States (see Fig. 15.3).[8] During the same period, it was 4.9% in Chile, 3.4% in Brazil and 3.7% in Argentina. As for the per capita GDP, it has increased by 1.6% per year on average in Mexico during this period, as

[7] The growth rate of the GDP was on average 6.5% a year between 1960 and 1980.

[8] Source: FMI, *World Economic Outlook Database*. Taking the years 1990–2008 as period of reference, we obtain an average GDP growth rate of 3.2% for Mexico, as compared with 5.4% for Chile, 2.6% for Brazil, and 4.1% for Argentina.

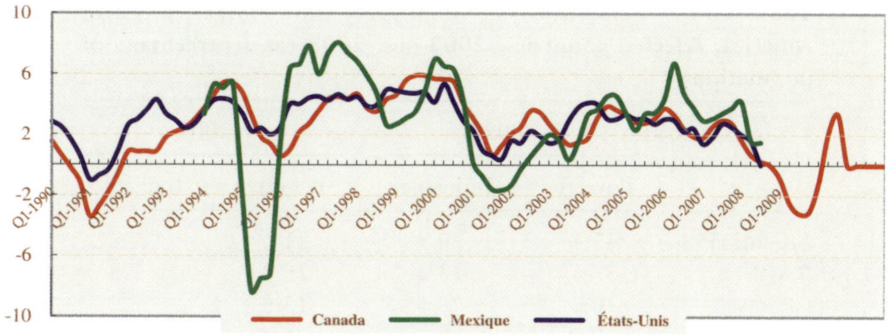

Figure 15.3. GDP Growth rate compared to the same quarter of previous year, Q1-1990–Q4-2009.

compared with 3.5% in Chile, 1.9% in Brazil and 2.5% in Argentina. Given Mexico's potential for growth, and also its goals in terms of job creation, augmentation of revenues and reduction of poverty, these numbers are very disappointing (see Table 15.6).[9]

Second, it should be noted that Mexico's economy, even more than Canada's, has become very dependent on the United States economy. There are two reasons for this: the extraverted character of Mexico's development and its political choices, dating back to the 1980s, in favour of competitive integration within the global economy. Thus, in 1980, exports of merchandise represented only 11% of GDP, as compared with 28% for Canada; in 1990, they represented 16% of the GDP, while in 2000 they had increased to 27% and in 2008, to 28%.[10] These figures don't explain everything, since Canada, too, experienced an increase in its extraversion rate during the same period, stabilizing today around 35% after having reached a peak of 44% in 2000. Just like Mexico's, Canada's economy follows that of the United States, but the cyclical amplitude is much

[9] Results are most contrasted in the area of agriculture. Although agricultural productivity has gone up considerably, bringing rural exodus in its wake as well as a drastic decline in jobs, still wages have scarcely increased, and greater poverty in rural areas is even observed.

[10] Source: United Nations. ComTrade.

Table 15.6. Persons living in poverty and indigence. Latin America, selected countries, 2002 and 2008 (as a percentage of population)

	2002		2008	
	Poverty	Indigence	Poverty	Indigence
Argentina*	45.4	20.9	21	7.2
Brazil	37.5	13.2	25.8	7.3
Chile*	20.2	5.6	13.5	3.2
Costa Rica	20.3	8.2	16.4	5.5
Mexico	39.4	12.6	34.8	11.2
Peru	54.7	24.4	36.2	12.6
Uruguay	15.4	2.5	14	3.5

Source: ECLAC, *Social Panorama of Latin America*, 2009.
Note: *2007.

less pronounced, both on the rise and on the decline. Hence a second explanatory factor: economic growth, like trade, relies to a large extent on the activity of the *maquiladoras*,[11] which are mainly concentrated along the border with the United States, importing parts and equipment and re-exporting finished or semi-finished products, as indicated in Table 15.7 (INEGI, 2007).

[11] The *maquiladora* program was created in the 1960s to stimulate industrial activity along the border with the United States. It allowed enterprises to import products exempt of customs duties, provided that these products were worked on in order to be re-exported in modified form. The program really took off in the 1980s. Another program, PITEX (Program for Temporary Imports to Promote Exports) was created in 1990 to allow enterprises located in the centre and in the south of Mexico to benefit from analogous advantages and thus be able to compete with the *maquiladora* industries. As a result of its rules of origin, NAFTA modified these programs. The *maquiladora* program authorised any foreign enterprise to import under the privilege of the franchise; this advantage was extended during NAFTA's first phase of implementation, between 1994 and 2001. Subsequently, North American standards were applied, which meant that non-NAFTA enterprises lost the privileges of the franchise. The two programs, PITEX and maquiladora, were merged in 2007 and the *maquiladora* industries were integrated into the manufacturing sector in 2008. In 2000, the *maquiladoras*, who could already sell up to 50% of their production on the domestic market, saw this possibility expanded to 85%.

Table 15.7. US Exports and imports with Canada and Mexico, 2008 text mission billions dollars and % of total

Rank		($)	(%)		($)	(%)
			Canada			
	Exports	222.4	100	Imports	334.8	100
1	Automotive products	42.0	18.9	Fuels and oil products	111.3	33.2
2	Machinery and Mechanical appliances	34.3	15.4	Automotive products	47.5	14,2
3	Fuels and oil products	15.9	7.2	Machinery and mechanical appliances	21.6	6.5
4	Electrical machinery and equipment	14.6	6.6	Plastics	10.7	3.2
5	Plastics	10.9	4.9	Electrical machinery and equipment	10.0	3.0
	Trade balance	−112.4				
	Oil products non included	−17.0				
			Mexico			
	Exports	131.5	100	Imports	216.3	100
1	Electrical machinery and equipment	17.8	13.6	Machinery and mechanical appliances	53.4	13.6
2	Fuels and oil products	15.9	12.1	Electrical machinery and equipment	42.6	12.1
3	Automotive products	12.9	9.8	Automotive products	32.1	9.8
4	Machinery and mechanical appliances	11.1	8.4	Fuels and oil products	24.7	8.4
5	Optical, medical, precision instruments	10.3	7.9	Plastics	7.35	7.9
	Trade balance	−84.8				
	Oil products non included	−53.3				

Source: *US International Trade Commission.*

A third finding is that although the composition of its trade has changed and the technological content of its exports increased in the last two decades, the productivity of Mexico's economy has only slightly progressed. Mexico, moreover, does not stand up well to comparison with other countries, starting with Canada, but also with Chile, Costa Rica or Brazil, judging by the competitiveness indicator of the World Economic Forum (as shown in Table 15.8).[12]

Finally, and as a consequence of the previous observations, the expected convergence with the United States is not happening (Pages-Serra, 2010). This is a huge disappointment. Although the same phenomenon may be observed in Canada and although economic growth, especially in the current decade, has caused poverty and extreme poverty to retreat, one can't help but notice that, not only has the gap between salaries in the United States and salaries in

Table 15.8. Global competitiveness index rankings, 2007, 2008, and 2009

	(Out of)	U.S	Canada	Chile	Costa Rica	Brazil	Mexico	China
Global rank								
2009	133	2	9	30	55	56	60	29
2008	134	1	10	28	59	64	60	30
2007	131	1	13	26	63	72	52	34
Components								
Basic requirements		28	10	32	62	91	59	36
Efficiency enhancers		1	4	33	58	42	55	32
Innovation and sophistication factors		1	12	43	37	38	67	29

Source: *World Competitiveness Report* 2009.

[12] See also the recent BID study, highlighting the link between weak productivity on one hand and weak expansion on the other. The study also shows the important role of services in the growth of both these elements. (Pages-Serra, 2010)

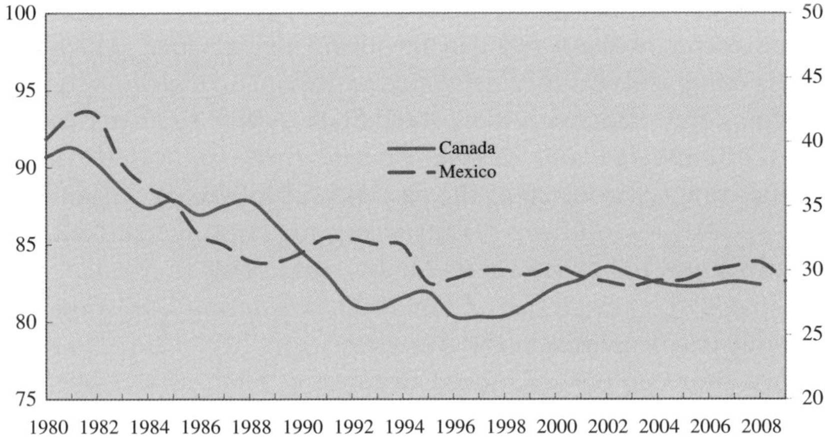

Figure 15.4. Relative GDP per capita on PPP basis. Canada and Mexico as % of US, 1980–2009.

Mexico remained unchanged for two decades, but the gap between the per capita GDP (PPP basis) of the US and that of Mexico is not getting any smaller either. The per capita GDP of Mexico is worth 30% of that in the US, as compared with 83% for Canada, as indicated in Fig. 15.4.

15.4.4. NAFTA Under Stress

Apart from the broadened, preferential and secure access to the 'supermarket' of the United States, two other categories of arguments took hold in the NAFTA debate in Canada and in Mexico. First, the political argument of a 'marriage of reason' (Weintraub, 1990), or of 'free trade by default' (Brunelle and Deblock, 1989); second, the economic arguments of scale economies (Canada) and of technological transfers (Mexico). In the United States, the debates were of a different nature. To the arguments set forth above, two others should be added: first, the creation of a vast market giving unrestricted access to natural resources, and second, the reorganisation of production networks to take advantage of the geographical proximity of a semi-developed economy. Once the early polemics had died down, the evolution of the three partners within NAFTA seemed to prove them right in favouring this alliance. Mexico and Canada congratulated themselves on having made the right choice by privileging free trade with the United States, while the latter congratulated themselves on having transformed an often difficult neighbouring relationship of the past into a profitable economic partnership, both for business ventures and for consumers. Today, this self-satisfaction has given way to doubt, particularly in Mexico, whose GDP dropped by more than 7% in 2009, registering one of the worst economic performances in the Americas.

Two more points are indeed disturbing. First, as we have noted previously, the three countries rely on each other much more for their exports than for their imports. Not only has this trend become more pronounced with the ascent of China as a competitive force to contend with, but it has also been observed that enterprises and, by the same token, jobs, are tending to migrate towards the new El Dorado embodied by Asia in general and by China in particular. Secondly, as NAFTA, at least in its present form, is showing its limitations, the debate is on again both in Canada and in Mexico about which new avenues should be taken to boost the economy and adapt to the changing architecture of the world's economy. Let us examine these two points.

15.4.5. Chinese Competition

While NAFTA may have been appropriate to the economic and political context of the 1990s, it is much less so today. The industrial model is based on a traditional scheme of relay subsidiaries and workshop subsidiaries (Michalet, 1998), and not on chains of value and production such as those found in Europe or in Asia (Dymond and Hart, 2008). This weakness is partly due to the gravitational pull exercised by the United States' economy on its two neighbours, and partly due to the limited effects of transmission and appropriation between American subsidiaries and their environment. These weak points and vulnerabilities, which have been emphasised many times, are reflected in the prevailing gaps of productivity between the United States on one hand and Canada and Mexico on the other. Having a stronger economic and financial base, Canada has made out more successfully than Mexico, notably through its foreign investments and by engaging itself in commercial services and the new economy. Nonetheless, like Mexico, Canada's manufacturing industry is doubly threatened by foreign competition: both in its main market, the United States, and in its own market, production conditions cannot compete with the conditions that prevail today in China (Rosales and Kuwayama, 2007).

An analogous problem exists from the United States perspective: not only has the reshaping of markets not really allowed American industries to become more competitive and to reconquer market shares from competing foreign companies that were already in place, as the latter benefit from the same NAFTA advantages as American businesses — the automobile industry being a perfect example of this — but, *de facto*, Chinese competition has brutally imposed itself in sectors that were delocalised in proximity to the American market, such as textiles and electric and electronic products. We can observe this quite clearly in Figs 15.5 and 15.6. In both cases, we clearly see that NAFTA initially played in favour of Mexico and of the other countries of Central America, but that this positive effect was short-lived. China's adherence to the WTO has given it unimpeded access to the United States market, with the result that Chinese products have now replaced Central American products on this same market.

The table relating to bilateral trade shares (Table 15.9) is even more significant. Certainly, it illustrates the vertiginous progress of Chinese imports amongst the imports of the three NAFTA countries, ultimately to the detriment of intra-regional imports. But it mostly shows that, unlike the United States, who, in spite of everything, somehow or other manages to maintain an honourable level of export to China, Mexico and Canada, are not seeing any progress in terms of their own exports towards this new and powerful trade partner. Not only does this beg the question, for the two countries, of 'what to

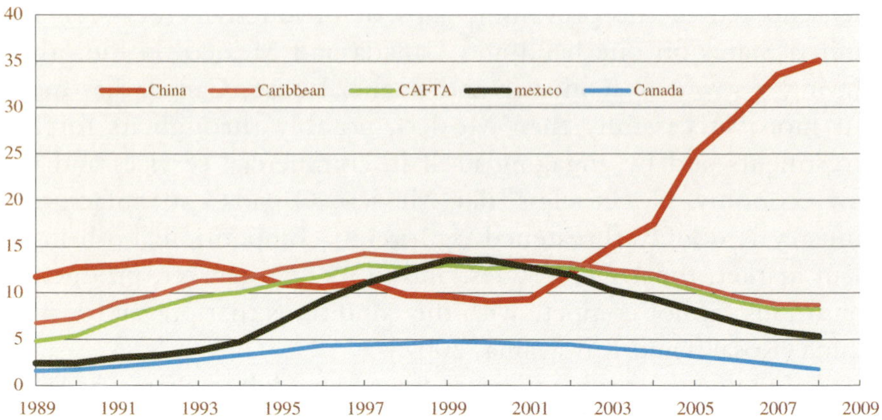

Figure 15.5. US Imports of textiles and apparels. Selected countries and regions, as a percentage of total.

Source: US. International Trade Administration.

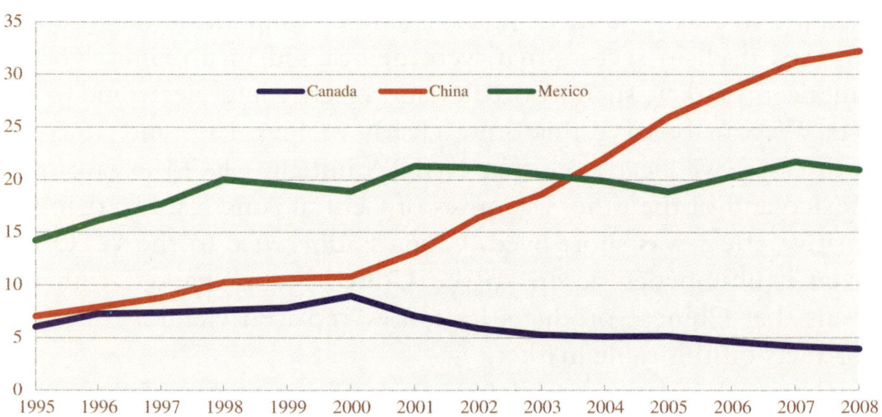

Figure 15.6. US Imports of electrical and electronic equipment: Canada, China and Mexico, as a percentage of total.

offer' China in exchange for the purchased products, what is more, it demonstrates that countries such as Mexico, who have chosen a path of industrial development through integration with the American market, today are seeing that development threatened, not by a North–North competition, but by a South–South one.

Table 15.9. Canada, Mexico and United States blateral trade as a percentage of total trade, 1996 and 2008

Canada	United States	Mexico	China
Exports	(%)	(%)	(%)
1996	79.9	0.5	1.1
2008	78.8	2.5	2.5
Imports	(%)	(%)	(%)
1996	65.4	2.5	2.1
2008	52.8	4.1	10.1
Mexico	**United States**	**Canada**	**China**
Exports	(%)	(%)	(%)
1996	77.2	4.6	0.2
2008	74.7	5.8	0.7
Imports	(%)	(%)	(%)
1996	60.6	1.0	0.8
2008	49.9	1.7	10.7
United States	**Canada**	**Mexico**	**China**
Exports	(%)	(%)	(%)
1996	18.3	9.1	1.9
2008	17.0	11.7	6.5
Imports	(%)	(%)	(%)
1996	19.6	9.0	6.6
2008	16.6	10.1	16.5

Source: United Nations COMTRADE.

15.5. TRADE OPTIONS

Canada and Mexico are faced today with a dilemma: as the free trade by default option is no longer satisfying, what other trade options are open to them?

In a certain way, it's the 'third option' debate resurfacing some 40 years later in a different form. Indeed, in the early 1970s, the Canadian government had, similarly to what Mexico had done a long time before, identified three options for trade and foreign policy. The first was the status quo, the second was free trade with the United

States and the third involved a geographic and sectoral diversification of trade, combined with what has been called the 'Canadianisation' of the economy. As the third option failed to yield the anticipated results, despite numerous efforts deployed in its favour, Canada finally turned towards the second option in the mid-1980s and was followed therein by Mexico.

The debate is of a different nature today, since it is the second option that represents the status quo. What options, then, are available to Canada and to Mexico henceforth? We can identify three main ones.

(1) The first involves bolstered bilateralism with the United States accompanied by a general bilateralisation of trade policies. This option seems to reflect the Zeitgeist and has garnered much support in Canada. It amounts to dropping Mexico in order to return to Canada's old ties of friendship with the United States (Hart, 2008), bolstering these ties while simultaneously orienting trade diplomacy towards widespread bilateralism. Against it, this option has two major drawbacks: for one, such a diplomacy requires huge efforts in exchange for fairly humble results, and secondly, Canada has become much less important to the United States, both from economic and political standpoints.[13]

(2) The second option would be to strengthen, improve and promote the evolution of NAFTA. The question has been raised on several occasions, namely to transform NAFTA into a Customs Union or a currency zone, or to establish capacity building mechanisms.[14] (Mace, 2004; Alexandroff *et al.*, 2008) Once again, the question as to the reopening of NAFTA was raised during the presidential campaign of 2008, this time by the

[13] Canada is integrated into the Bureau of Western Hemisphere Affairs section of the US State Department.

[14] The most interesting initiative came from President Vicente Fox in July 2000. Amongst other things, he proposed to transform NAFTA into a Customs Union, to coordinate policies to a greater extent, even to have a shared monetary policy, to facilitate the circulation of workers and resolve problems of clandestine immigration, and to establish a transfer fund program for the poorest regions. These proposals remained without echo.

Democrats.[15] The problem with this option is that NAFTA offers few possibilities for evolution, except at a technical level. A Security and Prosperity Partnership of North America (SPP) between the three countries was launched in 2005, and numerous work groups were established, but this partnership was mainly focused on security and border facilitation issues, energy supplies and shared regulations. The partnership, which has since been abandoned by the Obama Administration, completed NAFTA more than it constituted a new phase thereof.

(3) The third option involves targeting specific economic partnerships. The project of a Free Trade Area of the Americas (FTAA) had received enthusiastic support from Canada and Mexico (Daudelin, 2007). The objective for the two countries was simultaneously to maintain ties with the rest of the continent and to develop common positions towards the United States. As the Summit of Mar del Plata in 2005 ended on a note of profound division between the countries who were ready to pursue negotiations and those for whom the conditions had not been fulfilled, the project, for all intents and purposes, is forgotten, as evidenced by the final declaration of the fifth Summit of the Americas, held in Port of Spain in March 2009, in which no mention whatsoever is made of trade.[16] The problem is to determine with whom one should establish economic partnerships. Amongst others, Canada has opted for a reinforced dialogue with Europe and eventually with Latin America and India.[17] Mexico for its part seems to be

[15] See the dossier devoted to this topic in *The International Economy* magazine, 'Should NAFTA be Revisited? The Views of Twenty Experts', Summer 2008, pp. 24–35.

[16] The United States did, however, launch the Pathways to Prosperity in the Americas initiative, in the fall of 2008, to maintain contact with the group of countries who were favourable to pursuing negotiations. There have since been three meetings at the level of the ministers of foreign trade.

[17] Canada is currently negotiating with the European Union, Korea, the Dominican Republic, the CARICOM, the Central America Four, Panama, and Singapore. There have been exploratory discussions with India, Morocco, the Ukraine, and the Andean countries.

heading towards a revival of Latin American cooperation. This option has certain advantages, on condition, however, that Canada does not find the United States in its path and that it encounters reciprocal interest from its targeted partners, and that Mexico succeeds in renewing trust and finding its place in Latin America between Brazil and Venezuela.

As we can see, none of the three options is truly satisfying. Even the third one is nothing more than a second-best solution to the aborted FTAA negotiations. Some see a possible way out in a reboot of the Americas project in a different form, and others in the recovery of the domestic market, in the case of Mexico. The problem with the first avenue is that, for the time being, no one is talking about the integration of the Americas. Moreover, in addition to the continental divide between those countries who have chosen to follow the lead of the United States and the others, there is another division, namely between countries who are producing raw materials that are in high demand from China, and who thus are able to take advantage of favourable trade conditions, and the other countries. The domestic market avenue is more attractive, at least for Mexico, which has over 100 million inhabitants. However, one mustn't forget that NAFTA forecloses certain policies and prevents any return to economic nationalism. Another problem: considering that economic development, both in Canada and Mexico, is resolutely turned outwards and export led, any measures that could be taken to develop the domestic market, for example the increase of revenues in the case of Mexico, are likely to run into multiple problems of domestic supply and of international competitiveness.

15.6. CONCLUSION

To what extent, then, can we speak of NAFTA as a model? The jury is still out on this question, especially in light of the results. However, it was as such that the Agreement was initially presented — starting with the United States, which had placed great hopes on it, whether to propel trade negotiations from the bottom up, to create precedents in terms of market rules, to improve the competitiveness of its enterprises, or to turn Mexico into a case of exemplary development. This was true as well for Canada and Mexico, both of which had high expectations for what was supposed to be an exemplary model of successful integration within the world economy. We have chosen to focus our attention on Mexico and Canada. What results do we find?

As for the goals presented in the Agreement itself, we can say that they have, for the most part, been achieved; certain reservations, however, are called for. While trilateral trade and cross investments have certainly increased considerably over the past 15 years, one may wonder if NAFTA's effect has not been mainly to introduce a better business climate, to give enterprises greater freedom to maneuver, and thus, to strengthen certain tendencies that were already present. We have an illustration of this in the fact that exchanges between Canada and Mexico have scarcely developed since 1994. In this regard, the intra-regional trade figures are misleading. The share of intra-regional trade in the overall trade is of 50% for exports and 33% for imports, as compared with 67% and 63%, respectively, in the case of the European Union. These percentages, however, are mostly attributable to the strong dependency of Canadian and Mexican trade on the US. What's more, it would be far more accurate to speak of double bilateral relationships — United States/Canada and United States/Mexico — than of trilateral ones. And if we must speak of integration, it is the integration of two economies, Canada's and Mexico's, within a third, the economy of the United States, that one should speak of, and not of regional integration (Sydor, 2008).

Furthermore, from the viewpoints of growth and economic convergence, the results are extremely disappointing. While Mexico did benefit initially from the stimulus caused by the liberation of exchanges and the supposed "modernisation" reforms, gains in productivity have remained moderate and gains in trade are not disseminated throughout the whole country as one might have hoped. NAFTA carries part of the responsibility for this in that the Agreement does not recognise the asymmetrical nature of the relationship with Mexico, nor does it allow its government to take action to develop certain strategic industries. Possibilities do exist in a few sectors or in matters of regional development, but they are limited, and both Canada and the United States have always opposed Mexico's requests for the implementation of a regional development fund, such as there is in Europe. There is a bank, the North American Bank of Development, whose mandate is to finance certain common projects, notably along the border between the United States and Mexico, but this bank only involves the two countries and its scope is limited.

All the problems, however, do not come from NAFTA. In Canada and in Mexico, secure access to the United States market as well as a very favourable exchange rate during NAFTA's first decade have created bad habits and have not encouraged productive investment, which, furthermore, is too dependent on foreign investments. From another perspective, the opportunities created by NAFTA have often caused governments to labour under the impression that trade is a sufficient impetus to growth and development, while trade surpluses and good economic performance have sustained them in the belief that no economic policy was necessary, other than that of macro-economic stability. The absence of long-term economic strategies in Canada and in Mexico is patently clear, and all the more acute because the NAFTA model, far from fulfilling all its promises, now appears exhausted, if not threatened.

Finally, from the viewpoint of trade policy, one may speak of NAFTA as a trap from which it is difficult both for Canada and Mexico to extricate themselves, despite numerous efforts to that effect. Once again, however, these initiatives are quite recent. For a long time, neither country thought it wise to seek other trading partnerships, for fear of offending the 'American Friend', except — and even then — when it was a matter of following the lead of the United States so as not to lose the advantage of regional preference. Today, options are limited and, for the time being, no clear strategies are apparent, as trade interests are still too focused on the United States and advantages that may be offered to eventual partners are too limited. The option of a reinforced dialogue with the European Union in the case of Canada or, in that of Mexico, of a Community of States of Latin America and the Caribbean — excluding the US and Canada — as outlined by the conference of Latin

American leaders that took place in Cancun in February 2010 — are possible approaches. However, they require solid commitments and especially, a great deal of adroit diplomacy: in the past, the United States has never allowed Canada to overtake it on the transatlantic axis nor has it accepted being excluded from integration projects in the Americas. Has the American market moved from being a springboard that allows Canada and Mexico to conquer international markets to a trap from which it is quite difficult to pull out?

BIBLIOGRAPHY

Alexandroff, A. S., Hufbauer, G. C. and Lucenti, K. (2008). Still amigos: A fresh Canada–US approach to reviving NAFT, *Commentary*, 274, pp. 1–25.

Arès, M. (2005). 'Du triomphe à l'inquiétude. L'industrie maquila dans la tourmente', in Rioux, M. (ed.), *Mondialisation et pouvoir des entreprises*, Collection Économie politique internationale, Éditions Athéna, Montréal, pp. 215–234.

Arès, M. (2009). Maquiladoras et salaires au Mexique: revue de littérature, *Regards sur le travail,* Quebec, 6, 1, Fall, pp. 35–39.

Blecker, R. A. (2009). External Shock, Structural Changes and Economic Growth in Mexico, 1979–2007, *World Development*, 37(7), pp. 1274–1284.

Brunelle, D. and Deblock, C. (1989). *Le libre-échange par défaut*, Montreal, VLB éditeur.

Daudelin, J. (2007). Canada and the Americas: A Time for Modesty, *Behind the Headlines*, 64, 3, CIC, Ottawa, pp. 1–31.

Deblock, C. and Turcotte, S. (eds) (2003). *Suivre les États-Unis ou prendre une autre voie? Diplomatie commerciale et dynamiques régionales au temps de la mondialisation*, Éditions Bruylant, Bruxelles.

Deblock, C. (2010). 'Le bilatéralisme commercial Américain', in Remiche, B. and Ruiz-Fabri, H. (eds), *Le commerce international entre bi- et multilatéralisme*, Larcier, Brussels, pp. 115–173.

Dymond, B. and Hart, M. (2008). Navigating New Trade Routes: The Rise of Value Chains and the Challenges for Canadian Trade Policy, *Commentary*, 259, March, C. D. Howe Institute, Toronto, pp. 14–31.

Faux, J., Salas, C. and Schott, R. E. (2006). *Revisiting NAFTA: Still not working for North America's Workers*, EPI. Briefing Paper, September, Economic Policy Institute, Washington, DC.

Hart, M. (2008). *From Pride to Influence: Towards a New Canadian Foreign Policy,* UBC Press, Vancouver.

Hornbeck, J. F. (2004). NAFTA at Ten: Lessons from Recent Studies, *CRS Report for Congress*, RS21737, February.

Hufbauer, G. (2008). NAFTA's bad rap, *The International Economy*, Summer, pp. 19–23.

INEGI (2007). *Industria Maquiladora de Exportación*, Mexico, February.

Ito, T. (2010). NAFTA and Productivity Convergence Between Mexico and the US, *Cuadernos de Economia*, 47, May, pp. 15–55.

Mace, G. (2004). 'Quelles institutions pour l'ALENA?', in Deblock, C. and Brunelle, D. (eds), *L'ALENA. Le libre-échange en défaut,* Fides, Montréal, pp. 133–154.

Michalet, C.-A. (1998). *Le capitalisme mondial*, PUF, Paris.

Pacheco-López, P. (2008). Foreign Direct Investment, Exports and Imports in Mexico, *World Economy*, 28(8), pp. 1157–1172.

Pages-Serra, C. (2010). *The Age of Productivity: Transforming Economies from the Bottom Up*, IADB, Washington.

Rosales, O. and Kuwayama, M. (2007). Latin America Meets China and India: Prospects and Challenges for Trade and Investment, *CEPAL Review*, 93, December, pp. 81–103.

Schott. J. J. (2008), *The North American Free Trade Agreement: Time for a Change?* Peterson Institute for International Economics, Washington, DC.

Schwanen, D. (2003). *Free Trade and Canada —15 Years Later*, IRPP, Montreal.

Sydor, A. (2008). *Indice de l'intégration économique Canada-Américaine*, Ottawa, MAECI, Bureau de l'économiste en chef, Ottawa.

Viau, L. and Gagné, G. (2010). 'Ce que le Québec a gagné ou perdu suite à l'ALÉ ou les relations Québec/États-Unis vingt ans plus tard', in Lachapelle. G, (ed.), *Le destin Américain du Québec: Américanité, Américanisation et anti-Américanisme*, Presses de l'Université Laval, Québec, pp. 157–182.

Villarreal, A. M. (2009). U.S.–Mexico Economic Relations: Trends, Issues, and Implications, *CRS Report for Congress*, RL32934, April.

Villarreal, A. M. and Cid, M. (2008). NAFTA and the Mexican Economy, *CRS Report for Congress*, RL34733, November.

Waldkirch, A. (2008). *The Effects of Foreign Direct Investment in Mexico since NAFTA*, *MPRA Paper* 7975, March.

Weintraub, S. (1990). *A Marriage of Convenience. Relations between Mexico and the United States*, Oxford University Press, New York.

World Bank Group. (2004). *Mexico Makes Progress and Faces Challenges in Poverty Reduction Efforts*, New York, June.

Zeda, E., Wise, T. A. and Gallagher, K. P. (2009). Rethinking Trade Policy for Development: Lessons from Mexico Under NAFTA, *Policy Outlook*, Carnegie Endowment for International Peace, December.

Part Four

RELIGION, CULTURES, AND ETHNIC IDENTITIES

Chapter

16

The Religious Field in Latin America: Autonomy and Fragmentation

David Lehmann

16.1. INTRODUCTION

The subject of this chapter is the religious field, and its focus is therefore on the creation and shifting of the boundaries which define, delimit and subdivide the field — not religion in general. Inevitably, then, the institutional projection of Catholicism is at its centre, since our subject is dominated by the erosion of the hegemonic position of the Church and of Catholic culture and then their renewal in tandem with a broader trend in which religious renewal among the faithful is accompanied by secularization in society at large. The restructuring of the field takes the form of a loss of many (but not always all) state-sanctioned privileges and exemptions (*laïcité* or *laicidad*) and also a redrawing of Catholicism itself as a field. This redrawing is brought about by the changing demography of the priesthood, the increasing prominence of devotional and quasi-monastic movements, and the hierarchy's own preoccupation with securing the Church's moral and ideological frontiers. Although the episcopacy have increased their political influence in the recent period of democratization (Hagopian, 2009), their influence on social mores is evidently rather limited. Like evangelical churches, the bishops can deploy solid nuggets of votes, but that is no longer comparable to the pan-societal role they have carried for centuries.

Likewise, the account of evangelical churches concentrates on changing frontiers and, notably, changes in the regime of religious regulation which have opened up the public sphere for them, and also to their involvement in politics. A sign of secularization is precisely the possibility for religious organizations to become involved in politics for non-religious purposes like gaining influence and access to resources, without arousing fears of a theocratic offensive.

Inevitably other religious traditions take second place in this account, be it only for reasons of quantity and space. Non-Christian religious traditions have also benefited from growing social openness and erosion of Catholic hegemony. The Jewish population has become integrated and assimilated, but it has also suffered quantitative erosion from intermarriage and emigration to the US and Israel. Pockets of Muslims are able to exist in peace and sometimes there are unexpected conversions as in Chiapas. President Carlos Menem of Argentina was a Muslim until he converted. But the most important change in the non-Christian religious sphere has been the recognition afforded by the state to indigenous and African-derived religions (*'religiões de matriz Africana'* as they are sometimes called in Brazil). This is not precisely a direct recognition in the framework of religious regulation but rather an indirect recognition through the channels of *interculturalidad*, as folklore or local tradition and as identity rather than as a religion in the strict sense. Nonetheless, the Brazilian state of Rio Grande do Sul now recognizes marriages celebrated by an *umbanda* or *candomblé* officiant on the same basis as those celebrated by a priest, pastor, or Rabbi. '*Cultos afro*' seek recognition and both political and legal protection as heritage, as heirs to black culture, but also as a religion when they find themselves the objects of harassment and persecution by evangelical churches, especially neo-Pentecostals, who denounce them vociferously as pagans, doing the work of the

Devil. But in this chapter we keep to the Catholic and Pentecostal or evangelical churches, for it is those which are in contention for defining the field, the frontiers of religion, and indeed the very meaning of the word 'religion'.

16.2. RELIGION: POPULAR AND ERUDITE

Writing on Latin American religion must take as one of its building blocks the classic distinction between erudite or institutionalized religion and popular religion, which are also distinctive features of Catholicism throughout the Latin world. They are not watertight compartments, but rather different spheres which nevertheless are engaged in a constant dialectic, mutually influencing each other's rituals and symbolism, their heroes and monsters, saints and sinners. The distinctively Catholic character of the popular-erudite dialectic derives from the Church's millennial development of a worldwide hierarchical and institutional apparatus, including Holy Orders, educational and charitable institutions, and an omnipresent musical, architectural and monumental presence, coexisting with an infinity of local saints, festivals, confraternities, shrines, pilgrimages and superstitions, of which a small number blossom, for probably quite contingent reasons, into regional, national and even global cults (cf. Lourdes and of course, Guadalupe). The French sociologist Pierre Bourdieu[1] built his entire concept of religious capital around the polar opposites of a religion of superstition which barely merited the title of 'religion', and a religion orchestrated and deployed by an apparatus of power: the contrast between 'small-scale salvation operations' ('les petites enterprises du salut') with their 'ambiguous and enigmatic responses' ('réponses ambigües et énigmatiques') at one pole, and at the other 'more rational methods to gain access to divine will' in the hands of 'a trained priesthood' ('méthodes plus rationnelles pour connaître la volonté divine' and 'prêtres capables de les pratiquer') (Bourdieu, 1992, p. 302). This image, evoked first in the context of Ancient

[1] All translations of Bourdieu in this chapter are by David Lehmann.

Israel, is then transposed into a model of a (Catholic) Church whose apparatus of power is a relatively autonomous religious field' ('champ religieux relativement autonome') which engages in a 'process of systematization and moralization of religious representations and practices' ('processus de systématisation et de moralisation des pratiques et des repésentations religieuses') and to 'the religious ideology as an approximation to an expressly systematized system' ('l'idéologie religieuse comme (quasi) système expressément systématisé'), in which a good and just God replaces the unpredictable and capricious gods of magic (Bourdieu, 1992, p. 302). But, later, Bourdieu (1992, p. 327) deals with two sorts of challenge faced by any religious bureaucracy: one is the demand for immediate responses to immediate problems (characteristic of the culture of magic and taboo which religion itself has replaced): this model of what might be called the evolution of belief essentially leads to concessions: the Church can co-opt the world of superstition. Thus he quotes Van Gennep's *Manuel de Folklore Français Contemporain*, with its innumerable examples of 'exchanges between peasant culture and the culture of the Church — "liturgical feasts institutionalized as folklore like rogations" — pagan rituals incorporated into standard liturgy, saints endowed with magical powers and functions etc. — all of which mark the concessions which clerics have to make to profane pressures', be it only so as to retain the trust of the faithful who would be alienated by a radical 'modernization'. He uses the word 'concessions' to denote the market forces at play for a church which has to hold on to its flock, but contrasts these with the much more serious threat coming, so to speak, from the 'right', not from wandering preachers and healers, represented by a Prophet who challenges the apparatus in the name of the true faith from which the official bearers of orthodoxy, the prestigious hierarchy, have strayed or which they have betrayed. In response, in Bourdieu's stylized history of religion, the apparatus develops simplified and highly routinized procedures which can be applied by subordinate trained representatives without much explanation. And if they receive little explanation, this is precisely because the issues at stake — salvation, the afterlife, the reasons for this or that procedure — are hard to explain. Thus additional protective rings of ritual and of personnel are formed to protect the mysterious knowledge and power of the core apparatus itself (Bourdieu, 1992, p. 328). They may still not be enough in some circumstances, notably in times of crisis and when suitably gifted or daring individuals can take on the Prophet's mantle. But the point is that, to protect itself from those threats, the Church develops a formidable apparatus for the administration and domestication of the supernatural. Bourdieu really seems to believe that a Church — and he means a Church or similar apparatus, not religion in general — can shape the beliefs and values which command society and underwrite the state:

> its proper function is to contribute to the preservation of the symbolic order (i) by the imposition and inculcation of frameworks of perception, thought and action objectively attuned to the political structures, and thus apt to 'naturalize' these structures, conferring upon them thereby the ultimate legitimation. This is achieved by establishing and restoring a consensus on the ordering of the world through the propagation of common frameworks of thought and by solemnly affirming or reaffirming that consensus in religious festivals and ceremonies whose symbolic efficacy is itself reinforced by shared belief in their efficacy; (ii) by committing its [the Church's] specifically religious authority to confront in the symbolic sphere itself any prophetic or heretical attempts to undermine the symbolic order. (Bourdieu, 1992, pp. 328–329)

The Church, he tells us, neglects her symbolic deployment at her peril. But at the edges the symbolic and the practical are entangled with one another. Now turn to the following remark by the late Olivia Harris: 'To write about practical Christianity [in the Andes in this case] is always to face a conundrum: What to include and what to exclude?' (Harris, 2006, p. 52). That is, what counts as Christianity and what counts as religion in general? As her paper develops so Harris describes the continuing interaction between official and non-official practices within Andean Christianity and on its edges — but as she says, there is no consistent line. Five hundred years after the first campaigns of Christian conversion, the relationship between official and unofficial practices, even under the same church roof, continues, especially in regions with a prominent indigenous presence. In accordance with Bourdieu, the relationship between the official and the indigenous is one of permanent negotiation. Peasants (Harris avoids calling them '*indios*') attend Mass but do not take communion, which has no interest for them, let alone confession: instead they rush to be sprinkled with Holy Water. Attendance at life cycle rituals is for the purpose of ensuring health, of 'satisfying God's hunger' (Harris, 2006, p. 55) with no regard for the idea of a sacrament or of eternal life. For the peasants, payment for a Mass is essential because it ensures that an exchange has taken place and thus guarantees the benefit which otherwise would be just a promise. In Harris's account Spanish priests schooled in post-conciliar (i.e. post-Vatican II) modernism and social commitment are utterly disconcerted: one of them is described driving away in his overloaded jeep after unwillingly accepting the payments and enduring an interminable Mass — interminable no doubt because of the votive offerings, promises and exchanges which had to be dealt with individually (Harris, 2006, p. 56). These payments are not gifts because for those who make them, exchange is the essence of their relationship with the supernatural, whether the supernatural being is one of 'their' divinities or a Catholic one.

The bemused priest might have recalled the difficulties faced by his colonial predecessors in explaining to the ancestors of those peasants — or at least of their Mexican counterparts — that the effigies of a Virgin or of Jesus were only representations, and were not *themselves* possessed of supernatural powers (Gruzinski, 1990, p. 109). In 1525 the Franciscans unleashed a campaign of terror in New Spain, being forced, in Serge Gruzinski's words, to remove Christian images because 'images of Christ and the Virgin had been mingled with the idols and irresistibly absorbed into the autochthonous paganism' (Gruzinski, 2001, p. 61). His point is that images served and continue to serve many purposes and could not be immunized against magical manipulation any more than the people could be immunized against their own inclinations to imbue certain sorts of venerated objects, with magical, supernatural, or indeed contagious qualities, or with powers of pollution. The first generation who conquered Mexico with Cortés thought that they were destroying the indigenous belief system by destroying idols, but did not understand that supernatural forces were, and maybe still are, ubiquitous: for the indigenous saw the presence of the deities in all sorts of objects. Anthropomorphic representation was not part of their way of grasping the supernatural forces on whose appeasement — with food and human blood — their lives depended (Gruzinski, 1990, p. 93; Gruzinski, 2001, p. 58). A few years later Franciscan missionaries — undertaking a campaign similar to the those being conducted in Europe at the same time — could not understand how the monotheism they preached, or thought they were preaching, led Indians to attach the names of God and the Virgin Mary to almost any image that crossed their sight (Gruzinski, 1990, p. 107; Gruzinski, 2001, p. 66).

It is necessary to recall the richness and variety of popular religion in Latin America because the changes in the religious field since the mid-twentieth century involve substantial changes in the relationship between popular and institutionalized religion. Latin American popular religion not only survived the Counter-Reformation; it also subsequently prospered and adapted and showed more resilience than in Europe, both among indigenous peoples and among the rest of the population, especially the lower strata. While the religiosity observed by Harris bears a clear indigenous imprint, the link of popular religion with indigenous belief systems, cosmologies, or rituals has to be seen in combination with many other influences: lay people leading prayer groups saying the rosary in church; local saint's days organized by *cofradías*; infinite cures and untold numbers of healers; and assorted *agentes de salvação* (Brandão, 1980). Popular religion focuses on individuals' life cycles and on the life of their immediate circle, their locality or community; it mixes the sacred and the profane, if not in the same ceremony, certainly in the same event — the Saint's Day is also a market day, during which the official celebrations are followed by dancing and revelry, a bullfight, a cockfight and so on. The phrase 'and so on' conveys very well the unguarded or unbounded character of popular celebrations, and the proliferation of rituals and roles which they can encompass (Brandão, 1989), while the idea of exchange conveys the multiple social relationships which are cemented, or ruptured, by popular religious practices. The notion of exchange is derived from Bourdieu as well, and — probably unwittingly — Brandão, like me (Lehmann, 1996; Lehmann, 2009), also uses a notion similar to Bourdieu's quoted above when he describes what I have called the dialectic of the erudite and the popular, that is, the efforts of the Church to 'purify' or subordinate popular celebrations whose protagonists are, for their part, fulfilling their function as vehicles for the preservation of heritage. The public character of the celebration is not frivolous — in Brandão's words it exhibits a belief that the locality has been cleansed of the dust of sinfulness because it has recognized the majesty of divine judgment (Brandão, 1989, p. 14). Yet to some extent the words of Bourdieu have been fulfilled, in that, despite its departure from the detail of approved ritual, popular Catholicism has remained subordinate to the official Church, and has not developed any kind of dissidence nor has it produced a distinctive theology. The traditional popular religion which survives, in the context of contemporary massive urbanization and globalization, shows symptoms of detachment, occasionally reaching the edges of the surreal, as witness the disconcerting cult of Santísima Muerte — a cult which spreads beyond the local through networks of media and violent crime, exhibiting an autonomous deployment of quasi-Catholic imagery on an unprecedented scale — but this is like a parallel religion, not a saintly cult within the Catholic pantheon (Howe, Zaraysky *et al.*, 2009). This type of 'escape', in which a hegemonic apparatus of religious power loses control of its own symbolic resources, is a symptom of the changing religious field, as we shall see later.

The remainder of this chapter will describe and interpret the way in which this relationship was transformed in the late twentieth century. It will consider how the popular became independent of the erudite; how Liberation Theology or 'basista' Catholicism could be seen as yet another — maybe the last — strategy to capture and channel popular religion; how evangelical Christianity became a far more autonomous version of popular religion, cut off from the erudite and shorn of hegemonic potential; and finally how devotional movements within Catholicism itself represent perhaps a new stage in the gradual evolution of Catholicism from its centuries-old status as a hegemonic culture towards the conformation of a mere denomination (hopefully not a sect, as Hans Küng fears) which can, finally, live with modernity, demonstrating yet again that it is not necessary to be liberal to achieve that; indeed in the religious sphere at least the reverse may be the case if a religion is to thrive, not just survive. To complicate matters further, when finally the people do wake up to some sort of abstract notion of a rational divinity presiding over a moral order (which is how Bourdieu understands religion proper), they are quite likely to convert to Pentecostalism. Even then, however, the rationality and the moral austerity are nuanced by hopes and promises of immediate earthly gratification, and Pentecostal preachers are in certain churches more than ready to incorporate ideas of healing, possession and exorcism into their images of the diabolic. And those notions are also adopted by Catholic devotional and charismatic movements. So the rationalization of religion remains incomplete.

16.3. REINING IN AND RIDING THE PERIPHERY FROM ROMANIZATION TO JOHN PAUL II

In Latin America the Church hierarchy in the twentieth century undertook various campaigns to make popular religion more orthodox and also to encourage commitment and religious education among more nominal Catholics. Romanization in the 1930s reflected a concerted effort at centralization of power in the Vatican, especially power of appointment of bishops without government involvement (after reaching concordats with various states), as well as involvement in education and some political alliances. In Brazil, it inspired the 'neo-Christendom' strategy of Cardinal Leme, who cultivated a cordial relationship with Getulio Vargas. The Social Doctrine of the Church as first elaborated by Leo X in *Rerum Novarum* (1899) fed into corporatist ideas of the state and of state regulation of class conflict and industrial relations which inspired labour legislation in Chile in the 1920s (under Arturo Alessandri), in Vargas' Estado Novo and later in Argentina. During this period the Church hierarchy also showed itself adept at mobilizing popular religion in the interests of its own positions: this is graphically described by Alan Knight and also by Mary Kay Vaughan in her account of fierce struggles over education in post-*Cristiada* Mexico under Cárdenas. In the different regions Vaughan studied (Sonora, Puebla) we find the clergy uniting with the more conservative post-revolutionary politicians against the more radically anti-clerical and socialist educational initiatives, brandishing the threat that the new teachers would undermine traditional morals and place the virtue of their daughters at risk (Knight, 1994; Vaughan, 1997). This had less to do with the social doctrine than with a classic defence of the field. But precisely during this period the French public Catholic intellectual Jacques Maritain was heralding a change in the religious field in Europe and Latin America in his widely read *Humanisme Intégral* (1936). Maritain was an advocate of a corporatist arrangement of society in the image of medieval guilds as a way of overcoming the contradictions of capitalism, but he was also very unpopular in clerical circles on account of his hostility to Franco during the Spanish Civil War, and he remains a major figure as an advocate of a non-sectarian Catholic politics in the shape of what became Christian Democracy.

Through the romanizing and modernizing cycles popular religion was left alone, though occasionally it did erupt into conflict with the hierarchy or indeed with the state — notably in Brazil with various disconnected millenarian, messianic or simply socio-religious movements (Canudos, Contestado, Padre Cicero). These uprisings could be seen as examples of Bourdieu's dissident prophets: calling on the apparatus to heed to its roots and to its core traditions. Being popular movements, they were more concerned with traditions than with doctrine. To some extent the Cristero War was also such an instance, though in that case a sector of the clergy took an active part in military action, against the judgment, even the fury, of many bishops and of the Vatican itself. Jean Meyer in his celebrated, masterly and passionate account insists again and again on the betrayal by the hierarchy of the Cristero campesinos prepared to fight and die for Christ who looked to the long term, did not believe the Church in Mexico was in mortal danger and wanted peaceful coexistence with the state (Meyer, 1973–1974). At the same time the bishops took tighter control of lay organizations like the small Círculos Obreros Católicos and Acción Católica. Meyer exalts the popular religion of the Cristeros who, far from being superstitious idolaters, accepted implicitly the message that God sent his mother the Virgin of Guadalupe specifically to Mexico, and now took the chance to reach heaven by dying in defence of their faith.

Argentina, thanks to Lila Caimari (Caimari, 1994), presents us with the case which best illustrates shifting frontiers and mutations in the fields of politics and religion, or rather of the church and state, during the period from Leo XIII to John XXIII, that is from romanization to Vatican II. In 1894, the state had decreed 'educación laica, obligatoria y gratuita' and this remained in force until 1943 when the military government, which kept Argentina from allying with the Allies and maintained a deeply conservative line during the war, imposed the teaching of religion in schools and, equally importantly, entrusted it to the Church. During the 1930s, as elsewhere, Acción Católica had some success, following on from the Círculos Obreros Católicos founded in 1894, organizing summer camps for workers and young people, and publishing profusely, in the then standard project of 'rechristianizing society', but they still only had 35,000 members even by 1950. Caimari remarks that in the 1920s the Vatican lost an opportunity to promote an activist priest, Fr. de Andrea, to the Archbishopric of Buenos Aires, leaving the position open to a series of inexpressive figures. As the 1945 elections approached the Church leaders gravitated towards Perón not because they were particularly sympathetic to his anti-establishment, anti-oligarchic rhetoric, nor because they took kindly to his claim that his policies were inspired by the Papal encyclicals (i.e. the social doctrine going back to Leo XIII), but because they distrusted the *laicidad* of his liberal opponents, especially in the education field. They may not at first have noticed that Perón's invocation of that Papal inspiration heralded something deeper, expressed in his inclination to lecture the bishops on who and what was a good Christian, and his depiction of himself and his movement as bearers of the true Christianity (not Catholicism) in contrast to the formalisms of conventional religious observance. So his confirmation of religious education in schools, and a similarly friendly gesture in exempting the Catholic Church from the Registro Nacional de Cultos in 1946 were double-edged: it went together with the subordination of religious education to the Ministry of Education, although the teaching itself was in the hands of church appointees, and the content was deeply conservative, describing the Catholic Church as the only bearer of Christian truth and the Ten Commandments as forbidding the reading and propaganda of anti-Catholic books and parties. The co-optative agenda behind all this was bolstered by generous measures to fund and raise clerical salaries and double the number of beneficiaries. But even while the top hierarchy was tempted by the material benefits offered, and by the regime's appeal to its claim to monopolize the religious field, there was unrest elsewhere among the ranks of its followers. The Church's oligarchic friends were shocked by Peronism's aggressive rhetoric, especially when Evita moved front stage. The Sociedad de Beneficiencia — a venerable charity in the classic mould of aristocratic good works — was taken over by the state and handed to her Foundation; private (mostly Catholic) schools were obliged to accept workers' children or lose their state subsidy; in 1954 religious education in state schools was replaced by 'un moral de fondo y no de forma' (the same slogan) led by spiritual advisors from the Eva Perón Foundation (Caimari, 1994, p. 187) and promoting popular religion rather than devotional and moral instruction (Caimari, 1994, pp. 190–191); Eva as 'Jefa Espiritual de la Nación' proclaimed her love for 'el Cristo entre los descamisados' (Caimari, 1994, p. 189) and contrasted her social work, which was about justice, with the patronizing charity ('*limosna*') of the respectable classes. She even began to appropriate Christmas for the Peronist movement, speaking of how 'en esta noche una mujer, un hombre … llamaron inútilmente a las puertas del orgullo y de la soberbia', and finally, in her last Christmas message, quoting the Magnificat in a manner that could not but assimilate her own image to that of the Virgin Mary (Caimari, 1994, p. 228). These provocations, combined with the ever more martyr-like imagery surrounding her person as illness advanced, drove a deep wedge between the regime and the Catholic faithful in the upper classes and all the hierarchy save the top echelon. After her death, Perón did try to calm the atmosphere somewhat but it was too late: the hostility acquired all sorts of lurid connotations inspired by the regime's sponsorship of sports and rumours of his close involvement in teenage female sporting activities and by his increasing closeness to Pentecostal and Spiritist groups and organizations, especially after Evita's death (Caimari, 1994, p. 201). After his overthrow, the Cardinal who had given in to the regime's blandishments, measuring the good health of the Church only by its '*privilegios corporativos*' in the words of his critics, was removed to a sinecure in Rome. In the 1970s, when Perón returned, he had made his peace with the Church, but the Church for its part had not undergone any reform. Indeed, although Argentina gave birth to some very radical priests in the Third World Priests movement, the repression against them, especially within the Church, was fiercer than anywhere, and later the complicity of the hierarchy with the crimes of the 1976–1983 dictatorship became a cause for shock and scandal (Mignone, 1988).

Whereas in Europe the Church was baffled and embattled by socialism in Spain, France, Germany and Italy, and by fascism in Italy and Germany — though Spanish fascism was in a close alliance with the Church — in Latin America Church leaders fought off the challenge of Peronism and found an accommodation with the PRI in Mexico. Broadly, the Church gained both independence and influence vis-à-vis the state, and was under little external pressure to adapt to the permissiveness which had always troubled Church leaders and the socialist influences which were far more attenuated in Latin America than in Europe. So the moderately modernizing changes initiated with Romanization continued, until pressures for change which had built up in Europe (not much in Latin America) eventually came to a head at Vatican II.

A group of Latin American theologians and bishops (Gustavo Gutierrez, Msgr. Manuel Larraín of Chile and Helder Camara of Brazil) who had been very active at Vatican II brought the Council's message back to the continent. The translation of Vatican II into the Latin American context took several forms. The most intellectual was Liberation Theology which took the project of the social doctrine much further by denouncing the Church's posture as an ally of the ruling classes and by questioning the whole idea of a salvation which would only come after death. Liberation Theology also sought to play down the emphasis of traditional religiosity on an individual's personal relationship with the divine, drawing on the Gospel's teachings to emphasize the relationship with our neighbour, with the community, also, like Eva Perón, shifting the idea of charity, with its connotations of short-term alleviation, towards structural change as a more enduring way of caring for one's neighbour. Liberation Theology was vulnerable to the charge that it represented a version of Marxism, and some followers did indeed eventually 'convert' to Marxist parties or movements; but for the most part the defence was that Marxism was a method, and the leading theologian of liberation, Gustavo Gutierrez, ceased to make any reference to Marxism after the publication of his first book *Teologia de la Liberación: perspectivas* in 1967. It was in some ways a challenge to the transcendent in religion, and in other ways was viewed by some as a type of Protestantism. But it had broad international appeal and also broad intellectual appeal beyond the frontiers of the Church, of theology and of Catholicism or even religion. As has been said before (Lehmann, 1990; Lehmann, 1996), Liberation Theology brought about more change outside the Church than inside. The range of influence of Liberation Theology, or rather of ideas derived more or less directly and more or less faithfully from it, has been vast: from the Brazilian MST (Movimento dos Sem Terra) to some guerrilla ventures in Bolivia, Colombia and Guatemala (though here it was not precisely the influence of Liberation Theology); it also helped to bring the themes of participation and popular education onto the international development agenda, notably because among the Christian Base Communities (CEBs), which Liberation Theology inspired, the method of Paulo Freire, the world-renowned educator, gained much acceptance. Liberation Theology made a major contribution to the autonomy of the NGO field in the sphere of development policy and practice and to social movements through the work of inspired priests and nuns. They also gained support from the Bishops' Conferences, mostly, though not exclusively, in Brazil. These had not existed as decision-making bodies before Vatican II, but once formally established they provided a bureaucratic instance and also a channel for external funding for the Pastorals, which now tended to replace what were previously known as Missions: Brazilian examples include the Pastoral da Juventude, Pastor do Indigena, Pastoral da Terra, and there are similar institutions in other countries. These institutions were staffed mostly by lay activists with a sprinkling of ex-priests. The CEBs for their part have tended to rely on the logistical, educational and intellectual support of priests and nuns and some bishops for their organization — despite the rhetoric of autonomy and a 'People's Church', proclaimed by some of their most renowned advocates like the brothers Clodovis and Leonardo Boff (Hewitt, 1991; Mariz, 1993; Burdick, 1994). Their influence on Catholic schools and universities, whose intake was mostly upper middle class, seems to have been limited (Marin, 1995), and they have remained a minority phenomenon when compared with devotional movements such as Foccolari, Neocatecumenes, and above all the Catholic Charismatic Renewal. The vocation conferred upon the CEBs by the Boff brothers — both of whom were then members of religious orders — and others who saw in them the nucleus of an alternative to the hierarchical Church, was not taken up on a significant scale.

Liberation Theology reached the apogee of its influence at the Conference of Latin American Bishops (CELAM) in Medellin, Colombia, in 1968, which denounced the continent's structural injustice, social inequality, and external dependence. It could be seen as one attempt to transform the field of Catholicism, but in retrospect it lacked certain attributes necessary for the task: the comparison with the devotional movements, to which we shall come, is instructive because these are far less innovative ideologically, but seem to have a more durable effect. Historically, Catholicism has spoken more to society as a whole while Evangelicals speak almost exclusively to their own — but, as we shall see, recent tendencies within Catholicism appear to signal a much more inward-looking culture among its most dynamic elements than has traditionally been the case.

Although Liberation Theology's ideas had roots in Europe, in modern developments in Catholic and Protestant theology, they were often regarded, in Europe itself, as a result of the undoubted innovations of Gustavo Gutierrez in particular, as distinctively Latin American. And Gutierrez himself over time developed increasingly Latin themes as he paid more attention to indigenous issues and looked to the sixteenth-century Bishop Bartolomé de las Casas rather than modern theology and philosophy as his inspiration (Gutiérrez, 1993). Las Casas, nonetheless, has never ceased to attract controversy, and the question of his canonization apparently arose only in the year 2000.

At first, Liberation Theology had an ambivalent relationship with popular religion, divided between a disdain for superstition — seen as a distraction from the structural problems of society — and a certain reverence for the true, unblemished religiosity of the oppressed. Under the influence of Liberation Theology's ideas — which I term *basismo* — samba drums might be brought into church, for example, or a pilgrimage which once had celebrated a fiesta would be turned into a celebration of the migrant worker as an emblem of suffering (as in the *Romaria do Migrante* or Migrant's Pilgrimage near Campina Grande in the northeast of Brazil).[2] On the whole, though, one could say that Liberation Theology and *basismo* had little effect on the rituals and celebrations which punctuate the calendar of many parishes, or on the routine activities of *benzedeiras* and *curandeiras* who, for example, make up the fabric of religious life in the Brazilian hinterland (Brandão, 2007, Chapter 4). Thus Burdick quotes several black informants from his research in the suburbs of Rio de Janeiro who were offended by the Church's attempts in its Campanha da Fraternidade of 1988 to recognize the black population and the current and past discriminations they have suffered. In particular they were disconcerted by the occasional introduction of samba drums into Church 'there was misinterpretation', the samba drums were an

[2] The drums may have been an influence of the theology of inculturation rather than liberation — a theology promoted in the African context and also among the Latin American proponents of Teología Indígena.

accoutrement of *macumba* and thus introducing evil into church; a medium said 'if they hated me for so long' why do they 'want me now?' (Burdick, 1994, pp. 158ff.). It should be added, however, that these responses are not easy to evaluate, and may or may not be representative, since the subject is so easily caught up in the rhetoric of victimhood and in claims to exclusive ethnic voice.

Burdick also emphasizes the middle-, or lower middle-, class character of CEB participants and the somewhat academic character of their meetings. In my own studies in Salvador da Bahia in the early 1990s (Lehmann, 1996) I noted the presence of university students, but also people of extremely low incomes: for me the striking feature was that the meetings and discussion groups — known as Educação Popular — attracted a core group of faithful participants, but did not treat evangelizing — gathering in new adepts — as a priority. The contrast with the expansionary energy of their Pentecostal neighbours was overwhelming; also while the Pentecostals were self-financing, Educação Popular relied on foreign funding to keep going.

Vatican II, by opening the windows to allow fresh air to blow in, as John XXIII put it, did shake the structure because of its demographic as well as ideological sequel: the effects of a collapse of recruitment to the clergy and religious orders, in Latin America but also in the European countries which supplied so many of them, compounded an exodus of those who were inside. And of course the evangelical Christians were growing and after 1980 were also developing a high public profile, to which we shall return. Pope John Paul II reimposed Papal authority in pre-conciliar mode, when he decreed a withdrawal from political controversy and party alignment, and undertook a campaign of marginalization against Liberation Theology and *basismo*. His emissaries went around Latin America removing Liberation Theology theologians from teaching posts and positions of influence, dispatching them to obscure parishes and positions. Like Lenin his motto could have been 'better fewer, but better', with a focus on personal morality and a tightening of discipline within the structures of the Church. John Paul also signalled a desire to encourage popular religion, with its focus on local traditions, by promoting and approving record numbers of new beatifications and canonizations, reversing the traditionally sceptical response of the Vatican to popular beatification campaigns.

16.4. DEVOTIONAL AND CHARISMATIC MOVEMENTS AT THE TURN OF THE CENTURY

The Pope was also encouraging, more or less discretely, both older movements and orders which resisted, more or less discretely, the spirit of Vatican II, like Opus Dei and the Legionarios de Cristo, and newer types of religious renewal which Liberation Theology had simply not dreamed of and which caught its protagonists off guard. These renewal movements have only been visible since about 1980 but in that short period they have taken part in a multifaceted reshaping of Latin American Catholicism and have produced changes which would have seemed inconceivable in the immediate aftermath of Vatican II. This reshaping has yet to be registered on a significant scale in an academic literature which, *grosso modo*, turned from enthusiasm for Liberation Theology to a fascination for Pentecostalism.

From one point of view they represent a strategy to resist the pressures to democratize the Church's hierarchy, to resist the permissive society and to resist involvement with social movements identified largely with the left, by espousing conservative values and the religiosity of instant satisfaction, while at the same time raising, rather than lowering, the price to pay for religious recognition in terms of personal, carnal and financial sacrifice. That is, these movements emphasize healing and earthly fulfilment, but they make heavy demands on their followers' time and financial resources.

The movements are nonetheless highly diverse: too much so to be interpreted as a response to a single strategy; they are far too wealthy, often, for their existence to be explained by Vatican or even Episcopal support and they vary substantially in structure and ethos. This can be seen from a list only of a few of them: Opus Dei, the Legionarios de Cristo, the Cursillos de Cristiandad, Foccolari, Communione e Liberazione (CL) (mostly Italian), Sodalitium and

Schoenstatt, and the biggest of them all: the worldwide quasi-Pentecostal but Catholic movement, the Catholic Charismatic Renewal (CCR), born at a meeting at the Jesuit Duquesne University in the US in 1967, and eventually recognized by the Vatican in September 1993.[3] They all enjoy some kind of Papal recognition, expressed in numerous titles the Pope has at his disposal. Opus is a 'personal prelature', Legionarios a religious congregation and so on, but none originates in a papal or Episcopal initiative and many are lay-founded and lay-driven. Some of them are quite secretive (especially Opus Dei). Opus' website says it has 88,000 'fieles' of whom less than 2,000 are priests and 77% are married men and women. The remainder have taken vows of chastity and of these many live in Opus houses. Opus operates schools and universities in several countries (Universidad de los Andes in Chile; Universidad del Pacífico in Mexico and its original Universidad de Navarra in Spain) and as of 2010 includes several Chilean and Peruvian Bishops among its members — notably the Archbishop of Lima. The Legionarios are more of a mass organization: they too operate a network of universities: in Mexico under the Anahuac name and in Chile (Universidad Finis Terrae), as well as schools. According to their website, the Legion has 800 priests and 2,500 seminarists in training plus a large but unspecified number of followers in its affiliated Regnum Christi movement. In Chile at least, the Legion and Opus run schools which attract the children of the economic elite and have an explicit evangelizing agenda, notably to bring parents to religion through their children (Thumala Olave, 2007). Of Foccolari, Schoenstatt and the Neocatecumene little is published save on Wikipedia. Communione e

[3] The precise situation is that on 30 November 1990 the Pontifical Council for the Laity granted recognition to the Catholic Fraternity of Charismatic Covenant Communities and Fellowships and then in 1993 it recognized the International Catholic Charismatic Service (ICCRS) as a body for the promotion of the Catholic Charismatic Renewal'. This body has its seat in Rome and its president is elected by its Council from nominations approved by the Pontifical Council for the Laity. The ICCRS is the successor to a body first established in 1978 in Brussels by Cardinal Suenens.

Liberazione has had great success setting up student residences in Italian university towns; its ethos is devotional and also encourages students to engage in social work, and until the collapse of Christian Democracy it had a prominent role in Italian politics. Its presence in Latin America seems sketchy: it does run the Universidad Sede Sapientiae in Peru — though to what extent this is intended to spread the CL ideology is unclear.

This list does not include the many Jesuit schools and universities, such as the Universidad Iberoamericana in Mexico, which is at the heart of a network of Jesuit institutions of higher education. But the ethos of these institutions is different from those mentioned: they are not established with a missionary or evangelizing purpose and encourage a liberal atmosphere. They are expensive, though, and so their students tend to come from the upper middle classes, like those of the institutions operated by Opus and the Legionarios, with the exception of the Jesuits' Instituto Superior Intercultural Ayuuk, (an intercultural university) located in an indigenous community in Oaxaca, Mexico. Another example of such opening is the Catholic University of Rio de Janeiro (PUC-Rio), whose affirmative action programme run in cooperation with EDUCAFRO, a network of courses helping black and low-income applicants prepared for university entrance exams has brought a noticeable change in the racial profile of its student body.

Of these movements Renovación Carismática (RC) is the one which most resembles a mass movement, at least in Latin America. (In North America it seems to be more of a sect-like affair operating in small groups (Csordas, 1997)). In the early 1990s (Lehmann, 1996; Lehmann, 2003) intellectuals linked to or identified with TL and the Igreja Popular were contemptuous of what they saw as its conservative focus on personal religiosity and its middle class following but the fact is that the RC has grown rapidly and in diverse ways. Unlike Opus or the Legionarios, it is not a tight organization with clear boundaries but rather a movement animated by activists within the clergy and among the laity. It runs, or maybe just inspires, meetings of all sizes, from very small parish-based gatherings to mass meetings in football stadia and spectacles featuring celebrity preachers — like the so-called

Singing Priest of São Paulo (Clarke 1999). Like the Pentecostals, the RC has 'morphed' into numerous forms so it is no longer possible to describe a convergent archetype. On the one hand it is a mass movement which can gather tens of thousands in football stadiums and in processions on the Day of Pentecost (seven weeks after Easter), which harks back to the occasion when the Apostles of Jesus were gathered and tongues of fire descended upon them and they began speaking in other languages.[4] But the Catholic Charismatic Renewal has also inspired small communities devoted to a religious vocation and innumerable prayer groups. The RC also has a mediatic affinity which in Brazil strongly influenced the Church's efforts in this sphere. It was a Fr. Dougherty, who came from the US and introduced the CCR into Brazil in the 1970s, who revived the Church's media presence with its TV station Redevida — even though at first his initiatives had been brushed off by the National Bishops' Conference (CNBB). In the early 2000s it was claimed that 'the majority' of the programming on Brazil's 181 Catholic radio stations was produced by 'CCR members' (Chesnut, 2003, pp. 94–96). In 1993 the CCR in Brazil launched the Ofensiva Nacional, and by 2000 they had a prayer group in every parish in Brazil (Chesnut, 2003, p. 98).

The RC, unlike Opus and the Legionarios for example, is a movement whose open style and mediatic inclinations places it in a position to propagate its practices and motifs. Charismatics, we are told 'tend to adopt a Pentecostal-type ascetic code of conduct' especially among the popular classes, which is precisely where the other Pentecostals tend predominantly to be found (Chesnut, 2003, p. 96). Beyond events carrying the charismatic label, one also observes charismatic habits — like singing with arms outstretched — infiltrating services in parish churches. One concern for the Church is to maintain control of the RC,

[4] 'And when the day of Pentecost was fully come, they were all with one accord in one place. And suddenly there came a sound from heaven as of a rushing mighty wind, and it filled all the house where they were sitting. And there appeared unto them cloven tongues like as of fire, and it sat upon each of them. And they were all filled with the Holy Ghost, and began to speak with other tongues, as the Spirit gave them utterance', *Acts of the Apostles*, 2, 1–8.

so often Bishops will name a priest to oversee it, and priests require that meetings must take place in a church, not in other premises. Although benign, this is still a more formalized arrangement than would ever govern the Church's relationship with popular religion. On one of Pope John Paul II's visits to Brazil he was greeted in Rio's Maracana stadium by a vast crowd organized by the RC, and Benedict, his successor, was greeted in 2007 by a crowd organized by the Legionarios. Services run by the RC exhibit many similarities to Pentecostal services, but we have too narrow a base of observation to make any generalization.

These movements may or may not reflect a Church institution which has come to terms, finally, with modernity, but they surely reflect the penetration of Catholicism's culture by modernity, and although some find this surprising because they seem so conservative, it is by now widely agreed that many movements whose ethos is deeply conservative with respect to religiosity and personal morality are also modern in their forms of organization and in their independence from inherited structures of religious power. This is recognized by grand theorists like Eisenstadt and David Martin with respect to Pentecostals and fundamentalists (Martin, 1990; Eisenstadt, 1995; Eisenstadt, 2000), but has yet to be applied to renewal movements in Catholicism, Anglicanism, or Islam. The Catholic Charismatic Renewal uses phrases such as 'being in the world but not of the world, in the media but not of the media' — in short, 'to be modern without modernity' (Carranza, Mariz, *et al.*, 2009, p. 52) and this includes a prominent, even equal role for men and women and the admission of couples in religious communities (Carranza, Mariz, *et al.*, 2009, p. 162). One feature of their modernity is the focus on managing one's wellbeing, sometimes described as refashioning the self — making the individual responsible for self-transformation as opposed to waiting for supernatural intervention in response to prayer or offerings. They also seem to signify a profound change in the vast and varied institutional apparatus of Catholicism: although recognized in their different statuses by the Papacy or by local bishops, these are mostly movements in which the laiety plays a prominent role, deploying substantial resources which are not under the control of bishops and priests. The flexibility of such arrangements stands in contrast to the rigidity and complex procedures of the hierarchy. They bring quite a different sort of lay involvement from the intimacy and localism of popular religion for these are transnational organizations operating on a different scale, with elaborate formal organization, while the smaller communities seem to be made up of people who are fleeing their social networks rather than embedded within them in the classic location-based style of popular religion. In addition Opus and the Legionarios are also concerned to gain influence among political and economic elites and in the professions. Opus Dei, which first appeared in politics in Franco's Spain, also has a record of placing its people in high political and bureaucratic positions, as in the example of the new (2010) Minister of Education in Chile and President García's Minister of Defence in Peru. Opus is the nearest thing to a religious order: although its members are mostly drawn from the laity, they agree to subject themselves to certain disciplines and take vows, and the dividing lines between clergy and laiety and between men and women are very clearly drawn.

The redrawing of the religious field can be seen in these projects to create large-scale, global and lay organizations. Previously lay and popular religion had tended to be a local affair and often incorporated rituals which, though not strictly approved, were nonetheless tolerated by priests and bishops, as we saw in the Brazilian and Bolivian examples. Stereotypically, the hierarchical mind no doubt regarded popular religion as religion for the simple folk, which had no theological or structural repercussions. But the organizations mentioned seem to herald a new departure — albeit one that has been developing gradually over many decades, since Opus was founded before the Second World War and the Legionarios in 1941. Some constitute spaces for parallel or even slightly unorthodox religiosity but always under the watchful eye of priests or bishops. Opus and Legionarios have elaborate systems of recruitment and training and presumably also for fundraising, because they do not receive funding from bishops, although we do not know what the fallout has been from the shocking revelations, which dragged on over many years, regarding the founder of the Legionarios, Marcial Maciel. Indeed, it may well be that these apparently well endowed organizations can gain influence because they can contribute funds — a subject which is probably impossible to research. All this remains more a research agenda than a set of findings. Even in an extremely useful recent volume, the devotional movements receive scarce attention; they are mentioned by Catalina Romero (Romero, 2009), who deplores their influence but does not analyze it, while Christián Parker Gumucio's account of education is strong on statistics but does not note the importance of Opus and Legionarios in education as explained by Angelica Thumala (Parker Gumucio, 2009). Just as academic social science ignored the Pentecostals for a decade, paying more attention to the more ideologically and socially congenial *basista* Catholicism, so maybe now it is ignoring the devotional movements in Catholicism.

Organizational features apart, the religiosity promoted by these different movements puts paid to the claim that Evangelicals have, so to speak, seized the modernity banner and left Catholicism standing. The Catholic Charismatic Renewal promotes the religiosity of instant emotional gratification which is also the trademark of evangelical churches (Neitz, 1987), and although it may not have openly adopted the ethos of Prosperity Theology, parts of the movement must be open to that influence, given the powerful influence already exercised on the CCR by Pentecostalism. Opus and Legionarios are clearly distinct from any charismatic movement on account of their insistence on prolonged and thorough training, education, indoctrination perhaps, and socialization. This is at the antipodes of the quantity-driven dynamic of the CCR. But their cultivation of close relationships with business and modern management — as in various business schools sponsored by them — and their autonomy vis-à-vis the secular clergy illustrate a recognition of modernity. *Basista* Catholicism found it hard to espouse modernity without going to the brink of a rupture, amalgamating too readily the modern with the secular.

16.5. CHURCH AND POLITICS

These shifts in the type and source of Catholic influence may seem surprising in the light of broader trends towards less religious observance in society as a whole, but the causality is not quite what such expectations assume. As in other parts of the world, even while the ranks of the religiously observant decline, within those ranks there has been a decline in the influence of liberal and tolerant forms of religion in the Christian, Jewish and Muslim traditions. The more irredentist, the less compromising, the advocates of strict boundaries and anti-intellectual interpretations of sacred texts, the opponents of relativism and permissiveness, have gained in influence. In Latin America the redemocratization of the late twentieth century also seems to have helped the Church hierarchy to achieve a degree of political influence which may exceed anything it has enjoyed since the high tide of romanization. Although it is misleading analytically to allow the issue of abortion to dominate discussions about the Church and politics, the fact remains that during the Papacy of John Paul II it came to occupy an increasingly prominent and even dominant place at the centre of the Church's own concerns, often at the expense of other social issues (Hagopian, 2009). In Mexico episcopal campaigns against abortion have yielded a total prohibition in 17 out of 32 states leaving only the Federal District as a bastion of *laicidad* in which the infuriated, even incendiary attacks of the Archbishop in 2002 and again in 2007 still did not prevent the Federal District's legislature from adopting permissive legislation on both abortion and same-sex partnerships; in Nicaragua, Peru and Chile likewise governments and parliaments have adopted similar restrictive laws on abortion under fierce clerical pressure, and in Chile even sex education has been held back, together with AIDS-related TV advertisements. In Brazil abortion legislation is slightly more liberal, but still highly restrictive (Htun, 2009). In Argentina, Congress — encouraged by President Cristina Fernandez de Kirchner — legalized same-sex partnerships amid much predictable hoo-ha in 2010. This followed an earlier episode in 2005 when her husband, the previous President Kirschner, had forced the removal of the Army Chaplain, Bishop Baseotto, after his incendiary remarks calling for the Minister of Health to be 'thrown into the sea with a millstone round his neck' ('cuelguen una piedra de molino al cuello y arrojen al mar') in the context of a dispute about abortion.

But it should also be noted that the bishops are not alone in these campaigns since they have firm allies among Evangelicals who take the same line on matters of personal morality — the sort of convergence which explains why they do not direct very strong attacks against the Evangelicals even though they are all competitors in the religious field.

The Catholic Church remains, nevertheless, the most respected institution in all Latin American countries, enjoying a 70% approval rating in a 2004 Latinobarómetro poll (Htun, 2009, p. 358), though respect for its priests is, according to many observers, more tempered. The next best score went to the military with a '30 point gap'. Yet this is a Church which is distancing itself from the universalistic outlook which has characterized it for centuries and which was particularly noticeable in Latin America in the twentieth century. In the place of a Church which was laying out a design for the structure of society, for the structure of the state, for the accommodation of the social classes, for the preferential option for the poor, for *entente* between cultures, for world peace and development, this still widely admired institution is retrenching and entrenching itself behind the protective walls of dead certainty. It is indeed adopting the method espoused by other religious forces (for example ultra-Orthodox Judaism) which manage to adapt to modernity and expand their scope and influence even while closing in and appearing to reject change. In doing so the Church is helped by the movements which (a) originate with initiatives among the laiety or among priests operating independently of the Episcopal hierarchy, (b) have little to do with a heritage of popular religion, (c) have a global reach and (d) focus on personal religiosity and the control or monitoring of personal morality. These are, however, very general features and it is important to recall their diversity in ethos, organization, status, size and in the balance of lay and clerical following or membership. This new stage in the Church's encounter with modernity is achieved by making religion more uncompromising vis-à-vis the cultures and institutions representing competing value systems, such as science (in the form of genetic engineering), entertainment media (in the form of sexual permissiveness) and humanism, but also adopting modern methods of training, marketing and the disciplining of the body. In addition, a religiosity of experience in the culture of these movements is taking the place of popular religion's religiosity of heritage and memory, while their missionary activity serves to replace the decline of a cadre depleted by ageing and falling, even collapsing recruitment.

16.6. RELIGIOUS REGULATION AND *LAICIDAD*

The wave of constitution-making has opened up spaces for non-Catholics and non-Christians to various degrees and enabled evangelical churches to gain access to resources and positions in the state. This varies: in Brazil the opening is probably greatest; in Argentina semi-formal mechanisms and registration requirements remain an obstacle to the achievement of their full recognition and special status has been retained by the Catholic Church, which is exempt from the requirement of registration (Frigerio, 2007) and still receives government salaries for a few of its higher clergy. In Peru, in accordance with the 1980 Concordat, the Catholic Church receives exemptions and benefits including personal financial benefits for some bishops which are not counted as salaries and so are not taxed. But it would be wrong to imply that pentecostal churches suffer even a small amount of discrimination. They are not subject to legal discrimination, and some of them, especially the wealthy and fastest growing neo-Pentecostals, may operate in a shady fiscal niche. The widely recognized obscurity of the division between the finances of a church and those of its leader or leaders has only very rarely been the subject of political or legal controversy: the one famous example is that of the Brazil-based Universal Church of the Kingdom of God: in the early 1990s, under President Collor, it was accused of using funds derived from drug trafficking to finance the purchase of TV Record (the third largest TV network in Brazil), but although an investigation was launched it came to nothing — and the rumour was that the entire affair was an invention of the media giant TV Globo, who wanted to discredit a potential competitor (Birman and Lehmann, 1999). Nonetheless, it is hard not to ask questions of an organization which draws a massive income from cash donations made at its meetings. Those who rail against the legal exemptions of the Catholic Church might note that other religious organizations and their leaders, who control apparently massive and obscure fortunes, are never investigated for financial irregularities — only in Argentina have they been investigated, but for other reasons.[5]

16.7. POLITICAL INVOLVEMENT

We turn now to the movements which would normally be the first to come to mind when speaking of change in the religious field, namely Evangelical/Charismatic/Pentecostal Protestantism. Although the quantitative growth of these movements is impressive if not startling, the extent to which they have brought about profound change requires careful consideration.

The pattern and purpose of evangelical involvement in politics, which should certainly be seen as a shift in the boundaries of the religious field, differs markedly from that of the Catholic Church. The Catholic Bishops do not put up candidates nor do they any longer support particular parties or create parties of their own, as they did occasionally in the early part of the twentieth century, but, as in the past, they do regard intervention on issues of policy and principle as a legitimate activity. The Evangelicals, in contrast, who tend to quote a standard Lutherian injunction to retain political neutrality and respect the ruler whoever that might be, have principled positions on only a very restricted range of issues (against the death penalty, against privileges for the Catholic Church) but have drifted away from the injunction in order to gain representation, influence and access to

[5] In these matters academics have to rely on journalists, since they are not detectives or accountants. An example of journalistic reporting is an article in *Epoca* (29 March 2010) which describes the wealth of the Valdemiro Santiago , the leader of the apparently fastest-growing church in Brazil — Igreja Mundial — including two helicopters and a private jet. His associates say that the church and his wealth are growing so fast that he is forced to put assets in their names because, they seem to say, the authorities would never believe they could grow so fast. The Church is described as spending R$13 million per month on media transmissions inside and outside Brazil.

resources. Evangelical churches need channels to the state because they want to operate TV and radio stations, they want to obtain subsidies for social projects like drug rehabilitation and they want access to potential converts in prison. Vasquez Palacios dismisses Mexican evangelical churches as having 'not yet created a widespread social impact' (Vasquez Palacios, 2008, p. 59) and quotes Patricia Fortuny (from 1994) as saying that Mexican evangelical churches, 'lack a clear political project, oscillating according to the space the political system permits them' (Vasquez Palacios, 2008, p. 60). The churches I studied in Brazil would support their own members who stood for various parties, which were presumably pleased to receive a guaranteed nugget of votes. But with that came the danger of opportunism and floor-crossing: in the 1999 legislature 20 out of 45 Evangelicals on the government's side had switched parties by mid-2001, some because they abandoned Lula's coalition on their leader's instructions. Their total numbers declined precipitously from 57 to 28 in the 2006 elections because of their involvement in the scandals of Lula's first government, but significantly the most politically focused of the Pentecostal movements, the Igreja Universal do Reino de Deus (IURD — Universal Church of the Kingdom of God), which had overtaken the Assemblies of God in numbers of Congressmen, then took measures to discipline their representation. The Church at first had put forward candidates, in various parties, who were members but not pastors or bishops. But the scandals brought about a rethink. Brasil Fonseca (Brasil Fonseca, 2008) quotes an interview with the Church's leader in Congress in which he says that those representatives were sucked into the politics of personal interests, so the Church started putting forward more reliable people from its cadre, namely pastors and bishops, who made up 35 out of its 44 parliamentarians in 2001. It is claimed that the IURD can expect 70% of its members to vote for designated candidates at the first election, and in Rio de Janeiro it was found in a 1994 survey that 95% of those who identified with the Universal Church voted for its nominated candidates (Fernandes, 1998; Machado, 2006). Such figures explain why political parties with no particular religious interest readily make alliances with churches. In a system where voters may have several votes, it is not very costly for them to give one to their pastor, and pastors who can deliver even small, but secure, nuggets, will be sought out by the politicians. But today it is made clear by the leaders of the IURD to those who receive its support that if they underperform as parliamentarians they will not be re-elected (a rare threat in a political system where serial re-election for all save the President is regarded as almost a divine right (Ames, 2001)). This is a significant development, because it shows a Pentecostal group adopting the procedures of a modern institution. The IURD penetrates other non-religious spheres without trying to drown them in its embrace, and avoids projecting a sectarian image when operating outside its own controlled environment. Thus although the Church — or more likely its leader — owns TV Record, it operates it along standard secular and commercial lines, confining religious broadcasting to the hours after midnight. There are now organized *evangélico* groups for athletes, entrepreneurs, students, police officers and the military, and Pentecostal churches have been seen to offer a platform for Black activism and for a range of political ideas (Burdick, 2005; Burdick, 2009).

These last details could be significant because in the case of the IURD they reveal a Church which is operating effectively and in an institutionalized manner beyond its own boundaries in contrast with the usual Pentecostal tendency of churches to keep to their own flock and draw thick boundaries around them. But it may be a tendency peculiar to Brazil where Pentecostalism seems to have acquired the epidemiological characteristics of a social movement, penetrating into unfamiliar groups and institutional niches.

Pentecostal churches until quite recently were mostly creating institutions for their own growth and their own followers: what Putnam has called 'bonding social capital' (Putnam, 2000). But there are signs that this might be changing. Although the Catholic Church in our analysis is turning its face inwards, over its 2,000-year history it has played a major historical role in creating and contributing to the social capital which makes our societies function: the modern state, medical care, social welfare, schools and universities — the list is very long. This has created what Putnam calls bridging social capital.

Maybe Pentecostal churches, which have tended to focus on bonding social capital, tightening internal bonds, are now, in an inverse movement, beginning to look beyond their own, but it will take a long time. The IURD's charitable arm, the Associação Beneficente Cristã (ABC), seems to have a patchy record and a social scientist familiar with it says it tends to be active in places where the Church itself has a political or evangelical interest; it also tends to move its head office from place to place, thus undermining confidence in its independence. Indications that Pentecostals remain entrenched in the clientelist habits of Brazilian politics are not hard to find: for example during the tenure of the evangelical Garotinho couple as Governors of the state of Rio de Janeiro (Anthony Garotinho was succeeded as governor by his wife Rosangela Matheus in 2002) an income support programme for the elderly called '*cheque-cidadão*' was distributed largely through evangelical church networks (Machado, 2006, p. 99, 119–120).

16.8. WHICH FIELD? HOW MUCH AUTONOMY?

We have surveyed several very significant changes: the Catholic Church turning inwards yet adapting more to the modernity which its leaders still distrust, through the upsurge of charismatic and devotional movements and on account of the demographic crisis of the priesthood. And in an inverse direction, Pentecostal churches venturing into the public spheres of politics and the media and exploding out of the local chapel-focused world into neo-Pentecostal megachurchdom. For them modernity is hardly a problem. We also see that both of these trends are at the expense of the popular religion which for centuries has provided the locally-based, thaumaturgic, dialectical counterpoint to institutionalized Catholicism. So, is the Latin American religious field being divided into separate fields each with its own autonomy? We have already remarked that Bourdieu's account of the religious field, with its emphasis on hierarchies and the deployment of power, seems to take the Catholic Church as a model, but if we look to his account of the emergence of an autonomous field of literary and artistic production in nineteenth-century France (in *Les Règles de l'Art*) (Bourdieu, 1992), written 20 years later, we find a far more intricate, multilayered and dynamic account of how a field is constructed and transformed: he describes the interactions, the to-ings and fro-ings, and the ups and downs, as the avant-garde led by Flaubert, Baudelaire and others forged an autonomous field in which artists would no longer have to pay homage to the rich and famous; in which purely aesthetic criteria govern the standing and earning capacity of works and their authors; and in which reviews take an analytical, rather than biographical, descriptive or moralistic approach to their subject. Bourdieu also describes the way in which factions arose among the avant-garde, meeting each in their 'own' café, publishing with their 'own' publishers and of course in their own publications. The literary field, new or old, and the artistic field generally, also are shown to have their guardians, celebrated individuals and institutions with the power to decree who is a 'true writer' and who is a mere scribbler; who a true artist and who a mere copyist or society painter (producing 'art pompier', in the inimitable phrase, or society portraits). For our present discussion, it is important to note that Bourdieu does not describe a straightforward transition or a rupture: on the contrary he dwells at length on individuals who navigate between different spheres, as for example the 'artiste maudit' who makes a career out of being hated by the establishment, the divergences between those who would compromise for the sake of fame or money and others who would not, and in the end the essential role of outstanding figures, celebrities, champions, 'ces êtres bâtards et inclassables' ('bastard and unclassifiable beings') like Baudelaire and Flaubert themselves, who can deploy a symbolic capital from a combination of literary success, 'prestige sulfureux' and 'succès de scandale' (Bourdieu, 1992, p. 162) to open the way for an artistic revolution.

The resonances for religious change in the contemporary world are notable: the scandalous character of the Pentecostals and above all of the neo-Pentecostals; the uncertainties surrounding what counts as a religion (the Ayahuasca cult known as Santo Daime); and who counts as an authority in deciding that question, the shift in power within Catholicism from the hierarchy to devotional movements, the

Pentecostalization of some of Catholicism's most dynamic sectors — all these are symptoms of a field which is undergoing deep structural change and perhaps spawning new fields. The question of whether a totally new field has been created by the Pentecostals could be a tedious and purely academic one, but within that question there is a deeper one which is important, reflected in Bourdieu's use of the word 'logique'. In explaining how he came upon the usage of 'habitus' (drawn from the art historian Panofsky as he readily tells us), he says he was inspired by the world of *haute couture* which led him to the realization that one of the most fundamental features of all 'champs de production' (fields of production) was 'la logique proprement magique de la production du producteur et du produit comme fétiches' (Bourdieu, 1992, p. 257) ('the truly magical logic of the production of the producer and the product as fetishes'). In other words the autonomous field takes up its place as common sense: it imbues those who operate within it with a sense that its procedures and mental structures (or perhaps modes of thought) are self-evident ('comme allant de soi') and require no discussion or explanation. Note here how 'logique' and 'magique' seem almost indistinguishable. It is not entirely surprising that he invokes the fashion industry in the oxymoron of logic and magic: *haute couture* has a magical way of creating itself and its ways of doing things; an autonomous field is one where the deeply rooted logic of its operation ('la logique immanente de son fonctionnement') has penetrated the unconscious assumptions that govern everyday life (common sense). The 'logique' is not really logical at all — it is magical, because it is so hard to understand what holds a sub-culture together.

Like the field of literary production in its early formative period, evangelical Christianity has today gradually created a world with its own magical logic: it presents us with an array of habits and rituals which have come together with, broadly speaking, two particular structures, namely the Pentecostal and the neo-Pentecostal. Coherent and consistent as they might appear, these structures and their accompanying ways of life and thought have not been the outcome of a particular struggle in a particular forum. There is no Baudelaire, nor indeed a Luther or a Picasso, and that is what is forever puzzling about it. The culture of the classic Pentecostals — the Pentecostalism of chapels and storefronts — spread from place to place, country to country, with a small input from missionaries, but without a controlling centre, and yet it has reproduced the same ethos, the same rituals, the same dress codes from Africa to Latin America to Asia. The neo-Pentecostals may learn more purposively, having much larger organizations and training systems and enjoying access to international networks through conferences and education. But nevertheless, lacking a global hierarchy, the resemblance between their enterprises is surprising. Like the magic of Bourdieu's 'logique interne' these common features are obviously essential to the growth of Pentecostalism yet are very hard to explain in terms of a power struggle or an organizational strategy. Observing the attention they pay to the building of grandiose churches and meeting halls, of universities and media premises, one sees the ambition of founding institutions with a high public profile, and of projecting them into the collective imaginary. The latest such project in Brazil is the construction in São Paulo of the Third Temple of Solomon by the Universal Church of the Kingdom of God. The church's leader, Bishop Edir Macedo, says he was called by God to build this Temple and to this end he has purchased and cleared an entire street block in the Bras neighbourhood — a former industrial area now a twilight zone between residential and commercial use. As of August 2010 work was just beginning on the site and church members and workers assured me that the stone from Jerusalem was already on a ship on its way to Brazil. This enormous structure, taller than the city's cathedral, is in addition to the Catedral da Fé in Rio which must hold some 6,000 people and likewise is located in a middle- to lower middle-class area and has its entrance flanked by stone brought from Jerusalem. These particular neo-Pentecostal churches are present on the Internet, but it does not seem that they are intending to migrate to the Internet: they use it to communicate information and publicity, but also pay much attention to the printed word, in the Universal Church's case by distributing a free newspaper. Nonetheless, they surely reflect the creation of an autonomous field, marking a radical departure not just in religious style and creed, but more importantly, a change in what it means to adhere to a religion, in modes of religious socialization, in ideas about religious authority and the legitimate administration of the supernatural.

Are we then witnessing a transformation of the religious field in general? We have seen that the Catholic Church is in the midst of what would seem to be an important change, as lay devotional movements become more proactive in managing religious life. To be sure, they are not in the least ideologically dissident, but they do represent a shift in the management of religious life as well as a change in the erudite-popular dialectic which has characterized Catholicism throughout the Latin world. This shift parallels the rise of Pentecostalism because in both cases it is a detachment of religious life from heritage, from a sense of continuity with ancestral practices rooted to locality, to kinship and to neighbourhood.

But now neo-Pentecostal churches signal a deeper change: religion becomes a path to prosperity and to political power, the personal link between followers and the church official is absent, and the place of worship or prayer can also acquire the characteristics of a service centre, providing counselling, legal advice, Bible Schools, and, in the case of large-scale structures (the IURD's cathedrals), leisure areas, fast-food establishments and cafés. The personal link is far more ephemeral and tenuous, well captured by the Brazilian phrase, 'fast-food religion' or the title of a thesis on the Universal Church in South Africa: 'A church of strangers' (van Wyck, 2008). But the supernatural has not been displaced: on the contrary, in neo-Pentecostalism the manipulation of possession and exorcism is the centrepiece of ritual, if not the only ritual — for services do not usually follow a fixed liturgical sequence. It is a curiously amoral sort of religion in which submission to the Church and the financial sacrifice of contributing to Church funds brings immediate benefits — for 'only by giving will you receive' (a standard phrase in the Universal Church) — yet God's miracles are free — a perhaps crucial variation on the Grace of God (grace being the root of the word 'gratuity' or the French '*gratuit*'). These churches, of course, are entitled to the same exemptions and entitlements, such as tax-free status, as any other religious institution (or '*templo religioso*' in Brazil) but while their status has not been challenged legally, from a sociological point of view their innovative practices must raise the question whether they have redefined the notion of religion and of being religious.

There are also elements here of the hybridity and frontier-crossing which accompany the growth of a new field (reminiscent of 'ces êtres bâtards et inclassables'). The Universal Church builds vast cathedrals, to self-consciously mimic and compete with the Catholic Church; like all Pentecostal churches, draws on the same Holy Bible, but regards theology as the work of the Devil and uses the scripture as a source of morality tales, archetypes and exempla, rather than as a text. It has half-borrowed its logo — the white dove against the background of a red heart — from the Catholic image of the Sacred Heart, combining it with the classic symbol of the Holy Spirit. And of course, in radical contrast to classic Pentecostals, it has created a hierarchy of authority, with bishops at its head and the founder-leader Edir Macedo at the summit. Similar remarks apply to other neo-Pentecostal churches, such as those described by Ruth Marshall in Nigeria and by Paul Gifford in Kenya (Gifford, 1993; Gifford, 2004; Marshall, 2009), while Jean Comaroff, using mainly South African examples concerning this selfsame Universal Church, has announced that they herald an attempt to establish global theocracies (Comaroff, 2009).

We see how a habitus has been created, with its autonomous field. This field recombines elements from the established field in unpredicted ways which are still hard to comprehend: the 'mainstream' of religion — that is, the dominant institutions which had come to define not only themselves but the main features of any religion in Europe and Latin America — was moving in a liberal, quasi-secular direction and had discarded explicit references to the action of the supernatural in our daily lives, to ideas about evil and possession, while at the same time retaining the apparatus of power which had evolved to administer the supernatural over centuries. Now the neo-Pentecostals challenge those definitions and assumptions by restoring the action of the supernatural in daily life while adopting a completely different model of organization, revolving around the cult of personality of their leaders and dispensing with extended periods of theological education and priestly formation, and shifting the intimate exchanges which are at the heart of popular religion to the level of an abstract, disembodied relationship with the Church, while proclaiming that God's miracles are free.

From this perspective, classic Pentecostalism, despite its massive quantitative presence, can be thought of as not achieving the autonomy necessary to command great influence. Although neo-Pentecostals have obviously drawn on their older cousins for basic ideas about conversion, about mission, about the uses of the Bible, they have gone much further by engaging in open competition with Catholicism for prestige, for the conquest of public space, for the conquest of the media, especially with Universal Church's TV record (Birman and Lehmann, 1999), for the conquest of political power and for the capacity to legitimately define what counts as religion in the public sphere. Within the Catholic Church, by comparison, we have seen the beginnings of a reshaping of the field after several decades of attempts first to achieve a liberal modernization (Vatican II and Liberation Theology), then to roll the liberalization backwards, all the while preserving the structures of power — but now we observe new structures of religious activism which also share some features with Pentecostalism.

So the field of religion is being reshaped: the power to define what constitutes religion is passing into new hands, the relationship between religion and politics likewise, and the relationship between the apparatuses of power and the administration of the supernatural is also changing. The one thing which is clear is that even 10, let alone 20, years ago few would have predicted the developments described here. Amidst all this sound and fury, however, let us not forget that the time of religious hegemony is largely over: Kung may (I hope) exaggerate when he warns that the Catholic Church is becoming like a sect, but it is surely gradually becoming a 'church like any other', while the others are becoming more and more Pentecostal.

BIBLIOGRAPHY

Ames, B. (2001). *The deadlock of democracy in Brazil*, University of Michigan Press, Ann Arbour.

Birman, P. and Lehmann, D. (1999). Religion and the media in a battle for ideological hegemony, *Bulletin of Latin American Research*, 18, 2, 145–164.

Bourdieu, P. (1992). *Les Règles de l'Art: genèse et structure du champ littéraire*, Le Seuil, Paris.

Brandão, C. R. (1980). *Os Deuses do Povo: um estudo sobre a religião popular*, Brasiliense, São Paulo.

Brandão, C. R. (1989). *A cultura na rua*, Papirus, Campinas.

Brandão, C. R. (2007). *Os Deuses do Povo: um estudo sobre a religião popular*, new and unabridged ed., Editora da Universidade Federal de Uberlândia.

Brasil Fonseca, A. (2008). 'Religion and Democracy in Brazil: A Study of the Leading Politicians, in Freston, P. (ed.), *Evangelicals and democracy in Latin America*, Oxford University Press, New York, pp. 163–205.

Burdick, J. (1994). *Looking for God in Brazil*, University of California Press, Berkeley.

Burdick, J. (2005). Why is the Black Evangelical Movement Growing in Brazil?, *Journal of Latin American Studies*, 37, 2, 311–332.

Burdick, J. (2009). Collective Identity and Racial Thought in São Paulo's Black Gospel Music Scene, *Music and Arts in Action*, 1, 2, 16–29.

Caimari, L. (1994). *Perón y la Iglesia Católica: Religión, Estado y Sociedad en la Argentina (1943–55)*, Ariel, Buenos Aires.

Carranza, B., Mariz, C. *et al.*, (eds) (2009). *Novas comunidades católicas: em busca de um espaço pós-moderno*, Ideias e Letras, Aparecida.

Chesnut, A. (2003). *Competitive Spirits: Latin America's New Religious Economy*, Oxford University Press, New York.

Clarke, P. B. (1999). Top-star priests and the Catholic response to the 'explosion' of evangelical protestantism in Brazil: The beginning of the end of the 'walkout'?, *Journal of Contemporary Religion*, 14, 2, 203–216.

Comaroff, J. (2009). The Politics of Conviction: Faith on the Neo-Liberal Frontier, *Social Analysis*, 53, 1, 17–38.

Csordas, T. (1997). *Language, Charisma and Creativity*, University of California Press, Berkeley.

Eisenstadt, S. N. (1995). 'Fundamentalism, Phenomenology and Comparative Dimensions', in Marty, M. and Appleby, R. S. (eds), *Fundamentalisms Comprehended*, Chicago University Press, Chicago, pp. 259–276.

Eisenstadt, S. N. (2000). Multiple modernities. *Daedalus*, 129, 1, 1–29.

Fernandes, R. C. *et al.* (1998). *Novo nascimento: os Evangelicos em Casa, na Igreja e na Política*, ISER, Mauad.

Frigerio, A. (2007). 'Repensando el monopolio religioso del catolicismo en la Argentina', in Carozzi, M. J. and Ceriani, C. (eds), *Ciencias sociales y religión en América Latina: perspectivas en debate* Biblos/ACRSM, Buenos Aires, pp. 87–118.

Gifford, P. (1993). *Christianity and the state in Doe's Liberia*, Cambridge University Press, Cambridge.

Gifford, P. (2004). *Ghana's New Christianity: Pentecostalism in a Globalizing African Economy*, Hurst and Co., London.

Gruzinski, S. (1990). *La guerre des images: de Christophe Colomb à Blade Runner (1492–2019)*, Fayard, Paris.

Gruzinski, S. (2001). *Images at War: Mexico from Columbus to Blade Runner (1492–2019)*, Duke University Press, Durham, NC.

Gutiérrez, G. (1993). *Las Casas: in search of the poor of Jesus Christ*, Orbis Books, Maryknoll, New York.

Hagopian, F. (2009). 'Social Justice, Moral Values or Institutional Interests? Church Responses to the Democratic Challenge in Latin America, in Hagopian, F. (ed.), *Religious Pluralism, Democracy and the Catholic Church in Latin America*, University of Notre Dame Press, Notre Dame, pp. 257–331.

Harris, O. (2006). 'The Eternal Return of Conversion: Christianity as Contested Domain in Highland Bolivia', in Cannell, F. (ed.), *The Anthropology of Christianity*, Duke University Press, Durham, NC, pp. 51–76.

Hewitt, T. (1991). *Base Christian Communities and Social Change in Brazil*, University of Nebraska Press, Lincoln, NE.

Howe, F. C., Zaraysky, S. *et al.* (2009). 'Devotional Crossings: Transgender Sex Workers, Santisima Muerte, and Spiritual Solidarity in Guadalajara and San Francisco', in Lorentzen, L. A., Do, H. D., Gonzalez, J. J. and Bazan, L. (eds), *Religion at the Corner of Bliss and Nirvana: Politics, Identity, and Faith in New Migrant Communities*, Duke University Press, Durham, NC, pp. 3–38.

Htun, M. (2009). 'Life, Liberty and Family Values: Church and State in the Struggle over Latin America's Social Agenda', in Hagopian, F. (ed.), *Religious Pluralism, Democracy and the Catholic Church in Latin America*, University of Notre Dame Press, Notre Dame, pp. 335–364.

Knight, A. (1994). Popular Culture and the Revolutionary State in Mexico, 1910–1940. *Hispanic American Historical Review*, 74, 3, 393–444.

Lehmann, D. (1990). *Democracy and Development in Latin America: Economics, Politics and Religion in the Post-War Period*, Polity Press, Cambridge.

Lehmann, D. (1996). *Struggle for the Spirit: Religious Transformation and Popular Culture in Brazil and Latin America*, Polity Press, Oxford.

Lehmann, D. (2003). Dissidence and conformism in religious movements: What difference — if any — separates the Catholic Charismatic Renewal and Pentecostal churches?, *Concilium*, 3.

Lehmann, D. (2009). 'Religion and Globalization: A Comparative and Historical Perspective', in Woodhead, L., Kawanami, H. and Partridge, C. (eds), *Religions in the Modern World: Traditions and Transformations*, Routledge, Abingdon, pp. 345–363.

Machado, M. das. D. C. (2006). *Política e Religião: a participação dos Evangélicos nas eleições*, Editora FGV, Rio de Janeiro.

Marin, R. (1995). *Dom Helder Camara, les puissants et les pauvres: pour une histoire de l'Eglise des pauvres dans le Nordeste Bresilien, 1955–1985*, Editions de l'Atelier, Paris.

Mariz, C. L. (1993). *Coping with Poverty: Pentecostals and Christian Base Communities in Brazil*, Temple University Press, Philadelphia.

Marshall, R. (2009). *Political Spiritualities: The Pentecostal Revolution in Nigeria*, University of Chicago Press, Chicago.

Martin, D. (1990). *Tongues of Fire: The Pentecostal Revolution in Latin America*, Blackwell, Oxford.

Meyer, J. (1973–1974). *La Cristiada*, 3 Vols, Siglo XXI, Mexico D. F.

Mignone, E. (1988). *Witness to the Ttruth: The Ccomplicity of Church and Dictatorship in Argentina, 1976–1983*, Orbis Books, Maryknoll.

Neitz, M. J. (1987). *Charisma and Community: A Study of Religious Commitment within the Charismatic Renewal*, Transaction Books, New Brunswick.

Parker Gumucio, C. (2009). 'Education and Increasing Religious Pluralism in Latin America: The Case of Chile', in Hagopian, F. (ed.), *Religious Pluralism, Democracy and the Catholic Church in Latin America*, University of Notre Dame Press, Notre Dame, pp. 131–181.

Putnam, R. (2000). *Bowling Alone: The Collapse and Revival of American community*, Simon and Schuster, New York.

Romero, C. (2009). 'Religion and Public Spaces: Catholicism and Civil Society in Peru', in Hagopian, F. (ed.), *Religious Pluralism, Democracy and the Catholic Church in Latin America*, University of Notre Dame Press, Notre Dame, pp. 365–401.

Thumala Olave, M. A. (2007). *Riqueza y piedad: el catolicismo de la elite económica Chilena*, Debate, Santiago.

van Wyck, I. (2008). A church of strangers: The case of the Universal Church of the Kingdom of God (UCKG) in Durban, *Anthropology*, LSE, London.

Vasquez Palacios, F. (2008). 'Democratic Activity and Religious Practices of Evangelicals in Mexico', in Freston, P. (ed.), *Evangelical Christianity and Democracy in Latin America*, Oxford University Press, New York, pp. 37–62.

Vaughan, M. K. (1997). *Cultural Politics in Revolution*, University of Arizona Press, Tucson.

Chapter

17

Indigenous Peoples of Latin America Between Assimilation, Disappearance, *Mestizaje* and Re-emergence: The Argentine Case

Sabine Kradolfer

17.1. INTRODUCTION

The last decades of the twentieth century have proven to be of special significance in bringing about a reappearance of the indigenous peoples of Latin America at the forefront of the political, economic and social arenas, making visible their struggles and claims as well as, one might say, the simple fact of their existence. One of the most striking and internationally renowned examples of this resurgence of Indian identity within the political sphere is undoubtedly the emphasis placed on the Indian origins of Evo Morales at the head of the Bolivian state since 2006, and the mobilisation of indigenous rituals and symbols as a feature of his government. We think here in particular of the ceremonies of investiture officiated by the Amauta (Aymara sages), following the elections of 2006 and 2009 in the ruins of Tihuanaco, a few dozen kilometres from La Paz, during which this president was elevated to the rank of 'Supreme Head of the Indians' or 'spiritual leader'. The reclaiming and staging of his Indian identity by Evo Morales is not an isolated phenomenon. In recent decades, many indigenous groups or nations of Latin America have reasserted their identity in sometimes vastly different registers that borrow as much from 'tradition' as from '(post)modernity' and that manifest in a variety of ways. What Evo Morales demonstrated at Tihuanaco is part of a revival movement of major rituals, both in the Andes and in Mexico (Galinier and Molinié, 2006), in which thousands of people gather — as for example at the fortress of Sacsayhuamán above Cuzco, or in Teotihuacan near Mexico City — for solstice and equinox celebrations. Thus, we are witnessing a gradual breakdown in the dynamics of invisibility, marginalisation and/or negation of Amerindian populations that were once perpetuated by national states. For many natives, this strong revival of Indian cultures on the Latin American political scene has brought hope that new relationships with mainstream society can be established by redefining ways of doing politics and imagining the Nation (Dávalos, 2005).

This chapter, based on the Argentinian case study, will focus on the processes of social recomposition between indigenous and non-indigenous populations — that is to say, the 'Old World' people who came to settle in the Americas over five centuries ago. In their call for chapters, the coordinators of this book were interested in the processes of social recomposition currently experienced by the Latin American continent, which acknowledge a 'vision of the vanquished'. The basic question they raise is: 'Does this social recomposition lead to "hybrid cultures" or to a juxtaposition of autonomous cultures?' Between these two ways of looking at intercultural relations (that must be understood as 'ideal types' in the Weberian sense), we encounter a whole range of situations where cultures mingle, mix, interpenetrate and so on. Drawing from the particular example of the indigenous populations of Argentina, I wish to demonstrate the fluidity of these categories by investigating the processes that led, in that country as in many other Latin American nations, from an occultation of indigenous peoples to their reappearance (Bengoa, 2000). I will examine certain paradigmatic moments in the history of the Americas, as well as some illustrative cases, between assimilation, disappearance, *mestizaje* and return, that highlight the ways in which the indigenous peoples were viewed, first by the European settlers and later by the national states founded in the early nineteenth century. We will see how these classifications still influence the ways in which relations between indigenous and non-indigenous populations are envisaged today.

17.2. THE 'DISCOVERY' OF THE AMERICAS: FROM RADICAL OTHERNESS TO INTERMINGLING

The term 'New World', drawn from an account entitled 'Mundus Novus' by the Florentine Amerigo Vespucci, whose name would later be given to the American continent, was used from the very beginning of the sixteenth century to designate the lands that lie beyond the Atlantic Ocean — not only the Americas but also Oceania and Australia. This division of the world between 'Old' and 'New' already carries with it the seeds of what colonial relations were to become: from the newness, a different world would arise, conceived by the inhabitants of the Old World and created by them from scratch with their own frames of references and a view to extracting maximum benefits. As we know, their negative perception of inhabitants of the New World and/or their sense of superiority led to the physical destruction of a large portion of the Amerindian population (genocide) and to the imposition of European values (ethnocide, see Jaulin, 1970). As an example of the latter, their adherence to the sphere of Christianity allowed Amerindian populations to obtain recognition of their membership in humanity, while some humanists of the time, such as Oviedo, wanted to reduce them to the world of inanimate things:

> [...] For him, the Indians are not reduced to the level of horse or donkey (or even just below) but somewhere in the category of building materials, wood, stone or iron, in any case, of inanimate objects. (Todorov, 1982, p. 157)

Having escaped this classification and been granted membership into the society of men, the Indians had yet to be given a place deemed appropriate for them by the representations of the *conquistadores*. In this way, a new, dual colonial society was established, made up of two halves or 'republics' that were supposed to exist separately: the '*república de españoles*' consisting of the white population (born in Spain or America) and the '*república de indios*', with reference to indigenous societies. However, as stated by Stolcke: '[b]y the seventeenth century it was clear that the Crowns early project to establish two separate republics of Indians and Spaniards had failed' (Stolcke, 2005, p. 23). Indians were escaping from the reductions in which they had been confined and lived in proximity with the Spaniards, thus contributing to the sharp increase of *mestizaje*. The vice-royalty of Mexico (New Spain), like that of Peru, then began to construct its identity around the idea of miscegenation resulting from the countless mixes of different populations (white, black and indigenous), giving rise to a classification of groups based on the genealogy of their members.

Because they experienced a slower penetration of European populations, some frontier territories of the continent did not suffer the same colonial relations between the sixteenth and eighteenth centuries, nor did they undergo the same processes of *mestizaje* that were widespread in Mesoamerica, Brazil and the Andes. Although the indigenous hinterlands were seldom explored by Whites, contacts between 'Indians' and 'Spaniards' were frequent on the borders separating the two worlds. Quotation marks are used to refer to these categories of population, because here too, they are to be understood as ideal types. For example, in the Santa Cruz de la Sierra region, which today belongs to Bolivia, the majority of Spaniards were in fact of mixed blood and assimilated with the indigenous populations of Chané, Guarani, etc. (Coello, personal communication.)

Thus, a huge territory in the south of the continent remained under indigenous administration until the end of the nineteenth century. These populations were able to resist the foreign armies and to secure peace treaties, first with the Spanish Crown and later, after the national independencies, with the representatives of the Argentinian and Chilean states. From now on, I will focus my attention on the indigenous Mapuche inhabitants of the Pampas and Patagonia in order to analyse their relationships with the authorities of the new Argentine nation,[1] created in 1810, and to study how societies based on the division between Indian and 'White'[2] populations, a division that is still in force today, could establish themselves on both sides of the border.

17.3. EGALITARIANISM IN REPUBLICAN IDEOLOGY

Under the impetus of the Enlightenment philosophy, which inspired the new nation of Argentina, there was a strong willingness to integrate the Indians into the structures of the new state and to recognise them as free and equal citizens (Menni, 1995). At that time, the territories of the continent occupied by indigenous peoples extended southwards from the cities of Buenos Aires, San Luis and Mendoza to the southern most tip of the continent: Tierra del Fuego (see Fig. 17.1). Only a few coastal trading posts — such as Carmen de Patagones or Viedma (and later Bahía Blanca) — were established south of this border to allow non-indigenous people to trade with the natives. In this region, then, we witness the development of different

---

[1] Past and present Mapuche populations settled on both sides of the Andean Cordillera, upon territories that since the nineteenth century have been under Chilean administration on the west side and Argentinian administration on the east side. In this chapter, I focus on the Mapuche case study in Argentina (less studied than the one to the west of the Andes) and I will speak of the Chilean situation only when comparative elements are relevant to the discussion. The fact that the Mapuche have suffered from the confrontation and/or domination of two different national states for 200 years has led to the strengthening of local specificities and made it difficult to conduct a unified analysis of the whole Mapuche people (for some attempts, see Hernández, 2003; Ray, 2007).

[2] Here the term 'Whites' refers to the distinction made by the Mapuche between themselves and the *Huinca*, a word that means at the same time white, thief and foreigner. Furthermore, this distinction (Indians vs. Whites) is currently used in Argentina to separate the indigenous populations from the non-indigenous immigrant population.

Figure 17.1. Map of Argentina (© Instituto Geográfico Militar).

societies, established on either side of a boundary line and sovereign in their respective territories.

Throughout the nineteenth century, many meetings (called *parlamentos*) were held between Argentinian and Mapuche representatives, to sign peace agreements and treaties for the recognition of borders. Though never fully respected either by the Argentines or the Mapuche, these agreements reflect an equality of treatment between the two populations. According to Mandrini (1989–1990), the purpose of these agreements was primarily to determine the areas controlled by each society, rather than to establish an impermeable boundary or line of separation. Indeed, the 'boundary' line functioned both as a hub of inter-ethnic relations and as a filter for cultural influences (for the borders of indigenous territories in the mid-nineteenth century, see Fig. 17.2). The Argentine and indigenous societies did

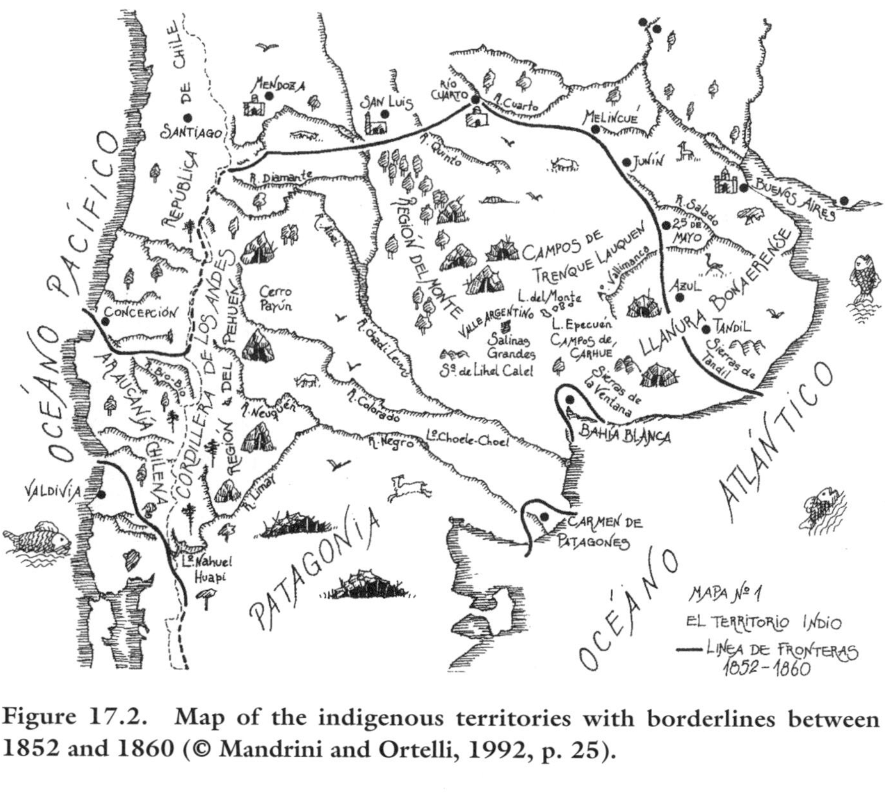

Figure 17.2. Map of the indigenous territories with borderlines between 1852 and 1860 (© Mandrini and Ortelli, 1992, p. 25).

not form two separate and isolated worlds since their economic and cultural exchanges were important. But contact was not limited to these exchanges. We know that some Whites — political refugees, fugitive criminals and prisoners captured in combat — lived in the indigenous settlements. In this sense, Zavala's observation in the context of the Colonial era also seems relevant to the Republican period:

> [...] under the term 'border', the Spaniards were alluding to a special kind of rapport established with the Mapuche, a relationship oscillating between hostility and negotiation, but not yet of consolidated domination. (Zavala, 1998, p. 186)

This situation of relative peace was shattered in 1832, when General Juan Manuel de Rosas undertook an expedition to push the frontier further south, so as to protect the *estancias* (ranches) from native raids. Once again, peace treaties were signed, and the Argentine government continued to support chiefdoms, giving military jobs to some 'cacique friends' and paying them a salary in livestock and goods of European origin. In return, the Mapuche had to agree not to leave their territories without prior authorisation from the Argentine government, and to contribute military contingents at that government's request in case of war. These new peace terms were to last about 20 years.

17.4. THE BRUTAL INCORPORATION OF THE MAPUCHE INTO THE ARGENTINE STATE

In the last quarter of the nineteenth century, under the pressure of demand for land from the *estancieros*[3] and for food by international markets and because of the international economic crisis, the government of President Nicolás Avellaneda (1874–1880) made the decision to advance onto the free indigenous territories of the Pampas,[4] thus

[3] In Argentina, large ranches for the extensive raising of livestock — *latifundia* — are called *estancias* and their owners, *estancieros*.

[4] At that time, the southern border of Argentina did not even reach the limits of today's Buenos Aires and Mendoza provinces; however, it extended southwards of the Córdoba and San Luis provinces.

ending Argentina's hitherto peaceful relations with the indigenous peoples. In 1879, Julio A. Roca led the *Campaña al Desierto* (Desert Campaign)[5] pushing back the southern border of Argentina to the rivers Neuquén and Río Negro where Patagonia begins. He continued the conquest of Patagonia between 1881 and 1883 with the *Campaña del Nahuel Huapi* (Nahuel Huapi Campaign) and *Campaña de los Andes* (Andean Campaign), persisting in the persecution of indigenous peoples until the last caciques gave themselves up in 1885. The damage to Indian Native societies caused by these military operations is considered a 'genocide' by some authors (Navarro Floria 1999, pp. 104–106).

A little earlier, in Chile, between 1866 and 1881, a military campaign named *Pacificación de la Araucanía*[6] (Pacification of the Araucania) had been carried out to incorporate the region still under Mapuche control to the national territory.[7] Survivors of these hostilities were brought together in *reducciones*, communal lands of reduced extension by comparison with the territories they had previously occupied. Land rights of the *reducciones* were regulated by allocating *títulos de merced* to the ancestors of the present-day inhabitants of these reserves. The other territories were made available for Chilean and European settlers.

As the processes to occupy the Mapuche territories on both side of the Andean Cordillera ran concurrently and in a concerted way, it is interesting to compare the very different names given by the two national states to designate their militaries campaigns. The word *pacificación* refers to a situation of aggression, although this region was living in a situation of relative peace, under Mapuche control, before its invasion by the Chilean armies. The real war began only when the

[5] This campaign lent its name to the whole conquest of the Pampa and of Patagonia (1875–1885), which was called '*Conquista del Desierto*' (Conquest of the Desert); I will come back later to this designation as 'desert', which raises a problem.

[6] Araucania is the name given to the region occupied by the Mapuche (who were also called Araucanians by the Spaniards) in present-day Chile.

[7] Some authors prefer to refer to this historical period as '*Ocupación de la Araucanía*' (Occupation of Araucania).

Chilean state decided to conquer these territories and confine its indigenous populations within reserves, to make the region more attractive for European settlers. The warlike image was attributed to the Mapuche (and not to the Chilean or Spanish armies), and we must go back to the sixteenth century to find its source in the epic poem by Alonso de Ercilla y Zúñiga *La Araucana* (1993), written between 1569 and 1589, in which the terrible fights that opposed the Spanish troops and the Mapuche are recounted. Furthermore, this image is still present nowadays and is fed by frequent violent confrontations between the Mapuche and the Chilean police or army.

By contrast, on the Argentinian side of the Andean Cordillera, the early processes of 'invisibilisation' of the indigenous national component can be traced to the *Conquista del Desierto*. It was not unusual during the last quarter of the twentieth century to hear that indigenous peoples had long since disappeared in Argentina (as was also the case in Uruguay), since it would seem that they had been absorbed into the melting pot of the population, but we can go back in time to this moment to analyse the beginnings of their 'disappearance' or 'invisibility'. These processes, in fact, began before the military surrender of the indigenous population, as indicated by the word 'desert' to describe the territories of the Pampas and Patagonia to be conquered.[8] In the name *Campaña del Desierto* (Desert Campaign) given to this period of confrontation in the official historiography,[9] the term 'desert' presents a double problem: partly the use of the term itself, and further by the way it was used by the *conquistadores* of the nineteenth century. The territories to which that word refers were not in fact affected by the drought — at least not the majority of them (only certain parts of Patagonia could be considered as semi-arid). In this regard, it is interesting to note that the concept of 'desert' at that time in Argentina applied not only to the arid regions but to tropical forests as well; it referred to spaces

[8] I would like to thank Pedro Navarro Floria for the abundant historical data and information that he provided me with and that will be discussed below.

[9] The Mapuche gave it the name of *Epoca de la Perdición* (Era of Ruin), or more simply *The Ruin*.

free of 'Western civilisation', and therefore conducive to the expansion of civilisation and progress. Of course, this reference to the absence of population applied to the 'civilised' white population only. Furthermore, had these areas been sparsely populated, it is legitimate to wonder why Roca had to raise a large army and undertake several military campaigns over several years. In reality, the main motivation for the campaigns led by this general was to seize new territories in order to exploit their wealth; regarding them as 'desert' became an effective argument to justify their occupation.

From that time on, native peoples were 'integrated' as Argentine citizens into the most marginalised sectors of society, and forced to submit to a legal system that ignored their customs, and to a school system that scorned their languages and cultures. Those who survived the fighting, the displacement of people to prison camps and slave labour, suffered another 'symbolic' loss, since they had to abandon their communal lifestyle, culture, language, etc. For several years, destitute Mapuche families kept on wandering through their former territories before coming together in small family units (called '*lof*' in Mapuche language) which practised a subsistence economy. The purpose of the conquest was achieved: 'civilisation' had conquered 'barbarism'. The ideal of the 'white nation' of nineteenth-century Argentina, that was Christian, modern, 'European' and 'civilised', had been achieved through a physical and symbolic removal of Amerindian populations.

17.5. THE (RE)EMERGENCE OF INDIGENOUS PEOPLES IN THE LATE TWENTIETH CENTURY

Paradoxically, little more than a century after the confrontations surrounding the *Conquista del Desierto*, the indigenous peoples do not seem to have disappeared from the Argentine territory; on 16 January 2005, one could even read the following headline in the daily *El Clarín*: '*El 56% de los Argentinos tiene antepasados indígenas*'[10] (Heguy, 2005). What had happened?

[10] 56% of Argentines have Indian ancestry.

During the last quarter of the twentieth century, in Argentina as in many other countries, the aboriginal issue gained increasing importance under the joint pressure of local context and the international scene. Locally, the return to democracy, the development of human rights movements and the debates a decade later surrounding preparations for the 500th anniversary of the 'discovery' of the Americas by Christopher Columbus, had an empowering effect. They enabled organisations defending aboriginal rights to start negotiating with the state on specific social and political rights.[11] Meanwhile, at the international level, we witness the creation of international forums (1982: UN Working Group on Indigenous Populations; 2002: UN Permanent Forum on Indigenous Issues; 2007: Expert Mechanism on the Rights of Indigenous Peoples) and of judicial frameworks (ILO Convention 169, 1989; UN Declaration on the Rights of Indigenous Peoples, 2007[12]) to regulate the problems faced by indigenous populations in their encounters with states and non-indigenous populations. Specifically, for this period in Argentina, there are three major elements to bear in mind:

1) For the first time, in 1985, federal law 23.302 'Indigenous policy and assistance to aboriginal communities' (which only came into effect very slowly) adopted a certain number of measures protecting indigenous people, provided, however, that they be gathered in 'communities'.
2) The indigenous peoples were officially recognised on 11 August 1994 with the adoption of a new national Constitution. Until

[11] For an analysis of power structures within Mapuche organisations and communities, see Kradolfer 2008. See Kradolfer 2007 for a discussion of the advantages derived nowadays from membership in an aboriginal community for negotiating specific rights with the state.

[12] The potential influence of this document, adopted at the UN General Assembly on 13 September 2007, on the aboriginal issue and on the elements described in this text, is related to the fact that it had been discussed within a specific UN working group since 1994 and had thereby already inspired some of the constitutional reforms of the 1990s.

that moment, the Constitution of 1853–1860 had specified in Article 67, paragraph 15 that the National Congress should: '[...] see to the safety of the borders, maintain peaceful relations with the Indians and facilitate their conversion to Catholicism' (Falaschi *et al.*, 1996, p. 237). By contrast, the new text specifies, in Article 75, paragraph 17, that the National Congress should:

> Recognise the previous ethnic and cultural existence of indigenous peoples in Argentina; guarantee respect for their identity and the right to bilingual and intercultural education; recognise the legal personality of indigenous communities, the possession and communal ownership of land traditionally occupied by them while regulating the transfer of other land suitable and sufficient for human development; no land may be alienable, transferable or susceptible of being charged or seized. Ensure their participation in managing natural resources and other issues that concern them. The provinces may exercise these powers simultaneously.

3) The ratification, on 3 September 2000, of ILO Convention 169, which had been adopted almost 10 years before, in 1992.

These legal elements, which recognise cultural diversity and the pre-existence of indigenous peoples in Argentina, respond both to external pressures (cf. supra) and to the demands of local indigenous organisations[13] and their support groups.[14] If we look in depth at the case of Mapuche organisations, we find that many of them have grown in cities (Briones, 1999; Kropff, 2005), proving that, contrary to popular belief, the Mapuche do not live only in rural communities.

---

[13] Such organisations appeared in Patagonia, for example, in the 1980s (Briones, 1999; Kropff, 2005).

[14] Associations for the Defence of Human Rights, along with other indigenous organisations throughout the continent and the world.

This finding is supported statistically in the context of the *Encuesta Complementaria de Pueblos Indígenas* (ECPI), which was carried out in 2004–2005 as a follow-up to the 2001 national census (*Censo Nacional de Población, Hogares y Viviendas*).[15] Before I go on, it should be noted that the previous census of the indigenous population (*Censo indígena nacional — CIN*)[16] was conducted in 1966–1968 (República Argentina y Ministerio del Interior 1966–1968).[17] It identified just under 29,000 Mapuche in the provinces of Patagonia. But, as noted by Radovish and Balazote, this data was incomplete:

> Because it used erroneous methodological criteria to define its census unit, the aforementioned census failed to register people living in scattered rural settlements and migrant people in urban areas. For this reason, CIN's result for total population must be considered far from reality. (Radovish and Balazote, 1992, p. 164)

During the 2001 census, in the Patagonian provinces of Neuquén, Río Negro, Chubut and Santa Cruz, no fewer than 76,606 people claimed to belong to the Mapuche people. It is estimated that 71% of this population is settled in urban areas, that is to say in communities of 2,000 or more inhabitants (INDEC 2001: s/p). As for those communities that are seen as embodying the archetypal essence of the Mapuche lifestyle, they make up only 60% of the Mapuche population in rural areas, with the remaining 40% of rural Mapuche dispersed throughout the territory (INDEC 2001: s/p). Another surprise of this census was the public resurgence of persons claiming to belong to indigenous people that had been considered extinct for decades, even centuries: the Huarpe, Ona, Charrúa or Quilmes.

---

[15] National Census on Population, Households and Settlements.

[16] Indigenous National Census.

[17] With regard to the general population censuses, only those of 1869, 1895 and 1914 took into account the ethnic variable.

17.6. CONCLUSION

The strength of the ethnic claims of the 1990s, in a nation-state that had attempted to construct its identity by promoting linguistic and cultural homogeneity and keeping native populations at the outskirts of its economic, political and social life, attests to the vitality of these cultures and their ability to develop other modes of articulation and incorporation within Argentine society than those that were imposed on them after the conquest of the last free territories in the late nineteenth century.

In Argentina, as in Latin America generally, one of the main challenges of the twenty-first century will certainly be to redefine the relationship between the nation-state and indigenous peoples in cultural terms. One must remember that the processes of historical construction of societies and the mechanisms of political and social reproduction (whether they transform or perpetuate existing structures) accord with social hierarchies and hegemonic power structures that tend to naturalise differences of status. Thus, whether we consider the construction of differences between national society and indigenous population in terms of race or culture, the construction mechanisms of hegemonies and hierarchies seem to come together within similar frames, although they remain closely related to the contexts in which different groups come together or confront each other. Furthermore, these hierarchies are reminiscent of the current discourse on immigration in developed countries where the views on cultural mix (*the melting pot*) have given way to those that Taguieff calls 'differential racism' or Stolcke (1995), 'cultural fundamentalism'. Henceforth, inferiorisation of the other is no longer the central element, because his difference is raised to an absolute and irreducible level, where any integration into the national cultural identity is rendered impossible.

BIBLIOGRAPHY

Bengoa, J. (2000). *La Emergencia Indígena en América Latina*, Fondo de Cultura Económica, México & Santiago de Chile.

Briones, C. (1999). *Weaving 'the Mapuche People': the Cultural Politics of Organizations with Indigenous Philosophy and Leadership*, Ph.D. thesis, University Microfilms International, Ann Arbor. Michigan.

Dávalos, P. (ed.) (2005). *Pueblos Indígenas, Estado y Democracia*, Consejo Latinoamericano de Ciencias Sociales, CLACSO, Buenos Aires.

de Ercilla y Zúñiga, A. (1993). *La Araucana*, Utz — UNESCO, Paris.

Galinier, J. and Molinié, A. (2006). *Les Néo-Indiens. Une Religion du IIIe Millénaire*, Odile Jacob, Paris.

Falaschi, C. (dir.) (1996). *Proyecto Especial de Investigación y Extensión UNC-APDH 'Defensa y Reivindicación de Tierras Indígenas'. Informe final*, Universidad del Comahue, Neuquén.

Hernández, I. (2003). *Autonomía o Cuidadanía Incompleta: El Pueblo Mapuche en Chile y Argentina*, Naciones Unidas — CEPAL, Santiago de Chile.

Heguy, S. (2005). Estudio de expertos de la UBA. El 56% de los Argentinos tiene antepasados indígena, *Clarín*, Buenos Aires, 16 January.

INDEC, 2001. *Encuesta Complementaria de Pueblos Indígenas (ECPI) 2004–2005 — Complementaria del Censo Nacional de Población, Hogares y Viviendas 2001*, Instituto Nacional de Estadística y Censos, Buenos Aires [Online], Available at: http://www.indec.gov.ar [Accessed 25 November 2010].

Jaulin, R. (1970). *La Paix Blanche. Introduction à L'ethnocide*, Seuil (Combats), Paris.

Kradolfer, S. (2007). Ser Mapuche en Argentina en el umbral del tercer milenio, *Revista del CESLA*, 10, pp. 37–52.

Kradolfer, S. (2008). Résister dans la division, *Tsantsa*, 13, pp. 80–88.

Kropff, L. (2005). 'Activismo Mapuche en Argentina: Trayectoria Histórica y Nuevas Propuestas', in Dávalos P. (ed.), *Pueblos Indígenas, Estado y Democracia*, Consejo Latinoamericano de Ciencias Sociales — CLACSO, Buenos Aires, pp. 103–132.

Mandrini, R. J. (1989–1990). Notas sobre el desarrollo de una economía pastoril entre los indígenas del suroeste bonaerense (fines del siglo XVIII y comienzos del XIX), *Etnía*, 34–35, pp. 67–87.

Mandrini, R. J. and Ortelli, S. (1993). *Volver al País de Los Araucanos*, Sudamericana, Buenos Aires.

Menni, A. M. (1995). *Relaciones Interétnicas en Argentina y Chile del Siglo XIX*, IREPS — APDH, Neuquén.

Navarro Floria, P. (1999). *Historia de la Patagonia*, Ciudad Argentina, Buenos Aires.

Radovich, J. C. and Balazote, A. (1992). 'El Pueblo Mapuche en la Actualidad', in Radovich, J. C. and Balazote, A. (eds), *La Problemática Indígena*, Centro Editor de América Latina, Buenos Aires, pp. 159–186.

Ray, L. (2007). *Language of the Land. The Mapuche in Argentina and Chile*, IWGIA, Copenhagen.

Stolcke, V. (2005). 'A New World Engendered: The Making of the Iberian Transatlantic Empires — XVI to XIX Centuries', in Pujadas, J. and Dietz, G. (eds), *Etnicidad en Latinoamérica: Movimientos Sociales, Cuestión Indígena y Diásporas Migratorias*, X congreso de la Federación de Asociaciones de Antropología del Estado Español, Sevilla, pp. 19–46.

Todorov, T. (1982). *La conquête de L'Amérique. La Question de L'autre*, Seuil, Paris.

Zavala, J. M. (2000). *Les Indiens Mapuche du Chili. Dynamiques Inter-Ethniques et Stratégies de Résistance, XVIIIème Siècle*. L'Harmattan, Paris.

Chapter

18

Afro-Latin Americans and the Limits of Equal Rights: 1810–1910–2010

Aline Helg

18.1. INTRODUCTION

This chapter shows how Afro-descended people have embodied the limits of equal rights in Latin America's multiethnic and multiracial societies in three key historical moments: 1) the independence process in the 1810s–1820s, when Latin American patriots fought for freedom from Spain and Portugal while at the same time maintaining slavery; 2) the period from 1889 to 1912, just after the abolition of slavery in Brazil and Cuba, when the elites in power granted legal freedom and equality to all but simultaneously championed positivism, pseudoscientific racism and European immigration;[1] 3) and finally the years from 1990 to 2010, when in several Latin American

[1] Some portions of the two first sections of this chapter have appeared with more details in Helg, A. (2008), 'Abolition and Afro-Latin Americans', in Holloway, T.H., (ed.), *Blackwell Companion to Latin American History*, Blackwell Publishing, Oxford, pp. 247–263.

countries from Colombia to Brazil, new constitutions recognised land rights and some autonomy to Native American and Afro-descended communities, while at the same time governments ignored or sponsored their forced displacement so that national and global corporations could exploit their territories.

18.2. THE INDEPENDENCE STRUGGLE AND ITS OUTCOME FOR FREE AND ENSLAVED PEOPLES OF AFRICAN DESCENT

When continental Spanish America initiated its process of independence in 1808, race mattered. For Spain, all people of African descent fell under the depreciative label of *castas*. Whereas whites, Indians and their *mestizo* offspring were credited with *limpieza de sangre* (blood purity), African slaves and their mixed or unmixed descendants were attributed a permanent 'depraved origin'. The 'stain of slavery' severely reduced their options as it hereditarily excluded them from the *limpieza de sangre* necessary for admission to secondary and higher education as well as for most civil, military and church positions. Yet, in many regions the pool of whites and *mestizos* was so small that some *castas* acceded to positions and trades legally closed to them. Moreover, much of the defence of the Atlantic coast was entrusted by Madrid to militiamen of African descent who, as a result, benefited from military privileges (Helg, 2004, pp. 100–105). Simultaneously, slavery was far from marginal. In Colombia and Venezuela about 10% of all inhabitants were slaves. In each Spanish American city, most domestic workers were slaves, as were the producers of Spanish American main exports, such as gold from the Pacific Coast, sugar from Peru and cocoa from Venezuela. Everywhere, however, slaves were outnumbered by *castas*, with the result that together free and enslaved people of African descent were an important component of society: between 6 and 10% in countries with an indigenous majority, such as Mexico, Peru and Ecuador; between 23 and 39% in Colombia, Argentina and Uruguay; and up to 60% in Venezuela. Everywhere, whites were a minority of the population (Andrews, 2004, p. 41).

The process of independence in continental Spanish America began in 1808, with the power vacuum created by the abduction of King Ferdinand VII by Napoleon Bonaparte. Yet, 1808 was just four years after the victory of the Haitian Revolution (1791–1804), which prompted shock waves throughout the Americas. For the first time, in 1792–1793 massive rebellion by free and enslaved people of African descent had forced a world power to abolish slavery and racial inequality in its colonies. What followed was the rise of former slave Toussaint Louverture to the governorship of Saint Domingue, the destruction of the colony's plantations, the elimination of its white population through exile or massacre, the successful resistance by freedmen and free people of colour to Napoleon's attempts to restore slavery and French domination and finally the independence of Saint Domingue, renamed Haiti, in 1804 (Geggus, 2002, pp. 5–29).

These dramatic events had a profound and long-lasting impact on Latin America. In 1808, in some Spanish colonies, such as Cuba and Puerto Rico, the Creole (i.e. native white) elite and planter class feared a revolution along Haitian lines so much that they remained faithful to Spain. In Venezuela, until 1814, the pro-independence movement embodied the interests of the Creole slave planters to such an extent that the royalists managed to mobilise *pardos* (free *castas*) and numerous slaves in the defence of Spain. Led by the Spaniard José Tomás Boves, the *llaneros* (cowboys) waged a race war reminiscent of the Haitian Revolution against the patriot elite and whites in general. At this point, Simón Bolívar, himself a slave-owning aristocrat, realised that Venezuela's independence could not be won without the support of the majority of African descent. He recast the war in new terms: a war to the death between Americans, regardless of race, and Spaniards. Nevertheless, only with Boves's death and the material support of Haiti did *pardos* and slaves begin to fight against Spain. In contrast, in Caribbean Colombia most free men of African descent, including those in the colonial militia, fought for independence. In the south of the continent as well, Afro-descended men were numerous in the patriot troops. The army of Gen. José San Martín, recruited in Río de la Plata, included not only a majority of *castas*, but hundreds of slaves, who were joined by hundreds more in Chile and

Peru as the liberation army progressed toward Lima (Blackburn, 1988, pp. 337–357).

The overrepresentation of men of African descent in the patriot armies had a direct impact on the sociopolitical systems adopted after independence. Most Spanish American nations became republics; they abolished the caste system and granted legal equality and qualified suffrage to all adult men *regardless of race*. This path-breaking racial inclusion erased the stain of slavery, which for centuries had legally maintained Afro-descended people in an inferior position. It contrasted sharply with the 1812 Constitution of the Spanish monarchy, which continued to exclude the latter from the new voting rights it granted to Indians and *mestizos* (Helg, 2004, pp. 242–245).

Despite legal equality of the free, post-independence governments were almost exclusively composed of whites who had access to higher education under Spain. Few *pardo* military men became high ranking officers, and even fewer achieved high political position under the republic they had contributed to forge. Many whites still feared a revolution along Haitian lines and promptly reacted to any attempt by people of African descent to organise and claim a more tangible equality than the one contained in constitutions and laws. Representative of this mindset was Bolívar's concern with what he labelled *pardocracia* (literally, the rule of the *pardos*), which would lead, according to him, to the extermination of whites. Bolívar believed that for many blacks and *pardos,* race was more important than the nation. This belief, added to his thirst for absolute leadership, could turn deadly for those who stood in his way. In 1817, Bolívar had the *pardo* Manuel Piar executed for challenging his supremacy by allegedly envisioning *pardocracia*, but he tamed with military advancement two white challengers. In 1828, he also secured the execution of Gen. José Padilla, a *pardo* who played a decisive role in the liberation of Venezuela and Colombia but protested continuing racial privileges and seized power to defend the 1821 Constitution against Bolívar's attempts to impose a semi-monarchical constitution. What sealed the fate of these men was not so much their partial African ancestry, exceptional among top political circles, but the fact that they did not silence it and used it to mobilise lower-class people. In contrast, a handful of Afro-descended leaders who integrated into white aristocratic circles without raising racial issues achieved elite recognition. A few others, such as Bernardo Rivadavia, first president of Argentina in 1825–1827, passed for white but were rumoured to have some African descent and often ridiculed for that reason (Helg, 2004, pp. 4, 195–218; Andrews, 1980, pp. 82–83).

Regarding slavery, the record of the new Latin American nations is much less imposing than on the subject of the legal equality of free men. In fact, there was hardly any correlation between independence and abolition. Although pro-independence discourse had often portrayed the colonised homeland as a chained slave, now in the name of private property a majority in the ruling elite refused to grant freedom to the enslaved. Most patriot leaders, often slaveholders themselves, did not perceive slavery as contradictory with a republic. During the early 1810s, they abolished the slave trade, partly on British insistence. However, only the revolutionary movements of Miguel Hidalgo and José María Morelos in Mexico decreed the full abolition of slavery (a decision reversed after their defeat), whereas patriots in Chile and Río de la Plata issued free womb laws[2] (Lynch, 1986). In 1816, Bolívar promised President Alexandre Pétion to abolish slavery in the territories he would liberate in return for Haiti's support. Although in 1818 Bolívar issued two edicts that abolished slavery in Venezuela, submitting former slaves to the service of arms equally with all male inhabitants, one year later Venezuela's Fundamental Law ignored these edicts and did not mention abolition (Helg, 2004, pp. 245–246).

After the end of the wars, only those slaves who could prove that they had fought with the patriot armies gained their freedom. In the early 1820s, with independence achieved, Chile and Central America, where slaves were few, ended slavery as a logical consequence of the principles of liberty and equality. Mexico followed in 1829, under the brief presidency of Gen. Vicente Guerrero, a man of

[2] The equivalent of US *post-nati* emancipation laws, the free womb laws granted freedom to slaves born to slave mothers after a certain date but subjected them to their mothers' owners until they reached adulthood.

Afro-indigenous ancestry who had been a commander in the Morelos insurgency (Carroll, 1991, pp. 110–111). Slavery was abolished in the Dominican Republic in 1822 under Haitian occupation (Sagás, 2000, pp. 29–31). In contrast, Venezuela and most other former Spanish colonies issued laws of manumission that only foresaw abolition in the long term. These laws confirmed the ban on the importation of new slaves, but allowed all kinds of transactions within the country. They emancipated slaves over 60 years of age and declared the freedom of the newborn (free womb), but submitted these children to unpaid labour for the owner of their slave mothers until they reached adulthood. Moreover, they did not repel the 1789 Spanish Código Negro (Helg, 2004, pp. 170–171).

Slavery outlived independence also because no powerful abolitionist movement formed in these new nations — even in those where free people of African descent comprised the majority of the population. When, 30 years later, in the 1850s, slavery was finally abolished in Argentina, Uruguay, Venezuela, Colombia, Ecuador, Peru and Bolivia (Paraguay followed in 1869), it had crumbled as a result of the ban on the slave trade, natural death, the upheaval of civil wars, flight and slaves' self-purchase. By then the British, in 1838, and the French, in 1848, had emancipated all the slaves of their colonies. Continental Spanish South America's abolition was, thus, belated and shows how Afro-descended people embodied then the limits of equal rights (Blackburn, 1988, pp. 358–375; Lombardi, 1971).

18.3. ABOLITION IN BRAZIL AND CUBA IN THE AGE OF POSITIVISM AND PSEUDOSCIENTIFIC RACISM

Unlike in continental Spanish America, Brazil achieved independence with little fighting during a phase of rapid expansion of slavery, when in 1822 the son of the king of Portugal crowned himself Emperor of Brazil. For its part, Cuba remained faithful to Spain, partly because its Creole elite feared rebellions along Haitian lines. Despite laws banning the slave trade, between 1811 and the end of the 1860s, slave traders delivered 1,150,000 Africans to Brazil and 550,000 to Cuba

(Eltis *et al.*, 2008). Both Brazilian and Cuban economies boomed thanks to sugar and coffee exports produced by slaves. But in both countries, overexploitation, abuse, demographic imbalance (most new African slaves were very young men), and poor living conditions made the number of slaves decline, even before the end of the illegal trade in the 1860s.

In Brazil, free people of African descent benefited from independence. The 1824 Imperial Constitution granted citizenship to all free male Brazilians, regardless of race. All discriminatory laws vanished, but the constitution limited the voting rights of *libertos* (free men born in slavery). By the time of Brazil's first national census, in 1872, free Afro-Brazilians had become the most numerous socioracial category (44% of the total population) (Da Costa, 2000, pp. 59–62; Klein, 1986, pp. 124–129). They were increasingly diverse: in addition to performing manual trades, some were teachers, journalists and writers. Quite unique in Latin America was the formation of a small Afro-Brazilian elite in some cities. Some mulattos (rather than blacks) studied at university and became medical doctors, lawyers and engineers. A few gained international fame, such as the engineer and abolitionist André Rebouças, or entered the nobility. Afro-Brazilians were also represented in state and national administrations, in the officer ranks of the army and in the clergy. Several were elected to the National Parliament and state legislatures, partly thanks to white aristocratic patronage (Klein, 1972, pp. 328–329).

In Cuba, on the contrary, the advancement of free people of African descent was strongly resisted by Spain and its Creole supporters. Free Afro-Cubans continued to be submitted to racist laws that excluded them from suffrage until the 1870s and brought them closer to the slaves under the single label of *raza de color* (race of colour). Ironically, however, Cuba's colour bar, which prohibited the absorption of some highly educated mulattos into the white planter-dominated elite as happened in Brazil, favoured the relative cohesion of the Afro-Cuban population and facilitated its mobilisation (Paquette, 1998; Helg, 1995, pp. 3–4).

The US Civil War (1861–1865), ending with the victory of the Union against the pro-slavery Confederacy, marked the end of the illegal slave trade and the dawn of slavery in the Americas. A few years after the abolition of slavery in the United States in 1865, Cuba and Brazil adopted laws of gradual slave emancipation (free womb, unpaid labour for children until adulthood, freedom for slaves older than 60 years, new manumission procedures), in 1870 and 1871 respectively. But these laws, which would have maintained slavery in the western hemisphere for another 60 years, that is, until 1930 or 1931, did not solve the crisis: slaves struggled more than ever to buy their freedom. Moreover, in Cuba, some Creole and Afro-Cuban leaders launched in 1868 the first war of independence, which considerably weakened slavery. Eventually, in 1880, Spain nominally ended slavery but replaced it with the *patronato* (patronage). Slaves, renamed *patrocinados*, were to gain freedom — after eight years of apprenticeship — in 1888. Slavery rapidly disintegrated as a result of slaves' continuing self-purchase and flight as well as natural death. With only 25,000 *patrocinados* left in 1886, the Spanish government abolished slavery in that year (Schmidt-Nowara, 1999, pp. 126–160; Scott, 1985, pp. 63–83, 111–172). In the meantime, in Brazil abolitionism, slave flight and insurgency threatened the country with civil war. As a result, Brazil too ended slavery earlier than stipulated by its own law of gradual emancipation and apprenticeship. On 13 May 1888, Princess Regent Isabel signed the Golden Law that finally ended legal slavery in Brazil — and thus, in the Americas (Holloway, 1977; Conrad, 1972; Toplin, 1972).

In Brazil, abolition was followed in November 1889 by a military coup that overthrew the Brazilian Empire and established the First Republic (1889–1930). Tragically, the national abolitionist movement vanished after the Golden Law, leaving freedmen and freedwomen with only the support of black brotherhoods and centres of syncretic worship as well as extended family networks. In addition, the new political system, far from being republican, excluded the majority of the Brazilian people and secured the domination of the planter oligarchy. Moreover, as most Latin American governments at the time, the Brazilian republic embraced pseudoscientific racism, social Darwinism and French philosopher Auguste Comte's positivism, as expressed by the words 'Order and Progress' on its national flag.

According to these philosophies, non-whites were racially inferior and unfit for free labour, and the best way toward progress was to whiten the country's population through massive European immigration. As a result, federal and state governments invested public funds in European immigrants (by paying their transatlantic passage) but refused to make any investment in Brazilians (by developing education and training or subsidising the transportation of workers from depressed areas to demanding regions). In other words, Europeans were being transported to Brazil to unfairly compete with Afro-Brazilians, and it was assumed that in the contest freedmen and darker Brazilians would lose.

And the planters fulfilled their dream. From 1888 to 1928 4 million whites came (primarily Italians, Portuguese and Spaniards), half of them to the coffee-producing state of São Paulo, where many industries were also created. Immigrants systematically displaced and marginalised Afro-Brazilians. They went to the most prosperous regions and received the most desirable jobs. Blacks were almost entirely excluded from contract work on coffee plantations, as well as from factories and commerce. Black artisans — who had dominated manual production until 1850 — virtually disappeared from the city. They found their opportunities restricted to domestic service and in petty jobs, such as porters, gardeners, newspapers vendors and day labourers (Holloway, 1980; Andrews, 1991, pp. 54–85).

After 1886, Afro-Cubans went through a similar process of marginalisation. However, some built on the Spanish-imposed concept of *raza de color* to unite blacks and mulattos, Cuban-born and African-born, free and former slaves alike and to foster racial pride. In 1887 mulatto journalist Juan Gualberto Gómez published a newspaper and organised already existing all-black clubs and societies into a federation that successfully coordinated anti-discriminatory actions island-wide and challenged Spanish authority (Helg, 1995, pp. 25–43).

Afro-Cuban veterans of the previous wars for independence, within Cuba and from exile, also prepared for the renewal of the anticolonial struggle. After launching a new war for independence in 1895, blacks and mulattos joined the Liberation Army against Spain en masse, galvanised by the leadership of mulatto Gen. Antonio Maceo and the hope to help build a nation founded on socioracial equality. However, the deaths of white anti-racist ideologue José Martí and General Maceo in the war led to the marginalisation of Afro-Cubans from the leadership of the army and the provisional government, now dominated by socially conservative whites, a few of whom even favoured annexation to the United States (Helg, 1995, pp. 56–78).

Blacks' marginalisation worsened with the 1898 US intervention in the war and military occupation of Cuba (1898–1902). Drawing on Cuba's deeply rooted patterns of racial differentiation, US officials imposed policies that often discriminated against Afro-Cubans. In 1902 the first elected Cuban government carried on several of the United States' occupation's policies. In addition, it promoted the whitening of Cuba's population through massive subsidised Spanish immigration. It also launched a campaign to repress traditions of African origin under the label of *brujería* (witchcraft) as a means of denigrating all Afro-Cubans. Simultaneously the government claimed that the 1901 Constitution, which stipulated the equality of all Cubans and granted universal male suffrage and Cuban citizenship to African-born freedmen, had resolved the 'black problem'. It did nothing to desegregate the public sphere and to help Afro-Cubans and the poor in general. No Afro-Cuban served in the upper level of the administration, and the government even publicly offended the few Afro-Cuban congressmen by not inviting their dark-skinned wives to presidential receptions (Helg, 1995, pp. 92–116).

Afro-Cubans began to protest marginalisation under the Republic. In 1908, a group of veterans formed the *Partido Independiente de Color* (Independent Party of Colour) which stands out as the first black party in the Americas. The party rapidly achieved nationwide membership, including day labourers, peasants, workers, artisans and a few middle-class individuals in a programme demanding full equality in the public and private spheres, social reform and proportional Afro-Cuban representation in public service. Seen as a threat to the new order, the party was banned in 1910 and annihilated in 1912, when hundreds of Afro-Cubans organised an armed protest against that ban in Oriente. The Cuban government sent the army and white volunteers against them to massacre between 3,000 and 6,000 blacks and mulattos — members and leaders of the *Partido Independiente de Color* as well as ordinary men, women and children, killed because of their race. The racist slaughter of 1912 dealt a long-lasting blow to Afro-Cubans, who subsequently struggled within existing political parties and labour unions rather than in their own organisations (Helg, 1995, pp. 142–159, 194–248).

As in Brazil and Cuba, from the 1880s to the 1920s, Positivism and pseudoscientific racism were influential throughout Latin America, drastically limiting people of African descent's options. The official ideology promoted white superiority and black inferiority as well as various stereotypes denigrating blacks. The population of African descent was universally portrayed as lazy, unfit for democracy and potentially criminal, and any attempt by blacks to mobilise was qualified as a threat of Africanisation or of another Haiti. In addition to Brazil and Cuba, Argentina and Uruguay were able to massively attract European immigrants to whiten and 'civilise' their population. As a result, in Buenos Aires, Afro-Argentines, who were 25% of the capital's population in 1838, had dropped to 2% in 1887 (Andrews, 1980, p. 4).

Nevertheless, throughout Latin America, ruling elites masked their racist policies by promoting images of their nations as 'racial democracies'. Up to the 1960s, they proudly contrasted Latin American legal equality with segregation in the American South. But they redefined equality as 'equality based on merits', which conveniently ignored the fact that all individuals, for historical reasons depending on their race, did not originate from equal conditions. Moreover, such a definition implied that merits could be fairly estimated within an ideological framework positing white superiority. Its ultimate function was to place the blame for blacks' continuing lower social position entirely on themselves: if most people of African descent were still poor despite the existence of legal equality, it was because they were *racially* inferior (Helg, 1995, pp. 105–106; Da Costa, 2000, pp. 234–246; Andrews, 1991).

Official discourses of racial equality confronted Afro-Latin Americans with an unsolvable dilemma. If they protested them, they exposed themselves to accusations of being racist and unpatriotic. If they subscribed to them, they had to simultaneously conform to negative views of blacks and remain subordinate. Indeed, such discourses made it offensive for people of African descent to proclaim their blackness along with their patriotism. In general, enfranchised Afro-Latin Americans solved this dilemma by conforming to white-dominated multiparty systems and by entrusting their representation to the less elitist party.

18.4. LAND RIGHTS AND AUTONOMY VERSUS AGRO-BUSINESS AND MINING INTERESTS

Up to today, throughout Latin America, people of African descent remain underrepresented in the upper spheres of power and over-represented in the lower strata of society. Yet, when compared with the 1910s, they have gained a lot. After the Great Depression, suffrage became less restricted, leading to the rise of socialism and populism. People of African descent began to demand racial equality and integration within political parties and unions more forcefully. They also increasingly protested European immigration. Yet, with the short-lived exception of the Frente Negra Brasileira in the 1930s, nowhere did they organise broad movements of black pride or black political parties, because they would have been accused of threatening the unity of the nation and repressed (Wright, 1990, pp. 98–100; Green, 2003; De la Fuente, 2001, pp. 189–199, 215–235; Butler, 1998, pp. 113–128). Nowhere either were they able to convincingly denounce anti-black racism, as in response the ruling elites could always raise the standard of Latin American inclusiveness against the scarecrows of American Southern segregation and lynching. Even the US Civil Rights Movement had little echo in Latin America, notably in Puerto Rico. As for Cuba, its leaders claimed shortly after the victory of the Revolution in 1959 that racism, as a product of slavery and US imperialism, had been erased by socialist reforms (Serviat, 1986).

Nevertheless, Afro-Latin Americans were successful in maintaining dissident subcultures that permitted collective self-affirmation. This was not a small victory after centuries of attempts by Eurocentric white elites to wipe out all African (and indigenous) derived cultures. In the 1930s, facing growing US imperialism, Latin American nations started to search for their roots and identity. In the process, some cultural expressions of African origin were recognised as essential parts of the national identity. These include African-derived music and dance, such as the Peruvian *zamacueca* and *marinera*, the *candombe*, ancestor of the Argentinian and Uruguayan *tango* and *milonga*, the Brazilian *samba* and *capoeira*, the Cuban *rumba* and *son*, the Dominican *merengue*, the Colombian *cumbia*, the Venezuelan *joropo*, the Mexican *son jarocho* — without forgetting the Central American *marimba* (a wooden xylophone introduced by African slaves). However, African-derived counter-religions, such as Cuban *santería* and *palo monte* and Brazilian *candomblé*, were not accepted by the elites before the 1970s (Moore, 1997).

Still, the incorporation of African-derived music and dance into Latin American national cultures did not challenge the socioracial order and racism. In fact, only in the 1980s did the fall of several dictatorships, the generalisation of universal suffrage in the western hemisphere and a lessening of political restrictions in Cuba allow for renewed consciousness among Afro-descended people of the discriminations they faced. Everywhere, Afro-Latin Americans began to take advantage of the small spaces for expression opening to them. In Cuba, shrinking state social programmes after the breakdown of the Soviet Union, the development of a tourist industry discriminating against Afro-Cuban employment, and the legalisation of remittances from the mostly white exile communities hit many blacks and mulattos (as well as many whites) hard. These men and women were left with few options other than absolute poverty or the resort to illegal means of acquiring the foreign currency vital to daily survival. Correspondingly, overt racism has been on the rise. Also, tourism has promoted a cottage industry of 'souvenirs' that display racial and sexual stereotypes questioning the effects of over 50 years of socialist education (De la Fuente, 2001, pp. 310–339).

Limited in their manifestation of distinctiveness, Afro-Cubans have expressed themselves through religion and the arts. Some are taking advantage of this aperture to publicly declare their faith in African-derived cults, to relate to Afro-diasporic cultural movements and to extend the national debate to the issue of racism (e.g. *Temas*, 1996, pp. 3–57).

In continental Latin America, some people of African descent are using the same strategies as Afro-Cubans. In addition, descendents of runaway slave communities (*quilombos* and *palenques*) and black populations of some specific areas have begun to borrow from indigenous nations to organise and claim territorial and ethnic rights. They have held international meetings; they also have built on the UN's policies against racism and in favour of indigenous self-determination, often with the backing of the Pastoral Afro-Americana founded by members of the Catholic Church in 1976.

Since the late 1980s, new constitutions in several Latin American countries have recognised the multiethnic and multiracial character of the nation and denounced existing racism despite legal equality. In Brazil, where 70% of all Afro-Latin Americans live, and where they represent 45% of the total population, Afro-descended organisations have shifted from cultural to more political goals. One century after abolition, in 1988, a new anti-discriminatory constitution was approved, and the Ministry of Culture created the Palmares Foundation, which, in addition to promoting African-derived cultures, registers and supports the legal recognition and land entitlement of Afro-Brazilian communities, descendants of former *quilombos.* In over 20 years of activity, the Foundation has certified 1,400 communities nationwide, principally in the states of Bahia and Maranhão — provoking some major conflicts with *fazendeiros* (Verán, 2003; Araújo, 2009).[3] Since 1996, the federal government has also launched 'compensatory policies to promote the social and economic advancement of

[3] The Brazilian terminology is 'comunidades remanescentes de quilombos'. See the official website of the Fundação Cultural Palmares, Ministry of Culture, Brazil. Available at: http://www.palmares.gov.br/ [Accessed 26 November 2010].

the black community', which have translated into some controversial affirmative action programmes (Andrews, 2004, pp. 187–188).

A very different path has been taken by Venezuela under the presidency of Hugo Chávez since 1999. Whereas politics have become increasingly polarised and sometimes racialised, with supporters of Chávez coming, like him, mostly from the popular classes of partial African and/or indigenous ancestry, and his opponents from the middle and upper classes of mostly European descent, the president has promoted social and nationalist reforms without addressing racism. The new Constitution adopted in 1999 recognises the cultural and collective land rights of the small indigenous communities, but does not mention Afro-Venezuelans, despite their mobilisation. Increasingly authoritarian, Chávez's government did little to directly address Afro-Venezuelan demands until March 2007, when thousands of urban and rural Afro-Venezuelans, under the leadership of the Network of Afro-Venezuelan Organizations (ROAV), demonstrated in Caracas. They requested that the 2010 census include racial and ethnic questions allowing Afro-Venezuelans to become as visible as indigenous Venezuelans. They also demanded some additions to the 1999 Constitution, notably the mention in its preamble of enslaved and free blacks' and *pardos*' major contribution to Venezuela's independence struggle and a chapter guaranteeing the protection of Afro-Venezuelans' culture, ancestral lands and ecology (Minority Rights Group International, 2007).

By making these requests, Afro-Venezuelan activists were only following a broad trend, in which people of African ancestry have built on indigenous struggles to gain ethnic and territorial recognition. For example, after the election of Rafael Correa to the presidency of Ecuador in early 2007, the national convention drafted a new constitution for the country that was approved by a large majority of Ecuadorians in 2008. This charter does not make distinctions between 'los pueblos ancestrales, indígenas, afroecuatorianos y montubios, which are all granted the same broad cultural, linguistic, anti-discrimination, territorial and governance rights (*Constitución de la República del Ecuador*, 2008).

Among the first Latin American nations to guarantee such rights to Afro-descended people was Colombia, in 1993. Three years earlier, in a rare moment of optimistic democracy, Colombians elected a constitutional assembly that included representatives of all political parties, former guerrilla fighters and delegates from indigenous communities. The constitution they drafted, adopted in 1991, promotes full liberty and equality, social rights and state protection against discrimination and violence. It declares Colombia to be a multiethnic and pluricultural state. Moreover, it grants two seats in the Senate to the indigenous peoples and recognises their communal rights to their ancestral lands and their traditional modes of governance (*Constitución política de Colombia*, 1991). However, the 1991 Constitution does not mention people of African ancestry, except in the Transitory Article 55. This article, adopted under grass-root pressure by a constitutional assembly comprising no delegates from Afro-Colombian associations, announced that within two years the government would issue a law focusing on the protection and rights of the country's black communities (Friedemann, 1992).

Indeed, in 1993 the Colombian Congress passed Law 70 of *Negritudes* (*sic*). This law recognises the ancestral collective property of rural black communities along the Pacific Coast; it protects their cultural identity, guarantees their economic development and gives them two special seats in the House of Representatives. It defines a 'black community' as 'the ensemble of families of Afro-Colombian descent who possess a specific culture, share a history, and have their own traditions and customs [...] that reveal and maintain an identity consciousness distinguishing them from other ethnic groups'. In other words, modelled after indigenous legislation, Law 70's definition of *negritudes* is limited and localised: it emphasises endogamy, cultural homogeneity and distinctiveness as well as rural location in the Pacific Basin (without mentioning historical origins: the African slave trade and slave labour in the region's gold mines). It automatically excludes peoples of mixed African ancestry from *negritud* as well as black communities in the cities, the valleys of Cauca and Patía, and the

Caribbean region (with the exception of the community of Palenque de San Basilio).[4]

Although the Law of Negritudes resulted in few concrete changes for most Afro-Colombians, it did offer the riverside dwellers of the Pacific Basin a legal instrument to transform the untitled lands already tilled by their ancestors into collective lands — a unique opportunity after centuries of abuse or state neglect they did not miss (Agudelo, 2002; Gros, 1994, p. 60). They organised, and in less than five years, black communities in Chocó realised a non-violent and unprecedented agrarian reform (in a nation ripe with civil wars that never had an agrarian reform): they managed to prove their ethnic identity and to obtain collective ownership titles for 3,500,000 hectares of ancestral lands out of a total of 5,000,000 (Sánchez, 2003; Almario, 2004, pp. 98–99).

However, this ethnic and agrarian reform occurred just when the Colombian government was launching the Plan Pacífico, designed to transform the region into a key centre of production and exports. Thus, Afro-Colombian land entitlement generated conflicts with major agro-industrial, fishing and mining enterprises, which in turn divided black communities. In 1996, the 'armed actors' of Colombia's undeclared internal war began to invade the very lands whose collective ownership by black — as well as indigenous — communities was being legally recognised. Schematically, in the north of the Pacific Basin, as the Fuerzas Armadas Revolucionarias de Colombia (FARC) were chased by the paramilitary Autodefensas Campesinas from

[4] There are important differences between the 1991 Constitution's indigenous rights and the 1993 Law 70's black communities' rights. First, it defines the lands of black communities as public (*baldías*), not as theirs; it considers blacks as settlers, not proprietors since time immemorial; it gives them the right to collective, not communal, property. Second, it does not grant black communities the right to local self-governance, as for the indigenous populations. Third, whereas the 1991 Constitution enables Indians, who make up only 3.4% of Colombia's population, to permanently secure two senatorial seats out of 100 and to obtain community ownership of 22% of the national territory, in 1996 the Constitutional Court nullified the stipulation of Law 70, giving black communities two special seats in the House of Representatives on technical grounds, without eliciting protest (Agudelo, 2002).

Córdoba and Urabá, many guerrilla groups forcibly took refuge in black and indigenous territories, where the paramilitary and the army pursued them. In the south, as the US-backed Plan Colombia targeted drug production and fumigated large areas in Putumayo, narco-producers, guerrillas, paramilitary forces, landless peasants and the army invaded the areas of Tumaco and Buenaventura. Black and indigenous communities ended up trapped in between, at the mercy of all armed actors. Some major agro-businesses, supported by the state and Plan Colombia, managed to obtain from community councils leasing contracts for the cultivation of African oil palm on their collective lands.

Since 2000, the paramilitary has won over the guerrillas in most of the Pacific Basin. Nevertheless, they continue to attack, murder, massacre and force non-submissive communities into flight. According to anthropologists, they use terror to carry out social and ethnic 'cleansing', as Afro-Colombian and indigenous traditional dwellers are compelled to abandon vast areas of land to white and *mestizo* colonisers from the interior. Simultaneously, the government of President Álvaro Uribe has ceased to finance projects aiming at the protection of the region's Afro-Colombian and indigenous cultures and unique biodiversity, whereas the weakened FARC continue to also harass and dislocate black and indigenous communities. As a result, the Pacific Basin is becoming one of Colombia's regions of major deforestation and production of illegal drugs, palm oil, mining and lumber (Restrepo, 2005, pp. 7–15; Almario, 2004, pp. 96–112). Abruptly and bloodily stopping a legal process of black (and indigenous) consciousness and empowerment, this massive irruption of armed actors and illegal production in the region is happening with practically no intervention of the Colombian state in defence of the 1991 Constitution and the 1993 Law of Negritudes.

As Gay McDougall, the UN Independent Expert on Minority Issues, stated in February 2010 in Bogotá: 'Despite the granting of collective titles to some 90% of Afro-Colombian ancestral lands, many communities are displaced, dispossessed and unable to live on or work their lands'. She expressed deep concern about 'mega-projects' involving major corporations encroaching on Afro-Colombians' land rights and concluded: 'In the face of such economic interests and mega-projects, it appears that the rights of communities are "inconvenient rights" and that the laws put in place to protect them are equally inconvenient' (UN News Service, 2010).

Indeed, in the Colombian Pacific lowlands as in many other frontier areas of the western hemisphere, Afro-descended people continue to embody the limits of equal rights in Latin America's multiethnic and multiracial societies.

BIBLIOGRAPHY

Agudelo, C. E. (2002). *Multiculturalismo en Colombia. Política, inclusión y exclusión de poblaciones negras*, Available at: http://www.iidh.ed.cr/comunidades/diversidades/docs/div_enlinea/MULTICULTURALISMOENCOLOMBIAcarlosagudelo.pdf [Accessed 26 November 2010].

Almario, O. (2004). 'Dinámica y consecuencias del conflicto armado Colombiano en el Pacífico: Limpieza étnica y desterritorialización de Afrocolombianos e indígenas y "multiculturalismo" de Estado e indolencia nacional', in Restrepo, E. and Rojas, A. (eds), *Conflicto e (in)visibilidad: Retos de los estudios de la gente negra en Colombia*, Editorial Universidad del Cauca, Popayán, pp. 73–120.

Andrews, G. R. (1980). *The Afro-Argentines of Buenos Aires, 1800–1900*, University of Wisconsin Press, Madison.

Andrews, G. R. (1991). *Blacks and Whites in São Paulo, Brazil, 1888–1988*, University of Wisconsin Press, Madison.

Andrews, G. R. (2004). *Afro-Latin America, 1800–2000*, Oxford University Press, New York.

Araújo, Z. (2009). 21 anos da Palmares: Tempo de Cidadania e Diversidade!, Jornal A Tarde, 19 August, Available at: http://www.palmares.gov.br/005/00502001.jsp?ttCD_CHAVE=803_[Accessed 26 November 2010].

Blackburn, R. (1988). *The Overthrow of Colonial Slavery, 1776–1848*, Verso, London.

Butler, K. D. (1998). *Freedoms Given, Freedoms Won: Afro-Brazilians in Post-Abolition São Paulo and Salvador*, Rutgers University Press, New Brunswick, NJ.

Carroll, P. J. (1991). *Blacks in Colonial Veracruz: Race, Ethnicity, and Regional Development*, University of Texas Press, Austin.

Conrad, R. E. (1972). *The Destruction of Brazilian Slavery, 1850–1888*, University of California Press, Berkeley.

Constitución de la República del Ecuador (2008). Online, Available at: http://www.asambleanacional.gov.ec/documentos/constitucion_de_bolsillo. pdf [Accessed 26 November 2010].

Constitución política de Colombia, 1991 (1994). Universidad Nacional Autónoma de México-Fondo de Cultura Económica, Mexico.

Da Costa, E. V. (2000 [1985]). *The Brazilian Empire: Myths and Histories*, University of North Carolina Press, Chapel Hill.

De la Fuente, A. (2001). *A Nation for All: Race, Inequality, and Politics in Twentieth-Century Cuba*, University of North Carolina Press, Chapel Hill.

Eltis, D., Behrendt, S. D., Richardson, D. *et al.* (eds) (2008 [1999]). *The Trans-Atlantic Slave Trade* [Electronic resource]*: A Database on CD-Rom*, Available at: http://wilson.library.emory.edu:9090/tast/assessment/estimates.faces [Accessed 26 November 2010].

de Friedemann, N. S. (1992). Negros en Colombia: Identidad e invisibilidad, *América Negra*, 3, pp. 25–35.

Fundação Cultural Palmares, Ministry of Culture, Brazil. Online, Available at: http://www.palmares.gov.br/ [Accessed 26 November 2010].

Geggus, D. P. (2002). *Haitian Revolutionary Studies*, Indiana University Press, Bloomington.

Green, W. J. (2003). *Gaitanismo, Left Liberalism, and Popular Mobilization in Colombia*, University Presses of Florida, Gainesville.

Gros, C. (1994). Noirs, Indiens et Créoles en Amérique latine et aux Antilles: Identité sociale et action collective, *Cahiers des Amériques Latines*, 17, pp. 53–64.

Helg, A. (1995). *Our Rightful Share. The Afro-Cuban Struggle for Equality, 1886–1912*, University of North Carolina Press, Chapel Hill.

Helg, A. (2004). *Liberty and Equality in Caribbean Colombia, 1770–1835*, University of North Carolina Press, Chapel Hill.

Helg, A. (2008). 'Abolition and Afro-Latin Americans', in Holloway, T. (ed.), *Blackwell Companion to Latin American History*, Blackwell Publishing, Oxford, pp. 247–263.

Holloway, T. (1977). 'Immigration and Abolition: The Transition from Slave to Free Labor in the São Paulo Coffee Zone', in Alden, D. and Dean, W. (eds), *Essays Concerning the Socio-Economic History of Brazil and Portuguese India*, University Presses of Florida, Gainesville, pp. 150–178.

Holloway, T. (1980). *Immigrants on the Land: Coffee and Society in São Paulo, 1886–1934*, University of North Carolina Press, Chapel Hill.

Klein, H. S. (1972). 'Nineteenth-Century Brazil', in Cohen, D. W. and Greene, J. P. (eds), *Neither Slave Nor Free. The Freedmen of African Descent in the Slave Societies of the New World*, Johns Hopkins University Press, Baltimore, pp. 309–324.

Klein, H. S. (1986). *African Slavery in Latin America and the Caribbean*, Oxford University Press, New York.

Ley 70 de 1993 (27 August) aprobada por el Congreso de la República (1993), or Ley 70 de Negritudes, Available at: http://www.acnur.org/biblioteca/pdf/4404.pdf [Accessed 29 December 2010].

Lombardi, J. V. (1971). *The Decline and Abolition of Negro Slavery in Venezuela, 1820–1854*, Greenwood Press, Westport, CT.

Lynch, J. (1986 [1973]). *The Spanish American Revolution, 1808–1826*, W. W. Norton, New York.

Minority Rights Group International (2007). *World Directory of Minorities and Indigenous Peoples — Venezuela: Overview*. Available at: http://www.unhcr.org/refworld/docid/4954ce6821.html [Accessed 26 November 2010].

Moore, R. D. (1997). *Nationalizing Blackness:* Afrocubanismo *and Artistic Revolution in Havana, 1920–1940*, University of Pittsburgh Press, Pittsburgh.

Paquette, R. L. (1988). *Sugar Is Made with Blood: The Conspiracy of La Escalera and the Conflict between Empires over Slavery in Cuba*, Wesleyan University Press, Middletown, CT.

Restrepo, E. (2005). De refugio de paz a la pesadilla de la guerra: el conflicto armado y el proceso organizativo en el Pacífico nariñense, *Revista de la Facultad de Ciencias Humanas y Sociales*, Universidad del Cauca, Popayán, 9, pp. 5–26.

Sagás, E. (2000). *Race and Politics in the Dominican Republic*, University Presses of Florida, Gainesville.

Sánchez, J. A. (2003). El conflicto está generando una contrarrevolución étnica, interview by Zapata, L., *Revista Semana*, Bogotá, 10 March, Available at: http://www.semana.com/noticias-on-line/conflicto-esta-generando-contrarrevolucion-etnica-entrevista-antropologo-colombiano-jhon-anton-sanchez/68732.aspx_[Accessed 29 December 2010].

Schmidt-Nowara, C. (1999). *Empire and Antislavery: Spain, Cuba, and Puerto Rico, 1833–1874*, University of Pittsburgh Press, Pittsburgh.

Scott, R. J. (1985). *Slave Emancipation in Cuba: The Transition to Free Labor, 1860–1899*, Princeton University Press, Princeton.

Serviat, P. (1986). *El problema negro en Cuba y su solución definitiva*, Empresa Poligráfica del CC del PCC, Havana.

Temas. Cultura, Ideología, Sociedad, 7 (1996). Departamento de Ciencia y Técnica del Ministerio de Cultura, Havana. Especially: Enfoque: De la etnia y la raza, pp. 3–57.

Toplin, R. (1972). *The Abolition of Slavery in Brazil*, Atheneum, New York.

UN News Service (2010). *UN human rights expert spotlights enduring plight of Afro-Colombians*, 15 February, Available at: http://www.unhcr.org/refworld/docid/4b7e652726.html [Accessed 26 November 2010].

Véran, J.-F. (2003). *L'esclavage en héritage (Brésil): Le droit à la terre des descendants de marrons*, Karthala, Paris.

Wright, W. R. (1990). *Café con leche: Race, Class, and National Image in Venezuela*, University of Texas Press, Austin.

Chapter

19

What Shall Become of Us Without Any Barbarians? Central American Gangs and the Utopia of Civilization in Latin America

Dennis Rodgers

'What shall become of us without any barbarians?'

Constantine Cavafy (1863–1933)

19.1. INTRODUCTION

2010 marks the bicentenary of the beginning of the Latin American struggles for independence, and is an eminently appropriate moment to reconsider some of the region's contemporary dynamics through the lens of the past. Certainly, as the British novelist Salman Rushdie pointed out in his excellent account of his travels through Nicaragua during the mid-1980s, history is always important to take into account in Latin America, where 'to understand the living..., it [is] necessary to begin with the dead' (Rushdie, 1986, p. 17). At the same time, however, simply juxtaposing the past and the present is not enough according to the American historian Harry Harootunian, particularly when this occurs — as it generally does — in a way that is underpinned by 'presumptions of continuity and the conviction ... that the present constitutes no problem other than supplying a platform from which the historian can look back on the past' (Harootunian, 2000, p. 15). Instead, we need to adopt a perspective whereby the past allows us to 'deconstruct ... the present' (Harootunian, 2000, p. 101). This is perhaps especially important with regards to a contemporary Latin America widely associated with violence and brutality (see, for example, Koonings and Kruijt, 1999; Moser and McIlwaine, 2004; Rosenberg, 1991), in stark contrast to the nineteenth-century visions that optimistically saw the region as 'the land of the future', as Hegel (2007, p. 86) famously put it in his 1831 *Philosophy of History.*

Understanding the underlying nature of this putatively paradoxical transformation requires exploding 'the continuity of universalizing conceptions of history' (Hanssen, 1998, p. 66), such as the one famously formulated by Domingo Sarmiento (1998 [1845]), based on the critical distinction between 'civilization' and 'barbarism'. At its most basic, positing that Latin America was fundamentally characterized by a progressive evolution whereby the former spread at the expense of the latter, Sarmiento's dichotomy is all the more relevant as it is arguably increasingly coming back into fashion, at least with regards to a paradigmatic aspect of the contemporary panorama of Latin American violence, namely the Central American gang phenomenon (see Rodgers and Jones, 2009). Certainly, gangs in the region are widely portrayed as a form of modern-day 'barbarism', but a closer examination of their underlying dynamics suggests that such an analysis is potentially flawed, and points to a fundamental transformation in the nature of both 'civilization' and 'barbarism' in contemporary Latin America, at least relative to the way they were defined by Sarmiento. This chapter begins by situating the Central American gang phenomenon, before then considering how it has been portrayed as a form of modern-day 'barbarism' emblematic of the region's dystopian social reality. It then goes on to consider this in light of Sarmiento's classic dichotomy, before concluding with some thoughts about the latter's contemporary relevance.

19.2. GANGS OF CENTRAL AMERICA

Although Central America has long been associated with violence, from the genocidal brutality of colonialism to the chronic civil wars and filibustering of the nineteenth century, as well as, perhaps most emblematically, the protracted revolutionary struggles against authoritarianism and imperialism during the 1970s and 1980s, contemporary levels of chronic brutality in the region are unprecedented (Call, 2000; Koonings and Kruijt, 1999; Londoño *et al.*, 2000; Moser and McIlwaine, 2004; Pearce, 1998; UNODC, 2007). This paradoxical situation is commonly attributed to the regional gang phenomenon, variably referred to as *maras* or *pandillas*. There is certainly no question that gangs have become highly emblematic of the violent social reality of contemporary Central America (Rodgers, 2009). At the same time, however, although they are often portrayed as a new phenomenon linked to the region's post-conflict circumstances from the early 1990s onwards, their origins in fact go back to the 1940s, and more specifically to the large-scale processes of urbanization that Central American countries underwent during this period. Gangs emerged principally in squatter settlements, as informal vigilante and self-protection groups in what were uncontrolled areas of rapidly growing cities. As such, they were an epiphenomenon of the first major regional push towards capitalist modernization, and their dynamics were not that different from those of the nineteenth-century New York gangs famously described by Herbert Asbury (1988 [1927]) — whose work was the basis for Martin Scorsese's 2002 film, *Gangs of New York* — or indeed gangs in many other parts of the world (see Hagedorn, 2008).

These initial gang manifestations waxed and waned with economic cycles — as well as political factors, including in particular repressive authoritarian rule, but also military conflict and conscription — until the early 1990s, when they suddenly came to the fore in much greater numbers and more violently than previously. The end of the Central American civil wars between 1990 and 1996 led to the demobilization of large numbers of youth who had acquired significant martial skills on an unprecedented scale. Although not all of these joined gangs, collectively they constituted a bigger demographic pool of likely gang members than had existed previously. Drawing institutionally on what was effectively a traditional form of youth collective action, many of these demobilized youth came together as gangs in an attempt to provide a measure of order for themselves and their local communities in broader postwar contexts of flux, heightened insecurity, and the emergence of local 'governance voids' (Koonings and Kruijt, 1999). From these relatively fluid and organic beginnings, these *pandillas* rapidly began to develop particular behaviour patterns that persisted over time, and which included semi-ritualized forms of gang warfare regulated by strict codes and expectations, generally revolving around territorial defence concerns, including in particular protecting local neighbourhood inhabitants from the vagaries of broader chronic insecurity. They also became much more institutionalized than past gangs, which had tended to be generationally ephemeral, and gave themselves names that persisted over time — examples from Nicaragua include *los Dragones* or *los Comemuertos* ('Eaters of the Dead'), for instance — despite gang member turnover, as successive generations 'matured out' (see Rodgers, 2006a).

The other major type of Central American gang, the *mara*, is linked to a particular two-way migratory pattern. Formally, there are just two *maras*, the *Dieciocho* and the *Salvatrucha*, which only operate in El Salvador, Guatemala, and Honduras within Central America, although they have reportedly begun to extend into Mexico as well. The origins of the *maras* lie in the 18th Street gang in Los Angeles, a gang founded by Mexican immigrants in the 1960s, although it rapidly began to accept Hispanics indiscriminately. The 18th Street gang grew significantly during the late 1970s and early 1980s as a result of the influx of mainly Salvadoran and Guatemalan refugees, many of whom sought to incorporate into the gang as a defence mechanism against the widespread discrimination that they experienced. In the latter half of the 1980s, a rival — possibly splinter — group founded by a second wave of Salvadoran refugees emerged, known as the *Mara Salvatrucha* (a combination of 'Salvadoreño' and 'trucha', meaning 'quick-thinking' or 'shrewd' in Salvadoran slang). The *Dieciocho* and the *Salvatrucha* rapidly became bitter rivals, frequently fighting each other, and were heavily involved in the looting that accompanied the 1992 Rodney King riots, which led the State of California to implement strict anti-gang laws.

Combined with the 1996 US Congress' Illegal Immigration Reform and Immigrant Responsibility Act, according to which non-US citizens sentenced to a year or more in prison were to be repatriated to their countries of origin after serving their sentence, this led to almost 70,000 felons being deported to Central America between 1998 and 2008, in addition to 200,000 illegal immigrants. Central America's northern triangle — El Salvador, Guatemala, and Honduras — received over 90% of the deportations from the US. Many of these deportees were members of the 18th Street and *Salvatrucha* gangs who barely knew the countries they had just arrived in, and unsurprisingly reproduced the structures that had provided them with support in the US. Deportees rapidly began to found local *clikas*, or chapters, of their gang in their communities of origin, which in turn quickly attracted local youth and either supplanted or absorbed local *pandillas.*[1] At the same time, it is important to note that the *mara* phenomenon is not simply a foreign problem

[1] It is important to note that Nicaragua does not have *maras*, mainly because less than 3% of Central American deportees are Nicaraguan, and most Nicaraguans who emigrate to the US settle in Miami, where contrarily to the more 'open' gangs of LA, the local gang scene is dominated by African-American and Cuban-American gangs that do not let Nicaraguans join (Rocha, 2006). This is also a major reason why Nicaraguan *pandillas* are not as violent as *maras*, insofar as the transnational transposition of US gang culture to El Salvador, Guatemala, and Honduras has had much more brutal consequences than the rise of home-grown, vigilante-style gangs. In effect, the *maras* are much less embedded within a local institutional context than *pandillas*, and therefore less rule-bound.

imported by deportees, but rather has evolved and grown in response to domestic political economy factors, including in particular state repression in the form of the (in)famous *Mano Dura* laws (see Jütersonke *et al.*, 2009). Indeed, deportation rates have in fact dropped over the past few years, and the *mara* phenomenon is now clearly locally self-sustaining. Contrarily to sensationalistic media reports, however, although each local *mara clika* is explicitly affiliated with either the *Mara Dieciocho* or the *Mara Salvatrucha*, and while *clikas* from different neighbourhoods affiliated with the same *mara* will often join together to fight other groupings claiming allegiance to the opposing *mara*, neither *über-mara* is a federal structure, and much less a transnational one, with their 'umbrella' nature more imagined and symbolic of a particular historical origin than demonstrative of any real unity, be it of leadership or action.

This imaginary aspect of their transnationalism notwithstanding, *maras* and *pandillas* are a very real phenomenon. Official police statistics suggest that there are at least some 70,000 *pandilla* and *mara* members operating in Central America, although the estimates of NGOs and academics suggest that the number could be as high as 200,000 (UNODC, 2007, p. 60). Even the lower figure would, however, mean that there are a greater number of gang members than military personnel in Central America, as Nicaragua and Honduras have armies of about 12,000 soldiers each, El Salvador 13,000 soldiers, and Guatemala 27,000 (see Millett and Perez, 2005, p. 59). These gangs clearly contribute a significant share of the violence afflicting the cities of these countries. Reliable information is extremely scant, however, with official statistics in particular especially problematic due to chronic underreporting, deficient data collection, and issues of political interference (see Huhn *et al.*, 2006, pp. 8–13). Nevertheless, Mo Hume (2007) claims that *maras* in El Salvador are thought to commit between 30 and 50% of all murders that occur in the country — which is reputed to be among the most violent in the world — while Ailsa Winton (2004, p. 85) notes that in Guatemala the ubiquity of gangs is such that 'there seems little need for the perceived severity of the problem to be verified by actual data'.

At the same time, although levels of violence in contemporary Central America are higher than those associated with the multiple civil wars and revolutionary conflicts that characterized the region during the 1970s and 1980s, and gangs are certainly key agents within the new political economy of violence, in contrast to sensationalist accounts linking them to migrant trafficking, kidnapping, and international organized crime, the various qualitative studies of Central American gangs that have been carried out over the past decade suggest that *pandillas* and *maras* are mainly involved in small-scale localized crime and delinquency such as theft, muggings, and racketeering. As Claire Ribando notes:

> Gangs are generally considered to be distinct from organized criminal organizations because they typically lack the hierarchical leadership structure, capital, and manpower required to run a sophisticated criminal enterprise. Gangs are generally more horizontally organized, with lots of small subgroups and no central leadership setting strategy and enforcing discipline. Although some gangs are involved in the street-level distribution of drugs, few gangs or gang members are involved in higher-level criminal drug distribution enterprises run by drug cartels, syndicates, or other sophisticated criminal organizations. (Ribando, 2007, pp. 1–2)

There is mounting evidence, however, that this is changing, and that both *pandillas* and *maras* are becoming increasingly either directly linked to, or supplanted by, such higher-level criminality (Rocha, 2007a; Rodgers, 2006a). I have linked this critical evolution in other writing to the intensifying exclusion that is a key feature of contemporary Central American cities as a result of the urban elite's retreat into gated communities and the more general political economy phenomenon of 'urban involution' — eloquently described by Mike Davis in his 2006 book, *Planet of Slums* — whereby the vast majority of the impoverished urban masses have been increasingly left unemployable in the face of economic restructuring due to the global rise of disembedded and delocalized capital accumulation processes. Drug trafficking has become one of the few viable livelihood opportunities in the poor neighbourhoods and slums of Central American cities, and their inhabitants are increasingly fighting each other to control what must inevitably be an exclusive economic activity. Gangs are, of course, ideally positioned, sociologically speaking, to dominate these veritable internecine 'slum wars', as organizations with quasi-monopolies over the local deployment of violence, and they are widely reported to drive localized regimes of terror that contrast strongly with their past community vigilante ethos, in order to ensure that they do not face competition or disruption of their new businesses (see Rodgers, 2009).

19.3. BARBARIANS AT THE GATE? THE SYMBOLIC CONSTRUCTION OF GANGS

Even if Central American gangs are not necessarily as violent as they are often perceived to be, they are clearly held up as a major contemporary regional security threat, whether by policy-making circles, academics, law enforcement officials, or the general population at large (see Jütersonke *et al.*, 2009). As Roxana Martel Trigueros (2006) and Mo Hume (2008, p. 63) both point out, the existence of such 'hegemonic epistemologies' has critical consequences for the way in which contemporary Central American gangs are symbolically constructed. Gang members are, for example, regularly depicted as evil and deranged sociopaths by the media (see Huhn *et al.*, 2006), sex-crazed personifications of Darwinist natural selection by academics (Rubio, 2007), and even the primary actors of 'another kind of war ... being waged ... within the context of a "clash of civilizations"' by policy-makers (Manwaring, 2008, p. 1). The latter description obviously has its intellectual roots in Samuel Huntington's (1996) infamous vision of global geopolitics, effectively harking back to the imagined medieval fault-line between supposedly civilized Christendom and putatively barbarian Islam, a perspective that is implicitly echoed in the persistent — but spurious — association of *pandillas* and *maras* with international terrorism — and more specifically al-Qaeda — in Central American media.

This implicit association with barbarism is arguably critical, and in fact frequently becomes explicit, as is well epitomized by political discourses such as the one delivered to the Salvadorean nation by the then President Francisco Flores on 23 July 2003, that directly associated gangs with barbarism and used this to justify the introduction of extreme forms of militarized repression: 'These groups have descended to dangerous levels of moral degradation and barbarism .... We are convinced that the combination of means proposed will give Salvadoran society the necessary instruments to fight this battle against criminals and their terrorism' (cited in Nowak, 2010, p. 40). This is an extreme example of this particular association, but it is one that is increasingly heard in a range of contexts in Central America, including, perhaps rather incongruously, in churches. For example, during a sermon that I attended in November 2009 at the local Catholic parish church near the poor *barrio* Luis Fanor Hernández, in Managua, Nicaragua, where I have been carrying out research on gangs since 1996, the priest delivered a homily based on the writings of Pope Leo the Great (*San León Magno*), famous for having prevented the barbarian Huns from ransacking Rome in 452 AD. He ended his speech admonishing his congregation to remember how Pope Leo had persuaded the leader of the Huns, Attila, to turn back through the demonstration of his unwavering faith in God whenever they felt that 'the delinquents that are the barbarians of today threaten to overwhelm your lives'.

At one level, this sort of social construction of gangs is by no means exceptional. The 'barbarian' label clearly serves to distinguish the legitimate from the illegitimate or, in other words, that which is acceptable versus that which must be suppressed and subjugated. Indeed, this is a process that has been a repeated feature of Latin American history, for example with indigenous people, communists, and now gang members (an interesting filiation to think about more broadly). The reinvocation of the label 'barbarian' is arguably a particularly powerful one, however, because the notion has a long history in the Latin American context, going back to Domingo Sarmiento's famous *Civilizacíon y Barbarie: Vida de Don Facundo Quiroga*. In this work, first published in 1845, Sarmiento proposed 'the dialectic between civilization and barbarism as the central conflict in Latin American culture' (González Echevarría, 2003, p. 2), and presented an account of the career of an Argentine *caudillo*, Juan Facundo

Quiroga, who was one of the dominant political figures of the country during the 1820s and 1830s. Argentina had yet to cohere as a unified entity at the time, and Sarmiento argued that this was because of the 'barbarism' of regional strongmen such as Facundo, whom he portrayed as 'a wild beast', 'destitute of learning', who 'delighted in exciting fear', 'arranging all his actions so as to produce terror in those around him' (Sarmiento, 1998, pp. 98–99).

Interestingly — in view of the sermon I attended in Managua — Sarmiento (1998, p. 95) even compares Facundo to Attila the Hun, but what makes his book especially striking is that he contended that, 'in Facundo Quiroga I do not only see simply a *caudillo*, but rather a manifestation of Argentine life as it has been made by colonization and the peculiarities of the land' (Sarmiento, 1998, p. 38). In particular, Sarmiento (1998, p. 10) associated 'barbarism' with 'the constant insecurity of life outside the towns [that] ... stamps upon the Argentine character a certain ... violence', and opposed this to life in the country's major cities, including in particular Buenos Aires, 'the only city in the vast Argentine territory which is in communication with European nations' (Sarmiento, 1998, p. 12). Sarmiento saw Europe as a template (and the source) for modernization and progress — i.e. 'civilization' — in postcolonial Latin America, rejecting all indigenous or autochthonous practices as violence-inducing 'barbarism'. In effect, his book is a manifesto concerning the nature of progress in Latin America, and he implicitly suggests that the region's future trajectory is one that will lead to its increasing 'civilization' through 'Europeanization'.

Thinking about Central American gang violence and its contemporary association with 'barbarism' in this light, it is clear that a significant difference between the beginning of the nineteenth century and that of the twenty-first is that while the former's barbarism was associated with 'the colonial past' (Stavans, 1998, xxii), contemporary barbarism in the form of gangs is more a consequence of present-day global geopolitical and political economy shifts — such as large-scale transnational population movement and 'urban involution'. These, however, are in many ways fundamental reflections of modernity, and would therefore theoretically be more readily associable with 'civilization' rather than 'barbarism' within Sarmiento's scheme of things. This putative paradox suggests one of two things. On the one hand, it may well be that the dichotomy between brutal barbarity and peaceful civilization is perhaps no longer as clear-cut as Sarmiento once assumed it to be. On the other hand, it could also be that contrarily to the past, contemporary Central America's modernity — i.e. its 'civilization' — may not be quite as progressive as Sarmiento assumed this historical state of affairs to inherently be. The exclusive and covertly repressive nature of contemporary oligarchic regimes characteristic of the region today — see Rodgers (2006b) — in fact makes both propositions eminently plausible.

Indeed, one could go even further and argue that a key feature of the contemporary moment in Central America is the emergence of an externally-shaped, violence-inducing 'civilization' that is intimately linked — rather than opposed — to present-day forms of 'barbarism' in the shape of gangs. Owing to the scarcity of alternative (legal/legitimate) economic opportunities, survival for the poor in Central America, including for gang members, effectively amounts to 'ruthless Darwinian competition', with tensions emerging over 'the same informal scraps, ensur[ing] self-consuming communal violence as yet the highest form of urban involution' (Davis, 2004, p. 28). Within this context, Central American gangs can perhaps be seen as something of an emergent vanguard — because youth, as Ziad Doueiri (1998), maker of the powerful film *West Beyrouth* (1998), has pointed out, 'have a stronger instinct for survival than adults[,] ... no doubt ... because [they] adapt better and faster to exceptional circumstances' — attempting to resist a contemporary social order characterized by historically unprecedented levels of social, economic, and spatial inequality. As such, they are epiphenomena of broader social and economic circumstances that have either been actively fostered, or negligently permitted to endure and worsen, by Central American states, and in this sense, the societies in the region today arguably hardly deserve the label of 'civilization'.

This is perhaps even more obviously the case in view of the veritable regional 'war on gangs' that Central American states have declared during the past decade. The opening salvo of this campaign was El Salvador's adoption of a *Mano Dura* ('Iron Fist') policy promulgated by the Salvadoran President Ricardo Maduro in July 2003, which advocated the immediate imprisonment of youth simply for having gang-related tattoos or flashing gang signs in public, something that became punishable with two to five years in jail, and applicable to gang members from the age of 12 onwards. Between July 2003 and August 2004, 20,000 youths were arrested, although 95% were eventually released without charge when the *Mano Dura* law was declared unconstitutional by the Salvadoran Supreme Court for violating the UN Convention on the Rights of the Child (UNCRC). A new *Mano Super Dura* package of anti-gang reforms was rapidly pushed through, which respected the provisions of the UNCRC but stiffened the penalties for gang membership to up to five years in prison for ordinary gang members, and nine years for gang leaders (Aguilar, 2006). Although under the new law the police need to have some proof of active delinquent behaviour in order to arrest an individual, El Salvador's carceral population has doubled over the past five years, from 6,000 to 12,000 prisoners, 40% of whom are gang members (Hume, 2007).

Honduras implemented a comparable policy called *Cero Tolerancia* ('Zero Tolerance') almost simultaneously in August 2003, which was also partly inspired by Rudy Giuliani's (in)famous eponymous policy in New York. Among the measures that this package promoted was the reform of the penal code and the adoption of legislation that established a maximum 12-year prison sentence for gang membership, a penalty which was later increased to 30 years, as well as provisions for better collaboration between the police and the Honduran army in urban patrolling. Guatemala likewise adopted its *Plan Escoba* ('Operation Broomsweep') in January 2004, which, although not as draconian as the Salvadoran *Mano Dura* and the Honduran *Cero Tolerancia*, still contained new provisions allowing minors to be treated as adults, and the deployment of 4,000 reserve army troops in troubled neighbourhoods in Guatemala City. Nicaragua, similarly, regularly implemented a range of anti-gang initiatives from 1999 onwards, although these were of a significantly 'softer' nature, partly because of the less violent nature of the *pandillas* compared to the *maras*.[2] Although these crackdowns have been very popular with the general public in all the Central American countries, they have also been vigorously opposed by human rights groups who are concerned with the potential abuse of gang suspects. More ominously, organizations such as Human Rights Watch and Amnesty International have presented evidence — corroborated by the US State Department in 2005 — of the existence of paramilitary death squads in Honduras and El Salvador that are deliberately targeting gang members, and often youth more generally, moreover in collusion with state authorities (Faux, 2006).

At a more regional level, Central American states have also begun to engage in unprecedented forms of cooperation in order to deal with gangs, which a September 2003 regional summit of heads of state declared to be 'a destabilizing menace, more immediate than any conventional war or guerrilla'. In January 2004, El Salvador, Guatemala, Honduras, and Nicaragua agreed to lift legal barriers to the cross-country prosecution of gang members, whatever their nationality, while in March 2005, Presidents Tony Saca of El Salvador and Oscar Berger of Guatemala agreed to set up a joint security force to patrol gang activity along their common border. The Central American states have also sought to involve the US, which was initially resistant to participate in anti-gang initiatives until June 2004, when the Honduran minister of Security, Oscar Alvarez, rather ludicrously claimed that a suspected Saudi member of al-Qaeda, Yafar Al-Taya, had arrived in Salvador in order to meet with gang leaders. Although clearly a completely unfounded assertion, by December 2004, the FBI had created a special task force focusing on Central American gangs, and in February 2005 announced the creation of a liaison office in San Salvador to coordinate regional information-sharing and anti-gang efforts. Following a new (and no less ludicrous) claim by Oscar Alvarez to have thwarted

---

[2] At the same time, it is important to note that although the Nicaraguan police force has gained a reputation for focusing on 'preventative' rather than 'repressive' anti-gang policies, the evidence of its practices on the ground tends to belie this (see Rocha, 2007b).

a Colombian FARC-*mara* plot to kill President Ricardo Maduro in April 2005, the region's military leaders formally called on the US Southern Command for assistance in the creation of a multinational force to tackle organized crime and youth gangs, although this has yet to be implemented.

While it has been widely reported that the different anti-gang initiatives seemed to initially reduce crime quite significantly, the evidence suggests that this was a temporary state of affairs, if ever true. There are increasing numbers of reports that the widespread repression of gangs is leading to their becoming more organized and more violent (Aguilar and Miranda, 2006, p. 42). This is something that was well illustrated by the tit-for-tat violence that certain *maras* engaged in with the Honduran government following the implementation of *Mano Dura*. On 30 August 2003, one month after the promulgation of the new anti-gang legislation, gang members attacked a bus in the northern city of San Pedro Sula in broad daylight, killing 14, and leaving 18 wounded, as well as issuing a note to President Ricardo Maduro ordering him to withdraw the law. The following month, in the town of Puerto Cortes, a young woman's head was found in a plastic bad with a note addressed to President Maduro saying that this was a response to the extrajudicial assassination of a gang member by the police. Over the course of the following year, more than 10 decapitated corpses were left in various cities with messages from gang members to the Honduras president, each time in response to a putative extrajudicial killing, and on 23 December 2004, in Chamalecon, gang members again attacked a bus and killed 28, once again leaving a message claiming revenge for the May 2004 deaths of 105 gang members in a prison following a suspect fire. Similarly gruesome events have been reported in El Salvador and Guatemala.

Despite such events, and notwithstanding a rhetorical turn promoting the adoption of less repressive policies, there is little evidence to suggest that Central American states are really changing their stance vis-à-vis gangs (Jütersonke *et al.*, 2009). To a large extent, this is because the design and implementation of social policy within any given set of circumstances will inevitably mirror the political dispensations and economic dynamics of the context in question. As such, arguably the single biggest obstacle to developing a more effective approach to gang violence in Central America is the deeply entrenched oligarchic nature of the societies in the region alluded to above. Central American governments are, to a large extent, undertaking their visible and widely-publicized crackdowns on gangs in order to avoid taking action regarding much trickier issues relating to exclusion, inequality, and the lack of job creation. Or put another way, gangs have become convenient scapegoats on which to blame the isthmus' problems and through which those in power maintain an unequal *status quo.* At the same time, however, they arguably also simultaneously embody the risks of violent social action that will inevitably erupt in the face of attempts to preserve an unjust society.

19.4. CONCLUSION

The gangs of contemporary Central America and the repressive policies that have been put in place by regional states to deal with them squarely raise the question of what constitutes 'civilization' and what is 'barbarism', as well as the social processes that these are respectively associated with in contemporary Central America society. If the social and political structures of the latter are to be considered 'civilized', and the gangs as 'barbarians', we can certainly ask ourselves a question along the line of the epitaph by the Greek poet Constantine Cavafy reproduced at the beginning of this chapter, which is, where would we be without any 'barbarians'? As Franz Fanon observed in his 1961 classic *The Wretched of the Earth*, although the gangster is often 'a thief, a scoundrel or a reprobate', he can also 'light … the way for the people' (1990, p. 54), particularly when his violence is directed against domination and injustice. Seen in this light, Sarmiento's critical distinction between 'civilization' and 'barbarism' becomes less a utopian blueprint for the progressive development of Latin American society, and more a revealing *longue durée* lens through which to expose the dystopian nature of the region in 2010 as compared to the 'brave new world' of 1810, and to force upon us a clear-eyed understanding of the way in which progress and utopia are often extremely tenuous notions.

BIBLIOGRAPHY

Aguilar, J. (2006). Los efectos contraproducentes de los Planes Mano Dura, *Quórum*, 16, pp. 81–94.

Aguilar, J. and Miranda, L. (2006). 'Entre la articulación y la competencia: Las respuestas de la sociedad civil organizada a las pandillas en El Salvador', in Cruz, J. M. (ed.), *Maras y Pandillas en Centroamérica: Las Respuestas de la Sociedad Civil Organizada*, UCA Editores, San Salvador, pp. 37–144.

Asbury, H. (1988 [1927]). *The Gangs of New York: An Informal History of the Underworld*, Arrow Books, New York.

Call, C. (2000). *Sustainable Development in Central America: The Challenges of Violence, Injustice and Insecurity*, CA 2020 working paper no. 8, Institut für Iberoamerika-Kunde, Hamburg.

Davis, M. (2004). Planet of slums: Urban involution and the informal proletariat, *New Left Review*, 26, pp. 5–24.

Davis, M. (2006). *Planet of Slums*. Verso, London.

Doueiri, Z. (1998). *West Beyrouth* (information sheet), Trigon-film, Versoix.

Fanon, F. (1990 [1961]). *The Wretched of the Earth*, Penguin, London.

Faux, F. (2006). *Les Maras, Gangs d'Enfants: Violences urbaines en Amérique Centrale*, Autrement, Paris.

González Echevarría, R. (2003). '*Facundo*: An Introduction', in Sarmiento, D. F. (ed.) *Facundo: Civilization and Barbarism*, University of California Press, Berkeley, pp. 1–16.

Hagedorn, J. M. (2008). *A World of Gangs: Armed Young Men and Gangsta Culture*, University of Minnesota Press, Minneapolis.

Hanssen, B. (1998). *Walter Benjamin's Other History: Of Stones, Animals, Human Beings, and Angels*, University of California Press, Berkeley.

Harootunian, H. (2000). *History's Disquiet: Modernity, Cultural Practice, and the Question of Everyday Life*, Columbia University Press, New York.

Hegel, G. (2007). *The Philosophy of History*, Cosimo, New York.

Huhn, S., Oettler, A. and Peetz, P. (2006). *Construyendo inseguridades: aproximaciones a la violencia en centroamérica desde el análisis del discurso*, GIGA working paper no. 34, German Institute of Global and Area Studies, Hamburg.

Hume, M. (2007). Mano Dura: El Salvador responds to gangs, *Development in Practice*, 17(6), pp. 739–751.

Hume, M. (2008). The Myths of Violence: Gender, Conflict, and Community in El Salvador, *Latin American Perspectives*, 35(5), pp. 59–76.

Huntington, S. P. (1996). *The Clash of Civilizations and the Remaking of World Order*, Simon & Schuster, New York.

Jütersonke, O., Muggah, R. and Rodgers, D. (2009). Gangs, Urban Violence, and Security Interventions in Central America, *Security Dialogue*, 40(4–5), pp. 373–397.

Koonings, K. and Kruijt, D. (eds) (1999). *Societies of Fear: The Legacy of Civil War, Violence and Terror in Latin America*, Zed Books, London.

Londoño, J.-L., Gaviria, A. and Guerrero, R. (eds) (2000). *Asalto al Desarrollo: Violencia en América Latina.* Inter-American Development Bank (IADB), Washington, DC.

Manwaring, M. G. (2008). *A Contemporary Challenge to State Sovereignty: Gangs and Other Illicit Transnational Criminal Organizations (TCOs) in Central America, El Salvador, Mexico, Jamaica, and Brazil*, Strategic Studies Institute, US Army War Collage, Carlisle.

Martel Trigueros, R. (2006). Las Maras Salvadoreñas: Nuevas Formas de Espanto y Control Social, *Revista ECA: Estudios Centroamericanos*, 696, pp. 957–979.

Millett, R. L. and Perez, O. J. (2005). New Threats and Old Dilemmas: Central America's Armed Forces in the 21st Century, *Journal of Political and Military Sociology*, 31(1), pp. 59–80.

Moser, C. and McIlwaine, C. (2004). *Encounters with Violence in Latin America: Urban poor perceptions from Colombia and Guatemala*, Routledge, London.

Nowak, M. (2010). *The Politics of Violence: State Discourse on Violence in El Salvador, 2003–2009*, MA dissertation, Graduate Institute of International and Development Studies, Geneva.

Pearce, J. (1998). From civil war to 'civil society': Has the end of the Cold War brought peace to Central America?, *International Affairs*, 74(3), pp. 587–615.

Ribando, C. M. (2007). Report for Congress: Gangs in Central America, *Congressional Research Service*, report RL34112, 2 August.

Rocha, J.-L. (2006). Mareros y Pandilleros: ¿Nuevos Insurgentes, Criminales?, *Envío*, 293, pp. 39–51.

Rocha, J.-L. (2007a). *Lanzando piedras, fumando 'piedras'. Evolución de las pandillas en Nicaragua 1997–2006*, cuaderno de investigación no. 23, UCA Publicaciones, Managua.

Rocha, J.-L. (2007b). Mapping the Labyrinth from within: The Political Economy of Nicaraguan Youth Policy Concerning Violence, *Bulletin of Latin American Research*, 26(4), pp. 533–549.

Rodgers, D. (2006a). Living in the Shadow of Death: Gangs, Violence, and Social Order in Urban Nicaragua, 1996–2002, *Journal of Latin American Studies*, 38(2), pp. 267–292.

Rodgers, D. (2006b). The State as a Gang: Conceptualising the Governmentality of Violence in contemporary Nicaragua, *Critique of Anthropology*, 26(3), pp. 315–330.

Rodgers, D. (2009). Slum wars of the 21st century: Gangs, Mano Dura, and the new Urban Geography of conflict in Central America, *Development and Change*, 40(5), pp. 949–976.

Rodgers, D. and Jones, G. A. (2009). 'Introduction: Youth violence in Latin America — An overview and agenda for research', in Jones, G. A. and Rodgers, D.

(eds), *Youth Violence in Latin America: Gangs and Juvenile Justice in Perspective*, Palgrave Macmillan, New York.

Rosenberg, T. (1991). *Children of Cain: Violence and the Violent in Latin America*, Penguin, New York.

Rubio, M. (2007). *De la Pandilla a la Mara: Pobreza, Educación, Mujeres y Violencia Juvenil*, Universidad Externado de Colombia, Bogotá.

Rushdie, S. (1987). *The Jaguar Smile: A Nicaraguan Journey*, Penguin, New York.

Sarmiento, D. F. (1998). *Facundo: Or, Civilization and Barbarism*, Penguin, London.

Stavans, I. (1998). 'Introduction', in Sarmiento, D. F. (ed.), *Facundo: Or, Civilization and Barbarism*, Penguin, London, pp. vii–xxxii.

UNODC (2007). *Crime and Development in Central America: Caught in the Crossfire*, United Nations Publications, Vienna.

Winton, A. (2004). Young People's View on How to Tackle Gang-Violence in 'Post-Conflict' Guatemala, *Environment and Urbanization*, 16(2), pp. 83–99.

Index